A Handbook of
PERSONNEL
MANAGEMENT
PRACTICE

A Handbook of

PERSONNEL MANAGEMENT PRACTICE

Third Edition

Michael Armstrong

NP

KOGAN
PAGE

To Bridget, Virginia, Clare and Patrick

First published in 1977 and reprinted in 1978, 1979, 1980, 1981 (twice). Second edition first published in 1984, and reprinted 1984, 1985, 1986. Third edition published in 1988 and reprinted 1989 and 1990 by Kogan Page Ltd, 120 Pentonville Road, London N1 9JN.

British Library Cataloguing in Publication Data

Armstrong, Michael, 1928 –
   A handbook of personnel management practice. – 3rd ed.
   1. Personnel management
   I. Title
   658.3   HF5549

   ISBN 1-85091-336-6

Library of Congress Cataloging-in-Publication Data
   Armstrong, Michael, 1928 –
   Handbook of personnel management practice/
   Michael Armstrong. – 3rd ed. p. cm.

   ISBN 0-89397-314-9.
   1. Personnel management – Handbook, manuals, etc.
   I. Title.
   HF5549.A8977 1988
   658.3–dc19   88-9905

Printed in England by Clays Ltd, St Ives plc

Contents

Part VI – Reward Management   **339**

Part VIII – Employee Relations   555

Appendices

List of figures

List of tables

Foreword

It is four years since the second edition of this handbook was published. It is a remarkable fact that in this relatively brief period the world of personnel management has changed far more than in the seven years that elapsed between the first and second editions.

The introductory chapter to this edition reviews the factors that have contributed to this change, including economic developments, the growth of the 'enterprise culture', the rapid expansion in the use of new technology, internationalism, the emphasis on excellence and the cult of corporate culture. The overall impact of these changes on organizations, productivity, employment, employee relations and pay are also discussed in the introduction.

Although personnel management may seem to be booming as a profession, the number of books and articles questioning the role of the personnel function indicate that there are still many doubts about the ambiguous nature of its place in the organization. The fact that a major chapter in Shaun Tyson and Alan Fell's book could be called 'The crisis in personnel management' is revealing. The new emphasis on human resource management as a more powerful and possibly more credible approach to personnel management is significant.

To reflect these changes, a considerable proportion of this third edition contains entirely new material. It includes:

- taking a much broader view of the basis of personnel management with particular reference to strategic planning and the development of more comprehensive personnel objectives and policies (Chapter 1);
- expanding the analysis of the role of the personnel function and the context within which personnel management takes place to take account of the impact of the changing scene and a number of significant research studies in personnel management that have been conducted recently (Chapters 2 and 3);
- analysing in depth the concept of human resource management to see what it has to offer as a new approach and to establish

whether or not it is a case of 'the emperor's new clothes' or 'old wine in new bottles' (Chapter 4);

● assessing the significance of corporate culture with its emphasis on shared values and a management style which aims to create a climate of 'mutuality' (Chapter 5);

● expanding the section on organization behaviour, dealing with motivation and commitment in order to re-assess the contribution of some of the pioneers in this field and to study the relevance of the new ideas that are being developed (Chapter 8);

● devoting a separate chapter to techniques of job analysis so that they can be covered in more detail and proper recognition given to the key part played by job analysis in personnel management (Chapter 9);

● challenging the received view that job design is about job enrichment and opening up other, possibly more rewarding, techniques such as high-performance work design (Chapter 11);

● describing in greater detail the use of models in human resource planning (Chapter 13);

● considering different ways of preparing personnel specifications and expanding the use of selection tests (Chapter 14);

● examining in detail the rapid development in computerized personnel information systems, including databased personnel management, expert systems and the wide range of applications available in almost every field of personnel management (Chapter 19);

● taking an entirely new look at salary administration and wage payment systems and:
   − considering them as a whole rather than as separate entities for white or blue-collared workers (in the spirit of harmonization that is beginning to prevail);
   − adopting the words 'reward management' to establish the view that the system should be about 'paying for performance and achievement' (PPA) and not about 'administration' as a bureaucratic routine;
   − emphasizing a contingency approach which designs systems to suit the situation rather than imposing prefabricated solutions;
   − stressing the need for flexibility in paying for performance and providing employee benefits;
   − rethinking the role of profit sharing (Chapters 20 to 27);

● developing the concept of 'performance management' to underline new approaches to the use of appraisal systems as means of improving organizational performance (Chapter 28);

● introducing new systems of 'career management' which require organizations to exercise more care over planning careers and providing help in the shape of counselling and mentoring programmes to develop skills and potential (Chapter 31);

- considering the major changes in the field of employee relations, taking account of the important research that has been carried out under the auspices of the Economic and Social Research Council into workshop industrial relations, and reviewing the impact of 'new realism' and 'non-strike' or 'pendulum' agreements (Chapter 32);
- providing comprehensive examples of personnel policies (Appendix A).

The concluding chapter of the handbook takes a look into the future, where the impact of new technology will change organization structures and employment patterns (eg multi-skilling and contract workers) and the pressure is likely to be increasingly on the flexible and individual treatment of 'single-status' employees using a human resource management approach which is devoted to taking a strategic view of the organization's most important resource.

A final word: an important section of this handbook discusses organizational behaviour as a theoretical framework for the following parts dealing with personnel policies and procedures. In those sections, the starry-eyed enthusiasm of the 1960s for the benefits of behavioural science has been tempered with a touch of the realistic 1980s. But, as Douglas McGregor said, and he was one of the wisest writers on this or, indeed, any other subject, 'there's nothing so practical as a good theory'.

Be that as it may, the writer has been fortunate in that within his firm – a highly successful publishing business – he has been given but has also seized the opportunity to put into practice what he has preached in such areas as reward management, computerized personnel information systems (including the use of models), psychological testing, project teams, team building training, quality circles and team briefing. Above all, he has introduced a human resource management approach to running a successful business, where human resource planning is an integral part of corporate planning and where the core values and personnel policies of the firm have been defined and communicated and are being acted upon. In BCA, we have seen the future and it works!

Introduction

Personnel management –
the changing scene

Personnel management is defined by the Institute of Personnel Management as 'the effective use and development of people's skills, knowledge and experience to achieve the goals of the organization'.

Aim of this book

The aim of this book is to start from this broad definition and present an integrated picture of personnel management as a key function in any organization and as a function which concerns all managers. Personnel management is not treated simply as something that personnel managers do. It is considered instead in relation to the needs of the business as a whole, where every manager is involved in obtaining, organizing, motivating, developing and interacting with the human resources he or she controls.

The book takes a contingency view of personnel management; that is, what personnel specialists do and how they do it depends on or is contingent upon the organizational context within which they operate, the corporate culture and the forces which affect processes within the organization and influence the behaviour of the individuals and groups who work in it. Personnel management is considered as a strategic process which recognizes that the quality of the human resources available to an organization is the key to its success and that the basic processes of human resource planning and development must constitute an integral part of the enterprise's strategic plan.

Dynamism

Personnel management will also be treated as a dynamic process; responding rapidly to change but, importantly, initiating change and helping to manage it. Personnel management has to cope with the turbulent times in which we live. In the four years that have gone by since the second edition of this handbook was published there have been a number of significant changes. Some of these have been imposed from outside, others have taken place within organizations or in the profession of personnel management itself. These are summarized below as a background against which the various themes of the book will be developed.

The changing scene – primary factors

The economy

Over the last few years, the picture world-wide has been one of economic recession. In the UK high levels of unemployment continue. There is a shift from the manufacturing industries into the finance sector and the services industries. The North-South divide has been accentuated. London, the South East and the Thames Valley dominate the British economy. Inflation, however, has been brought under control. Incomes policies are dead but the Government and the Confederation of British Industry are still concerned that increases in earnings are exceeding increases in gross national product.

The enterprise culture

Throughout the prime wealth-producing nations of the world, but particularly in Britain, the emphasis is on enterprise. The new enterprise culture is about wealth-creation through entrepreneurship, competition, individualism, a more aggressive, outward-looking stance to economic development, the survival of the fittest, and self-help. In this connection, Samuel Smiles lives again. He wrote in 1859: 'The spirit of self-help is the root of all genuine growth in the individual; and, exhibited in the lives of many, it constitutes the true source of national vigour and strength. Help from without is often enfeebling in its effect, but help from within invariably invigorates...and where men are subject to over-guidance and over-government, the inevitable tendency is to render them comparatively helpless.'

New technology

New technology, especially information technology, is making a profound impact on what organizations do, how they do it, and indeed, where they do it. Jobs, methods of working, organization structures and skill requirements are all affected.

Internationalism

The trend is towards internationalism. The multi-nationals thrive, Japanese firms expand in Britain. A cadre of super-international executives exists – they travel the world, bringing new ideas with them. What happens elsewhere is studied intensively. 'What is the secret of the success of the Japanese?' is a question that is being constantly asked. A seminal book on *The Art Of Japanese Management* was written by Richard Pascale and Anthony Athos in 1981 in an attempt to answer that question.

The emphasis on excellence

The drive to study the secrets of success of international and national companies led to *In Search of Excellence* by Tom Peters and Robert Waterman which spawned a number of look-alikes. The emphasis is on achievement, leadership, 'people programmes' (looked at from the point of view of the enterprise rather than the people themselves) and the importance of corporate cultures and core values. The movement is pragmatic and the influence of the behavioural scientists has declined noticeably.

The cult of culture

Corporate culture as a concept which strongly influences the ways in which organizations function has emerged as a key issue. All managers, but especially personnel managers, are being urged to analyse, understand and do whatever they can to manage the culture of their organization.

The changing scene – impacts

Organizations

To survive in an enterprise culture, organizations have had to learn how to operate more flexibly. The trend is towards organic organizations where the form is determined by the culture, the technology and the need for dynamism, rather than by a mechanistic view of how organizations ought to function. Organization structures are becoming flatter, teamwork is more important, and the spirit of enterprise pervading the economy has resulted in an emphasis on profit centres and a trend towards decentralization and delegation of authority. Organizations are having to become leaner and fitter to survive.

Productivity

Genuine productivity, not productivity 'deals', has become a key issue. This is being seen not just as a matter of paying people more to work harder (which has not always been successful), but as a function of how the enterprise organizes itself to carry out its work and how it makes the best use of the skills and capacities of its employees.

Employment

Old skills and crafts are disappearing. New ones linked to information technology and other technological developments have emerged. The trend is towards flexibility and multi-skilling at all levels in the organization. More and more managers are becoming generalists rather than specialists.

Many companies have had to recognize that fluctuations in demand and the need to respond rapidly to external opportunities or threats have forced them to abandon the traditional concept of a permanent full-time work force. More out-workers are being used and this process is helped by the phenomenal growth in the ownership of personal computers and the development of electronic mailing systems. Job sharing, in the sense of two people splitting the work between them to do one job, has not taken root universally, but it does exist. Short-term contracts are becoming more common.

The number of white collar jobs is increasing and at the same time there has been a drive towards the harmonization of the terms and conditions of employment for blue and white collar staff.

Following legislation, equal pay for work of equal value is at last being recognized as a matter to which management must pay more attention. Progress towards full equal opportunities has been slower although the proportion of women in employment has been increasing.

Employee relations

There has been a shift towards employee relations concerning all staff away from industrial relations concerned only with trade union members. This reflects a preference for an individualistic (enterprise) ideology rather than a collectivist one.

Trade unions no longer walk in the corridors of power as they did in the 1970s and unsympathetic union legislation has tried, with some success, to restrict their impact although in early 1988 there were plenty of signs that militancy still exists, in spite of 'new realism' in some union quarters. But in the UK, union membership is in decline and young people are becoming less convinced of the value of trade unionism for them. 'Macho'-management techniques, however unpleasant they have been, have occasionally worked, as at Wapping. Plant rather than centralized bargaining is on the increase. Pendulum or so-called 'no strike' agreements are being made and more long-term settlements have been negotiated.

The Japanese system of single status organizations with one trade union (if any) and considerable emphasis on involvement and commitment has attracted a lot of attention. Any business starting in a green field site is likely to prefer this pattern of employee relations to the traditional divisive and confrontational approach.

Pay

The emphasis is now on performance-related pay. A more flexible approach to remuneration is being adopted. Rigid salary structures with fixed incremental scales, while not yet things of the past, are beginning to disappear. The need to design pay structures which fit the corporate culture and can operate flexibly in the face of rapid change has been recognized. The essentially static techniques of 'salary administration' are being replaced by the dynamic concept of 'reward management'.

The crisis in personnel management

The crisis in personnel management was the title of the first chapter in Shaun Tyson and Alan Fell's book *Evaluating the Personnel Function* published in 1986. They quoted the following comments to illustrate their point:

- Failure to understand the function has led to the appointment of amateurs, or failures, to a task which requires considerable analytical and personal skills.
- A practising personnel director has written that 'at present a kind of generalized inferiority complex pervades the personnel field'.
- In many companies, personnel departments face growing disenchantment, and a steady decline in their influence.
- Little agreement exists on what Human Resource Management is or what it should be.
- Personnel management has constantly to establish its credibility before being able to contribute.
- Personnel management in the UK has failed to generate, or be associated with, an overall set of social, political and economic objectives which are acceptable to the major economic decision makers.
- There has even been a questioning, in the light of cost-cutting exercises, of the very role of personnel management, particularly in the public sector.

This somewhat pessimistic view about personnel management is confirmed by the remarkable number of books on the personnel manager as distinct from personnel management that have been published in recent years. Personnel managers or personnel academics seem to spend more time contemplating their navels than members of any other profession. This is in spite of the fact that more and more personnel specialists are achieving board status.

The rise in human resource management

To the distress of some personnel managers, human resource management has emerged as a new concept for dealing with people in organizations. Essentially, human resource management, or HRM, takes a strategic view of the management of people as a major although sometimes intractable resource. It looks at employees mainly from the point of what they can do or can be encouraged to do, for the organization, as distinct from what the organization can or should do for them.

Personnel managers are distressed or suspicious about HRM either because it seems to usurp their traditional role or because it is over-concerned with organizational values rather than with the needs of the members of the organization. Personnel professionals are also cynical about HRM either as an American import or as 'old wine in new bottles'.

However, in spite of these reactions, HRM is becoming a force to be reckoned with, and rightly so, if it ensures that personnel managers become partners in the business rather than retaining a purely service role.

Part I
Personnel Management – An Overview

In this part, personnel management is considered as an integral part of the overall process of management for which all managers as well as personnel specialists are responsible. Personnel management processes are analysed from the point of view of the objectives, strategies, policies and activities needed to meet organizational requirements. Personnel management is then examined within the context of the environment in which it operates – the environment that, from a contingency point of view, will strongly influence the role and activities of the personnel function.

Finally, the concept of human resource management (HRM) will be examined. It will be emphasized that while HRM is not a fundamentally different approach to personnel management, it does provide a different perspective which emphasizes the need to think strategically about people as a key resource. HRM is presented as a broader and at the same time more unified approach to personnel management, not as its replacement.

Chapter 1
The Basis of Personnel Management

Definition of personnel management

Personnel management is concerned with:

- obtaining, developing and motivating the human resources required by the organization to achieve its objectives;
- developing an organization structure and climate and evolving a management style which will promote co-operation and commitment throughout the organization;
- making the best use of the skills and capacities of all those employed in the organization;
- ensuring that the organization meets its social and legal responsibilities towards its employees, with particular regard to the conditions of employment and quality of working life provided for them.

Aim of personnel management

The overall aim of personnel management is to make an effective contribution to the objectives of the organization and to the fulfilment of its social responsibilities.

The constituents of personnel management

What happens in personnel management is contingent or dependent on two major factors:

1. Organizational context – the type and size of the organization, its purpose, objectives and culture.
2. The external environment.

These influence the following constituents of personnel management which are dealt with in the four sections of this chapter.

9

- *Objectives* – what the organization aims to do about its human resources.
- *Strategies* – the longer term plans on how the organization intends to achieve its objectives.
- *Policies* – the guidelines, derived from the personnel objectives and associated with its strategies, on the approaches and methods the organization uses in conducting its human resource management programmes.
- *Activities* – the personnel programmes, practices and procedures carried out by the organization to implement its personnel strategies in line with agreed personnel policies.

Personnel objectives

Definition

Personnel objectives are the aims, goals and targets that have been set for the way in which an organization manages its human resources. They are developed within the framework of corporate objectives.

Corporate objectives

Corporate objectives in public sector or non-profit making organizations will be related to the implementation of political programmes, the provision of services, the achievement of the overall purpose of the organization and the achievement of cost-effectiveness in the management of operations and their administration.

In the private sector, corporate objectives are developed under four headings:

1. The purpose or mission of the company
According to Theodore Levitt,[1] there are four prime business purposes:

(a) To create and keep customers.
(b) To produce and deliver goods and services that people want and value at prices and under conditions that are reasonably attractive relative to those offered by others.
(c) To produce revenue in excess of costs in sufficient regularity to attract and hold investors in the enterprise.
(d) To keep at least abreast and sometimes ahead of competitive targets.

2. Economic or financial targets
Overall corporate economic or financial objectives may be set as one fundamental goal, for example: 'Increase the return on shareholders' capital (ROSC) by x per cent within the next five years'. From this basic

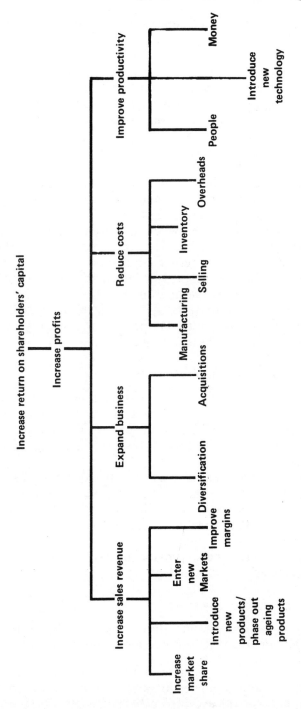

Figure 1.1 Hierarchy of corporate objectives

objective a hierarchy of subsidiary objectives may be derived as shown in Figure 1.1.

3. Ownership

Ownership objectives are set in terms of whether or not the company should remain private or go public, remain independent and resist strongly a takeover bid or merger proposal, or accept the logic of the right sort of merge.

4. What business are we in?

'What business are we in?' is Peter Drucker's[2] famous question. It leads to a definition of the markets and customers for which the company should be providing goods or services. It is answered by looking at the business from the point of view of the customer and then relating the particular strengths and weaknesses of the company to market opportunities. The internal and external appraisals carried out as part of the corporate planning process provide information which will help to define what the business should be at a future date. This definition will lead to strategies for product innovation, diversification, acquisition and expansion to increase market share. The personnel strategy of the organization will be integrated with these strategies.

The role of personnel objectives

The role of personnel objectives is to further the achievement of corporate objectives. But in formulating the latter, human resource considerations should exert a major influence – the organization cannot afford to get its programmes for human resource planning, management and development wrong.

Personnel objectives need to be formulated as a means of shaping corporate strategies in so far as they involve the utilization of human resources, on which, of course, effective organization entirely depends. Finance is required as well but this is obtained and used and generated by people.

Personnel objectives also provide the basis for the formulation of personnel strategies and policies.

Formulating personnel objectives

The formulation of personnel objectives is, or should be, an analytical process. The factors which should be considered are:

- *Corporate objectives* under the four headings mentioned earlier: purpose, targets, ownership and the business the company is in.
- *Core values* – the accepted beliefs on what is best or good for the organization and what should or ought to happen. They define

how management intends to conduct the business and to treat the people who work in it.

● *The nature of the business* – the type of work carried out, its technology and the sort of people it employs.

● *The climate of employee relationships* in the organization.

Hierarchy of personnel objectives

Personnel objectives and the means for achieving them will depend on their context. There are no universal objectives, just as there are no absolute principles governing personnel policies and practices. There are only certain basic headings and guidelines which provide a framework within which the organization does what it needs to do in the way which best suits itself.

Personnel objectives can be set out in the form of a hierarchy as in Figure 1.2. This states the overall and the main objectives concerned with organization, human resources, relationships and responsibility. Beneath each of these main objectives are listed possible sub-objectives. This is not a universally applicable list. It begs a number of questions: for example, what is an 'effective organization'? What is 'effective effort'? To what extent is it appropriate to pursue the objective of achieving a 'co-operative climate of relationships'?

Effectiveness has to be defined, and it may be necessary and even desirable to accept a degree of conflict in working through problems of relationships. A bland, and, on the surface, smooth-running organization is not necessarily an effective one in achieving the objectives of its owners, its management, its work-people and the unions.

A hierarchy such as the one illustrated in Figure 1.2 has its uses, however, as an indication of the main areas for concern in developing appropriate personnel strategies, policies and programmes.

Personnel strategies

What is strategy?

The historic origin of the concept of strategy lies in the military area, where it is a broad and rather vaguely described 'grand' concept of a campaign for the application of large-scale forces against an enemy. Strategy is contrasted to *tactics*, which are specific schemes for the employment of allocated resources.

The bridge in business usage was provided by von Neumann and Morganstern[3] in their theory of games. The theory provides a unifying viewpoint for all types of conflict situations regardless of whether their origin is in war, politics or business. As Igor Ansoff put it in his important book *Corporate Strategy*,

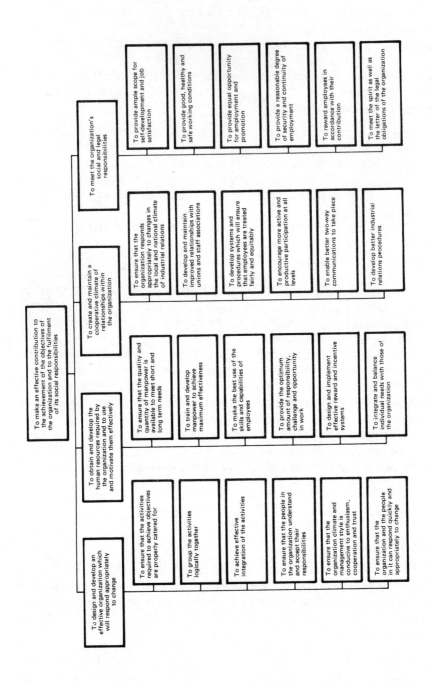

Figure 1.2 Hierarchy of personnel objectives

A *pure* strategy is a move or a series of moves by a firm, such as a product development programme in which successive products and markets are clearly delineated. A *grand* or *mixed* strategy is a statistical decision rule for deciding which particular pure strategy the firm should select in a particular situation.[4]

Business writers have used various definitions of strategy. Some borrow from game theory to define strategy as a set of specific programmes such as product-market entries.[5] Others have defined it in the military sense as the broad overall concept of the firm's business.[6]

The words *strategy* and *policy* are sometimes used loosely and have become almost interchangeable. Ansoff distinguishes between *policy* as a contingent decision made in accordance with defined decision rules to be applied in specified circumstances, and *strategy* as a *rule for making decisions* under conditions of partial ignorance, when alternatives cannot be arranged and examined in advance.

As usually defined, however, a business strategy is a broad statement of where in the longer term the business is going. A strategy is a statement of intent which provides the basis for the development and implementation of action plans and programmes. Business strategies in general and personnel strategies in particular are formulated as part of the corporate planning process.

Corporate planning

Definition
Corporate planning may be defined as the systematic analysis of internal strengths and weaknesses and of external opportunities and threats in order to formulate objectives and develop strategies and action plans to achieve them.

The need to plan
The discipline of corporate planning has evolved as a response to change. The major challenge to most organizations is change and the way they react to and manage change largely decides their future survival and growth. The extreme attitudes that can be adopted to change are:

(a) make a serious effort to look ahead as far as possible so that change can be anticipated and exploited, when it provides an opportunity, or dealt with, when it constitutes a threat;

(b) make little or no attempt to look ahead further than the more or less obligatory short-term budgeting period, and to rely on opportunism and flexibility to enable rapid adjustments to be made to change when it occurs.

There are, of course, organizations which have followed the second course and thrived, but these are the exceptions which operate in volatile conditions and can attract and retain the type of management and staff who can cope with these conditions. In other organizations, the rapidity of change and the shorter time available to deal with new situations has forced them to plan ahead further and more systematically than in the past.

Not that this is easy in times of economic uncertainty. Winston Churchill summed up the problem precisely when he said: 'It is wise to plan ahead but difficult to look farther than you can see.' In present circumstances, it may not be possible to produce corporate plans with time spans as long and maybe as unrealistic as they were in the heady days when corporate planning first became fashionable. However, the basic validity of the process is not challenged if it is seen as a systematic attempt to assess all the factors governing the future of the organization. Further analysis can relate these factors together as a framework for action and a reference point which can be used as a help in shaping alternative plans, if circumstances change, which they inevitably will.

Aims of corporate planning
The aims of corporate planning are to:

1. Define and plan the long-term future of the company as a whole.
2. Increase the rate of growth of the enterprise in the long run.
3. Ensure that the organization can meet the challenge of change and can profit from new opportunities.

The process of corporate planning
Corporate planning consists of the following stages:

1. *Setting objectives* which define what the company is and what it is setting out to do, in terms of growth in sales revenue and profit and in return on capital employed.
2. *Preparing* long-range forecasts based upon present strategies. These will identify any gaps between the objectives and targets as set out in stage 1 and indicate the extent to which new or revised strategies are required.
3. *Defining broad strategies* to achieve objectives, bearing in mind any gaps revealed by the analysis at stage 2.
4. *Creating* financial, marketing, capital investment, acquisition, diversification, product development and human resource plans to implement strategies.
5. *Monitoring results* against the plans and amending strategies or taking corrective action as necessary.

The first three stages – objectives, forecasts and strategies – are carried out in the light of a SWOT analysis which conducts:

(a) internal appraisals of the strengths and weaknesses of the company;
(b) external appraisals of the opportunities and threats facing the company now and in the longer term.

These processes are illustrated in Figure 1.3 and provide the framework within which personnel or human resource strategies are prepared.

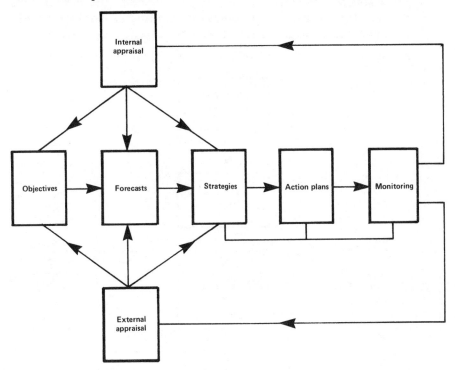

Figure 1.3 The process of corporate planning

Why have personnel strategies?

An organization is essentially a social unit, operating within a given but changing environment, which seeks to direct the energies of people it employs to achieve its objectives of survival and growth. As a social unit, an enterprise depends upon the abilities and efforts of those who work in it. The attainment of the overall objectives of an organization is therefore dependent upon the achievement of its personnel objectives. In consequence, personnel strategies have to be prepared as an integral part of the total corporate planning process as described above. They cannot stand in isolation, and to fulfil this role effectively they must be defined.

Personnel strategy areas

Personnel strategies can be divided into three main areas:

1. *Human resource management strategy* which is concerned with the acquisition, motivation and development of the human resources required by the organization.

2. *Organization development strategy* which is concerned with developing an effective and healthy organization.
3. *Employee relations strategy* which is concerned with relationships between the company and bodies representing its employees and with participation, involvement and communication systems.

The inter-relationships between these strategy areas are shown in Figure 1.4.

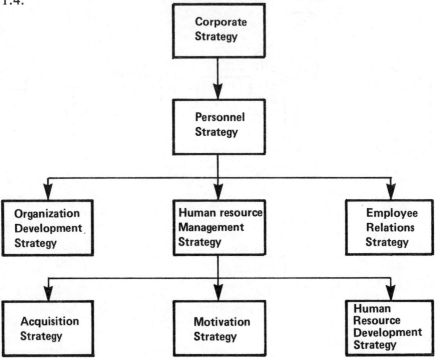

Figure 1.4 Personnel strategy areas

Human resource management strategies

The human resource management strategy answers three fundamental questions which should be posed during the preparation of the corporate plan:

1. How are we going to acquire and retain the number and quality of people required to meet the forecast needs of the organization for human resources?
2. How are we going to ensure that we have a well motivated and fully committed work force?
3. What actions will be needed to train, develop and fit people for greater responsibility and to respond to change and the creation of demands for different skills and abilities?

Acquisition and retention strategies
The starting point in the development of a personnel strategy is usually the identification of the long term human resource requirements of the organization. These have to be assessed in general terms to provide the basis for the more detailed human resource planning processes described in Chapter 13. The aim of the acquisition and retention strategies should be to ensure that on the one hand the achievement of corporate objectives will not be inhibited by human resource shortages or inefficiencies, while on the other hand, impending surpluses can be dealt with in good time with the minimum individual hardship and disruption to employee relations.

At this stage only broad questions need to be answered concerning:

1. Human resource requirements –
   (a) how many employees are needed?
   (b) what kind of abilities and skills will be required?
2. Availability –
   (a) what is available now inside the company?
   (b) what can be made available from inside and outside the company?
3. Retention –
   (a) what is the company's experience in retaining staff?
   (b) what are the problems and how can they be overcome?
4. Human resources utilization –
   (a) how well are human resources used in the company?
   (b) what is the scope for increasing productivity?

Motivation strategy
Motivation strategies should aim to increase the effective contribution of the members of the organization to the achievement of its objectives. In Likert's words, the task is to produce

'attitudes of identification with the organization and its objectives and a high sense of involvement in achieving them by harnessing effectively all the major motivational forces which can exercise significant influence in an organizational setting and which, potentially, can be accompanied by co-operative and favourable attitudes'.[7]

Motivation strategy is concerned with the reward management system, and in particular the type and scale of financial incentives that are to be provided. But it will also be concerned with other methods which should yield favourable attitudes. These will include job design, participation, objective setting, career development, and any other activities which relate to the individual's need to achieve and maintain a sense of personal worth and importance. Motivation is also affected by the quality of leadership in an organization, and the selection, training and development of effective leaders should be part of the strategy.

A strategy also needs to be developed to increase commitment. As Geoff White[8] points out, commitment is a wider concept than motivation or job satisfaction. It is both voluntary and personal. It cannot be imposed. To develop commitment, the strategy has to embrace all aspects of the ways in which employees are treated including not only motivation, but also leadership, job design, communications, training, participation and involvement. The strategy for commitment therefore links together other key human resources strategies, especially those concerned with organization development, employee relations, communications and the reward system. Approaches to improving commitment are discussed in more detail in Chapter 8.

Human resource development strategies
The human resource development strategy is concerned with the longer term programmes that the organization needs to improve operational performance at all levels in accordance with the additional demands that will be placed on people in the future. The strategy will cater for continuous development programmes which will be linked closely with the programmes designed for the organization as a whole to implement its product, technological and market development strategies.

Organization development strategies

The aim of the organization development strategy of an enterprise should be to ensure that an effective organization is maintained which will respond appropriately to changes in its internal and external environment and will make the best use of the individual and collective capacities of its members.

As defined by Sadler and Barry, organizational development is a

'never-ending process of continually redefining people's roles, their relationships with each other, and their organizational groupings in an attempt to keep pace with the changing nature of the task, changes in the external environment and the changing needs of the people themselves'.[9]

The principles and practice of organization development are discussed in Chapter 12, and at this stage it is only necessary to summarize the main strategic areas in which organization development takes place. These are:

● To analyse the implications of change and decide what actions are required to ensure that the organization will continue to function effectively when subjected to pressures resulting from change. The strategies will include changes in organization structure as well as culture management programmes and changes in organization climate and management style.
● To take steps to ensure that proper integration takes place of the increasingly diversified activities that are likely to result from change.

- To work with teams on team development.
- To manage conflict.
- To work in planning and objective-setting processes for individuals and teams.

Employee relations strategies

The aim of the employee relations strategy of an enterprise is to develop policies, systems and procedures which maximize the degree to which management and employees will co-operate to their mutual benefit, and minimize the causes and effects of unnecessary conflict or restrictive practices.

The employee relations strategies will be concerned with improving relationships and establishing and maintaining the rules and procedures which govern the management and discussions of issues affecting the company and its employees. It will encompass strategies for union recognition or, possibly, de-recognition, and for any collective bargaining arrangements. It will also cover the strategies for negotiations and for involving employees in the affairs of the company and for communicating to them information about its performance and future.

Evaluating strategies

Personnel strategies have to be evolved and balanced within the context of the constraints imposed by limited financial or manpower resources or by external economic and market pressures. Priorities have to be established for the allocation of resources before work can be programmed, and these must be related to an estimate of the contribution alternative strategies will make to achieving personnel objectives. For example, if it is thought that the main objective is to improve the quality and efficiency of human resources, then priority will have to be given to human resource planning programmes which aim to develop new sources for obtaining staff, or to improve the utilization of existing staff. At this stage, cost-benefit considerations are important and the fundamental question to be answered is: 'what is the benefit of this strategy in terms of, say, increased productivity, compared with the cost of implementing it?'

It is, however, notoriously difficult to produce realistic cost-benefit calculations on personnel matters. This applies even to training, where it might be thought that it should not be too hard to relate the cost of inputs in the shape of training programmes to the value of outputs in the shape of improved productivity. Because it may be difficult to distinguish the contribution of other inputs on the effect of external circumstances, it may be necessary to evaluate training in terms of intermediate objectives to which no financial value can be attached. Precise evaluation is therefore difficult, if not impossible. But some attempt should be made to relate the cost of the inputs implied by the strategies to the likely outputs, even if the latter cannot always be quantified. In its simplest terms this might be expressed as follows:

1. Forecast changes in technology indicate that we shall need x additional science graduates by 19... .
2. To meet this requirement, the steps that should be taken are (a), (b), (c), etc.
3. The resources required for this programme are y at a cost of £z.

Other programmes may have to be justified in somewhat more general terms, for example:

1. In department x efficiency is reduced to the extent of y because of low productivity and high staff turnover.
2. An important contributory cause to this situation is the method of working in the department which involves a high degree of specialization; and, consequently, a lack of flexibility.
3. A restructuring programme which includes re-designing a number of jobs in the department is required and the introduction of a large measure of multi-skilling; this programme would consist of stages (a), (b), (c), etc.
4. The cost of the programmes will be £z and the results should be an increase in productivity and reduction in staff turnover. The target is to increase productivity of x% and reduce staff turnover by y%.

Some programmes will have to be justified in even more abstract language. But this does not matter too much. The important thing to do is to subject the strategic planning process to the discipline of identifying problems, threats and opportunities in the light of an analysis of internal and external constraints, and then relating possible courses of action to agreed objectives and estimating, so far as this is possible, the costs and consequences of these actions.

Personnel policies

What are personnel policies?

Personnel policies are continuing guidelines on the approach the organization intends to adopt in managing its human resources. They define the philosophies and values of the organization on how people should be treated and from these are derived the principles upon which managers are expected to act when dealing with personnel matters. Personnel policies therefore serve as reference points when human resource management programmes are being developed and when decisions are being made about people. They help to define 'how things are done around here'.

Relationships of personnel policies to personnel objectives, strategies and procedures

Personnel policies should be distinguished from objectives, strategies and procedures. In essence:

- *personnel objectives* define ends;
- *personnel strategies* lay down the direction to be followed in achieving ends;
- *personnel policies* control the means of achieving ends;
- *personnel procedures* implement the policies.

Objectives lead both to strategies and policies, but guidelines on how these strategies should be achieved are needed in the shape of personnel policies. In turn, agreed policies are extended into personnel procedures which enable them to be implemented. The interconnections between objectives, strategies, policies and procedures are shown in Figure 1.5.

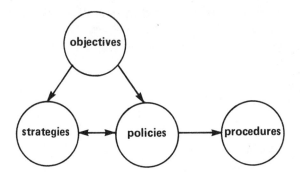

Figure 1.5 Interconnections between personnel objectives, strategies, policies and procedures

Why have personnel policies?

It is necessary to develop a coherent approach to managing people which binds together the various personnel strategies of the organization. This is the main function of personnel policies, or employment policies, as they are sometimes described.

Company personnel or employment policies are frameworks within which actions take place. They promote consistency and equity in the way in which people are treated. Because they provide guidance on what managers should do in particular circumstances they facilitate decentralization and delegation. And, while they should fit the corporate culture, they can also help to shape it.

Do policies need to be formalized?

All organizations have personnel policies. Some, however, exist implicitly as a philosophy of management and an attitude to employees that is expressed in the way in which personnel issues are handled; for example, the introduction of new technology. The advantage of explicit policies in terms of consistency and understanding may appear to be obvious, but there are disadvantages: written policies can be inflexible, platitudinous or both. To a degree, policies have often to be expressed in abstract terms and managers do not care for abstractions. But they do prefer to know where they stand – people like structure – and formalized personnel policies can provide the guidelines they need.

Formalized personnel policies can be used as the basis for induction, supervisory and management training which help those undergoing it to understand the philosophies and values of the company and how they are expected to behave within that context.

Personnel policy areas

Personnel policies can be expressed as overall statements of the philosophy of the organization and of its values. The specific policy areas, which may be contained in the overall statement or issued as separate documents, are:

(a) employment
(b) equal opportunity
(c) pay
(d) development and training
(e) participation
(f) employee relations
(g) new technology
(h) health and safety.

The main points that could be covered in each of these policies are summarized below. Examples of company policy statements are given in Appendix A.

Overall policy

The overall policy defines how the organization fulfils its social responsibilities for its employees and sets out its attitudes towards them. It is an expression of its values or beliefs about how people should be treated. In *In Search of Excellence*, Tom Peters and Robert Waterman wrote that if they were asked for one all-purpose bit of advice for management, one truth that they could distill from all their research on what makes a company excellent, it would be to: 'Figure out your value system. Decide what the company *stands* for.'[10] In *Leadership and Administration*, Philip Selznick emphasized the key role of values in organizations, when he wrote: 'The formation of an institution is marked by the making of value commitments, that is, choices which fix the assumptions of policy makers as to the nature of the enterprise, its distinctive aims, methods and roles.'[11]

The values expressed in an overall statement of personnel policies may explicitly or implicitly refer to the following concepts:

1. *Equity* – treating employees fairly and justly by adopting an 'even-handed' approach. This includes protecting individuals from any unfair decisions made by their superiors, providing equal opportunities for employment and promotion and operating an equitable payment system.
2. *Consideration* – taking account of individual circumstances when making decisions which affect the prospects, security or self-respect of employees.
3. *Quality of working life* – consciously and continually aiming to improve the quality of working life as a means of increasing motivation and improving results. This involves increasing the sense of satisfaction people obtain from their work by, so far as possible, reducing monotony, increasing variety and responsibility and avoiding placing people under too much stress.
4. *Working conditions* – providing healthy, safe and, so far as practicable, pleasant working conditions.

It may be difficult to express these policies in anything but generalized terms and, although ideals of social justice and welfare are important, it should be remembered that, as Sadler and Barry expressed it: 'Organizations in general and business enterprises in particular, are established to achieve specific sets of objectives and not to satisfy the needs of their members.'[9]

Increasingly, however, organizations are having to recognize that they are subject to external as well as internal pressures which act as constraints on the extent to which they can disregard the higher standards of behaviour that are expected of employers.

Employment policies

Employment policies cover the following areas:

1. *Human resource planning* – a commitment by the company to planning ahead in order to maximize the opportunities for employees to develop their careers within the organization and to minimize the possibility of compulsory redundancy.
2. *Quality of employees* – an organization may deliberately set out in its policy statement that, as a company which is dedicated to the pursuit of excellence and professionalism in all it does, it believes in recruiting people who have the ability or potential to meet the high standards of performance that will be expected of them.
3. *Promotion* – the policy would state the company's wish to promote from within wherever this is appropriate as a means of satisfying its requirements for high quality staff. The policy

would, however, recognize that there will be occasions when the organization's present and future needs can only be met by recruitment from outside. The point could be made that a vigorous organization needs infusions of fresh blood from time to time if it is not to stagnate. In addition, the policy might state that employees will be encouraged to apply for internally advertised jobs and will not be held back from promotion by their managers, however reluctant the latter may be to lose them.

4. *Equal opportunity* – the importance of this subject is so great that a separate policy is justified. But a reference could still be made in the general employment policy statement to the fact that 'this is an equal opportunity company'.

5. *Redundancy* – the redundancy policy could state that it is the company's intention to use its best endeavours to avoid involuntary redundancy through its human resource re-deployment and re-training procedures. A statement could also be made to the effect that if redundancy is absolutely unavoidable those affected will be given fair and equitable treatment, the maximum amount of warning, and every help that can be provided by the company to obtain suitable alternative work.

6. *Discipline* – the disciplinary policy should state that employees have the right to know what is expected of them and what could happen if they infringe the company's rules. It would also make the point that, in handling disciplinary cases, the company will treat employees in accordance with the principles of natural justice.

7. *Grievances* – the policy should state that employees have the right to raise their grievances with their manager, to be accompanied by a representative if they so wish and to appeal to a higher level if they feel that their grievance has not been resolved satisfactorily.

Equal opportunity policy

The equal opportunity policy should spell out the company's determination to give equal opportunities to all, irrespective of sex, race, creed or marital status. It could also state that the company will use its best endeavours to provide equal opportunities to disabled people.

Pay policy

The pay policy could cover such matters as:

(a) paying market rates
(b) paying for performance
(c) gain-sharing – sharing in the gains (added value) or profits of the company
(d) providing an equitable pay system

(e) equal pay for work of equal value, subject to over-riding market considerations.

Development and training policy

The development and training policy should express the company's commitment to the continuous development of the skills and abilities of employees in order to maximize their contribution and to give them the opportunity to advance their careers.

Involvement and participation policy

The involvement and participation policy should spell out the company's belief in involvement and participation as a means of generating the commitment of all employees to the success of the enterprise. This policy could also refer to the basis upon which the company intends to communicate information to employees.

Employee relations policy

The employee relations policy will set out the company's approach to the rights of employees to represent their interests to management through trade unions, staff associations or some other form of representative system.

New technology policy

A new technology policy could be incorporated in the employment policy, but in most organizations these days the introduction of new technology is so significant that it justifies a separate policy statement. Such a statement would refer to consultation about the introduction of new technology and to the steps that would be taken by the company to minimize the risk of compulsory redundancy.

Health and safety policy

Health and safety policies cover how the company intends to provide healthy and safe places and systems of work.

Formulating policies

Personnel policies are based on the values held in the company about how its human resources should be treated. These shared values act as an informal control system that tells people what is expected of them. They need, however, to be expressed in the form of personnel policies which provide more explicit guidance to the approach required in specific areas of human resource management.

The core values are a function of the corporate culture and it is therefore the culture that will ultimately determine the scope of personnel policies.

All corporate values are different. They are contingent on the culture and they have to match it. An example of a statement of core values is given in Appendix B.

The following steps should be taken when formulating or revising personnel policies:

1. *Gain understanding of the corporate culture and its shared values.* This is an analytical process and is discussed in Chapter 5.
2. *Analyse existing policies – written and unwritten.* Personnel policies will exist in any organization, even if they are implicit rather than expressed formally.
3. *Analyse external influences.* Company personnel policies are subjected to the influence of employment legislatures and the official codes of practice issued by such bodies in Great Britain, as ACAS (The Advisory, Conciliation and Arbitration Service). The codes of practice issued by the professional institutions, especially the Institute of Personnel Management, should also be consulted.
4. *Seek manager's views.* Check with managers, preferably starting at the top, on their views about personnel policies. This goes hand-in-hand with the analysis of corporate culture and values.
5. *Seek the views of employees.* Conduct an attitude survey to obtain the views of employees about the company's existing personnel policies.
6. *Seek the views of union representatives.* Find out from unions or staff representatives what they think about policies.
7. *Prepare draft policies.* Analyse the information obtained in the first six steps and prepare draft policies.
8. *Consult.* Discuss and agree policies with management and union representatives.

Personnel activities

Fundamental activities

Organizations can survive and thrive only if they obtain, retain and develop the quantity and quality of human resources they need. The fundamental activities of personnel management are therefore to plan and implement programmes to achieve objectives in those areas. The programmes constitute the basic personnel strategy and Figure 1.6 is a model of the process.

The total process

The fundamental activities of planning and implementing programmes for obtaining, retaining and motivating and developing people are linked to three other activity areas:

1. *Organizing* – the design of structures and jobs.

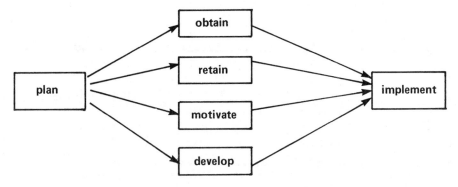

Figure 1.6 Personnel activities – basic model

2. *Managing* – performance, productivity and employee relationships.
3. *Administrating* – the personnel services concerned with recruitment, pay and benefits, health and safety and welfare. The process is illustrated in Figure 1.7.

Activity areas

The total process of personnel management as described in Figure 1.7 can be analysed into the following specific activity areas:

Organization

- *Organization design* – developing an organization structure which caters for all the activities required and groups them together in a way which encourages integration and co-operation and provides for effective communication and decision-making.
- *Job design* – deciding on the content of a job: its duties and responsibilities and the relationships that exist between the job holder and his or her superior, subordinates and colleagues.
- *Organization development* – planning and implementing programmes designed to improve the effectiveness with which an organization functions and responds to change.

Employee resourcing

- *Forecasting human resource requirements* – making plans to achieve forecasts, taking steps to improve productivity.
- *Recruitment and selection* – obtaining the number and type of people the organization needs.

Employment

- *Employment practices and procedures* – conditions of service, deploying and redeploying people, dealing with grievances and

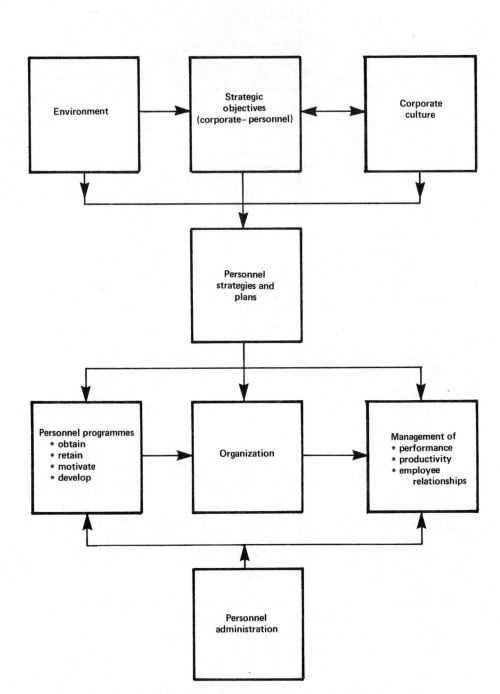

Figure 1.7 The process of personnel management

problems such as discipline and redundancy, ensuring that employment legislation and personnel policies in such areas as equal opportunity are implemented.

- *Health and safety* – administering health and safety programmes.
- *Welfare* – providing welfare services and helping with personnel problems.
- *Information systems* – personnel records and computerized personnel information systems.

Human resource development

- *Performance management* – assessing and improving performance.
- *Training* – systematically developing the knowledge and skills required to perform adequately a given job or task.
- *Management development* – ensuring that the organization has the effective managers it requires to meet its present and future needs.
- *Career management* – planning the careers of people with potential.

Reward management

- *Job evaluation* – establishing the relative value of jobs in a pay structure.
- *Pay* – developing and administering pay structures and systems.
- *Paying for performance* – relating rewards to effort and results.
- *Employee benefits* – pensions, sick pay, etc.

Employee relations

- *Industrial relations* – co-operating and negotiating with trade unions and staff associations.
- *Participation* – jointly involving management and employees in making decisions on matters of mutual interest.
- *Communications* – creating and transmitting information of interest to employees.

Relationships between activities and objectives

The considerable degree of interdependence between those activities is illustrated in Figure 1.8 and the contribution personnel activities make to achieving personnel objectives is shown in Figure 1.9.

Personnel management – theory and practice

In this chapter a theoretical model of personnel management has been presented. This is useful as a framework for analysing the role of the

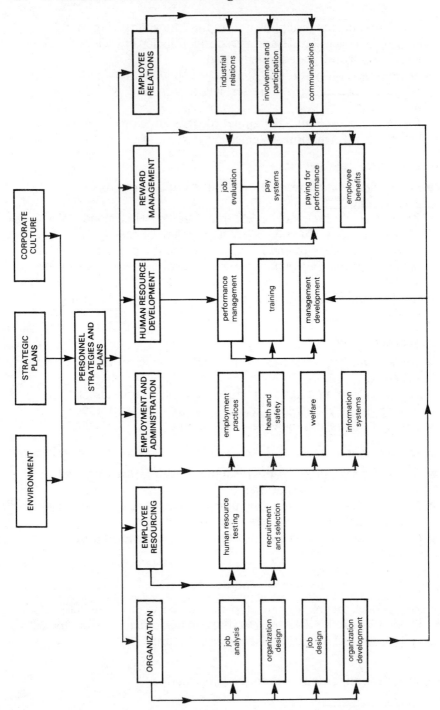

Figure 1.8 Personnel activities – interrelationships

Category	Activity	Organizations	Human resources	Relationships	Responsibilities
Employee relations	Communications	●		●	
	Involvement & participation	●		●	
	Industrial relations			●	
Reward management	Employee benefits				●
	Paying for performance		●		
	Pay systems		●		●
	Job evaluation		●		
Human resource development	Management development		●		
	Training	●	●	●	
	Performance management		●		
Employment and administration	Information systems		●		●
	Welfare				●
	Health and safety				●
	Employment practices		●		●
Employee resourcing	Recruitment and selection		●		
Human resource planning	Productivity plan		●		
	Retention plan		●		
	Acquisition plan		●		
	Supply forecasting		●		
	Demand forecasting		●		
Organization	Organization development	●		●	
	Job design	●			
	Organization design	●			
	Job analysis	●	●		
		Organizations — To design and develop an effective organization which will respond appropriately to change	**Human resources** — To obtain, retain and develop the human resources needed by the organization and to use and motivate them effectively.	**Relationships** — To maintain a corporate culture which creates a co-operative climate of relationships within the organization.	**Responsibilities** — To meet the organization's legal and social responsibilities

Figure 1.9 How personnel activities contribute to the achievement of personnel objectives

personnel functions and the personnel techniques and procedures that can be used. It does not, however, correspond with reality, which is, of course, infinite in its variety and cannot be slotted conveniently into the ready-made compartments provided by the model.

Personnel management in practice needs to be explained by answering two questions:

1. What do personnel managers actually do and how do they do it?
2. What is the context within which personnel managers operate and how does this affect their role?

These questions are answered in the next two chapters.

References

1. Levitt, Theodore *The Marketing Imagination*. The Free Press, New York, 1983.
2. Drucker, Peter *The Practice of Management*. Heinemann, London, 1955.
3. von Neumann, J and Morganstern, O *Theory of Games and Economic Behaviour*. Princeton University Press, Princeton, 1953.
4. Ansoff, H Igor *Corporate Strategy*. McGraw-Hill, New York, 1965.
5. Gilmore, E F and Brandenburg, R G 'Anatomy of Corporate Planning', *Harvard Business Review*, November-December, 1962.
6. Chandler, A D *Strategy and Structure*. The MIT Press, Cambridge, Mass., 1962.
7. Likert, R *New Patterns of Management*. McGraw-Hill, New York, 1969.
8. White, Geoff *Employee Commitment*. Advisory, Conciliation and Arbitration Service, Work Research Unit Occasional Paper 38, October, 1987.
9. Sadler, P J and Barry, B A *Organizational Development*. Longman, London, 1970.
10. Peters, T J and Waterman, R H *In Search of Excellence*. Harper & Row, New York, 1987.
11. Selznick, Philip *Leadership and Administration*. Row, Evanston, 1957.

Chapter 2
Role of the
Personnel Function

Overall role

The role of the personnel function should be to provide advice, services and functional guidance which will enable management to deal effectively with all matters concerning the employment of people and the relationships between the management of the organization and the people it employs.

The overall aim of the personnel function should be to make an effective contribution to the achievement of the objectives of the organization and to the fulfilment of its social and legal responsibilities. The particular aim should be to ensure that the personnel objectives of the organization are achieved, and the performance of the personnel function should be judged on the extent to which these objectives are met and on the efficiency with which advice, services and guidance are provided.

The personnel function is not the conscience of management. To state the reverse would be to adopt the arrogant posture that only personnel managers have a social conscience. But personnel managers are involved in the procurement, deployment and motivation of human resources on a full-time basis. Line managers may be equally concerned, but have other considerations to think about. It is the duty of personnel managers to alert line managers (line managers in this context include the managers of other functional departments as well as operational managers) to the human implications of what is happening to the organization and of what they are doing. They do this, not because they are inherently more aware of the implications, but because it is their job to use their time and analytical skills to consider all aspects of the utilization of human resources, while it is the job of line managers to be concerned about their own function as well as the people in it.

It must be emphasized, however, that all managers are concerned about human resources, not just personnel managers. The role of the personnel department is to help management to do this part of their job better and to provide services which it is more economical to group together under a functional head, where expertise is required which is unlikely to be shared equally amongst line managers.

In this chapter, attention is first given to the advisory, service and guidance aspects of the personnel function as a whole. The particular role of the personnel manager or specialist within the function is then examined, consideration being given to the extent to which personnel management can be described as a profession. The knotty problem of how to evaluate the effectiveness of the personnel function in carrying out its role is then discussed. Finally, a brief mention is made of organizational factors.

This chapter aims to outline the essence of what personnel departments and managers do. But how they operate will depend upon the organizational context, and this will be dealt with in Chapter 7.

Advisory role

The personnel function advises on personnel policies, procedures and methods and on the approach that should be adopted to deal with personnel and industrial relations problems.

Advice on policy

Advice is given in the following policy areas:

- *Social responsibility* – the philosophy of the organization towards the people it employs, covering such areas as equity, consideration of individual needs and fears, the quality of working life.
- *Employment* – the level of personnel the company wishes to employ, the provision of equal opportunity and reasonable security.
- *Pay* – the level of pay and other benefits for employees and the extent to which pay systems are negotiated and disclosed.
- *Promotion* – the attitude of the company to providing long term career prospects and to promoting from within the organization.
- *Training* – the scope of training schemes and the extent to which the company proposes to subsidize education and training.
- *Industrial relations* – policies on union recognition, closed shops, the role of shop stewards and the approach to dealing with grievances, discipline and redundancy.

These are all policies which should be decided at the highest level by top management. They are not determined by the head of the personnel function but it is his job to persuade the chief executive and his colleagues to give proper thought to these matters and to formulate draft policies for their consideration.

To do this job effectively, the personnel function has to carry out research and keep in touch with current developments in legislation, social thought, the behavioural sciences and the views of the trade unions. It must be aware of what is happening in the outside world, but it must be equally capable of relating environmental changes to the situation within the organization. As much as anything, the personnel function should be concerned with advising on the policies required to manage change as it affects the people in the organization and the way in which they work together. The personnel function has therefore to keep closely in touch with trends within the company, measuring its employees' level of morale, motivation, commitment and general satisfaction with the company as employers. This requires the maintenance and analysis of records and statistics on labour turnover, absenteeism, sickness, accidents, disciplinary problems, disputes, grievances and productivity. Judicious use should be made of these statistics to persuade management that a change in policy is required.

Advice on procedures and systems

The advice on procedures and systems should cover all those aspects of personnel administration with which top management and line management will be directly concerned. The personnel function develops procedures and systems for the approval and use of line management in the following areas:

- *Human resource planning* – the preparation of manpower budgets; forecasting future deficits and surpluses, specifying requirements; recording and analysing information on labour turnover, absenteeism and movements between different levels and parts of the organization.
- *Recruitment* – requisitioning; the preparation of job specifications; advertising; interviewing; selection; fixing terms and conditions of employment.
- *Employment* – induction arrangements; fixing hours of work and shift and night duties; overtime arrangements; recording working hours; leave of absence; holiday arrangements and pay; flexi-time arrangements; promotion, transfer and redundancy procedures; fulfilling employment legislation requirements.
- *Training* – selecting personnel for courses; administrative arrangements on courses; following-up training; recording training carried out and the costs of training.
- *Performance appraisal* – appraisal forms; reporting arrangements; counselling methods.
- *Wages and payment by result systems* – fixing and altering wage rates and premium or other special payments; job evaluation; fixing and amending bonus or piece rates; payment of day rate; average earnings or lieu rates in particular circumstances (eg on transfer, new work, waiting time, special duties, or when a piece rate is in dispute).
- *Salary administration* – fixing salary levels on appointment,

transfer or promotion; job evaluation; reviewing salaries; salary budgets.

● *Employee benefits* – arrangements for sick pay, pensions and other fringe benefits.

● *Industrial relations* – procedural agreements, including negotiating rights, closed shop arrangements, bargaining units, election of shop stewards and their rights, disputes procedure, disciplinary procedure, arrangements with regard to the *status quo.*

● *Joint consultation* – terms of reference; election arrangements; preparation of agenda and publication of minutes.

● *Communications* – briefing employees; using media.

● *Health and safety* – safety rules and regulations; arrangements for reporting incidents; inspection procedures.

● *Welfare* – arrangements for counselling and sick visiting.

The procedural aspects of personnel management, however, have to be treated with caution. One of the most dangerous traps a personnel manager can fall into is that of developing a massive bureaucratic machine which is resented by line management and ultimately defeats its own purpose by being ignored or by-passed. Personnel managers, like other managers in staff or service functions, are always liable to the accusation of empire-building. And too often this accusation is justified. At one time personnel managers who had not gained the respect of line managers could be dismissed as 'do-gooders'. It is even worse to be dismissed as 'bureaucratic do-gooders', and worst of all is the fate of being regarded as 'theoretical bureaucratic do-gooders'. Perhaps no one could fall into all three traps at once, but some personnel people seem to move in this direction by exhibiting a tendency to leap on to the latest personnel or behavioural science bandwagon without properly evaluating its practical use as seen through the eyes of line management. Drucker commented on this characteristic of personnel managers as long ago as 1955 when he wrote:

> The constant worry of all personnel administrators is their ability to prove that they are making a contribution to the enterprise. Their preoccupation is with the search for a 'gimmick' that will impress their management associates. Their persistent complaint is that they lack status.[1]

Unfortunately, this comment is just about as true today as it was then.

Service role

The personnel function provides services to line management, especially in the fields of employment, recruitment, training, salary administration, employee relations, health and safety and the management of personnel information systems. These services are provided for one or more of the following reasons:

- members of the personnel department have particular skills;
- line managers need to be relieved of some aspects of personnel administration;
- it is more convenient and, possibly, economical to have a centralized function providing common services for a number of other departments.

Functional guidance role

The functional guidance role of the personnel department is to interpret and help to communicate personnel policies and procedures approved by top management, and, on behalf of top management, to provide guidance to managers which will ensure that the policies and procedures are implemented and maintained.

This is perhaps the most difficult and delicate of all the roles that the personnel function carries out. It is not there to usurp or to interfere unduly with the legitimate authority of line management. But it is perfectly proper for top management to delegate some of its control duties to functional departments. The finance function controls budgets, the commercial function controls the wording of legal contracts and, in the same sense, the personnel function controls the implementation of personnel policies and procedures in order to ensure that they are consistently applied throughout the organization.

The word 'control' should really be in inverted commas. It is exercised in a very special sense. What, in effect, the personnel manager says is that 'this is the personnel policy of the company, ignore it at your peril'. He can seldom forbid anyone to do anything, except where it contravenes the law or a negotiated procedure, but he can refuse to authorize something – say a pay increase – if it is in his power to do so. And he can refer a matter to higher authority (the joint superior of the two managers concerned) and request that the action be delayed until a ruling has been made.

The principal matters upon which the personnel function might exercise control include:

- the application of contractual conditions of employment;
- alterations to rates of pay and pay structures;
- the implementation of agreed procedures; negotiating; grievance, discipline, redundancy, promotion and transfer;
- expenditure on recruitment and training;
- the quality and style of recruitment advertisements;
- the fulfilment of legal requirements concerning employment, health and safety.

In some companies the personnel department also exercises control over staff establishments. This is appropriate as long as the control is limited to ensuring that increases in establishment or replacements have been properly authorized, but it is not the job of personnel to fix establishment levels.

Research on the role of the personnel function

Although the existence of a wide variety of factors influencing the role of personnel managers make any generalizations about their work suspect, it is possible to obtain some insight into the range and diversity of activities carried out by reference to three research projects that have been undertaken recently, the results of which are summarized below.

The Role and Effectiveness of Personnel Managers – Guest and Horwood, 1980[2]

Guest and Horwood compared a manufacturing company and a health service organization by checking 85 separate tasks under the following 12 activity classifications:

1. Direction and policy determination.
2. Planning and research.
3. Industrial relations and collective bargaining.
4. Pay and benefit determination.
5. Payment administration.
6. Organization design and/or development.
7. Manpower planning and/or control.
8. Personnel information and records.
9. Employee development and training.
10. Recruitment and selection.
11. Employee communications.
12. Health, safety and welfare.

The most common tasks performed in both organizations were:

1. Managing subordinate personnel staff.
2. Providing advice to line managers on law.
3. Processing job applications.
4. Interviewing candidates.
5. Taking part in selection decisions.
6. Making offers of employment.

In both organizations personnel managers were primarily attending to industrial relations tasks, while their subordinates were more concerned with recruitment and selection. The personnel managers, however, were generalists covering many different activities. But while there were some similarities between the two organizations, there were also many differences. Job titles and job descriptions varied considerably. In the public sector organization personnel specialists were more involved in policy-making and planning than in the private sector company, where they concentrated mainly on advisory, executive and administrative activities.

The Changing Nature of Personnel Management – Mackay and Torrington, 1986[3]

The research carried out by Mackay and Torrington in 1984 and 1985 into what personnel managers do in 350 organizations revealed a highly variable pattern of the areas in which personnel specialists exercised most discretion, the proportion of the personnel managers in the sample who spent time in the areas and the amount of time they spent on each of them. The results of this survey are summarized in Table 2.1. As might be expected, recruitment and selection, employee relations and training are the three most important areas.

Areas of responsibility*	% of personnel managers who spent time in each area	% of personnel managers who spent 20% or more of their time in each area
1 Recruitment & selection	89	25
2 Employee relations	88	37
3 Training	80	15
4 Discipline & grievance	79	5
5 Appraisal	62	2
6 Health, safety & welfare	69	4
7 Redundancy & dismissal	71	3
8 Organization & management development	64	9
9 Job evaluation	49	2
10 Pay administration	65	8
11 Manpower planning	69	7
12 Changes in work organization	70	6

*ranked in descending order according to amount of discretion exercised

Table 2.1 *What personnel managers do*

(*Source:* Mackay, L and Torrington, D[3] *The Changing Nature of Personnel Management.* Institute of Personnel Management, 1986)

Evaluating the Personnel Function – Tyson and Fell, 1986[4]

Tyson and Fell evolved three models of personnel management from their research:

1. *The 'clerk of works' model.* In this model all authority for action is vested in line managers. 'Personnel policies are formed or created after the actions which created the need'. Policies are not integral to the business and are short-term and *ad hoc*. Authority is vested in line managers and personnel activities are largely routine – employment and day-to-day administration.

2. *The 'contracts manager' model.* In this model policies are well established, often implicit, with a heavy industrial relations emphasis, possibly derived from an employer's association. The personnel department will use fairly sophisticated systems, especially in the field of employee relations. The personnel manager is likely to be a professional or very experienced in industrial relations. He (or, more unlikely, she) will not be on the board and, although having some authority to 'police' the implementation of policies, acts mainly in an interpretive, not a creative or innovative, role.

3. *The 'architect' model.* In this model explicit personnel policies exist as part of the corporate strategy. Human resource planning and development are important concepts and a long-term view is taken. Systems tend to be sophisticated. The head of the personnel function is probably on the board and his or her power is derived from professionalism and perceived contribution to the business.

Of course, like all models, these provide a somewhat simplistic view of the different roles of personnel managers. They overlap in many organizations and exist in different ways in different parts of large or diversified companies. But there is a continuum between those situations where personnel management is a routine administrative, relatively lowly and reactive function to those where it is sophisticated, high powered and proactive. Where a personnel function is placed on the continuum depends partly on the extent to which those at the top really believe in a 'human resource management' approach which recognizes that people are *the* resource and have to be dealt with strategically. It also depends on the professionalism, sheer ability and determination to exercise authority and power of whoever heads the personnel function. These are all matters relating to the organizational context and are discussed in the next chapter.

What personnel managers do

As providers of services and, to a degree, functional guidance, personnel managers are administrators. They are there to get things done effectively, although there are serious problems in measuring effectiveness, and these are referred to later in this chapter.

As providers of advice and, in some other areas, guidance, personnel specialists are problem-solvers. Karen Legge[5] and others, such as Tom Lupton[6] and Ann Crichton,[7] see this as their main role. Indeed, in stressing this aspect of the job they seem to underestimate the existence of administration as an important though unglamorous activity in any personnel department.

Personnel managers may:

(a) *innovate,* ie devise and propose new policies, techniques and procedures;
(b) *administrate,* ie manage the activities for which the personnel department is responsible such as recruitment, training, pay administration, health and safety and record keeping;
(c) *solve problems,* ie general problems related to achieving corporate and personnel objectives and specific problems concerning disputes, grievances and disagreements with colleagues and superiors.

The activities carried out by personnel managers will include some but not necessarily all of those mentioned in the previous chapter. They may or may not be involved in the strategic planning process and in formulating personnel objectives and policies. Their role varies immensely in accordance with the organizational context.

Activity sample

It is not possible, for the reasons given above, to describe the typical activities of a personnel department. The following, however, is a sample of what happened in a busy personnel department in a fairly typical week in addition to the routine functions of recruitment, welfare and record keeping, using a computerized system.

1. A vacancy for a cost accountant has been outstanding for six months. Two offers have been rejected and one appointee resigned after six weeks for personal reasons. The agencies have no more applicants on their books and the manager doing the recruiting has come to the Personnel Department in a state of distress and frustration.
2. The Senior Financial Manager has approached Personnel about two other vacancies for qualified accountants (circa £17,500). One has been outstanding for six months, the other has just arisen. They are difficult to fill as salaries are below market rate.
3. A senior manager complains that a manager appointed in his department about two months ago is not proving satisfactory.
4. Mrs Smith is complaining that she was held up by Personnel and was too late applying to DHSS for full National Insurance deductions. She claims, therefore, that she will be delayed 12

months in obtaining sick pay because of the company's inefficiency.

5. Four months ago a redundancy was avoided (embarrassing for a growing company) by re-deploying a member of staff. Her manager is now complaining that she is not suited to the new job and wants to know what arrangements Personnel will make.

6. The senior representative of the union has confirmed with you that it is company policy for staff to see their own job descriptions on request. She has now told you that several people have been refused by their managers.

7. An employee with six weeks' service goes to the agency who placed her to complain that she is being persecuted by colleagues because of her colour. The agency staff telephone to warn us.

8. Following an urgent set of re-grading applications, jobs in the Finance Department have been graded higher when a professionally qualified accountant is required. This caused some concern with line management who eventually accepted the need for the qualification. Finance have now submitted a further job description which says this job could be carried out by someone who is not professionally qualified but who has the experience of a qualified accountant. The job is organizational at the same level as qualified accountants.

9. The company has an agreement with the union to consult prior to altering prices of food to employees. Two incidents upset the staff representatives:

   (a) A letter from the catering company to the Office Manager was opened in the wrong office and refers to an agreement to raise drink prices by 2p per cup.

   (b) Rolls and sandwiches were increased in price by the catering company's restaurant manager because he thought, wrongly, that consultations had been carried out.

10. The Distribution Director has run into problems with the union in changing rates in the bonus scheme and wants advice on how to force the changes through without causing serious unrest.

11. The Operations Director wants to 'front load' staff time to the earlier part of the week when the pressure of work is greatest. He seeks advice on how hours can be flexed to achieve this and so reduce overtime costs.

12. The Managing Director has 'discovered' quality circles and wants to know what the company should do about them.

How personnel managers do it

Personnel specialists carry out their advisory and administrative tasks in essentially the same way as any manager. They ensure that systems and procedures are operated or implemented properly and within predetermined time scales and budgets, and they maintain records and communicate information. This applies to such typical activities as recruitment, performance appraisal, training and salary administration, although in each case setting up the systems, evaluating their effectiveness and amending them in the light of experience or because of changed circumstances will involve problem-solving.

As problem solvers, personnel managers do three things:

1. They *define* the nature of the problem or, in the words of McFarland[8] conceptualize it – becoming aware of the difficulty or the non improvement and analysing the circumstances leading to and surrounding the situation.
2. They *diagnose* the cause(s) of the problem or the reason(s) for the situation arising. This process of diagnosis accompanies the process of definition and it is often iterative, ie possible explanations may highlight the need for further analysis which will lead to a different diagnosis which may indicate that more data is required, and so on.
2. They *decide* on a course of action, having weighed up the relative merits of a number of alternatives.

The emphasis throughout the process is on analysis. And this analysis has to cover the organizational context in which it is all happening. It ought therefore to be carried out against the background of an understanding of organizational processes that are taking place, ie organizational behaviour.

To a degree, personnel managers have to accept that what they do, and how to do it, will be contingent on a number of variable and often uncertain factors. Contingency theory as discussed in the previous chapter and as expounded by Lawrence and Lorsch[9] suggests that 'organizational variables are in a complex inter-relationship with one another and with conditions in the environment' and that these environmental contingencies, which include the technological character of the work, will act as both constraints and opportunities and influence the organization's internal structures and processes. How this contingency approach can be used in personnel management is discussed in the next chapter.

Meanwhile, it is worth re-emphasizing that the personnel managers in their analytical and diagnostic capacity need, in Karen Legge's words, 'a body of knowledge or frame of reference on which to base their diagnosis'.[5] Most commentators have suggested that this body of knowledge should be based on behavioural science. It is interesting to note, however, that some commentators, including Legge, do not appear to admit that the knowledge required includes an understanding of the range of techniques that can be used, selectively, to solve problems. Be that as it may, there *is* a body of knowledge available to personnel practitioners and this leads naturally to a consideration of the extent to which, because of this fact, personnel management can be regarded as a profession.

Personnel management as a profession

If the term is used loosely, personnel managers are professional because they display expertise in doing their work. A professional occupation such as medicine or the law could, however, be defined as one which gives members of its association exclusive rights to practise their profession. A profession is not so much an occupation as a means of controlling an occupation. Personnel management is not in this category.

A 'profession' may alternatively be identified using the following less rigid criteria:

(a) skill based on theoretical knowledge; the provision of training and education;
(b) a test of the competence of members administered by a professional body;
(c) a formal professional organization which has the power to regulate entry to the profession;
(d) a professional code of conduct.

By these standards personnel management could be regarded as a profession, especially in the UK where the Institute of Personnel Management carries out all the functions of a professional body.

A third approach to the definition of a profession is to emphasize the service ethic – the professional person is there to serve others. This, however, leads to confusion when applied to personnel managers. Whom are they trying to serve? The organization and its values, or the people in the organization and their needs (organizational values and personal needs do not necessarily coincide)? As Tyson and Fell have commented: 'In recent years the personnel manager seems to be encouraged to make the line manager his client, whilst trying simultaneously to represent wider social standards, and to possess a sense of service to employees. This results in confusion and difficulty for the personnel executive.'[4] In the face of this difficulty, the question has to be asked, why bother? The answer was suggested by Watson[10] who claimed the adoption of a professional image by personnel managers is a strategic response by personnel specialists to their felt lack of authority. They are in an ambiguous situation and sometimes feel they need all the help they can get to clarify and, indeed, strengthen their authority and influence.

If a profession is defined rigidly as a body of people who possess a particular area of competence, who control entry so that only members of the association can practice in that area, who unequivocally adopt the 'service ethic' and who are recognized by themselves and others as belonging to a profession, then personnel management is not a profession. This is the case even when a professional institution like the Institute of Personnel Management exists with the objective of acting as a professional body in the full sense of the word, an aim which it does its best to fulfil.

On the basis of their research, Guest and Horwood[11] expressed their doubts about the professional model of personnel management as follows:

> 'The (research) data also highlights the range of career types in personnel management. Given the diversity of personnel roles and organizational contexts, this is surely something to be welcomed. It is tempting but wrong to view personnel managers as homogeneous. Their different backgrounds and fields of operations raise doubts about the value of a professional model and of any attempt to view personnel problems as amenable to solution through a primary focus on professionalism'.

However, a broader definition of professionalism as the practice of specific skills based upon a defined body of knowledge in accordance with recognized standards of behaviour would entitle personnel management to be regarded as a profession. Sir Peter Parker, Chairman of British Rail for many years, had no doubts on this subject: 'I am an ardent advocate of professionalism in personnel management. There must be a core of disciplined expertise at the heart of its effectiveness.'[12] But he was not saying that personnel management is a 'profession'.

The debate continues, but it is an academic one. What matters is that personnel managers need expertise and have to use it responsibly. In other words, they should act professionally but do not *have* to be members of a professional association to do that. Such associations, however, have an important part to play in setting and improving professional standards.

Evaluating the personnel function

It is not easy to evaluate the personnel function – to measure its contribution to achieving the organization's objectives. Guest and Horwood[2] have commented on 'the considerable effort involved in attempting to define and evaluate effectiveness, either for the personnel function or indeed for individual roles'.

It is facile to say that people are the most important resource in an enterprise and that therefore the department that specializes in people is important. The head of an advertising agency once said that his 'inventory goes up and down in the lift'; but that did not mean that he attached any importance to the role of the personnel manager – if he had one – in looking after that inventory. This is the difficulty. People may be regarded as the vital resource – at least plenty of lip service is paid to this concept by company chairmen in their annual statements – but many managers find it difficult to appreciate where the personnel department fits in, except in the simplest terms as a procurement and fire-fighting function.

Chief executives are often perfectly happy with their personnel manager if he runs an efficient recruitment service ('he always gets his man – or woman'), keeps labour turnover down, is good at calming down shop stewards, keeps the company out of legal difficulties, and generally seems to please management and keep the workers happy. All this is highly desirable but somewhat subjective. If a personnel department can do all that, it is doing reasonably well, within limits, but it will still be difficult to measure the extent to which the work is contributing to profitability. Perhaps the most that can be said in many companies is that the personnel department has a role in providing the basis upon which profitability can be built up – ie the people; and it is also concerned in a negative way in helping to avoid situations where productivity is diminished – by minimizing disputes and removing causes of dissatisfaction.

The personnel function should, of course, do much more than that. Its true role is to make a positive contribution to organizational health and effectiveness by ensuring that well trained and well motivated people are there to work effectively and co-operatively together in the achievement of objectives which are recognized to be mutually beneficial to management and workers. This is the strategic role of personnel in the fields of organization development, manpower planning, management development, motivation and industrial relations. It is the key policy-formulating function and it is the one that is most difficult to evaluate. It is much easier to assess the effectiveness of the maintenance functions at office and shop floor level where the local personnel officer is there to provide efficient recruitment, employment, training, negotiating and record keeping services.

The personnel function is best evaluated under the headings of its three roles: advisory, service and guidance. The first and last roles present the greatest difficulties.

Evaluating the advisory role

For the personnel department's advisory role, the first level of evaluation will be made by management on the basis of whether the advice on policy sounds practical and is delivered in a positive, persuasive and straightforward manner. They will expect the personnel manager to anticipate problems and come up with realistic answers to them. Whether proposals are made orally or in writing they must be succinct and well argued; they must define the problem, explain why it must be solved, describe how it should be solved – by whom and when – set out clearly the costs involved, and end with a clear statement of the benefits that should result from the proposal. This provides at least some basis for evaluating the function from a cost/benefit point of view. There is nothing that damages the reputation of a personnel manager more than being woolly in his proposals; especially if he is the sort of individual who is so steeped in behavioural science and organization development jargon that he cannot put a proposition into language that management understands, let alone finds acceptable.

The second level of evaluation is, of course, whether the advice works. Unfortunately, in the personnel field, this evaluation will be largely subjective, except where specific advice is given on dealing with a specific problem; for example, how to handle a labour dispute or to deal with a discipline issue.

Advice on procedures can be evaluated by monitoring the effectiveness of the procedures. Do they run smoothly? Are managers using them properly? Do they produce the expected results? The procedural aspect of the advisory role overlaps with the service role, but when developing procedures, the personnel manager can be set targets such as the date when they should be in operation, the results they should obtain, and the costs of using them. Performance can then be measured against those targets.

The advisory aspect of personnel management is often concerned with projects designed to implement strategies and procedures. Where work can be set up on a project basis it is always easier to acquire a cost/benefit analysis before starting the project, to set precise time and targets and cost budgets for completing the project, to lay down procedures for reporting on progress, performance and costs, and to ensure that continuous steps are taken to measure cost-effectiveness. A project approach along these lines provides the most promising basis for evaluating the advisory aspects of personnel performance. The problem of evaluating the personnel manager's advisory role is, as Legge has said, that 'useful advice has a habit of becoming the property of the recipient and, unlike bad advice, its origins lost in the allocation of praise.'[5]

Evaluating the service role

The service role should be the easiest to evaluate. Standards can be set and the personnel department can be required to operate within a defined budget in meeting these standards. In this way cost-effectiveness can be measured, in theory at least. The difficulty is in selecting areas where realistic standards can be defined.

Some of the possible areas where quantitative standards or targets can be determined include:

- recruitment – speed in filling vacancies, advertising costs, recruitment cost per head, number of unfilled vacancies;
- employment – reduction in wastage rates and absenteeism;
- training – throughput of training schemes, time taken to develop and introduce new courses, impact of training on performance;
- management development – availability of trained managers to provide for management succession;
- industrial relations – number of disputes, extent to which disputes

are resolved, time taken to progress a grievance through the procedure at each stage;
- communications – speed with which briefing groups are convened; speed with which information is generally disseminated amongst employees;
- personnel costs – expenditure in relation to budget, cost of personnel function per employee.

In all or any of these areas, however, quantification may be impossible. In these circumstances, evaluation is inevitably carried out in qualitative terms. Subjective judgements are made about the efficiency of the service and the speed, willingness and degree of success achieved by members of the personnel function. The successful personnel manager is the one who can persuade top management and his management colleagues that he is providing them with a good service. This success is more likely to be achieved if the personnel manager can demonstrate that he is willing and able to help. It is less likely to happen where the personnel manager is too 'pushy' and attempts to steamroller his colleagues into trying out his latest idea.

The value of the personnel function in all areas is often best demonstrated by providing a small service cheerfully and efficiently and thus preparing people to accept that they are likely to benefit from an extension of the service. The Fabian approach of making progress one step at a time has much to commend it in the personnel world. It may, for example, be far easier to convince management of the virtues of a comprehensive training programme if a number of pilot-scheme courses are run to which senior managers are invited as observers and speakers.

Evaluating the guidance role

The guidance role can only be evaluated by top management who can observe the way in which the personnel department exercises functional control in accordance with the powers delegated to it. Information on effectiveness in providing control can be established by analysing the extent to which pay-roll costs or numbers of employees exceed budget, managers ignore personnel procedures in taking action, sub-standard employees are engaged, and the company is subjected to legal actions and references to industrial tribunals.

The overall evaluation of the personnel manager

Personnel managers can be evaluated under each of the headings described above, that is, their achievements in carrying out their three main roles – advisory, service and guidance. But, as Tyson and Fell suggest, 'There is a strong agreement in favour of assessing the performance of personnel managers by assessing their interpersonal behaviour...

Personnel managers, often without formal authority, have a need to influence manager colleagues and work people in order to sustain personnel policies, to motivate others and to control personnel systems.'[4]

An organization may strenuously pursue the ideal of assessing performance according to the results achieved compared with the results required (management by objectives). Ultimately, however, the assessment of personality and behaviour is the most commonly used measure, and this certainly applies to personnel managers whose work is so much concerned with interpersonal relationships.

A group of personnel specialists were asked by Tyson and Fell[4] to describe from their experience how they were evaluated by their board, by line managers and by themselves and produced the following criteria, which are largely behavioural:

1. *Board* – Personnel specialists should:
   - be able to sell themselves to management;
   - have an appreciation of the business;
   - control personnel costs; and
   - create high quality manpower resources.
2. *Line managers* – Personnel specialists should:
   - have the ability to solve line manager's personnel problems;
   - be judged by the speed of their communications;
   - be available;
   - be visible; and
   - be judged on the accuracy of their advice.
3. *Personnel specialists* should judge themselves by:
   - their satisfaction of client demands;
   - achievement of specific objectives;
   - involvement in central policy-making;
   - their ability to anticipate the needs of their clients.

This does not mean, however, that the evaluations should not be as objective as possible – against agreed standards – and should not relate to the achievement of specified objectives wherever possible. An example of an 'accountability statement' for a personnel manager which sets out the headings under which performance will be assessed is given in Appendix C.

Organization

The organization of the personnel department will clearly depend upon the organizational context within which it operates and the role assigned to the function.

There are two basic principles of organization, however, that should apply within any company. First, the head of the personnel function should be a member of the top policy-forming body of the enterprise – the board or executive committee – and should be directly responsible to the chief executive. Only thus can he make his proper contribution to the formulation of personnel policies and strategies which are clearly within the context of and supportive to the overall objectives, policies and strategies of the firm. Without taking a full part in policy deliberations and without having ease of access to the chief executive, the personnel function too easily becomes a peripheral body.

Second, the personnel organization should ensure that the day-to-day services required by management in the different divisions and departments can readily be made available. In a large divisionalized organization this may require the appointment of divisional personnel managers or factory personnel officers who may report directly to divisional or company line management. They would have a functional relationship with the chief personnel executive on the implementation of corporate personnel policies and the handling of issues such as union negotiations which may have corporate implications.

References

1. Drucker, P F *The Practice of Management*. Heinemann, London, 1955.
2. Guest, D and Horwood, R *The Role and Effectiveness of Personnel Managers: A Preliminary Report*. Department of Industrial Relations, London School of Economics, 1980.
3. Mackay, L and Torrington, D *The Changing Nature of Personnel Management*. Institute of Personnel Management, London, 1986.
4. Tyson, S and Fell, A *Evaluating the Personnel Function*. Hutchinson, London, 1986.
5. Legge, Karen *Power, Innovation and Problem Solving in Personnel Management*. McGraw-Hill, Maidenhead, 1978.
6. Lupton, T *Industrial Behaviour and Personnel Management*. Institute of Personnel Management, London, 1969.
7. Crichton, A *Personnel Management in Context*. Batsford, London, 1968.
8. McFarland, D E *Personnel Management: Theory and Practice*. Macmillan, New York, 1968.
9. Lawrence, P R and Lorsch, J W *Developing Organizations*. Addison-Wesley, Reading, Mass., 1969.
10. Watson, T *The Personnel Managers*. Routledge and Kegan Paul, London, 1977.
11. Guest, D and Horwood, R 'Perceptions of Effectiveness in Personnel Management', *Personnel Management*, May 1981.
12. Parker, P 'How I See the Personnel Function', *Personnel Management*, January 1983.

Chapter 3
Personnel Management in Context

The significance of context

Personnel managers, as well as those who write about personnel management, can fall into the trap of treating the subject in isolation. It is too easy to divorce personnel management from the context in which it operates – the organization and its environment.

It is interesting to observe how changes in the environment – economic pressures and the climate of opinion – have changed the role of personnel managers over the years. At one time personnel management was seen as a welfare activity – providing tea and sympathy. Then in the immediate post-war years, personnel management blossomed as a profession, advocating and deploying 'scientific' techniques for recruitment, job evaluation, and performance appraisal and training. Then, in the expansive 1960s, the behavioural scientists took over: organization development, job enrichment and concerns for the creation of organizational health, job satisfaction and involvement became pre-eminent. Management by objectives became a popular cult. The euphoria of the swinging (or socially conscious) 1960s spilled over into the early 1970s. But increasingly, as economic gloom took over, life became more real and earnest for personnel practitioners. They became aware that what mattered was survival as well as growth and job satisfaction. They became involved in tough redundancies. They had to take part in even tougher confrontations with trade unions as top management decided that enough was enough so far as union discruption was concerned. Participation and involvement was no longer the key to success. Productivity was what mattered. And this was *real* productivity, not the give-away productivity bargaining that had been indulged in previously. Personnel departments took part in and were subjected to cost-cutting exercises. And quality improvement by means of quality circles became the latest gimmick – if the Japanese can do it, why can't we?

In the 1980s, as described in the introduction to this handbook, Britain became a market economy and the enterprise culture dawned. Individualism, entrepreneurship and the pursuit of excellence became all-important.

The trades unions' dominating position was eroded. Payment for performance and personal contracts as a means of replacing collective bargaining were advocated strongly by Government spokesmen and leading industrialists. The emphasis on productivity and profitability increased.

Personnel management has had to change and the human resource management movement, which is described in the next chapter, is a symptom of this process. Personnel managers were no longer able to be self-righteous about what was good for their enterprise. As Legge[1] pointed out, personnel management specialists and textbook writers have tended to decide what was right for the organization on theoretical grounds without basing their views on a proper analysis of the situation or context in which their policies and procedures have to exist. It has been suggested by Legge and others that this analysis should be carried out on the basis of an understanding of contingency theory as described in the next section of this chapter.

Contingency theory

Contingency theory was developed originally in sociology under the name of structural functionalism. It emphasized the interdependence of organizations with their environment (cf. Gluckman[2]). The empirical studies of Woodward,[3] Burns and Stalker[4] and Lawrence and Lorsch,[5] applied the theory to work organizations.

In its crude, deterministic form, contingency theory implies that the internal structure and its system are a direct function of the environment, as illustrated in Figure 3.1. This model has been criticized as being simplistic and Silverman[6] has developed his more sophisticated 'action theory' approach. This suggests a much more complex set of relationships between the contingent factors, which might be external (market, economic) or internal (technical, cultural), management plans and actions. This is illustrated in Figure 3.2.

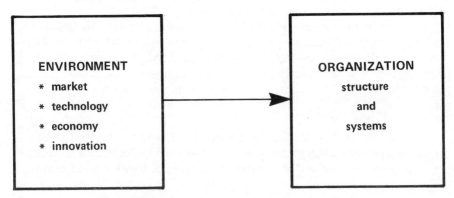

Figure 3.1 Deterministic contingency model

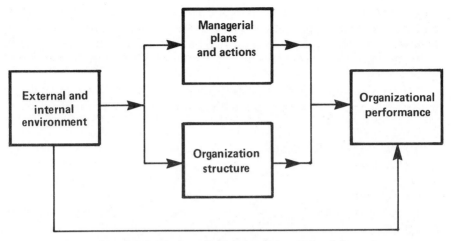

Figure 3.2 Action theory contingency model

Contingency theory tells us that definitions of aims, strategies and policy areas, lists of activities and analyses of the roles of departments can be no more than generalizations. What actually happens depends on six factors:

1. *Organization context* – purpose, environment, structure, performance, people, corporate culture.
2. *Attitudes* to personnel management.
3. *Constraints* – the problems and limitations created by organization context and relationships between personnel and other managers.
4. *Ambiguity* – the essentially ambiguous nature of the role of personnel managers who frequently do not know exactly where they stand. (This is a function of the first three factors and is explored more thoroughly later in this chapter.)
5. *Power* – the limitations of the power of personnel managers, which is also an aspect of their ambiguous situation.
6. *Policy formulation* – the extent to which personnel managers have the power to influence the formulation and implementation of policies.

These factors are discussed in turn in the rest of this chapter, which is completed with suggestions about what personnel managers can do when faced with the problems and limitations created by them.

Organization context

Charles Handy[7] has suggested six factors of crucial importance in the development of organizations and resulting behaviour patterns: history and ownership; size; technology; goals and objectives; the environment; and people. These provide a good basis for analysing organization behaviour but they need to be modified and extended if they are to help in understanding organization context from the viewpoint of personnel management.

The factors which particularly influence personnel objectives, policies, activities and the role and organization of the personnel function are:

(a) purpose
(b) external environment
(c) internal environment
(d) size
(e) structure
(f) performance
(g) people
(h) corporate culture and climate
(i) management style.

These factors are interconnected, as shown in Figure 3.3. They are described below.

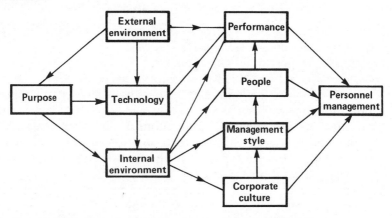

Figure 3.3 Factors affecting personnel management

Purpose

Organizations exist to achieve a purpose. In the public sector or in a non-profit making organization the purpose may be defined as the provision of certain services for national or local government, the community, or the members of the organization.

The purpose of a business will be to create and satisfy customer demands for goods or services, to provide customers with value for money and to generate an acceptable rate of return on the investment of its owners. As Drucker said, 'a business cannot be defined or explained in terms of profit'[8] and profit-making is not the sole purpose of a company. But unless shareholders are satisfied that they are getting a reasonable return on their investment and unless sufficient cash is generated to finance trading and development, the business will not survive or grow.

The steps taken to achieve the purposes of the organization may conflict with the needs of its employees. Douglas McGregor[9] has pointed out that the biggest challenge to personnel managers is to integrate the needs of the organization with the needs of those who work in it. It is not an impossible challenge, and there are a number of ways in which it can be met, as described later in this book. But none of these approaches will work unless personnel managers understand what the organization is setting out to achieve just as clearly as they understand what individuals need and want.

The external environment

Organizations will be affected by factors in their external environment such as competition, changes in markets, economic forces, government policies, public opinion and trade unions. Turbulence in the environment can create conditions which significantly alter personnel policies and practices, the most obvious example being shortage of work leading to cutbacks and redundancies. Change is perhaps the biggest challenge facing personnel managers. Techniques for managing change are discussed in Chapter 7 but without an understanding of what is happening outside the organization, these techniques will be ineffective.

The internal environment

The internal environment consists of the characteristics of the organization itself, namely its technology, its size and its structure.

Size

On the whole, large organizations are more formalized, and specialist functions such as personnel departments are more likely to exist. Size, however, brings with it problems of integration and communication with which personnel managers have to contend. Schumacher's proposition 'small is beautiful' has its attractions to anyone concerned with managing and motivating people.

Structure

The structure of an organization is related to its technology and size, which will influence the degree of formality in defining roles and relationships, the extent to which the organization is de-centralized and the numbers of levels of management or supervision that exist. In turn, these factors will influence the procedural aspects of personnel management (eg the use of formal job descriptions) and the ways in which people are managed and communications take place.

Performance

Performance in achieving purpose will be largely determined by the people in the organization, but will also be subjected to environmental influences. Clearly, personnel management is an entirely different affair in troubled times when costs are being cut and morale is suffering than when business is booming. Personnel managers must be prepared to adjust their methods accordingly.

People

Purpose and technology will determine what sort of people the organization employs and will therefore influence personnel policies and techniques. The personnel manager dealing with scientists in a high technology company has a quite different job from the personnel manager of a large mechanical bakery. The basic activities of recruitment, training, pay administration and employee relations may have the same names and share some basic concepts, but their application will be entirely different.

History, external influences and the feelings of management and employees will affect the degree to which the latter are organized into trade unions or staff associations. The strength of unions, if they exist, and the attitudes of management towards them will exert major influences on the role and activities of a personnel manager.

Corporate culture

The corporate culture is the system of assumptions about what is important to the organization, and what it should do and how it should do it. As Katz and Kahn put it:

> Every organization develops its own culture and climate; with its own taboos, folkways and mores. The climate or culture of the system reflects both the norms and values of the formal system and their reinterpretation in the informal system. Organizational climate reflects also the history of internal and external struggles, the types of people the organization attracts, its work processes and physical layout, the modes of communication, and the exercise of authority within the system.[10]

The corporate culture will be influenced by, but in turn will also influence, the factors mentioned above. It will also affect organizational behaviour in three areas:

1. Core values.
2. Organization climate.
3. Management style.

Core values

Core values are beliefs in what is best or good for the organization and what should or ought to happen. They are expressed by reference to both ends (goals) and means (action plans for achieving goals). A belief in these values and in the organization as a whole will be developed if something that is worth doing is being done well. Pride in the product and pride in the company may exist because of a long tradition of achievement and quality. But identification and loyalty are not inevitable; they have to be fostered.

Values will only be got across if they are believed in, acted upon and pursued relentlessly. The responsibility for presenting them should start at the top, but it should be shared among all managers and supervisors. You may not wish to go quite as far as the Japanese (in Japan, at 8 am every working day 87,000 Matsushita employees sing the company song and recite the company's code of values), but it has to be accepted that their belief in getting the total identification of employees with their company has paid off.

Organization climate

The climate or atmosphere of an organization is an expression of the way in which people behave and interact with one another. It will be influenced by the culture and the norms and values of management about how people should be treated with regard to justice, equity and the extent to which they are involved as partners in the enterprise. However, the attitudes of workpeople to their jobs and the company and the behaviour of trade unions will also contribute to the climate. The degree to which there is commitment, co-operation, suspicion or open hostility will be related to established values or behavioural norms. In the case of trade unions, norms may have been brought into the organization from outside, but the internal environment and the behaviour of management will determine the extent to which the external values thrive within the company.

Personnel managers must know their way around this maze if they are going to exert any influence or get anything worthwhile done. And every move they make to change a policy or to introduce a new technique must be thought through against the background of their understanding of the organization's culture and climate. These issues are explored more thoroughly in Part II of this book which deals with organizational behaviour.

Management style

The role of management is to ensure that the organization achieves its purpose. To this end, management sets objectives, budgets and targets, prepares plans to achieve objectives, obtains the resources required by the plans (people, finance, plant, etc), directs the use of these resources and monitors performance, taking corrective action if plans are not achieved.

Obtaining and using resources effectively is one of the key tasks of management. And people are obviously a major resource, alongside finance.

So managers will be concerned with leading, motivating and developing their staff. However, they are there to achieve results and in this process they will be encouraged, indeed commanded, in Robert Heller's words, 'to do the most possible with the least possible'.[11] They may attach a lot of importance to how they manage their staff but they will know that in the last analysis it is 'the bottom line that counts', ie the profits they achieve are *the* measure of their performance.

This emphasis on results in the minds of general or line managers, especially those responsible for achieving output or sales targets, can present a problem to personnel managers. The latter will be regarded as peripheral if they cannot demonstrate that what they are doing will make a direct and, preferably, measurable impact on the results the line manager is expected to achieve.

The way in which managers set about achieving results – their management style – will vary between organizations. The degree to which they are autocratic, democratic or permissive will depend partly on themselves and partly on the context in which they work, which includes technology and the climate of the organization. Personnel managers will, however, have to be prepared to cope with different management styles and ones with which they have little sympathy. They will want to bring influence to bear on changing inappropriate styles but should never underestimate the size of the problem in doing so.

Attitudes to personnel management

Attitudes to personnel management and personnel managers by management in general or chief executives and line managers in particular can be positive, negative or indifferent. Personnel managers themselves vary considerably in their perception of the role of personnel management and their own contribution to the organization. Clearly, this range of attitudes as described below affects the context within which personnel specialists operate.

Attitudes of management in general

Way back in the 1950s Peter Drucker could quote, almost with approval, a cynic's opinion that the personnel specialist's work was 'partly a file clerk's job, partly a social worker's job and partly fire fighting to head off union trouble or to settle it'.[8] And that arch-iconoclast, Robert Townsend, headed his section on personnel management in *Up the Organization* with the words 'Sack the personnel department'.[12]

More recently, Peter Prior, Chairman of H P Bulmer, expressed the following doubts about personnel managers:

All too often, personnel people have claimed to have approached the problems of the individual through social science but, with the greatest respect, the present state of human and industrial relations in many critical areas of British business says little for the success of their efforts'.[13]

Negative views were also put forward by Kingsley Manning writing in *Management Today*:

> The challenge and the opportunity for the personnel function remain as great as ever. The people a firm employs are still its largest cost and most important asset. Though the importance of getting the best performance out of that asset has not changed, personnel management as a discipline has yet to meet that challenge and make the significant impact it surely should.
>
> The failure to do so raises fundamental questions about the whole personnel function. Of all the major areas of management, personnel has the weakest conceptual base and the poorest technology. It is not surprising that personnel departments often exhibit little unity of purpose; but this effectively ensures that the departments contribute little to the company's decision-making process. If personnel management is to rise to the challenge of the turbulent 1980s it must review its most basic concepts and practices. What is needed is the sort of analytic and creative thinking that has been demonstrated so successfully in disciplines like marketing and finance.[14]

These opinions contrast strongly with those of John Crosby, President of the Institute of Personnel Management. In the October 1987 edition of *Personnel Management* he wrote:

> Personnel managers have every reason to be optimistic about the future in the context of the ever-growing public awareness of the importance of human resources (fostered actively by the Institute), the continuing and changing work challenges that face them and the steady increase both in their reputation and growing strength.

Attitudes of chief executives

The positive views of John Crosby about personnel management have certainly been shared by many chief executives, as the following quotations show:

> Skills of a very high order of professionalism, such as the Institute of Personnel Management exists to foster, will be increasingly required of the personnel function. These personnel skills will touch every point of the business and so I see the personnel function being drawn more and more into the general management of the business.
>
> We take it for granted that the finance specialist, the production specialist, the engineer, the materials and equipment specialist, the marketing expert will have their say in general management decisions. All too often the personnel contribution in the past has been a reactive one rather than a harnessing of human resources to maximize achievement. The time has come for this to change to a more positive role.   *Lord Ezra, Chairman, National Coal Board*[15]

> It is relevant here to quote part of a policy statement issued by our board: 'Involvement means that all employees are able to make known their views and ideas about the pattern of their everyday work, to contribute to decisions that affect its development and change, and are made aware of the wider issues affecting their well-being and security.
>
> This greater involvement of all employees in the content and purpose of their jobs

should apply whatever their particular role and working group. It should create an understanding of the individual contribution of all employees to achieving the prime objective of the company.

The most important role of personnel is probably to develop and enhance the commitment of managers and supervisors to this end, in ways compatible with collective bargaining arrangements agreed with recognized trade unions; and to help in providing the necessary training, education and communication of relevant commercial, financial and production information.

If personnel management is about people at work and their effective contribution to the business, personnel managers can have little fear about the importance of their future role and of the task that lies ahead of them.

Sir Alex Jarrett, Chairman, Reed Paper Group[16]

Summing up on the things I expect from personnel, there are two or three themes that recur. One of these is professionalism: another is the need to be outward-looking and in touch with other industries and society at large. The third is the need to operate on two distinct timescales. Personnel must develop long-term policies and strategies and it must also be in there pitching when day-to-day problems arise, when tough negotiations are being faced, when the line managers need their skill and experience to the full. In a sense, there is the creative, philosophical role, the preventative role and the day-to-day role. The job is not purely fire-fighting but we must recognize that even with the best long-term strategies, some fires will inevitably break out.   *Sir Peter Parker, Chairman, British Rail*[17]

Support from the top, especially in large progressive companies with strong leadership, often means that initiatives concerning human resource management are taken there. If personnel directors are part of the top team and as such are involved in strategic issues, they will have a significant role to play.

But top-down initiatives do not always work. A case study of what happened after an organizational development programme was launched by top management in ICI showed that middle managers were generally hostile or indifferent to the project, which consequently made little impact.

Chief executives can be the visionaries and the idealists in an organization – they should be able to conceptualize what sort of organization they want and they may feel that a human resource management type approach is the right way to go about it. But they need the support of line managers as well as the personnel function.

Attitudes of line managers

It is often the middle managers who are cynical about the core values expressed by top management and about the efforts of personnel specialists to get them accepted through ambitious, long-term or, as perceived by line management, not immediately relevant 'people programmes'. This attitude is understandable. It is, after all, the middle management who have to do the hard, slogging work, who get most of the kicks and not so many of the half-pence, and who have to be concerned with the here-and-now rather than looking beyond the blue horizon. Their attitude to the personnel department will be hostile or indifferent if it does not give them the practical help they want or spends too much time pursuing irrelevant or, as they would see it, high-faluting ideas. Karen Legge[1] quoted some fairly typical comments:

> The trouble with the Personnel Department here is that they try to introduce gimmicky new theories through general management channels. They should stick to welfare – that's what personnel's job is – looking after routine welfare matters.
> *Assistant Works Manager (Engineering)*

> The Personnel Department have little understanding of line management's problems. *Work Study Manager*

She also quoted a works director expressing a fairly common attitude, which in effect questions the need for an over-specialized personnel function:

> We're all personnel managers here. We have to be, as the only resource we've got is people.

A general works manager interviewed by Legge put the personnel department firmly in its place by saying:

> The Personnel Department here is, as it should be, a service to the line. For example, if we want more labour they get it, train it, and arrange for it to be paid. They provide information for negotiations too, but I do the real negotiating.

And one of the personnel specialists seen by Mackay and Torrington said, sadly: 'At least half of them (the line managers) see us as an encumbrance.'[18]

Line managers can, of course be positive about the personnel function, either because they understand without being told that their life is made easier if expertise is available to help solve their personnel problems or because they have been convinced by the members of the personnel department that the latter are useful. For example, an assistant works manager said to Karen Legge that:

> The personnel department is important in that both the industrial relations officer and the personnel superintendent are anchor men who provide continuity of experience and interpretation of company policy.

The challenge to personnel managers is that they have not only to be an integral part of the top management team as business partners, but have also to earn the respect and co-operation of middle managers and supervisors. These can be two different worlds and there is, of course, the third world – the workers in the offices and laboratories and on the shop floor with whom members of the personnel function are in constant contact and who will have their own views about what they expect from the staff of that department. Personnel managers may, therefore, have to exist in three worlds at once and this can be the cause of constraints on what they can do and ambiguities about their role.

Attitudes of personnel managers

When asked by Mackay and Torrington[18] which activities they thought were most central to the personnel function, 26.6 per cent of the personnel managers participating in the survey named employee relations. The next most frequently named activity was the organization and its survival (22.6 per cent). Advice to line management (12.9 per cent), recruitment and selection (11.7 per cent) and training (11.4 per cent) were the next three most frequently named key activities.

Personnel management can be a highly rewarding occupation and, as the Mackay and Torrington survey showed, many personnel managers enjoy their central function of employee relations, or that of exerting influence and providing advice which increases organizational effectiveness. The following are typical comments about what they enjoy:

> Well, in spite of myself, I enjoy the euphoria of good negotiations.
> *UK Personnel Director*

> Getting involved in the development of the organization and the development of the business – the politics if you like.   *Personnel Manager*

Some have doubts, like a personnel director who said:

> I don't think British industry will be too badly off without a personnel function. After all, what is it?

Tony Watson reported the fact that relationships with line managers were the major problem for his sample of personnel managers. As one of them said of line managers:

> They come along and dump a 'people problem' on us. When we try to get them to do something or see something in a wider perspective, they say 'That's your pigeon – that's personnel – now't to do with us'.[19]

And a personnel director said to Kingsley Manning recently:

> Ten years ago, my department seemed to make all the running, virtually nothing happened without our involvement. But now we have to fight just to know what's going on.[14]

Personnel managers, like any other managers, are satisfied at work if they are achieving worthwhile goals. Some do, and some do not. The fault may lie in their environment although it could lie in themselves. But all personnel specialists have to work within constraints and in ambiguous situations. The good ones learn how to live within or break through the barriers and how to tolerate ambiguity.

Constraints on personnel management

As Keith Thurley has said, personnel managers, in Britain at least, are often 'working against the grain of British culture and values' and 'it is judged that attempts to break out of this situation by developing overall strategies are difficult due to the constraints under which organizations have to work'.[20]

A hostile or turbulent environment which changes the role or affects the performance of the organization can restrict the positive things that personnel managers can do. What some managements regard as fringe activities, eg training, are the first in troubled times to be cut. Personnel departments go into reverse, removing rather than recruiting people. General and line managers become more hard-nosed.

There are, however, more fundamental and permanent constraints on what personnel departments can do. Legge wrote that it is easy to state that good personnel management should aim for 'the optimum utilization of the organization'.[1] In reality, however, this aim is difficult to define for the following reasons:

1. The goals and objectives of organizations are often hard to pin down and the targets for personnel aims and policies are therefore less clear.
2. Even when primary organizational goals can be defined (eg maximize profit) the secondary goals required to achieve them may not be obvious. In other words, while it is sometimes relatively easy to define ends there is often conflict over the best means to achieve these ends.
3. The concept of 'optimization' is not so clear as it seems. There are many interests in organizations, eg management and workers, not to speak of the state, the owners and the public. These groups may legitimately have different interests which are incompatible with one another and consequently difficult if not impossible to reconcile (the concept of the plurality of legitimate groups in organizations).
4. Although managers confess to aim for optimization, in practice they are often forced into choosing the just adequate or 'good enough' course of action. This is because choice is limited by constraints operating in or on the organization, limited knowledge, and the perceived need to avoid uncertainty and make decisions that will at least work even if they are not necessarily the 'best' decisions.
5. The ends (primary goals) and the means (secondary goals) will be influenced by the context of the organization – its environment, role, structure, management style, technology, etc. What is required and works well in one organization will not necessarily be appropriate or work in another setting.
6. The power of the personnel function to influence policies may be constrained by the values of the organization and the part the function is allowed to play in the decision-making process.

Variations in the organizational context and its values and environmental changes means that there is no fixed pattern for what personnel managers do or how they do it. This and a number of other factors contribute to the ambiguity inherent in the role of personnel management.

The ambiguous nature of personnel management

Personnel managers, in Thurley's words, are 'specialists in ambiguity'.[20] This arises partly because of the equivocal nature of the attitudes of line managers to personnel specialists, but also because the latter are often unsure about where they stand. Ambiguity in the role of the personnel function can result in confusion between ideals and reality. Tyson[21] sees a contrast between the ideologies and actual realities of organizational life to which personnel managers as 'organization men or women' have to conform.

This ambiguity is reflected in the comments about the role of the personnel function made by writers on personnel management. For example, Mackay and Torrington suggest that:

> Personnel management is never identified with management interests, as it becomes ineffective when not able to understand and articulate the aspirations of the work force.[18]

In complete contrast, Tyson and Fell believe that:

> Classical personnel management has not been granted a position in decision making circles because it has frequently not earned one. It has not been concerned with the totality of the organization but often with issues which have not only been parochial but esoteric to boot'.[22]

Karen Legge, recognizing the ambiguity inherent in the personnel role, distinguishes between two types of personnel professionals: the convergent innovators who seek to introduce changes congruent with senior manager's value systems, and the divergent innovators who would establish the relevance of different values and try to convert managers to them.

This ambiguity has been compounded because of the wide variety of approaches managements in different organizations use in the treatment of their human resources. Williamson and Ouchi[23] distinguished between 'hard' and 'soft' contracting. In 'hard contracting', relationships are formalized, jobs are task-specific and legalistic interpretations are made of the employment contract. A more authoritarian or 'macho' approach to management is likely in these circumstances. On the other hand, 'soft contracting' aims to create harmonious units based on tacit understanding and a reciprocal sense of obligation. Personnel managers who believe in a soft-contracting approach could find themselves in a hard-contracting situation and have to choose between going along with it, getting out, or working quietly against the grain (not easy).

The debate on human resource management (HRM) versus personnel management, which is fully discussed in the next chapter, has been generated by but has also contributed to this ambiguity. HRM is management orientated, and sees people as a key resource to be used to further the organization's objectives. Traditional personnel management, however, is more people orientated, taking the view that if their needs are satisfied, the organization as well as its members will benefit. Personnel managers can sometimes find themselves being pulled in both directions. It does not make their life any easier.

Power

Power in organizations depends on three main factors as analysed by Handy:[7]

- *Position* – the right to do something because of position or rank in an organization. The value of position as a source of power depends on the value placed on that position within the organization. It is also related to the resources controlled by the position holder.
- *Expertise* – the power that is vested in someone because of acknowledged expertise: 'authority goes to the one who knows'. This power can only be given by those over whom it is exercised.
- *Personal* – the most elusive form of power, which resides in the person and in his personality and is fanned by success and self-confidence or can evaporate in defeat.

Personnel managers hope that their power will rest on position and expertise with an admixture of personal charisma. But, as Handy comments: 'Too often personnel departments of organizations are forced to rely on position or resource power when their expert power proves to be unrecognized.' Legge established that, because the position power held by personnel management in company decision-making is often ambiguous,

... the personnel management considerations involved in production, marketing, and finance decisions were not so much overruled as went by default. In other words, non-specialists, while formally recognizing the importance of effectively utilizing human resources, lacking as they did the expertise to develop a systematic view of what this entailed in terms of personnel strategies and action, *in practice* tended to underestimate the importance of the human resource variables in decision-making on issues that were not explicitly 'personnel management'. While in theory they recognized that the effective use of manpower was of vital importance to their organizations, in practice the very pervasiveness of manpower management meant that, being taken for granted, it was neglected as a dimension to most problems under discussion and emerged as an issue worthy of concentrated consideration only if a specifically 'manpower' crisis threatened. Hence, although theoretically strategic to the organization, personnel management, even in its broadest sense, often was not perceived or treated as such.[1]

Policy formulation and implementation

Constraints, ambiguity and restricted power combine to limit the extent to which personnel managers can influence personnel policies in the sense that these define the organization's approach to its employees.

Brewster, Gill and Richbell, in their paper on the application of industrial relations policies,[24] distinguished between the *instigators* of policies (usually top management, who may or may not be advised by a personnel specialist), the *implementors* of policies (the line managers) and the *facilitators* (industrial relations specialists). In their research in a variety of companies they observed differences between 'espoused' policies – what the instigators intended to happen – and operational policies – what the implementors saw as their priorities and put into practice. Espoused and operational personnel policies were not always the same because personnel specialists were often not directly involved in their implementation: 'The personnel manager is frequently left on the touch-line – there to give advice but not allowed to play.' The line manager tends to assess the various demands upon him and acts in accordance with his own abilities and limitations. As Brewster and Richbell commented in a later article:

> Sometimes it seems as though a great many very talented personnel specialists are wasting an awful lot of time. They carefully watch developments in the industrial relations, political and labour market environments, they develop sensible, well thought-out personnel policies that would make their company one of the most progressive and highly respected of employers. And then they see their efforts continually frustrated and subverted by a management team that seems determined to ignore most of what the personnel department does.[25]

What should the personnel manager do?

At first sight, the results of the Brewster, Gill and Richbell research make depressing reading. Personnel managers must sometimes wonder what they *can* do, never mind what they should do, to cope with the complexity and changeability of their organizational context, the indifferent or even negative attitudes of line managers and the constraints placed upon the personnel function.

But all is not lost. The personnel specialist can not only cope, he can triumph over these adversities as long as he does not rely upon his position and expertise to prescribe what the organization must do.

Alan Fowler gave some good advice at an Institute of Personnel Management's conference:

> Efficient and effective personnel departments display certain characteristics. They are recognized and used as the central repository of all knowledge on personnel matters – not only of the organization itself, but concerning legislation, the industry, trends, etc. They take a positive advisory role, offering ideas and advice rather

than simply answering questions. They show a willingness to delegate and decentralize many personnel functions which can be part of uniform company policy and to bend rules to get things done. Their officers have a genuine interest in operational matters and are as keen as other line managers and directors to get all-round efficiency; at the same time they show an ability to involve others in personnel work.[26]

To make the approach suggested by Fowler work, personnel managers must develop and apply analytical skills to gain an understanding of the organizational context, the attitudes of their fellow managers, the constraints they have to live with *and* themselves – their own abilities, values and attitudes. It will help if the personnel specialist has adequate status and access to information and resources to exert influence and implement decisions. The use of collaborative problem-solving methods will achieve even better results. But understanding is the most important thing to achieve. As Brewster and Richbell put it:

> The realization of personnel policies demands an understanding of how policies are implemented within the organization. It should not be assumed that simply having a policy accepted at the formal level is the end of the exercise. There is a need to see 'policy' from the point of view of its implementors – frequently line and general managers – and to develop a deeper awareness of the many pressures and demands that make the implementation of espoused personnel policies difficult for them. Line managers do not decide to accept or reject policies arbitrarily; rather, they are, most of the time, trying to conform with the values and priorities of senior executives.[25]

To summarize, personnel managers need to ensure that:

- ideas for improvement or innovation are thoroughly tested against an analysis of the characteristics and true needs of the organization;
- ideas are sold to management on the basis of the practical and, wherever possible, measurable benefits that will result from their implementation (it is not the idea itself that is saleable but the result it can achieve) – persuasive ability is a major requirement for success in personnel management;
- new procedures or techniques are pilot-tested to make sure they work in practice and to provide evidence of the benefits they produce;
- the procedures or techniques are presented with great care to management as providing direct help to them in running the organization or their department more effectively than before;
- unobtrusive assistance, guidance and encouragement is provided in implementing new techniques – not from the stance of a would-be professional who knows it all, but from the point of view of a colleague who can give practical help in achieving something worthwhile;
- a human resource management approach as described in the next chapter is adopted;

● they develop the skills which are basic to effective personnel management, namely, diagnostic skills (for use in a contingency approach), and job analysis, interviewing, counselling, negotiating and communicating skills.

References

1. Legge, K *Power, Innovation and Problem-solving in Personnel Management*. McGraw-Hill, Maidenhead, 1978.
2. Gluckman, M (ed) *Closed Systems and Open Minds*. Oliver and Boyd, London, 1964.
3. Woodward, J *Industrial Organization*. Oxford University Press, Oxford, 1965.
4. Burns, T and Stalker, G M *The Management of Innovation*. Tavistock Publications, London, 1961.
5. Lawrence, P R and Lorsch, J W *Organization and Environment*. Harvard University Press, Cambridge, Mass., 1967.
6. Silverman, D *The Theory of Organization: a Sociological Framework*. Heinemann, London, 1970.
7. Handy, C B *Understanding Organizations*. Penguin Books, Harmondsworth, 1974.
8. Drucker, P *The Practice of Management*. Heinemann, London, 1955.
9. McGregor, D *The Human Side of Enterprise*. McGraw-Hill.
10. Katz, D and Kahn, R L *The Social Psychology of Organizations*. John Wiley and Sons, New York, 1964.
11. Heller, R *The Naked Manager*. Barrie and Jenkins, London, 1972.
12. Townsend, R *Up the Organization*. Michael Joseph, London, 1970.
13. Prior, P 'Toll the Knell for Leadership. The Personnel Man Cometh', *Personnel Management*, October, 1981.
14. Manning, K 'The Rise and Fall of Personnel', *Management Today*, March, 1983.
15. Ezra, Lord Derek 'How I see the Personnel Function', *Personnel Management*, July, 1982.
16. Jarrett, Sir Alex 'How I see the Personnel Function', *Personnel Management*, June, 1982.
17. Parker, Sir Peter 'How I see the Personnel Function', *Personnel Management*, January, 1983.
18. Mackay, L and Torrington, D *The Changing Nature of Personnel Management*. Institute of Personnel Management, London, 1986.
19. Watson, A *The Personnel Managers*. Routledge and Kegan Paul, London, 1977.
20. Thurley, K 'Personnel Management in the UK – A Case for Urgent Treatment'. *Personnel Management*, February, 1983.
21. Tyson, S 'Taking Advantage of Ambiguity', *Personnel Management*, April, 1983.
22. Tyson, S and Fell, A *Evaluating the Personnel Function*. Hutchinson, London, 1986.
23. Williamson, D E and Ouchi, W G 'The Markets and Hierarchies Programme of Research: Origins, Implications and Prospects', in Francis, A, Turk, J and Willmar, P (eds), *Power, Efficiency and Institutions*. Heinemann, London, 1983.
24. Brewster, C J, Gill, C G and Richbell, S 'Developing an Analytical Approach to Industrial Relations Policy', *Personnel Review*, Vol 10, No 2, 1981.
25. Brewster, C T and Richbell, S 'Getting Managers to Implement Personnel Policies', *Personnel Management*, December, 1982.
26. Fowler, A, as reported in *IPM Digest*, November, 1982.

Chapter 4
Human Resource Management

Definition

Human resource management has been defined variously as:

- 'A strategic approach to the acquisition, motivation, development and management of the organization's human resources'.[1]
- 'The strategic management of the organization's most expensive and least tractable asset'.[2]
- Having two themes: 'First, that every aspect of employee management must be wholly integrated with general business management and reinforce the desired corporate culture. Secondly, that a dominant emphasis on the common interests of employer and employed in the success of the business will release a massive potential of initiative and commitment within the workforce'.[3]
- 'Human resource management is a more comprehensive approach to the organization of people at work. With a base in the behavioural sciences, human resource management is concerned about the motivation and development of the individual employee and the performance and productivity of the organization . . . (it) is a holistic view wherein all activities are designed in a unified and interlocking manner'.[4]
- Human resource management is directed mainly towards management needs for human resources (not only employees) to be provided and deployed. There is greater emphasis on planning, monitoring and control, rather than on problem solving and mediation. It is totally identified with management interests and is relatively distant from the workforce as a whole'.[5]

Principles of human resource management

Human resource management (HRM) is an approach to the management of people, based on four fundamental principles:

71

1. Human resources are the most important assets an organization has and their effective management is the key to its success.
2. Organizational success is most likely to be achieved if the personnel policies and procedures of the enterprise are closely linked with, and make a major contribution to, the achievement of corporate objectives and strategic plans.
3. The corporate culture and the values, organizational climate and managerial behaviour that emanate from that culture will exert a major influence on the achievement of excellence. This culture must be managed, which means that continuous effort, starting from the top, will be required to get the values accepted and acted upon.
4. Continuous effort is required to achieve integration – getting all the members of the organization involved and working together with a sense of common purpose. This point was originally made by Douglas McGregor when he defined his principle of integration as: 'The creation of conditions such that the members of the organization can achieve their own goals best by directing their efforts towards the success of the enterprise'.[6] Methods of achieving integration are discussed in Chapter 12.

The roots of HRM

The pioneers

The roots of HRM go back to the pioneering work of Peter Drucker and Douglas McGregor in the 1950s. Drucker, in *The Practice of Management*, virtually invented management by objectives. He wrote that: 'An effective management must direct the vision and effort of all managers towards a common goal';[7] this concept of visionary goal-directed leadership is fundamental to HRM.

Douglas McGregor advocated management by integration and self-control, partly as a form of management by objectives, but more importantly as a strategy for managing people which affects the whole business. He believed that a management philosophy needed to be built up based on attitudes and beliefs about people and the managerial role of achieving integration. He did not see this process as simply one of deploying personnel techniques, manuals and forms. A key role of the personnel function, as he saw it, was 'to devise means of getting management to examine its assumptions, to consider the consequences of its present strategy and to compare it with others'.

He, like Drucker, therefore, paved the way to the HRM philosophy that human resource policies and programmes must be built into the strategic objectives and plans of the business and must also aim to get everyone involved in the achievement of these objectives and plans.

The behavioural science movement

The behavioural science movement came into prominence in the 1960s. It was founded by writers such as Maslow,[8] whose hierarchy of human needs place self-fulfilment or self-actualization at the top of the pyramid, and Likert,[9] who developed his integrating principle of supportive relationships. This stated that organization members should, in the light of their values and expectations, view their work as supportive and as contributing to the building and maintenance of their sense of personal worth and importance.

Another important figure in the behavioural science movement was Argyris, who believed that organization design should plan for integration and involvement and that individuals should feel that they have a high degree of self-control over setting their own goals and over the paths to defining those goals.

The most influential member of the behavioural science school, however, was Herzberg,[10] who advocated job enrichment as a means of increasing organizational effectiveness, claiming that such improvements should centre on the work itself as a source of motivation – if people feel that the job is stretching them, they will be moved to perform it well.

The behavioural science movement had a somewhat idealistic flavour about it, but it did make two useful contributions to HRM. First, it underlined the importance of integration and involvement and second, it highlighted the idea that management should accept as a basic value the need consciously and continuously to improve the quality of working life as a means to obtaining increased motivation and improved results.

The organization development movement

The concepts of the behavioural scientists provided the impetus for the organizational development (OD) movement of the 1960s and 1970s, whose beliefs were summarized by Bennis as follows:

1. A new concept of man based on increased knowledge of his complex and shifting needs which replaces an oversimplified, innocent, push-button idea of man.
2. A new concept of power, based on collaboration and reason, which replaces a model of power based on coercion and threat.
3. A new concept of organization values, based on humanistic-democratic ideas, which replaces the mechanistic value system of bureaucracy.[11]

The OD movement advocated the implementation of programmes designed to improve the effectiveness with which an organization functions and responds to change, with particular emphasis on how people carry out their work and interact with one another. The management of change and team development are often important parts of an organization development programme.

Like the behavioural scientists they usually were, OD practitioners tended to be idealistic, but the good ones saw the organization as a whole and based their plans on a systematic analysis of its circumstances and the changes and problems affecting it. This total approach to organizational behaviour exerted a strong influence on many of those who, in the late 1970s and early 1980s, began to concentrate on corporate culture as a central issue in the management of human resources.

The corporate culture analysts

The interest in corporate culture has derived partly from the organizational behaviour specialists but, importantly, the main thrust behind the cult of culture has come from empirical studies of the ingredients that make for corporate success.

One of the seminal works was *The Art of Japanese Management* by Richard Pascale and Anthony Athos.[12] This study of the secrets of Japanese business success attributed much of it to the creation of powerful organizational cultures, from which are derived the shared values between management and workers which emphasize 'mutuality' – a common interest in corporate excellence.

Another influential work was *In Search of Excellence* by Peters and Waterman.[13] They found that companies whose only articulated goals were financial did not do nearly as well as companies that had broader sets of values. They quoted with approval Andrew Pettigrew, a British researcher, who saw the process of shaping culture as the prime management role. He said: 'The (leader) not only creates the rational and tangible aspects of organizations, such as structure and technology, but also is the creator of ideologies, language, beliefs, rituals and myths',[14] and found that the value sets of the excellent companies integrate the 'notions of economic health, serving customers and making meanings down the line'. Peters and Waterman also noted that the excellent companies were people orientated, by a wide range of 'people programmes'. Like Drucker, they warned against the 'gimmick trap' (for example, quality circles) if it is not part of an overall approach which has the absolute backing of top management and is truly representative of the corporate culture and its values.

Reservations about HRM

The concept of HRM has been enthusiastically embraced by a lot of chief executives and management gurus, especially in the United States. So much so, that it has been disparaged by some people as a fad or no more than 'flavour of the month', like other managerial nostrums such as organizational development, job enrichment and similar applications of the behavioural sciences. Over-enthusiasm can kill or at least maim a fundamentally good idea.

In an article in *Personnel Management* Alan Fowler,[3] while approving of much of the HRM approach, said that the message tends to be beguilingly simple: 'Don't bother too much about the techniques or content of personnel management, it says. Just manage the context. Get out from behind your desk, by-pass the hierarchy, and go and talk to people. That way you will unlock an enormous potential for improved performance'. But Fowler points out that commitment needs competence, and this includes the use of the skills of marketing, financial, production, data processing *and* personnel professionals. He also says, quite rightly, that there is a danger of implying that the HRM culture as prescribed is right for all organizations; but there is ample evidence that different situations can call for different organizations and different management styles. There is no one simple way of doing anything when dealing with organizations and people.

Some people also express reservations about the manipulative aspects of HRM. They say that, adapting the principle of 'what is good for General Motors is good for America', chief executives with a mission for HRM believe that 'what is good for the business must be good for everyone in it'. They could be right, but not always so, and all the forces of internal persuasion and propaganda may be deployed to get people to accept values with which they are not in accord and which may in any case be against their interests.

As Fowler pointed out, HRM also seems to ignore the existence of trade unions. As a system of management it starts at the top and cascades to all levels of management and staff through various processes of communication backed by specific devices such as team briefing. The emphasis is rightly on participation, but it takes two to play at that game. However hard management tries to get its message across about identification and commitment, there may still be the belief in the offices and on the shop floor that the collective interests of the work force need to be protected by trade unions or staff associations.

This could be correct: in some ways an organization is a plural society, containing many related but separate interests and objectives which must be maintained in some kind of equilibrium. Management has to work with trade unions to build harmonious relationships and to develop agreed systems of rules and procedures which will facilitate this process and resolve, with the minimum amount of damage to either party, the conflicts that will almost inevitably arise. HRM in some of its forms does not seem to recognize that this need exists.

All these are valid points, but they do not destroy the basic principles of HRM. What the reservations do tell you is that you have to be cautious about applying the HRM message too simplistically; you must avoid trying to impose an HRM type culture which is not relevant to the circumstances of the organization, or does not take sufficient account of the possibility that the values of management and workers may be too far apart to be integrated with ease.

Application of HRM

As a strategic approach to the management of the organization's human resources, HRM is devoted to shaping an appropriate corporate culture, and introducing programmes which reflect and support the core values of the enterprise and ensure its success. HRM is proactive rather than reactive, ie always looking forward to what needs to be done and then doing it, rather than waiting to be told what to do – about recruiting, paying or training people or dealing with employee relations problems as they arise.

The concepts of the pioneers, the behavioural scientists and the organization development specialists are built into the values underlying the programmes and will influence the techniques used in them. These techniques will include many familiar to personnel managers, such as manpower planning, selection, performance appraisal, salary administration, training and management development. These will be overlaid by special programmes designed to improve communications and increase involvement, commitment and productivity. All of them will be incorporated into a coherent approach which will link the various 'people programmes', referred to by Peters and Waterman, in a way which makes a major contribution to the achievement of the organization's objectives by being completely integrated with its strategic plans.

References

1. Armstrong, M 'Human resource management: a case of the emperor's new clothes?', *Personnel Management*, August, 1987.
2. Stanton, M, Lecture on communications management, July, 1987.
3. Fowler, A 'When chief executives discover HRM', *Personnel Management*, January, 1987.
4. Tyson, S and Fell, A *Evaluating the Personnel Function*. Hutchinson, London, 1986.
5. Mackay, L and Torrington, D *The Changing Nature of Personnel Management*. Institute of Personnel Management, London, 1986.
6. McGregor, D *The Human Side of Enterprise*. McGraw-Hill, New York, 1966.
7. Drucker, P *The Practice of Management*. Heinemann, London, 1955.
8. Maslow, A H *Motivation and Personality*. Harper & Row, New York, 1954.
9. Likert, R *New Patterns of Management*. McGraw-Hill, New York, 1966.
10. Herzberg, F *et al*, *The Motivation to Work*. Wiley, New York, 1959.
11. Bennis, W *Organizational Development*. Addison-Wesley, Reading, Mass., 1960.
12. Pascale, R and Athos, A *The Art of Japanese Management*. Simon and Schuster, New York, 1981.

13. Peters, T and Waterman, R *In Search of Excellence*. Harper & Row, New York, 1982.
14. Pettigrew, A 'The creation of corporate culture'. Paper delivered in Copenhagen in 1976.

Part II
Organizational Behaviour

The study of organizational behaviour is the study of how organizations function, in terms of their structure and processes, and how the people within organizations act, individually or in groups.

Personnel managers perform their jobs within complex systems called organizations. Managers in general, and personnel managers in particular, exist to influence behaviour in a desired direction. Skills in the analysis and diagnosis of patterns of organizational behaviour are therefore important. They help in the definition of organizational context, and, as Nadler and Tushman have said:

> The manager needs to be able to *understand* the patterns of behaviour that are observed, to *predict* in what direction behaviour will move (particularly in the light of managerial action), and to use this knowledge to *control* behaviour over the course of time... Effective managerial action requires that the manager be able to diagnose the system he or she is working in.[1]

The purpose of this part of the book is to outline a basic set of concepts and to provide analytical tools which will enable the personnel manager to diagnose organizational behaviour and to take appropriate actions. The actions will include the use of techniques to design organizations and jobs, to develop more effective organizations and people, to manage change and conflict, to motivate people to work and to deal with problems concerning individuals or groups. These techniques should be developed and operated in the knowledge of the processes at work in the organization as they affect and are affected by the behaviour of the people in it.

Chapter 5 addresses the overriding concept of corporate culture as it manifests itself in the forms of assumptions, beliefs, values, organizational climate and management style.

Chapter 6 considers how organizations are structured, taking into account the human factors involved. In Chapter 7 the way in which organizations function is examined by studying the various processes that take place within them – change, leadership, power, conflict, stress and group behaviour. Chapter 8 deals with the factors that influence individual behaviour at work – motivation and how people adapt to their roles.

79

Reference

1. Nadler, D A and Tushman, M L *A Congruence Model for Diagnosing Organizational Behaviour*. Resource Book in Macro-Organizational Behaviour, R H Miles (ed), Goodyear Publishing, Santa Monica, 1980.

Chapter 5
Corporate Culture

The importance of culture

Corporate culture in the shape of a pattern of shared beliefs pervades all organizations. It underlies much of the way in which things get done. It encompasses the company's goals and dominant ideologies. It can be expressed through its myths, heroes, stories, jargon, rites and rituals. It is also expressed in corporate values – what is good for the organization and what should or should not happen; organizational climate – the working atmosphere of the organization as perceived and experienced by its members; and management style – the way in which managers behave and exercise authority.

Personnel managers have to live within the corporate culture. They must understand it as a basis for diagnosing and solving problems and for developing new policies or procedures. And they may well be involved in managing the culture in times of change or during crises.

This chapter starts by defining corporate culture. It then discusses how it is formed, its constituents and how it manifests itself. The chapter is concluded with an analysis of how culture can be managed.

Definition of corporate culture

Corporate culture has been defined as the personality of an organization, but there is much more to it than that. Professor Ed Schein of the MIT, who is a leading expert on corporate culture, has defined it more formally:

> The pattern of basic assumptions that a given group has invented, discovered or developed in learning to cope with the problems of external adaption and integration, and that have worked well enough to be considered valid, and, therefore, to be taught to new members as the correct way to perceive, think and feel in relation to these problems.[1]

Corporate culture can also be defined as: 'A system of shared values (what is important) and beliefs (how things work) that interact with a

company's people, organizational structures and control system to produce behavioural norms (the way we do things about here).' (Dr Nicholas
Georgiadis, 'Cultural Change in British Airways', MCE paper, Lisbon
1987.)

The word 'culture' has many meanings and connotations and Schein
suggests that it should be reserved for the deeper level of assumptions and
beliefs that are shared by members of an organization, that operate sub-
consciously, and that define in a basic 'taken-for-granted' fashion an
organization's view of itself and its environment. He wrote that:

> Culture is not the overt behaviour or visible artifacts that one might observe if one
> were to visit the company. It is not even the philosophy or value system which the
> founder may articulate or write down in various 'charters'. Rather it is the assump-
> tions which lie behind the values and which determine the behaviour patterns and
> the visible artifacts such as architecture, office layout, dress codes and so on.[2]

Many writers on corporate culture, management consultants and managers adopt a narrow definition of culture that emphasizes the shallower
levels rather than the deeper perspective adopted by the academics. The
popularizers discuss culture in terms of visible behaviour patterns and the
'rules of the game.' They take the last phrase in Nick Georgiadis' definition and simply describe corporate culture as 'the way things are done
around here.' They seem to have T S Eliot on their side when he wrote in
Notes Towards the Definition of Culture:

> 'What we believe in is not merely what we formulate and subscribe to . . . behaviour
> is also belief.'[3]

What Eliot is of course saying is that culture manifests in beliefs *and* behaviour and in turn is influenced and modified by behaviour. You cannot
have one without the other but you certainly cannot concentrate entirely
on behaviour, as the more simplistic commentators do. If you want to
change behaviour you have to go back to its roots in the form of, in
Schein's words, 'The assumptions which lie behind the values and which
determine the behaviour patterns.'[2] This view was confirmed by Michael
Thomas who wrote in *Personnel Management* that organization culture
is 'something more profound even than 'attitude' and something which
makes the members of a given group behave more like each other than
non-members'.[4]

However, the nature of the basic concept of corporate culture does not
diminish its significance. It is by no means unreal, even to someone as
down-to-earth as Alan Sugar, Chairman of Amstrad, who said in an
address in 1987 to the City University Business Centre: 'It is essential to
retain a strong corporate culture and philosophy, otherwise the business
can drift and become confused and lost in direction.'

How corporate culture is formed

Culture is learned. Ed Schein suggests that there are two ways in which this learning takes place. First, the trauma model, in which members of the organization learn to cope with some threat by the erection of defence mechanisms. Second, the 'positive reinforcement' model, where things which seem to work become embedded and entrenched. Learning takes place as people adapt to and cope with external pressures, and as they develop successful approaches and mechanisms to handle the technologies of their organization.

Environmental influences will make a strong impact on the corporate culture. The organization has to exist in an external environment which could be turbulent or steady, and could either drive the enterprise in certain directions whether it likes it or not, or could be managed so that the business goes where it wants to go. The type of activity the organization carries out will largely determine its technology and the way it goes about its business, and these will in turn affect the way the corporate culture develops and is manifested within the organization.

Against this background, corporate culture is created by organizational members, with the values, philosophy, beliefs, assumptions and norms of top management playing a dominant role.

The constituents of corporate culture

Corporate culture contains assumptions about the nature of the business and its markets and customers, the way in which business should be carried out, how work should be organized, the sort of people the organization needs and how they should be treated.

A corporate culture can be strong or weak, and a strong culture is not necessarily a good one – it could be the wrong culture and it could be difficult to change. A weak culture, even a practically non-existent culture, may be acceptable if the organization functions well. Within one organization there may be a dominant culture, but there will certainly be many sub-cultures in different departments or locations.

Corporate cultures are different: that at Mars is totally dissimilar to that at Cadbury's; IBM and ICL are quite unalike; no one could have anything to do with Allied Dunbar or the Prudential and not become quickly aware that they are fundamentally different. But you would be hard put to it to attribute the relative levels of success achieved by each of these pairs to particular cultural attributes.

To an extent, the interest in the concept of corporate culture has been encouraged by attempts to uncover the secrets of Japanese success. Pascale and Athos in *The Art of Japanese Management*[5] emphasized the advantages of the Japanese culture in the shape of its ability to help them manage ambiguity, uncertainty and imperfection, and in its emphasis on interdependence as the most approved mode of relationship. Although there may be many good things about Japanese corporate culture which we could usefully apply in our own organizations, it is not necessarily a model which we should slavishly copy. As Pascale and Athos pointed out: 'The dozen high-performing companies identified in our study of Japanese and American firms included six that were American. The prime determinant of their success was not society or culture; it was management. United Airlines and IBM were among these firms, and in a variety of ways they outperformed their Japanese counterparts.'

How corporate culture manifests itself

Corporate culture manifests itself in organizational behaviour – how managers and individual employees or groups behave in the context of the organization. In other words, it becomes 'the way things are done around here'. The culture influences behaviour in three areas:

1. *Corporate values:* (as defined in Chapter 3) beliefs in what is best or good for the organization and what should or ought to happen. They are expressed by reference to both ends (goals) and means (action plans for achieving goals).
2. *Organization climate:* the working atmosphere of the organization as perceived and experienced by its members. This will encompass how people feel about and react to the characteristics and quality of the corporate culture and its values.
3. *Management style:* the way in which managers behave and exercise authority. They may be autocratic or democratic, tough or easygoing, formal or informal. It also describes the way in which managers behave. Michael Maccoby[6] suggests that there are four basic types of manager:

   The craftsman: an independent perfectionist whose passion is for quality and for doing things better.

   The jungle fighter: a power-hungry predator who likes to be feared. Will fail where success depends on teamwork.

   The company man: a courteous, loyal careerist who believes in performance and people – but wants security even more than success.

   The modern gamesman: a fast-moving, flexible winner who loves change. Competes for the pleasure of the contest and for the sheer exhilaration of victory.

According to Maccoby, the ideal type is the creative gamesman – a lion with a heart who is flexible enough to behave appropriately in a variety of situations and is mentally tough but also compassionate.

The style managers adopt will be affected by the organization's culture and values. It depends to a degree on the individual's attitudes, but will also be affected by the leadership situations in which people are placed and, most importantly, by the example given by more senior managers, especially the person at the top. The chief executive by his own behaviour can exert a great influence on the management style throughout the organization.

A management style that is more likely to encourage commitment and co-operation will lean in the direction of being democratic, relaxed, friendly, informal and open. But this does not mean that it should not be tough and direct when the occasion demands it – and it should always be decisive.

Rites and rituals

Terence Deal and Alan Kennedy believe that:

'Strong culture companies communicate exactly how they want their people to behave. They spell out standards of acceptable decorum – so people who visit or work in any of their places of business can know exactly what to expect. They call attention to the way in which procedures – for example, strategic planning and budgeting – are to be carried out, so the fault if the procedures fail is substantive, not just a failure to follow a prescribed process. Often they also establish ways, or at least the settings, in which their people can play and have fun – so that people will know they belong to a functioning and complete society. In short, strong culture companies create the rites and rituals that exercise the most visible and pervasive influence "in the way we do things around here".'[7]

Culture management

Because corporate culture is based on taken-for-granted assumptions and beliefs about what is good and not good for the organization, it is a somewhat elusive concept. There may not be a single culture but a number of cultures spread throughout the organization; and this does not make 'managing' the culture any easier. In any case, there is no such thing as a 'good' or 'bad' culture, but only cultures which are appropriate or inappropriate. If you have an appropriate culture, its management consists of no more than maintaining the existing values, climate and management style; change is not necessary.

Corporate cultures can, however, have significant effects on behaviour. These can be fundamental if incorrect assumptions about the market and the company's position in it lead to an unsuitable strategic plan. Even when the correct strategies have been adopted, their implementation may be hindered if the wrong assumptions are made about how to sell the product or service, how to organize the people in the business, or how to manage, motivate, develop, reward and communicate with these people. Cultural change programmes may be required if the wrong assumptions have created an inappropriate culture and this is affecting performance.

Can corporate culture be managed?

Corporate culture is a key factor in achieving success but it is not easy to get at. Because it will have evolved over the years through a number of learning processes, a deeply rooted culture may be difficult to change – old habits die hard. The answer to the question, 'Can it be managed?' is, 'Yes, but with difficulty'.

However, you also have to answer the question, 'Should it be managed?' because there are a number of alternative approaches to culture management, as put forward by Howard Schwartz and Stanley Davies.[8] These are:

- Ignore the culture.
- Manage round it.
- Attempt to change elements of the culture to fit the strategy.
- Change the strategy.

You can also take the culture you have got and do your best to maintain what is good about it while attempting to change counter-productive aspects of behaviour.

Deal and Kennedy said in *Corporate Cultures* that there are only five reasons to justify large-scale cultural change:

1. If your company has strong values that do not fit a changing environment.
2. If the industry is very competitive and moves with lightning speed.
3. If your company is mediocre or worse.
4. If your company is about to join the ranks of the very largest companies.
5. If your company is small but growing rapidly.

Deal and Kennedy say that if none of these reasons apply, don't do it. Their analysis of 10 cases of attempted cultural change indicated that it will cost between 5 and 10 per cent of what you already spend on the people whose behaviour is supposed to change and even then you are likely to get only half the improvement you want. They warn that it costs a lot (in time, effort and money) and will take a long time.

How should corporate culture be managed?

A culture management programme involves the following steps, which are described in more detail later in this section:

1. Identify basic assumptions and beliefs and challenge them if necessary.

2. Define or re-define the core values – stated or unstated.
3. Analyse the organizational climate.
4. Analyse the management style.
5. Plan and implement on the basis of steps 1 to 4 what aspects of the culture (as defined by assumptions, values, climate and management style) need to be changed and what aspects should be maintained or reinforced.

A key part is played in this process by the chief executive who, with the support of his team, achieves excellence by defining the organization's mission, getting his vision of what needs to be done across to everyone, defining and promulgating what he believes to be the right organizational values, exercising leadership in order to motivate the members of the organization, and ensuring that they are involved in and committed to achieving its objectives.

Personnel specialists should be closely involved in the analytical work. They should also play a major part in the culture management programme (Step 5) as described below.

The approaches that can be adopted to manage corporate culture and help to achieve cultural change are:

1. *Reorganization* to facilitate integration, to create departments or jobs which are responsible for new activities or to eliminate unnecessary layers of management.
2. *Organization development* to improve the effectiveness with which an organization functions and responds to change. OD programmes are concerned with achieving better co-ordination, teamwork and commitment and with the management of change and conflict.
3. *Communications* to get the message across about the values and to achieve the objectives for a communications change programme set up in Book Club Associates in 1987, which were to:
   - increase the identification of staff with the firm and therefore to enhance their commitment;
   - provide the opportunity for all levels of staff to become more involved in the firm's affairs;
   - generate ideas from staff to develop the business, improve the levels of customer service and increase productivity.
4. *Training* to help form new attitudes to such matters as customer service, quality, managing and motivating people or productivity; to increase commitment to the firm and its values; to review and challenge assumptions; and to improve skills or teach new skills.
5. *Recruitment* to set out deliberately to change the type of people recruited to fit the desired culture or to reinforce the existing culture by drawing up related job specifications and finding candidates who meet those specifications.

6. *Management by objectives* to ensure that managers know what they are expected to do.
7. *Performance management* to ensure that managers, supervisors and staff are assessed on the basis of the results they achieve and that performance improvement programmes consisting of self-development, coaching, counselling and training are used to capitalize on strengths or overcome weaknesses.
8. *Reward management* to enhance the cultural assumption that rewards should be related to achievement by introducing performance-related bonus schemes and remuneration systems.

References

1. Schein, E H 'Coming to a New Awareness of Corporate Culture'. *Sloan Management Review*, Winter 1984.
2. Schein, E M *Organizational Dynamics*, Summer 1983.
3. Eliot, T S *Notes Towards the Definition of Culture*. Faber & Faber, London, 1948.
4. Thomas, M 'In Search of Culture', *Personnel Management*, September, 1985.
5. Pascale, R T and Athos, A G *The Art of Japanese Management*. Simon & Schuster, New York, 1981.
6. Maccoby, M *The Gamesman*. Bantam, New York, 1978.
7. Deal, T E and Kennedy, A *Corporate Cultures*. Addison-Wesley, Reading, Mass., 1982.
8. Schwartz, H and Davies, D *Matching Corporate Culture and Strategy*. MAP Concept Paper, Cambridge, Mass., 1983.

Chapter 6
Organization Structure

Organizations exist to get work done. The organization itself is an entity which is there for a purpose. This determines what it sets out to do, but *what* it actually does and *how* it does it will be influenced by a number of external and internal forces, including the environment and the history of the organization.

The process of organizing can be described as the design, development and maintenance of a system of co-ordinated activities in which individuals and groups of people work co-operatively under authority and leadership towards commonly understood and accepted goals. The key word in that definition is 'system'. Organizations are systems which, as affected by their environment, have a structure which has both formal and informal elements.

All organizations have some form of structure, which has been defined by John Child as comprising 'all the tangible and regularly occurring features which help to shape its members' behaviour'.[1] This chapter deals with the considerations that affect the structure of organizations. It does this by reviewing the various organization 'models' developed by the theorists on this subject. These concepts are intended to provide a background against which the design of organizations and jobs as discussed in Part III of this book can be carried out.

Basic considerations

Organizations vary in their complexity, but in every case it is necessary to divide the overall management task into a variety of activities and to establish means of co-ordinating and controlling these activities. This design process leads to the development of a formal organization structure consisting of units and positions between which there are relationships involving the exercise of authority and the communication and exchange of information.

The structure must be appropriate to the organization's purpose and to the situation in which it exists. As Lupton says: 'Organizations are seen as patterns of human tasks and relationships, shaped so as to allow at least survival, at most growth and development, in environments which constrain, but which also offer opportunities.'[2]

Personnel managers are, or should be, involved in the design and development of organizations. They should base their contribution on an understanding of the forces shaping their own organization. To do this they need tools which will help them to analyse and appreciate what is happening. These tools are provided in the form of 'models' developed by a number of writers and researchers on organization development.

The original model derived from the work of the *classical school* of organization theorists, who believed that the design of the structure should conform to certain general principles. The *human relations school*, however, emphasized that the way organizations function and how, therefore, they should be structured, is primarily dependent on how people behave, interact and create the informal organization. The *bureaucratic model* developed by Weber suggested that there were circumstances in which organizations did require formal hierarchies and clear definitions of responsibilities. The *systems* and *contingency schools* stressed correctly that the way organizations functioned and were structured was closely related to their environment, technology and the amount of change and differentiation to which they were subjected.

It should be remembered, however, that while these models either contribute to our understanding of the different forms of organization or provide a basis for tackling organizational problems, they do not add up to a universal theory of organization. As Perrow wrote: 'We know enough about organizations now to recognize that most generalizations that are applicable to all organizations are too obvious or too general to be of much use for specific predictions.'[3] And the earliest models produced by the scientific management or so-called 'classical' school fell into this trap, which is why, as will emerge later, the contingency approach seems to have most to offer.

Scientific management

The scientific management or classical school as represented by Fayol, Taylor and Urwick believed in control, order and formality. Organizations need to minimize the opportunity for unfortunate and uncontrollable informal relations, leaving room only for the formal ones. From these overriding principles the following concepts are derived:

1. *Structure.* Formal structures are required to provide orderly relationships between functions. The basic structure contains the line organization, which exercises delegated authority in performing the functions of the enterprise, and the staff organization which offers advice and provides services required by the line

organization. Structural considerations include the span of control, which relates to the number of subordinates an executive can manage and the number of levels in the hierarchy.

2. *Specialization.* As the human organization grows, work must be broken down along lines as natural as possible to provide well defined areas of specialization. This is the classical economic theory of the division of labour and all other scientific-management principles are derived from it.

3. *Co-ordination.* The need for specialization creates the need for co-ordination. The many different functions performed by the members of an organization must be co-ordinated or tied together so that they contribute jointly to the end result. To achieve this members have to carry out their work as and when required so that each contribution fits the contribution of others.

4. *Authority.* Organizations achieve order and regularity by the use of authority implemented through a defined hierarchy or chain of command.

5. *Continuity.* Organizations should be designed to achieve continuity, stability and predictability. This must be done by minimizing disruptions caused by personality and individual idiosyncrasy. The organization consists of replaceable members and its design should not be affected by the people who happen to be employed in it.

The scientific management model has been attacked vigorously because it is too rigid and because it makes no allowance for situational factors such as the environment or technology. Neither does it take account of change or human factors, including the informal organization. But this approach, with its emphasis on organization charts and manuals, job descriptions, clear definitions of responsibility and authority and limited spans of control, still thrives. As Lupton pointed out: 'The attraction of the classical design from the point of view of top management is that it seems to offer them control.'[2] Managers like to think they are rational and this has all the appearance of a rational approach. Many line managers when asked to describe their organizations will draw hierarchical charts, produce job descriptions and use such expressions as chain of command, levels of authority, line and staff and span of control. This is the language of classical theory and it is not inherently wrong — most people prefer some structure and find it difficult to tolerate ambiguity. But it must not be applied too rigidly. There are other considerations.

The human relations school

The scientific management school reigned supreme until the late 1930s and still holds sway in the 1980s, as mentioned above. But in 1938 a business executive named Chester Barnard suggested that organizations are co-operative systems, not the products of mechanical engineering. He stressed natural groups within the organization, upward communication, authority from below rather than from above, and leaders who function-ed as a cohesive force. Barnard also emphasized the importance of the informal organization – the network of informal roles and relationships which, for better or worse, strongly influences the way the formal struc-ture operates. He wrote: 'Formal organizations come out of and are necessary to informal organization: but when formal organizations come into operation, they create and require informal organizations.'[4] Much more recently, Child[1] has pointed out that it is misleading to talk about a clear distinction between the formal and the informal organization. Formality *and* informality can be designed into structure. Unofficial policies do exist in organizations but they are not to be confused with informality. Organization designers recognize the relevance of informal relationships but do not implement unofficial structures.

In 1938 Roethlisberger and Dickson[5] reported on the Hawthorne Studies – the first large-scale investigation of productivity and industrial relations, which took place at the Hawthorne plant at Western Electric. This highlighted the importance of informal groups, work restriction norms and decent, humane leadership.

It was widely, if unfairly, believed that supporters of the human rela-tions school approach only wanted organizations to be nice to people. But by largely ignoring organizational needs, that is the impression they often made.

The behavioural science school

In the 1960s a number of behavioural scientists emerged who would not like to be described as part of the human relations school, but did in fact subscribe to some of the fundamental beliefs of that school, although these beliefs were refined and re-presented on the basis of further study and research. The most notable contributors to this post-war develop-ment were McGregor, Likert and Argyris.

Douglas McGregor

Douglas McGregor is best known for his classification of assumptions about human nature into Theories X and Y. Theory X is the traditional view that the average human being dislikes work and wishes to avoid re-sponsibility and that, therefore, 'most people must be coerced, controlled, directed, threatened with punishment to get them to put forward adequate effort towards organizational objectives.'[6] The more progressive, some would say optimistic, assumptions contained in Theory Y are that, given the chance, people will not only accept but also seek responsibility: 'The capacity to execute a relatively high degree of imagination, ingenuity and creativity in the solution of organizational problems is widely, not narrowly, distributed in the population.'

The central principle of organizations that McGregor derived from Theory Y is that of integration – the process of recognizing the needs of both the organization and the individual and creating conditions which will reconcile their needs so that members of the organization can work together for its success and share in its rewards: 'Man will exercise self-direction and self-control in the service of objectives to which he is committed.'

Rensis Likert

Rensis Likert derived his concept of organizations based on supportive relationships from the programmes of research at the University of Michigan where he was director. The initial studies distinguished between job-centred and employee-centred supervisors and established that employee-centred supervisors were higher producers than the job-centred ones. The studies also distinguished between general and close supervision and showed that general rather than close supervision is more often associated with a high rather than a low level of productivity.

From his analysis of high-producing managers Likert found that their operations were characterized by attitudes of identification with the organization and its objectives and a high sense of involvement in achieving them. This situation was created by 'harnessing effectively all the major motivational forces which can exercise significant influence in an organizational setting and which, potentially, can be accompanied by co-operative and favourable attitudes.'[7]

The integrating principle of supportive relationships was derived from this analysis. This principle states that:

> The leadership and other processes of the organization must be such as to ensure a maximum probability that in all interactions and all relationships with the organization each member will, in the light of his background, values and expectations, view the experience as supportive and one which builds and maintains his sense of personal worth and importance.[7]

Chrys Argyris

The research carried out by Argyris into personality development in organizations suggested to him 'that the formal organization creates in a healthy individual feelings of failure and frustration, short time perspective and conflict'.[8] He further concluded that the formal work organization requires many members to act in immature rather than adult ways: 'At all levels there is behaviour that is not productive in the sense of helping the organization achieve its objectives. For example, at the lower levels we found apathy, indifference and non-involvement. At the upper levels we found conformity, mistrust, inability to accept new ideas, and fear of risk taking.'[9]

To overcome this problem Argyris wants the individual to feel that he has a high degree of self-control over setting his own goals and over defining the paths to these goals. The strategy should be to 'develop a climate in which the difficulties can be openly discussed, the employee's hostility understood and accepted, and a programme defined which everyone can participate in attempting to develop new designs. Wherever this is impossible, the attempt will be made to design new work worlds that can be integrated with the old and that help the employee obtain more opportunity for psychological success.'[9] Lest this seems too idealistic (a tendency shared by all members of the human relations school) Argyris stresses the need for some structure to provide 'the firm ground on which to anchor one's security'. Organization design has therefore to plan for integration and involvement, although these processes will probably have to take place within the traditional pyramidal structure.

Other contributions to the behavioural science movement

The behavioural science movement, pioneered by the writers mentioned above, but furthered by people such as Herzberg and Blake, continued to emphasize that in organizations the proper study of mankind is man. The research conducted by Herzberg and his colleagues[10] suggested that improvements in organization design must centre on the individual job as the positive source of motivation. If the individual feels that the job is stretching him he will be moved to perform it well. (Herzberg's theories are dealt with in more detail in Chapter 8.)

Blake[11] concentrates on management style – the way in which managers manage, based on their beliefs and values. He suggests that there are two factors: 'concern for people' and 'concern for production' (this is in line with the distinction made by the Ohio State University researchers Halpin and Winer[12] between leadership styles based on 'consideration' or 'initiating' structure). Blake's managerial grid presents a matrix of 81 styles based on nine degrees of concern for people and nine degrees of concern for production. A manager scoring 9 for people and 1 for production would be a 9/1 manager – the softy who lets production slide in case he offends anyone; someone who scores 1 for people and 9 for production would be too tough, the no-nonsense man who gets the staff out of the door and doesn't care whom he hurts in the process. Ideally, one should be 9/9 but most people are probably 5/5 or thereabouts. Blake believes that the process of analysing managerial style along the lines of discussing how to progress to 9/9 is the best way to seek organizational efficiency.

The concepts of these and other behavioural scientists provided the impetus for the organization development movement whose beliefs were summarized by Bennis as follows:

(a) A new concept of man based on increased knowledge of his complex and shifting needs which replaces an oversimplified, innocent, push-button idea of man;
(b) a new concept of power, based on collaboration and reason, which replaces a model of power based on coercion and threat;
(c) a new concept of organization values, based on humanistic-democratic ideals, which replaces the mechanistic value system of bureaucracy. [13]

Views on the behavioural science school

No one can quarrel with the values expressed by the human relations school and those behavioural scientists associated with it – we are all in favour of virtue. But there are a number of grounds on which the more extreme beliefs of the school can be criticized:

1. It claims that its concepts are universally applicable, yet organizations come in all shapes and sizes, types of activity and context.
2. It ignores the real commercial and technological constraints of industrial life. Instead, it reflects more of an ideological concern for personal development and the rights of the individual rather than a scientific curiosity about the factors affecting organizational efficiency.
3. It overreacts against the excessive formality of the scientific management school by largely ignoring the formal organization and attaching too much importance to informal work-group processes.
4. Its emphasis on the need to minimize conflict overlooks the point that conflict is not necessarily undesirable, and may rather be an essential concomitant of change and development.

To be fair, not all behavioural scientists were so naive. Although McGregor's Theory Y was somewhat idealistic, he at least recognized that 'industrial health does not flow automatically from the elimination of dissatisfaction, disagreement, or even open conflict. Peace is not synonymous with organizational health; socially responsible management is not co-extensive with permissive management.' [6]

The bureaucratic model

Meanwhile, as Perrow put it:

In another part of the management forest, the mechanistic school was gathering its forces and preparing to outflank the forces of light. First came the numbers men – the linear programmers, the budget experts, the financial analysts . . . Armed with emerging systems concepts, they carried the 'mechanistic' analogy to its fullest – and it was very productive. Their work still goes on, largely untroubled by organizational theory; the theory, it seems clear, will have to adjust to them, rather than the other way around . . . Then the works of Max Weber, not translated until the 1940s . . . began to find their way into social science thought. [14]

Max Weber coined the term 'bureaucracy' as a label for a type of formal organization in which impersonality and rationality are developed to the highest degree. Bureaucracy, as he conceived it, was the most efficient form of organization because it is coldly logical and because personalized relationships and non-rational, emotional considerations do not get in its way. The ideal bureaucracy, according to Weber, has the following features:

- maximum specialization;
- close job definition as to duties, privileges and boundaries;
- vertical authority patterns;
- decisions based on expert judgement, resting on technical knowledge and on disciplined compliance with the directives of superiors;
- policy and administration are separate;
- maximum use of rules;
- impersonal administration of staff.

At first, with his celebrations of the efficiency of bureaucracy, Weber was received with only reluctant respect, even hostility. Most writers were against bureaucracy. But it turned out, surprisingly, that managers are not. They prefer clear lines of communication, clear specifications of authority and responsibility and clear knowledge of whom they are responsible to. Admittedly, in some situations, as Burns and Stalker point out,[15] they might want absolute clarity but they can't get it. On the other hand there are circumstances when the type of work carried out in an organization requires a bureaucratic approach in the Weberian, not the pejorative 'red tape', sense. The apparently conflicting views of the human relations and bureaucratic schools of thought had to be reconciled. Much of what they said was right, but it was insufficiently related to context. The first step was to look at how organizations worked as systems related to their environment – this was taken by the systems school. At the same time a number of researchers were looking at organizations primarily in relation to their environment; they constitute what may be termed the contingency school.

The systems school

The systems approach to organizations as formulated by Miller and Rice[16] states that organizations should be treated as open systems which are continually dependent upon and influenced by their environments. The basic characteristic of the enterprise as an open system is that it transforms inputs into outputs within its environment.

As Katz and Kahn wrote: 'Systems theory is basically concerned with problems of relationship, of structure and of interdependence.'[17] As a result there is a considerable emphasis on the concept of transactions across boundaries – between the system and its environment and between the different parts of the system. This open and dynamic approach avoided the error of the classical and human relations theorists who thought of organizations as closed systems and analysed their problems with reference to their internal structures and processes of interaction, without taking account of external influences and the changes they impose or of the technology in the organization.

The socio-technical model

The basic idea of the organization as a system was extended by the Tavistock Institute researchers into the socio-technical model of organizations. The basic principle of this model is that in any system of organization, technical or task aspects are interrelated with the human or social aspects. The emphasis is on interrelationships between, on the one hand, the technical processes of transformation carried out within the organization, and on the other hand, the organization of work groups and the management structures of the enterprise.

The socio-technical model originated from two major studies carried out by members of the Tavistock Institute: first, the Longwall study in the mines of Durham and, second, the study of the textile mills in Ahmedabad, India. In the mining study it was found that two very different forms of organization were operated in the same seam and with identical technology. The conventional Longwall system combined a complex formal structure with simple work roles. The miner was committed to only one task and entered into a very limited number of unvarying social relations that were sharply divided between those within the particular task group and those who were outside. With those 'outside' he shared no sense of belongingness and recognized no responsibility to them for the consequences of his actions. The composite Longwall system, in contrast, combined a simple formal structure with complex work roles. The miner in this system had a commitment to the whole group task and consequently found himself drawn into a variety of tasks in co-operation with different members of the work group. As Trist wrote:

> That two such contrasting social systems can effectively operate the same technology is clear enough evidence that there exists an element of choice in designing a work organization. However, it is far from a matter of indifference which form of organization is selected . . . The technological system and the effectiveness of the total production system will depend upon the adequacy with which the social system is able to cope with these requirements. [18]

The research demonstrated that the composite system showed superiority over the conventional in terms of production and costs. It enabled miners to operate more flexibly and thereby cope better with changing conditions.

It made better provision for the personnel needs of miners and reduced stress as measured by absenteeism.

The analysis of the Longwall study suggested that when changes are being made in technology, it is necessary to choose carefully from among the alternatives available for the division in labour, the working practices and the reward system. While the aim should be to exploit the new technology, care should be taken not to threaten the existing social system.

The textile studies in India conducted by A K Rice were concerned with the re-design of an organization and based upon the socio-technical model. The reorganization was based on the following principles:

1. There is an optimum level of grouping activities which can be determined only by an analysis of the requirements of the technological system.
2. Grouping should be such that the workers are primarily related to each other by way of the requirements of task performance and task interdependence.
3. Supervisory roles should be designed after analysing the system's requirements for control and co-ordination. The aim should be to create unified commands which correspond to natural task groupings. This should free the supervisor for his tasks of planning, co-ordinating and controlling, first by enabling him to detect and to manage the boundary conditions which relate his individual commands to the larger system, and second by maximizing the autonomous responsibility of the work groups for internal control and co-ordination.

The contingency school

The contingency school consists of writers such as Burns and Stalker, Joan Woodward, Lawrence and Lorsch, and Perrow who have analysed a variety of organizations and concluded that their structures and methods of operation are a function of the circumstances in which they exist. They do not subscribe to the view that there is one best way of designing an organization or that simplistic classifications of organizations as formal or informal, bureaucratic or non-bureaucratic are helpful. They are against those who see organizations as mutually opposed social systems (what Burns and Stalker refer to as the 'Manichean world of the Hawthorne studies')[15] which set up formal against informal organizations, and against those who impose rigid principles of organization irrespective of the technology or environmental conditions.

Burns and Stalker

Burns and Stalker based their concept of mechanistic and organic organizations on research into a number of Scottish firms in the electronics industry. They emphasized the rate of change in the environment of the organization as being the key factor in determining how it could operate.

In stable conditions a highly structured or 'mechanistic' organization will emerge with specialized functions, clearly defined roles, strict administrative routines and a hierarchical system of exercising authoritarian control. In effect, this is the bureaucratic system. However, when the environment is volatile, a rigid system of ranks and routines will inhibit the organization's speed and sensitivity of response. In these circumstances the structure is, or should be, 'organic' in the sense that it is a function of the situation in which the enterprise finds itself rather than conforming to any predetermined and rigid view of how it should operate. Individual responsibilities are less clear cut and members of the organization must constantly relate what they are doing to its general situation and specific problems.

Perhaps the most important contribution made by Burns and Stalker was the stress they placed on the suitability of each system to its own specific set of conditions. They concluded their analysis by writing:

> We desire to avoid the suggestion that either system is superior under all circumstances to the other. In particular, nothing in our experience justifies the assumption that mechanistic systems should be superseded by organic in conditions of stability. The beginning of administrative wisdom is the awareness that there is no one optimum type of management system.

Woodward

Woodward's ideas about organization derived from a research project carried out in Essex designed to discover whether the principles of organization laid down by the classical theorists correlate with business success when put into practice. She found considerable variations in patterns of organization which could not be related to size of firm, type of industry or business success. She also found that there was no significant correlation between adherence to the classical principles relating to matters such as span of control or number of levels in the hierarchy, and business success. After further analysis, she concluded:

> When, however, the firms were grouped according to similarity of objectives and techniques of production, and classified in order of the technical complexity of their production systems, each production system was found to be associated with a characteristic pattern of organization. It appeared that technical methods were the most important factor in determining organizational structure and in setting the tone of human relationships inside the firms. The widely accepted assumptions that there are principles of management valid for all types of production systems seemed very doubtful.[19]

Woodward's main contribution to organization theory is, therefore, her belief that different technologies demand different structures and procedures and create different types of relationships.

Lawrence and Lorsch

Lawrence and Lorsch[20] developed their contingency model on the basis of a study of six firms in the plastics industry. Organization, as they define it, is the process of co-ordinating different activities to carry out planned transactions with the environment. The three aspects of environment upon which the design of the organization is contingent are the market, the technology (ie the tasks carried out) and research and development. These may be differentiated along such dimensions as rate of change and uncertainty. This process of reacting to complexity and change by *differentiation* creates a demand for effective *integration* if the organization as a whole is to adapt efficiently to the environment. This concept of differentiation and integration is, in fact, the greatest contribution of Lawrence and Lorsch to organization theory.

They suggested that:

> As organizations deal with their external environments, they become segmented into units, each of which has as its major task the problem of dealing with a part of the conditions outside the firm... These parts of the system need to be linked together towards the accomplishment of the organization's overall purpose.

Their research showed that the two organizations with the most successful records had, in fact, achieved the highest degree of integration of the six, and were also amongst the most highly differentiated. The differentiation of the various units was more in line with the demands of the environment for those two organizations than for the others.

One of the most important implications of the Lawrence and Lorsch model for organization designers is that, although differentiation demands effective integration, this must not be achieved by minimizing differences and producing a common bland outlook. Instead, integration should be achieved by allowing each department to be as different in its outlook and its structure as its tasks demand – that is to be highly distinctive – but to use mediating devices such as committees, *ad hoc* project groups and assigned 'integrators' who stand midway between the functions with which they are concerned and are not dominated by any of them. Integration can therefore be achieved by structural means as well as by organizational development interventions designed to increase trust and understanding between groups and to confront conflict.

Perrow

The model developed by Perrow[3] recognizes the importance of structure and the inevitable tendency towards routinization, standardization and bureaucracy in organizations. In accordance with the views of other members of the contingency school, he suggests that different structures can exist within the same firm and that a bureaucratic structure is as appropriate for some tasks as a non-bureaucratic structure is for other tasks.

Application of organization theory

The different schools of organization theory provide a number of ways of analysing organizations from the point of view of the formal structure, individual behaviour, the organization as a system and the environmental influences which affect the shape and climate of an organization. The most pragmatic approach is provided by the contingency school. They say: first ensure that you understand the environment, the technology and the existing systems of social relationships, and then design an organization which is *contingent* upon the circumstances of the particular case. There is always some choice, but the designer is trying to achieve the best fit he can. But in making his choice, he should be aware of the structural, human and systems factors which will influence the design, and of the context within which the organization operates. He must also take into account the culture of the organization, the processes that take place in it, namely change and the exercise of leadership and power, and the effect all this has on relationships (conflict), on individuals (stress) and on groups within the organization. The impact of corporate cultures was considered in Chapter 5 and the other factors are discussed in the next chapter.

References

1. Child, J *Organization, A Guide to Problems and Practice*. Harper and Row, London, 1977.
2. Lupton, T '"Best Fit" in the design of organizations', *Personnel Review*, **4**, 1, 1975.
3. Perrow, C *Organizational Analysis. A Sociological View*. Tavistock Publications, London, 1970.
4. Barnard, C *Functions of the Executive*. Harvard University Press, Cambridge, Mass., 1938.
5. Roethlisberger, F J and Dickson, W J *Management and the Worker*. Harvard University Press, Cambridge, Mass., 1939.
6. McGregor, D *The Human Side of Enterprise*. McGraw-Hill, New York, 1966.
7. Likert, R *New Patterns of Management*. McGraw-Hill, New York, 1961.
8. Argyris, C *Personality and Organization*. Harper, New York, 1957.
9. Argyris, C *Integrating the Individual and the Organization*. John Wiley, New York, 1964.
10. Herzberg, F *et al, The Motivations to Work*. John Wiley, New York, 1959.
11. Blake, R R and Mouton, J S *The Managerial Grid*. Gulf Publishing, Houston, 1964.
12. Halpin, A W and Winer, B J *A Factorial Study of the Leader Behaviour Description*. Ohio State University, 1957.
13. Bennis, W *Organization Development*. Addison-Wesley, Reading, Mass., 1969.
14. Perrow, C *The Short and Glorious History of Organizational Theory*. Resource Book in Macro-Organizational Behaviour, R H Miles (ed), Goodyear Publishing, Santa Monica, 1980.
15. Burns, T and Stalker, G M *The Management of Innovation*. Tavistock Publications, London, 1961.

16. Miller, E and Rice, A K *Systems of Organization*. Tavistock Publications, London, 1967.
17. Katz, D and Kahn, R L *The Social Psychology of Organizations*. John Wiley, New York, 1964.
18. Trist, E L *et al, Organizational Choice*. Tavistock Publications, London, 1963.
19. Woodward, J *Industrial Organization*. Oxford University Press, 1965.
20. Lawrence, P R and Lorsch, J W *Organization and Environment*. Harvard University Press, Cambridge, Mass., 1967.

Chapter 7
How Organizations Function

Organizations are subject to change and have to be restructured. As they grow, differentiation takes place. Adaptive mechanisms such as integration have to be deployed. Different approaches to defining roles and managing people may be required. These processes of change, leadership and power result in conflict and stress. To understand and manage these processes it is necessary to analyse the situation in terms of the different types of culture and the circumstances in which one or other is appropriate, as discussed in Chapter 5. It is also necessary to review the impact of group behaviour before considering and acting on the factors that determine organizational effectiveness and performance.

Change

The problem

Change is the only thing that remains constant in organizations. As Alfred Sloan said:

> The circumstances of an ever-changing market and an ever-changing product are capable of breaking any business organization if that organization is unprepared for change – indeed in my opinion if it has not provided procedures for anticipating change.[1]

Change is imposed by the external environment, eg the economy, the market, government. But it can also arise internally from the introduction of new tasks, technologies and systems.

People resist change because it is seen as a threat to familiar patterns of behaviour as well as to status and financial rewards. Woodward made this point clearly:

> When we talk about resistance to change we tend to imply that management is always rational in changing its direction, and that employees are stupid, emotional or irrational in not responding in the way they should. But if an individual is going to be worse off, explicitly or implicitly, when the proposed changes have been made, any resistance is entirely rational in terms of his own best interest. The interests of the organization and the individual do not always coincide.[2]

103

If not properly managed, change can decrease morale, motivation and commitment and create conditions of conflict within an organization.

Managing change

Resistance to change will be less if:

- those affected by change feel that the project is their own, not one imposed on them by outsiders;
- the change has the wholehearted support of top management;
- the change is seen as reducing rather than increasing present burdens;
- the change accords with well-established values;
- the programme for change offers the kind of new experience which interests participants;
- participants feel that their autonomy and security are not threatened;
- participants have jointly diagnosed the problem;
- the change has been agreed by group decisions;
- those advocating change can understand the feelings and fears of those affected and take steps to relieve unnecessary fears;
- it is recognized that new ideas are likely to be misunderstood and ample provision is made for the discussion of reactions to proposals to ensure complete understanding of them.

In carrying out the process of managing change the three mechanisms suggested by Lewin[3] can be used:

1. *Unfreezing* – altering the present stable equilibrium which supports the present behaviour and attitudes. This process must take account of the inherent threat that change presents and motivate those affected to attain the natural state of equilibrium by accepting change.
2. *Changing* – developing new responses based on new information.
3. *Refreezing* – stabilizing the change by integrating the new responses into the personality of those concerned.

Leadership

The function of the leader is to achieve the task set for him with the help of his group. The leader and his group are therefore interdependent.

Main roles

The leader has two main roles. First he must achieve the task. Secondly, he has to maintain effective relationships between himself and his group and the individuals in it – effective in the sense that they are conducive to achieving the task. These two roles were first identified by the Ohio State researchers (Halpin and Winer)[4] who identified the two dimensions of leadership behaviour:

- Initiating structure – specifying ways and means of accomplishing the goals of the group and co-ordinating the activities of its members.
- Consideration – motivating the members of the group to accept the group goals and to work at the group task while at the same time maintaining internal harmony and satisfaction.

In fulfilling his role the leader has to satisfy the following needs:

1. *Task needs.* The group exists to achieve a common purpose or task. The leader's role is to ensure that this purpose is fulfilled. If it is not he will lose the confidence of the group and the result will be frustration, disenchantment, criticism and, possibly, the ultimate disintegration of the group.
2. *Group maintenance needs.* To achieve its objectives the group needs to be held together. The leader's job is to build up and maintain team spirit and morale.
3. *Individual needs.* Individuals have their own needs which they expect to be satisfied at work. The leader's task is to be aware of these needs so that where necessary he can take steps to harmonize them with the needs of the task and the group.

As John Adair[5] pointed out, these three needs are interdependent. The leader's actions in one area affect both the others; thus successful achievement of the task is essential if the group is to be held together or the individual is to be motivated to give his best effort to the job. Action directed at meeting group or individual needs must be related to the needs of the task. It is impossible to consider individuals in isolation from the group or to consider the group without referring to the individuals within it. If any need is neglected, one of the others will suffer and the leader will be less successful.

Exercising leadership

The kind of leadership exercised will be related to the nature of the task and the people being led. It will also depend on the environment and, of course, on the leader himself. Analysing the qualities of leadership in terms of intelligence, initiative, self-assurance and so on has only limited value. The qualities required may be different in different situations. It is more useful to adopt a contingency approach and take account of the variables the leader has to deal with; especially the task, the group and his own position in the group.

Fiedler, in particular, concentrated upon the relationship between the leader and his group and the structure of the task as determinants in the choice of the most effective style of leadership. His research indicated that the leaders of the most effective groups tended to maintain greater distance between themselves and their subordinates than the leaders of less effective groups. He found that an 'initiating structure' approach was most effective when the situation was either very favourable or unfavourable to the leader, while 'consideration' was more appropriate when the situation was only moderately favourable. Fiedler also emphasized the 'situational' aspects of leadership:

> Leadership performance then depends as much on the organization as on the leader's own attributes. Except perhaps for the unusual case, it is simply not meaningful to speak of an effective leader and an ineffective leader; we can only speak of a leader who tends to be effective in one situation and ineffective in another.[6]

Leadership style

The most effective leaders fit their style to the situation, which includes their own preferred style of operating and personal characteristics as well as the nature of the task and the group.

Leadership style is the way in which managers exercise their leadership role – it characterizes their approach to managing people. Leadership styles tend to be defined in terms of extremes:

authoritarian   – democratic
autocratic   – participative
job-centred   – people-centred
close, directive – general, permissive

In fact, most managers develop an approach somewhere between the two extremes. There is no one style appropriate to all situations. Managers must be prepared to adjust their style according to the circumstances. This does not imply inconsistency. Effective managers adopt the same approach in similar situations.

A continuum of leadership behaviour based on the work of Tannenbaum and Schmidt[7] (Figure 7.1) suggests that there are five basic styles: tell, sell, consult, join and delegate. These styles move from the authoritarian to the democratic, but it is not suggested that one is better than the other. There will be circumstances when a manager has to *tell* someone to do something; in other circumstances he may have to sell the idea or consult his subordinates in one way or another. The job of the leader is to analyse the situation and apply the most appropriate style in accordance with his knowledge of his own capabilities and limitations.

Power

Organizations exist to get things done and in the process of doing this

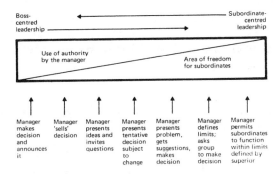

Figure 7.1 Continuum of leadership behaviour

people or groups will exercise power. Directly or indirectly the use of power in influencing behaviour is a pervading feature of organizations, whether it is exerted by managers, specialists, informal groups or trade union officials.

Sources of power

Power is clearly linked to position and rank. But to a certain degree it has to be earned. Managers give orders to their subordinates but they will get more out of them if they obtain their willing co-operation rather than their grudging submission. Power is bestowed upon managers, but they also have to justify their use of it. There are, however, other sources of power, namely:

- *Access to people with power.* Proximity or a direct line obviously gives people more scope to exert influence, actual or perceived. That is why secretaries are important.
- *Control over information.* 'Knowledge is power' or, alternatively, 'authority goes to the one who knows'. If people are in the know, they are in a better position to control events or, if they want to play politics, to put a spoke in other people's wheels.
- *Control over results.* Power goes to those who can control what the organization achieves. When trade unions strike, they are exercising this sort of power.
- *Control over resources.* If control is exercised over resources such as money, manpower, equipment or services that anyone else needs, the person in that position will have power.
- *Control over rewards and punishments.* People have power if they can give rewards or punishments or influence others who control them.
- *Expertise.* People gain and keep power if they can convince others that they are the experts.

● *Identification*. Power can be achieved over others if they identify with what is being done or with the individual concerned. This is what charismatic leaders do by enthusiasm, dedication, getting people involved and by sheer force of personality.

Using power

John Kotter[8] interviewed over 250 managers who were in a position to use power. He found that the successful ones had the following characteristics:

1. They use their power openly and legitimately. They are seen as genuine experts in their field and consistently live up to the leadership image they build for themselves.
2. They are sensitive to what types of power are most effective with different types of people. For example, experts respect expertise.
3. They develop all their sources of power and do not rely too much on any particular technique.
4. They seek jobs and tasks which will give them the opportunity to acquire and use power. They constantly seek ways to invest the power they already have to secure an even higher positive return.
5. They use their power in a mature and self-controlled way. They seldom if ever use power impulsively or for their own aggrandizement.
6. They get satisfaction from influencing others.

Conflict

The sources of conflict

Conflict is inevitable in organizations because they function by means of adjustments and compromises among competitive elements in their structure and membership. These elements produce conflict of two kinds: horizontal conflict between functions, departments and groups, and vertical conflict between different levels in the hierarchy.

Conflict also arises when there is change, because it may be seen as a threat to be challenged or resisted, or when there is frustration – this may produce an aggressive reaction: fight rather than flight. Conflict is not to be deplored. It is an inevitable result of progress and change and can and should be used constructively.

Conflict between individuals raises fewer problems than conflict between groups. Individuals can act independently and sort out their differences. Members of groups may have to accept the norms, goals and values of their group. The individual's loyalty will usually be to his own group if it is in conflict with others.

Approaches to managing conflict

The basic assumptions about conflict made by Blake, Shepart and Mouton[9] are that:

- conflict is inevitable, agreement is impossible;
- conflict is not inevitable, yet agreement is not possible;
- although there is conflict, agreement is possible.

The third assumption is clearly the most hopeful. There are three approaches that can be adopted if this assumption is held:

1. *Peaceful co-existence.* People are encouraged to work happily with one another. There is the maximum amount of information, contact and exchange of views, and people move freely between groups. This is a pleasant ideal but it may lead to smoothing over real differences and is not practicable in all circumstances.
2. *Problem-solving.* The joint development of solutions to the problem and the sharing of responsibility to see that the solutions work. This is clearly the best approach. It emphasizes the need to find a genuine solution to the problem, rather than simply accommodating different points of view.
3. *Compromise.* Splitting the difference by negotiation or bargaining. This approach assumes that there is no right or best answer and is essentially pessimistic, although it may be inevitable if the other two approaches are tried and do not work.

Stress

Unfortunately, stress is a feature of organizational life associated with getting work done, relating to other people, being subjected to change, supervision and the exercise of power.

Causes of stress

The main causes of stress are:

- the work itself – over-pressurized, actual or perceived failure;
- role in the organization – ambiguity in what is expected of the individual or conflict between what he wants to do and can do;
- poor relationships within the organization – with the boss, colleagues or subordinates;
- impact of the organization – lack of information, little effective consultation, restrictions on behaviour, office politics;
- feelings about job or career – lack of job security, over-promotion or under-promotion;
- external pressures – clash between demands made by the

organization and those made by the family or other external interests. Home interface problems of excessive hours (why *should* managers be expected by means of cultural pressures to start early and stay late), lots of travelling, company moves etc, can be extremely stressful and organizations tend to ignore these problems.

Coping with stress

How people deal with stress will depend on their personality, tolerance for ambiguity and ability to live with change. Some people revel in highly pressurized jobs. Others cannot cope. Motivation also comes into it. Motivation is a form of pressure. People can be too highly motivated and pressure becomes stress when they cannot achieve what they are setting out or expected to do.

Stress can be coped with by adaptive behaviour. An overworked manager may adapt successfully by delegating some work, but someone else may accept the overload with the result that his performance deteriorates. And, as Torrington and Cooper[10] point out, a manager who adapts successfully to role ambiguity will seek clarification with his superior or colleagues, but a manager who cannot adapt will withdraw from some aspect of his work role.

Managing stress

The three basic ways in which stress can be managed by an organization are:

- job design – reducing the scope for placing people under stress and clarifying roles;
- placement and career development – placing people in jobs with which they can cope and advancing their careers in accordance with their capabilities;
- motivation – using methods of motivation and leadership which do not place undue demands on people.

Some refinements to these basic methods have been suggested by Torrington and Cooper. These include:

- using performance reviews as a basis for discussion between the superior and the subordinate about the latter's progress in a job;
- counselling – giving the individual the chance to talk over his problems with a member of the personnel department or the company medical officer;
- training – helping people to understand and to carry out their jobs better.

Additionally, Cooper[11] has suggested a number of other ways of alleviating stress, namely:

- stress awareness training focussing on the physical, emotional and behavioural problems which may be stress related;
- sabbaticals;
- keep fit programmes;
- a conscious policy of recognizing and alleviating home interface problems.

Group behaviour

Organizations consist of groups of people working together. Interactions take place within and between groups and the degree to which these processes are formalized will vary according to the organizational context. To understand and influence organizational behaviour it is necessary to understand how groups behave. In particular this means considering the nature of:

- formal groups
- informal groups
- the processes that take place within groups
- the factors that make for group effectiveness.

Formal groups

Formal groups are set up by organizations to achieve a defined purpose. People are brought together with the necessary skills to carry out the tasks and a system exists for directing, co-ordinating and controlling the group's activities. The structure, composition and size of the group will depend largely on the nature of the task; although tradition, organizational culture and management style may exert considerable influence. The more the task is routine or clearly defined the more structured the group will be. In a highly structured group the leader will have a positive role and may well adopt an authoritarian style. The role of each member of the group will be precise and a hierarchy of authority is likely to exist. The more ambiguous the task the more difficult it will be to structure the group. The leader's role is more likely to be supportive – he will tend to concentrate on encouragement and co-ordination rather than on issuing orders. The group will operate in a more democratic way and individual roles will be fluid and less clearly defined.

Informal groups

Informal groups are set up by people in organizations who have some affinity for one another. It could be said that formal groups satisfy the needs of the organization while informal groups satisfy the needs of their members. One of the main aims of organization design and development should be to ensure, so far as possible, that the basis upon which activities are grouped together and the way in which groups are allowed or encouraged to behave satisfy both these needs. The values and norms established by informal groups can work against the organization. This was first clearly established in the Hawthorne studies which revealed that groups could regulate their own behaviour and output levels irrespective of what management wanted. An understanding of the processes that take place within groups can, however, help to make them work for, rather than against, what the organization needs.

Group processes

As mentioned above, the way in which groups function will be affected by the task and by the norms in the organization. An additional factor will be size. There will be a greater diversity of talent, skills and knowledge in a large group, but individuals will find it more difficult to make their presence felt. According to Handy,[12] for best participation and for highest all-round involvement, the optimum size is between five and seven. But to achieve the requisite breadth of knowledge the group may have to be considerably larger, and this makes greater demands on the skills of the leader in getting participation.

The main processes that take place within groups are:

Interaction

There are three basic channels of communication within groups, as illustrated below:

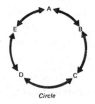

Wheel   Circle   All-channel

These patterns were defined by Leavitt,[13] and he and subsequent researchers found the following to be true:

- Wheel groups, where the task is straightforward, work faster, need fewer messages to solve problems and make fewer errors than circle groups, but they are inflexible if the task changes.
- Circle groups are faster in solving complex problems than wheel groups.
- All-channel groups are the most flexible and function well in complex open-ended situations.

The level of satisfaction for individuals is lowest in the circle, fairly high in the all-channel and mixed in the wheel, where the leader is more satisfied than the outlying members.

Task and maintenance functions

The following functions need to be carried out in groups:

- task – initiating, information seeking, diagnosing, opinion-seeking, evaluating, decision-managing;
- maintenance – encouraging, compromizing, peace-keeping, clarifying, summarizing, standard-setting.

It is the job of the group leader or leaders to ensure that these functions operate effectively. Leaderless groups can work, but only in special circumstances. A leader is almost essential – whether official or self-appointed. The style adopted by the leader will affect the way the group operates. If he is respected, this will increase the group's cohesiveness and its ability to get things done. An inappropriately authoritarian style will create tension and resentment. An over-permissive style will mean that respect for the leader will diminish and the group will not function so effectively.

Group ideology

In the course of interacting and carrying out its task and maintenance functions, the group develops an ideology which affects the attitudes and actions of its members and the degree of satisfaction which they feel.

Identification

An individual will identify with his group if he likes the other members, approves of the purpose and work of the group and wishes to be associated with the standing of the group in the organization. Identification will be more complete if the standing of the group is good.

Group effectiveness

An effective group is likely to be one in which the structure, leadership and methods of operation are relevant to the requirements of the task. The Tavistock Institute Longwall and Ahmedabad studies referred to in Chapter 6 emphasized the importance of commitment to the whole group task and the need to group people in a way which ensures that they are related to each other by way of the requirements of task performance and task interdependence.

In an effective group, its purpose is clear and its members feel that the task is important both to them and the organization (the concept of saliency). According to McGregor[14] the main features of a well-functioning creative group are as follows:

1. The atmosphere tends to be informal, comfortable, relaxed.
2. There is a lot of discussion in which initially everyone participates, but it remains pertinent to the task of the group.
3. The task or objective of the group is well understood and accepted by the members. There will have been free discussion of

the objective at some point until it was formulated in such a way that the members of the group could commit themselves to it.

4. The members listen to each other. Every idea is given a hearing. People do not appear to be afraid of being considered foolish by putting forth a creative thought even if it seems fairly extreme.

5. There is disagreement. Disagreements are not suppressed or overridden by premature group action. The reasons are carefully examined, and the group seeks to resolve them rather than to dominate the dissenter.

6. Most decisions are reached by a kind of consensus in which it is clear that everybody is in general agreement and willing to go along. Formal voting is at a minimum; the group does not accept a simple majority as a proper basis for action.

7. Criticism is frequent, frank and relatively comfortable. There is little evidence of personal attack, either openly or in a hidden fashion.

8. People are free in expressing their feelings as well as their ideas both on the problem and on the group's operation.

9. When action is taken, clear assignments are made and accepted.

10. The leader of the group does not dominate it, nor on the contrary does the group defer unduly to him. There is little evidence of a struggle for power as the group operates. The issue is not who controls but how to get the job done.

These characteristics together present an ideal which might be striven for but is seldom attained. The extent to which it is possible or even desirable for them to be achieved will depend on the situation. A mechanistic or bureaucratic type of enterprise – where this is appropriate to the technology – cannot allow its formal organizational units to function just like this, although it should try to ensure that any committees, task forces or project teams that are set up do exhibit these forms of behaviour.

Organizational effectiveness

An organization could be said to be effective if it achieves its purpose. But at what cost? It is necessary to be concerned not only with what an organization achieves but how it achieves it. The behavioural scientists who wrote about organization development, such as Richard Beckhard,[15] were concerned about organizational behaviour in terms of what they referred to as an organizational health. Beckhard has defined a healthy organization as having the following characteristics:

1. The total organization, the significant sub-parts, and individuals manage their work against goals and plans for the achievement of these goals.

2. Form follows function (the problem, or task or project, determines how the human resources are organized).
3. Decisions are made by and near the source of information, regardless of where these sources are located on the organization chart.
4. The reward system is such that managers and supervisors are rewarded (and punished) comparably for (a) short-term profit or production performance, (b) growth and development of their subordinates, and (c) creating a viable working group.
5. Communication laterally and vertically is relatively undistorted. People are generally open and confronting. They share all the relevant facts, including feelings.
6. There is a minimum amount of inappropriate win/lose activity between individuals and groups. Constant effort exists at all levels to treat conflict and conflict situations as problems subject to problem-solving methods.
7. There is a high 'conflict' (clash of ideas) about tasks and projects, and relatively little energy spent in clashing over inter-personal difficulties because they have been generally worked through.
8. The organization and its parts see themselves as interacting with each other *and* with a *larger* environment. The organization is an 'open system'.
9. There is a shared value, and management strategy to support it, of trying to help each person (or unit) in the organization to maintain his (or its) integrity and uniqueness in an inter-dependent environment.
10. The organization and its members operate in an 'action research' way. General practice is to build in feedback mechanisms so that individuals and groups can learn from their own experience.

This is an ideal view of how organizations should behave, and it seems to represent the philosophy adopted by most organization development practitioners. But there is some danger in adopting these values as ends in themselves and neglecting the fact that organizations exist to serve a purpose. The values are important because they can promote the effectiveness of an organization as well as its health.

Although these values are important because they can promote the effectiveness of an organization as well as its health, consideration must also be given to the factors affecting organizational performance and the achievement of excellence.

Factors affecting organizational performance

John Child[16] examined the factors affecting organizational performance on the basis of research in 82 British companies. He found that where the following propositions were operating, performance was better:

1. In conditions of environment variability, successful organizations will tend to have structures with the following characteristics: (a) arrangements to reduce and structure uncertainty; (b) a relatively high level of integration achieved through flexible, rather than formalized, processes. This is in accordance with contingency theory whereby different approaches to organization design are conducive to high performance, depending on whether or not the environment in which the organization operates is variable and complex in nature, or stable and simple.
2. Organizations that increase their degree of formalization to parallel their growth in size will tend to achieve higher levels of performance. Child found that in each industry the more profitable and faster growing companies were those that developed a bureaucratic type organization when they had more than about 2000 employees.
3. Organizations that group their basic activities into divisions once these activities become diversified will tend to achieve higher levels of performance.
4. Organizations that carefully design their work flow control and support technology will tend to achieve higher levels of performance.
5. Organizations that adopt forms of administrative structure consistent with the expectations and perceived needs of their employees will tend to achieve higher levels of performance. This proposition may be a truism but it emphasizes the need to understand the *perceived* needs and expectations of employees. This means looking at the factors affecting their behaviour as individuals – their motivation and the way they adapt to their roles. These matters are considered in the next chapter.

Achieving excellence

One of the most influential books on management in recent times has been *In Search of Excellence* by Tom Peters and Robert Waterman[17] which was described in its sub-title as 'lessons from America's best-run companies'. The analytical framework they used was based on the seven elements, described as the 'seven Ss', which Richard Pascale and Anthony Athos used in *The Art of Japanese Management*.[18] These were:

1. *Strategy:* the plan to reach identified goals.
2. *Structure:* the characteristics of the organization structure – functional, decentralized etc.
3. *Systems:* the routine for processing and communicating information.

4. *Staff:* the categories of people employed.
5. *Style:* how managers behave in achieving the organization's goals.
6. *Skills:* the capabilities of key people.
7. *Superordinate goals:* the significant meanings or guiding concepts that an organization imbues in its members (ie values).

A distinction was made between the 'hard' elements – strategy, structure and systems – on which UK and American companies concentrate, and the remaining 'soft' elements which Pascale and Athos claimed the Japanese manage particularly well.

Using these factors in their research into 75 highly regarded companies Peters and Waterman identified the following eight attributes which characterized the excellent innovative companies:

1. *A bias for action:* the excellent companies get on with it. They are analytical in their decision making but this does not paralyse them, as it does in some companies.
2. *Close to the customer:* they get to know their customers and provide them with quality, reliability and service.
3. *Autonomy and entrepreneurship:* leaders and innovators are fostered and given scope.
4. *Productivity through people:* they really believe that the basis for quality and productivity gain is the rank and file. They do not just pay lip service to the slogan 'people are our most important asset'. They do something about it by encouraging commitment and getting everyone involved.
5. *Hands-on, value driven:* the people who run the organization get close to those who work for them and ensure that the organization's values are understood and acted upon.
6. *Stick to the knitting:* the successful organizations stay reasonably close to the businesses they know.
7. *Simple form, lean staff:* the organization structure is simple and corporate staff are kept to a minimum.
8. *Simultaneous loose-tight properties:* they are both decentralized and centralized. They push decisions and autonomy as far down the organization as they can get, into individual units and profit centres. But, as Peters and Waterman say, 'they are fanatic centralists around the few core values they hold dear'.

References

1. Sloan, A P *My Years with General Motors.* Doubleday, New York, 1964.
2. Woodward, J 'Resistance to Change', *Management International Review*, Vol 8, 1968.
3. Lewin, K *Field Theory in Social Science.* Harper and Row, New York, 1951.

4. Halpin, A W and Winer, B J *A Factorial Study of the Leader Behaviour Descriptions.* Ohio State University, 1957.
5. Adair, J *The Action Centred Leader.* McGraw-Hill, London, 1973.
6. Fiedler, F E *A Theory of Leadership Effectiveness.* McGraw-Hill, New York, 1967.
7. Tannenbaum, R and Schmidt, W H 'How to Choose a Leadership Pattern', *Harvard Business Review*, May-June 1973.
8. Kotter, J P 'Power, Dependence and Effective Management', *Harvard Business Review*, May-June 1973.
9. Blake, R R, Shepart, H A and Mouton, J S *Managing Intergroup Conflict in Industry.* Gulf Publishing, Houston, 1964.
10. Torrington, D P and Cooper, C L 'The Management of Stress in Organizations and the Personnel Initiative', *Personnel Review*, Summer 1977.
11. Cooper, C L 'What's New in Stress?', *Personnel Management*, June 1984.
12. Handy, C B *Understanding Organizations.* Penguin Books, Harmondsworth, 1976.
13. Leavitt, H J 'Some Effects of Certain Communication Patterns on Group Performance', *Journal of Abnormal Psychology*, 1951.
14. McGregor, D *The Human Side of Enterprise.* McGraw-Hill, New York, 1966.
15. Beckhard, R *Organization Development: Strategy and Models.* Addison-Wesley, Reading, Mass., 1969.
16. Child, J 'What Determines Organization Performance?', *Organizational Design, Development and Behaviour, A Situational View.* K O Magnusen (ed), Scott Foreman, Glenview, Illinois, 1977.
17. Peters, T and Waterman, R *In Search of Excellence.* Harper & Row, New York, 1982.
18. Pascale, R and Athos, A *The Art of Japanese Management.* Simon and Schuster, New York, 1981.

Chapter 8
The Individual at Work – Motivation, Commitment and Roles

Introduction

The ways in which people behave at work depend on five factors:

1. The organization context, which includes its culture, values, climate, structure and management style; especially, in the latter case, the effectiveness with which leadership is exercised.
2. The attitudes of their fellow workers – the influence of the group on individual behaviour.
3. Their needs, goals and drives – ie, their motivation to work.
4. The commitment to the organization and its values.
5. How, in the light of all these factors, they adjust to their roles in the organization.

The organizational context and group influences were dealt with in the previous three chapters. This chapter is concerned with people as individuals working with others in organizations. It concentrates mainly on motivation, a subject which is often treated simplistically but which is in fact one of considerable complexity. The process of motivation can be and has been analysed in all sorts of ways. There have been a number of motivational schools which have generated a multitude of theories. The method adopted in this chapter of finding a route through the jungle is to:

(a) introduce the subject by a brief definition of the basis of motivation;
(b) trace the development of motivation theory by the various schools;
(c) summarize the key motivation theories emerging from these schools;
(d) in the light of this summary, develop a general theory of the process of motivation;
(e) explore the practical use of motivation theory.

The chapter then goes on to consider the wider subject of commitment.

Finally, the ways in which people adjust their behaviour to their roles are explored bearing in mind that behaviour will be affected by motivation, commitment and the other organizational factors discussed in earlier chapters.

The basis of motivation

Motivation is about what makes people act or behave in the way they do. When we observe people behaving in a particular manner, we ask: how can we motivate them?

At work we can observe some people working harder or more effectively than others. We can experience difficulties in recruiting or retaining staff and obtaining the sort of effort and commitment we want from them. Managerial action is required if these difficulties prevent the organization from achieving its objectives.

Motivation is inferred from or defined by goal-directed behaviour. It is anchored in two basic concepts: (a) the *needs* that operate within the individual and (b) the *goals* in the environment toward or away from which the individual moves. In its simplest form, the process of motivation is initiated by the conscious or unconscious recognition of an unsatisfied need. A goal is then established which, it is thought, will satisfy that need, and a course of action is determined that will lead towards the attainment of the goal. But, as goals are satisfied, new needs emerge and the cycle continues.

This basic model is illustrated in Figure 8.1.

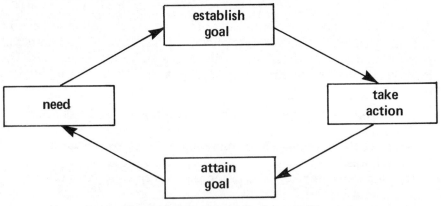

Figure 8.1 Basic motivation model

Schools of motivation theory

The theory of motivation is an eclectic one, derived from a number of schools of thought. To obtain an initial perspective of this complicated subject it is helpful to summarize the main approaches that have been developed adopting the four classifications used by Schein:[1]

1. Rational-economic man.
2. Social man.
3. Self-actualizing man.
4. Complex man.

Since Schein developed these classifications a fifth has emerged which may be described as 'Japanese man in search of excellence'.

Rational-economic man

According to this view, man is primarily motivated by economic rewards. It assumes that a person will be motivated to work if rewards and penalties are tied directly to his performance; thus the awards are contingent upon effective performance. This approach has its roots in the scientific management methods of Taylor who wrote: 'It is impossible, through any long period of time, to get workmen to work much harder than the average men around them unless they are assured a large and permanent increase in their pay.'[2]

This approach has been described by 'the law of effect' or 'the principle of reinforcement'. This states that if a person undertakes an action and this action is followed by a reward, the probability that the action will be repeated is increased. On the other hand, if the person undertakes an action which is ignored or followed by a punishment, that behaviour is less likely to be repeated.

Motivation using this approach has been and still is widely adopted and can be successful in some circumstances. But it is based exclusively on a system of external controls and fails to recognize a number of other human needs. It also fails to appreciate the fact that the formal control system can be seriously affected by the informal relationship existing between workers.

This rational motivational model is illustrated in Figure 8.2.

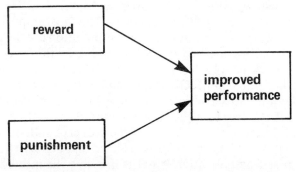

Figure 8.2 The rational motivational model

Social man

Elton Mayo[3] and his colleagues observed this shortcoming and developed an approach which emphasized man's social needs. The need for belonging was seen as providing the basic motivation for individuals to work. The social controls set up by cohesive work groups can be a powerful countervailing force to management's efforts to use financial rewards and organizational controls to achieve what it wants. This concept rapidly developed into the human relations school which believed that productivity was directly related to job satisfaction and that an individual's output will be high if he likes his co-workers and is given pleasant supervision.

To a certain extent, this approach is akin to paternalism, where it is assumed that people can be induced to work out of a feeling of gratitude for the system.

This human relations model is illustrated in Figure 8.3.

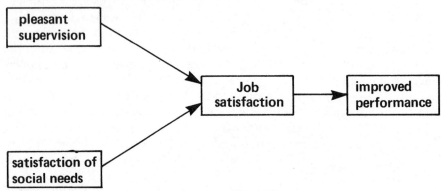

Figure 8.3 The human relations model

Self-actualizing man

The social man/human relations school was seen by many psychologists as somewhat naive, especially in its apparent assumption that a contented individual is necessarily highly productive. Man was seen by people such as Murray, Maslow, Alderfer, McGregor, Argyris and Herzberg to be motivated by a number of different needs. The most important of these needs from the point of view of long-term motivation are the higher order needs for self-fulfilment, actualization and growth. These needs are linked to the work people do and are not subject to an external control system. The key point in McGregor's Theory Y – 'that people will exercise self-direction and self-control in the achievement of organizational objectives to the degree that they are committed to those objectives'[4] – is fundamental to this concept. Argyris[5] also sees each individual person as having a potential which can be fully realized and believes that such self-realization or self-actualization benefits not only the individual but also those around him and the organization in which he works.

The other significant contributor to this school was Herzberg,[6] whose basic theme is that opportunities for self-actualization are the essential requirements of both job satisfaction and high performance.

The behavioural scientists who developed the self-actualizing model made a distinction between:

- *Intrinsic motivation* – the self-generated factors which influence people to behave in particular ways or to move in particular directions.
- *Extrinsic motivation* – what is done to or for people to motivate them.

They tended to belittle the importance of the extrinsic motivators (rewards and punishments) although they accepted, with some reluctance, that they could have a direct, albeit short-lived, effect on motivation and performance. Instead, they emphasized the role of the intrinsic motivators (responsibility, achievement etc) as creators of job satisfaction and therefore improved performance.

These relationships are illustrated in Figure 8.4.

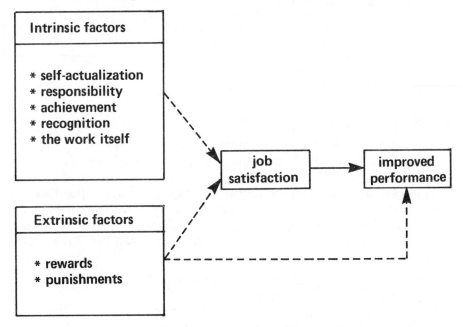

Figure 8.4 The self-actualizing motivation model

Complex man

None of the models described before is completely wrong; their only fault is that they over-simplify. Motivation is a complex affair, first, because people are complicated, with a multitude of needs and expectations; secondly, because the situations in which people work vary and affect motivation in different ways; and thirdly, because these situations are in a constant state of change. The models make the assumption that satisfaction always increases motivation, which cannot be sustained, and they do not take sufficient account of expectations, ability loads, the perceived value of the reward and what is called role perception – feelings about what individuals want to do or think they are required to do.

The concept of complex man was originated by Schein.[1] Its basis is an open-system theory which essentially states that human beings are constantly interacting with and are affected by their environment. Open-system theory was originally formulated by Von Bertalanffy who wrote that:

> A living organism is an open-system which continually gives up matter to the outer world and takes in matter from it, but which maintains itself in the continuous exchange in a steady state.[7]

Allport[8] further developed this definition by setting out the following features of an open system:

- Intake and output of both matter and energy.
- Achievement and maintenance of steady (homeostatic) states so that the intrusion of outer energy will not seriously disrupt internal form and order.
- Increase in order over time owing to an increase in complexity and differentiation of parts.
- Extensive transactional commerce with the environment.

The concept was developed by Lawrence and Lorsch[9] who suggested that an individual can usefully be conceived as a system of biological needs, psychological motives, values and perceptions. The individual's system operates so as to maintain its internal balance in the face of the demands placed upon it by external forces and it develops in response to his basic needs to solve the problems presented by the external environment. But each individual system will have unique characteristics because, as Lawrence and Lorsch say:

1. Different individual systems develop with different patterns of needs, values and perceptions.
2. Individual systems are not static, but continue to develop as they encounter new problems and experiences.

Two American researchers, Porter and Lawler[10] developed a model (Figure 8.5) which describes these complex relationships. This suggests that there are two factors determining the effort people put into their job:

1. The values of the rewards to individuals in so far as they satisfy their needs for security, social esteem, autonomy and self-actualization.

2. The probability that rewards depend on effort, as perceived by the individual – in other words, his or her expectations about the relationships between effort and reward.

Thus, the greater the value of a set of awards and the higher the probability that receiving each of these rewards depends upon effort, the greater the effort that will be put forth in a given situation.

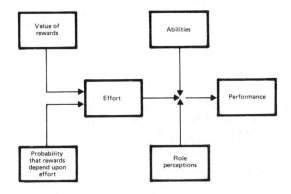

Figure 8.5 Motivation model (Porter and Lawler)[10]

But effort is not enough. It has to be effective effort if it is to produce the desired performance. The two additional variables to effort which affect task achievement are:

● ability – individual characteristics such as intelligence, manual skills, know-how;
● role perceptions – what the individual wants to do or thinks he or she is required to do. These are good from the viewpoint of the organization if they correspond with what it thinks the individual ought to be doing. They are poor if the views of the individual and the organization do not coincide.

This complexity was increased by the contribution of Brehm[11] who developed reactance theory, the concept that people react strongly when attempts are made to threaten their freedom or the degree to which they can control their destiny. They do not like to be imposed upon, and motivational devices originating from management – whether to increase intrinsic or extrinsic motivation – may not always be welcomed.

A further correction to the simple view that motivation is mainly about the satisfaction of instinctive needs as suggested by Maslow[12] and others was provided by the field research projects conducted by Goldthorpe[13] and Blackburn and Mann.[14] These indicated a number of environmental factors that contribute to the orientation adopted by people to work (these are discussed in more detail later in this chapter).

Japanese man and the pursuit of excellence

Attempts made to explain the secret of Japanese business success by such writers as Ouchi[15] and Pascale and Athos[16] have led to the belief that the best way to motivate people is to get their full commitment to the values of the organization by leadership and involvement. This might be called the 'hearts and minds' approach to motivation and, amongst other things, it popularized such devices as quality circles.

The baton was taken up by Peters and Waterman[17] and their many imitators. Peters summarized this view as follows:

> Trust people and treat them like adults, enthuse them by lively and imaginative leadership, develop and demonstrate an obsession for quality, make them feel they own the business, and your work force will respond with total commitment.[18]

It seems to work in Japan and in the 'excellent' companies cited by Peters and Waterman (although not all of those managed to maintain themselves on their pinnacle of excellence). It is much more direct and obvious than some of those produced by other schools. But it over-simplifies the issues and does not take sufficient account of the reactance effect. Unless the national or corporate culture supports this approach, employees may passively or actively resist attempts to force togetherness down their collective throats. As was noted in Chapter 4, the concept of human resource management is weakened to the extent that it relies on this method of motivation.

Motivation theories

The motivation schools produced a number of theories to explain the process of motivation and its effect on behaviour. The key theories are discussed in more detail in the next eight sections of this chapter as follows:

- *Homeostasis theory* which derives from open system theory and explains the tendency people have to move towards equilibrium. It provides a basis for the other theories of motivation.
- *Needs theory* which explains behaviour as a means of satisfying needs.
- *Goals theory* which emphasizes the importance of setting and achieving goals in the process of motivation.
- *Reinforcement theory* which explains how people learn to adapt their behaviour in response to experience, including trial and error, reward and punishment.
- *Expectancy theory* which describes the influence of expectations on behaviour.
- *Orientation theory* which studies motivation from the viewpoint of orientations.

● *Reactance theory* which explains how people may react to what is done to or for them.
● *Satisfaction/performance theory* which deals with the relationship between satisfaction and performance.

Homeostasis theory

The human organism, like all other living organisms, is constantly in a state of disequilibrium. It expends energy to stay alive and must replenish this energy. Automatic mechanisms exist to maintain a normal body temperature. This is called the homeostatic principle and it underlies all behaviour and motivation. The drive to satisfy unsatisfied needs is actuated by the constant move towards equilibrium.

Another concept which has some affinity with the principle of homeostasis is the desire to master one's immediate environment. Individuals subjectively organize their environment by reference to past experience, present needs and future expectations. This develops into a pattern which is taken for granted until some external influence affects it. The individual then engages in interpretative or problem-solving activity in an attempt to absorb or resist the change.

Needs theory

An unsatisfied need creates tension and a state of disequilibrium. To restore the balance a goal is identified which will satisfy the need, and a behaviour pathway is selected which will lead to the achievement of the goal. All behaviour is therefore motivated by unsatisfied needs.

Not all needs are equally important for a person at any one time – some may provide a much more powerful drive towards a goal than others, depending on the individual's background and present situation. Complexity is further increased because there is no simple relationship between needs and goals. The same need can be satisfied by a number of different goals and the stronger the need and the longer its duration, the broader the range of possible goals. At the same time, one goal may satisfy a number of needs – a new car provides transport as well as an opportunity to impress the neighbours.

A number of needs models have been formulated and these are described below.

Murray's list of needs

Henry Murray produced one of the first and most influential lists of human needs in the 1930s. He defined 20 'psychogenic needs' or social motivators as follows:

1. *Abasement* – to submit passively to external force.
2. *Achievement* – to accomplish something difficult.
3. *Affiliation* – to draw near and enjoy, co-operate or reciprocate with another person or other persons.
4. *Aggression* – to overcome opposition forcefully.
5. *Autonomy* – to resist coercion and restraint.
6. *Counteraction* – to make up for failure by resumed action.
7. *Defendence* – to defend the self against assault, criticism and blame.
8. *Deference* – to admire and support a superior.
9. *Dominance* – to influence, direct or control the behaviour of others.
10. *Exhibition* – to make an impression, to be seen and heard.
11. *Harm avoidance* – to avoid pain, injury, illness and death.
12. *Infavoidance* – to avoid humiliation.
13. *Nurturance* – to give sympathy and gratify the needs of a helpless object, to support, console, protect, help and comfort.
14. *Order* – to put things in order, to achieve balance, neatness, tidiness and precision.
15. *Play* – to act for 'fun' without purpose.
16. *Rejection* – to separate oneself from an object.
17. *Sentience* – to seek and enjoy sensuous impressions.
18. *Sex* – to form and foster a sexual relationship.
19. *Succourance* – to have one's needs gratified by the sympathetic aid of an allied object.
20. *Understanding* – to be interested in theory, to speculate, formulate, analyse and generalize.

Maslow's hierarchy of needs

The most famous classification of needs is the one formulated by Maslow.[12] He suggested that there are five major need categories which apply to people in general, starting from the fundamental physiological needs and leading through a hierarchy of safety, social and esteem needs to the need for self-fulfilment, the highest need of all. Maslow's hierarchy is as follows:

1. *Physiological* – the need for oxygen, food, water and sex.
2. *Safety* – the need for protection against danger and the deprivation of physiological needs.
3. *Social* – the need for love, affection and to be accepted as belonging to a group.
4. *Esteem* – the need to have a stable, firmly based high evaluation of oneself (self-esteem) and to have the respect of others (prestige). These needs may be classified into two subsidiary sets: first, 'the desire for achievement, for adequacy, for confidence in

the face of the world, and for independence and freedom' and second, the desire for reputation or status defined as respect or esteem from other people, and manifested by recognition, attention, importance or appreciation.

5. *Self-fulfilment* (self-actualization) – the need to develop potentialities and skills, to become what one believes one is capable of becoming.

Maslow's theory of motivation states that when a lower need is satisfied the next highest becomes dominant and the individual's attention is turned to satisfying this higher need. The need for self-fulfilment, however, can never be satisfied. He said that man is a 'wanting animal'; only an unsatisfied need can motivate behaviour and the dominant need is the prime motivator of behaviour. Psychological development takes place as people move up the hierarchy of needs, but this is not necessarily a straightforward progression. The lower needs still exist, even if temporarily dormant as motivators, and individuals constantly return to previously satisfied needs. The schematic representation of the progressive development of needs is shown in Figure 8.6.

One of the implications of Maslow's theory is that the higher order needs for esteem and self-fulfilment provide the greatest impetus to motivation – they grow in strength on satisfaction, while the lower needs decline in strength on satisfaction. But the jobs people do will not necessarily satisfy their needs, especially when they are routine or de-skilled.

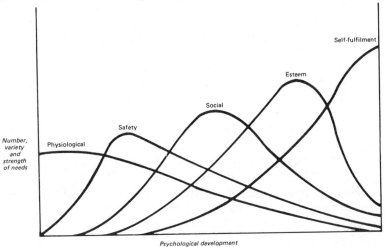

Figure 8.6 Progressive development of needs (Maslow)[12]

Alderfer's ERG theory

ERG theory (the needs for existence, relatedness and growth) as formulated by Alderfer[19] is about the subjective states of satisfaction and desire.

Satisfaction concerns the outcome of events between people and their environment. It is a subjective reaction which refers to the internal state of people who have obtained what they are seeking and is synonymous with getting and fulfilling. Desire is even more subjective because it refers exclusively to the internal state of a person related to needs, wants, preferences and motives. ERG theory adopts an 'open system' approach to understanding the human personality. This approach suggests that human beings are open systems which are constantly engaging in transactions with their environment which inevitably affect their behaviour.

From this basis, Alderfer devised a theory of human needs which postulated three primary categories:

1. *Existence needs* which reflect the requirement people have for material and energy exchange and the need to reach and maintain a homeostatic equilibrium with regard to the provision of certain material substances. Hunger and thirst represent deficiencies and are existence needs. Pay, fringe-benefits and working conditions are other types of existence needs.
2. *Relatedness needs* which acknowledge that people are not self-contained units but must engage in transactions with their human environment. The basic characteristic of relatedness needs is that their satisfaction depends on a process of sharing or mutuality. Acceptance, understanding, confirmation and influence are elements of the relatedness process.
3. *Growth needs* emerge from the tendency of open systems to increase in internal order and differentiation over time as a consequence of going beyond the environment. Growth needs impel people to make creative or productive efforts for themselves: 'satisfaction of growth needs depends on a person finding the opportunities to be what he is most fully and to become what he can.'[19]

ERG theory assumes that these three categories of needs are active in all living persons. All people are alike in that they possess some degree of each need, but they differ in the strength of their needs. The theory does not suggest a hierarchy of needs through which people progress from lower level to higher needs as in Maslow's theory (Maslow himself had doubts about the validity of a strictly ordered hierarchy). The three primary needs in ERG theory are related to one another but in a more complex way, as follows:

- The less existence needs are satisfied the more they will be desired.
- The less relatedness needs are satisfied, the more existence needs will be desired.
- The more existence needs are satisfied, the more relatedness needs will be desired.

- The less relatedness needs are satisfied, the more they will be desired.
- The less growth needs are satisfied, the more relatedness needs will be desired.
- The more relatedness needs are satisfied, the more growth needs will be desired.
- The more growth needs are satisfied, the more they will be desired.

Thus, any desire can have several types of satisfaction, and any satisfaction also affects more than one desire.

Each of the three basic ERG needs can be defined in terms of a target towards which efforts at gratification are aimed and in terms of a process through which, and only through which, satisfaction can be obtained. These targets and processes are summarized in Table 8.1.

Needs	Target	Process
Existence	Material substances	Getting enough
Relatedness	Significant other people or groups	Mutual sharing of thoughts or feelings
Growth	Environmental settings with which people contend and which enable them to engage problems which utilize their capacities fully and to develop additional capacities	People becoming more differentiated and integrated as human beings

Table 8.1 *ERG needs – targets and processes*

ERG theory builds on Maslow's theory but removes some of the ambiguities in Maslow's five need categories, where safety needs can either be concerned with material matters or interpersonal affairs, and esteem can be either interpersonal or self-confirmed. The Maslow and ERG categories are compared in Table 8.2.

ERG theory is also more related to the reality of motivation as a highly complex process and the process of refining need categories to three areas makes it possible to relate each of them to more specific targets and processes. This helps in diagnosing problems arising from the lack of need satisfaction and in formulating methods of dealing with these problems.

Maslow categories	ERG categories
Physiological	Existence
Safety – material	
Safety – interpersonal	
Love (belongingness)	Relatedness
Esteem (interpersonal)	
Esteem (self-confirmed)	Growth
Self-actualization	

Table 8.2 *Comparison of Maslow and ERG need categories*

Herzberg's two-factor model

The two-factor model of satisfiers and dissatisfiers was developed by Herzberg following an investigation into the sources of job satisfaction and dissatisfaction of accountants and engineers. As Vroom comments, the methods used by the researchers were neither correlational (between satisfaction and productivity) nor experimental. It was assumed that people have the ability and the motivation to report accurately the conditions which made them satisfied and dissatisfied with their jobs. Accordingly, the subjects were asked to tell their interviewers about the times during which they felt exceptionally good and exceptionally bad about their jobs and how long their feelings persisted. It was found that the stories told about 'good' periods most frequently concerned the content of the job. Achievement, recognition, advancement, responsibility, and the work itself were the most frequently coded themes in such stories. On the other hand, stories concerned with 'bad' periods most frequently concerned the context of the job. Company policy and administration, supervision, salary and working conditions more frequently appeared in these stories than in those told about 'good' periods. The main implications of this research, according to Herzberg, are that:

> The wants of employees divide into two groups. One group revolves around the need to develop in one's occupation as a source of personal growth. The second group operates as an essential base to the first and is associated with fair treatment in compensation, supervision, working conditions and administrative practices. The fulfilment of the needs of the second group does not motivate the individual to high levels of job satisfaction and to extra performance on the job. All we can expect from satisfying (this second group of needs) is the prevention of dissatisfaction and poor job performance.[6]

These groups form the two factors in Herzberg's model: one consists of the satisfiers or motivators, because they are seen to be effective in motivating the individual to superior performance and effort. The other consists of the dissatisfiers which essentially describe the environment and serve primarily to prevent job dissatisfaction, while having little effect on positive job attitudes. These were named the *hygiene* factors in the medical use of the term, meaning preventive and environmental.

Herzberg's theory has been strongly attacked. The research method has been criticized because no attempt was made to measure the relationship between satisfaction and performance. It has been suggested that the two-factor nature of the theory is an inevitable result of the questioning method used by the interviewers. It has also been suggested that wide and unwarranted inferences have been drawn from small and specialized samples and that there is no evidence to suggest that the satisfiers do improve productivity. In an extended critique of the theory, Opsahl and Dunnette stated that the data on feelings about salary 'seem inconsistent with the interpretations and lend no substantial support to hypotheses of a so-called differential role for money in leading to job satisfaction or job dissatisfaction.'[20]

In spite of these criticisms (or perhaps because of them, as they are all from academics) the Herzberg theory continues to thrive; partly because for the layman it is easy to understand and seems to be based on 'real-life' stories rather than academic abstractions, and partly because it fits in well with the highly respected ideas of Maslow and McGregor in its emphasis on the positive value of the intrinsic motivating factors. It is also in accord with a fundamental belief in the dignity of labour and the Protestant ethic – that work is good in itself. As a result, Herzberg has had immense influence on the job enrichment movement which seeks to design jobs in a way which will maximize the opportunities to obtain intrinsic satisfaction from work.

McClelland's achievement – affiliation – power needs

An alternative way of classifying needs was developed by McClelland[21] who based it mainly on studies of managerial staff. He identified three needs as being most important:

1. *The need for achievement*, defined as the need for competitive success measured against a personal standard of excellence.
2. *The need for affiliation*, defined as the need for warm, friendly, compassionate relationships with others.
3. *The need for power*, defined as the need to control or influence others.

Different individuals have different levels of these needs. Some have a greater need for achievement, others a stronger need for affiliation, and still others a stronger need for power. While one need may be dominant, however, this does not mean that the others are non-existent.

These needs may be given different priorities at different levels of management. High need for achievement is particularly important for success in many junior and middle management jobs where it is possible to feel direct responsibility for task accomplishment. But in senior management positions a concern for institutionalized as opposed to personal power becomes more important. A strong need for affiliation is not helpful at any level. However, as Guest points out: 'Those making a bid for power should take note of one of McClelland's findings. In a 20-year follow up of Harvard graduates who had scored high on the need for power, 58 per cent had high blood pressure or had died of heart failure.'[22]

A general theory of needs

In general, it is probably best to go back to Murray and accept that people have a wide range of needs, many of which are latent until stimulated by the environment. Murray's classification, however, does not provide very specific guidance on what should be done about motivation at work.

Maslow and Herzberg have produced simple classifications which have become enormously popular. But in their different ways they are flawed, and they have not been supported by research.

Alderfer also presents a simplified model of needs but it is more realistic than Maslow's and has been supported by research, although caution in interpretation of research is necessary because of the difficulty of providing acceptable measures of needs.

As Guest[22] points out, the four needs which have potentially important implications in work settings, are the needs for achievement, power, affiliation and autonomy. These embrace two of the ERG needs (relatedness and growth), and McClelland's extensive research concentrated on the first three. They are, of course, included in the other classifications but this formulation is more useful as a guide to motivation strategy.

Goal theory

Goal theory as developed by Locke[23] states that motivation and performance will be higher when individuals are set specific goals, when goals are difficult but accepted and when there is feedback on performance. Participation in goal setting is important as a means of getting agreement to the setting of higher goals. Difficult goals must be agreed and their achievement reinforced by guidance and advice. Finally, feedback is vital in maintaining motivation, particularly towards the achievement of even higher goals.

Goal theory is in line with the concept of management by objectives. The latter approach, however, has often failed because it has been tackled bureaucratically without gaining the real support of those involved and, importantly, without ensuring that managers are aware of the importance of the processes of agreement, reinforcement and feedback, and are skilled in practising them.

Reinforcement theory

As experience is gained in taking action to satisfy needs, people perceive that certain actions help to achieve their goals while others are less successful. Some actions bring rewards, others result in failure or even punishment. Reinforcement theory as developed by Hull[24] is derived from the previously mentioned law of effect. It suggests that successes in achieving goals and rewards act as positive incentives and reinforce the successful behaviour which is repeated the next time a similar need emerges. The more powerful, obvious and frequent the reinforcement, the more likely it is that the behaviour will be repeated until, eventually, it can become a more or less unconscious reaction to an event. Conversely, failures or punishments provide negative reinforcement which suggests that it is necessary to seek alternative means of achieving goals.

The degree to which experience shapes future behaviour does, of course, depend first on the extent to which an individual correctly perceives the connection between the behaviour and its outcome and, secondly, on the extent to which he is able to recognize the resemblance between the previous situation and the one that now confronts him. Perceptive ability varies between people as does the ability to identify correlations between events. For these reasons, some people are better at learning from experience than others, just as some people are more easily motivated than others.

It has been suggested that theories based on the law of effect or the principle of reinforcement are limited because they imply, in Allport's phrase, a 'hedonism of the past'.[25] They assume that the explanation of the present choices of an individual is to be found in an examination of the consequences of his past choices. Insufficient attention is paid in the theories to the influence of expectations, and no indication is given of any means of distinguishing in advance the class of outcomes which would strengthen responses and those which would weaken them.

Expectancy theory

The assumption of the needs-goal concept is that people will direct their efforts towards the goals which they value. But, as Cooper says: 'The existence of a valued goal is not a sufficient condition for action; people will act only when they have a reasonable expectation that their actions will lead to desired goals.'[26] The concept of expectancy was defined by Vroom as follows:

> Whenever an individual chooses between alternatives which involve uncertain outcomes, it seems clear that his behaviour is affected not only by his preferences among these outcomes but also by the degree to which he believes these outcomes to be possible. An expectancy is defined as a momentary belief concerning the

likelihood that a particular act will be followed by a particular outcome. Expectancies may be described in terms of their strength. Maximal strength is indicated by subjective certainty that the act *will* be followed by the outcome, while minimal (or zero) strength is indicated by subjective certainty that the act *will not* be followed by the outcome.[27]

The strength of expectations may be based on past experiences (reinforcement), but individuals are frequently presented with new situations – a change in job, payment system or working conditions imposed by management – where past experience is an inadequate guide to the implications of the change. In these circumstances, motivation may be reduced.

Motivation is only likely when a clearly perceived and usable relationship exists between performance and outcome, and the outcome is seen as a means of satisfying needs. This explains why extrinsic motivation – for example, an incentive or bonus scheme – only works if the link between effort and reward is clear and the value of the reward is worth the effort. It also explains why intrinsic motivation arising from the work itself can be more powerful than extrinsic motivation; intrinsic motivation outcomes are more under the control of the individual who can place greater reliance on his past experiences to indicate the extent to which positive and advantageous results are likely to be obtained by his behaviour.

Orientation theory

Orientation theory examines the factors which are instrumental, ie serve as a means, in directing people's choices about work. An orientation is a central organizing principle which underlies people's attempts to make sense of their lives. In relation to work, as defined by Guest: 'An orientation is a persisting tendency to seek certain goals and rewards from work which exists independently of the nature of the work and the work content.'[22]

Orientation theory is primarily developed from field work carried out by sociologists rather than laboratory work conducted by psychologists. Goldthorpe and his colleagues studied skilled and semi-skilled workers in Luton, and in the *Affluent Worker*[13] they stressed the importance of instrumental orientation, that is, a view of work as a means to an end, a context in which to earn money to purchase goods and leisure. According to Goldthorpe, the 'affluent' worker interviewed by the research team valued work largely for extrinsic reasons:

> Considerations of pay and security appear most powerful in binding men to their present job . . . Workers in all groups within our sample tend to be particularly motivated to increase their power as consumers and their domestic standard of living, rather than their satisfaction as producers and the degree of their self-fulfilment in work.[13]

He went on to emphasize the economic returns as the key factor:

> The workers have in effect chosen in favour of work which enables them to achieve a higher level of economic return . . . a decision has been made to give more weight to the *instrumental* at the expense of the expressive aspects of work.

However, it should be recognized that while pay may be the dominant factor in the *choice* of employer, there is no evidence that the level of pay determined the degree of satisfaction with the work itself.

In their research carried out with blue collared workers in Peterborough, Blackburn and Mann[14] found a wider range of orientations. They suggested that different ones could come into play with varying degrees of force in different situations. The fact that workers in practice had little choice about what they did contributed to this diversity – their orientations were affected by the choice or lack of choice presented to them and this meant that they may be forced to accept alternative orientations.

But Blackburn and Mann confirmed that pay was a key preference area, the top preferences being:

1. Pay.
2. Security.
3. Workmates.
4. Intrinsic job.
5. Autonomy.

And they commented that: 'An obsession with wages clearly emerged . . . A concern to minimize unpleasant workers was also widespread.' Surprisingly perhaps, they also revealed that 'the most persistent preference of all was for outside work', a fairly clear desire for a combination of 'fresh air and freedom'.

The orientation approach stresses the role of the social environment outside work as a key factor affecting motivation. It therefore corrects the over-emphasis of Maslow and others on instinctive needs and links closely with the work of Murray and McClelland, who both recognize the importance of environmental factors.

Another study carried out by McDougall,[28] although not strictly based on orientation theory, did in effect look at the orientation of managers in a large British company to pay and the other rewards obtained from their work.

Managers were asked to rate the importance to them of each of 31 tangible or intangible rewards which might be associated with their jobs. An analysis of the replies into six motivational groups showed that the largest group, comprising 25 per cent of the managers, was mainly interested in material reward expressed in money, fringe benefits and opportunities for advancement. This group was younger and potentially more mobile than the others and included a high proportion of production staff and accountants. The groups, however, varied considerably in their preference, which led the research team to conclude that it is dangerous to make any generalized assumptions about values and motives when considering the role of money and the type of remuneration system a company ought to provide.

These research projects and a number of other studies demonstrate that 'it is never fair, never wise, never safe to generalize' about the motivation to work. It varies between people generally because of their different orientation as affected by their environment and the choices they have about what they do. It also varies between different levels and types of managers and workers.

Reactance theory

Reactance theory as formulated by Brehm starts from the premise that 'to the extent a person is aware of his needs and the behaviour necessary to satisfy these needs, and providing he has the appropriate freedom, he can choose behaviour so as to maximize need satisfaction.'[11]

If, however, this freedom to act is threatened, people will react, that is, they will, in accordance with the principle of homeostasis, be motivationally aroused to the avoidance of any further loss of freedom. In essence, as Brehm says:

> Given that a person has a set of free behaviours, he will experience reactance whenever any of these behaviours is eliminated or threatened with elimination, and when a free behaviour of an individual is eliminated (or threatened) his desire for that behaviour or for the object of it will increase.[11]

In other words, individuals are not passive receivers and responders. Instead, they actively strive to make sense of their environment and to reduce uncertainty by seeking to control factors influencing rewards. Management may have all sorts of wonderful ideas about motivating employees, but they will not necessarily work unless they make sense to the people concerned in terms of their own values and orientations.

Satisfaction/performance theory

Job satisfaction

The term 'job satisfaction' refers to the attitudes and feelings people have about their work. Positive and favourable attitudes towards the job indicate job satisfaction, and negative and unfavourable attitudes towards the job indicate job dissatisfaction.

Morale is often defined as being equivalent to job satisfaction. Thus Guion defines morale as 'the extent to which the individual's needs are satisfied and the extent to which the individual perceives that satisfaction as stemming from his total work situation'.[29] Other definitions stress the group aspects of morale; for example, Gilmer suggests that morale 'is a feeling of being accepted by and belonging to a group of employees through adherence to common goals'.[30] And he, like others, distinguishes between morale as a group variable, related to the degree to which group members feel attracted to their group and desire to remain a member of it, and job attitude as an individual variable related to the feeling the employee has about his job.

Factors affecting job satisfaction

The following factors affect job satisfaction:

1. *The intrinsic motivating factors.* These relate to job content, especially variety, challenge, responsibility, control over work methods, control over work pace, the opportunity to use skills and abilities and influence in decision-making.
2. *The extrinsic factors.* These relate to pay and the context in which the work is carried out.
3. *The quality of supervision.* The Hawthorne studies[31] resulted in the claim that supervision is the most important determinant of worker attitudes. The Ohio State Leadership Studies[32] later identified two major independent dimensions of leadership behaviour (while other studies distinguished between employee orientation and production orientation). The first dimension was called 'consideration' and includes supervisory behaviour 'indicative of friendship, mutual trust, respect and warmth'. The second dimension was termed initiating structure, which includes behaviour in which the supervisor organizes and defines group activities and his relation to the group. A number of subsequent studies have suggested that the display of consideration of supervisors has increased employee satisfaction and resulted in lower labour turnover, less absenteeism and fewer grievances. But they have not shown that there is a direct relationship between consideration, satisfaction and productivity. Herzberg, however, claimed that the importance of supervision has been over-rated and it seems clear that considerate supervision is only one out of many factors that can affect attitudes and satisfaction.
4. *The work group.* Elton Mayo believed that 'a man's desire to be continuously associated in work with his fellows is a strong, if not the strongest, human characteristic'.[3] And it is true that social interaction can be highly rewarding to most people, and that experiences with one's fellow workers can be a major satisfaction at work. Research has shown that larger groups where less interaction is possible have lower cohesiveness or morale than smaller groups. The social isolation which exists on assembly lines is a known cause of dissatisfaction.

5. *Success or failure.* Success will obviously create satisfaction, especially if it enables the individual to prove to himself that he is using his skills effectively. And it is equally obvious that the reverse is true of failure.

Job satisfaction and performance

It is a commonly held and apparently not unreasonable belief that an increase in job satisfaction will result in improved performance. The whole human relations movement was based on the belief that productivity could be increased by making workers more satisfied. The first real blow to this view came from the Survey Research Centre studies in an insurance company[33] and a railroad.[34] No differences were found in either study between the satisfaction with wages, satisfaction with job status, or satisfaction with fellow workers in high and low productivity sections.

A review of the extensive literature on this subject by Brayfield and Crockett[35] concluded that there was little evidence of any simple or appreciable relationship between employee attitudes and the effectiveness of their performance. An updated version of their analysis by Vroom[27] covered 20 studies, in each of which one or more measures of job satisfaction or employee attitudes was correlated with one or more criteria of performance. The median correlation of all these studies was 0.14, which is not high enough to suggest any marked relationship between satisfaction and performance. Our own observations confirm the results of this analysis. We are constantly coming across people who are perfectly content to do the minimum that will keep them in employment.

It has been suggested that it is not increases in satisfaction that produce improved performance but improved performance that increases satisfaction. This is certainly true in the sense that individuals are motivated to reach certain goals and will be satisfied if they achieve those goals through improved performance. But individual goals can be satisfied in other ways besides working harder or better. Improved performance is not a necessary or the only factor in improving satisfaction. As Brayfield and Crockett suggested:

> Productivity is seldom a goal in itself but is more commonly a means to goal attainment. Therefore . . . we might expect high satisfaction and high productivity to occur together when productivity is perceived as a path to certain important goals and when these goals are achieved. Under other conditions, satisfaction and productivity might be unrelated or even negatively related.[35]

Increases in satisfaction may therefore reduce staff turnover, absenteeism and grievances but they do not necessarily result in increases in productivity. Satisfaction and performance are often related but the precise effect on one another depends upon the working situation and the people in it. Motivation is not simply a matter of increasing job satisfaction. The common sense view that people are only motivated when they have something to strive for accords with Maslow's suggestion that only an unsatisfied need motivates behaviour. A measure of dissatisfaction and a desire for more achievement or power may be the best motivator for some people. But it will all depend on the people concerned and the environment in which they are working.

Motivation and performance

Although there is some doubt about the relationship between perform-ance and satisfaction, it seems obvious that the link between motivation and performance is a positive one: increased motivation results in more effort and improved performance. But there are two qualifications to this point of view. First, there is the effect of ability, and second, there are the possible detrimental effects of too much motivation. There is also the whole question of the impact of such factors as rewards and the individu-al's understanding of the kinds of activities and behaviour he should engage in to perform his job successfully (role perceptions).

Motivation and ability

However keen someone is to do something, he will not be able to do it unless he has the required abilities. Vroom suggested on the basis of a number of experiments that:

> The effects of motivation on performance are dependent on the level of ability of the worker, and the relationship of ability to performance is dependent on the motivation of the worker. The effects of ability and motivation on performance are not additive but interactive. The data presently available on this question suggest something more closely resembling the multiplicative relationship depicted in the following formula:
>
> Performance =   (Ability x Motivation)[27]

This formula expresses more than the truism that you cannot perform a task without some ability *and* some motivation. The emphasis is on the multiplicative relationship between the two factors, from which it fol-lows that when ability is low increases in motivation will result in smaller increases in performance than when ability is high. Similarly, when moti-vation is low, increases in ability will result in smaller increases in per-formance than when motivation is high.

The implication is that it is as necessary to concentrate on improving ability by means of good selection and training as it is to concentrate on improving motivation by some manipulation of the extrinsic and intrinsic factors affecting it. At the same time, more is to be gained from increas-ing the motivation of those who are high in ability than of those who are low in ability, and more is to be gained from increasing the ability of those who are highly motivated than of those who are relatively less well motivated.

Effects of high motivation

There is a second qualification to the concept that higher motivation always results in greater productivity. It is possible for someone to be too highly motivated; to want something so much that he becomes over-anxious and therefore prone to indecision and error or to ignoring relevant information. Vroom proposed three hypothetical relationships between the amount of motivation and performance, as shown in Figure 8.7. He suggests that while it is possible for performance to improve steadily as in the straight line on Figure 8.7, it is equally possible that the rate at which performance increases diminishes until there is no further increase, as in the dotted line. Another plausible relationship is shown by the broken line, where performance reaches its maximum point under moderate levels of motivation and then drops off under high levels of motivation. The latter view is supported by a number of research studies.

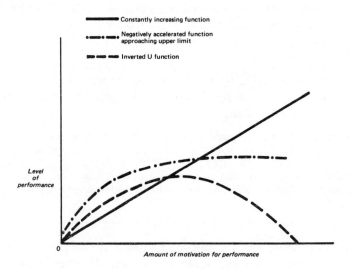

Figure 8.7 Hypothetical relationships between motivation and performance

Motivation/performance model

The work of Lawler and Porter on the relationships between motivation and performance has been developed by Schwab and Cummings[36] (Figure 8.8). The refinements introduced into this model are derived in part from expectancy theory and are, first, that performance results in intrinsic or extrinsic rewards which, through a feedback loop, affect perceptions about the relationships between effort and reward and hence the amount of effort. Second, the model suggests that satisfaction is affected not only by the existence of reward but also by perceptions about the extent to which the reward is fair and equitable. By a feedback process this determines the value of the reward, which also influences the amount of effort. The model clearly shows the interactive nature of performance and satisfaction. Satisfaction is contingent upon the receipt of equitable rewards following performance, but it also influences perceptions about the value of rewards and, therefore, effort and performance.

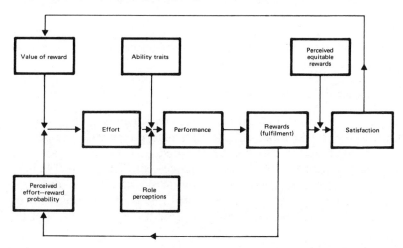

Figure 8.8 Motivation model (Schwab and Cummings)[36]

A general theory of motivation

A general theory of motivation can be derived from the various schools and theories described above. This general theory covers the following areas:

(a) the process of motivation involving homeostasis, reinforcement and the needs-goals model;
(b) the specific influences of needs and goals on motivation;
(c) the relevance of the extrinsic and intrinsic factors on motivation;
(d) the importance of expectations as motivating forces;
(e) the influence of orientations and reactions on motivation;
(f) the relationship between motivation and performance;
(g) the key factors to consider when motivating people.

The process of motivation

- *Basis* – the basic of motivation is the process of recognizing a need and taking action to satisfy it by reaching a goal.
- *Complexity* – motivation is a complex process because people have different needs and varied perceptions about them.
- *Homeostasis* – individuals are in essence open systems constantly

interacting with their environment and at the same time striving for equilibrium. Consequently, they have a wide variety of goals and of perceptions about the actions which are likely to help them achieve those goals. Motivation is very much a matter of perceptions which will be influenced by past experiences and the present environment.

● *Reinforcement* – success in achieving goals and rewards act as positive incentives and reinforces the successful behaviour, which is repeated as similar needs arise.

The influence of needs

In response to stimuli from the environment, needs emerge which upset equilibrium. To restore equilibrium in accordance with the principle of homeostasis, these needs must be satisfied.

The basic needs are related to existence – survival, security and maintaining a reasonable standard of living in relation to expectations. Another powerful need is for relationships or affiliations with others. But the key motivating needs are for growth and freedom, that is:

● achievement
● power
● autonomy.

Money, however, may be a dominant motivating force because it can be instrumental in satisfying a multitude of needs especially those concerned with existence, growth, achievement, power and autonomy.

The influence of goals

Individuals at work are motivated by having specific goals and they perform better when they are aiming for difficult goals which they have accepted and when they receive feedback on performance.

Extrinsic and intrinsic motivating factors

Motivation at work can be either extrinsic – provided by the employer in the context of the job, or intrinsic – derived from the content of the job. Extrinsic rewards provided by the employer, including pay, can be important in attracting and retaining employees and, in the short term, increasing effort and minimizing dissatisfaction. Intrinsic rewards related to responsibility, achievement and the work itself may have a longer-term and deeper effect in creating and increasing satisfaction.

The importance of expectations

The degree to which people are motivated will depend not only upon the perceived value of the outcome of their actions – the goal or reward – but also upon their perceptions of the likelihood of obtaining the reward, ie their expectations. They will be highly motivated if they can control the means to attain their goals.

Higher effort or motivation will therefore exist when employees perceive a link between effort, performance and rewards. The extent to which better performance will be achieved depends partly on the strength of the need and the attractiveness of the goal but, also, and to a large extent, on their expectation of reaching the goal. In addition, employees must have the necessary knowledge and skills and an understanding of the requirements of their job or role.

The influence of orientations and reactions

Organizations may have expectations about how their motivating strategies will improve performance as well as helping to attract and retain employees. But the situation may not be under as much control as they would wish because of the influence of:

- *Orientations* – independently of what the company attempts to do in the way of motivating its employees, people have orientations or preferences for what they want to get out of work which are influenced by their environment and the choice of activities or work that is available to them.
- *Reactance* – individuals are not passive receivers and responders, they attempt to control their own environment irrespective of what the organization wants them to do, and react against any threat to whatever autonomy they possess or think they possess.

The relationship between motivation and performance

The basic requirements for job satisfaction may include comparatively higher pay, an equitable payment system, real opportunities for promotion, considerate and participative supervision, a reasonable degree of social interaction at work, interesting and varied tasks and a high degree of control over work pace and work methods. The degree of satisfaction obtained by individuals, however, will depend largely upon their own needs and expectations and the environment in which they work.

But research has not established any strongly positive connection between satisfaction and performance. A satisfied worker is not necessarily a high producer, and a high producer is not necessarily a satisfied worker. Some people claim that good performance produces satisfaction rather than the other way round, but their case has not been proved.

The key motivating factors

The overriding consideration in motivation is that the members of an organization contribute to the organization in return for the inducements that the organization offers them. In the words of Simon: 'Individuals are willing to accept organization membership when their activity in the organization contributes, directly or indirectly, to their own personal goals'.[37] The task of the organization is to analyse its own circumstances and the particular needs and requirements of its employees to determine the mix of extrinsic and intrinsic motivating factors needed to attract and retain good quality staff and to obtain consistently high standards of performance from them.

If management wishes to increase productivity it has to bear in mind, in the words of Georgopoulos:

> Individual productivity is, among other things, a function of one's motivation to produce at any given level; in turn such motivation depends upon (a) the particular needs of the individual as reflected in the goals towards which he is moving, and (b) his perception regarding the relative usefulness of productivity behaviour as an instrumentality, or as a path to the attainment of these goals.[38]

Thus the individual's main concern is to assess the benefits that will accrue to him from doing what the organization wants him to do, and the penalties that may result from a failure to act as the organization requires. The organization has to make assumptions about what people want in deciding how they should be motivated. This is the problem of motivation. Many such assumptions are invalid because they are based on generalizations and an inadequate understanding of the process of motivation. Even if attitude surveys are used to assess needs and wants they can easily produce misleading results because of the difficulties of administration and interpretation. (Attitude surveys are considered in more detail later in this chapter.) Finally, there is the problem that all managers meet – it is easy to observe behaviour, it is much more difficult to interpret and attach reasons for that behaviour when it has been motivated by a set of hidden needs and goals.

Motivation strategies

Simplistic approaches

There are three basic approaches which have been advocated by motivation experts. Each has its merits, but because they are often put forward as the only answer to all motivation problems, they are essentially simplistic. The three approaches are:

1. *Carrot and stick:* people work for rewards. They will work hard if you pay them well and will work harder if you pay them more. If they do not perform satisfactorily, then you punish them.
2. *Motivate through the work itself:* give people fulfilling work and their level of job satisfaction, and therefore performance, will be high.

3. *The one-minute manager system:*[39] set goals with your
   subordinates and give them positive feedback when they do something right and negative feedback when they do something wrong.

Managers, according to their inclinations, take up these nostrums
because they seem easy: a quick fix in a complex world. There is nothing
wrong with any one of them – for the right people, in the right place at the
right time – but the complexity of the process of motivation and the infinitely varying demands made by different situations do not admit any
'quick fixes'. Motivation strategy will only be effective if it uses the contingency approach, which means basing it on a thorough analysis of the
situation. Attitude surveys and behaviour modification techniques can
be used for this purpose. A diagnosis of the problem areas follows from
this analysis and leads to the choice of the mix of motivation techniques
that are suitable to the situation and to the diagnosis.

Attitude surveys

Attitude surveys can provide general information on attitudes and feelings as a basis for formulating policies. Attitude surveys can also be used
to:

- provide particular information on the preferences of employees,
  for example, on a union recognition issue;
- give warning on potential trouble spots;
- diagnose the cause of particular troubles;
- compare morale in different parts of the organization;
- evaluate training;
- assess how organizational and other policy changes have been
  received;
- observe the effects of policies and actions over a period of time;
- provide people with the opportunity to express their views –
  attitude surveys are therefore in themselves a means of increasing
  job satisfaction as long as feelings of frustration do not arise
  because of lack of action on the part of management after the
  survey;
- provide an additional means of communication, especially if the
  survey includes some discussions with employees on their
  attitudes and what actions they would like management to take.

Approach

The approach is first to identify the individual's needs and then to assess
the extent to which these needs are being met. This means using two
questionnaires. The first questionnaire would ask people how they feel
about various things for *any* job they might do, not just their present job.
Thus, against the heading of 'good wages' they would be asked to indicate how they feel by ticking the appropriate heading – absolutely top

priority, very important, fairly important, not very important. The second questionnaire would ask them to express their feelings about different aspects of their present job. For example, indicating against 'pay' whether their feelings about it are very good, good, neither good nor bad, bad, very bad.

Methods of conducting attitude surveys

There are three methods of conducting attitude surveys:

1. By the use of *structured questionnaires* issued to all or a sample of employees. The questionnaires may be standardized ones such as the Brayfield and Rothe Index of Job Satisfaction, or they may be developed specially for the organization. The advantage of using standardized questionnaires is that they have been thoroughly tested and in many cases norms are available against which results can be compared. Additional questions specially relevant to the company can be added to the standard list. A tailor-made questionnaire can be used to highlight particular issues but if it is thought to be essential, it is advisable to obtain professional help from an experienced psychologist who can carry out the skilled work of drafting and pilot-testing the questionnaire and interpreting the results. Questionnaires have the advantage of being relatively cheap to administer and analyse, especially when there are large numbers involved.

2. By the use of *interviews*. These may be 'open-ended' or depth interviews where the discussion is allowed to range quite freely. Or they may be semi-structured in that there is a checklist of points to be covered, although the aim of the interviewer is to allow discussion to flow around the points so that the frank and open views of the individual are obtained. Alternatively, and more rarely, interviews can be highly structured so that they become no more than the spoken application of a questionnaire. Individual interviews are to be preferred because they are more likely to be revealing and are easier to analyse. But they are expensive and time consuming. Group discussions are a quicker way of reaching a large number of people, but the results are not so easy to quantify and some people may have difficulty in expressing their views in public.

3. By a combination of *questionnaire and interview*. This is the ideal approach because it will combine the quantitative data from the questionnaire with the qualitative data from the interviews. It is always advisable to accompany questionnaires with some depth interviews, even if time permits only a limited sample. An alternative approach is to administer the questionnaire to a group of people and then discuss the reactions to each question with the group. This ensures that a quantified analysis is possible but

enables the group, or at least some members of it, to express their feelings more fully.

Assessing results

It is an interesting fact that when people are asked directly if they are satisfied with their job, most of them (70 to 90 per cent) will say they are. This is regardless of the work being done and often in spite of strongly held grievances. The probable reason for this phenomenon is that while most people are willing to admit having grievances – in fact, if invited to complain, they will complain – they may be reluctant to admit, even to themselves, to being dissatisfied with a job which they have no immediate intention of leaving. Many employees have become reconciled to their work, even if they do not like some aspects of it, and have no real desire to do anything else. So they are, in a sense, satisfied enough to continue, even if they have complaints. Finally, many people *are* satisfied with their job overall, although they will grumble about many aspects of it.

Overall measures of satisfaction do not, therefore, always reveal anything interesting. It is more important to look at particular aspects of satisfaction or dissatisfaction to decide whether or not anything needs to be done. In these circumstances, the questionnaire will only indicate a line to be followed up. It will not provide the answers. Hence the advantage of individual meetings or group discussions to explore in depth any issue raised.

Behaviour modification

Behaviour modification is concerned with creating the circumstances to ensure appropriate behaviour. Using information from attitude surveys or any other means of analysing job satisfaction, morale or productivity, behaviour modification techniques can form the basis of the other motivating techniques described below. Behaviour modification is primarily concerned with individuals and consists of five stages as described by Guest:[22]

1. *Pinpoint* – specify the behaviour to be changed in terms of what people are expected to do.
2. *Record* – establish basic data on current performance.
3. *Identify* influences on behaviour: such as training, guidance, instructions.
4. *Arrange* for reinforcement of desired behaviour which takes the form of 'social' reinforcement from the supervisor such as praise and careful feedback of results.
5. *Evaluate* – record new performance data.

Motivation techniques

The motivation techniques that can be used to modify and improve performance are:

- Use money as a reward and an incentive.
- Spell out requirements.
- Motivate through the work itself.
- Reward and recognize achievement.
- Exercise leadership.
- Build up teamwork.
- Train and develop people.
- Eliminate the negatives.

Each of these methods is discussed below.

Money

Money, in the form of pay or some other sort of remuneration, is the most obvious extrinsic reward. Money provides the carrot which most, if not all, people want.

Doubts have been cast on the effectiveness of money by Herzberg because while the lack of it can cause dissatisfaction, its provision does not result in lasting satisfaction. There is something in this, especially for people on fixed salaries or rates of pay who do not benefit directly from an incentive scheme. They may feel good when they get an increase – apart from the extra money, it is about as tangible a form of recognition as you can find – but this feeling of euphoria can rapidly die away. Other dissatisfactions from Herzberg's list of hygiene factors, such as working conditions or the quality of management, loom larger in their minds, or they fail to get the satisfaction they need from the work itself.

Nevertheless, money provides the means to achieve a number of different ends. It is a powerful force because it is linked directly or indirectly to the satisfaction of many needs. In Maslow's hierarchy, it clearly satisfies the basic needs for survival and security, if it is coming in regularly. It can also satisfy the need for self-esteem (as noted above, it is a visible mark of appreciation) and status – money can set you in a grade apart from your fellows and can buy you things they can't to build up your prestige. Money satisfies the less desirable but still prevalent drives of acquisitiveness and cupidity.

Money may in itself have no intrinsic meaning, but it acquires significant motivating power because it comes to symbolize so many intangible goals. It acts as a symbol in different ways for different people, and for the same person at different times.

Money can therefore provide positive motivation in the right circumstances, but Herzberg is correct in pointing out that pay systems can demotivate. Another researcher in this area was Elliott Jaques,[40] who emphasized the need for such systems to be perceived as being fair and equitable. In other words, the reward should be clearly related to effort or level of responsibility and people should not receive less money than they deserve compared with their fellow workers. Jaques called this the 'felt-fair' principle.

To use money effectively as a motivator and to avoid it acting as a de-motivator it is necessary to:

- Pay competitive rates to attract and retain people.
- Provide the rate for the job which must reflect the value of the work to the company and be paid fairly and equitably.
- Relate pay to performance or results wherever possible, thus providing a direct incentive.

Remember that incentive or bonus schemes only work as motivators if it is felt that: (1) the reward is worth having in relation to the effort; (2) the reward is commensurate with the effort; and (3) the worker can confidently expect that his effort will be followed by the reward – quickly and consistently.

Spell out requirements

Motivation is not simply a matter of providing rewards and incentives. People have to know what they are expected to do and what will happen to them if they do not do it. They need to be clear about their roles, the objectives they have to achieve and the required standards of performance and behaviour. They can be made aware of the rewards in the shape of money, advancement or improved status that will result from compliance with these expectations (the carrot); but they must be equally aware of the sanctions that will be applied if they fail (the stick).

Motivating through the work itself

Given an equitable and competitive pay structure which, so far as possible, offers effective financial incentives, an organization can increase identification and provide for long-lasting motivation by developing an intrinsic reward system. Intrinsic rewards are contained in the content of the job and give satisfaction by enabling people to feel a sense of accomplishment, to express and use their abilities, and to exercise their own decision-making powers. Motivation through the work itself is mainly a matter of job design and job enrichment as described in Chapter 11.

Reward and recognize achievement

A pay system can be geared to providing appropriate rewards for achievement, but people can also be motivated by giving them more responsibility (an intrinsic reward) as well as opportunities for promotion and increased status (extrinsic rewards). Tangible rewards are best, as long as they have been earned and people appreciate that fact. Praise for work well done is, however, an important motivator although, again, it must be earned. It is devalued if it is given too liberally.

The key messages for motivators from expectancy and goal theory, however, are that:

- the goals and values of employees must be systematically identified;
- rewards should be provided on an individual basis tied to achievements rather than on a general basis – overall pay rises have little motivational impact;
- rewards should be publicized so that everyone appreciates the link between performance and rewards, thus enhancing expectation;
- employees should be provided with the knowledge, skills and understanding required to direct motivation to improved performance.

Exercise leadership

Leadership plays a key role in motivation. It promotes commitment and identification, but it also provides a sense of direction. It can clarify roles and objectives, develop a sense of purpose and foster team spirit. Inspirational leadership from charismatic figures who get everyone to accept what are sometimes called 'superordinate goals' – ie aims above and beyond the call of duty – can be appropriate in some circumstances, for example in crises. But cool, quiet, restrained leaders who carry people with them just because they clearly know where they are going can be very effective.

Build up teamwork

A cohesive team will carry all its members along with it, although it should be remembered that teams do not always go in the direction management wants. Many an incentive scheme has been ruined by workers who have restricted earning levels and ganged up against rate busters because they felt that otherwise, management would tighten up the rates. Team development or building activities are described in Chapter 12.

Train and develop people

Systematic training and development programmes as described in Chapter 29 will provide motivation by giving people the opportunity to enhance their skills and to achieve positions of greater responsibility. Sending someone away on a course can be a good way of showing him that he is valued. Company training programmes, especially residential ones, can help to build commitment and identification.

Eliminate the negatives

Herzberg's two-factor model of satisfaction and dissatisfaction may not be based on adequate research but it does make it clear that, while motivating techniques such as those described above should accentuate the positives it is also necessary to eliminate, or at least minimize, the negatives. These will include an inequitable pay structure, poor working conditions, poor communications, lack of involvement, lack of recognition, little scope for advancement or widening experience, inadequate management or supervision and unduly restrictive bureaucratic practices.

Putting the motivation package together

All these methods of motivation can and should be used. But they need to be deployed judiciously to meet organizational needs and to lead to behaviour modification in the direction required by the organization. They include motivators that satisfy extrinsic needs such as pay and those that cater for intrinsic needs such as recognition and achievement. Ultimately, motivation is an individual matter and it is essential to train managers in the skills of identifying what factors will motivate their staff and the motivating and counselling techniques they should use.

Commitment

Commitment, as described by White,[41] denotes three areas of feeling or behaviour related to the company in which a person works:

1. Belief in, and acceptance of, the organization itself and/or its goals and values.
2. Willingness to exert effort on behalf of the organization beyond what is contracted for. This might include giving private time to work, postponing a holiday, or making some other personal sacrifice for the organization without the expectation of immediate personal gain.
3. Desire to maintain membership of the organization.

It is possible to distinguish between passive (intention to stay) and active (desire to achieve) commitment. White suggests four possible groups as shown in Figure 8.9.

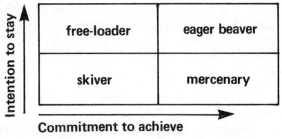

Figure 8.9 Commitment psychology

Commitment and motivation

Commitment is a wider concept than motivation and tends to be more stable over a period of time. It is less responsive to transitory aspects of an employee's job. It is possible to be dissatisfied with a particular feature of a job while retaining a reasonably high level of commitment to the organization as a whole.

In relating commitment to motivation it is useful to distinguish, as do Buchanan and Huczynski,[42] three perspectives.

1. The goals towards which people aim. From this perspective, goals such as the good of the company, or effective performance at work, may provide a degree of motivation for some employees, who could be regarded as committed in so far as they feel they own the goals.
2. The process by which goals and objectives at work are selected, which is quite distinct from the way in which commitment arises within individuals.
3. The social process of motivating others, usually, in a working context, to perform effectively. From this viewpoint, strategies aimed at increasing motivation will also affect commitment. It may be true to say that, where commitment is evident, motivation is likely to be strong, particularly if a long-term view is taken of effective performance.

Commitment and performance

The link between commitment and performance, like that between job satisfaction and performance, is not always clear. Strong commitment to the work is, however, likely to result in conscientious and self-directed application to do the job, regular attendance, nominal supervision and a high level of effort. Commitment to the organization will certainly be related to the intention to stay, in other words, loyalty to the company.

Developing commitment

Commitment to the organization will increase if people identify with its values, aims and activities, believe that if the organization thrives, so will they, and feel that they are treated fairly and humanely by the company. As with motivation, there is no one method available to increase commitment. It will be developed by the use of an appropriate mix of the following approaches:

- induction programmes for new employees which creates favourable attitudes from the start;
- communications programmes which inform employees of the company's aims, values and achievements;

- the implementation of personnel policies which emphasize equity, equal opportunity and justice;
- involvement programmes which help employees to feel that they are an important part of the organization;
- a management style which ensures that managers are both visible and approachable;
- organization development programmes which emphasize teamwork, help people to understand and accept the reasons for change and resolve conflict situations.

Roles

An individual at work – and elsewhere – occupies a role in relation to other people (his 'role set'). He will have expectations about the behaviour he should exhibit. If he lives up to these expectations he will have successfully performed the role.

An individual's performance in a role will be a product of the interaction between his own personality and the situation he is in. Situational factors are important, but the role he performs will both shape and reflect his personality. Stress and inadequate performance will result when roles are ambiguous, incompatible or in conflict with one another.

Role ambiguity
When an individual is unclear about what his role is, what he is expected to do or how he is getting on he may become insecure or lose confidence in himself.

Role incompatibility
Stress and poor performance may be caused by someone's role having incompatible elements, as when there is a clash between what other people expect from the role and what the individual believes it is.

Role conflict
Role conflict results when even if the role is clearly defined and there is no incompatibility between expectations, the individual has to carry out two antagonistic roles. For example, conflict can exist between the role of the individual at work and his role at home.

Implications of motivation and role theory

Motivation theory helps us to understand why people behave in the way they do and what we can do about it. There are, however, no easy answers. Motivation is a complex process. The relationship between satisfaction and performance is not so clear as some people would have us believe. Motivation can be extrinsic or intrinsic but the relative importance of these to an individual will depend on his personality and his expectations, and the latter are not always predictable. Motivation theory does not, therefore, provide us with all the answers. But it does give us a set of analytical tools which we can use to assess the situation and consider what actions are most likely to be appropriate in the circumstances.

The importance of role theory is that it emphasizes the fact that people at work are placed in situations where they have to play roles which are not always ones that suit them and which can result in stress and poor performance. However well motivated someone is, he may get into difficulties because his role is ambiguous or incompatible with what he wants to do or can do.

Motivation theory shows the importance of establishing the right mix of extrinsic and intrinsic rewards which meet the expectations of people at work. Role theory adds to this concept the need for people to be fitted, so far as possible, into jobs that suit them, to be trained in how to use their skills, and to be managed in a way which enables them to deploy their capacities effectively in their jobs.

References

1. Schein, E H *Organizational Psychology*. Prentice-Hall, New Jersey, 1965.
2. Taylor, F W 'The Principles of Scientific Management', *Scientific Management*, Harper, New York, 1947.
3. Mayo, E *The Human Problems of an Industrial Civilization*. Macmillan, London, 1933.
4. McGregor, D *The Human Side of Enterprise*. McGraw-Hill, New York, 1960.
5. Argyris, C *Personality and Organization*. Harper & Row, New York, 1957.
6. Herzberg, F W, Mausner, B and Snyderman, B *The Motivation to Work*. John Wiley, New York, 1957.
7. Von Bertalanffy, L 'Theoretical models in biology and psychology'. In Krech, D and Klein, G S (eds) *Theoretical Models and Personality Theory*. Duke University Press, Durham, 1952.
8. Allport, G 'The open system in personality theory', *Journal of Abnormal and Social Psychology*, 1960, **61**, pp 301-311.
9. Lawrence, P R and Lorsch, J W *Developing Organizations*. Addison-Wesley, Reading, Mass., 1969.
10. Porter, L W and Lawler, E E *Managerial Attitudes and Performance*. Irwin-Dorsey, Homewood, Illinois, 1968.
11. Brehm, J W *A Theory of Psychological Reactance*. Academic Press, New York, 1966.
12. Maslow, A H *Motivation and Personality*. Harper & Row, New York, 1954.
13. Goldthorpe, J H, Lockwood, D C, Bechoter, F and Platt, J *The Affluent Worker: Industrial Attitudes and Behaviour*. Cambridge University Press, 1968.
14. Blackburn, R M and Mann, R *The Working Class in the Labour Market*. Macmillan, London, 1979.
15. Ouchi, W G *Theory 2*. Addison-Wesley, Reading, Mass., 1981.
16. Pascale, R T and Athos, A G *The Art of Japanese Management*. Simon & Schuster, New York, 1981.

17. Peters, T J and Waterman, R H *In Search of Excellence*. Harper & Row, New York, 1982.
18. Peters, T J *A Passion for Excellence*. Collins, London, 1985.
19. Alderfer, C P *Existence, Relatedness and Growth*. The Free Press, New York, 1972.
20. Opsahl, R C and Dunnette, M D 'The role of financial compensation in industrial motivation', *Psychological Bulletin*, Vol 56, 1966, pp 94-118.
21. McClelland, D C *Power, The Inner Experience*. Irvington, New York, 1975.
22. Guest, D 'What's new in motivation?', *Personnel Management*, May, 1984.
23. Latham, G P and Locke, F A 'Goal setting – a national technique that works', *Organizational Dynamics*, **8**, 1979.
24. Hull, C *Essentials of Behaviour*. Yale University Press, New Haven, 1951.
25. Allport, G 'The historical background of modern social psychology'. In G Lindzey (ed) *Handbook of Social Psychology*. Addison-Wesley, Cambridge, Mass., 1954.
26. Cooper, C *Job Motivation and Job Design*. Institute of Personnel Management, London, 1975.
27. Vroom, V H *Work and Motivation*. John Wiley & Sons, New York, 1964.
28. McDougall, C 'How well do you reward your managers?', *Personnel Management*, March, 1973.
29. Guion, R M 'Industrial morale (a symposium) – The problems of terminology', *Personnel Psychology*, Vol 11, 1958, pp 59-64.
30. Gilmer, B *Industrial Psychology*. McGraw-Hill, New York, 1961.
31. Roethlisberger, F J and Dickson, W J *Management and the Worker*. Harvard University Press, Cambridge, Mass., 1939.
32. Halpin, A W and Winer, B J 'A factorial study of the leader behavioural description'. In R M Stogdill and A E Coons (eds) *Leader Behaviour: Its Description and Measurement*. Ohio State University, Columbus, 1957.
33. Katz, D, Maccoby, N and Morse, N C *Productivity, Supervision and Morale in an Office Situation*. Survey Research Centre, University of Michigan, Ann Arbour, 1950.
34. Katz, D, Maccoby, N, Gurin, G and Floor, L G *Productivity Supervision and Morale Among Railroad Workers*. Survey Research Centre, University of Michigan, Ann Arbor, 1951.
35. Brayfield, A H and Crockett, W H 'Employee attitudes and employee performance', *Psychological Bulletin*, Vol 52, 1955, pp 346-424.
36. Schwab, D P and Cummings, L L 'Theories of performance and satisfaction', *Industrial Relations*, Vol 9 (4), 1970.
37. Simon, H A *Administrative Behaviour*. Macmillan, New York, 1957.
38. Georgopoulos, B S, Mahoney, G M and Jones, N W 'A path-goal approach to productivity', *Journal of Applied Psychology*, Vol 41, pp 345-353.
39. Blanchard, K and Johnson, S *The One Minute Manager*. Willow Books, London, 1983.
40. Jaques, E *Equitable Payment*. Heinemann, London, 1961.
41. White, G *Employee Commitment*. Advisory, Conciliation and Arbitration Service, Work Research Unit Occasional Paper 38, October, 1987.
42. Buchanan, D A and Huczynski, A A *Organizational Behaviour*. Prentice Hall, New York, 1985.

Part III
Organizational Planning and Development

This part deals with the analyses that have to be carried out and the plans that must be made in order to develop an effective and healthy organization. The starting point is to find out what work has to be done. This means analysing the content of jobs and the process of job analysis provides a base for a number of personnel activities and procedures. It also produces the information required to analyse organizational requirements and, therefore, define what needs to be done, who does it and how the various parts of the organization are structured so that work is directed, co-ordinated and controlled in a way which ensures the achievement of organizational objectives.

Organizational design is concerned with the overall structure: the allocation of responsibilities, the grouping of activities and the definition of lines of communication and control. Within this structure, attention has to be paid to the design of individual jobs so that they make sense in terms of the work that has to be carried out and, importantly, provide, so far as possible, for the motivation of job holders through giving them opportunities for achievement, responsibility and the utilization of the skills they possess or can be helped to acquire.

Finally, attention has to be paid to the way in which the organization functions with regard to how individuals and groups of people work together. Organization development programmes aim to improve the methods by which the processes of coping with change, conflict and the problems of working effectively with other people are managed.

Chapter 9

Job Analysis and Job Descriptions

Definition

Job analysis

Job analysis is the process of collecting, analysing and setting out the following information about a job:

- *Job content* – tasks and operations to be performed and duties to be carried out.
- *Job requirements* – the knowledge, skills, abilities and personality required to perform the job satisfactorily.
- *Job responsibilities* – the level of responsibility the job holder has to exercise, in terms of impact on end results, the amount of discretion allowed to make decisions, the complexities of the job, the difficulty and scale of the problems to be solved, the quantity and value of the resources to be controlled, including people, money, plant and equipment, and the type and importance of the contacts made with other people.
- *Job motivating factors* – the particular features of the job that are likely to motivate or de-motivate job holders if, in the latter case, nothing is done about them.
- *Job features* – other features of the job, including promotion and career prospects, opportunities to acquire new skills or expertise, mobility, unsocial hours, working conditions and health and safety considerations, including ergonomic factors relating to the design or use of the equipment or work station.

Job description

A job description sets out clearly and succinctly the job holder's overall role or responsibilities, specific tasks or accountabilities and reporting relationships. Its content is based on job analysis.

Use of job analysis

Job analysis provides the essential information required to design and operate a number of key personnel procedures and techniques. It is one of the most fundamental and important skills that personnel managers have to exercise.

The ten main uses of job analysis are as follows:

1. *Organization and job design* (Chapters 10 and 11).
2. *Human resource planning* – defining future requirements (Chapter 13).
3. *Recruitment and selection* – preparing personnel specifications (Chapter 14).
4. *Ergonomic design* – ensuring that ergonomic considerations are taken into account in selecting and using equipment, devising work procedures and routines and setting up work stations (Chapter 16).
5. *Computerized personnel information systems* – indicating what needs to be stored on the database (Chapter 19).
6. *Job evaluation* – deciding on the relative value of jobs in a job hierarchy (Chapter 21).
7. *Pay comparisons* – ensuring that when market rate surveys are carried out like is compared with like in dealing with specific jobs (Chapter 22).
8. *Payment by results and bonus schemes* – providing the data on task and output requirements needed to devise incentive schemes (Chapters 25 and 26).
9. *Performance management* – setting out the factors in the job that will be taken into account in setting objectives, targets and standards of performance and in reviewing the results achieved (Chapter 28).
10. *Human resource development* – providing the basis for deciding on the knowledge and skills required in jobs (skills analysis) as an aid to the preparation of training and management development programmes, including the design of assessment centres (Chapters 29 and 30).

The process of job analysis

The process of job analysis as described below consists of two stages:

(a) data collection;
(b) the preparation of job descriptions.

Data collection

Basic steps

The basic steps required to collect information about jobs are as follows:

1. Obtain documents such as existing organization, procedure or training manuals which give information about the job.
2. Ask managers for fundamental information concerning the job, the overall purpose, the main activities carried out, the responsibilities involved and the relationships with others.
3. Ask the job holders similar questions about their jobs. It is sometimes helpful to get them to keep a diary or a detailed record of work activities over a week or two.
4. For certain jobs, especially those involving manual or clerical skills, observe job holders at work. Even with managers or professional staff it is helpful, if time permits, to spend time with them.
5. Attempt to carry out some of the tasks yourself to get a 'feel' for what is done. Clearly this step can only be taken for jobs where it is possible for a newcomer to do some of the work with safety and without special training.
6. Write the job description as described later in this chapter.

Methods of data collection

The principal methods of data collection are:

- questionnaires;
- checklists;
- observation;
- interviews.

Questionnaires

Questionnaires to be completed by job holders and approved by the job holder's supervisor are useful when a large number of jobs are to be covered. They can also save interviewing time by recording purely factual information and by helping the analyst to structure questions in advance to cover areas which need to be explored in greater depth.

Questionnaires should provide the following basic information:

- the job title of the job holder;
- the job title of the job holder's manager or supervisor;
- the job titles and numbers of staff reporting to the job holder (best recorded by means of an organization chart);
- a brief description (one or two sentences) of the overall role or purpose of the job;

- a list of the main tasks or duties that the job holder has to carry out; as appropriate, these should specify the resources controlled, the equipment used, the contacts made and the frequency with which the tasks are carried out.

These basic details can be supplemented by questions designed to elicit from the job holder some information about the level of his responsibilities and the demand made upon him by the job. Such questions are difficult to phrase and answer in a meaningful way. The replies may be too vague or misleading and usually have to be checked with the job holder's supervisor and in subsequent interviews. But they at least give the job holder an opportunity to express his feelings about the job and they can provide useful leads for development in discussion. These questions can cover such aspects of the job as:

- the amount of supervision received and the degree of discretion allowed in making decisions;
- the typical problems to be solved and the amount of guidance available when solving the problems;
- the relative difficulty of the tasks to be performed;
- the qualifications and skills required to carry out the work.

The advantage of questionnaires is that they can produce information quickly and cheaply for a large number of jobs. But a substantial sample is needed and the construction of a questionnaire is a skilled job which should only be carried out on the basis of some preliminary field work. It is highly advisable to pilot test questionnaires before launching into a full-scale exercise. The accuracy of the results also depends on the willingness and ability of job holders to complete questionnaires and many people find it difficult to express themselves in writing about their work, however well they know and do it. Examples of questionnaires are shown in Appendix D.

Checklists

A checklist is similar to a questionnaire but response requires fewer subjective judgments and tends to be of the either YES or NO variety. Checklists can cover as many as 100 activities and job holders tick those tasks that are included in their jobs.

Like questionnaires, checklists need to be thoroughly prepared and a field trial is essential to ensure that the instructions for completion are adequate and that the responses make sense. Checklists can only be used where a large number of job holders exist. If the sample is below 30 the results can be erratic.

Rating scales are an improvement on the relatively crude checklist. Like the checklist, they present job holders with a list of activities. But instead of simply asking them to mark those they carry out, scales are provided for them to give a rating from one to, typically, seven, according to the amount of time spent and, sometimes, the importance of the job. These scales could look like those given in Table 9.1.

	Job analysis rating scale	
Activity description	*Time spent — The activity occupies:*	*Importance of activity*
Dealing with requests for information by telephone	1 Hardly any time (less than 10%)	1 Extremely unimportant
	2 A small proportion of the job (10%-24%)	2 Very unimportant
	3 Rather less than half the job (25%-44%)	3 Not very important
	4 About half the job (45%-54%)	4 Fairly important
	5 A fairly large proportion of the job (55%-74%)	5 Important
	6 A very large proportion of the job (75%-89%)	6 Very important
	7 Almost the whole of the job (90% or more)	7 Extremely important

Table 9.1 *Example of a job analysis rating scale*

There are a number of general purpose rating scales or inventories available, the most widely used of which is the Positional Analysis Questionnaire developed by McCormick, Jeanneret and Mecham.[1] This was based on studies of over 3700 jobs from which six major work factors were identified:

1. The input of information.
2. Mental processes, for example decision making.
3. Work input, for example the use of machine controls.
4. Relationships with people.
5. Work environment.
6. Other characteristics.

Scales were devised under each heading to measure specific requirements for almost 200 job elements. Each scale describes the activity and has 'benchmark' descriptions for each rating point as in the example given in Table 9.2.

Near Visual Discrimination (visual discrimination of objects within arm's reach)	
7	Inspects precision watch parts for defect
6	Proofreads newspaper articles before publishing
5	Reads electric house meters
4	Makes entries on sales tickets
3	Observes position of knife when carving beef
2	Paints house walls
1	Sweeps street with push broom
0	Makes no near visual discrimination

Table 9.2 *Position Analysis Questionnaire – Example of benchmark scale for an element (McCormick)*

Smith and Robertson[2] comment that the Position Analysis Questionnaire approach has the advantage of being generally applicable, comprehensive and having benchmarks. However, it is time consuming to administer and requires some specialist knowledge.

Observation

Observation means studying job holders at work, noting what they do, how they do it and how much time it takes. It is appropriate for situations where a relatively small number of key jobs need to be analysed in depth, but it is time consuming and is difficult to apply in jobs which involve a high proportion of unobservable mental activities, or in highly skilled manual jobs where the actions are too speedy to observe accurately.

Interviews

To obtain the full flavour of a job it is necessary to interview job holders and to check the findings with their superiors. The aim of the interview should be to obtain all the relevant facts about the job, covering the areas listed above in the section on questionnaires.

To achieve this aim job analysts follow these guidelines:

1. Work to a logical sequence of questions which help the interviewee to order his thoughts about the job.
2. Pin people down on what they actually do. Answers to questions

are often vague and information is given by means of untypical instances.

3. Ensure that job holders are not allowed to get away with vague or inflated descriptions of their work. If, for example, the interview is part of a job evaluation exercise they would not be human if they did not present the job in the best possible light.

4. Sort out the wheat from the chaff: answers to questions may produce a lot of irrelevant data which must be sifted before preparing the job description.

5. Obtain a clear statement from job holders about their authority to make decisions and the amount of guidance they receive from their superior. This is not easy. If asked what decisions they are authorized to make most people look blank because they think about their job in terms of duties and tasks rather than abstract decisions.

6. Avoid asking leading questions which make the expected answer obvious.

7. Allow the job holder ample opportunity to talk by creating an atmosphere of trust.

The advantages of the interviewing method are that it is very flexible, can provide in-depth information and is easy to organize and prepare. But interviewing can be time consuming and expensive and the results are not always easy to analyse.

Job descriptions

Job descriptions should be based on a detailed job analysis and should be as brief and as factual as possible. The headings under which the job description should be written and notes for guidance on completing each section are set out below.

Job title
The existing or proposed job title should indicate as clearly as possible the function in which the job is carried out and the level of the job within that function. The use of terms such as 'manager', 'assistant manager' or 'senior' to describe job levels should be reasonably consistent between functions with regard to gradings of the jobs. But this does not mean that all posts described, say, as manager, should be in the same grade. It is quite possible for someone correctly described as a manager in one function to have a less responsible job than a manager in another function.

Reporting to
The job title of the manager or supervisor to whom the job holder is directly responsible should be given under this heading. No attempt should

be made to indicate here any functional relationships the job holder might have to other managers.

Reporting to him

The job titles of all the posts directly reporting to the job holder should be given under this heading. Again, no attempt should be made here to indicate any functional relationships that might exist between the job holder and other staff.

Overall responsibilities

This section should describe as concisely as possible the overall purpose of the job. The aim should be to convey in no more than two or three sentences a broad picture of the job which will clearly identify it from other jobs and establish the role of the job holder and the contribution he should make towards achieving the objectives of the company and his own function or unit.

No attempt should be made to describe the activities carried out under this heading, but the overall summary should lead naturally to the analysis of activities in the next section.

When preparing the job description, it is often better to defer writing down the definition of overall responsibilities until the activities have been analysed and described.

Main tasks

The steps required to define the main tasks of the job are as follows:

1. Identify and list the tasks that have to be carried out. No attempt should be made to describe how they are carried out, but some indication should be given of the purpose or objectives of each task.
2. Analyse the initial list of tasks and, so far as possible, simplify the list by grouping related tasks together so that no more than, say, seven or eight main activity areas remain.
3. Decide on the order in which tasks should be described. The alternatives include:
   - frequency with which they are carried out (continually, hourly, daily, weekly, monthly, intermittently);
   - chronological order;
   - order of importance;
   - the main processes of management that are carried out; for example, setting objectives, planning, organizing, co-ordinating, operating, directing and motivating staff, and controlling.
4. Describe each main task separately in short, numbered paragraphs. No more than one or at most two sentences should be used for the description, but, if necessary, any separate tasks carried out within the task should be tabulated (a, b, c, etc) under the overall description of the activity. A typical sentence describing a task should:

● start with an active verb to eliminate all unnecessary wording. Use verbs which express the actual responsibility to recommend, to do, to ensure that someone else does something, or to collaborate with someone, for example, prepares, completes, recommends, supervises, ensures that, liaises with;

● state what is done as succinctly as possible;

● state why it is done: this indicates the purpose of the job and gives a lead to setting targets or performance standards.

5. Amplify as appropriate with examples and details of any quantitative measures of the amount of work involved. The frequency with which the work is carried out and, when it can be estimated, the proportion of time involved should also be stated wherever possible.

6. Group related tasks under descriptive headings to enable a quick appreciation to be obtained of the range of activities. For example, all the work a manager does in connection with manpower and facilities planning could be placed under the heading 'planning'.

Examples of job descriptions are given in Appendix C (expressed as a 'statement of accountability') and Appendix E.

References

1. McCormick, E J, Jeanneret, P R and Mecham, R C 'A study of job characteristics and job dimensions based on the Position Analysis Questionnaire (PAQ)', *Journal of Applied Psychology*, Vol 56, pp 347-68, 1972.
2. Smith, M and Robertson, I T *Systematic Staff Selection*. Macmillan, London, 1986.

Chapter 10
Organization Design

Much of personnel management in its broadest sense is concerned with providing answers to questions such as 'who does what?', 'how should functions and people be grouped together?', 'what lines and means of communication need to be established?' and 'how should people be helped to understand their roles in relation to the objectives of the organization and the roles of their colleagues?'.

Organization design deals with the structural aspects of organizations; it aims to analyse roles and relationships so that collective effort can be explicitly organized to achieve specific ends. It is necessary to divide the overall management task into a variety of activities and to establish means of co-ordinating and controlling these activities. This design process leads to the development of an organization structure consisting of units and positions between which there are relationships involving the exercise of authority and communication and exchange of information. Organization design may thus lead to the definition and description of a more or less formal structure but it cannot ignore the existence of the informal organization – the network of informal social roles and relationships, as described in Chapter 6.

It may be appropriate to think in terms of organization re-design or modification. Organizations are in a constant state of change and anyone with responsibilities for organization has to be able to move fast. But action should be based upon an understanding of the objectives, activities, decision-making processes and relationships within the organization. And this must be developed against the background of an understanding of the historical background to the organization – how it got to where it is; the personalities involved – who exerts influence, how and why; the power relationships between people; the reward system; the economic and cultural environment; and the dynamics of the organization – what is happening to it and where it is going.

The first stage in an organization design review is therefore an analysis of the present and future circumstances of the enterprise. This is followed by the detailed planning and implementation stages. Within each stage a number of steps are carried out as shown in Figure 10.1.

Organization analysis

Organization analysis is the process of defining the aims, objectives, activities and structure of an enterprise in the light of a study of its external environment and internal circumstances. The aims of the analysis are to assess the strengths and weaknesses of the organization and to determine the activities it should carry out prior to designing its structure and planning how it should be implemented. Clearly, the scale of the study will vary according to the size and complexity of the organization under review, but the general approach to organization analysis discussed here is appropriate in most circumstances.

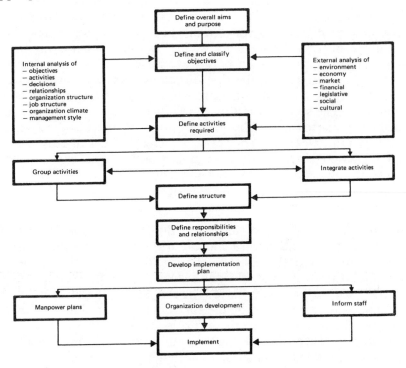

Figure 10.1 Organization survey programme

Organization analysis should move from the general to the particular. The general stages are: first, to obtain a broad understanding of the overall aims and purpose of the enterprise and second, to define and analyse the environment in which the organization exists and the changes that are taking place in it. The initial stages are followed by the more detailed step by step analysis of these aspects of the organization:

● objectives
● activities

- decisions
- relationships
- organization structure
- job structure
- organization climate
- management style
- manpower resources.

Each of these general and particular aspects of organization analysis is discussed below.

Defining overall aims and purpose

The initial stage is to define the overall aims and purpose of the enterprise. In a profit-making concern this means answering Drucker's famous question 'what business are we in?' as well as identifying the basic aims of growth, survival, corporate excellence and social responsibility.

When analysing aims, the first question to answer is whether or not they seem to be relevant to the present and future circumstances of the enterprise. The second question is whether or not the aims provide an adequate guide to the establishment of the more specific objectives which will determine where the enterprise is going. Neither of these questions can be answered in full until the organization's external environment and its specific objectives have been analysed.

Analysing the external environment

The external environment consists of the economic, market, financial, legislative, social and cultural climate within which the enterprise operates. The analysis of the environment should determine first, the extent to which it is turbulent or stable, and second, the rate and direction of any changes that may be taking place. The constraints, threats and opportunities imposed or presented by the environment should then be assessed. For the whole enterprise, this means looking at economic and market indicators as well as considering the implications of legislation and social change. For individual functions within the enterprise, it will mean looking at particular external influences. For example growth in white collar trade unionism may affect the role and the organization of the personnel function.

Analysing objectives

Objectives are the specific aims or targets to be achieved if the organization is to fulfil its purpose. In a profit-making concern these would be set out under such headings as profits, level of investment, future ownership, product development, market standing, manufacturing facilities, personnel policies and social responsibilities. The objectives of departments or individuals would then be determined by reference to their function or role. These could be expressed quantitatively (eg profit, volume), or qualitatively (eg level of service, quality of advice).

In a non-profit-making organization the objectives would be defined by reference to the areas in which services are provided for the government, for members of the organization or for the public. Thus a professional institution might set out its objectives under such headings as developing and maintaining high professional standards, improving the technical competence of its members, providing information and other services for its members and representing the interests of the profession to the government and the public at large.

The analysis of objectives should concentrate on establishing the extent to which they are clearly defined, understood and relevant.

Analysing activities

Activity analysis establishes what work is done and what needs to be done if the enterprise is to achieve its objectives. The analysis should start with a broad look at the basic functions and technologies of the enterprise. Is it profit-making or non-profit-making? Is it primarily an administrative service, a manufacturing or a selling organization? To what extent does the work involve planning, research and development, administration, selling or production? Is the work continuous or subject to constant changes, as in project or case work? What type of production system is used: unit, mass, process, batch or flow? To what extent is the work routine or innovative? How much numerical analysis is used? To what extent are systems computerized?

The analysis of activities should establish what is and what is not being done, who is doing it, where it is being done and how much is being done. The most important points to be established are that everything is being done that needs to be done and nothing is being done that does not need to be done. Whether or not the activities are being done in the right place and by the right people can be established when looking at the structure of the organization.

Analysing decisions

The analysis of activities and tasks leads naturally into the analysis of decisions. This will establish how work is being delegated or decentralized and how and where interrelated decisions are being made.

Decision analysis is most helpful when it cuts across vertical and horizontal boundaries: vertical between levels of management in the hierarchy; horizontal between individuals in different functions who jointly contribute to making corporate decisions.

Decision analysis moves horizontally across functions but may also incorporate some vertical analysis of the division of responsibility between managers and their subordinates. The aim is to establish who ultimately has the authority to make the operating decision. The analysis should also show who is responsible for formulating the policy guidelines which determine the boundaries within which the decision is made, and who is contributing to the decision by providing information and advice. It should help, therefore, to identify information flows and areas where co-operation is required as well as clarifying the responsibilities and authorities for decision-taking.

Questions on decisions should concentrate on the extent to which decisions are being made in the right place and on the degree to which there is adequate information, communications and consultation during the process of decision-making.

Analysing relationships

Relationships should be analysed from the point of view of the communications that take place between people and units in the organization and the contacts that are regularly made by individuals inside and outside the company with colleagues, customers and outside bodies. The analysis should provide information which can be used to assess whether the grouping of activities, lines of communication, information system and organization climate generally are conducive to effective management, co-operation and decision-making. The relationship analysis should also cover the power structure of the organization – who exerts influence, who gets things done.

Analysing the organization structure

The structural aspects of the organization that should be analysed are:

(a) how activities are grouped together;
(b) the span of control of managers and supervision;
(c) the number of levels in the hierarchy.

Grouping activities
The analysis should establish which activities are carried out by the different functions and in the different organizational units. The two main points to be covered are: first, the extent to which the activities are grouped logically together and second, whether or not there is any unnecessary duplication of activities.

The analysis of how activities are grouped should also consider the need to integrate closely related activities to avoid problems of co-ordination and communication and to enable those responsible for the function or group of activities to have adequate control of all the resources they require.

Span of control
Spans of control should be analysed in order to find out if they are too

wide or too narrow. However, the organization designer must avoid falling into easy assumptions about what is an optimum span. It is an almost instinctive reaction to say that more means worse. But there have been many instances where what might appear to be over-extended spans of control have worked perfectly well because the manager was a good delegator.

Very small spans of control can work badly. In one instance, the chief executive had only two direct subordinates. But they formed themselves into armed camps and because the chief executive identified himself with the operational wing of the enterprise (there is a tendency towards polarization in these situations), the other administrative and financial wing was left out in the cold. As a result, operational decisions were made without proper regard to their financial implications and the enterprise rapidly became insolvent.

The organization designer must also beware of imposing mechanistic span of control assumptions. If work alters rapidly or if it is carried out by frequently changing project teams, span of control in the classical sense may no longer be a valid concept when analysing structures. In these circumstances, the analyst must concentrate more on establishing that the project teams or task forces are set up properly in the sense that they know what they are there to do and are in a position to do it – because they have the resources they need and, when necessary, are able to integrate their work with others.

Management levels
The number of management levels in the hierarchy should be studied to establish whether communications are being affected by the existence of too many barriers or whether unnecessary layers of management have been inserted in the structure.

Analysing job structure

The analysis of the organization structure concentrates on the grouping of activities into units and on the relationships between these units. The next stage is to look at the structure of the individual jobs within those units in terms of the range of tasks to be carried out, the demands made on the job holders, the amount of authority and responsibility they are given and their relationship with other people.

The analyst should find out if tasks have been grouped logically together into jobs, whether job holders have been given sufficient responsibility and authority and if they understand what they are expected to do. The design of individual jobs is dealt with in Chapter 11.

Analysing organization climate

In general, organization climate is the working atmosphere of the enterprise. In particular, it is the ways in which the following aspects of behaviour in the organization manifest themselves:

- teamwork and co-operation
- commitment
- communications
- creativity
- conflict resolution
- participation
- confidence and trust between individuals and groups and between management and their staff.

These are a reflection of the norms and values of the organization as they have evolved over time and they constitute the headings under which the climate should be analysed.

The analysis should look at the current situation, but it should also examine its antecedents and the likely ways in which it might develop in the future. The importance of examining organization climate is that the study will help to explain how the structure has evolved into its present state as well as identifying the factors that have to be taken into account in changing the structure and in implementing change. These are the human factors which determine the health of the organization and they must be appreciated at this stage of a survey.

Analysing management style

The analysis of management style should concern itself with questions on the degree to which management is authoritarian, democratic or *laissez-faire*, the way in which rewards and punishments are meted out, and methods of delegating authority and communicating information. The traditional or prevailing style, whether it is open and democratic, or closed and authoritarian, will have influenced the way in which the organization has been structured and must be taken into account when considering changes.

Analysing manpower resources

Management and manpower resources need to be analysed from two points of view: first, the extent to which the existing structure has been built round the personalities and strengths or weaknesses of the key people in the organization; second, the availability of the quality and quantity of people required to enable any necessary changes in organization structure to take place.

All but the most bureaucratic or mechanistic type of organizations will allow the structure to adapt itself to the people available – to a certain degree. This may be unavoidable and it could be desirable in the more organic type of organization where room has to be provided for entrepreneurs, innovators and others with special administrative and technical skills. But it can go too far, and the analyst must try to assess if the structure has been unnecessarily distorted by empire-building or by weakly accommodating people whose skills are by no means unique. This information is required because the designer may have to accept that pure logic has to bow to necessity. But he should not accept it too readily. The case has to be made.

Organization design leads into organization planning – assessing implications of structural changes on future manpower requirements and taking steps to meet those requirements. The organization analyst has therefore to take an inventory of existing manpower resources in terms of numbers and skills, and, for management and other key jobs, in terms of strengths, weaknesses and potential. This may be a purely statistical exercise, or in some situations it may mean making or obtaining individual assessments of people.

Organization planning

Organization planning is the process of converting the analysis into the design. It determines structure, relationships, roles, manpower requirements and the lines along which changes should be implemented. There is no one best design. There is always a choice between alternatives. Logical analysis will help in the evaluation of the alternatives but the law of the situation will have to prevail. The final choice will depend upon the present and future circumstances of the organization. It will be strongly influenced by personal and human considerations – the inclinations of top management, the strengths and weaknesses of management generally, the availability of people to man the new organization and the need to take account of the feelings of those who will be exposed to change. Cold logic may sometimes have to override these considerations. If it does, then it must be deliberate and the consequences must be appreciated and allowed for when planning the implementation of the new organization.

It may have to be accepted that a logical re-grouping of activities cannot be introduced in the short term because no one is available with the experience to manage the new activities, or because a capable individual is so firmly entrenched in one area that to uproot him would cause serious damage to his morale and would reduce the overall effectiveness of the new organization. This frequently happens when planning a highly structured organization, where one of the most difficult tasks facing the designer is that of reconciling ideal requirements with the practical realities of the situation. But it can also happen in non-structured situations, although the problem may not be so well recognized. The designer may wish to develop a more loosely defined organic type of organization, but he could find that many people like structure and feel threatened if the well-defined framework within which they live their lives is taken away from them. The organic concept may have to be modified and some structure left behind.

The worst sin that an organization designer can commit is that of imposing his own ideology on the organization. His job is to be eclectic in his knowledge, sensitive in his analysis of the situation and deliberate in his approach to the evaluation of alternatives.

Having planned the organization and defined structures, relationships and rules it is essential to consider how the new organization should be implemented. It may be advisable to stage an implementation over a number of phases, especially if new people have to be found and trained. It will be even more necessary to address the often significant problems of introducing organizational change.

Introducing organizational change

Management may feel that it has perfectly valid reasons for introducing organizational change, for example to:

(a) respond to changes in the environment – market or technological;
(b) deal with the new arrangements required following an acquisition, merge or takeover;
(c) eliminate overlapping areas of activity;
(d) cater for the introduction of new activities or the elimination of old ones;
(e) gain economies of scale by amalgamating activities;
(f) facilitate better co-ordination, control or communications;
(g) decentralize operations to place decision making closer to the point of action, to reduce the size of an unwieldy head office and/or to cut down on bureaucracy;
(h) conversely, centralize operations to provide for better control from the top;
(i) accommodate management changes;
(j) 'shake up the business a bit' – managements have been known to articulate a belief that change is a stimulus in itself. There could be some truth in this in a stagnant organization, but 'change for change's sake' is a dangerous doctrine.

The problem of organizational change

Those affected by organizational change may not perceive it the same way. They have seen it all happen before. They may call it organization by whim not by design. They will have seen fashions for centralization and decentralization come and go. And they may quote wisely amongst themselves the old saying: 'organize – re-organize – disorganize'. If they are classicists they may even be able to quote someone else who felt about re-organizations as they do – Gaius Petronus Arbiter, a Roman governor of Nero's time who complained:

> We trained hard, but it seemed that every time we were beginning to form up into teams, we would be reorganized. I was to learn later in life that we tend to meet any new situation by reorganizing, and a wonderful method it can be for creating the illusion of progress while producing confusion, inefficiency and demoralization.

These fears and reactions may seem to management to be unreasonable, but they exist, and they can seriously prejudice the success of a reorganization, however carefully it has been planned and executed.

Reasons for adverse reactions to organizational change

Adverse reactions to reorganization from the point of view of those affected by it are not unreasonable. It constitutes change, about which most people are wary, if not overtly hostile. The reasons for resistance to change are quite clear: it is a combination of a fear of the unknown, a reluctance to change familiar and comfortable working habits, a belief in general that change is always for the worse, and a feeling in particular that the individuals affected by it are going to lose out in a number of specified ways.

The most frequently expressed or felt fears about organizational change are:

- loss of job;
- reduction of career prospects;
- down-grading of work and possible reduction in present or future rates of pay;
- loss or erosion of carefully built up empires;
- loss of status;
- reduction in responsibility and job interest;
- need to learn new skills, which could be difficult;
- new and unknown bosses, or even new and *known* bosses if their bad reputations come before them;
- break-up of well-established work groups and friendships;
- transfer to new, unknown (or known and disliked) locations or departments.

The list is formidable but not exhaustive. There are plenty of other adverse reactions people can have to organizational change, and, whether or not they are justified, every attempt must be made to prevent them happening before they arise or, if this is impossible, at least to deal with them swiftly if they emerge.

Gaining acceptance for organizational change

Prevention is always better than cure and the following ten preventive steps should be taken to minimize hostility, although, people being what they are, some fears will probably remain in their minds, whatever is done to eliminate them.

1. Base the change on a thorough organizational analysis.
2. Involve those concerned in the analysis – explain why it is carried out and seek their views on what improvements are required.
3. If the change is forced on the company, explain why it is happening and, if at all possible, allay fears at this stage about adverse effects.
4. Consult people on alternative methods of dealing with the situation. Try to get them to 'own' the solution as theirs, and not something imposed upon them by an unfeeling management.
5. Accentuate the positive benefits – if they exist – to those affected by change. They could include increased responsibility, more clearly defined duties, the removal of barriers to communication, new challenges and opportunities, greater security in a more effective or prosperous organization, or the chance to learn new skills.
6. If the changes may adversely affect individuals or groups of people, attempt to mitigate them in advance by offering, if the worst comes to the worst, generous redundancy settlements involving voluntary redundancy where possible, 'outplacement' benefits, ie redundancy counselling and help to find alternative work, generous relocation allowances, retraining facilities, guarantees, if feasible, on loss of pay or status, and a measure of choice about relocations or transfers.
7. Be prepared to modify the ideal solution in response to any reasonable fears expressed by those concerned – show willingness to listen and to act accordingly.
8. Take particular care in defining the new organization and the responsibilities of those concerned. Involve everyone affected in drawing up job descriptions. Set up training schemes to develop new skills and communications programmes to get the message across about changes.
9. Get groups together with their existing or new bosses to discuss the changes and their implications and agree jointly on how they are going to be managed.
10. Consider the use of third parties or 'change agents' to facilitate change and get involved in discussions on what is happening, why it is happening and what everyone should do about it.

Who does the work?

Organization design may be carried out by line management with or without the help of members of the personnel function or internal consultants, or it may be done by outside consultants. Personnel management should always be involved because organization design is essentially about people and the work they do – subjects on which personnel managers should be capable of giving sound advice. The advantage of using outside consultants is that an entirely independent and dispassionate view is obtained. They can cut through internal organizational pressures, politics and constraints and bring experience of other organizational problems they have dealt with. Sometimes, regrettably, major changes can only be obtained by outside intervention. But there is a danger of consultants suggesting theoretically ideal organizations which do not take sufficient account of the problems of making them work with existing people. They do not have to live with their solutions as do line and personnel managers. If outside consultants are used, it is essential to involve people from within the organization so they can ensure that they are able to implement the proposals smoothly.

Chapter 11
Job Design

What is job design?

Job design is the process of deciding on the content of a job in terms of its duties and responsibilities; on the methods to be used in carrying out the job, in terms of techniques, systems and procedures; and on the relationships that should exist between the job holder and his superiors, subordinates and colleagues.

Job design has two aims: first, to satisfy the requirements of the organization for productivity, operational efficiency and quality of product or service, and second, to satisfy the needs of the individual for interest, challenge and accomplishment. Clearly, these aims are interrelated and the overall objective of job design is to integrate the needs of the individual with those of the organization.

The process of job design must start from an analysis of what work needs to be done – the tasks that have to be carried out if the purpose of the organization or an organizational unit is to be achieved. This is where the techniques of work study, process planning, organization and methods and organizational analysis are used. Inevitably, these techniques are directed to the first aim of job design: the improvement of organizational performance. They concentrate on the work to be done, not the worker. They may lead to a high degree of task specialization and assembly line processing, of paper work as well as physical products. This in turn can lead to the maximization of individual responsibility and the opportunity to use personal skills.

It is necessary, however, to follow Drucker and distinguish between efficiency and effectiveness. The most efficient method may maximize outputs in relation to inputs in the short run, but it may not be effective in the longer term in that it fails to achieve the overall objectives of the activity. Short term profits may be achieved by efficient stock control which minimizes inventory levels; in the long run, however, customer dissatisfaction because of delays in providing spares may have a detrimental effect on sales which wipes out the initial profits. Similarly, in job design, the pursuit of short term efficiency by imposing the maximum degree of task specialization may reduce longer term effectiveness by demotivating job holders and increasing labour turnover and absenteeism.

Job design has therefore to start from work requirements because that is why the job exists – too many writers on job design seem to imply that job design is *only* concerned with human needs. When the tasks to be done have been determined it should then be the function of the job designer to consider how the jobs can be set up to provide the maximum degree of intrinsic motivation for those who have to carry them out. Consideration has also to be given to the third implied aim of job design: to fulfil the social responsibilities of the organization to the people who work in it by improving the quality of working life, which, as stated in Wilson's report on this subject, 'depends upon both efficiency of performance and satisfaction of the worker'.[1]

Factors affecting job design

Job design is fundamentally affected by the technology of the organization and the changes that are taking place in that technology and the environment in which the organization operates. Job design has therefore to be considered within the context of organizational design, as described in Chapter 10, but it must also take into account the following factors:

- the process of intrinsic motivation;
- the characteristics of task structure;
- the motivating characteristics of jobs;
- the implications of group activities.

The process of intrinsic motivation

The case for using job design techniques is based on the premise that effective performance and genuine satisfaction in work follow mainly from the intrinsic content of the job. This is related to the fundamental concept that people are motivated when they are provided with the means to achieve their goals. Work provides the means to earn money, which as an extrinsic reward satisfies basic needs and is instrumental in providing ways of satisfying higher level needs. But work also provides intrinsic rewards which are under the direct control of the worker himself.

Characteristics of task structure

Job design requires the assembly of a number of tasks into a job or a group of jobs. An individual may carry out one main task which consists of a number of interrelated elements or functions. Or task functions may be split between a team working closely together or strung along an assembly line. In more complex jobs, individuals may carry out a variety of connected tasks, each with a number of functions, or these tasks may be allocated to a group of workers or divided between them. Complexity in a job may be a reflection of the number and variety of tasks to be carried out, or the range and scope of the decisions that have to be made, or the difficulty of predicting the outcome of decisions.

The internal structure of each task consists of three elements: *planning* (deciding on the course of action, its timing and the resources required), *executing* (carrying out the plan), and *controlling* (monitoring performance and progress and taking corrective action when required). A completely integrated job will include all these elements for each of the tasks involved. The worker, or group of workers, having been given objectives in terms of output, quality and cost targets, decides on how the work is to be done, assembles the resources, performs the work, and monitors output, quality and cost standards. Responsibility in a job is measured by the amount of authority someone has to do all these things.

The ideal arrangement from the point of view of intrinsic motivation is to provide for fully integrated jobs containing all three task elements. In practice, management and supervisors are concerned with planning and control, leaving the worker responsible for execution. To a degree, this is inevitable, but one of the aims of job design is often to extend the responsibility of workers into the functions of planning and control.

Motivating characteristics of jobs

Three characteristics have been distinguished by Lawler[2] as being required in jobs if they are to be intrinsically motivating.

1. *Feedback*. Individuals must receive meaningful feedback about their performance, preferably by evaluating their own performance and defining the feedback. This implies that they should ideally work on a complete product, or a significant part of it which can be seen as a whole.
2. *Use of abilities*. The job must be perceived by individuals as requiring them to use abilities they value in order to perform the job effectively.
3. *Self-control*. Individuals must feel that they have a high degree of self-control over setting their own goals and over defining the paths to these goals.

Techniques of job design

The five job design techniques are:

1. *Job rotation* which involves the movement of employees from one task to another to reduce monotony by increasing variety.
2. *Job enlargement* which involves combining previously fragmented

tasks into one job, again to increase the variety and meaning of repetitive work.

3. *Job enrichment* which was defined by Paul and Robertson as follows:

> Job enrichment seeks to improve both task efficiency and human satisfaction by building into people's jobs, quite specifically, greater scope for personal achievement and recognition, more challenging and responsible work, and more opportunity for individual advancement and growth.[3]

Job enrichment increases job responsibility by adding what Frederick Herzberg calls 'vertical job-loading factors'. Herzberg's seminal 1968 article 'One more time: how do you motivate employees?' was re-published in 1987.[4] It presents compelling arguments in favour of job enrichment and, in spite of the criticisms that have subsequently been made of this technique of job design, Herzberg still believes in it passionately.

4. *Autonomous group working* which creates self-regulating groups who work without direct supervision. They are allocated an overall task and given discretion over how the work is done. This technique provides for intrinsic motivation by giving people autonomy and the means to control their work. It is in line with socio-technical systems theory which, as described in Chapter 6, suggests that the best results are obtained if grouping is such that workers are primarily related to each other by way of the requirements of task performance and task interdependence. It is claimed by advocates of autonomous group working that this approach 'offers a more comprehensive view of organizations than the rather simplistic individual motivation theories which underpin job rotation, enlargement and enrichment.'

5. *High-performance work design* which, as described by Buchanan in his article for *Personnel Management* – 'Job enrichment is dead: long live high performance work design!'[5] – is a means of improving performance in an environment where positive and demanding goals are set. It starts from the principles of autonomous group working and develops an approach which enables groups to work effectively together in situations where the rate of innovation is high, operational flexibility is important, and there is therefore the need for employees to gain and apply new skills quickly with the minimum of supervision.

Of these five techniques, it is generally recognized that, although job rotation and job enlargement have their uses in relieving monotony and extending skills, they do not go to the root of the requirement for intrinsic motivation.

Job enrichment has certainly achieved a lot of publicity as the approach most likely to succeed, and is considered in more detail below. But it has been subject to some criticism and, although the autonomous working group technique has not been widely favoured, there is a growing movement in support of high-performance work design – in the right circumstances. This technique is also discussed below.

Job enrichment

Job enrichment aims to maximize the interest and challenge of work by providing the employee with a job that has these characteristics:

- It is a complete piece of work in the sense that the worker can identify a series of tasks or activities that end in a recognizable and definable product.
- It affords the employee as much variety, decision-making responsibility and control as possible in carrying out the work.
- It provides direct feedback through the work itself on how well the employee is doing his job.

Job enrichment is not just increasing the number or variety of tasks, neither is it the provision of opportunities for job rotation. It is claimed by advocates of job enrichment that these approaches may relieve boredom, but they do not result in positive increases in motivation.

Job enrichment techniques

There is no one way of enriching a job. The technology and the circumstances will dictate which of the following techniques or combination of techniques is appropriate:

- increasing the responsibility of individuals for their own work;
- giving employees more scope to vary the methods, sequence and pace of their work;
- giving a person or a work group a complete natural unit of work – ie reducing task specialization;
- removing some controls from above while ensuring that individuals or groups are clearly accountable for achieving defined targets or standards;
- allowing employees more influence in setting targets and standards of performance;
- giving employees the control information they need to monitor their own performance;
- encouraging the participation of employees in planning work, innovating new techniques and reviewing results;
- introducing new and more difficult tasks not previously handled;
- assigning individuals or groups specific projects which give them more responsibility and help them to increase their expertise.

Steps to job enrichment

When developing job enrichment the following steps are usually recommended:

- Select those jobs where better motivation is most likely to improve performance.
- Set up a controlled pilot scheme before launching the full programme of job enrichment – do not try to do too much too quickly.
- Approach these jobs with a conviction that they can be changed – it is necessary to challenge assumptions at this stage, especially about the ability of people to take on responsibility and the scope for changing established work methods.
- Brainstorm a list of changes that may enrich the jobs, without concern at this stage for their practicability.
- Screen the list to concentrate on motivation factors such as achievement, responsibility and self-control.
- Ensure that the changes are not just generalities like 'Increase responsibility' but list specific differences in the way in which the jobs are designed and carried out.
- Do not be too concerned about achieving a high degree of participation from employees in changing their jobs. Improvement is to be achieved by changing the *content* of jobs, not making employees feel happier because they have been consulted.
- Make the maximum use of line management and supervision in enriching jobs, but make sure that they have the training, guidance, encouragement and help they need.
- Bear in mind that job enrichment may develop into a major change programme and appreciate that change may be resisted and will have to be introduced with care.
- Set precise objectives and criteria for measuring success and a time-table for each project, and ensure that control information is available to monitor progress and the results achieved.

Impact of job enrichment

The advocates of job enrichment have been so dedicated to their cause that one cannot help feeling sometimes that their enthusiasm for the philosophy of their movement has clouded their judgement of its real benefits to the organization, let alone to the individuals who are supposed to have been 'enriched'.

There have been plenty of case studies which have indicated success, although this has often been measured in subjective terms. Volvo is the famous example, although ICI has carried out a number of job enrichment programmes in the UK, and in the United States there are the well known examples of American Telephone and Telegraph and Texas Instruments. In Robert Ford's report on the AT & T programme he said that 'of the 19 studies, nine were rated outstandingly successful'. He goes on to admit that:

> No claim is made that these 19 trials cover a representative sample of jobs and people within the Bell system. For example, there were no trials among the manufacturing or laboratory employees, nor were all operating companies involved. There are more than a thousand different jobs in the Bell system, not just the nine in these studies.[6]

Douglas McGregor has said that 'unless there is opportunity *at work* to satisfy these higher level needs (esteem and self-actualization) people will be deprived, and their behaviour will reflect this deprivation'.[7] But extensive research into the effects of job enrichment has not found this belief to be universally applicable. For example, Reif and Schoderbek's[8] study of 19 United States companies who had introduced job enrichment revealed that only four thought their experience was very successful. They found that only 15 per cent of the companies had attempted to enrich unskilled jobs, and in follow-up interviews three major reasons emerged why it was more difficult to get unskilled workers to accept job enrichment: (a) the unskilled preferred the *status quo*; (b) the unskilled seemed to prefer highly specialized work, and (c) the unskilled showed a lack of interest in improvements in job design which require learning new skills or assuming greater responsibility. A representative comment was: 'Most unskilled workers prefer the routine nature of their jobs, and it has been my experience that they are not eager to accept responsibility or learn new skills.' Numerous studies quoted by Reif and Luthans[9] have pointed out that repetitive work can have positively motivating characteristics for some workers. Maurice Kilbridge[10] found that assembly line workers in television factories did not necessarily regard repetitive tasks as dissatisfying or frustrating.

A study by Hulin and Blood[11] of all relevant research on job enrichment concluded that the effects of job enrichment on job satisfaction or worker motivation are generally overstated and in some cases unfounded. They argue convincingly that many shop floor workers are not alienated from the work environment but are alienated from the work norms and values of the middle class, especially its belief in the work-related elements of the Protestant ethic and in the virtue of striving for the attainment of responsible positions.

Fein's study of worker motivation came up with essentially the same conclusion. He states:

> Workers do not look upon their work as fulfilling their existence. Their reaction to their work is the opposite of what the behaviouralists predict. It is only because workers *choose* not to find fulfilment in their work that they are able to function as

healthy human beings. By rejecting involvement in their work which simply cannot be fulfilling, workers save their sanity . . . The concepts of McGregor and Herzberg regarding workers' needs to find fulfilment through their work are sound *only for those workers who choose to find fulfilment through their work* . . . Contrary to their postulates, the majority of workers seek fulfilment outside their work.[12]

High-performance work design

High-performance work design, as described by Buchanan, requires the following steps:

1. Management clearly defines what it needs in the form of new technology or methods of production and the results expected from its introduction.
2. Multi-skilling is encouraged – that is, job demarcation lines are eliminated as far as possible and encouragement and training is provided for employees to acquire new skills.
3. Equipment is selected which can be used flexibly and is laid out to allow freedom of movement and vision.
4. Autonomous working groups are established, each with around a dozen members and with full 'back-to-back' responsibility for product assembly and testing, fault-finding and some maintenance.
5. Managers adopt a supportive rather than an autocratic style with groups and group leaders (this is the most difficult part of the system to introduce).
6. Support systems are provided for kit-marshalling and material supply which help the groups to function effectively as productive units.
7. Management set goals and standards for success.
8. The new system is introduced with great care by means of involvement and communication programmes.
9. Thorough training is carried out on the basis of an assessment of training needs.
10. The payment system is specially designed with staff participation to fit their needs as well as those of management.

In the case quoted by Buchanan (Digital Equipment Corporation), management felt that the autonomous work groups had demonstrated, amongst other things:

- an ability to change;
- communication helped by layout changes;
- product identification and 'ownership' for actions;
- greater flexibility through multi-skilling;
- better priority setting.

References

1. Wilson, N A B *On the Quality of Working Life*. Her Majesty's Stationery Office, London, 1973.
2. Lawler, E E 'Job Design and Employee Motivation', *Personnel Psychology*, Vol 22, 1969, pp 426-35.
3. Paul, W J and Robertson, K B *Job Enrichment and Employee Motivation*. Gower Press, London, 1970.
4. Herzberg, F 'One more time: How do you motivate employees?', *Harvard Business Review*. September-October 1987.
5. Buchanan, D 'Job enrichment is dead: long live high performance work design!', *Personnel Management*, May 1987.
6. Ford, R *Motivation Through the Work Itself*. American Management Association, New York, 1969.
7. McGregor, D *Leadership and Motivation*. The MIT Press, Cambridge, Mass., 1966.
8. Reif, W E and Schoderbek, P F *Job Enlargement*. University of Michigan, Ann Arbor, 1969.
9. Reif, W E and Luthans, F 'Does Job Enrichment Pay Off?', *California Management Review*, Vol XV, No 1, 1973.
10. Kilbridge, M D 'Do Workers Prefer Larger Jobs?', *Personnel*, Sept-Oct 1960.
11. Hulin, C L and Blood, M R 'Job Enlargement, Individual Differences and Worker Responses', *Psychological Bulletin*, Vol 69, No 1, 1968.
12. Fein, M *Approaches to Motivation*. Hillsdale, New Jersey, 1970.

Chapter 12
Organization Development

What is organization development?

Organization development is concerned with the planning and implementation of programmes designed to improve the effectiveness with which an organization functions and responds to change. The programmes will be based on a variety of behavioural science concepts and techniques, but these will be carefully integrated so that a coherent approach is used to change for the better the ways in which people carry out their work and interact with others.

Organization development should be distinguished from management development, although the two often overlap. Management development (as discussed in Chapter 30) is mainly aimed at the improvement of the performance and potential of individuals, while organization development is more concerned with improving the overall effectiveness of the organization; in particular, the way its various processes function and how people work together.

Methods of organization development

Organization development programmes are usually characterized by three main features:

1. They are managed, or at least strongly supported, from the top but may make use of third parties or 'change agents' to diagnose problems and to manage change by various kinds of planned activity of 'intervention'.
2. The plans for organization development are based upon a systematic analysis and diagnosis of the circumstances of the organization and the changes and problems affecting it.
3. They use behavioural science knowledge and aim to improve the way the organization copes in times of change with such processes as interaction, communications, participation, planning and conflict.

Organization development programmes can consist of any one or a mix of these activities, and this is why it is difficult to describe 'OD', as it is familiarly known, in a satisfactorily comprehensive way. In some companies an OD programme is no more than a glorified management development package, using a few team-building exercises, informal training courses and, perhaps, dabbling in some interactive skills training such as transactional analysis. In others the programme embraces a number of different but related activities, all designed to achieve a measurable improvement in the performance of the organization.

Analysis and diagnosis

The success of an organization development programme depends upon the thoroughness and accuracy of the initial analysis and diagnosis of the problems and opportunities faced by the organization. This should lead to a definition of the objectives of the programme and the preparation of action plans. A model of this process is shown in Figure 12.1.

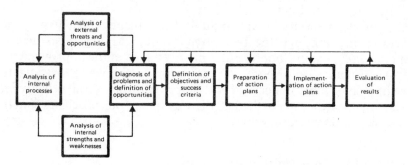

Figure 12.1 Organization development – planning model

A satisfactory diagnosis of problems and opportunities depends upon a thorough analysis of the internal processes of the organization as they are affected by change imposed externally or from within. When carrying out their diagnosis, most organization development practitioners take a normative view. In other words, they establish in their minds norms of behaviour or values to which they think the organization should conform. A list of typical values produced by Richard Beckhard was set out in Chapter 7. The OD consultant then analyses the differences between actuality and his norms, and these are the gaps to be filled by the OD programme of interventions. The analysis is carried out by observations and by means of largely unstructured interviews and group meetings. A more structured approach is to use a questionnaire to uncover attitudes and opinions as well as indicating how the various processes of interaction, planning, participation and consultation operate. Questionnaires can be fairly simple, as in the example shown on page 194 used by Douglas McGregor at Union Carbide.

In *Organizational Development*[1] Sadler and Barry give another example of a simple questionnaire which they used for diagnostic purposes in a printing works. More elaborate questionnaires have been produced by Likert[2] and, for ICI, by Maugham, Shaw and Wilson.[3]

The writer's own experience of using questionnaires suggests that the best approach is to design a special questionnaire following a brief pilot study conducted by means of a small sample of unstructured interviews. This does not frighten the participants or top management, who can be worried by what appears to be an over-detailed and time-consuming exercise. A short, specially designed questionnaire can easily be completed and discussed during interviews and group meetings and saves the inevitable difficulties of explanation when a longer questionnaire has to be distributed and completed in advance. Brevity also makes for easier analysis.

Planning organization development programmes

The steps required after the diagnosis has been completed are to:

- define the objectives of the programme – as specifically as possible;
- establish criteria for measuring the ultimate effectiveness of the programme and for monitoring its progress during intermediate stages;
- prepare the action plan.

When preparing the action plan it should be remembered that there will be a number of alternative choices, depending on the situation. At one end of the scale it may simply be a matter of introducing new systems or structures. This could be accomplished by information, education and discussion. At the other end of the scale, the requirement may be for a fundamental change in attitudes and values. Many OD practitioners are wary of any suggestion that their job is to change attitudes. To them it smacks of manipulation and borders on the unethical. But people's attitudes to change may be unconstructive and even if they cannot be changed, at least they can be given the opportunity to recognize for themselves why their attitudes might have to be modified. In between these extremes are the situations where there is a specific problem, but the solution requires a rather more pronounced change in behaviour or modification of attitudes than is necessary in a simple change of systems or structures.

The plan will have to consider which of the various organizational development processes should be used. These include team development activities, inter-group relations work and educational programmes and are examined in more detail in the next section of this chapter. It is usual to combine a number of these, and a typical approach would be to start with a general education programme such as laboratory training, Coverdale or Blake's grid, continue with on-the-job team building or inter-group relations work and add, as required, further educational programmes to follow up the initial activities. Such a sequence is illustrated in Figure 12.2.

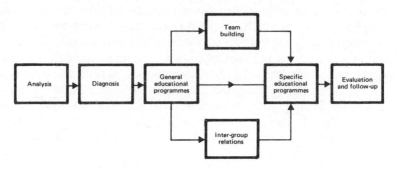

Figure 12.2 Organization development programme

In large organizations, varied environments produce a multitude of different development problems. The extent to which the programme is to cover the whole organization or selected parts of it has therefore to be considered. It may be decided that the educational phase at least should cover all management, supervision and key technical and administrative staff, and this approach has been adopted by British companies such as Esso and Unigate. Obviously this is a massive investment and it is wise to start with a pilot scheme. Alternatively, the plan might be to tackle the organization on a divisional or functional basis, although provision could be made for extending the activities across interrelated functions or for including both head office and divisional departments to assist with integration. The scope of the programme must depend upon the diagnosis of the problem, the resources available and the degree to which management is committed to the value of organization development.

Organization development activities

Organization development activities can be classified into five main areas:

1. Implementing changed systems or structures.
2. Achieving co-ordination and integration.
3. Team development.
4. Inter-group relations.
5. Educational programmes.

Implementing changed systems and structures

The need to introduce new systems or structures may have been established at the diagnosis stage. Their introduction would have to take account of potential resistance to change and should therefore try to ensure that staff will understand, accept and 'own' the change. Two examples of this type of activity with which the writer was concerned are first, a Civil Service department where, because the role of the department was changing, a fundamental change to the structure was required. The broad outlines of the revised structure were discussed extensively with the members of the department. When they had been agreed, the management and supervisors of each of the new units were brought together for a week to discuss how the work should be organized and what their staff requirements were. During the week various educational activities were carried out to give the participants an insight into the main organization issues. The second example was in a manufacturing company where the introduction of a new performance review system was used as a reason for setting up a number of 'workshops' for managers and supervisors in which they agreed what was required, helped to design the system and received training in its operation.

Co-ordination and integration

The co-ordination and integration of activities in an organization does not just happen; it has to be worked at. People tend to head off in different directions – to go their own sweet way. They will not necessarily co-operate with one another. Good co-ordination is partly a structural matter. It is helpful if activities are grouped logically together, lines of communication are short and well-defined, and managers do not have unwieldly spans of control, but there are additional approaches you can adopt to achieve better integration. These include:

1. *Voluntary integration:* encourage people to communicate with each other and to integrate their activities without reference to higher authority, except where a decision is needed to resolve differences of opinion.
2. *Meetings:* set up meetings or committees to deal with planning and operational matters requiring integration. To avoid the dangers inherent in 'management by committee' you should ensure that meetings concentrate on resolving policy issues where joint decisions are required, rather than attempting to usurp the normal role of management.
3. *Project teams:* set up teams or working parties to deal with specific issues or problems outside the normal routine; for example, product development, quality control and systems development. Getting people from different departments to work

together is a good way of increasing understanding and developing a sense of common purpose.

4. *Communications:* improve the quality of communications throughout the organization. This is partly a matter of attitude (there has to be the will to communicate and to listen to communications), partly a matter of structure (too many levels of management or too many separate units or departments will inhibit communications), and partly a matter of the systems and techniques used (the more effective use of the spoken or written word). All this is easier said than done. You cannot force people to communicate; you can only encourage them and try to remove barriers of misunderstanding.

5. *Training:* train people to make them more aware of the need to integrate and to improve communication and leadership techniques. Courses attended by members of different departments can increase understanding. Team-building training, which concentrates on helping people to work better together in groups, is useful.

6. *Understanding of roles:* help interrelated functions, units and individuals to be aware of their respective roles. This can be achieved by various informal means, as mentioned above. You can also produce more formal definitions and circulate them to all concerned, but this seldom works: it is just possible that the missives will be read by the recipients, although it is most unlikely that they will take any notice of impersonal exhortations. Management by exhortation is the last refuge of the incompetent manager.

7. *Planning:* set up planning procedures which involve people in different units and at different levels in jointly formulating policies and preparing plans.

8. *Management information:* install management information systems which help to identify areas where joint action is required.

Team development

Team development activities are aimed at improving the ways in which work groups function. The need might emerge naturally from a systems or structures review, or it might result from a specific study of group processes in the organization and the resulting diagnosis that teamwork within groups needs to be improved. Douglas McGregor's definition of well functioning groups was given in Chapter 7. He felt they should be developed along the following lines:

1. A group meeting in which issues are explored under the guidance of a group leader and agreement is reached on what the team development exercise is expected to achieve.

2. The presentation by the leader of his understanding of what needs to be done in such areas as structure, systems, relationships and methods of operation and communications.
3. Contributions from each member of the group on matters affecting him in the areas referred to by the leader.
4. A joint discussion to resolve any areas of disagreement.
5. The joint preparation of detailed action plans to improve team-work and communications.

This approach could be made slightly less structured by confining the group leader's role to the organization of discussion, and allowing the group to develop its own ideas without too much prompting from the leader. Team development work may be related to general issues or specific projects and it may be combined with educational activities of one kind or another as described under the headings 'Group exercises' and 'Group dynamics' in Appendix K. A team development scale used for self-assessment is shown in Table 12.1.

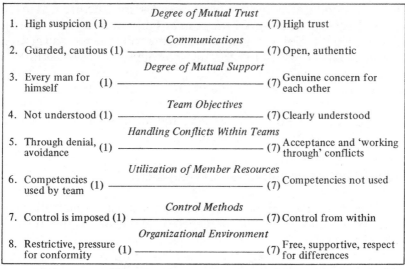

Table 12.1 *Team development scale (used by groups for self-assessment)*

Inter-group relations

Inter-group relations activities deal with conflict situations, or problems relating to communication or roles which may lead to conflict. They may also be concerned with the conflicts or misapprehensions that arise when two companies or departments have to be merged.

Conflict resolution is the basis of most inter-group relations work. The simplest and crudest approach is a confrontation meeting in which the two parties get together with a third party on the side-lines to help them work through their differences.

A more refined version of this approach is to get the third party to hold discussions with each of the groups separately to agree on the issues and on an agenda for discussion. This can be time-consuming, but in the writer's experience the time is well spent. Fairly long discussions with the separate parties in which they do all the talking are of value in themselves as a means of relieving feelings and bringing hidden issues out into the open. It is especially in this area that the OD specialist has to be able to gain confidence and trust – and be a good listener.

Educational activities

Educational activities in organization development programmes aim to improve skill, especially in the processes of teamwork, interaction, problem-solving, objective-setting and planning. Some knowledge may have to be imparted on the basic factors affecting the processes, but this is incidental. The emphasis should be on active learning by experiencing and analysing the various processes.

The educational activities can be more or less unstructured, as in laboratory or 'T-group' training. Or they can be built round a series of projects as in Coverdale Training, which could be described as semi-structured – the participants are asked to carry out in groups a series of set tasks, but they are given the maximum amount of scope to discover for themselves the processes at work and to analyse the lessons they have learned. A slightly more structured approach is provided by the managerial grid series of programmes devised by Blake and Mouton. These activities are described in more detail in Appendix K.

Management of organization development

One of the basic tenets of the OD movement is that an organization development programme should be 'managed from the top'. If this means that the chief executive should personally take charge of planning the programme and should actively participate in its implementation, then it is an unrealistic requirement in all but the smallest organizations. If it means that the chief executive should give active rather than passive support, then it is more feasible. Such support is clearly desirable, and the writer's own knowledge of OD programmes that have failed suggests that one of the prime reasons for failure has been because an experiment has been forced on to the company by an outsider or by an internal staff specialist without gaining the real interest of top management.

The implications of the 'managed from the top' view are that OD can only succeed if it is organization-wide. Ideally, of course, it should cover the whole enterprise, but practical experience has shown that programmes covering separate functions or units have been quite successful, as long as the head of the function really believes in them.

Almost by definition, OD programmes need to be run by a third party. In the jargon of the OD trade – and like all new movements, it abounds in jargon – the third party is the 'change agent' who makes 'interventions' in the 'client system'. It is usually assumed that the third party should be a qualified behavioural scientist. He may come from outside or inside the organization.

An external consultant should be able to bring to the organization a wide range of experience and knowledge. He is not involved in the day-to-day politics of the enterprise and can be seen as objective and dispassionate. He should be able to act as a true catalyst – bringing about change without being changed himself. The internal consultant or adviser has the advantage that he knows something about the processes at work in the organization and should be able to reach management easily. He may be able to work more continuously than the outsider and can play a key role in implementing agreed actions following an OD programme – something the external consultant may not be given the time to do. But the internal consultant may find it difficult to keep in touch both with top and middle management in order to maintain the confidence of all concerned – a prophet is not always honoured in his own country. The external adviser may well be in a better position because he is engaged by top management but is also given ample opportunity to use his skills to make himself acceptable to middle management.

The choice depends on the situation. If the enterprise has trained people available or thinks that it is worth recruiting them, then there is much to be said for an internally managed programme. Otherwise, it may be best to get outside help, but the consultant should preferably work closely with members of the organization who will be responsible for implementation.

The factors required for success when introducing OD are:

- the credibility of the advocates who must show that they know what they are talking about, must be able to refer to successful experience in the field and must look and sound like the sort of people those taking part in the programme will trust;
- a presentation to management which will show that the specialist appreciates their problems and can describe them in language they understand;
- a description of the proposed activities which will indicate what is going to take place, why this approach is being adopted, the results that should be achieved and how these results should help to overcome the problems and benefit the organization;
- a clear indication of the time and resources required and the cost of the programme, so that this can be measured against the potential benefits;

- the avoidance at all times of the use of OD jargon – terms such as 'change agent', 'intervention', 'client system', 'experiential learning' and 'confrontation meeting' may be convenient shorthand to the specialist, but mean nothing to the typical manager and are usually positively off-putting;
- a continuing programme of communication and discussion with line managers which is aimed at convincing them that organization development will work for them;
- the programme must take account of the values of the organization as well as that of the interventionist.

Does organization development work?

Organization development programmes are based on a set of values. The first question to ask in evaluating OD is: 'Are these values appropriate to the organization?' Organization development has lost a degree of credibility in recent years because the messianic zeal displayed by some practitioners has been at variance with the circumstances and real needs of the organization. Values have been imposed and have therefore been resisted. As Adrian McLean has commented:

It is becoming increasingly apparent that there exists a considerable discrepancy between OD as practised and the prescriptive stances taken by many OD writers . . . The theory of change and change management which is the foundation of most OD programmes is based on over-simplistic generalizations which offer little specific guidance to practitioners faced with the confusing complexity of a real change situation.[4]

The somewhat naive beliefs of many behavioural scientists who started the OD movement have shifted in recent years to a contingency approach as advocated by Karen Legge and Tom Lupton. This emphasizes the need to decide from the start how the process of planned change should be evaluated and then recognize that viewpoints for values will change during the course of the programme. As Lupton and Warnington state: 'Not only the strategy but the specific goal itself is likely to change as the strategy develops and better understanding of the dynamics of the system is achieved through the monitoring process.'[5]

The future of organization development

In his persuasive article on the future of OD, McLean concluded:

There seems to be a growing awareness of the inappropriateness of some of the fundamental value stances, models and prescriptions inherited from the 1960s. Writers are facing up to the naivety of early beliefs and theories in what might be termed a climate of sobriety and new realism. There is an increasing recognition of the existence of human traits other than those of trust, love, openness and sharing. Such traits as competitiveness, political ambition, distrust and dislike are coming to be seen as endemic and enduring features of organizational life. The signs are that more recent theories and concepts are beginning to incorporate these new perspectives.[4]

This new climate of realism coupled with a contingency approach means that OD still has something to offer because it recognizes that change and other organizational processes should not be allowed to drift. They must be managed.

There are a number of management approaches available but they are all based on analysis followed by diagnosis. Evaluation is based not on a rigid set of values but a viewpoint which is developed in the light of an assessment of the situation.

Knowledge of the contribution of the behavioural sciences to the understanding of the processes of change, conflict, interaction, group dynamics, motivation and role playing will help but will not dictate the choice of the most appropriate method in the circumstances. Less reliance will be placed on the OD packages developed in the 1960s. A more empirical approach is required which will use individual sessions and group meetings to increase understanding of what needs to be done so that those concerned will do it for themselves. Argyris summarized this approach when he defined the three primary tasks of the OD practitioner or interventionist as being to:

- generate and help clients to generate valid information that they can understand about their problems;
- create opportunities for the clients to search effectively for solutions to their problems, to make free choices;
- create conditions for internal commitment to these choices and apparatus for the continual monitoring of the action taken.[6]

References

1. Sadler, P J and Barry, BA *Organizational Development*. Longmans, Green and Co, London, 1970.
2. Likert, R *The Human Organization*. McGraw-Hill, New York, 1967.
3. Maugham, I L, Shaw, D and Wilson, B *Managing Change*. British Institute of Management, London, 1971.
4. McLean, A 'Organization Development: A Case of the Emperor's New Clothes?', *Personnel Review*, Vol IV, No 1, 1981.
5. Lupton, T and Warnington, W A *A systems approach to determining the criteria for successful change in the context of a particular action research programme*. Manchester Business School Working Paper No 6, 1974.
6. Argyris, C *Intervention Theory and Method: A Behavioural Science View*. Addison-Wesley, Reading, Mass., 1970.

Part IV
Employee Resourcing

Employee resourcing is about ensuring that the organization knows and gets what it wants in the way of the people needed to run the business now and in the future. It starts from an initial analysis of the strategic objective of the company and continues with an analysis of the human resources required to achieve them.

Human resource planning uses demand and supply forecasting techniques to set out needs in both quantitative (how many people) and qualitative (what sort of people) terms. It provides the basis for resourcing programmes which use recruitment procedures and selection techniques to ensure that requirements are met in accordance with quality, quantity and time specifications.

Chapter 13
Human Resource Planning

Aims and activities

The aims of human resource planning are to ensure that the organization:

- obtains and retains the quantity and quality of people it needs;
- makes the best use of its human resources;
- is able to anticipate the problems arising from potential surpluses or deficits of people.

Human resource planning consists of six interrelated areas of activity:

1. *Demand forecasting* – estimating future manpower needs by reference to corporate and functional plans and forecasts of future activity levels.
2. *Supply forecasting* – estimating the supply of manpower by reference to analyses of current resources and future availability, after allowing for wastage.
3. *Forecasting requirements* – analysing the demand and supply forecasts to identify future deficits or surpluses with the help of models, where appropriate.
4. *Productivity and cost analysis* – analysing productivity, capacity, utilization and costs in order to identify the need for improvements in productivity or reductions in cost.
5. *Action planning* – preparing plans to deal with forecast deficits or surpluses of manpower, to improve utilization and productivity or to reduce costs.
6. *Budgeting and control* – setting human resource budgets and standards and monitoring the implementation of the plans against them.

Although these are described as six separate areas, and are analysed as such in later sections of this chapter, they are, in fact, closely interrelated and often overlap. For example, demand forecasts are estimates of future requirements, and these can only be prepared on the basis of assumptions about the productivity of employees. But the supply forecast will also have to consider productivity trends and how they might affect the supply of people.

A flow chart of the process of human resource planning is shown in Figure 13.1.

Demand forecasting

Demand forecasting is the process of estimating the future quantity and quality of people required. The basis of the forecast should be the annual budget and longer term corporate plan, translated into activity levels for each function and department. In a manufacturing company the sales budget would be translated into a manufacturing plan giving the numbers and types of products to be made in each period. From this information the number of hours to be worked by each skill category to make the quota for each period would be computed. A plan for a van sales operation would start from the sales plan setting out a programme for establishing new rounds. In an insurance company, forecasts of new business would be translated into the number of proposals that would have to be processed by the underwriting department. In a mail order company,

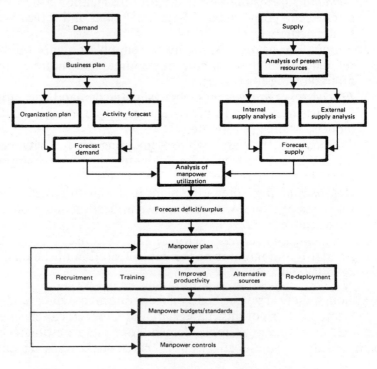

Figure 13.1 The process of human resource planning

forecasts would be made of the number of orders that have to be processed, assembled and dispatched.

Details are required of any organization plans which would result in increased or decreased demands for staff. For example, setting up a new regional organization, creating a new sales department, decentralizing a head office function to the regions.

The planning data would refer to expected changes in productivity or manpower levels arising from changes in working methods or procedures, automation or mechanization. These could be set out as a crude percentage increase in productivity which could be used to adjust the required hours for a given level of output. Or they might give specific instances of cases where the manning for a machine, a production line, a clerical section or a sales office is to be increased or decreased.

Demand forecasting methods

There are four basic demand forecasting methods:

1. Managerial judgement.
2. Ratio-trend analysis.
3. Work study techniques.
4. Modelling.

These are described separately below, although in many cases a combination of, say, managerial judgement and statistical techniques would be used.

Managerial judgement

The most typical method of forecasting used in smaller companies, or those who do not have access to work study data, is managerial judgement. This simply requires managers to sit down, think about their future workloads and decide how many people they need. It might be done on a 'bottom-up' basis with line managers submitting proposals for agreement by senior management.

Alternatively, a 'top-down' approach can be used in which company and departmental forecasts are prepared by top management, possibly acting on advice from the personnel and organization and methods (O & M) departments. These forecasts are reviewed and agreed with departmental managers. A less directive approach is for top management to prepare planning guidelines for departmental managers setting out the planning assumptions and the targets they should try to meet. The personnel and organization and methods of work study departments then discuss and agree budgets with departmental managers.

Perhaps the best way of using managerial judgement is to adopt both the 'bottom-up' and 'top-down' approach. Guidelines for departmental managers should be prepared which indicate broad company assumptions about future activity levels which will affect their departments. Targets are also set where necessary. Armed with these guidelines, departmental managers prepare their forecasts to a laid-down format. They are encouraged to seek help at this stage from personnel, O & M, or work study. Meanwhile, the personnel department, in conjunction as necessary with planning, O & M and work study departments, prepares a company human resource forecast. The two sets of forecasts can then be reviewed by a human resource planning committee consisting of functional heads. This committee reconciles with departmental managers any discrepancies between the two forecasts and submits the final amended forecast to top management for approval. This is sometimes called the 'right-angle method'.

An example of a staff forecast form using managerial judgement is shown opposite in Figure 13.2.

Ratio-trend analysis

In its crudest form, ratio-trend analysis is carried out by studying past ratios between, say, the number of direct and indirect workers in a manufacturing plant, and forecasting future ratios, having made some allowance for changes in organization or methods. Activity level forecasts are then used to determine direct labour requirements and the forecast ratio of indirects to directs is used to calculate the number of indirect workers needed. For example, Table 13.1 shows how ratio-trend analysis could be used to forecast the number of inspectors required in an assembly plant. Similar techniques could be used to develop fairly crude ratios between activity levels and numbers of staff.

	Year	No. of Employees		Ratio Inspector : Production
		Production	*Inspector*	
Actual	- 3	1500	150	1 : 10
	- 2	1800	180	1 : 10
	Last year	2000	180	1 : 11
Forecast	Next year	2200*	200†	1 : 11
	+2	2500*	210†	1 : 12
	+3	2750	230†	1 : 12

* calculated by reference to forecast activity levels
† calculated by applying forecast ratio to forecast activity levels

Table 13.1 *Demand forecast – inspectors*

Table 13.2 shows how an analysis of actual and forecast ratios between the number of routine proposals to be processed by an insurance company underwriting department and the number of underwriters employed could be used to forecast future requirements.

Category of staff . . . . Year		
Staff members and movements	*No. of staff to be provided*	*Remarks*
1. Number of staff at 1.1..... (excluding known resignations) 75	—	Age groups: Under 25 30 25 - 34 20 35 - 44 15 45 and over 10

2.(a) Expected retirements,
    transfers out and
    promotions during year 8
(b) Less expected transfers in,
    promotions and new
    appointments already made 3
	5	(dates to be specified)

3.(a) Number of staff
    required at 1 January,
    next year 80
(b) Less present staff 75
	5	Increase in number to be substan-
		tiated by O & M report

4. Expected staff losses due to
   normal wastage of existing
   staff 15
	15	Estimated by age groups:
		Under 25 12
		25 - 34 2
		35 - 44 1
		45 and over —

5. Expected losses of staff to be recruited in the period 5	5	Short service staff turnover at 20% of 25 (events 2. + 3. + 4 above)
6. Total staff to be provided during period	30	5 to be recruited by 1 February — others to be programmed later

Figure 13.2 Staff forecast form

	Year	No. of underwriters	No. of proposals per week	Ratio Underwriters : Proposals
Actual	- 3 - 2 Last Year	10 10 12	2,000 2,500 3,600	1 : 200 1 : 250 1 : 300
Forecast	Next Year +2 +3	14 16 18	4,200 4,800 5,400	1 : 300 1 : 300 1 : 300

Table 13.2 *Demand forecast – underwriters*

These techniques, although crude, are easy to understand and use. Their value depends upon accurate records and realistic estimates of future activity levels and effect of improved performance or changed methods.

Work study techniques

Work study techniques can be used when it is possible to apply work measurement to calculate how long operations should take and the amount of labour required. The starting point in a manufacturing company is the production budget prepared in terms of volumes of saleable products for the company as a whole, or volumes of output for individual departments. The budgets of productive hours are then compiled by the use of standard hours for direct labour, if standard labour times have been established by work measurement. The standard hours per unit of output are then multiplied by the planned volume of units to be produced to give the total planned hours for the period. This is divided by the number of actual working hours for an individual operator to show the number of operators required. Allowance may have to made for absenteeism and forecast levels of idle time. The following is a highly simplified example of this procedure:

(a)	Planned output for year	20,000 units
(b)	Standard hours per unit	5 hours
(c)	Planned hours for year	100,000 hours
(d)	Productive hours per man/year (allowing normal overtime, absenteeism and down time)	2,000 hours
(e)	Number of direct workers required (c/d)	50

Work study techniques for direct workers can be combined with ratio-trend analysis to calculate the number of indirect workers needed. Clerical staff requirements may also be estimated by these methods if clerical work measurement techniques can be used.

Modelling

Mathematical modelling techniques using computers can help in the preparation of demand forecasts. These are discussed later in this chapter (pages 220 to 223).

Supply forecasting

Human resources comprise the total effective effort that can be put to work as shown by the number of people and hours of work available, the capacity of employees to do the work and their productivity. Supply forecasting measures the number of people likely to be available from within and outside the organization, having allowed for absenteeism, internal movements and promotions, wastage and changes in hours and other conditions of work. The supply analysis covers:

● existing human resources;
● potential losses to existing resources through labour wastage;

● potential changes to existing resources through internal promotions;
● effect of changing conditions of work and absenteeism;
● sources of supply from within the firm.

The information required and the methods of analysis that can be used are considered below. As in the case of demand forecasting, the process of supply forecasting can be greatly facilitated by the use of human resource modelling techniques as described later in this chapter (pages 220 to 223).

Analysing existing human resources

The basic analysis should classify employees by function or department, occupation, level of skill and status.

The aim should be to identify from this analysis 'resource centres' consisting of broadly homogenous groups for which forecasts of supply need to be made. There is endless scope for cross analysis in preparing human resource inventories, but beware of collecting useless data; it is necessary to subject the analytical scheme to rigorous analysis, and for each category ask the questions: 'Why do we need this information?' and 'What are we going to do with it when we get it?'

Some detailed analysis may be essential. For example, the review of current resources may need to cut across organizational and occupational boundaries to provide inventories of skills and potential. It may be important to know how many people the organization has with special skills or abilities; for example, chemists, physicists, mathematicians, economists or linguists. From the point of view of management succession planning and the preparation of management development programmes it may be equally important to know how many people with potential for promotion exist and where they can be found.

An analysis of staff by age helps to identify problems arising from a sudden rush of retirements, a block in promotion prospects, or a preponderance of older employees. Age distribution can be illustrated graphically as in Figure 13.3 which shows that a large number of staff will retire shortly and that the proportion of employees in the older age brackets is unduly high.

Length of service analysis may be even more important because it will provide evidence of survival rates, which, as discussed later, are a necessary tool for use by planners in predicting future resources.

The analysis of current resources should look at the existing ratios between different categories of staff; for example, supervisors to employees, skilled to semi-skilled, direct to indirect, clerical to production. Recent movements in these ratios should be studied to provide guidance on trends and to highlight areas where rapid changes may result in manpower supply problems.

Wastage or staff turnover

Staff wastage should be analysed in order to forecast future losses and to identify the reasons for people leaving the organization. Plans can then be made to attack the problems causing unnecessary wastage and to replace uncontrollable losses. The human resource planner therefore has to know how to measure wastage and how to analyse its causes.

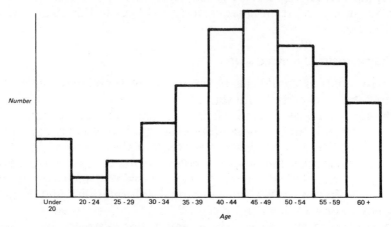

Figure 13.3 Analysis of age distribution

Measuring turnover or wastage
This can be done in various ways:

Turnover Index. This is the traditional formula for measuring wastage:

$$\frac{\text{Number of leavers in a specified period (usually 1 year)}}{\text{Average number of employees during the same period}} \text{ x } 100$$

This method is in common use because it is easy to calculate and to understand. It is a simple matter to work out that if last year 30 out of an average force of 150 skilled fitters left (20% turnover), and this trend continues, then the company will have to recruit 110 fitters during the following year, in order to increase and to hold the labour force at 200 in that year (50 extra fitters, plus 40 to replace the 20% wastage of the average 200 fitters employed, plus 20 to replace wastage of the 90 recruits).

This wastage formula is simple to use. But it can be positively misleading. The main objection to the measurement of turnover in terms of the proportion of those who leave in a given period is that the figure may be inflated by the high turnover of a relatively small proportion of the work force, especially in times of heavy recruitment. Thus, a company employing 1,000 people might have had an annual wastage rate of 20%, meaning that 200 jobs had become vacant during the year. But this could have been spread throughout the company, covering all occupations and long as well as short service employees. Alternatively it could have been restricted to a small sector of the work force – only twenty jobs might have been affected although each of these had to be filled ten times during the year. These are totally different situations, and unless they are appreciated, inaccurate forecasts would be made of future requirements and inappropriate actions would be taken to deal with the problem. The turnover index is also suspect if the average number of employees upon which the percentage is based is unrepresentative of recent trends because of considerable increases or decreases during the period in the numbers employed.

Stability Index. This measure is considered by many to be an improvement:

$$\frac{\text{Number with 1 year's service or more}}{\text{Number employed 1 year ago}} \times 100$$

This index provides an indication of the tendency for longer service employees to remain with the company, and therefore shows the degree to which there is a continuity of employment. But this too can be misleading because the index will not reveal the vastly different situations that exist in a company or department with a high proportion of long-serving employees in comparison with one where the majority of employees are short service.

Length of Service Analysis. This disadvantage of the stability index may be partly overcome if an analysis is also made of the average length of service of people who leave, as in Table 13.3 overleaf.

This analysis is still fairly crude, because it only deals with those who leave. A more refined analysis would compare for each service category the numbers leaving with the numbers employed. If, in the example shown, the total numbers employed with less than three months' service was 80 and the total with more than five years was 80, the proportion of leavers in each category would be, respectively, 50% and 10% – much more revealing figures, especially if previous periods could be analysed to reveal adverse trends.

Survival Rate. Another method of analysing turnover which is particularly useful for human resource planners is the survival rate: the proportion of employees who are engaged within a certain period who remain with the firm after so many months or years of service. Thus an analysis of trainees who have completed their training might show that after two years, ten of the original 'cohort' of twenty trainees were still with the company, a survival rate of 50%.

Occupation	Leavers by Length of Service 19.....						Total no. leaving	Average no. employed	Index of labour turnover
	less than 3 months	3 - 6 months	6 months - 1 year	1 - 2 years	3 - 5 years	5 or more years			%
Skilled	5	4	3	3	2	3	20	200	10
Semi-skilled	15	12	10	6	3	4	50	250	20
Unskilled	20	10	5	3	1	1	40	100	40
Totals	40	26	18	12	6	8	110	550	20

Table 13.3 *Analysis of leavers by length of service*

The distribution of losses for each entry group or 'cohort' can be plotted in the form of a 'survival curve' as shown in Figure 13.4.

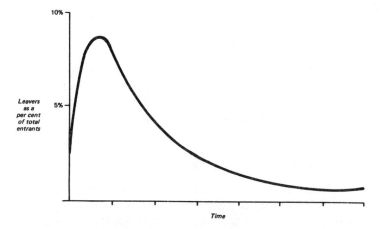

Figure 13.4. A survival curve

The basic shape of this curve has been found to be similar in many situations, although it has been observed that the peak of the curve may occur further along the time scale and/or may be lower when it relates to more highly skilled or trained entry cohorts. Table 13.4 would tell the human resource planner that he has to allow for half the number of recruits in any one year to be lost over the next five years, unless something can be done about the factors causing wastage. Thus, to achieve a requirement of 50 trained staff in five years' time, 100 people would have to be engaged this year.

Entry cohort	Original strength	No. surviving to end of year after engagement				
		Year 1	*Year 2*	*Year 3*	*Year 4*	*Year 5*
A	40	35	28	26	22	20
B	32	25	24	19	18	17
C	48	39	33	30	25	23
D	38	32	27	24	22	19
E	42	36	30	26	23	21
Average survival rate	100%	83%	71%	62%	55%	50%

Table 13.4 *Survival rate analysis*

Half-Life Index. A simpler concept derived from survival rate analysis is that of the half-life index, which is defined as the time taken for a group or cohort of starters to reduce to half its original size through the wastage process (five years in the above example). Comparisons can then be made for successive entry years or between different groups of employees in order to show where action may have to be taken to counter undesirable wastage trends.

Choice of Measurement. It is difficult to avoid using the conventional labour turnover index as the easiest and most familiar of all methods of measurement. But it needs to be supplemented with some measure of stability – an analysis of turnover or wastage as part of a human resource planning exercise requires detailed information on the length of service of leavers to identify problem areas and to provide a foundation for supply forecasts.

Analysing the effect of promotions and transfers

The supply forecast should indicate the number of vacancies that will have to be filled to meet the demand forecast. Vacancies arise because people leave but the exit of a senior manager may produce a chain reaction of replacements. Transfers between departments and divisions may also have to be allowed for.

In a large organization, persistent patterns of promotion or transfer may develop and it may be possible to predict the proportions of employees in particular categories who are likely to be promoted or moved in the future by starting with a forecast of the chain reaction factor, to give a broad indication of the number of displacements that may occur. For example, where there are three levels of management:

3rd line management	:	1 promotion	=	3 moves
2nd line management	:	5 promotions	=	10 moves
1st line management	:	25 promotions	=	25 moves
Total promotions/moves		**31**		**38**

But this is very crude, and in most companies management succession planning has to be worked out specifically by reference to known retirements and transfers.

Assessing changes in conditions of work and absenteeism

This assessment should cover factors operating within the firm such as changes in: normal weekly hours of work; overtime policies; the length and timing of holidays; retirement policy; the policy for employing part-timers; and shift systems.

The effect of absenteeism on the future supply of employees should also be allowed for, and trends in absenteeism should be analysed to trace causes and identify possible remedial actions.

Analysing sources of supply

Internal sources will include the output from established training schemes or management development programmes and the reservoirs of skill and potential that exist within the organization. But the availability of people from outside as well as inside the enterprise is a vital factor when preparing development plans. Too often, corporate or functional plans make assumptions about the availability of people locally or nationally, which could easily be proved wrong after a brief investigation. It is particularly necessary to identify at an early stage any categories of employees where there might be difficulties in recruiting the numbers required, so that action can be taken in good time to prepare a recruiting campaign, to tap alternative sources, or to develop training or re-training programmes to convert available staff to meet the company's needs. The factors which can have an important bearing on the supply of manpower are listed below.

Local factors

1. Population densities within reach of the company.
2. Current and future competition for staff from other employers.
3. Local unemployment levels.
4. The traditional pattern of employment locally, and the availability of people with the required qualifications and skills.
5. The output from the local educational system and government or other training establishments.
6. The pattern of immigration and emigration within the area.
7. The attractiveness of the area as a place to live.
8. The attractiveness of the company as a place to work in.
9. The availability of part-time employees.
10. Local housing, shopping and transport facilities.

National factors

1. Trends in the growth of the working population.
2. National demands for special categories of employees – graduates, professional staff, technologists, technicians, craftsmen, secretaries.
3. The output of the universities, polytechnics and professional institutions.
4. The effect of changing educational patterns – children staying longer at schools, or different emphases in university or school curriculae.
5. The impact of national government training schemes.
6. The impact of government employment regulations such as, in Britain, the Employment Protection Act, the Sex Discrimination Act or the Equal Pay Act.

Forecasting human resource requirements

Human resource requirements are forecast by relating the supply to the demand forecasts and establishing any deficits or surpluses of employees that will exist in the future. Table 13.5 shows how demand and supply forecasts can be scheduled over a period of five years to indicate the number of fitters to be recruited.

		Year 1	Year 2	Year 3	Year 4	Year 5
Demand	1. Numbers required at beginning of year	120	140	140	120	120
	2. Changes to requirements forecast during year	+20	Nil	- 20	Nil	Nil
	3. Total requirements at end of year (1+2)	140	140	120	120	120
Supply	4. Numbers available at beginning of year	120	140	140	120	120
	5. Gains from transfers and promotions in	5	5	--	--	--
	6. Losses through:					
	(a) retirements	3	6	4	1	3
	(b) wastage	15	17	18	15	14
	(c) transfers and promotions out	2	4	6	3	--
	(d) total losses	20	27	28	19	17
	7. Total available at end of year (4+5-6)	105	118	112	101	103
Requirement	8. Deficit (d), or surplus (s): (3-7)	25(d)	22(d)	8(d)	19(d)	17(d)
	9. Losses of those recruited during year	3	6	2	4	3
	10. Additional numbers required during year (8+9)	28	28	10	23	20

Table 13.5 *Forecast of recruitment needs for fitters*

The first year of the forecast could be the labour budget for the year and the forecast would be updated annually, or more frequently if there are rapid changes in demand. In some situations it might be impossible to forecast as far ahead as five years, and in others there might be no point in doing so because no action could be taken by the company more than one or two years in advance.

An example of a more detailed one-year staff budget for a sales organization is shown in Table 13.6.

The reconciliation of demand and supply forecasts shows how many people may have to be recruited or made redundant and this forms the basis for the manpower plan proper – drawing up recruitment campaigns and training programmes or preparing for redundancy.

	Current establish-ment	New appoint-ments during year	Forecast losses of existing staff during year				Requirements during year			Losses of staff recruited during year	Number to be recruited during year
			Retire-ment	Wastage	Promo-tion out	Total	Total (2+6)	By promotion	By recruitment		
	(1)	(2)	(3)	(4)	(5)	(6)	(7)	(8)	(9)	(10)	(11)
General Sales Manager	1	–	1	–	–	1	1	1	–	–	–
Regional Sales Managers	6	1	1	–	1	2	3	3	–	–	–
Area Sales Managers	18	2	–	2	3	5	7	6	1	–	1
Sales Representatives	165	10	1	15	6	22	32	–	32	3	35

Table 13.6 *Sales staff budget: year commencing* . . . .

In situations where a considerable quantity of demand and supply data has to be analysed and a number of assumptions about the future need to be evaluated, use of human resource modelling techniques is advisable.

Human resource modelling

Definition

A model is a representation of a real situation. It depicts inter-relationships between the relevant factors in that situation and, by structuring and formalizing any information about these factors, presents reality in a simplified form.

Uses of modelling – in general

Models can help to:

    (a) increase the decision maker's understanding of the situation in which a decision has to be made and the possible outcomes of that decision;

    (b) stimulate new thinking about problems by, among other things, providing answers to 'what if' questions (sensitivity analysis);

    (c) evaluate alternative courses of action.

Application of human resource models

Human resource modelling techniques can be used to prepare general human resource forecasts, to understand, predict and measure wastage and to assist in career evaluation. If a computerized personnel information system exists, as described in Chapter 19, the information contained on the database can be exploited swiftly to provide detailed analyses of massive quantities of data which can be turned into projections of future demand and supply flows and forecasts of staff requirements.

The 'what if' questions that can be answered by a model include the impact on human resource requirements of alternative activity level forecasts or variations in assumptions about wastage rates, promotions and transfers, or changing patterns in the use of skills arising from the introduction of new technology or changes in marketing strategy.

Data required

The data required for setting up and operating human resource models is essentially the same as that used for demand and supply forecasting. But it may have to be organized on a more systematic basis to fit the modelling process.

The main headings under which data will need to be assembled are:

1. *The human resource system.* This describes how people move into and out of the organization or any of its units and how they progress between the various organizational levels or grades. A highly simplified representation of the system is illustrated in Figure 13.5.

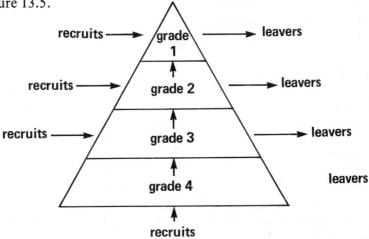

Figure 13.5 A human resource system

2. *Stocks.* Stocks – the number of people employed in each grade – are analysed in age or length of service bands.
3. *Flows.* Leavers, recruits and promotion flows are also analysed by grade and age or length of service.
4. *Assumptions.* Alternative assumptions can be made about the future behaviour of the system so that the implication of the different outcomes can be evaluated. These assumptions might include a 'push' analysis of flows where the organization 'pushes' people through the system as their career progresses without having fixed grade sizes (this type of system uses salary progression curves rather than salary ranges, as discussed in Chapter 23). In a graded system the assumptions will be concerned with targets for grade sizes expressed as a growth or shrinkage percentage rate per grade, or target numbers from the operational plan.
5. *Careers analysis.* A 'careers prospectus' can be built up by analysing data on promotions between grade and career progression curves, and by projecting trends. The model can link this data to information on the database about the potential of current employees so that future stocks for promotion can be estimated.

The data on stocks and flows can be recorded on a form like the one illustrated in Figure 13.6.

Grade	Age ranges			
Grade 4	16-24	25-34	35-44	45-65
Stocks at beginning of year				
Recruits during year				
Recruits leaving during year				
Leavers during year				
Promotions to grade 3				
Promotions from grade 5				
Stocks at end of year				

Figure 13.6 Stocks and flows data schedule

Using models

Models such as those produced by the Institute of Manpower Studies (Microprospect, IMS – Monitor, IMS-WASP, IMS-CAMPLAN) can be obtained to use on a computerized personnel information system as described in Chapter 19. The advice given by the Institute of Manpower Studies in operating their models includes the following points:

● Understand why a model is being used, what outputs are required and what assumptions have to be included.
● In making assumptions about the manpower system, flows and targets, start by asking what happens if current practices continue to be operated and then consider possible changes in market conditions, the use of new technologies, etc.
● Use time series data, ie trend analysis, wherever possible to provide the basis for extrapolations.
● Although disaggregation, ie splitting mass data into sub-divisions, can apparently lead to greater accuracy, this could be spurious if it involves manipulating very small numbers.
● Do not push the data further than it will go. When dealing with

small or doubtful numbers smooth or aggregate where necessary or sensible.
- Cross-check assumptions about wastage rates with other companies to ensure they are reasonable.
- Carry out sensitivity analysis, ie the study of assumptions in order to predict alternative outcomes, depending on the assumption.
- Look first for significant results in the model's output, especially changes in work force composition and unusually large or small flows.

Productivity and costs

Planning is just as concerned with making the best use of people as with forecasting and getting the numbers required. An increase in activity levels can be catered for by improving productivity as well as by recruiting more staff. This means looking at productivity and employment costs as well as the possibility of treating human resources as assets rather than liabilities, to be invested in, maintained and allocated on the same rational basis that is used for all other assets.

Productivity

Fundamentally, productivity represents the output of goods and services which can be obtained from a given input of employees. Within the firm, productivity should be monitored by using such measures as employment costs per unit of output, employment costs as a ratio of sales value, sales value per employee, tons of product handled per man hour, or labour costs as a percentage of added value (the difference being production costs and sales value). Internal and external comparisons may then reveal areas where improvement is required by mechanization, automation, improved management or other means.

Employment costs

Employment costs can be grouped under seven headings as follows:

1. *Remuneration costs:*
   (a) pay – basic, bonuses, profit-sharing, overtime and shift payments, merit pay, other supplementary pay;
   (b) direct fringe benefits – pensions, life insurance, holidays, car, luncheon vouchers/subsidized meals, share ownership schemes, housing schemes, housing assistance, education loans;
   (c) statutory costs – national insurance and pension fund contributions, training board levies (offset by grants), employer's liability insurance.

2. Recruitment costs:

    (a) preparation of job specifications and advertisements;
    (b) advertising and general promotional activities;
    (c) sifting applications, interviewing and corresponding with applicants;
    (d) selection testing;
    (e) medical examinations;
    (f) induction.

3. Training costs:

    (a) remuneration and expenses of trainees and trainers;
    (b) preparing and maintaining training programmes;
    (c) training materials, equipment and premises;
    (d) lower efficiency of trainees until fully trained.

4. Relocation costs:

    (a) travel, accommodation and disturbance allowances;
    (b) housing assistance;
    (c) hostel charges.

5. Leaving costs:

    (a) loss of production between leaving and replacement;
    (b) statutory redundancy payments, less rebates;
    (c) *ex gratia* payments.

6. Support costs:

    (a) indirect fringe benefits – social and sports facilities, medical, welfare, rehabilitation and convalescent schemes, canteens, preferential purchase schemes, house magazines, music-while-you-work, library;
    (b) long-service awards;
    (c) suggestion schemes;
    (d) safety facilities;
    (e) car parking.

7. Personnel administration costs: personnel department costs, other than those allocated under other headings.

It may be difficult to collect and allocate expenses under all these headings, but the more detailed the analysis the better the control that can be exercised over manpower costs.

Action planning

The human resource plan should be prepared on the basis of an analysis of human resource requirements and a study of the implications of the information on productivity and costs. The main elements, depending on circumstances, will consist of:

1. *The recruitment plan* which will set out:

    (a) the numbers and types of people required and when they are needed;
    (b) any special supply problems and how they are to be dealt with;
    (c) the recruitment programme.

2. *The re-development plan* which will set out programmes for transferring or re-training existing employees.

3. *The redundancy or 'down-sizing' plan* which will indicate:

    (a) who is to be made redundant and where and when;
    (b) the plans for re-development or re-training, where this has not been covered in the re-development plan;
    (c) the steps to be taken to help redundant employees find new jobs;
    (d) the policy for declaring redundancies and making redundancy payments;
    (e) the programme for consulting with unions or staff associations and informing those affected.

4. *The training plan* which will show:

    (a) the number of trainees or apprentices required and the programme for recruiting or training them;
    (b) the number of existing staff who need training or re-training and the training programme;
    (c) the new courses to be developed or the changes to be made to existing courses.

5. *The productivity plan* which will set out:

    (a) programmes for improving productivity or reducing employment costs by such means as:
        – improving or streamlining methods, procedures or systems;
        – mechanization or automation;
        – productivity bargaining;
        – training;
        – the use of financial incentives; payment by result schemes, bonuses, profit-sharing;

- the development of other methods of improving motivation and commitment: organization development programmes, re-designing jobs, increased participation;

(b) productivity or efficiency targets such as:
- remuneration or total employment costs as a percentage of sales revenue;
- sales per employee;
- net profit after tax as a percentage of remuneration cost;
- remuneration or labour cost per unit of output;
- employment costs as a percentage of added value;
- standard hours as a percentage of actual hours worked.

6. *The retention plan* which will describe the actions required to reduce avoidable wastage under the following headings:

(a) pay problems – increasing pay levels to meet competition; improving pay structures to remove inequities, altering payment systems to reduce excessive fluctuations; introducing procedures for relating rewards more explicitly to effort or performance;

(b) employees leaving to further their career – providing better career opportunities and ensuring that employees are aware of them; extending opportunities for training; adopting and implementing 'promotion from within' policies and introducing more systematic and equitable promotion procedures; deliberately selecting employees who are not likely to want to move much higher than their initial job;

(c) employees leaving due to conflict – introducing more effective procedures for consultation, participation and handling grievances; improving communications by such means as team briefing; using the conflict resolution and team-building techniques of organization development programmes;. re-organizing work and the arrangement of offices or workshops to increase group cohesiveness; educating and training management in approaches to improving their relationships with employees;

(d) the induction crisis – improving recruitment and selection procedures to ensure that job requirements are specified accurately and that the people who are selected fit the specification; ensuring that candidates are given a realistic picture of the job, pay and working conditions, developing better induction and initial training programmes;

(e) shortages – improving recruitment, selection and training for the people required; introducing better methods of planning and scheduling work to smooth out peak loads;

(f) changes in working requirements – ensuring that selection and promotion procedures match the capacities of individuals to the demands of the work they have to do; providing adequate training or adjustment periods when working conditions change; adapting payment by result systems to ensure that individuals are not unduly penalized when they are only engaged on short runs;

(g) losses of unstable recruits – taking more care to avoid recruiting unstable individuals by analysing the characteristics of applicants which are likely to cause instability and using this analysis to screen results.

In each of the six areas of the human resource plan it will be necessary to estimate the costs involved so that they can be assessed against the potential benefits. It will also be necessary to indicate who is responsible for implementing the plan, for reporting on progress and for monitoring the results achieved.

Control

The human resource plan should include budgets, targets and standards. It should also clarify responsibilities for implementation and control and establish reporting procedures which will enable achievements to be monitored against the plan. These may simply report on the numbers employed against establishment (identifying both those who are in-post and those who are in the pipeline) and on the numbers recruited against the recruitment targets. But they should also report employment costs against budget and trends in wastage and employment ratios. Procedures and forms for preparing and presenting personnel statistics are discussed in Chapter 18 on personnel records.

Chapter 14
Recruitment and Selection

The recruitment and selection process

The overall aim of the recruitment and selection process should be to obtain at minimum cost the number and quality of employees required to satisfy the manpower needs of the company. This chapter discusses three stages of recruitment and selection:

1. *Defining requirements* – preparing job descriptions and specifications; deciding terms and conditions of employment.
2. *Attracting candidates* – reviewing and evaluating alternative sources of applicants, inside and outside the company; advertising; using agencies and consultants.
3. *Selecting candidates* – sifting applications, interviewing, testing, assessing candidates; offering employment, obtaining references; preparing contracts of employment.

The last section of the chapter covers induction and follow-up procedures for new employees.

The flow of work and main decisions required in a recruitment and selection procedure are shown in Figures 14.1 and 14.2.

Defining requirements

The number and categories of manpower required should be specified in the recruitment programme, which is derived from the manpower plan. In addition, there will be demands for replacements or for new jobs to be filled, and these demands should be checked to ensure that they are justified. It may be particularly necessary to check on the need for a replacement or the level or type of employee that is specified.

In a large organization it is useful to have a form for requisitioning staff, as illustrated in Figure 14.3. However, even when a requisition form is completed, it may still be necessary to supplement the brief information contained in the form about the job, and it will almost certainly

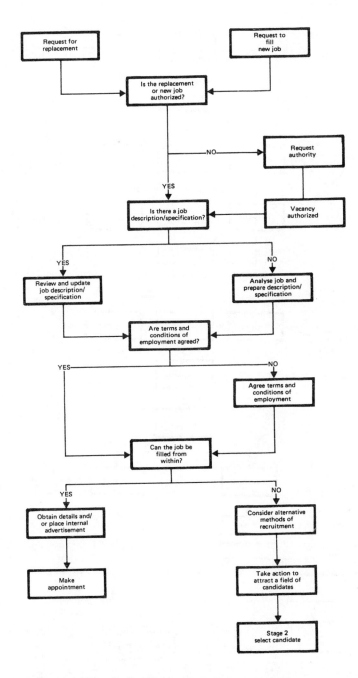

Figure 14.1 Recruitment flow chart – stage 1:
preliminary stages

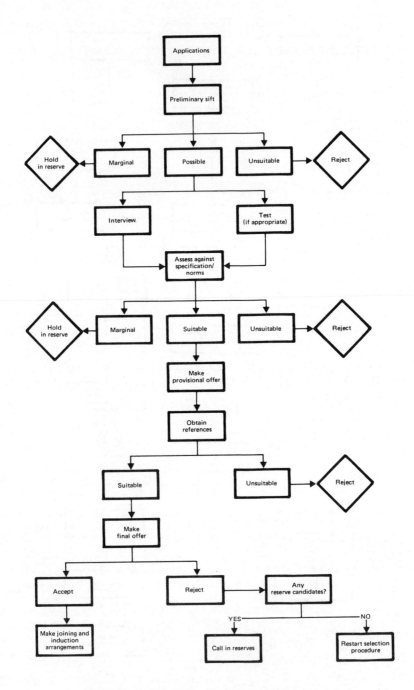

Figure 14.2 Recruitment flow chart – stage 2:
interviewing and selection stages

STAFF REQUISITION			
To Personnel Department	From	Department	Date

REQUIREMENTS	
Job title	Permanent ☐ Temporary ☐
Salary grade	Date needed
	If temporary, specify the period from to
Brief outline of main duties	Education and qualifications required
	Experience required
	Special skills, mental or personality requirements
	Age limits (if any)
	Who will supervise the employee?
	Whom will the employee supervise?

IF A REPLACEMENT, COMPLETE THE FOLLOWING			
Employee replaced	Job title	Salary	Date terminated
Reason for termination			
Performance ☐ Above average ☐ Satisfactory ☐ Unsatisfactory		Would you re-engage? ☐ Yes ☐ No	

IF INCREASE IN ESTABLISHMENT, COMPLETE THE FOLLOWING		
What has created the need for an increase?		
Explain why it is not possible to avoid this increase by organizational or other re-arrangements		
Increase in establishment approved	Signed	Date

Figure 14.3 Staff requisition form

be necessary to check on the specification. If a requisition form is not available, then the job has to be analysed and a job description and job specification prepared. Existing descriptions and specifications should be checked to ensure that they are up-to-date. It is also necessary to establish or check on the terms and conditions of employment at this stage.

Job descriptions

A job description defines the overall purpose or role of the job and the main tasks to be carried out. A good job description is vital to the success of a selection procedure because it is the foundation upon which all the other processes are based. The personnel or job specification and, in turn, the advertisement and the interviewing, testing and assessment procedures will all be derived from it.

The main points to be included in a job description are:

- the location of the job – division, department, branch or section;
- the title of the job;
- the job title of the individual to whom the job holder is responsible;
- the job grade;
- the job titles of any individuals responsible to the job holder and the numbers of employees he or she supervises;
- a brief description of the overall purpose of the job;
- the main tasks carried out by the job holder – these should be listed separately in chronological order or in order of importance;
- details of the equipment or tools used or any special requirements to deal with people, inside or outside the company;
- the location of the job and the amount of travelling that may be required;
- special circumstances such as shifts or night work, considerable overtime or weekend working, heavy lifting, exceptionally monotonous work, unpleasant or dangerous working conditions.

Personnel specifications

Personnel specifications, also known as recruitment or job specifications, define the qualifications, experience and personal qualities required by the job holder and any other necessary information on the special demands made by the job, such as physical conditions, unusual hours, or travelling away from home. They should also set out or refer to terms and conditions of employment such as salary, fringe benefits, hours and holidays.

The information on qualifications, experience and qualities should be derived from an analysis of the knowledge and skills needed to carry out the job. These should therefore be specified: for example, the skills a machine operator requires to operate a machine or group of machines;

the ability to read engineering drawings needed by a tool room fitter; the knowledge of double entry book-keeping an accounts clerk may have to possess; or the persuasive ability needed by a salesman. The list should be as exact as possible so that at the interviewing stage the interviewer can ask direct questions about what the applicant knows or can do.

The biggest danger to be avoided at this stage is that of overstating the qualifications required. Perhaps it is natural to go for the best, but setting an unrealistically high level for candidates increases the problems of attracting applicants, and results in dissatisfaction amongst recruits when they find their talents are not being used. Understating requirements can, of course, be equally dangerous, but it happens much less frequently.

When the requirements have been agreed, they should be analysed under suitable headings. There are various ways of doing this; the most familiar being the seven-point plan developed by Alec Rodger[1] and the five-fold grading system produced by Munro Fraser.[2] Other more complex methods include job component analysis and repertory grids.

The seven-point plan (Rodger)
The seven-point plan covers:

1. *Physical make-up* – health, physique, appearance, bearing and speech.
2. *Attainments* – education, qualifications, experience.
3. *General intelligence* – fundamental intellectual capacity.
4. *Special aptitudes* – mechanical, manual dexterity, facility in the use of words or figures.
5. *Interests* – intellectual, practical – constructional, physically active, social, artistic.
6. *Disposition* – acceptability, influence over others, steadiness, dependability, self-reliance.
7. *Circumstances* – domestic circumstances, occupations of family.

The five-fold grading system (Munro Fraser)
The five-fold grading system covers:

1. *Impact on others* – physical make-up, appearance, speech and manner.
2. *Acquired qualifications* – education, vocational training, work experience.
3. *Innate abilities* – natural quickness of comprehension and aptitude for learning.
4. *Motivation* – the kinds of goals set by the individual, his consistency and determination in following them up, his success in achieving them.
5. *Adjustment* – emotional stability, ability to stand up to stress and ability to get on with people.

Job component analysis

Job component analysis uses position analysis questionnaires (described in Chapter 9 on job analysis) to identify job elements which can be specifically linked to human characteristics. Shaw and McCormick[3] describe how each rating can be given a weight which reflects its relevance to a particular characteristic. The weighted ratings are then added up to produce an estimate of the level of the characteristics needed.

Repertory grids

Repertory grids are derived from the personal construct theory developed by Kelly[4] who postulated that people behave like scientists, exploring their environments, and on the basis of these explorations they construct mental maps of the world. These maps consist of the elements (the objects) and the constructs (the qualities which the objects have). Repertory grids are a procedure and a statistical technique which can be used to make the maps explicit. This process was described by Smith and Robertson[5] as follows:

> Producing a personnel specification and a job analysis is analogous to producing these mental maps: the analyst is the scientist, the elements are the tasks from a conventional job analysis, and the constructs are the characteristics included in the personnel specification. An unpublished example by Smith concerned the production of a job specification for supervisors in the knitting and hosiery industry. The Industry Training Board had previously conducted a conventional job analysis from which 29 common 'supervisor' tasks could be identified. A sample of 34 supervisors were interviewed in order to obtain the characteristics which supervisors needed in order to perform these tasks.
>
> The interview procedure followed the triadic method of elicitation commonly used in repertory grid methodology. Three of the tasks were chosen at random and the supervisor was asked to nominate which task was the odd man out in terms of the qualities and characteristics people need in order to do the tasks. Once they had nominated the odd man out they were asked to specify the quality or characteristic which made it the odd man out. This process was repeated until 10 to 12 different qualities had been elicited. This elicitation process has the advantages that the supervisor can answer in any terms he wishes; the investigator does not suggest any responses, yet the method samples the supervisor's ideas and forces him to make comparisons and contrasts. At the close of the interview the supervisor was asked to rate every task on every quality using a seven point scale. The data obtained from 34 supervisors could be cast into a 29 x 340 matrix which could be subjected to a principal component analysis. The results shown in Table 14.1 indicate that the job of supervisor required seven major characteristics.

Qualities	% of variance
Sympathetic but firm personality	18
Ability to communicate clearly	13
Ability to plan and organize	8
Ability to solve problems	7
Knowledge of the industry and the firm	6
Ability to maintain safety and discipline	5
Trouble-shooting	5

Table 14.1 *Qualities required of supervisors in the knitting industry*

Choice of method

Of these systems the seven-point plan has the longer pedigree. The five-fold grading scheme is simpler, in some ways, and places more emphasis on the dynamic aspects of the applicant's career. Both provide a good framework for interviewing although a more simple approach used by many interviewers is to start from the analysis of the knowledge and skills required and go on from there to define the minimum and the optimum education, qualifications, training and experience needed to succeed in the job. This leads on naturally to a specification of the personal and physical attributes required and to a definition of other requirements such as age limits, location of work, travelling, night or shift work. This information can be recorded on a personnel specification form as shown in Figure 14.4. The more complex systems can be used in circumstances where the jobs themselves are fairly complicated and the numbers to be recruited or trained are large.

Attracting candidates

Attracting candidates is primarily a matter of identifying, evaluating and using the most appropriate sources of applicants. However, in cases where difficulties in attracting or retaining candidates are being met or anticipated, it may be necessary to carry out a preliminary study of the factors that are likely to attract or repel candidates – the strengths and weaknesses of the organization as an employer.

Analysis of recruitment strengths and weaknesses

The analysis of strengths and weaknesses should cover such matters as the national or local reputation of the company, pay, fringe benefits and working conditions, the intrinsic interest of the job, security of employment, opportunities for education and training, career prospects, and the location of the office or plant. These need to be compared with competition so that a list of what are, in effect, selling points, can be drawn up as in a marketing exercise, in which the preferences of potential customers are compared with the features of the product so that those aspects which are likely to provide the most appeal to the consumers can be emphasized. Candidates are, in a sense, selling themselves, but they are also buying what the company has to offer. If, in the latter sense, the labour market is a buyer's market, then the company which is selling itself to candidates must study their needs in relation to what it can provide.

The aim of the study might be to prepare a better image of the company for use in advertisements, brochures or during interviews. Or it might have the more constructive aim of showing where the company needs to improve if it is to attract more or better candidates. The study could make use of an attitude survey to obtain the views of existing employees. One

Part 1: JOB DESCRIPTION	
Department	Section
Job title	Job grade
Reporting to (job title)	
Reporting to job holder (job titles)	
Overall purpose of job	
Main activities/tasks	
Special requirements (tools and equipment used, external contacts, etc.)	
Other features of job: shift or night work, travelling, working conditions, etc.	
Location of job	

Figure 14.4(a) Personnel specification form (part 1)

Part 2: JOB REQUIREMENTS
Knowledge and skills
Education, qualifications and special training
Experience
Personality requirements
Physical requirements
Other requirements Age Travel Hours Other

Figure 14.4(b) Personnel specification form (part 2)

such survey mounted by the writer in an engineering company wishing to attract science graduates elicited the response that the main concern of the graduates was that they would be able to use and develop the knowledge they gained at university. As a result, special brochures were written for each major discipline giving technical case histories of the sort of work graduates carried out. These avoided the purple prose used in some brochures (which the survey established was distinctly off-putting to most students) and were found to be a most useful recruitment aid. Steps were also taken to encourage research managers to make proper use of the graduates they recruited.

Sources of candidates

The main sources of candidates are:

- internal, by means of a search or 'trawl', as the Civil Service puts it more expressively, or by internal advertisements;
- external advertisements;
- employment agencies – private or government;
- education and training establishments;
- other external sources, unsolicited letters or casual callers, and recommendations from employees.

One source may suffice, or it may be necessary to tap a number of alternative sources. It depends upon the type of job to be filled, the relative difficulty of attracting candidates, the area in which the company operates and the history of success or failure in using different methods.

Clearly, if the job can be filled from inside, so much the better. Failing that, unsolicited inquiries and/or personal recommendations are to be preferred, if they are known to work and if the cost of maintaining an employment office to deal with inquiries is taken into account.

From a cost point of view, an approach to government employment agencies, schools, universities, or ex-servicemen employment agencies may be preferred to advertising or to the use of private agencies or consultants. But the effectiveness of the alternative sources must be taken into account as well as the indirect costs of using them or of having to put up with a longer waiting period before recruits can be obtained. External advertising may have to be used as the only reliable method of attracting candidates or to supplement other sources, but it is essential to evaluate such advertising properly in terms of cost per reply from each insertion.

The first choice of method may depend on the type of job, and typical methods for different categories of jobs are shown below:

Job Category	Typical Sources
1. Juveniles	Schools, youth employment agencies
2. Clerical and secretarial staff	Private employment agencies

Job Category	*Typical Sources*
3. Manual workers	Government employment and training centres
4. Professional staff	Advertisements, including the professional institutions themselves, where they operate an employment service and the Professional and Executive Recruitment Service (UK)
5. Graduates	Direct from universities, polytechnics and business schools
6. Managerial staff	Advertisements, consultants, the Professional and Executive Recruitment Service.

Advertising

Advertising is the most obvious method of attracting candidates. Nevertheless, the first question to ask is whether an advertisement is really justified. This means looking at the alternative sources mentioned above and confirming, preferably on the basis of experience, that they will not do. Consideration should be given as to whether it might be better to use an agency or a selection consultant. When making the choice, refer to the three criteria of cost, speed and the likelihood of providing good candidates. The objectives of an advertisement should be to:

- *attract attention* – competing for the interest of potential candidates against other employees;
- *create and maintain interest* – the advertisement has to communicate in an attractive and interesting way information about the job, the company, the terms and conditions of employment and the qualifications required;
- *stimulate action* – the message needs to be conveyed in a manner which will not only focus people's eyes on the advertisement but will also encourage them to read to the end and stimulate action in the form of a sufficient number of replies from good candidates.

To achieve these aims six things need to be done:

1. Analyse requirement.
2. Decide who does what.
3. Write the copy.
4. Design the advertisement.
5. Plan media.
6. Evaluate response.

Analyse requirement

First it is necessary to establish how many jobs have to be filled and by when. Then turn to the job description and specification to obtain information on responsibilities, qualifications and experience required, age limits, and any other data needed to draft the advertisement.

The next step is to consider where suitable candidates are likely to come from, the companies, jobs or education establishments they are in and the parts of the country where they can be found.

Finally, think about what is likely to attract them about the job or the company so the most can be made of these factors in the advertisement. Consider also what might put them off; for example, the location of the job, so that objections can be anticipated. Analyse previous successes or failures to establish what does or does not work.

Decide who does what

When planning a campaign or when recruiting key people there is much to be said for using an advertising agency. An agency can provide expertise in producing eye-catching headlines and writing good copy. It can devise an attractive house style and prepare layouts which make the most of the text, the logo and any 'white space' around the advertisement. Moreover, it can advise on ways of achieving visual impact by the use of illustrations and special typographical features. Finally, an agency can advise on media, help in response analysis and take up the burden of preparing blocks and placing advertisements.

The following steps should be taken when choosing an advertising agency:

1. Check experience in handling recruitment advertising.
2. See examples of its work.
3. Check with clients on the level of service provided.
4. Meet the staff who will be working on the advertisements.
5. Check the fee structure.
6. Discuss methods of working.

Write the copy

A recruitment advertisement should start with a compelling headline and then contain information on:

● the company
● the job
● the person required
● the benefits provided
● the location
● the action to be taken.

The headline is all important. The simplest and most obvious approach is to set out the job title in bold type. To gain attention it is advisable to quote the salary (if it is worth quoting) and to put 'plus car' if a company car is provided. Salaries and cars are major attractions and should be stated clearly. Applicants are rightly suspicious of phrases such as 'salary will be commensurate with age and experience'. This usually means either that the salary is so low that the company is afraid to reveal it, or that salary policies are so incoherent that the company has no idea what to offer until someone tells them what he wants.

The name of the company should be given. (Do not use box numbers – if you want to be anonymous use a consultant.) Add any selling points such as growth or diversification and any other areas of interest to potential candidates. The essential features of the job should be conveyed by giving a brief description of what the job holder will do and, as far as space permits, the scope and scale of activities. Create interest in the job but do not oversell it.

The qualifications and experience required should be stated as factually as possible and age limits (if any) should be given. There is no point in overstating requirements and seldom any point in specifying exactly how much experience is wanted. This will vary from candidate to candidate and the other details about the job and the salary should provide them with enough information about the sort of experience required. Be careful about including a string of personal qualities such as drive, determination and initiative. These have no real meaning to candidates. Phrases such as 'proven track record' and 'successful experience' are equally meaningless. No one will admit to not having either of them.

The advertisement should end with information on how the candidate should apply. 'Brief but comprehensive details' is a good phrase. Candidates can be asked to write, but useful alternatives are asking them to telephone or to come along for an informal chat at a suitable venue.

Remember that the Sex Discrimination Act 1975 makes it unlawful to discriminate in an advertisement by favouring either sex, the only exceptions being a few jobs which can only be done by a man or a woman. Advertisements must therefore avoid sexist job titles such as salesman or stewardess. They must refer to a neutral title such as 'sales representative' or amplify the description to cover both sexes by stating 'steward or stewardess'. It is accepted, however, that certain job titles are unisex and therefore non-discriminatory. These include director, manager, executive and officer. It is best to avoid any reference to the sex of the candidate by using neutral or unisex titles and referring only to the 'candidate' or the 'applicant'. Otherwise you must specify 'man or woman' or 'he or she'.

The Race Relations Act 1976 has similar provisions making unlawful an advertisement which discriminates against any particular race. As long as race is never mentioned or even implied in an advertisement, you should have no problem in keeping within the law.

Design the advertisement

The main types of advertisement are:

1. *Classified/run-on,* in which copy is run-on, with no white space in or around the advertisement and no paragraph spacing or indentation. They are cheap but suitable only for junior or routine jobs.
2. *Classified/semi-display,* in which the headings can be set in capitals, paragraphs can be indented and white space is allowed round the advertisement. They are fairly cheap and semi-display can be much more effective than run-on advertisements.
3. *Full display,* which are bordered and in which any typeface and illustrations can be used. They can be expensive but obviously will make the most impact for management, technical and professional jobs.

Professional advice in designing display advertisements is desirable. The aim should be simplicity. Logos, illustrations, pre-set headings and borders and different typefaces can all help to achieve impact, but avoid creating too cluttered an impression. Use of 'white spaces' can be very effective.

Plan media

An advertising agency can advise on the choice of media (press, radio, television) and its cost. *British Rates and Data* (BRAD) can be consulted to give the costs of advertising in particular media.

The quality papers are best for managerial, professional and technical jobs. The popular papers can be used to reach less qualified staff such as sales representatives and technicians. Local papers are obviously best for recruiting clerical, secretarial and manual workers. Professional and trade journals can reach your audience directly, but results can be erratic and it is often best to use them to supplement a national campaign.

Avoid Saturdays and be cautious about repeating advertisements in the same medium. Diminishing returns can set in rapidly.

Evaluate response

Measure response to provide guidance on the relative cost effectiveness of different media. Cost per reply is the best ratio.

Using agencies

Most private agencies deal with secretarial and clerical staff. They are usually quick and effective but quite expensive. London agencies charge a fee averaging 15 per cent of the first year's salary for finding someone. It can be cheaper to advertise, especially when the company is in a buyer's market. Shop around to find the agency which suits the company's needs at a reasonable cost.

Agencies should be briefed carefully on what is wanted. They will produce unsuitable candidates from time to time but the risk is reduced if they are clear about your requirements.

Using selection consultants

Selection consultants generally advertise, interview and produce a short-list. They provide expertise and reduce workload. The company can be anonymous if it wishes. Most selection consultants charge a fee based on a percentage of the basic salary for the job, ranging from 15 to 20 per cent. The following steps should be taken when choosing a selection consultant:

1. Check reputation with other users if there are any doubts.
2. Look at the advertisements of the various firms. An idea of the quality of a consultancy and the type and level of jobs with which it deals can thus be gained.
3. Check on special expertise. The large accountancy firms, for example, are obviously skilled in recruiting accountants.
4. Meet the consultant who will work on the assignment to assess his quality.
5. Compare fees, although the differences are likely to be small, and the other considerations will usually be more important.

When using a selection consultant do the following:

1. Brief them clearly on their terms of reference.
2. Give every assistance to the consultant in defining the job and the company's requirements. He will do much better if he knows what type of person is most likely to fit well into the company.
3. Check carefully the proposed programme and the draft text of the advertisement.
4. Clarify the basis upon which fees and expenses will be charged.
5. Ensure that arrangements are made to deal directly with the consultant who will handle the assignment.

Using executive search consultants

Use an executive search consultant or 'head hunter' for senior jobs where there are only a limited number of suitable people and a direct lead to them is wanted. They are not cheap. Head hunters charge a fee of 30-50 per cent of the first year's salary, but they can be quite cost effective.

Head hunters first approach their own contacts in the industry or profession concerned; the more numerous the contacts the better the head hunter. Some may be interested in the job themselves, others may provide leads to people who can be approached. If this fails, the consultant will telephone likely people, even if there is no indication that they are interested. Those who receive unexpected calls from a head hunter are often flattered or interested enough to agree to see him. A fairly relaxed and informal meeting then takes place and the consultant forwards the names of suitable and interested candidates to his client.

There are some good and some not-so-good executive search consultants. Do not use one unless a reliable recommendation is obtained.

Selecting candidates

Sifting applications

Assuming that the vacancy or vacancies have been advertised and that a fair number of replies have been received, the typical sequence of steps required to process and sift applications is as follows:

1. List the applications on a standard control sheet such as the one illustrated in Figure 14.5.

Ref.		Vacancy					
Media							
No.	Media Ref.	Name	Address	Grading	Acknow-ledge	Inter-view	Final letter
1							
2							
3							
4							
5							
6							
7							
8							
9							
10							

Figure 14.5 Recruitment control sheet

2. Send a standard acknowledgement letter to each applicant unless an instant decision can be made to interview or reject. If there is

insufficient information in the initial letter, the applicant could be asked to complete and return an application form. To save time, trouble, expense and irritation, it is best to make a decision on the initial letter rather than ask for a form.

3. Compare the applications with the key criteria in the job specification: qualifications, training, experience, age and location, and sort them initially into three categories:
   - possible
   - marginal
   - unsuitable.

4. Scrutinize the possibles again to draw up a shortlist for interview. This scrutiny could be carried out by the personnel or employment specialist, and, preferably, the manager.

5. Invite the candidates to interview, using a standard letter where large numbers are involved. At this stage candidates should be asked to complete an application form, if they have not already done so.

6. Review the remaining possibles and marginals and decide if any are to be held in reserve. Send reserves a standard 'holding' letter and send the others a standard rejection letter. This should express thanks to the candidate for the interest he has shown and inform him briefly, but not too brusquely, that he has not been successful. A typical reject letter might read as follows:

> Since writing to you on . . . we have given careful consideration to your application for the above position. I regret to inform you, however, that we have decided not to ask you to attend for an interview. We should like to thank you for the interest you have shown.

Application forms

Application forms are required as a means of setting out the information on a candidate in a standardized format. They provide a basis both for the interview and for the subsequent actions in offering an appointment and in setting up personnel records. An example of a form is given in Figure 14.6(a), (b), (c) and (d).

Interviewing arrangements

The interviewing arrangements will depend partly on the procedure being used, which may consist of individual interviews, an interviewing panel, a selection board or some form of group selection procedure. The main features of these alternative procedures are described later in this section but, in most cases, the arrangements for the interviews should conform broadly to the following pattern:

- The candidate who has applied in writing or by telephone should

BCA
BOOK CLUB ASSOCIATES

APPLICATION FOR EMPLOYMENT

SURNAME	FIRST NAMES	
ADDRESS	MAIDEN NAME (IF APPLICABLE)	
	DATE OF BIRTH	
	COUNTRY OF BIRTH	
TELEPHONE (HOME)	MARITAL STATUS	
TELEPHONE (WORK)	NUMBER OF CHILDREN	
POSITION APPLIED FOR		
WHERE DID YOU LEARN OF THIS VACANCY?		

Figure 14.6(a) Application form

EDUCATION AND TRAINING
QUALIFICATIONS

What academic and/or professional qualifications do you hold?
(Use initials to indicate this e.g. C.S.E., 'O' Level, B.Sc., A.C.A. etc.)

SECONDARY EDUCATION

Dates		Name of school or college	Give details of major subjects studied, examinations taken and results
From	To		

EDUCATION BEYOND SECONDARY LEVEL

Dates		Name of college/university or other institution (Indicate if part-time or by home study)	Give details of major subjects studied, examinations taken and results
From	To		

TRAINING

Give details of any specialised training received and/or courses attended

OTHER SKILLS

Other qualifications and skills (including languages, current driving licence, keyboard skills, etc.)

Figure 14.6(b) Application form

EMPLOYMENT HISTORY

Give details here of all positions held since completing your full time education. Start with your present or most recent position and work back.

Dates		Name of employer, address and nature of business. Include any service with the Armed Forces.	Position and duties	Starting and leaving salary and any other benefits	Reason for leaving or wanting to leave
from	to				

Figure 14.6(c) Application form

INTERESTS

Please describe your leisure interests.

ADDITIONAL INFORMATION AND COMMENTS

Do you have any permanent or persistent health problems? Please give details.

Have you ever worked for Book Club Associates? Please give details.

Please state salary required.

When would you be able to start work, if you were offered a position?

Please give the names and addresses of *two* persons who are in a position to comment on your professional/work ability. (References will not be taken up without your knowledge)

Name _____   Name _____

Address _____   Address _____

_____   _____

_____ Telephone no. _____   _____ Telephone no. _____

Position _____   Position _____

Add any comments you wish to make to support your application.

I confirm that the information given on this application form is correct.

Signature of applicant _____ Date _____

Figure 14.6(d) Application form

be told where and when to come and whom to ask for. The interview time should be arranged to fit in with the time it will take to get to the company. It may be necessary to adjust times for those who cannot get away during working hours. If the company is difficult to find, a map should be sent with details of public transport. The receptionist or security guard should be told who is coming. Candidates are impressed to find that they are expected.

● Applicants should have somewhere quiet and comfortable in which to wait for the interview, with reading material available and access to cloakroom facilities.

● The interviewers or interviewing panel should have been well briefed on the programme. Interviewing rooms should have been booked and arrangements made, as necessary, for welcoming candidates, for escorting them to interviews, for meals and for a conducted tour round the company.

● Comfortable private rooms should be provided for interviews with little, if any, distractions around them. Interviewers should preferably not sit behind their desks as this creates a psychological barrier.

● During the interview or interviews, time should be allowed to tell the candidate about the company and the job and to discuss with him conditions of employment. Negotiations about salaries and other benefits may take place after a provisional offer has been made, but it is as well to prepare the ground during the interviewing stage.

● Candidates should be told what the next step will be at the end of the interview. They may be asked at this stage if they have any objections to references being taken up.

● Follow-up studies should be carried out of the performance of successful candidates on the job compared with the prediction made at the selection stage. These studies should be used to validate the selection procedure and to check on the capabilities of interviewers.

Individual interviews

The individual interview is the most familiar method of selection. It involves face-to-face discussion and provides the best opportunity for the establishment of close contact – *rapport* – between the interviewer and the candidate. If only one interviewer is used, there is more scope for a biased or superficial decision, and this is one reason for using a second interviewer or an interviewing panel.

Interviewing panels

Two or three people gathered together to interview one candidate may be described as an interviewing panel. The most typical situation is when a personnel man and line managers see the candidate at the same time. This has the advantage of enabling information to be shared and reducing overlaps. The two interviewers can discuss their joint impressions of the candidate's behaviour at the interview and modify or enlarge any superficial judgements.

Selection boards

Selection boards are more formal and, usually, larger interviewing panels convened by an official body because there are a number of parties interested in the selection decision. Their only advantage is that they enable a number of different people to have a look at the applicants and compare notes on the spot. The disadvantages are that the questions tend to be unplanned and delivered at random, the prejudices of a dominating member of the board can overwhelm the judgements of the other members, and the candidates are unable to do justice to themselves because they are seldom allowed to expand. Selection boards tend to favour the confident and articulate candidate, but in doing so they may miss the underlying weaknesses of a superficially impressive individual. They can also underestimate the qualities of someone who happens to be less effective in front of a formidable board, although he would be fully competent in the less formal or less artificial situations that would face him in the job.

Group selection

A group selection procedure involves gathering a number of candidates together (ideally six to eight) in the presence of a group of interviewers/ observers (ideally two or three). The candidates are subjected to a series of exercises and tests which are supplemented by individual or panel interviews.

The group exercises may be of the 'analogous' type in which the group is given a case study to discuss, which includes features and problems similar to those they would meet if they joined the organization. Or the group may be asked to discuss a general social or economic problem. They may even be sat down and asked to agree amongst themselves what they are going to discuss.

Members of the group may be tested on leadership qualities by being asked to take turns in leading the group, or the groups may not have appointed leaders, so that leadership qualities can emerge in discussion.

The observers will rate or rank participants in respect of a set of factors such as:

- ability to think in a logical manner about the problem posed;
- realistic, practical approach to the problem;
- confidence in putting his views to the group;
- willingness to follow and consider other people's opinions;
- tendency to emerge as a leader in the group;
- willingness to accept criticisms of his ideas.

Ranking on each of these characteristics is sometimes preferred to rating on a numerical scale because of the difficulty of ensuring that the raters maintain a uniform standard of judgement.

In addition to the group discussions, candidates may be tested on their ability to express themselves in writing by being given paper exercises. Their ability to express themselves and to present a case orally may be tested by asking them to deliver 'lecturettes' or to make a presentation of a proposal to the group based on the study of a brief.

Individual abilities and qualities can be discussed by administering a battery of intelligence, personality and aptitude tests.

Group selection procedures are time-consuming and expensive to run but they appear to be a more comprehensive method of making selection decisions, ie they have 'face validity'. This is because they expose candidates to a number of more or less realistic situations and enable interviewers to see them in action with others as well as individually. A number of studies have been carried out on their *true* validity – that is, their value as a means of predicting future performance in the job, and one conducted for the Civil Service Commission showed that the selection procedure as a whole had a considerable degree of validity when judged in the light of follow-up information about the performance of successful candidates.

But Vernon sounded the following warning on group selection procedures:

> They are likely to be somewhat superior to the conventional interview method of assessing people, because they provide a more prolonged and varied set of situations in which to observe and interpret. But they are just as dependent as the interview on the skill, experience and impartiality of the observer and they should be applied with all the more caution because they engender in the observers an undue measure of confidence in the accuracy of their judgements.[6]

The interview

The purpose of the interview is to obtain and assess information about a candidate which will enable a valid prediction to be made of his future performance on the job in comparison with the predictions made for any other candidates. Interviewing therefore involves processing and evaluating evidence about the capabilities of a candidate in relation to the job specification. Some of the evidence will be on the application form but this must be supplemented by the more detailed or specific information about experience and personal characteristics that can be obtained in a face-to-face meeting. Further evidence may be obtained from selection tests or from references but the interview remains the main source of information.

An interview has been described as a conversation with a purpose. It is a conversation because the candidate should be drawn out to talk freely with his interviewer about himself and his career. But the conversation has to be planned, directed and controlled to achieve the main purpose of the interview, which is to make an accurate prediction of the candidate's future performance in the job for which he is being considered.

Interviewers, however, have other aims. One is to provide the candidate with information about the job and the company. An interview is basically an exchange of information which will enable both parties to make a decision: to offer or not to offer a job; to accept or not to accept the offer. A further aim is to give the candidate a favourable impression of the company. This should encourage the good candidate to join and should leave the rejected candidates without any ill-feelings.

A good interviewer knows what he is looking for, then knows how to set about finding it. Finally, he has a method for recording his analysis of the candidate against a set of assessment criteria.

Knowing what to look for
Knowing what to look for is a matter of knowing the job specification and the information needed to confirm whether or not the candidate meets the specification under each of its headings: qualifications, experience, knowledge, skills, physical and personality characteristics, personal circumstances.

Knowing how to find it
Knowing how to find the information required is a matter first of planning the interview and then of conducting it in a way which will obtain all the data needed to make a balanced decision.

The interview should be planned around the candidate's application form to cover each of the headings on the job specification. It is therefore essential to read the application form thoroughly before the interview to decide on the line of questions and any areas where probing may be required. The aim is to establish exactly what the applicant knows and can do or to fill any gaps in his employment record. A biographical approach is usually best, starting with the applicant's education (especially younger candidates) and then moving progressively and naturally through his work experience, job by job, discussing for each job: why he took it, what he did, what knowledge and skills he acquired and why he left it. Clearly, the interview should concentrate on the most recent experience. There is no point in dwelling for long on the earlier experience of someone who has been in employment for a number of years.

The information required in an interview can seldom be obtained in less than 20 minutes, but it is usually unproductive to extend the information-gathering part of the interview beyond 30 to 40 minutes. Allowance has also to be made for the information-giving part of the interview and for the candidate's questions. For a managerial interview, a longer period may be necessary to discuss recent experience and ambitions more thoroughly. Time must also be allowed for information about the company and the job, and for the candidate to ask questions. The best approach is to start with a few welcoming remarks and explain how the interview is to be planned. Then carry out the biographical interview before telling the candidate about the job and discussing conditions of employment, including pay and fringe benefits. There is no point in giving a lengthy dissertation about the company or the work to someone who is clearly unsuitable or uninterested. Allow time at the end for questions and round off the interview by telling the candidate what the next step will be. It is normally better not to announce the final decision during the interview. It may be advisable to obtain references and, in any case, time is required to reflect on the information received. Moreover, some candidates, especially senior staff and students, do not like to think that snap decisions are being made about them, even if they are favourable. These points are summarized in Table 14.2.

Do	Don't
☐ plan the interview	☐ start the interview unprepared
☐ establish an easy and informal relationship	☐ plunge too quickly into demanding questions
☐ encourage the candidate to talk	☐ ask leading questions
☐ cover the ground as planned	☐ jump to conclusions on inadequate evidence
☐ probe where necessary	
☐ analyse career and interests to reveal strengths, weaknesses, patterns of behaviour	☐ pay too much attention to isolated strengths or weaknesses
☐ maintain control over the direction and time taken by the interview	☐ allow the candidate to gloss over important facts
	☐ talk too much

Table 14.2 *Do's and dont's of interviewing*

Assessment of criteria

The criteria for assessing candidates and the method of recording assessments should either be standardized for regular recruitment exercises or, if a one-off recruitment is being carried out, they should be drawn up in advance of the interviewing stage.

The criteria should obviously be those used in drawing up the job specification: for example, the seven points or the five factors in the two schemes referred to earlier in this chapter.

Admirable though these systems may be when they are used by a skilled personnel practitioner or a trained manager, they sometimes prove too complex for the typical line manager or selection board. It may therefore be necessary to devise a simplified set of criteria for their use which can be expressed in terms a layman can understand with the minimum of training.

In any situation in which non-specialists are making selection decisions it is best to use criteria which can be defined simply in familiar language and can easily be related to a job specification. The following criteria, which were mentioned earlier in this chapter when discussing job specifications, are used by managers in practice even if they do not necessarily analyse them under precisely similar headings:

- qualifications and training;
- experience;
- knowledge and skills – as required by experience, training and education or the natural abilities the individual possesses;
- overall impression – appearance, manner and speech, physique, health (physical characteristics);
- personality characteristics – leadership, drive, dependability, persistence, self-reliance, sociability.

An interview record form using these criteria is illustrated in Figure 14.7.

Vacancy	Candidate					
Factor	*Comments*	Rating				
		A	B	C	D	E
Qualifications and training						
Experience						
Knowledge and skills						
Personality characteristics						
Overall impression						
Recommendation						
A = Very much above average; B = Above average; C = Average; D = Below average; E = Very much below average.						

Figure 14.7 Interview assessment form

Whatever assessment criteria are used, it is essential to follow up interviews to find out if the assessments and predictions have been validated by performance on the job. This is the only way in which interviewers can ever find out how effective they are. It takes time and trouble, and valid criteria are not always easy to identify, but it is well worthwhile.

Psychometric tests

The purpose of a selection test is to provide an objective means of measuring individual abilities or characteristics. These involve the application of standard procedures to subjects which enable their responses to be quantified. The differences in the numerical scores represent differences in abilities or behaviour.

A good test has the following four characteristics:

1. It is a *sensitive measuring instrument* which discriminates well between subjects.
2. It will have been *standardized* on a representative and sizeable sample of the population for which it is intended so that any individual's score can be interpreted in relation to that of others.
3. It is *reliable* in the sense that it always measures the same thing. A test aimed at measuring a particular characteristic, such as intelligence, should measure the same characteristic when applied to different people at the same or a different time, or to the same person at different times.
4. It is *valid* in the sense that it measures the characteristic which the test is intended to measure. Thus an intelligence test should measure intelligence (however defined) and not simply verbal facility. A test meant to predict success in a job or in passing examinations should produce reasonably convincing (statistically significant) predictions.

The main types of psychometric tests used for selection are intelligence tests, aptitude and attainment tests, and personality tests.

Intelligence tests

Intelligence tests are the oldest and most frequently used psychological tests. The first test was produced by Binet and Simon in 1905, and shortly afterwards, Stern suggested that the test scores should be expressed in the form of intelligence quotients, or IQs. An IQ is the ratio of the mental age as measured by a Binet-type test to the actual (chronological) age. When the mental and chronological age correspond, the IQ is expressed as 100. It is assumed that intelligence is distributed normally throughout the population, that is, the frequency distribution of intelligence corresponds to the normal curve shown in Figure 14.8.

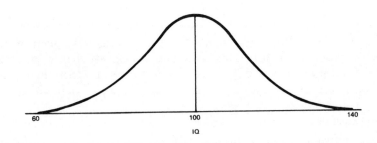

60   100   140
                        IQ

Figure 14.8 A normal curve

The most important characteristic of the normal curve is that it is symmetrical – there are an equal number of cases on either side of the mean, the central axis. Thus the distribution of intelligence in the population as a whole consists of an equal number of people with IQs above and below 100.

The difficulty with intelligence tests is that they have to be based on a theory of what constitutes intelligence and then have to derive a series of verbal and non-verbal instruments for measuring the different factors or constituents of intelligence. But intelligence is a highly complex concept. There is no agreed definition of it amongst psychologists and the variety of theories about intelligence and the consequent variations in the test instrument or battery available makes the choice of an intelligence test a difficult one. For general selection purposes, a test which can be administered to a group of candidates is the best, especially if it has been properly validated and it is possible to relate test scores to 'norms' in such a way as to indicate how the individual taking the test compares with the rest of the population, in general or in a specific area.

Aptitude and attainment tests

Aptitude tests are designed to predict the potential an individual has to perform a job or specific tasks within a job. They can cover such areas as clerical aptitude, numerical aptitude, mechanical aptitude and dexterity.

All aptitude tests should be properly validated. The usual procedure is to determine the qualities required for the job by means of a job analysis. A standard test or a test battery is then obtained from a test agency. Alternatively, a special test is devised by or for the company. The test is then given to employees already working on the job and the results compared with a criterion, usually supervisor's ratings. If the correlation between test and criterion is sufficiently high, the test is then given to applicants. To validate the test further, a follow-up study of the job performance of the applicants selected by the test is usually carried out. This is a lengthy procedure, but without it no real confidence can be attached to the results of any aptitude test. Many do-it-yourself tests are worse than useless because they have not been properly validated.

Attainment tests measure abilities or skills that have already been acquired by training or experience. A typing test is the most typical example. It is easy to find out how many words a minute a typist can type and compare that with the standard required for the job.

Personality tests

The term 'personality' is all-embracing in terms of the individual's behaviour and the way it is organized and co-ordinated when he or she interacts with the environment. There are many different theories of personality and, consequently, many different types of personality tests. These include self-report personality questionnaires and other questionnaires which measure interests, values or work behaviour.

Self-report personality questionnaires are the ones most commonly used. They adopt a 'trait' approach, defining a trait as a fairly independent but enduring characteristic of behaviour which all people display but to differing degrees. Trait theorists like Cattell or Guilford identify examples of common behaviour, devise scales to measure these and then obtain ratings on these behaviours by people who know each other well. These observations are analysed statistically using the factor analysis technique to identify distinct traits and to indicate how associated groups of traits might be grouped loosely into personality 'types'. There are a number of questionnaires to choose from and reference should be made for further guidance on what is available to *Testing, A Practical Guide* by Toplis, Pulewicz and Fletcher (Institute of Personnel Management, 1987), which covers the whole subject of tests very thoroughly.

'Interest' questionnaires are sometimes used to supplement personality tests. They assess the preferences of respondents for particular types of occupations and are therefore most applicable to vocational guidance but can be helpful when selecting apprentices and trainees.

'Value' questionnaires attempt to assess beliefs about what is desirable or 'good' or what is undesirable or 'bad'. The questionnaires measure the relative prominence of such values as conformity, independence, achievement, decisiveness, orderliness and goal-orientation.

Specific work behaviour questionnaires cover behaviours such as leadership (Fleischman's Leadership Opinion Questionnaire) or selling (The Poppleton-Allen Sales Aptitude Test).

Personality tests can provide interesting supplementary information about candidates which is free from the biased reactions that frequently occur in face-to-face interviews. But they have to be used with great care. The tests should have been developed by a reputable psychologist or test agency on the basis of extensive research and field testing and they must meet the specific needs of the user.

Choosing tests
It is essential to choose tests which meet the four criteria of sensitivity, standardization, reliability and validity. It is very difficult to achieve the standards required if a company tries to develop its own test batteries unless it employs a qualified psychologist or obtains professional advice from a member of the British Psychological Society. This organization, with the full support and understanding of the reputable test suppliers, exercises rigorous control over who can use what tests and the standard of training required and given. Particular care should be taken when selecting personality tests – there are a lot of charlatans about.

Do-it-yourself tests are always suspect unless they have been properly validated and realistic norms have been established. Generally speaking, it is best to avoid using them.

The use of tests in a selection procedure

Tests are most likely to be helpful when they are used as part of a selection procedure for occupations where a large number of recruits are required, and where it is not possible to rely entirely on examination results or information about previous experience as the basis for predicting future performance. In these circumstances it is economic to develop and administer the tests and a sufficient number of cases can be built up for the essential validation exercise.

Intelligence tests are particularly helpful in situations where intelligence is a key factor but there is no other reliable method of measuring it. It may, incidentally, be as important to use an intelligence test to keep out applicants who are too intelligent for the job as to use one to guarantee a minimum level of intelligence. A validation exercise with which the author was concerned on tests for van salesmen established that applicants above a certain level of intelligence should be rejected, unless they have promotion potential, because they could not settle down in the job.

Aptitude and attainment tests are most useful for jobs where specific and measurable skills are required, such as typing or computer programming. Personality tests are potentially of greatest value in jobs such as selling where 'personality' is important and where it is not too difficult to obtain quantifiable criteria for validation purposes.

Tests should only be administered by staff who have been thoroughly trained in what the tests are measuring, how they should be used and how they should be interpreted.

It is essential to evaluate all tests by comparing the results at the interview stage with later achievements. To be statistically significant, these evaluations should be carried out over a reasonable period of time and cover as large a number of candidates as possible.

In some situations a battery of tests may be associated, including various types of intelligence, aptitude and personality tests. These may be a standard battery supplied by a test agency, or a custom-built battery may be used. The biggest pitfall to avoid is adding extra tests just for the sake of it, without ensuring that they make a proper contribution to the success of the predictions for which the battery is being used.

Offers and references

After the interviewing and testing procedure has been completed a provisional decision to make an offer orally by telephone or in writing can be made. This will normally be 'subject to satisfactory references' and the candidate should, of course, be told that these will be taken up. If there is more than one eligible candidate for a job it may be advisable to hold one or two people in reserve. Applicants can often change their minds, especially those whose only purpose in applying for the job was to carry out a 'test marketing' operation, or to obtain a lever with which to persuade their present employers to value them more highly.

References

The purpose of a reference is to obtain in confidence factual information about a prospective employee and opinions about his character and suitability for a job.

The factual information is straightforward and essential. It is simply necessary to confirm the nature of the previous job, the period of time in employment, the reason for leaving (if relevant), the salary or rate of pay and, possibly, the attendance record.

Opinions about character and suitability are less reliable and should be treated with caution. The reason is obvious. Previous or present employers who give references tend to avoid highly detrimental remarks either out of charity or because they think anything they say or write may be construed as slanderous, or libellous (references are, in fact, privileged as long as they are given without malice and are factually correct).

Personal referees are, of course, entirely useless. All they prove is that the applicant has at least one or two friends.

Written references save time, especially if they are standardized. They may take the form of an invitation to write a letter confirming the employment record and commenting on the applicant's character in general. If brief details about the job are included (these may be an extract from the advertisement – they should certainly not be an over-elaborate job description), the previous employer can be asked to express his views about the suitability of the individual for the job. But this is asking a lot. Unless the job and companies are identical, how well can any existing or ex-employer judge the suitability of someone he may not know particularly well for another job in a different environment?

More precise answers may be obtained if a standard form is provided for the employer to complete. The questions asked on this form should be limited to the following:

    (a) What was the period of employment?
    (b) What was the job title?
    (c) What work was carried out?
    (d) What was the rate of pay or salary?
    (e) How many days' absence over the last twelve months?
    (f) Would you re-employ (if not, why not)?

Question (f) is the key one, if it is answered honestly.

Telephone references may be used as an alternative or an addition to written references. The great advantage of a telephone conversation is that people are more likely to give an honest opinion orally than if they have to commit themselves in writing. It may also save time to use the telephone.

Employer references are necessary but they are unreliable. A satisfactory reference has to be treated at its face value – all one can be reasonably certain about is that the factual details will be correct. A very glowing reference may arouse suspicion, and it is worth comparing it with a reference from another employer (two employment references are desirable in any case). Poor or grudging references must create some alarm if only because they are so infrequent. But allowance should be made for prejudice and a check should be made, by telephone if possible.

Confirming the offer

The final stage in the selection procedure is to confirm the offer of employment after satisfactory references have been obtained and the applicant has passed the medical examination required for pension and life assurance purposes or because a certain standard of physical fitness is required for the work. The contract of employment should also be prepared at this stage.

Contracts of employment

The basic information that should be included in a written contract of employment will vary according to the level of job, but the following checklist sets out the typical headings:

- job title;
- duties, including a phrase such as 'The employee will perform such duties and will be responsible to such person, as the Company may from time to time direct';
- date when continuous employment starts and basis for calculating service;
- rate of pay, allowances, overtime and shift rates, method of payment;
- hours of work including lunch break and overtime and shift arrangements;
- holiday arrangements:
    - days paid holiday per year;
    - calculation of holiday pay;
    - qualifying period;
    - accrual of holidays and holiday pay;
    - details of holiday year;
    - dates when holidays can be taken;
    - maximum holiday that can be taken at any one time;
    - carry over of holiday entitlement;
    - public holidays;

- sickness:
    - pay for time lost;
    - duration of sickness payments;
    - deductions of national insurance benefits;
    - termination due to continued illness;
    - notification of illness (medical certificate);
- length of notice due to and from employee;
- grievance procedure (or reference to it);
- disciplinary procedure (or reference to it);
- works rules (or reference to them);
- arrangements for terminating employment;
- arrangements for union membership (if applicable);
- special terms relating to rights to patents and designs, confidential information and restraints on trade after termination of employment;
- employer's right to vary terms of the contract subject to proper notification being given.

Induction

Induction is the process of receiving and welcoming an employee when he first joins a company and giving him the basic information he needs to settle down quickly and happily and start work. Induction has three aims:

- to smooth the preliminary stages when everything is likely to be strange and unfamiliar to the new starter;
- to establish quickly a favourable attitude to the company in the mind of the new employee so that he or she is more likely to stay;
- to obtain effective output from the new employee in the shortest possible time.

Company induction

The first stage in induction is when the employee arrives at the company. He or she should be welcomed by a responsible person (not simply a commissionaire or a junior wages clerk) who can provide basic information about the company and terms and conditions of employment. Some of the information will confirm what the employee has already been told, some will be new, but there is a limit to how much can be conveyed at this stage.

An employee handbook is useful for this purpose. It need not be too glossy, but it should convey clearly and simply what new staff need to know under the following headings:

- a brief description of the company – its history, products, organization and management;
- basic conditions of employment – hours of work, holidays, pension scheme, insurance;

- pay – pay scales, when paid and how, deductions, queries;
- sickness – notification of absence, certificates, pay;
- leave of absence;
- works rules;
- disciplinary procedure;
- grievance procedure;
- promotion procedure;
- union and joint consultation arrangements;
- education and training facilities;
- health and safety arrangements;
- medical and first-aid facilities;
- restaurant and canteen facilities;
- social and welfare arrangements;
- telephone calls and correspondence;
- travelling and subsistence expenses.

If the organization is not large enough to justify a printed handbook, the least that can be done is to prepare a typed summary of this information.

Company induction procedures, however, should not rely on the printed word. The member of the personnel department or other individual who is looking after new employees should run through the main points with each individual or, when larger numbers are being taken on, with groups of people. In this way, a more personal touch is provided and queries can be answered.

When the initial briefing has been completed the new employee should be taken to his place of work and introduced to his manager or supervisor for the departmental induction programme. Alternatively, he may go straight to a training school and join the department later.

Departmental induction

The departmental induction programme should, wherever possible, start with the departmental manager, not the immediate supervisor. The manager may limit his remarks to a general welcome and a brief description of the work of the department before handing the new employee over to his supervisor for the more detailed induction. But it is important for the manager to be involved at this stage so that he is not seen as a remote figure by the new employee. And at least this means that the new starter will not be simply a name or a number to him.

The detailed induction is probably best carried out by the immediate supervisor who should have five main aims:

- to put the new employee at ease;
- to interest the employee in the job and the company;
- to provide basic information about working arrangements;

- to indicate the standards of performance and behaviour expected from the employee;
- to tell the employee about training arrangements and how he or she can get on with the company.

Follow up

It is essential to follow up newly engaged employees to ensure that they have settled in and to check on how well they are doing. If there are any problems it is much better to identify them at an early stage rather than allowing them to fester.

Following up is also important as a means of checking on the selection procedure. If by any chance a mistake has been made, it is useful to find out how it happened so that the selection procedure can be improved. Misfits can be attributed to a number of causes, for example: an inadequate job description or specification, poor sourcing of candidates, weak advertising, poor interviewing techniques, the use of inappropriate or invalidated tests, or prejudice on the part of the selector. If any of these are identified, steps can be taken to prevent their recurrence.

References

1. Rodger, A *The Seven-Point Plan*. National Institute of Industrial Psychology, London, 1952.
2. Munro Fraser, J *A Handbook of Employment Interviewing*. Macdonald and Evans, London, 1954.
3. Shaw, J M and McCormick, E J *The Prediction of Job Ability Requirement Using Attribute Data Based upon the Position Analysis Questionnaire*. Report prepared for USA Office of Naval Research. Purdue University, Purdue, 1976.
4. Kelly, G A *The Psychology of Personal Constructs*. Norton, New York, 1955.
5. Smith, M and Robertson, I T *Systematic Staff Selection*. Macmillan, London, 1986.
6. Vernon, P E 'The Validation of Civil Service Board Selection Procedures', *Occupational Psychology*, Vol 24, 1950, pp 75-95.

Part V
Employment and Personnel Administration

This handbook emphasizes the importance of strategic considerations in formulating personnel policies and planning personnel programmes to achieve defined objectives. The fact remains, however, that much of personnel management is about dealing with the problems that will always arise when people work together and have to be managed and the various services and facilities needed to ensure that both they and the organization feel that their needs are being satisfied.

Employment practices are concerned with the ways in which day-to-day matters relating to personnel management are dealt with. These include procedures for handling grievances, discipline, redundancies and transfers. The personnel department has also to provide a number of important services aimed at ensuring that the organization meets its social and legal responsibilities for its employees with regard to providing a healthy and safe working environment, looking after the welfare of individuals and making social facilities available for employees in accordance with their needs.

Finally, the function of the Personnel Department is to keep personnel records and, increasingly, to develop and maintain a computerized personnel information system. This operates from a database that provides the means for achieving efficiency in personnel administration as well as the opportunity to make decisions which are founded on a deeper understanding of what is happening now and may occur in the future.

Chapter 15
Employment Practices and Procedures

Employee resourcing is not just about organizing, obtaining, appraising and training people. It is also about dealing with specific issues and problems concerning their employment, often on a day-to-day basis. Practices and procedures should be developed in the following areas:

1. Grievances.
2. Discipline.
3. Redundancy.
4. Transfers.
5. Promotions.

This chapter considers the basic principles which should be taken into account in each area. The precise practice to be followed will, of course, depend on the circumstances in the organization. For example, a large bureaucratic-type organization is likely to adopt a fairly rigid procedure for promotions, involving internal advertisements, formal reviews and appointment boards, all of which may be related to a career planning system. In a smaller, informal organization the procedures will be much more flexible. But the principles of giving people equal opportunity for promotion and assessing their capabilities fairly will be the same in each case.

Grievances

It is often said that the best way to settle grievances is to get the facts and then settle on an equitable solution. This is easier said than done. The problem is frequently hedged around with matters of opinion, and it is essential to attempt to penetrate the facade – the ostensible problem or grievance – and reach the real feelings. In any case facts are always subject to interpretation and feelings are, by definition, subjective. It will not be possible to reach behind the facade or achieve the co-operation of the individual in solving the problem if an autocratic or directive approach is adopted – ie *telling* someone what is wrong and how to improve. More co-operation and more information will be obtained if the following non-directive approach is used:

1. *Listen with intelligence and sympathy.* People in difficulty cannot fail to benefit if they are allowed to discuss their problems with a sympathetic listener: attentive silence is often the interviewer's best contribution.
2. *Define the problem.* Ideally, interviewees define the problems for themselves with the aid of sympathetic listening and brief, well-directed questions. It is essential to get the problem clearly stated and accepted as a problem by interviewees as well as interviewers. A considerable amount of listening and questioning may be necessary before the point becomes clear since strong emotions and clarity of expression seldom go together. When you think you understand the interviewee's viewpoint it is often helpful to ask a summarizing question – 'is that what you mean?' – without passing any moral judgement at this stage.
3. *Stay alert and flexible.* Plan the interview in advance to decide broadly how you will tackle it, but be prepared to change direction in the light of new information.
4. *Observe behaviour.* While listening to the words being spoken, take note of gestures, manner, tone and inflexion, pauses and others ways of responding.
5. *Conclude the interview.* Try to get the interviewees to summarize their problem and suggest a possible solution. If this response is not forthcoming, help them either by a summarizing question or a crystallizing statement, such as 'Am I right in thinking that your problem boils down to this ... ?'

The aim should be to get to the root of the matter and, if there is no justification for being aggrieved, let individuals work it out for themselves with prompting from the interviewer as necessary. If there is something in the complaint, time and trouble should be taken to identify causes rather than just dwelling on symptoms.

Individuals should be given the right to appeal if they feel that their complaint has not been adequately dealt with. A grievance procedure should allow people to take their case through higher levels of authority to the chief executive of the organization if they want. An example of a grievance procedure is given in Appendix G.

Discipline

In the UK the way in which disciplinary problems are handled is very much influenced by the statute law on unfair dismissal as interpreted by case law and backed up by the code of disciplinary practice and procedures in employment. Although only applicable in the UK, the regulations are based on principles of natural justice which are, or should be, universal.

When handling disciplinary problems it is advisable to be aware of what these accepted principles of natural justice are and, building on this foundation, understand:

- the basic provisions of the law, such as the law of unfair dismissal;
- the general approach that should be used to deal with disciplinary matters as set out in the code of practice;
- the particular approaches to be used in dealing with specific branches of discipline or with cases of unsuitability, especially incapability, misconduct, absenteeism and lateness.

Natural justice

There are three basic principles which should govern the way in which you handle potential discipline problems:

1. Individuals should know the standards of performance they are expected to achieve and the rules to which they are expected to conform.
2. They should be given a clear indication of where they are failing or the rules broken.
3. Except in cases of gross misconduct, they should be given an opportunity to improve before disciplinary action is taken.

Four further principles governing how disciplinary cases should be dealt with have been defined in case law:

1. Individuals should know the nature of the accusation against them.
2. They should be given the opportunity to state their case.
3. The disciplinary tribunal should act in good faith.
4. Employees should be allowed to appeal.

The law of unfair dismissal

The law of unfair dismissal in the UK applies generally to employees with more than one year's service. Under this law, dismissals are fair if the principal reason was one of the following:

- incapability, which covers the employee's skill, aptitude, health and physical or mental condition;
- misconduct;
- failure to have qualifications relevant to the job;
- a legal factor which prevents the employee continuing work;
- refusal to join a trade union where a closed shop exists and it cannot be shown that the employee objects on grounds of deeply held personal conviction to joining the union;
- redundancy, where this has taken place in accordance with a customary or agreed procedure;

● employees broke or repudiated their contract by going on strike (as long as they were not singled out for this treatment).

Dismissals are unfair in the following circumstances:

1. The employer fails to show that he has good reasons to dismiss the employee (one of the admissible reasons listed above).
2. The employer has not acted reasonably in the circumstances. This can arise when the employer has not followed the principles of natural justice set out earlier, especially those concerning proper warnings, the opportunity for the employee to state his case and the right to appeal.
3. 'Constructive' dismissal takes place, ie the employer's conduct is such that the employee would be entitled to regard the contract of employment as having been repudiated by the employer. But the employee is only entitled to leave and claim constructive dismissal if the employer is in breach of some express or implied term of the contract and the breach is so serious that it goes to the root of the contract.

Examples of constructive dismissal are:

● giving unjustified warnings;
● using extremely provocative or denigratory language;
● forcing the employee to resign;
● failing to provide a safe system and place of work;
● forcing an employee to do work clearly outside his or her contract.

When assessing whether or not a dismissal is fair, an industrial tribunal asks itself the following questions:

1. Was the manner of the dismissal correct, ie did the employer follow a proper procedure, giving fair warning of the consequences of continued misconduct or incapability?
2. Was the employer's decision to dismiss based on sufficient evidence?
3. Did the employee's offence or misbehaviour merit the penalty of dismissal or would a lesser penalty have been appropriate in the circumstances?
4. Were there any mitigating circumstances which the employer should have taken into account?

Approach to handling disciplinary cases

The approach should be clearly governed by the principles of natural justice and the legal considerations set out above. There should be a disciplinary procedure which is understood and applied by all managers and supervisors.

A disciplinary procedure should provide for a three-stage approach before action is taken:

1. Informal oral warnings.
2. Formal oral warnings which, in serious cases, may also be made in writing. These warnings should set out the nature of the offence and the likely consequences of further offences.
3. Final written warnings which should contain a statement that any recurrence would lead to suspension, dismissal or some other penalty.

The procedure should provide for employees to be accompanied by a colleague or shop steward at any hearing. There should also be an appeal system and a list of offences which constitute gross misconduct and may therefore lead to instant dismissal. An example of a disciplinary procedure is given in Appendix H.

Managers and supervisors should be told what authority they have to take disciplinary action. It is advisable to have all final warnings and actions approved by a higher authority. In cases of gross misconduct, supervisors and junior managers should be given the right to suspend, if higher authority is not immediately available, but not to dismiss. The importance of obtaining and recording the facts should be emphasized. Managers should always have a colleague with them when issuing a formal warning and should make a note for file of what was said on the spot.

Incapability

Incompetence can be shown to exist by comparing actual against expected performance. But where measurement is difficult, as in managerial jobs, it can still be shown if a responsible employer has come to the conclusion over a reasonable period of time that a manger is incompetent. Employees should normally be given a reasonable period to improve. But, if there is clear evidence of inherent and irredeemable incapability such that an opportunity to improve is most unlikely to have any effect, the employer can fairly and lawfully dismiss the employee without going through the whole procedure, although the complaint should have been brought to the attention of the employee over a period of time.

It is often not possible to judge performance against clearly defined standards. A gradual decline in overall competence is particularly difficult, and, if someone has been allowed to get away with it in the past, it becomes progressively more difficult to do anything. That is why it is better for everyone's sake to take action at the time, if only to give a warning, rather than to let things slide. A soft approach now can lead to real problems in the future.

Those problems which are hardest to solve arise when 'the face doesn't fit' or attitudes to work are incompatible. Who is to blame if the boss cannot get on with his subordinates or *vice versa*? How is it possible to substantiate accusations that someone is unco-operative or upsets colleagues? What is the point of warning someone that things must improve or else, when the problem is one of an inherent personality characteristic which individuals may not accept as being a defect and, even if they did, could not do much about changing? In any case, people who are vaguely accused of being unco-operative frequently respond with remarks like 'everyone is out of step but me'.

Criticisms of behaviour are difficult to make and even more difficult to back up. The only way to do it is to produce evidence of the effects of such behaviour on performance – of individuals or of other people – and make them recognize the fault and work out for themselves how to overcome it. And it is no good making blunt accusations. The best approach is to spot unsatisfactory behaviour when it starts and discuss it informally, using the non-directive interviewing techniques mentioned earlier.

Redundancy

Redundancy, or what is now sometimes called, 'down-sizing', is the saddest and often the most difficult problem concerning people personnel managers ever have to deal with. There are five things which can be done to make it less painful:

1. Plan ahead to avoid redundancy.
2. Use other methods of reducing numbers or man hours to avoid or minimize the effects of redundancy.
3. Call for voluntary redundancy.
4. Develop and apply a proper redundancy procedure.
5. Provide help in finding new jobs, ie 'outplacement', as it is now called.

Plan ahead

Planning ahead means anticipating future reductions in manpower needs and allowing natural wastage to take effect. A forecast is needed of the amount by which the labour force has to be reduced and the likely losses through labour turnover. Recruitment can then be frozen at the right moment to allow the surplus to be absorbed by wastage.

The problem is that forecasts are often difficult to make, and in periods of high unemployment natural wastage rates are likely to be reduced. It is possible therefore to overestimate the extent to which they will take up the slack. It is best to be pessimistic about the time it will take to absorb future losses and apply the freeze earlier rather than later.

Ideally, steps should be taken to transfer people to other safer jobs and re-train them where possible.

Use other methods

The other methods which can be used to avoid or at least minimize redundancy include, in order of severity:

- calling in outside work;
- withdrawing all sub-contracted labour;
- reducing or preferably eliminating overtime;
- developing work-sharing: two people doing one job on alternate days or splitting the day between them;
- dismissing part-timers;
- temporary lay-offs.

Voluntary redundancy

Asking for volunteers – with a suitable pay-off – is one way of relieving the number of compulsory redundancies. The amount needed to persuade people to go is a matter of judgement. It clearly has to be more than the statutory minimum, although one inducement for employees to leave early may be the belief that they will get another job more easily than if they hang on until the last moment. Help can be provided to place them elsewhere.

One of the disadvantages of voluntary redundancy is that the wrong people might go, ie good workers who are best able to find other work. It is sometimes necessary to go into reverse and offer them a special loyalty bonus if they agree to stay on.

Outplacement

Outplacement is the process of helping redundant employees to find other work or start new careers. It may involve counselling which can be provided by firms who specialize in this area.

Redundancy procedure

If forced into redundancy the problems will be reduced if there is an established procedure to follow. This procedure should have three aims:

- to treat employees as fairly as possible;
- to reduce suffering as much as possible;
- to protect management's ability to run the business effectively.

These aims are not always compatible. Management will want to retain their key workers. Trade unions, on the other hand, will want to adopt the principle of last in, first out, irrespective of the value of each employee to the company.

The following points should be included in any redundancy procedure:

1. Early warnings and consultation with unions and staff: in the UK

firms are required by law to inform the union and the Department of Employment if 10 or more employees are to be made redundant, giving at least 30 days' notice.

2. Means to be adopted to avoid or reduce redundancies, eg cutting back overtime and the use of temporary staff, short-time working, transfers to other jobs with an appropriate trial period (four weeks required in law).

3. The basis of selection for redundancy. The starting point may be the principle of last in, first out, but the right has to be reserved to deviate from this principle where selection on the basis of service would prejudice operational efficiency.

4. The basis of compensating for redundancy, ie payments made by the company which are additional to the statutory minimum.

5. The help the company will give to redundant employees to find other work.

An example of a redundancy procedure is given in Appendix I.

Transfer procedures

Re-deployment in response to changing or seasonal demands for labour is a necessary feature in any large enterprise. The clumsy handling of transfers by management, however, can do as much long-lasting harm to the climate of employee relations as ill-considered managerial actions in any other sphere of personnel practice.

Management may be compelled to move people in the interests of production. But in making the move, managers should be aware of the fears of those affected so that they can be alleviated as much as possible.

The basic fear will be of change itself – a fear of the unknown and of the disruption of a well-established situation: work, environment, colleagues and workmates, travelling arrangements. There will be immediate fears that the new work will make additional and unpalatable demands for extra skill or effort. There will be concern about loss of earnings because new jobs have to be tackled or because of different pay scales or bonus systems. Loss of overtime opportunities or the danger of shift or night work may also arouse concern.

Transfer policies should establish the circumstances when employees can be transferred and the arrangements for pay, resettlement and re-training. If the transfer is at the company's request and to suit the convenience of the company it is normal to pay the employee's present rate or the rate for the new job, whichever is higher. This policy is easiest to apply in temporary transfers. It may have to be modified in the case of longer term or permanent transfers to eliminate the possibility of a multi-tiered pay structure emerging in the new location, which must cause serious dissatisfaction amongst those already employed there.

When transfers are made to avoid redundancy in the present location the rate for the job in the new department should be paid. Employees affected in this way would, of course, be given the choice between being made redundant or accepting a lower paid job.

The policies should also provide guidelines on how requests from employees for transfer should be treated. The normal approach should be to give sympathetic hearing to such requests from longer serving employees, especially if the transfer is wanted for health or family reasons. But the transferred employee would have to accept the rate for the job in his new department.

The procedures for handling transfers may have to include joint consultation or discussions with workers' representatives on any major transfer programme. If regular transfers take place because of seasonal changes it is best to establish a standard procedure for making transfers which would include payment arrangements. Individual transfers would be managed by departmental supervisors, but they should be made aware of company policies and procedures and the need to treat the human problems involved with care and consideration.

Promotion procedures

The aims of the promotion procedures of a company should be, first, to enable management to obtain the best talent available within the company to fill more senior posts and, second, to provide employees with the opportunity to advance their careers within the company, in accordance with the opportunities available and their own abilities.

In any organization where there are frequent promotional moves and where promotion arrangements cause problems, it is advisable to have a promotion policy and procedure which is known to both management and staff. The basic points that should be included in such a procedure are:

- promotion vacancies should be notified to the personnel department;
- specified vacancies should be advertised internally unless there is a recognized successor or, because of unusual requirements, there is no suitable candidate within the company;
- departmental managers should not be allowed to refuse promotions within a reasonable time unless the individual has been in the department for less than, say, one year, or the department has recently suffered heavy losses through promotions or transfers;
- promotion opportunities should be open to all, irrespective of race, creed, sex or marital status.

An example of a promotion procedure is given in Appendix J.

Chapter 16
Health and Safety

Health and safety policies and programmes are concerned with protecting employees – and any other people affected by what the company produces or does – against the hazards arising from their employment or their links with the company.

Occupational health programmes deal with the reactions of work people to their working environment and with the prevention of ill-health arising from working conditions and circumstances. They consist of two main elements – occupational medicine, which is a specialized branch of preventive medicine concerned with the diagnosis and assessment of health hazards and stresses at work; and occupational hygiene which is the province of the chemist and the engineer engaged in the measurement and physical control of environmental hazards.

Safety programmes deal with the prevention of accidents and with minimizing the resulting loss and damage to persons and to property. They relate more to systems of work than to the working environment, but both health and safety programmes are concerned with protection against hazards and their aims and methods are closely interlinked.

This chapter therefore treats health and safety as two aspects of the same problem, although the particular considerations affecting occupational hygiene or accident prevention are treated separately, as are special areas of the subject such as fire precautions.

Health and safety programmes need to be considered against the background of the factors that affect health and safety at work, and the chapter begins with an analysis of these factors and a discussion of the basic principles that influence policies and procedures. This is followed by a description of the elements of the overall health and safety programme, and the chapter then deals with each of these elements, namely:

- the identification and analysis of health and safety hazards and problems;
- health and safety policies;
- the organization of health and safety;
- occupational health programmes and procedures;

● accident-prevention programmes and procedures;
● the prevention of fire and explosions;
● education and training in health and safety precautions;
● the measurement and control of health and safety performance.

Factors affecting health and safety

The work and writings of a number of distinguished practitioners and researchers in health and safety have resulted in a range of basic principles, concepts and approaches which need to be understood by anyone concerned with the development and implementation of health and safety programmes.

The first and most influential of the practitioners was H W Heinrich[1] who developed his axioms of industrial safety to underline his thesis that the conventional approach to prevention, by concentrating on injuries that had happened rather than on accidental occurrences that might be predicted, looked at only a fraction of the total problem and looked at it backwards. From this analysis a considerable body of literature has developed advocating the techniques of 'damage control' and 'total loss control'. The basic message of these approaches, which were mainly North American in origin, is that the employer who wants to prevent injuries in the future, to reduce loss and damage, and to increase efficiency, must look systematically at the total pattern of accidental happenings – whether or not they caused injury or damage. He must then plan a comprehensive system of prevention rather than rely on the *ad hoc* patching-up of deficiencies which injury accidents have brought to light.

Principles of health and safety management

An analysis of the contributions of various schools of thought on health and safety matters suggests that there are five basic principles which should determine the approach to be used in health and safety management.

1. Industrial disease and accidents result from a multiplicity of factors, but these have to be traced to their root causes, which are usually faults in the management system arising from poor leadership from the top, inadequate supervision, insufficient attention to the design of health and safety into the system, an unsystematic approach to the identification, analysis and elimination of hazards, and poor education and training facilities.
2. The most important function of health and safety programmes is to identify potential hazards, provide effective safety facilities

and equipment, and to take prompt remedial action. This is only possible if there are:
- comprehensive and effective systems for reporting all accidents causing damage or injury;
- adequate accident records and statistics;
- systematic procedures for carrying out safety checks, inspections and investigations;
- methods of ensuring that safety equipment is maintained and used;
- proper means available for persuading managers, supervisors and work-people to pay more attention to health and safety matters.

3. The health and safety policies of the organization should be determined by top management who must be continuously involved in monitoring health and safety performance and in ensuring that corrective action is taken when necessary.
4. Management and supervision must be made fully accountable for health and safety performance in the working areas they control.
5. All employees should be given thorough training in safe methods of work and should receive continuing education and guidance on eliminating health and safety hazards and on the prevention of accidents.

Health and safety programmes

The essential elements of a health and safety programme are:
- analysis – of health and safety performance, problems and potential hazards;
- development – of policies, organization, procedures and training systems;
- implementation – of the programme by means of training schemes, inspections, investigations and audits;
- evaluation – of control information and reports and of the effectiveness of the organization and training systems. This evaluation should provide feedback to be used for improving performance.

The constituents of the health and safety programme are shown in Figure 16.1.

Health and safety programmes are the responsibility of top management but they should enlist the support of middle management, supervisors and work-people in conducting the initial analysis and in developing and implementing the programme. Assistance and guidance can be provided internally by specialist health and safety advisers and externally by

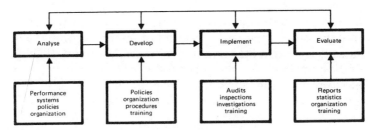

Figure 16.1 Health and safety programme

the government inspectorate (in the UK the Health and Safety Executive), bodies concerned with health and safety such as, in the UK, the Royal Society for the Prevention of Accidents, or employers' associations, some of whom have strong safety departments. But advisory services do not detract from the ultimate responsibility of management for health and safety performance.

Analysis of health and safety performance

Health and safety programmes must be based on an analysis of the facts on the organization of health and safety as it exists, on the procedures used and results obtained.

The facts should be analysed under the following headings:

- policies – the extent to which health and safety policies are defined and implemented;
- the organization – the role and effectiveness of management, supervision and work-people, health and safety staff and safety committees;
- systems and procedures – for carrying out inspections and investigations, reporting and recording accidents, ensuring at the design or development stage that equipment, facilities, plant, processes or substances are not dangerous, providing safety equipment, educating and training employees;
- performance – the health and safety record of the company as shown by statistics, reports, special investigations and sample checks.

Such an analysis will involve discussions with managers, supervisors, work-people, shop stewards, factory inspectors and insurers, as well as a review of standard procedures and an examination of safety records.

Health and safety policies

Written health and safety policies are required to demonstrate that top management is concerned about the protection of their employees from hazards at work and to indicate how this protection will be provided. These are therefore: first, a declaration of intent; secondly, a definition of the means by which that intent is to be realized; and, thirdly, a statement of the guidelines that should be followed by management and workpeople in implementing the policy. The policies should provide a base for organization, action and control as shown in Figure 16.2.

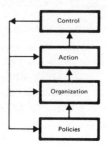

Figure 16.2 The role of health and safety policies

The policy statement should consist of three parts:

1. The general policy statement.
2. The description of the organization for health and safety.
3. Details of the arrangements for implementing the policy.

The general policy statement

The general policy statement should be a declaration of the intention of the employer to safeguard the health and safety of his employees. It should emphasize four fundamental points: first, that the safety of employees and the public is of paramount importance; second, that safety will take precedence over expediency; third, that every effort will be made to involve all managers, supervisors and employees in the development and implementation of health and safety procedures; and fourth, that health and safety legislation will be complied with in the spirit as well as the letter of the law. (See Appendix A.)

Organization

This section of the policy statement should describe the health and safety organization of the company through which high performance standards are set and achieved by people employed at all levels in the organization.

The statement should underline the ultimate responsibility of top management for the health and safety performance of the company. It should then indicate how key management personnel are to be held accountable for performance in their areas. The role of safety committees and safety representatives should be defined and the duties of the specialists who advise on health and safety matters, such as the safety adviser and the medical officer, should be summarized.

Health and safety arrangements

The description of health and safety arrangements should indicate how the general policy statement is to be put into effect. It should cover:

- procedures for reporting accidents, illness and safety and health hazards; fire precautions; first aid;
- arrangements for monitoring the atmosphere and maintaining high standards of hygiene with regard to potentially harmful substances;
- arrangements for instructing work-people in safe working methods and for training employees in health and safety matters;
- good housekeeping requirements covering storage facilities, adequate space for machinery and plant, the provision of gang-ways, and welfare arrangements;
- special rules for work done at a height, in confined spaces, on certain electrical equipment or unguarded machinery;
- the maintenance of equipment and the provision of proper inspection and testing arrangements;
- general rules on safe working habits;
- special rules for internal transport drivers;
- arrangements for checking new machinery and materials;
- safety inspections;
- the provision of personal protective equipment, and rules as to its use;
- suggestions on safety matters.

Health and safety organization

Health and safety concerns everyone in an establishment, although the main responsibility lies with management and supervision for formulating and implementing safety policies and procedures.

The role of management

The role of management is to develop health and safety policies and procedures with the help of its medical and safety advisers. Management must then ensure that the procedures are implemented by making supervisors accountable for health and safety performance in their areas and by providing them with the help, guidance and training they need to carry out their responsibilities. Management must also set up information and control systems so that the health and safety performance can be monitored and corrective action initiated when required.

It is essential to have a director with specific responsibility for health and safety matters. His job is to advise the board on policies, to ensure that the agreed policies are implemented and to report back to the board on health and safety performance. He should also be responsible for the overall management of the health and safety organization.

The role of supervision

Supervisors can exert the greatest influence on health and safety. They are in immediate control of employees and work processes and it is up to them to keep a constant watch to reveal potentially unsafe practices or conditions. But they need all the support and encouragement they can get from higher management to fulfil these responsibilities. If the emphasis from above is purely on output and cost reduction, supervisors can hardly be blamed if they neglect safety precautions. Exhortations on safety from management or safety advisers are useless unless it can be demonstrated that health and safety considerations will be given priority if there is any conflict between them and the output and cost budgets.

Supervisors need training and guidance on their safety functions. This can be provided by the safety and training departments, if any, but the existence of well-defined safety rules and procedures should also help.

The role of the medical adviser

Medical advisers have two functions: preventive and clinical. The preventive function is the most important, and this covers advising on health precautions, conducting inspections and inquiries, establishing health standards and holding medical examinations. Their clinical function is to deal with industrial accidents and diseases and to advise on the steps necessary to recover from injury or illness. It is not their job to usurp the role of the family doctor, but their special knowledge of the factory should enable them to give more relevant advice on matters concerning health at work.

Only larger companies can afford full-time medical officers, but any company with more than 100 employees should be able to call on the part-time advice of a local doctor who is interested and able to help.

The role of the safety adviser

The main functions of the safety adviser should be to:

- advise on health and safety policies and standards, rules and procedures;
- advise on the health and safety aspects of the design and use of plant and equipment;
- advise on the use of safety equipment and protective clothing;
- plan and carry out safety audits and inspections;

● conduct investigations into accidents;
● maintain safety records and statistics;
● liaise continually with management, supervision and safety
representatives;
● liaise with the health and safety inspectorate.

The role of the safety committee

Safety committees should be concerned with reviewing unsafe practices
and conditions and making suggestions on methods of improving health
and safety performance. Like all such committees, they are most effective when they can be involved in real issues and can see their recommendations put into effect. That is why they should take part in formulating
health and safety policies, procedures and rules, carrying out safety audits and inspections, investigating accidents and analysing accident reports
and statistics.

Occupational health programmes

Occupational health programmes are concerned with the identification
and control of health hazards arising from toxic substances, radiation,
noise, fatigue and the stresses imposed upon body and mind at work.

Basic approach

In each of these areas the same basic approach is necessary. The first stage
is to identify the substances, conditions or processes which are actually or
potentially dangerous. The second stage is to evaluate how the hazard
arises by studying the nature of the substance or condition and the circumstances in which the danger occurs. This means establishing the point at
which a substance or an environmental condition is in danger of becoming
harmful in terms of the intensity of exposure and the duration of exposure.
It also means that the effect of working methods and processes on the
human body and mind has to be examined. Industrial hygiene research
into these matters should be carried out by specialist medical advisers
working closely with process engineers and chemists. In particularly
hazardous environments, research and advice may be required from
members of the growing profession of occupational hygienists.

The final stage is to develop methods for minimizing the risk by exercising control over the use of dangerous substances or over the environment in which the hazard occurs. Control of occupational health and
hygiene problems can be achieved by:

● eliminating the hazard at the source by means of design and process
engineering which may, for example, ensure that harmful concentra-
tions of toxic substances are not allowed to contaminate the worker;

- isolating hazardous operations or substances so that workers do not come into contact with them;
- changing the process or substances used to promote better protection or to remove the risk;
- providing protective equipment, but only if changes to the design, process or specification cannot completely remove the hazard;
- training workers to avoid risk by eliminating dangerous practices or by using the protective equipment provided;
- maintaining plant and equipment to minimize the possibility of harmful emissions;
- good housekeeping to keep premises and machinery clean and free from toxic substances;
- regular inspections to ensure that potential health risks are identified in good time. (Procedures for conducting safety inspections which also cover occupational health hazards are discussed below.)
- pre-employment medical examinations and regular checks on those exposed to risk;
- ensuring that ergonomic considerations (ie those concerning the design and use of equipment, machines, processes and work stations) are taken into account in design specifications, establishing work routines, personnel specifications and training.

Toxic substances

Many toxic substances are present in working environments in the form of dusts (eg lead oxide), liquids (eg carbon disulphide) and gases (eg chlorine) and can be absorbed into the body through the lungs, mouth or skin. The increasing use in industry of potentially harmful chemical substances is producing new and more subtle hazards against which constant vigilance is necessary.

The work of environmental hygienists in the control of toxic substances must be firmly based on medical intelligence. But chemists, engineers and doctors should be part of one team working on the scientific assessment of the risks and the precise quantification of preventive standards in the form of agreed maximum levels of exposure expressed in threshold limit values (in the UK these are published by the Health and Safety Executive for a wide variety of substances used in industry).

It is the job of line management in a factory to ensure that they get information and advice from their own specialists or those who can be made available from government agencies. This should enable the company to identify and list hazards from toxic substances and decide on the control actions required. These could be any combination of the control steps listed above but, in addition, specific instructions and training should be made available for each operator exposed to risk on what should be done to avoid contamination and disease.

Environmental controls need to cover dust, fumes, gases, smoke and vapour in addition to the materials used in manufacturing processes. These create health risks, but they also result in pollution to the atmosphere, and control over pollution is a legal requirement as well as a social responsibility.

Radiation

Radiation hazards are familiar enough to have generated an ultra-cautious attitude to the use of radioactive substances, resulting in the imposition of elaborate controls. This is an area where expert advice is essential for any employer who is not familiar with the subject so that protection can be provided by monitors, remote control systems, special clothing, and rigid control over the doses of radiation any person is allowed to receive.

Noise

Noise is an aspect of occupational health which is probably more neglected than any other. Yet excessive noise can cause fatigue, speech interference, loss of hearing and emotional stress. Any of these could be instrumental in producing lasting physical damage or in increasing the likelihood of an accident.

A noise control programme should be based on a survey of the factory to identify the areas of noise and determine the abatement methods that can be used. The main problem is that noise reduction is something which should be catered for at the design stage – once the plant has been installed it becomes an expensive business to attack noise.

Fatigue

Fatigue is the inevitable result of continued exertion – either mental or muscular. The factors that increase fatigue are badly designed machines, high temperature or humidity, excessive noise, inadequate lighting or glare, the nature of the floor upon which workers have to stand, and the absence of training in how to perform tasks with the least amount of exertion.

Fatigue induces carelessness and is therefore a potential cause of accidents. It can be attacked by paying attention to all the factors listed above when designing plant and fitting out factories or offices, carrying out work study exercises and designing training programmes.

Physical and mental stress

Physical and mental stress can result from fatigue or from the strains and pressures built into the system of work. This problem also needs to be tackled at the design stage so that the machine (or office procedure) can be designed to fit the person rather than the person made to fit the machine.

This is the science of ergonomics and some large companies such as Pilkingtons employ full-time ergonomists who join teams in the design stages of factory programmes and advise on the physical and mental factors that should be heeded when developing office systems and procedures. It is a highly technical and important discipline and it is sad that so little attention is paid to it when training design or system engineers.

Musculo-skeletal conditions such as tenosynovitis need to be minimized by ergonomic design, selection screening and training. Strain through the use of VDUs has also to be eliminated so far as possible.

The avoidance of strain from lifting heavy objects or from bad posture is also a matter of designing a safe work system. But this is an area where intensive training and constant propaganda are required to reduce risks.

Medical checks

The importance of preventive medicine in industry can hardly be over-emphasized. It is the role of the medical adviser in co-operation with occupational hygienists, engineers, chemists and ergonomists to identify health risks and establish general threshold limits for exposure to the risks and individual standards of health and physique for employees.

The aim should be to develop health standards for each occupation and use these as selection and placement criteria when carrying out pre-employment medical examinations, which are a must in any situation where there are health risks.

A continuing programme of preventive medicine is required which should include checks on the extent to which employees are being exposed to health hazards, inspections to review and revise exposure threshold limits and health standards, and regular examinations for anyone at risk. It is essential to produce a detailed programme for this purpose, and the medical adviser should be required to keep top management informed of his programme and the results of his work.

Accident prevention

The prevention of accidents is achieved by:

- identifying the causes of accidents and the conditions under which they are most likely to occur;
- taking account of safety factors at the design stage – building safety into the system;
- designing safety equipment and protective devices and providing protective clothing;
- carrying out regular inspections and checks and taking action to eliminate risks;
- investigating all incidents resulting in damage to establish the cause and to initiate corrective action;

- developing an effective health and safety organization;
- maintaining good records and statistics which will identify problem areas and unsatisfactory trends;
- conducting a continuous programme of education and training on safe working habits and methods of avoiding accidents.

Identifying the causes of accidents

The process of identifying causes is mainly one of conducting inspections, checks and investigations, as described below. Some consideration should be given, however, to the general factors that induce accidents, as these will indicate the approach that should be used at the design and inspection stages.

Fundamentally it is the system of work to which human beings are exposed that is the cause of accidents. Carelessness, fatigue, lack of knowledge, inexperience, inadequate training or poor supervision may, in different degrees, be the immediate causes, but all these factors are related to the basic system of work.

The causes of accidents can therefore be divided into two main areas:

1. Those related to the system at work which are the basic reason for most accidents.
2. Those related to immediate individual factors, which in most cases arise from the system of work, but which might not have happened if there had been no human failure at or near the point of time when the accident occurred.

System of work factors
The main factors in the system of work which induce accidents are:

- unsafely designed machinery, plant and processes;
- congested layouts;
- unguarded or inadequately guarded machinery;
- defective plant, materials or working conditions; rough, sharp or obstructive objects; slippery or greasy conditions; decayed, corroded, frayed or cracked containers, wires, conveyor belts or piping; badly maintained machinery;
- poor housekeeping – congestion; blocked gangways or exits; inadequate disposal arrangements for swarf or other waste products; lack of storage facilities; unclean working conditions;
- overloading of machines, transport vehicles or conveyor belts;
- inadequate lighting, glare;
- inadequate ventilation or systems for removing toxic fumes from the working environment;
- lack of protective clothing or devices.

It should be noted that although these factors are all connected with the system of work they all result from a human failure at some time.

Immediate factors
The immediate, direct and personal factors causing accidents are:

- using unsafe equipment;
- using equipment unsafely – deliberately or through fatigue;
- unsafe loading and placing of materials or parts on machines or transport systems;
- operating without sufficient clearance;
- operating at an unsafe speed;
- making safety devices inoperative to reduce interference and speed up work;
- distractions from other people, noise or events taking place in the workshop;
- failure to use protective clothing or devices.

Any of these factors may result from personal failures such as carelessness, recklessness, laziness, impatience, lack of consideration, or inadequate knowledge, training, skill or supervision.

Building safety into the system

The hazards to employees who operate and maintain machines arise from the belts and pulleys, gears, projecting parts, shaft ends, clutches and other moving parts used to stamp, to press, to cut or to shape materials. Transmission and transportation arrangements and the layout of plant and processes are also hazardous areas.

The prevention of accidents should be a major factor when designing plant or work processes. It is much more effective and economical to build safety into the system at the design stage rather than try to add makeshift safety devices later. It is equally important to specify the procedures and methods to be used in operating machines safely.

Designers should obtain feedback on accidents that may have been caused by a design fault, so that accidents can be eliminated by modification to existing and future designs.

Safety inspections

The purpose of safety inspections is to locate and define the faults in the system and the operational errors that allow accidents to occur. It is essential to develop a systematic and thorough programme of inspections and spot-checks which will cover all parts of the factory at regular intervals. The five steps required are described below:

- *The first step* is to define the general points that should be covered in any area in which an inspection takes place. These should be included in a checklist.
- *The second step* is to divide the plant into areas (which may or

may not follow existing departmental boundaries) and list the specific points to which attention should be given.

● *The third step* is to determine methods of inspection. These can take four forms.

1. Checklists are prepared of the points to be covered and a programme is planned to deal with them at regular intervals or over a series of inspections covering particular areas or safety points. This may be described as the audit approach, and the aim is to carry out a comprehensive review of all aspects of health and safety. Figure 16.3 is an example of the layout of a form that can be used for this purpose.

Audit area		Audited by		Date	
Check points	Symptoms	Causes	Action recommended	Responsibility for action	Date for completion

Figure 16.3 Safety audit form

2. Spot-checks can be made in each area on a random sample basis or to cover special problems, such as the inadequate use of protective clothing. In their simplest form these may simply enumerate the unsafe acts or conditions observed by the inspector or inspection team and thus identify areas where more detailed investigations are required. A numerical count of this nature can also be done on a comprehensive basis prior to a thorough inspection. An example of the layout of a sample inspection form is shown in Figure 16.4.

Area	Check carried out by			Date
	Number of observations			
Unsafe act or condition	Department A	Department B	Department C	Department D

Figure 16.4 Safety sample inspection form

3. Supervisors can be required to make daily checks of safety points in the areas under their control which should list the problem

conditions and indicate the action to be taken either by the supervisor himself, management, or the safety adviser. An example of a supervisor's checklist is shown in Figure 16.5.

Department	Supervisor		Date
Item	Condition	Immediate action taken	Future action proposed

Figure 16.5 Supervisor's daily checklist

4. Regular inspections, as required by legislation or by insurance companies, of boilers, pressure vessels, pipe-lines, dangerous processes, lifts, hoists, etc.

   The best approach is to use all four methods. The comprehensive audit can be a continuous Forth Bridge-type operation, but spot-checks should be used to supplement the audit and keep supervisors and work-people alert. The supervisor's checklist is also required to formalize the inspection procedures and this should be regarded as one of his key responsibilities. Statutory or insurance company inspections are obligatory, of course.

● *The fourth step* is to define the responsibility for planning, conducting and acting on safety inspections. A safety adviser or the manager responsible for health and safety can prepare the checklists and programmes, although this should be done in consultation with managers, supervisors and work-people. The inspections themselves should involve everyone concerned with safety; they should not be left to the safety adviser. This means that managers and supervisors and safety representatives should physically check conditions in their working areas. They may do this individually, but it is best done by a joint team working under the aegis of a health and safety committee. The safety adviser will still, of course, carry out his own investigations, but the prime responsibility for completing the pre-planned programme and taking action should rest with line management and the people working in the factory.

● *The fifth step* should be to set up systems of reporting on the results of inspections and on the action taken or proposed. It is essential that top management should take a direct interest in the inspection programme and that control procedures should be installed to ensure that audits, spot-checks and inspections do take place. The safety adviser can help top management to exercise control, but the ultimate responsibility is theirs.

Accident reports and investigations

A standard system for reporting accidents should be used which will classify all incidents under appropriate headings, indicate the likely cause of the accident and suggest any remedial action that should be taken. It is necessary to have a standard classification system for accidents under headings such as those listed below:

1. *Type of accident*
   - falls of persons
   - falls of material
   - flying material
   - handling (manual)
   - handling (mechanical)
   - stepping on or striking against stationary objects
   - hand tools
   - railways and vehicles
   - escapes of gas, fumes, etc
   - escapes of steam, hot water, liquids, etc
   - machinery in motion
   - electricity
   - welding, brazing, burning, etc
   - fires
   - explosions
2. *Location of the injury*
   - head and neck
   - eyes
   - back
   - upper limb
   - lower limb
   - hand
   - fingers
   - foot and toes
   - body system
3. *Severity of the injury*
   - fatal injury
   - permanent injury, total disablement
   - permanent injury, partial disablement
   - temporary injury, total incapacity for work
   - temporary injury, capable of carrying out alternative work
   - temporary injury, able to continue work.

An example of a simple report form is shown in Figure 16.6.

Accident-reporting systems can only work if supervisors and medical or first-aid staff are trained in how to prepare reports. It is also necessary to emphasize, and to keep on emphasizing, the importance of the reports as a means of identifying causes and preventing the recurrence of accidents in order to ensure that they are completed accurately, comprehensively and in good time.

Department		
Name of injured	Date of injury	
	Date/time of return to work	
Where and how did the accident occur?		
Nature of injury		
Name(s) of witnesses		
Classification of accident		
Type of accident	Location of accident	Severity of injury
Measures taken and proposed to avoid repetition		
Signed _____ Date _____		

Figure 16.6 Accident report form

A report is useless unless it can contribute to increased understanding of health and safety problems and to the formulation of action programmes. In the case of minor and isolated incidents, it may not be necessary to follow up every report, although statistical trends should be kept under review to reveal areas where accidents are increasing and thus show the need for a special investigation.

More serious incidents must, of course, be investigated by the safety adviser or manager responsible for safety. Line management and supervisors should also be involved in the investigation of accidents in their areas, and safety representatives should be included in major investigations. The aim of the investigation should be to decide what needs to be done to avoid future incidents. It should not simply be a matter of apportioning blame. The results of the investigation, however, may well be used as evidence in later inquiries or court actions and it is essential to document all the circumstances, record the observations of eye witnesses, take photographs and ensure that defective machines or parts are isolated.

Prevention of fire and explosion

The prevention of fire and explosions is achieved by adopting the same basic procedures as those used in preventing accidents. The steps required are to appraise the risks and to develop the basic precautionary measures.

Appraising the risks

The appraisal should be carried out in conjunction with the local fire brigade, the Health and Safety Inspectorate, insurers, architects and process engineers.

Developing precautionary measures

After the initial survey of the premises and plant, it is necessary to list the precautions required to minimize risk. These precautions can be classified under these headings:

- preventive maintenance programme
- regular inspections to identify potential risks
- safety rules
- detection and warning devices
- procedures and devices for dealing with fires and explosions, for evacuating the premises and for calling in outside help.

In each of these areas expert advice from specialists in the prevention of fires and explosions should be obtained.

Education and training

Health and safety conditions at work do not simply happen. They have to be planned for and managed, and an essential part of this process is the education and training of managers, supervisors and work-people.

Educational programmes

The aim of educational programmes should be to ensure that everyone is fully aware of the hazards they meet at work and the potential consequences of hasty or thoughtless actions. They should be designed to create and maintain interest, using all the formal and informal means of communication available – safety bulletins, posters and notices, films and slides, talks and discussions.

Educational programmes should be continuous – they should not rely on intermittent spurts of activity, although they can include campaigns to deal with specific problems such as strains from lifting heavy objects. The message should be delivered straight to the people who need to hear and learn from it. This is why generalized campaigns are less effective than those aimed at people in their own workshop by the supervisors with whom they are in contact every day.

This can be done informally, but it is better to have an organized programme which supervisors can be trained to administer. Such a programme is the 'Safety Contact Scheme' developed by the Distillers Company, the essential elements of which are as follows:

● Supervisors are required to contact each employee in their section at least once in every four-week period to discuss with them a safety topic which has been selected for them by management.
● The supervisors are trained in how to run the contact sessions and given carefully prepared notes for guidance on the subject matter which summarize the main points to be made and provide illustrations which help to get the message across.
● After each contact the supervisor records it on a record card which is inspected regularly by his manager to ensure that the programme is being followed.

Health and safety training

Health and safety training programmes should be derived from an analysis of training needs. This should refer to the hazards generally present in the company as well as the specific hazards associated with individual jobs.

Managers, supervisors, safety advisers and safety representatives should be trained in such techniques as conducting inspections and investigations, collecting and analysing statistical data and communicating with people on health and safety matters.

Employees should be provided with general induction training as well as training in the hazards present in specific occupations.

Induction training
Induction training should aim to give new employees a general understanding of what they must do to avoid risks and how the safety policies and facilities of the company will help them to avoid occupational illnesses and accidents. The points that should be covered include:

(a) the health and safety policies of the company, with particular reference to the duties of employees to work safely;
(b) the organization of the safety function;
(c) the arrangements for safety training;

(d) the main hazards that the employee is likely to face and what he should do about them;

(e) methods of working including posture to be adopted to minimize risks to health or safety;

(f) the unsafe practices that he should avoid;

(g) the use of protective clothing and safety equipment;

(h) the safety rules and procedures of the company;

(i) the procedure for reporting accidents;

(j) evacuation procedures in case of fire or explosion;

(k) first-aid facilities.

Job training

Job safety training should be based on an analysis of the special hazards presented by a job. The job should then be broken down into its constituent parts, and the safety points to which the operator must pay attention should be defined for each part.

Measurement and control of health and safety performance

Effective measurement and control is primarily a matter for action by management and supervision with the help of health and safety advisers. The procedure for carrying out surveys and inspections and for investigating incidents referred to earlier in this chapter provides the best means of monitoring performance and identifying where preventive or corrective action needs to be taken.

These measures, however, should be supplemented by safety statistics – not as an end to themselves (which they too often are) but as a basis for comparisons, inside and outside the company, and as a means of identifying undesirable trends which may not be revealed so clearly by the normal inspection procedures.

Statistical measures

The most commonly used measure in the UK is the 'incidence rate', which is the number of reportable injuries (involving absence for over three days) per 1000 manual workers employed, thus:

$$\text{Incidence rate} = \frac{\text{Number of reportable injuries in period}}{\text{Average number of manual employees in period}} \times 1000$$

Other measures include the 'frequency rate', which is the number of disabling injuries per 1,000,000 man-hours and the 'severity rate', which is the days lost through accidents per 1,000,000 hours worked.

The problem with these indices is that they only deal with reportable accidents, and in smaller companies the number of such accidents may be so small that the statistics will not provide a reliable indication of trends. It may be better in these circumstances to measure the incidence of all accidental injuries, or even of all accidents causing damage.

Measuring the cost

These statistics also ignore the cost of accidents and those who advocate the 'total loss control' approach emphasize the need to look at accidents from the point of view of their cost to the company as a whole as well as their effect on the individuals who sustain them. This approach, they claim, will provide a much greater incentive for commercially minded managements to take action.

The costs of accidents, other than the cost of insurance and special medical and safety facilities, can be allocated under the following headings:

1. Wages paid to injured workers who are off work.
2. Wages paid to workers who are not personally involved in the accident but lose time as a result of it.
3. Damage to machines, equipment, materials and buildings.
4. Loss of production because of damage or because workers are less effective when they return to work after an accident.
5. Salaries paid to managers, supervisors and other staff concerned in dealing with the accident and investigating its cause.
6. Other costs, including public liability claims, additional overtime, and the cost of renting equipment.

If these costs can be analysed (which could prove difficult) it is possible to work out a 'cost severity rate', which is the total cost of accidents per 1,000,000 man-hours worked, thus:

$$\text{Cost severity rate} = \frac{\text{Total cost of accidents over a period}}{\text{Total man-hours of production and maintenance during the period}} \times 1,000,000$$

Conclusion

Inspection, investigations, reports and statistics are all necessary to the improvement of health and safety performance. But they depend for their effectiveness entirely upon the willpower of the managers and supervisors concerned, who in turn will depend upon the leadership exercised by top management. That is why the Robens Committee report on Safety and Health at Work emphasized that:

> Promotion of safety and health at work is an essential function of good management. We are not talking about legal responsibilities. The job of a director or senior manager is to manage. The boardroom has the influence, power and resources to take initiatives and to set the pattern.[2]

References

1. Heinrich, H W *Industrial Accident Prevention.* McGraw-Hill, New York, 1959.
2. *Safety and health at work: report of the Committee 1970-72* Cmnd 5034, Her Majesty's Stationery Office, London, 1972.

Chapter 17
Welfare

Why welfare?

Welfare includes such activities as private advice on any type of personal problem; assistance with problems of health or sickness; special responsibilities for young people, elderly and retired staff and the provision of sports and social facilities. The first question to be answered is why any organization should be concerned with these matters.

The case against welfare

The arguments against are obvious. Welfare implies 'do-gooding'; the personnel management fraternity have spent many years trying to shake off their association with what they, and others, like to think of as at best peripheral and at worst redundant welfare activities. Welfare is provided for by the state services – why should industrial, commercial or public sector organizations duplicate what is already there? The private affairs of employees and their out of work interests should not be the concern of their employers. It is selfish to maintain large playing fields and erect huge sports pavilions if they are going to be used by a minute proportion of staff for a very limited period of time – the space and facilities could be better used by the community. The argument that the provision of welfare services increases the loyalty and motivation of employees has long been exploded. If welfare services are used at all, they are taken for granted. Gratitude is not a prime motivating factor.

The case for welfare

The case against welfare is formidable; the last point is particularly telling and there is some validity in each of the others – although there are limitations to their validity. Welfare state services are in theory available to all, but the ability of social workers to give individual advice, especially on problems arising from work, is limited in terms both of time and knowledge. It is all too easy for people to fall into the cracks existing in the edifice of the welfare state.

The case for welfare has to rely mainly on the abstract grounds of the social responsibility of organizations for those who work in them. This is not paternalism in the Victorian sense – turkeys at Christmas – or in the Japanese sense, where the worker's whole life centres around his employer. Rather, it is simply the realization that in exchange for offering his services, an employee is entitled to rather more than his pay, his statutory fringe benefits and healthy and safe systems of work. He is also entitled to consideration as a human being, especially when it is remembered that many of his personal problems will arise in the context of work and are best dealt with there. People's worries arise from work – about security, pay, health, relationships with others. But they also bring their personal problems to work; and many of these cannot be solved without reference to the situation there – they may require time off to deal with aged parents or sick wives, or advice on how to solve their problems and so minimize interference with their work.

The argument for welfare services at work was well put by A O Martin when he wrote:

> Staff spend at least half their waking time at work or in getting to it or leaving it. They know they contribute *to* the organization when they are reasonably free from worry, and they feel, perhaps inarticulately, that when they are in trouble they are due to get something *back* from the organization. People are entitled to be treated as full human beings with personal needs, hopes and anxieties; they are employed as *people*; they bring themselves to work, not just their hands, and they cannot readily leave their troubles at home.[1]

The social argument for welfare is the most compelling one, but there is also an economic argument. Increases in morale or loyalty may not result in commensurate or, indeed, in any increases in productivity, but undue anxiety can result in reduced effectiveness. Even if welfare services cannot increase individual productivity, they can help to minimize decreases. Herzberg's two factor model in effect placed welfare amongst the hygiene factors, but he did not underestimate the importance of 'hygiene' as a means of eliminating or at least reducing causes of anxiety or dissatisfaction.

A further practical argument in favour of welfare is that a reputation for showing concern helps to improve the local image of the firm as a good employer and thus assists in recruitment. Welfare may not directly increase productivity but it may add to general feelings of satisfaction with the firm and cut down labour turnover.

A case for welfare therefore exists and the real question is not 'why welfare?' but 'what sort of welfare?'. This question needs to be answered in general terms before discussing the type of welfare services that can be provided and how they should be organized.

What sort of welfare?

Welfare services fall into two categories:

1. Individual or personal services in connection with sickness, bereavement, domestic problems, employment problems, elderly and retired employees.
2. Group services, which consist of sports and social activities, clubs for retired staff and benevolent organizations.

Principles of personal casework

Individual services require personal casework and the most important principle to adopt is that this work should aim to help the individual to solve his own problems. The employer, manager or welfare officer should not try to stand between the individual and his problem by taking it out of his hands. Emergency action may sometimes have to be taken on behalf of the individual, but if so, it should be taken in such a way that he can later cope with his own difficulties. Welfare action must start on the basis that disengagement will take place at the earliest possible moment when the individual can, figuratively, stand on his own two feet. This does not mean that follow-up action is unnecessary, but this is only to check that things are going according to plan, not to provide additional help unless something is seriously wrong.

Personal services should be provided when a welfare need is established, and a welfare need exists where it is clear that help is required, that it cannot be given more effectively from another source, and that the individual is likely to benefit from the services that can be offered.

In an organizational setting, an essential element in personnel casework services is confidentiality. There is no point in offering help or advice to someone if he thinks that his personal problems are going to be revealed to others, possibly to the detriment of his future career. This is the argument for having specialized welfare officers in organizations large enough to be able to afford them. They can be detached in a way that line managers and even personnel managers cannot be.

Principles for providing group services

Group services, such as sports or social clubs, should not be laid on because they are 'good for morale'. There is no evidence that they are. They are costly and should only be provided if there is a real need and demand for them, arising from a very strong community spirit in a company or lack of local facilities. In the latter case, the facilities should be shared in an agreed and controlled way with the local community.

Individual welfare services

Sickness

These services aim to provide help and advice to employees absent from work for long periods because of illness. The practical reason for providing them is that they should help to speed the return of the employee to work, although it is not part of the welfare function to check up on possible malingerers. The social reason is to provide employees with support and counsel where a welfare need exists. In this context, a welfare need will exist where the employee cannot help himself without support and where such aid is not forthcoming from the state medical or welfare services or the employee's own family.

Welfare needs can be established by keeping in touch with an absent employee. This should not be done by rushing round as soon as anyone has been absent for more than, say, ten days or has exhausted his sickness benefit from work. It is generally better to write to sick absentees, expressing general concern and good wishes for a speedy recovery and reminding them that the firm can provide help if they wish, or simply asking them if they would like someone to visit them – with a stamped addressed envelope for their reply. Such letters should preferably be sent by the employee's line manager.

There will be some cases where the employee is reluctant to request help or a visit and the company may have to decide whether a visit should be made to establish if help is required. This will be a matter of judgement based on the known facts about the employee and his circumstances.

Visits can be made by the line manager, a personnel officer or a specialized full- or part-time welfare officer. Alternatively, arrangements can be made for a colleague to pay the visit. The aims of the visit should be first, to show the employee that his company and colleagues are concerned about his welfare; second, to alleviate any loneliness he may feel; and third, to provide practical advice or help. The latter may consist of putting him in touch with suitable organizations or ensuring that they are informed and take action. Or more immediate help may be provided to deal with pressing domestic problems.

Bereavement

Bereavement is a time when many people need all the help and advice they can get. The state welfare services may not be able to assist and families are often non-existent or unhelpful. Established welfare organizations in industry, commerce or the public sector attach a lot of importance to this service. The advice may often be no more than putting the bereaved employee or the widow or widower of an employee in touch with the right organizations, but it is often extended to help with funeral arrangements and dealing with will and probate matters.

Domestic problems

Domestic problems seem the least likely area for welfare services. Why should the company intervene, even when asked, in purely private matters? If, for example, an employee gets into debt, that is surely his affair. What business is it of the company?

These are fair questions. But an employer who has any real interest in the welfare of his staff cannot ignore appeals for help. The assistance should not consist of bailing people out of debt whenever they get into trouble or acting as an amateur marriage guidance or family casework officer. But, in accordance with the basic principle of personal casework already mentioned, employees can be counselled on how to help themselves or where to go for expert advice. A counselling service at work, whether operated by full-time welfare officers or by others on a part-time basis, can do an immense amount of good simply by providing an opportunity for employees to talk through their problems with a disinterested person. There is a limit to how much can or should be done in the way of allowing employees to pour out their troubles on willing shoulders but, used with discretion, it is a valuable service.

Employment problems

Employment problems should normally be solved by discussion between the individual and his boss or through the company's grievance procedure. There may be times, however, when employees have problems over interpersonal relations, or feelings of inadequacy, about which they want to talk to a third party. Such counselling talks, as a means of relieving feelings and helping people to work through their problems for themselves, can do a lot of good, but extreme caution must be displayed by the company official who is involved. He must not cut across line management authority but, at the same time, he must preserve the confidentiality of the discussion. It is a delicate business and where it affects superior/subordinate relationships, it is one in which the giving of advice can be dangerous. The most that can be done is to provide a counselling service which gives employees an opportunity to talk about their problems and allows the counsellor to suggest actions the employee can take to put things right. The counsellor must not comment on the actions of anyone else who is involved. He can only comment on what the employee who seeks his help is doing or might do.

Elderly and retired employees

Welfare for elderly employees is primarily a matter of preparing them for retirement and dealing with any problems they have in coping with their work. Preparation for retirement is a valuable service that many firms offer. This may be limited to advising on the classes and facilities local authorities provide for people prior to retirement, or when they have retired, or it may be extended to sponsoring special classes held during working hours. Some companies have made special provision for elderly employees by setting aside jobs or work areas for them. This has its dangers. Treating someone as a special case ahead of his time may make him over-aware of his condition or over-dependent on the services provided for him. There is everything to be said for treating elderly employees as normal workers, even though the health and safety services may take particular care to ensure that the age of the worker does not increase the danger of accident or industrial disease.

Retired employees, particularly those with long service, deserve the continuing interest of their former employer. The interest need not be oppressive, but continuing sick visiting can be carried out and social occasions can be provided for them.

Group welfare services

Group welfare services mainly consist of sports and social clubs, although some companies still support various benevolent societies which provide additional help and finance in times of need.

A massive investment in sports facilities is usually of doubtful value unless there is nothing else in the neighbourhood and, in accordance with the principles mentioned earlier, the company is prepared to share its facilities with the local community. In a large company in a large town it is very difficult to develop feelings of loyalty towards the company teams or to encourage people to use the sports club. Why should they support an obscure side when their loyalties have always been directed to the local club? Why should they travel miles when they have perfectly adequate facilities near at hand? In the writer's experience, such clubs are usually supported by small cliques who have little or no influence over the feelings of other employees, who leave the enthusiasts to get on with whatever they are doing.

The same argument applies to social clubs, especially those forced on to employees by paternalistically minded companies. It is different when they arise spontaneously from the needs of employees. If they want to club together then the company should say good luck to them and provide them with a reasonable amount of support. The subsidy, however, should not be complete. The clubs should generate their own funds as well as their own enthusiasm. Facilities can be provided within the firm's premises if they are needed and readily available. An investment in special facilities should only be made if there is a real likelihood of their being used regularly by a large proportion of employees. This is an area where prior consultation, before setting up the facility, and self-government, when it has been established, are essential.

Organization of welfare

It can be argued that the prime responsibility for welfare should rest with line managers on the principle that an officer's first concern should be the well-being of his troops. This is correct up to a point but the military analogy is not really valid. The basic unit in an army, the platoon, has a quite dissimilar function to that of the basic unit in an office or section, and the relationships between officers and their men have traditionally been quite different from those between a supervisor and his subordinate. Managers must be aware of personal problems and if people come to them for help and advice, so much the better. But this is a bonus and should not be relied upon. Line management may not be qualified to give advice or even direct people to where advice can be obtained, and employees may be reluctant to reveal personal problems which may prejudice their boss against them.

The obvious alternative is the personnel manager or local personnel officer. These people should be knowledgeable about how help can be provided and capable of exercising counselling skills. In smaller organizations it is inevitable that they should have a welfare role in addition to their normal personnel functions. But the welfare role is not necessarily consistent with their other responsibilities. Personnel managers are there to provide a service to management. This will involve providing certain services to employees, including welfare, but the interests of the company as a whole may have to prevail over the interests of an individual employee. A personnel officer is not therefore always in a position to give disinterested advice. In any case, he may not have the time to provide both the advice and the other personnel services.

In larger organizations the case for specialized welfare officers is that they should have the expertise and time to deal with individual casework and should be in a position to provide a sufficiently detailed counselling service. Clearly, they have to be aware of the fact that they only exist because the company exists. The advice and help they give cannot be contrary to the interests of the company as a whole, which will include the interests of colleagues or the individuals they have dealings with. But they can listen to people's problems and help them to help themselves without suffering from the conflicts of interest and shortages of time to which line and even personnel managers are prone. Their role is a delicate one, for reasons that have already been discussed, but they can have an important part to play in ensuring that the organization is able to meet its social responsibilities towards its employees.

Reference

1. Martin, A O *Welfare at Work*. Batsford, London, 1967.

Chapter 18
Personnel Records

The need

Personnel record and information systems are required for three main purposes:

1. To store for reference the personal details of individual employees.
2. To provide a basis for decision-making in every area of personnel work, especially:
   - manpower forecasting and planning;
   - recruitment and selection;
   - employment, including promotion, transfers, disciplinary procedures, termination and redundancy;
   - education and training;
   - pay administration;
   - health and safety.
3. To provide data for returns to government departments and agencies.

Personnel records and information procedures can be based on an entirely manual system but, increasingly, they are being computerized to a greater or lesser degree. The advent of micro-computers is accelerating this process. There are, however, certain basic principles and practices which apply to any system and these are considered in the first three sections of the chapter: requirements of a good record system, identifying information requirements and designing the system. The next section deals with basic forms and returns which may exist only as a manual system or may be linked to a computer. The use of computers is discussed in Chapter 19.

Requirements of a good record system

Personnel records, like any other records, must be simple, easy to maintain, comprehensive and relevant to the needs of the undertaking.

Simplicity and ease of maintenance are vital; records can be expensive to set up and maintain. A universal hatred of form filling and paper work generally will be enhanced to the total detriment of accuracy and utility if forms and records are complex, difficult to complete or hard to understand. This means designing forms so that entries can be made in logical and convenient sequence, left to right across the paper and from top to bottom. So far as possible, the method of completing the form should be self-explanatory – elaborate notes for guidance should be avoided. Plenty of space should be provided for each item; if different units of information are 'boxed' in, the form will be easier to complete and to read. Particularly vital pieces of information should be given prominence and may be placed in a more heavily defined box. Space should be provided for alterations and additions. One side of one sheet of paper is the ideal size although clearly, some records such as application forms may have to be longer.

It is also important to ensure that records are not unduly duplicated, and this may mean taking care when assessing the degree to which records should be centralized or decentralized (discussed below).

Accuracy partly depends upon ensuring that clear definitions are made of the information that has to be entered on the form. If there is any ambiguity about, for example, a job title, the resulting entry may produce misleading information later for manpower planning or training surveys. It is important to place accurate information on the record. It is equally important to remove redundant information from the card or dossier. Many employee dossiers are full of useless documents which take up unnecessary space and increase the difficulty of getting at essential information. A regular review of records is required to clear out useless data.

A comprehensive system of records covers all the information required about individual employees or needed for personnel decision-making. But the information must be relevant. Every piece of information must be challenged with the questions 'what purpose will this serve?', 'to what use will it be put?'. The first point to clear when setting up a record system is the objective of each item in terms of the decisions it will help to make, its contribution to the assembly of essential statistical information, or its importance as a reference point in dealing with matters affecting individual employees.

It is necessary to avoid gaps in information essential to decision-making. It is equally necessary to avoid gathering useless data or maintaining elaborate statistics to which no one ever refers. Too often, a 'one-off' request for information leads to the setting up of a permanent record or data collection system, although the information may never be requested again. Regular reviews should be made of all records and returns to ensure that they are serving a useful purpose and that they are generally cost-effective. It may be cheaper in some circumstances to maintain manual records rather than to computerize. It may be less time-consuming and costly to carry out a special exercise rather than to maintain a permanent record, just in case.

Identifying information requirements

The starting point should be an analysis of the decisions that the company makes or may need to make about individuals or groups of employees or the work force as a whole. This should be followed up by an analysis of the information required by government departments and agencies and by employers' associations.

Personnel decisions requiring statistical data

The main decisions for which statistical information or individual data may be required include:

- forecasting the future supply of manpower by analysing, for each category of staff, labour turnover, age distribution, absenteeism and promotions;
- forecasting the future demand for manpower by ratio-trend analysis (calculating current ratios of manpower to activity levels and forecasting future ratios by reference to projected activity levels) and other statistical means;
- the introduction of productivity improvement or cost reduction campaigns based upon analyses of present manpower productivity levels and costs (eg manpower cost per unit of output, or the ratio of manpower costs to sales turnover or profit);
- planning recruitment campaigns on the basis of analyses of the results of previous campaigns, especially sources of recruits, media costs and success rates, and the relative pulling power of different inducements and recruitment methods;
- introducing new or improved interviewing and testing techniques on the basis of comparisons between interview and test assessments and subsequent performance;
- identifying people with particular skills or potential for new appointments or promotion;
- improving disciplinary procedures or amending works rules by analysing disciplinary cases;
- introducing new or improved time-keeping methods or considering the introduction of flexi-time by reference to time-keeping records;
- planning redundancies – consulting unions, transferring or re-training employees, selecting employees for redundancy, helping to place redundant employees;

- planning training programmes – subjects to be covered, types of courses and numbers of courses – by reference to analyses of future changes in manpower (numbers and skills), performance review records and job and training specifications;
- taking steps to improve job satisfaction and morale by reference to statistics on labour turnover, absenteeism, sickness, accidents, discipline cases and grievances;
- changing pay systems on the basis of statistics of wage drift, fluctuations in earnings, the proportion of employees on average earnings rather than payment – by results, cost per unit of output, fluctuations in earnings, the number and consequences of arguments over job rates;
- reviewing pay structures and levels of pay by reference to statistics of earnings in the company, rates of pay elsewhere, and the distribution of rates in each pay grade (eg compa-ratios for salary structure analysis as described in Chapter 27);
- controlling merit reviews by analysing the distribution of merit awards in relation to budgets and guidelines and by assessing the implications of salary attrition (see Chapter 27);
- taking steps to improve employee relations by analysing the causes of disputes;
- determining the information that should be communicated to unions and employees about the company or to assist in negotiations and joint consultation;
- improving health, safety and fire precautions by analysing reports on industrial disease, accidents and dangerous occurrences, monitoring returns on exposure to health hazards in relation to predetermined threshold limits and studying reports on health, safety and fire inspection, spot-checks and audits.

Personnel returns

The personnel returns required may include (in Great Britain):

- manpower and earnings statistics to the Department of Employment or employers' associations;
- training statistics to industrial training boards;
- health and safety statistics to the Health and Safety Executive.

Individual data

Individual information should include:

- the application form giving personal particulars;
- interview and test record;
- job history after joining the firm including details of transfers, promotions and changes in occupation;

- current pay details and changes in salary or pay;
- education and training record with details of courses attended and results obtained;
- details of performance assessments and reports from appraisal or counselling sessions;
- absence, lateness, accident, medical and disciplinary records with details of formal warnings and suspensions;
- holiday entitlement;
- pensions data;
- termination record, with details of exit interview and suitability for re-engagement.

Collective data

Collective information may include:

- numbers, grades and occupations of employees;
- absenteeism, labour turnover and lateness statistics;
- accident rates;
- age and length of service distributions;
- total wage and salary bill;
- wage rates and salary levels;
- employee costs;
- overtime statistics;
- records of grievances and disputes;
- training records.

Designing the system

The type and complexity of the personnel records and information system must obviously depend upon the company and its needs. Small companies may only need a basic card index system for individual employees and a simple set of forms for recording information on numbers employed, labour turnover and absenteeism. But a larger company will almost certainly need a more complex system because more information has to be handled, many more decisions have to be made, and the data changes more often. Card indexes are not enough, because supplementary records may be needed to give more detailed information about individual employees.

The key decisions to be made when designing the system concern:

- the design of the basic records, forms and input material;
- the use of computers;
- the extent to which records should be centralized or decentralized;
- the procedures and programme for collecting, recording, updating and disseminating information.

The design of basic records and forms

The basic records and forms must be designed in accordance with the principles of simplicity, clarity, cost-effectiveness and relevance discussed earlier. Examples of typical forms and statistical returns are given at the end of this chapter and can be found elsewhere in this book.

Centralization and decentralization of records

In a small company, or one in which operations are concentrated on one site, the issue of centralization and decentralization may not be an important one. Although, even in the latter case, there may be problems of duplication if departments insist on keeping records of their own employees in addition to those maintained centrally.

The advantages of centralization are that there is less expenditure on space and equipment, company statistical analyses can more easily be prepared and duplication is avoided. The disadvantages are that local departments or units may not have ready access to the information they need while there may be delays in obtaining the data required by central records.

The advantages of decentralization are that departments have the information they need on the spot, and delays in transmitting data are reduced. The disadvantages are additional costs because of space requirements and duplicated efforts and possible loss in effectiveness at the centre because of difficulties in analysing the total situation in the company.

In a divisionalized company, where these problems are likely to be most pressing, the answer is usually a compromise. Divisions maintain all their own personnel records but a standardized set of returns is devised for transmission to the central personnel information office to be processed by the computer or manually so that the group statistical analyses and returns can be prepared. In this situation, the aim should be to keep the central returns to a minimum, possibly only covering basic data on manpower numbers and trends, and earnings.

Procedures

The procedures to be used in collecting, analysing, disseminating and updating information should be laid down at the design stage so that everyone knows what to do and when to do it. Decisions should be made at this stage as to whether data should be *event triggered* or *time triggered.*

Event triggered data are recorded when pre-specified events occur, giving information about the occurrence or non-occurrence of a particular event, eg an accident, or someone leaving, which is important for control purposes. *Time triggered* recordings are generated at pre-specified intervals of time, eg earnings surveys.

The procedures for disseminating information should list who initiates the report, to whom it goes and, where appropriate, what action should be taken. Updating procedures may include reviews of the relevance and accuracy of data as well as systems to ensure that changes in data are recorded quickly and accurately.

Examples of forms and statistical returns

The following are examples of basic forms and statistical returns:

Type of Form	Figure No.
Basic personnel record card	18.1
Quarterly return – employment, labour turnover and earnings	18.2
Monthly analysis of leavers	18.3
Monthly/annual summary of absence	18.4

Name		Date joined
Date of birth	Marital status	No. of children
Address		Home telephone no.
Qualifications		
Languages		

Previous employment		
Company	Position	Dates

Present employment		
Department	Position	Dates
Date left	Reason for leaving	

Front

Salary — Performance — Potential Record			
Date	Salary	Performance rating	Potential rating

Training received	
Date	Course

Reverse

Figure 18.1 Basic personnel record card

QUARTERLY RETURN – EMPLOYMENT, LABOUR TURNOVER AND EARNINGS

Occupation	Number on pay-roll			Labour turnover annual rate %			Average weekly earnings		
	This quarter	Increase(+) or decrease(-) since:		This quarter	Increase(+) or decrease(-) since:		This quarter	Increase(+) or decrease(-) since:	
		Last quarter	Same quarter last year		Last quarter	Same quarter last year		Last quarter	Same quarter last year
Total									

Quarter ending

Figure 18.2 Quarterly return – employment, labour turnover and earnings

MONTHLY ANALYSIS OF LEAVERS

Month of _____ 19 ____ Department _____ Occupation(s) _____

Reasons for Leaving

Length of service	Sex	Discharge		Personal better-ment	Dissatisfaction with:				Domestic reasons	Retire-ment	Death	Unknown	Total
		Unsuit-able	Discipline Redun-dancy		Pay Work	Working conditions	Hours	Manage-ment	Other factors					
Less than 1 month	M													
	F													
1 - 3 months	M													
	F													
4 - 12 months	M													
	F													
1 - 5 years	M													
	F													
Over 6 years	M													
	F													
Total	M													
	F													

Labour turnover rate expressed as an annual rate%*

	This month	Last month	Same month last year
Male			
Female			
Total			

* Monthly labour turnover rate expressed as an annual rate%.

$$= \left[\frac{\text{Number of leavers during month}}{\text{Average number employed during month}} \right] \times 100 \times 12$$

Figure 18.3 Monthly analysis of leavers

MONTHLY/ANNUAL SUMMARY OF ABSENCE

Year	Department/company					Occupation(s)			
Month	Hours of absence						Total planned hours (including overtime)	% lost of planned hours (including overtime)
	Sickness or accident		Other absence		Total absence (including lateness)			
	Certified	Uncertified	Authorized	Unauthorized (inc. lateness)				
January								
February								
March								
April								
May								
June								
July								
August								
September								
October								
November								
December								
Total for year								

Figure 18.4 Monthly/annual summary of absence

Chapter 19
Computerized Personnel
Information Systems

Background

The rapid expansion of information technology in recent years, especially in the use of micro-computers, and the development of new facilities for using databases more flexibly and for networking, have combined to produce what Colin Richards-Carpenter of the Institute of Manpower Studies (IMS) has described as 'the astonishing growth in computer applications within the personnel field.'[1] This growth has produced increasingly sophisticated packages covering almost every aspect of human resource management.

Against this background, this chapter deals with:

1. The overall role of the computerized personnel information system (CPIS).
2. CPIS applications in such areas as personnel records, human resource planning, salary modelling and expert systems.
3. Selecting the system.
4. Developing the system.
5. Operating the system.

The role of the computerized personnel information system (CPIS)

The role of a CPIS is to:

- Improve administrative efficiency by speeding up the provision of data, by reducing the resources required to carry out routine administration, and by freeing resources for the higher value activities which are fundamental to the success of business management.
- Provide decision support – information which gives a factual basis for decisions concerning the planning, acquisition, development and utilization and remuneration of human resources.

Achieving the role

A CPIS achieves its role by:

1. *Data capture* – maintaining a database of personnel records and other information.
2. *Administrative actions* – using the database to:

   - produce listings of employees by age, length of service, job category, job grade, rate of pay, etc;
   - generate reports analysing distribution in such areas as relationships between age or service and job grade or pay;
   - initiate and print internal memoranda and documents such as notification of pay increases or contracts of employment;
   - produce external letters such as offers of employment;
   - use electronic mailing facilities to transmit data and correspondence between terminals.

3. *Decision support* – using the database to answer 'what if' and other *ad hoc* inquiries and to carry out modelling and trend analysis and to produce projections.

Applications

The main applications for which a CPIS can be used are described below under the following headings:

- personnel records
- integrated systems
- human resource planning
- recruitment
- reward management
- organization planning and development
- performance management
- human resource management
- absence control
- equal opportunity monitoring
- competency modelling
- expert systems.

Personnel records

The database

The personnel record system is essentially the electronic file, but it also provides the database for the whole CPIS.

A database is a collection of integrated data stored so that it can be accessed by authorized users with simple 'user friendly' dialogs, ie information retrieval devices. The physical database is the form in which data are actually held in the storage media. From this can be developed one or more logical databases which comprise the database as viewed by the user. The structure of the data in a logical database need not be the same as in the physical database. The two main types of database are:

1. *The relational database.* This comprises a collection of relations between different items of data which can be manipulated and reconfigured by the database management system. This provides a high degree of flexibility in the use of the system.
2. *The hierarchical or network database.* This is a database which allows records to be related to one another in a predetermined network. In this system, the data structure is defined at the outset and after that the links between records are automatically forged. The advantages claimed for this type of database are that it is easier for the user to operate the system, no duplicate information needs to be kept, mass updates are immediately reflected throughout the database and it is quicker to operate than a relational one, particularly as the database expands. But a hierarchical database could be less flexible than a relational one.

Types of records

The main types of personnel records as described below are:

- personal details
- job details
- employment contracts
- salary details
- performance appraisal
- contacts and addresses
- employee transactional data.

Personal details

Personal details contain all the information which is personal to the employee such as sex, a 'known as name', marital status, etc. An example of a personal details screen as provided by Percom's PMS system, which uses a hierarchical database, is shown in Figure 19.1.

The Percom system provides a standard screen for these personal details and also what they call a 'window', which enables additional information to be held. In this example, the top half comprises the standard screen which includes a range of personal information, including ethnic origin and union membership, and two free fields to record other personal duties such as first aider, fire officer, shop steward, registered disabled. The

```
┌11:19──────────────────────────PERSONAL DETAILS──────────────────────22/03/88┐
│                                                                              │
│Surname     P.................  Initials   ...   Reference No      .........  │
│Forenames   ..............      .............................  Title    ....  │
│Known as    ..............      Prev Sname ....................  Sex      .   │
│Birthdate   /  /     Age __    Mar Status ..    Children   0. Mobility .       │
│Eth Orig    ../...   Nationality .../...         Union       ..........       │
│Join Date   /  /     Int Tel No .............    Car Reg     ...........       │
│Address     ............................         Post Code   ..........        │
│            ............................         Telephone   ............       │
│            ............................         Free Field1 ...............    │
│            ............................         Free Field2 ...............    │
│                                                                              │
├──────────────────────────────────────────────────────────────────────────────┤
│Newman          CE   : `073                                                    │
│Njie            A    : 255                                                     │
│O'Brien         JR   : 204                                                     │
│O'Neill         PM   : 228                                                     │
│Parrott         JA   : 229                                                     │
│Pataki          L    : 249                                                     │
│Patel           M    : 221                                                     │
│Peluso          L    : 226                                                     │
└──────────────────────────────────────────────────────────────────────────────┘
```

Figure 19.1 A personal details screen – Percom PMS system

lower half of the screen caters for data which can usefully be stored in this basic record such as job, salary and grade details.

Job details

This screen (Figure 19.2) gives details of the job the employee occupies rather than the employee, ie the establishment record. Each job is identified by a code number and can be classified into larger generic groups. In

```
┌00:07──────────────────────────JOB DETAILS──────────────────────────01/01/80┐
│                                                                              │
│Job No  PD.... Job Family Code  DIR...   Job Title   Production Director......│
│Dept    PROD.. Production                Div  MFG    Manufacturing            │
│Company SI     Sunrise Industries Plc    CstC AB123. Automation Budget 123    │
│Grade   DIR... Date 10/06/83 ITB         JobT D..... Director                 │
│Rep to  MD.... Managing Director_____  Loc  WAR    Warrington               │
│        036____ Powell_____    Int Tel No  157.........  FTE 1.0000 │
│Free Field1    ..................        Free Field3 ..........               │
│Free Field2    ..................        Free Field4 ..........  Vac No ......│
│                                                                              │
├──────────────────────────────────────────────────────────────────────────────┤
│Surname  Peters              Initials FG   Reference No          090          │
│Assignment Date      06/04/1986                                               │
│                                                                              │
│                                                                              │
│                                                                              │
│                                                                              │
│                                                                              │
└──────────────────────────────────────────────────────────────────────────────┘
```

Figure 19.2 A job details screen – Percom PMS system

this example the production manager is in the job type 'manager' and the family 'technical manager'. Other information includes reporting relationships, location and a vacancy number so that the user can flag it for establishment report purposes. The window shows the name of the job holder and the comment screen (Figure 19.3) can be used as a note pad to record any other items of information about the employee that cannot be held elsewhere.

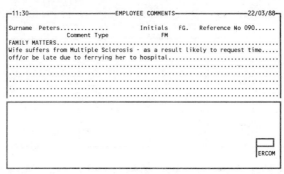

Figure 19.3 Employee comments screen – Percom PMS system

Employment contract

An example of the information that can be shown on an employment screen is shown in Figure 19.4.

Figure 19.4 Employment contract screen – Percom PMS system

Salary details

A salary detail screen is illustrated in Figure 19.5. The standard screen gives details of salary review dates, job grade, basic salary, earnings, and, in the free fields, bonuses or other payments. There is scope to record the total cost of employment, including National Insurance contributions and allowances. The window shows the employee's salary history.

Performance appraisal

The performance appraisal screen shown in Figure 19.6 holds information

```
┌─11:21─────────────────────SALARY DETAILS────────────────22/03/88─┐
│ Surname   Peters.............      Initials FG.   Reference No 090......
│
│ Review Date             /  /       Reason   AR. Next Review      01/01/88
│ NI No    XT237837C...              Personal Grade    ...... (.)
│ Job Grade DIR___                   Grade Point      0
│ Basic Salary/Wage    26375.0000    Period A Currency ST.  Payroll Code S
│ Earnings 1           21500.00      Earnings 2                 23000.00
│ Free Field 1             0.0000    Free Field 3          ..............
│ Free Field 2             0.00      Free Field 4          ..............
│
├──────────────────────────────────────────────────────────────────┤
│ 01/01/1987    AR       26375.0000     JG DIR      PG
│ 01/10/1986    AR       25000.0000     JG DIR      PG
│ 30/06/1985    AR       20000.0000     JG MGT2     PG
│ 30/06/1984    AR       19750.0000     JG          PG
│ 13/08/1983    PRO      17500.0000     JG          PG
│ 15/06/1983    AR       15000.0000     JG          PG
│ 13/06/1982    AR       13500.0000     JG          PG
└──────────────────────────────────────────────────────────────────┘
```

Figure 19.5 Salary details screen – Percom PMS system

relating to both performance and potential (accessible to the employee under the British Data Protection Act). The appraisal history can be shown in the window.

```
┌─11:28───────────────────PERFORMANCE APPRAISAL──────────────22/03/88─┐
│Surname  Peters.............       Initials  FG.   Reference No 090......
│
│Last Appraisal Date    /  /        Appraised By  H Flaxman...............
│Next Appraisal Date  14/05/87
│Performance Rating    08           Performance Profile    High...........
│Potential Rating      08           Potential Profile      Superior.......
│
│Remarks   Adapting well to new role as manager.......................
│
├──────────────────────────────────────────────────────────────────┤
│
│
│
│ 14/05/1986            H Flaxman                              08
│ 14/05/1985            S Newton                               C
│
└──────────────────────────────────────────────────────────────────┘
```

Figure 19.6 Performance appraisal screen – Percom PMS system

Contacts and addresses

If the personnel department wants to keep additional addresses relating to their employees such as those for the previous employer, an emergency contact, next of kin, spouse's work place, and bank, these can be held in a contacts and addresses file as shown in Figure 19.7.

```
┌─11:29──────────────────CONTACTS / ADDRESSES──────────────22/03/88─┐
│ Surname Peters.............     Initials FG.   Reference No 090......
│
│ Address Type BNK. Address   Midland Bank.................
│                             44 Hatton Road...............
│                             Warrington...................
│                             Lancs........................
│                   Post Code WE3 5RD...
│ Telephone     0295-38599... / .............
│ Contact Name  Mr H Arnold............. Relationship      Bank Manager...
│ Free Field1   30-20-40...........    Free Field2 0198842.............
├──────────────────────────────────────────────────────────────────┤
│
│
│
│
│                                                        ┌─┐
│                                                        └─┘
│                                                        ERCOM
└──────────────────────────────────────────────────────────────────┘
```

Figure 19.7 Contacts and addresses file – Percom PMS system

Employee transactional data

A computerized record system can also be used to hold all these special items of information that companies need about their employees such as qualifications, special skills, training, absence, medical records and discipline. In the Percom system, what is termed a flexiscreen is used for this purpose, as illustrated in Figure 19.8, where the screen displays the somewhat unhappy medical record of Mr Peters. Additional data can be

```
┌─11:31──────────────────EMPLOYEE TRANSACTIONAL DATA────────────22/03/88─┐

 Surname  Peters.............        Initials FG.    Reference No 090......

 Trans Group     AA                  Group Name   Absence_____
 Trans Type      SI....              Type Name    Sickness_____


 Start     End      Code             Reason            NoWkDays  SSP Days  SM Au
 ----------------------------------------------------------------------------
 ./../.. 03/03/88 06.... Broken Hand..............    12.00      9.00    M. KL


 ┌────────────────────────────────────────────────────────────────────────┐
 │ 17/02/1988 03/03/88 06    Broken Hand              12.00      9.00    M  KL │
 │ 02/01/1985 03/01/85 02    Upset Stomach             1.00      0.00    S     │
 │ 24/10/1984 30/10/84 01    Influenza                 5.00      2.00    S  KL │
 │ 21/08/1984 23/08/84 04    Stiff Back                3.00      0.00    S  KL │
 │ 17/07/1984 22/07/84 01    Heavy Cold                4.00      1.00    S  KN │
 │ 10/05/1984 18/05/84 02    Back Pain                 7.00      4.00    S  KN │
 │ 21/03/1984 25/03/84 02    Gastroenteritis           5.00      2.00    M  KN │
 └────────────────────────────────────────────────────────────────────────┘
```

Figure 19.8 Employee transactional screen

expanded on a supplementary screen as shown in Figure 19.9 which contains detailed records of qualifications which can be linked to a skills inventory (see below).

```
┌─11:32──────────────EMPLOYEE SUPPLEMENTARY DATA────────22/03/88─┐

 Surname  Peters.............      Initials FG.   Reference No 090......

 Supplement Type EDQ               Description  Education Qualifications
 ------------------------------------------------------------------------
 Level   HND.......    .......... CSE     .. O Level 7..        0.00
 School  12/09/66  End Dt  16/06/72  A Level 3. S Level ...     0.00
 Univ    04/10/72  End Dt  06/05/75  OND    .. HND    ...       0.00
 Degree  BSc Engineering............. RSA    .. C&Quild ...     0.00
 Univ/Co Lincoln College-Oxford....... Other  ..        ...     0.00

 ┌──────────────────────────────────────────────────────────┐
 │                                                          ┌┐ │
 │                                                          └┘ │
 │                                                      ERCOM  │
 └──────────────────────────────────────────────────────────┘
```

Figure 19.9 Employee supplementary data screen –
Percom PMS system

Integrated systems

A database approach to using the computer in personnel management means making the most of any personnel data stored in the mainframe computer or in any other mini- or micro-computers in the organization. The database can be the starting point for the various applications described below, but it can also be used to integrate three main areas of administration: people, payroll and pensions. An integrated database system such as the one developed by Peterborough Software allows payroll, pension and statutory sick pay applications to use the data stored on the computerized personnel information system. The advantages of swifter and cheaper administration arising from linking these areas is obvious.

Human resource planning (manpower planning)

Human resource flows

A CPIS can be used to model the effects on groups of people within the organization of change over time in the numbers and structure of each group and movements into, through and out of each group. A model such as MICROPROSPECT developed by the Institute of Manpower Studies looks at the organization using a manpower system consisting of grades and flows. The user has considerable freedom in defining the number and type of flows required whether into, through or out of each level of the system, ie:

- flows in – recruitment, transfers in;
- flows out – transfers out, retirement, resignation (uncontrolled losses), early retirement (controlled losses).

The user can control the way in which the flow is operated by specifying recruitment as numbers to be 'pushed' in, percentages to be 'pulled out' to meet a target, or proportions by age or length of service bands.

Wastage monitoring and control

Computer models can monitor and help in the control of wastage. They can therefore provide a critical input to other areas of human resource decision making such as policies on recruitment, promotion, redeployment, training and career planning.

The Institute of Manpower Studies' WASP model offers the following modules which can be specified by either using age or length of service bands:

1. *Cohort* – wastage or survival rates for the same group of people over a specified period of time.

2. *Census* – a cross-sectional analysis of current wastage patterns for a particular group of people.
3. *Plot* – a display of up to four sets of data, eg wastage rates and services.
4. *Projections* – the age or length of service distribution for a group of people projected into the future under specified influences of policies.
5. *Compare* – a statistical comparison of two wastage patterns for two groups of people or the same group of people over time.

Human resource management

The CPIS can be used to provide an integral system for gearing human resources to business needs. The process of scheduling human resources to meet output in processing targets is becoming increasingly complex with the availability of more flexible ways of deploying people. They include multi-skilling (employees who are capable of carrying out different tasks and are not subject to trade union-imposed constraints in doing so), the use of contract workers, the use of out-workers (people working at home or in another centre, a process which is facilitated by computer networking and electronic mailing), twilight shifts, more part-timers, job sharing, etc.

Human resource planning is an interactive process which is always using output from one part of the process to influence another part of the process. Thus, assessments of the demand and supply of people, scheduling policies and possibilities, and the scope for flexing work loads and the use of people will all influence the human resource supply policies adopted by the organization.

A CPIS provides the best basis for modelling this whole interrelated and iterative process which is illustrated in Figure 19.10.

Profiling

Profiling is a particular aspect of employee scheduling concerned with the matching of staff to workloads and ensuring that the right number of people are available to meet fluctuations in activity levels over time. Profiling techniques are used where there are measurable volumes of work that can be costed and forecast with reasonable accuracy. Profiling can be linked with staff budgeting control in the sense that the use of staff resources is both constrained and influenced by the cash budget and performance and staff establishment targets.

Profiling models such as the one developed by the Department of Health and Social Security in association with the Institute of Manpower Studies can be used to:

● monitor and analyse staff usage;

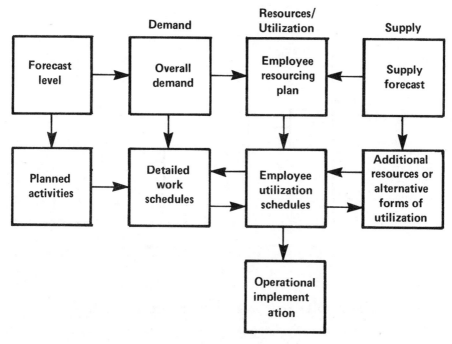

Figure 19.10 The CPIS human resource planning process

- disentangle the interactive effects between staff in-post targets and other staffing constraints;
- test the effects of moving some activities to different times of the year and analyse their predicted impact on the staffing profile;
- monitor movements in expenditure on pay and other employee benefits and carry out sensitivity tests on the impact of different salary assumptions;
- forecast future staff requirements;
- synchronize the recruitment of permanent and temporary staff with forecast workloads;
- flex staff budgets on the basis of revised activity level forecasts;
- control staff budgets.

The profiling model can generate bar charts such as the one illustrated in Figure 19.11 which shows staff surpluses and shortfalls over a year. The model can then be used to work out the implications of alternative resourcing strategies such as rescheduling training or overtime. In this example (Figure 19.12) the model has been used to indicate how the shortage in Period 6, the holiday month, could be eliminated by such means.

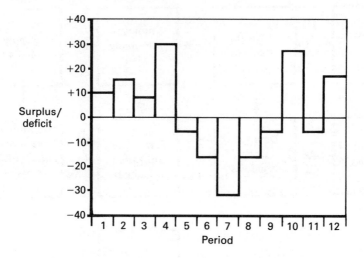

Figure 19.11 Staff usage profile before adjustment

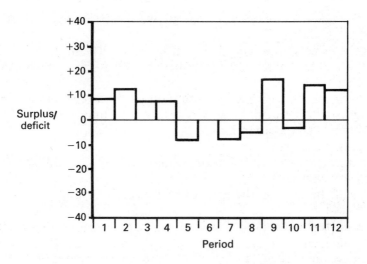

Figure 19.12 Staff usage profile after adjustment

Recruitment

A CPIS recruitment system can carry out four basic administrative tasks:

1. Storage of applicant's details.
2. Retrieval and amendment of those details.
3. Letter writing (linking the system to word processing facilities) – acknowledgements, invitations to interview, offers and rejections.
4. Management reports, analysis of response by media and monitoring recruitment costs.

Automated recruitment control packages such as the one developed by Hall Associates will not only automate recruitment correspondence (coupling the CPIS with word processors) but will also enable users to determine instantly who has applied for which post, track progress in recruiting for a specific post and match and process internal candidates from the organization's own human resources bank.

The Percom personnel recruitment system maintains three sets of records:

1. Applicant records with personnel details.
2. Vacancy records with job and recruitment details.
3. Applicant processing, which enables information extracted from the database to be put directly into the text of the letter for reproduction on a word processor. The *ad hoc* enquiry facility enables users to match applicants with vacancies so that short-lists can be made, to list applicants by source, vacancy and ethnic origin, to diarize follow-up actions, to calculate recruitment costs and to carry out statistical analyses of the number of applications, interviews, offers, rejections, and the cost effectiveness of the recruitment source or medium or the internal recruiter.

Reward management

A CPIS can be used for salary modelling and to carry out a number of salary administration activities.

Salary modelling

Salary models provide the answers to 'what if' questions such as, 'How much would it cost if we gave x per cent to this part of the company, y per cent to another part of the company, and implemented the following special package across these job functions?' A typical model such as PERSIS developed by IBM will start from a database that defines the physical elements of the cost of salaries, such as the number of staff, average pay level for each group of employees, starting and leaving rates, overtime rates and so on. The model takes the personnel database with its movements of job level, promotions, starters, leavers etc, and uses parameters such as the expected level of promotions and range increases contained in the salaries policy files to calculate the cost of the salary review in a particular year, taking into account such factors as attrition (the erosion of the cost of salary increments over a period of time as a result of the average salary of leavers exceeding the average salary of joiners).

Salary administration

A CPIS can:

● Analyse and report on average salaries or salary distributions by job, grade, age or length of service – this could be expressed initially in the form of a scattergram as illustrated in Figure 19.13. Regression lines showing trends can then be plotted onto a vertical axis as shown in Figure 19.14 which divides the salary progression curves into deciles.

Figure 19.13 Scattergram of distribution of salaries by age

● Calculate compa-ratios to show how average salaries in a range differ from the target salary of the midpoint of the range – a compa-ratio is calculated as follows:

$$\frac{\text{average of all salaries in grade}}{\text{midpoint of range}} \times 100$$

● Calculate the effects of attrition.
● Estimate the costs of salary reviews.

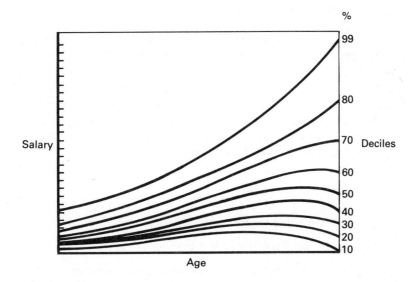

Figure 19.14 Distribution of salaries – regression (trend) lines

● Provide the basis for preparing and monitoring salary bands.
● Forecast future salary costs on the basis of given assumptions about numbers, promotions and pay levels.
● Administer pay reviews, producing review forms, analysing proposals against the budgets and agreed values of distributions of merit increases, calculating the implications of alternative review guide lines, generating instructions to adjust pay and letters to individuals informing them of their increase. If there are any formulae governing the relationship between merit assessments and merit increases, the CPIS can work these out.

Organization planning and development

The CPIS database can be used in more advanced applications to assist in:

● experimenting with and amending the organization structure in the face of changing market or technology demands;
● designing or redesigning new or existing jobs within the structure against which specific goals and performance standards can be developed;
● establishing selection profiles incorporating the standards against which potential job holders can be assessed so that the right people can be appointed or promoted into jobs.

Performance management

A CPIS can help to operate a performance appraisal and management system, generating appraisal forms, analysing and reporting on the result of performance reviews showing the distribution of people with different degrees of potential or performing at different levels, and highlighting individuals with particular skills or who are specially promising. This system can be linked to others to provide an integrated basis for creating and implementing human resource management policies (see competency modelling and expert systems below).

Human resource management

Training administration (computer-managed learning)

A CPIS can be used for training administration by:

- analysing the training recommendations contained in performance appraisal reports to identify collective and individual training needs;
- identifying suitable training courses to meet training needs;
- making arrangements for 'off the job' courses (booking facilities, inviting speakers);
- informing managers and staff about the arrangements for courses;
- handling correspondence about training courses;
- storing data on standard or individually tailored induction, continuation or development training programmes, including syllabi, routings, responsibilities for giving training, test procedures and progress reporting;
- generating instructions and notes for guidance for all concerned with providing or undergoing on-the-job training programmes;
- storing progress reports and monitoring achievements against training objectives;
- producing reports summarizing current and projected training activities and calculating the output of training programmes – this can be linked to human resource planning models including those designed to determine the input of apprentices or trainees required for training schemes;
- recording and monitoring training expenditure against budget.

Computer-based training

Computer-based training (CBT) is a form of individualized learning and, as such, is a manifestation of educational technology. It uses the power of the computer to assist in the constant need to train and retrain workers in new processes and procedures. It also plays an important part in 'distance learning' in the fields of occupational training and higher education for institutions such as the Open University.

CBT starts with the process of instructional systems design (ISD). Each individual lesson is planned on the basis of careful job analysis, sequencing and testing. The experience gained in the 1960s in the development of teaching machines, feedback classrooms and programmed instruction has had a powerful influence on CBT.

CBT enables instructors to build into their sessions the adaptability that a truly interactive process of learning should provide. Using a computer, the author can devise an interactive sequence in which the responses the students make will determine their route through the training unit or programme – a route which will be unique to them alone.

CBT uses hardware as illustrated in Figure 19.15.

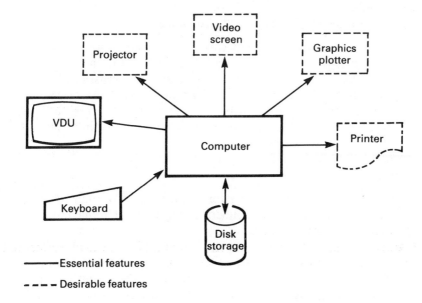

Figure 19.15 Computer-based training hardware

(Source: *The Personnel Training Databook*. Kogan Page, 1985)

Most CBT systems get trainees to study text on a visual display unit (VDU). They respond to problems which appear on the screen by typing an answer on a keyboard. More advanced systems use interactive video as described in Appendix K on training techniques.

Skills inventory

Many organizations need to store detailed information about the skills and experience of the individuals they employ. A separate skills inventory can be linked to a personnel database so that any individual changes in experience or additional training can be fed through automatically to it. This provides a basis for assessing the strengths and weaknesses of the organization in terms of available skills, and leads to the design of special training programmes to fill any gaps.

Career management

A CPIS can help in the implementation of career management policies and procedures which embrace both career planning and management development. The system does this by analysing the progression of individuals and comparing the results of that analysis first with assessments of organizational requirements as generated by the human resource planning models and, secondly, with the outputs of the performance management system.

The system developed by Royal Insurance:

● assesses the 'supply' side of career development as shown by salary progression (see Figures 19.13 and 19.14) and extrapolates on the basis of the last four years' average increases the progression of each individual for a period of five years ahead;
● identifies from their assessment those whose progression is such that they could move into the next level and also those who are 'plateauing out' or appear to be slipping;
● shows the number of vacancies likely to arise;
● lists possible candidates against those vacancies.

The output of this and similar systems can be used to plan for management succession and to devise collective or individual management development training programmes.

Career progression curves can be produced using computer techniques to show the percentage of those recruited or in-post at a certain age who are likely to finish their careers in a particular grade. A simplified product of this type of analysis is given in Figure 19.16 which shows that 50% of those engaged at a certain age who remain with the organization are likely to get no further than Grade 3 when they retire, while 30% will achieve Grade 2 and 20% Grade 1.

Absence control

Absence control can be carried out with the help of computerized time recording and attendance systems which:

● record clocking-in or out time and the hours actually worked;
● enable employees to record the time spent on particular jobs;
● get employees to explain the reason for late arrival or early departure or for any other absence;

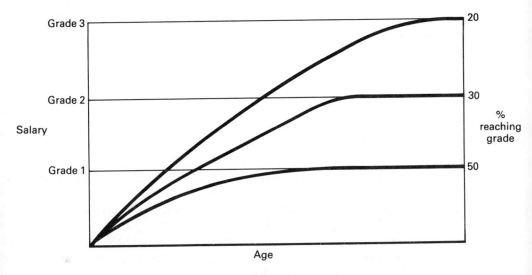

Figure 19.16 Career progression analysis

- can be linked to the payroll system for pay and bonus calculation purposes and to a flexible working hours system;
- provide supervisors with a statement on the first day back to work showing the length and reasons for absence. ˙

Advanced systems link information obtained from clocking-in or out direct to a screen in supervisors' offices so that they have instant information on how many people are at work and on the incidence of lateness.

Equal opportunity monitoring

The CPIS can store records of the racial composition of the labour force. This information can be analysed to produce data on the distribution of ethnic minorities by occupation, job grade, age, service and location. The sort of information the analysis could provide is the overall proportion of ethnic minority employees compared with the proportion in each job grade. Similar statistics can be produced for men and women. The analysis can be extended to cover career progression, splitting the results of the overall analysis into comparisons of the rate at which women and men of different ethnic groups progress.

Competency modelling

Competency modelling brings together organization planning and performance management data to establish the skills or competencies required to do particular jobs. This will assist in appointment, promotion and training decisions. Competency analysis looks both at what tasks have to be carried out and at the skills required. Profiles can then be developed by the computer and matched to assessments of current job holders or job applicants.

Expert systems

Expert systems are computer programs which contain knowledge about particular fields of human activity and experience, which, through linkages and rules built into the system design, can help solve human resource management problems. Unlike a database system which stores, sorts, manipulates and presents bits of information – ie data – expert systems store, sort, manipulate and present managers with ready-to-use knowledge of management practice, written in a language that management understands, as opposed to computerese.

The expert system developed in British Shipbuilders began by defining about seventy 'job dimensions', which are discrete activities from which a combination can be selected to provide a specification for any possible job. Each dimension can operate at from four to six levels of responsibility. The next stage was to define all the attributes that people needed to perform each of the dimensions at the different levels – fifty attributes were identified, each scaled at from five to six levels.

The software engineering that followed these analyses linked attributes with dimensions in such a way as to identify the optimum attribute level for each dimension level. Because of the numbers of possible combinations, this could only be done with the help of a computer. A user-friendly package was then developed for analysing any job, and models were produced to maintain, monitor and control vacancy procedures to help in performance appraisal, to evaluate jobs, to advise on training needs, to administer psychological tests and to produce organization charts.

Selecting the system

When selecting the computer system the considerations that should be taken into account are:

- what is to be computerized?
- bureau or in-house?
- mainframe, mini or micro?
- package or in-house development?
- the extent to which it has to be user-friendly.

What to computerize?

A CPIS can be used simply to provide administrative support, or its use can be extended to provide decision support in a number of areas. If it is to be no more than an electronic filing system this will obviously simplify the whole development programme, but it would be a pity to neglect all the other applications that could be derived from the database. Requirements for decision support should therefore be considered from an early stage. Another factor to be taken into account is the need for the system to be flexible so that it can expand and link with other systems.

Bureau or in-house?

Bureaux operate and maintain computers externally and charge out on a time-sharing basis. They are worth considering when large quantities of batch processing are involved which cannot be dealt with on company hardware, or where powerful computer facilities are needed but not in any great quantity. Bureaux are often used by small or medium sized companies for their payroll or for pensions administration.

Bureaux are, however, not so appropriate when the company wants an integrated administrative system and/or a decision support facility. Members of the personnel department must obviously have immediate access to data and the ability to obtain answers to enquiries and to use the computer in association with word processors as a memorandum, letter writing and report production facility. The full development of a CPIS is only possible if it is operated in-house.

Mainframe, mini or microcomputer?

Mainframes and minicomputers are more robust than micros, they hold more information, they process data faster and there is more software available (although this situation so far as micros are concerned is changing rapidly as software packages proliferate). Mainframes and minis therefore offer greater scope for the wider applications of database management.

Micros are, of course, less expensive and the personnel department can have sole use of one or more of them for its own purposes. They are at their best in applications involving calculations rather than heavy information. But they have plenty of potential as integrated administration systems provided that:

- the personnel department concerned is small enough to be happy with a single-user application;
- certain limits are placed on the amount of data to be stored (these limits are not very severe but could become relevant in a company employing thousands rather than hundreds of people);

- certain compromises concerning the robustness of the system are acceptable to the users;
- the software has been written in a highly efficient way.

Package or in-house development?

A package is a software system which is already fully written. It will have sufficient flexibility to be applicable in different organizations, although the software houses are increasingly marketing packages which are relevant for particular businesses. Packages are being developed in increasing numbers by a number of specialist firms.

The likelihood of finding an appropriate software package, even if the choice is somewhat bewildering, is enhanced by the fact that suppliers are dealing with data requirements that are common to many if not all organizations. Everyone wants to store such things as personal details, employment history and pay, benefits and job grade information.

In-house development seems to offer a more flexible approach at less cost, but these advantages may be illusory. As mentioned above, there is plenty of choice for packages which are increasingly flexible in use. And the cost of buying software, although seemingly high, may well be only one-tenth of the true cost of developing a system in-house.

User-friendly?

Whatever type of hardware or software is adopted the system must be user-friendly. That is, members of the personnel department without specialized computer skills or elaborate training must be able to input data, gain access to the information they require and use the system for administrative purposes or as decision support without difficulty.

Implementing the system

The ten steps required to implement a CPIS are:

1. *Determine objectives* – are they to save administrative costs, speed up processing, provide advanced decision support, or a combination of any of these?
2. *Carry out a feasibility study* to consider applications and their likely costs and benefits. This study could be carried out in-house or with the help of outside consultants or software houses who provide a consultancy service. The feasibility study will broadly analyse and define user requirements and ensure that all concerned are aware of what is being planned, how they will benefit from it and the contribution they will be expected to make to the development and application of the system.
3. *Prepare a requirements specification* which will set out in detail

what the system is expected to do and how the company would like to use it. This specification can be used to brief hardware and software suppliers before selecting the system.

4. *Select the system* in the form of the hardware and the software required. This may involve decisions on the extent to which existing hardware or systems (eg payroll systems) will be used. The need and scope for networking, that is linking users by means of terminals, and the employment of word processors will also need to be considered. At this stage caution has to be exercised not to limit the value of the CPIS by relying too much on the use of existing facilities. There are apparent attractions, not least cost savings, in using the mainframe or the payroll system, but these could restrict the development of a fully integrated system which can be used flexibly by the personnel department.

5. *Plan the implementation programme* to ensure that the objectives will be achieved within a given timescale and in line with the cost budget.

6. *Involve users* to ensure that everyone who will benefit from the system (line managers as well as members of the personnel department) can contribute their ideas and thus feel that it is *their* system rather than one imposed upon them.

7. *Control the project* against the implementation programme to ensure that it delivers what is required, on time and within the budget.

8. *Provide training* to all users to ensure that they can operate and get the most out of the system.

9. *Monitor performance* to ensure that the system lives up to expectations.

10. *Continually develop* the basic system to extend its use in administration and decision support.

Reference

1. Richards-Carpenter, C 'Achieving Practical Solutions – Current Concerns', *Computers in Personnel*. Institute of Personnel Management and Institute of Manpower Studies, 1987.

Part VI
Reward Management

Reward management is about designing, implementing and maintaining pay systems which are geared to the improvement of organizational performance. This aspect of personnel management used to be called salary administration, but this is now regarded as a limited description of one aspect of the whole subject of payment which is only concerned with administering the pay system and exercising control over the implementation of pay policies. The alternative phrase 'compensation management' is used in the US, and gaining recognition in the UK. It is generally used to represent a more up-to-date approach to creating and managing pay systems, but the use of the word 'compensation' seems to imply that work is an unpleasant necessity which people have to be compensated for doing rather than spending their time more rewardingly elsewhere. Reward management is the term used in this book because it describes a more positive approach to paying people for what they have done and can do for the enterprise and for themselves by contributing effectively to the achievement of organizational objectives.

In this part, the basis of reward management is examined first. Consideration is given to reward management strategies and policies, the factors affecting pay levels and the role of money as a motivator. The next two chapters (21 and 22) discuss the two criteria which determine pay levels: first, internal equity and the process of measuring and comparing levels of responsibility by means of job evaluation, and, secondly, methods of establishing market rates so that the organization can ensure that its pay structure remains competitive. One of the points made in this part is that the need for organizations to be more flexible and responsive to their environment means that pay levels are much more influenced by market conditions than before.

Chapter 23 reviews the various kinds of pay structures and their design. Current trends in the direction of increased flexibility are explored. The conventional graded salary structure is not yet a thing of the past, but many organizations are finding it necessary to offer their employees more scope to increase their rewards according to performance and achievement –

what might be called the RPA (rewards for performance and achievement) approach to remuneration.

This leads naturally into Chapters 24 and 25 which consider methods of rewarding performance either in a salary progression system, or by payment by results for manual workers, or by profit sharing or one of the other types of bonus schemes that are available.

Chapter 25 also reviews the other forms of remuneration and employee benefits which can be included in the total reward or remuneration package. Finally, salary administration procedures are considered in Chapter 26 as a means of ensuring that the pay system operates properly.

One of the recurring themes in this part was well expressed by Rosabeth Moss Kanter, who in her *Harvard Business Review* article in April 1987, 'Attack on Pay', delivered a broadside against traditional pay plans in which, as she wrote:

> Each job comes with a pay level that stays about the same regardless of how well the job is performed or what the real organizational value of that performance is. Pay scales reflect such estimated characteristics as decision-making responsibilities, importance to the organization, and number of subordinates. If there is a merit component, it is usually very small. The surest way – often the only way – to increase one's pay is to change employers or get promoted. A mountain of tradition and industrial relations practice has built up to support this way of calculating pay.

Perhaps things are not quite as bad as that in the UK, but there is still a need for increased flexibility so that PRA can operate for the good of the organization and its members. This means accepting Rosabeth Kanter's plea to create new forms for identifying, reorganizing, and ultimately rewarding contributions so that 'the iron cage of bureaucracy is rattled in ways that will eventually change the nature and the meaning of hierarchy in ways we cannot yet imagine'.

Her final words, with which the writer entirely agrees, were that we must:

> Analyze – and, if necessary, rethink – the relationship between pay and value to the organization. Keep in mind that organizational levels defined for purposes of co-ordination do not necessarily reflect contributions to performance goals, and de-couple pay from status and rank. And finally, be prepared to justify pay decisions in terms of clear contributions – and to offer these contributions more often to more stakeholder groups.

Chapter 20
The Basis of Reward Management

Reward management is concerned with the design, implementation and maintenance of remuneration systems which help the organization to achieve its objectives. To do this, the systems have to provide for competitive levels of remuneration and ensure that rewards are linked explicitly to contribution, performance and potential. They must also be effectively communicated and be perceived by employees as meeting their needs for recognition.

Many of the conventional approaches to salary administration operated in the 1970s are no longer valid in these days when enterprise is the key to success and, in the world of industry and commerce, competition is severe and only the fit survive. In a significant article in the *Harvard Business Review* Rosabeth Kanter wrote:

> Status, not contriubution, has traditionally been the basis for numbers on employee's pay-checks. Pay has reflected where jobs rank in the corporate hierarchy – not what comes out of them. Today this system is under attack. More and more senior executives are trying to turn their employees into entrepreneurs – people who earn a direct return on the value they help create, often in return for putting their pay at risk. In the process, changes are coming into play that will have revolutionary consequences for companies and their employees.[1]

It is this approach which has to be taken into account when defining the aims of reward management.

Overall aims of reward management

The primary aim of reward management is to underpin the drive to improve organizational performance. The achievement of excellence and, in the phrase of Peters and Waterman, 'productivity through people', depends on attracting and retaining the right calibre of people and then, having got them, providing them with both financial and non-financial incentives and rewards which will maintain and indeed increase their motivation. In short, the aims of reward management are to attract, retain and motivate people of the quality required by the enterprise.

The need to satisfy individual expectations

The achievement of this overall aim on the part of managements depends on their ability to convince employees that the reward system meets their needs. Where individual agreements are made on remuneration, mutual satisfaction depends on fixing a rate which is felt to be fair on both sides in relation to the contribution and market value of the employee. In the case of negotiated settlements, this takes the form of the effort bargain.

The need to conduct satisfactory effort bargains

The objective of employees is to strike a bargain with management about the relation between what they regard as a reasonable contribution, and what the employer is prepared to offer to elicit that contribution. This is termed the 'effort bargain' and may, in effect, be the basis of an agreement between management and unions which lays down the amount of work to be done for the agreed wage, not just the hours to be worked. Explicitly or implicitly, all employers are in a bargaining situation with regard to payment systems. A system will not be effective or workable until it is agreed as being fair and equitable by both sides.

The need to be competitive

High calibre people are in short supply. They will know their worth – the actual or potential value of their contribution – and expect to be rewarded accordingly. The reward system must be attractive and competitive for these people.

The need to recognize solid worth

The philosophy of reward management with its emphasis on performance may seem to favour the stars at the expense of everyone else. This must not be allowed to happen. Good, solid, dependable performance needs to be rewarded too.

Middle ranking managers, supervisors, office and laboratory staff and people working on the shop floor equally deserve to be paid according to their contribution, to get more if they do their job better, to receive extra rewards for special effort and to participate in the success of the organization which ultimately depends on their abilities, skills and effort.

The problem of equity

Rewards must be competitive, but it is necessary to aim for a reasonable degree of equity in remuneration, although complete equity in a competitive situation where market forces drive salary levels may be difficult to attain.

Specific aims of reward management

The overall aims of reward management can be specified in greater depth for three main areas: the organization, its individual employees and, collectively, any trade union or staff association that represents the employees.

Organizational aims

To fulfil its overall aim of helping the organization to attain its goals, the reward management system should be geared to the value of the contributions individuals make to reaching these objectives. It must be tailored to meet the organization's special needs and it should be capable of being easily modified in response to the change that will inevitably take place in a dynamic enterprise.

In particular the system should aim to:

- Ensure that the organization can recruit the quantity and quality of staff it requires.
- Encourage suitable staff to remain with the organization.
- Provide rewards for good performance and incentives for further improvements in performance.
- Achieve equity in the pay for similar jobs.
- Create appropriate differentials between different levels of jobs in accordance with their relative value.
- Operate flexibly enough to accommodate organizational changes and alterations in the relative market rates for different skills.
- Be simple to explain, understand, operate and control.
- Be cost-effective in the sense that the benefits of the system are obtained without undue expense.

Individual aims

Individuals want to feel that they are being treated fairly and would thus like to be paid according to their own valuation of their worth. Their valuation will be based on comparisons with the market rates for similar jobs elsewhere and with the pay received by other staff in the organization. They will expect their salary to increase in line with their own estimate of improvements in their performance and increases in responsibility. They will also want their salaries to keep pace with inflation and general increases in salary levels.

Collective aims

The objective of trade unions and staff associations must be to obtain the maximum benefits for their members without unduly prejudicing their future security. They will want their members' pay to keep ahead of inflation, to match or exceed market rates and to reflect any increases in the prosperity of the company.

Unions and staff associations will also want to obtain as much information as they can about salary policies and pay structures. They will want an equitable system, and some have objected to merit review schemes based on management discretion, because they are thought to be arbitrary and unfair. For this reason, fixed incremental payment schemes may be preferred. However, a number of unions, even within the public sector, have recently adopted a more open-minded approach and will negotiate merit pay systems with management. In these negotiations they will want to satisfy themselves that management will manage the system fairly.

Unions may approve of job evaluation schemes in principle, because they are seen to be the fairest way of grading jobs. They may want to participate in selecting and implementing a scheme but will not wish to prejudice their negotiating rights by agreeing to accept the results of the scheme in advance.

In dealing with trade unions, managements should remember that many now have powerful research departments who provide comprehensive information on pay levels and pay systems generally.

Achieving the aims

The role of top management

Reward management is a positive process designed to help the organization get results. It is not something which exists in isolation from the strategic plans of the enterprise. It is, or it should be, a matter of urgent and continuous concern to top management. Only they can decide where they want the company to go and what sort of people it needs to get there. Only they can distil the advice they are given and make the key decisions about the levels of remuneration the organization needs and how the reward management system should play a major part in improving performance. They can then turn the system over to the administrators to operate and maintain.

Reward management policies

Policies on how rewards should be managed need to be formulated to ensure that the development of the various components of the system are geared to achieving its overall aims. The policies should be thought through against the background of an understanding of (1) the main factors affecting reward levels in an organization, (2) the role of money as a motivator and, importantly, (3) the corporate culture.

Factors affecting reward levels

The factors affecting reward levels in an enterprise are:

1. *Individual worth:* the value of an individual's contribution and performance to the organization.
2. *External relativities:* market rates as affected by supply and demand, general movements in pay levels and particular areas of market pressure.
3. *Internal relativities:* salary relativities between jobs within the organization depending on the values attached to different jobs.
4. *Union pressures:* the influence of trade unions on pay increases and differentials exerted by means of whatever bargaining power they possess.

Individual worth

The value of the contributions made by individuals to achieving organizational goals should determine their rewards. Productivity through people is achieved by paying for performance. This process must not be constrained by the artificial barriers built into rigid salary structures.

External relativities

A salary or wage rate is a price indicating, like any other price, the value of the service to the buyer and seller: the employer and the employed. The going rate for a job (nationally or locally) is its market rate, and those who emphasize the importance of market forces will claim that a job is worth what the market says it is worth. There is much to be said for this point of view. If insufficient attention is given to market rates a company may be unable to attract and retain good quality staff. External equity is a fundamental aim of any reward system: most people look first at the salary level stated in advertisements when seeking a job. Within a company, staff will study advertised salaries to find out if they are being paid fairly in relation to the market and this provides data which will help them to decide whether to stay or to look around for another job.

The external value of a job – the market rate – is primarily determined by the laws of supply or demand. If people in a particular occupation are in short supply they are in a seller's market and can force up prices (ie pay levels). The opposite applies in a buyer's market where there is a surplus of labour. But the labour market is generally not a perfect market. Employers and unions can exert monopolistic pressures to counteract free market forces. People will not always be guided by purely economic factors. They will seek or accept substitutes for their present jobs for what may be largely subjective reasons, rather than on the grounds of an analysis of relative economic values. And one of the factors they will consider is the quality of life the organizations provide – job satisfaction, the work environment and, importantly, the opportunity to use their skills and develop their careers.

Those who claim the supremacy of market forces say that because reward systems are caused by the market, the systems themselves cannot be deemed unfair or inappropriate because they are at the mercy of the market – they are incapable of causing anything. In reality, because it can be difficult to link pay directly to performance, all the market does is to allow us to assume that people occupying equal positions tend to be paid equally, and that people with similar experience and education tend to be worth about the same. As Rosabeth Kanter put it: 'The process is circular . . . we know what people are worth because that's what they cost in the job market, but we also know that what people cost in the market is just what they're worth.'[1]

Be that as it may, no enterprise can afford to ignore the 'going rate' or, as it should properly be described, the going range, if it wants to attract and retain good quality staff. Although internal salary structures are not directly and instantaneously responsive to market forces at all points, the general structure must move up or down and differentials must expand or contract in response to the changing pressures of the market. The points of pressure are most likely to be at the intake points in a structure, for example, among newly qualified accountants, computer specialists or experienced brand managers.

Internal relativities

The value of a job within an organization is relative. There is no such thing as absolute value. The value of anything is always comparative.

Within an organization, pay levels will be affected by real or perceived differences between the value of jobs and the individual contributions made by job holders. Differentials have to be maintained although these may be distorted by the influence of accepted market differentials. It could be argued, however, that differentials established in a market from which a company recruits are right, simply because they are there, and internal differentials have to take account of what the market dictates.

Trade union pressures

To achieve their aims, as described earlier in this chapter, trade unions will exert pressure on pay levels. This impact on the reward system, will, of course, depend on their bargaining power. It is interesting to note that where staff associations have been fostered by management to keep unions out, they have often been able to enforce higher awards because the company has been over-anxious to preserve the staff association's independence against all comers from the real trade union movement.

In the new climate, unions are becoming much more involved in the whole process of productivity, quality and performance improvement. In many cases a more flexible approach is being encouraged by a new generation of more sophisticated negotiators who appreciate that this will benefit their members by increasing their prosperity and their security in a thriving organization.

The role of money as a motivator

Reward management policies are based implicitly or explicitly on assumptions about the role of money as a motivator. This is an area where often too much is taken on trust and rather simplistic views are adopted about what is, in fact, a very complex process (see Chapter 8).

The overriding consideration in motivation is that the members of an organization contribute to it in return for the inducements that the organization provides. Money is clearly a major inducement, but because of the complexity of the motivation process involving many different needs and goals, it is dangerously simplistic to adopt the old 'economic man' theory, viz. that money is the only motivator. Intrinsic rewards are also important.

Money as a motivator for those already in employment will only work if people are in a position to anticipate the rewards they will obtain in return for a certain degree of achievement. In other words, there must be a clear link between effort and reward. People will also be better motivated by money if they can exercise direct control over their rewards. Good incentive and bonus schemes, whose worthwhile and foreseeable rewards are attainable by actions which are under the control of the worker, can be effective motivators.

Motivation theory also supports the case for a fully disclosed pay system. How can money be a motivator if people do not know how much they can earn? This applies not only to the amount of bonus they can obtain if they achieve a defined level of performance but also how they can progress according to merit either within their existing salary scale or, through promotion, to even more rewarding jobs.

While it is dangerous to place too much reliance on money as a motivator it is still a powerful force because it is linked directly or indirectly to the satisfaction of all the basic needs. Although money itself has no intrinsic meaning it does acquire significant motivating power when it comes to symbolize intangible goals. Money in itself is a measure of achievement. Reward policies should, therefore, recognize the importance of money as a motivator, but overall human resource management policies should also ensure that the other intrinsic motivators such as job satisfaction, recognition and achievement can play their part.

Reward management policies

Influences

Reward management policies have to take into account all the factors affecting reward levels mentioned above. But they will vary according to the type of organization, its culture and its environment. There is no such thing as a 'right' policy. It all depends. For example, a large and bureaucratic company may feel most comfortable with a graded salary structure and highly formalized job evaluation, salary survey, performance review and salary administration procedures. A smaller, more loosely organized company, especially one which is growing and changing rapidly, will not want to overformalize its procedures. It will need flexibility to respond quickly to change. An autocratic style of management will result in control from the top, no participation in formulating policies and as little disclosure of information by the company as possible.

A more democratic style will produce more delegation of authority, participation and openness. A strong union or staff association may enforce consultation, full disclosure and a formally defined structure. An entrepreneurial company needing top-quality specialized staff who are in short supply and on whom heavy demands will be made, will be happy to pay well over the odds if by so doing it gets the people it wants. On the other hand, a company which offers security and prestige and is not in the market for lots of high-flyers may settle for rates of pay around the average. The main policy areas are discussed below.

Levels of reward

The policy on reward levels should determine whether or not the company needs to be a high-payer. This is sometimes called its pay posture, which will be the policy on where rates of pay and fringe benefit packages should lie in relation to what comparable companies pay for similar jobs. This policy will be linked to the one on market rates.

Fast-moving profitable companies will want the top people and, if they want to stay in front, will pay top rates, or at least in the upper quartile of the range of pay for similar jobs in comparable companies. They will go to great efforts to ensure that they maintain that position. Small concerns like advertising agencies working on high margins who depend entirely on the talent of their staff will pay exceptionally good salaries and provide magnificent benefits (Porsches for all). So much so, that the companies outside this particular magic circle cannot possibly compete.

Other organizations may seek to pay closer to the median – to keep pace with market rates. One never comes across companies who admit that it is their policy to pay below the median. Obviously, however, that is where half of them are, possibly because they are unaware of the fact, and not through any deliberate actions on their part.

Performance-related rewards

The extent to which performance governs rewards and how the two are linked together depend absolutely on the core values of the organization. Thrusting, thriving and growing companies have to be entrepreneurial. And they must encourage what Gifford Pinchot describes as an 'intra-preneurial' spirit. He defines this as taking hands-on responsibility for creating innovation of any kind within an organization. The intrapreneur may be the creator or inventor but is always the dreamer who figures out how to turn an idea into a profitable reality.

Intrapreneurship within an enterprise will flourish if people believe that the game is worth the candle, ie that potential rewards justify the effort or the risk that have to be put into achieving them. They must *expect* that the value of their contribution to the organization will be rewarded appropriately.

Market rate policy

How far should market rate pressures be allowed to affect or possibly distort a salary structure? They cannot be ignored completely, but there is an element of choice. It might be decided that the salaries for certain jobs have to keep pace with the market. These would be distinguished as special market rates in the salary structure ('red-circled') or put into a separate market group. The salaries of other jobs would primarily be fixed by internal comparisons, possibly using as upper and lower limits the chief executive's salary and the pay levels required to maintain a reasonable differential between first line supervision and the clerical staff or operatives they control. Alternatively, pay levels for all key jobs may be assessed by reference to market rates, which would also indicate differentials between functions and between levels in the hierarchy. The main factor in assessing the influence that external pay levels should be allowed to exercise internally is the degree to which there is open market competition for staff. The less the need to go to the market, the less the need to react to short-term pressures.

In formulating market rate policy it should be remembered that the company is probably operating in several different labour markets. There will be the local market for shop floor workers and clerical staff, the national market for managerial, professional and highly technical staff and, possibly, the international market.

Labour markets are becoming increasingly fragmented, between different sections of industry or commerce, for different occupations and in different areas. The market in London, for example, where the finance sector is concentrated and house prices are spiralling upwards, is quite different from anywhere else in the country.

Market rate policies have therefore to be flexible and continuously under review so that they can be adjusted swiftly to the needs of the organization and changes in the labour markets.

Equity

Equity is a perceived sense that salary policies are just and fair because pay matches individual contribution, capacity and the level of work carried out, pay differentials are related to finite differences in the degree of responsibility, and equal pay is received for equal work. Absolute equity is an unattainable ideal, but the policy should be to achieve as high a degree of equity as possible by adopting a systematic and analytical approach to establishing the value of jobs. It is, however, often difficult to reconcile the two aims of being equitable *and* competitive. It may be hard to avoid paying higher than internal rates for comparable jobs in order to attract the right people. Market forces sometimes have to be allowed to prevail.

This does not imply that elaborate job evaluation schemes are essential. It is possible to be both systematic and analytical, without calling on the aid of what is too often a pseudo-scientific job evaluation scheme. In this context, 'systematic' means a methodical collection of facts about market rates and content of the jobs, and 'analytical' means the resolution of the data into elements to increase the ease and accuracy with which comparisons can be made between different jobs. The choice of method is wide and the alternatives are discussed in Chapter 21.

Pay structure

The main policy questions to be answered about pay structures are:

- Is a formal structure required?
- If a formal structure is necessary, what sort of structure should it be?

Some companies do without a formal structure quite successfully. They decide on the starting rate for a job on some *ad hoc* basis and adjust it as and when required. They can operate flexibly and react quickly to events, and this may be desirable in a fluid situation. The obvious danger is that pay will be dealt with inconsistently and inequitably, unless there is rigid central control, which is not always possible or desirable. By its very name a pay structure implies a certain amount of rigidity. But this need not be so. A structure can and should be no more than an understood framework within which consistent administration policies can be applied. It is possible to design and operate pay structures which enable a sufficient degree of flexibility to be achieved but allow for an adequate amount of control in order to avoid inequities and excessive costs.

Communication

If money is a motivator, it is right and proper that people should be told what is available to them so that they can be motivated by it. If equity is the first consideration, the fairness of the system has to be seen to be believed.

The contribution of reward management strategies

Reward management strategies should be designed to support each of these policies by the following means:

1. Develop pay and benefit structures which will help the organization to get and keep the sort of people it needs.
2. Link reward strategies to the key human resource strategies for performance and career management.
3. Provide remuneration systems which pay for individual success and achievement.
4. Introduce schemes which relate individual rewards to the performance of the company, department or working group.

Reference

1. Kanter, R M 'The Attack on Pay', *Harvard Business Review* March-April 1987.

Chapter 21
Job Evaluation

Job evaluation is a system of comparing different jobs to provide a basis for a grading and pay structure. An analysis of market rates will provide the information needed to ensure that a reward management system is competitive, but it is still necessary to maintain a pay structure into which jobs can be slotted according to their relative value. This will be strongly influenced by market forces but attention has also to be paid to internal relativities in order to achieve, as far as possible, both appropriate differentials to reward different levels of contribution and equity in the form of equal pay for work of equal value.

A pay structure consists of a hierarchy and decisions have to be made on how and where jobs should be fitted into that hierarchy. The aim of this chapter is to assist in making those decisions by:

- Defining job evaluation.
- Setting out the aims of evaluation.
- In the light of these descriptions, considering the pros and cons of job evaluation.
- Developing a strategy for selecting a method of evaluation and introducing it.
- Reviewing in detail the implications of the equal pay for work of equal value legislation in the UK. Job evaluation schemes can be used to ensure that inequalities are not allowed to happen or to continue, but they can also be used to defend differentials as being based on a proper comparative analysis of job values. In cases where equal value claims are heard by industrial tribunals they can appoint independent experts to carry out job evaluations. The pressure for evaluations is therefore increasing where equal value claims are possible. These, however, are more likely to happen at junior levels – supervisors, clerical staff and manual workers.
- Outlining the developments taking place in job evaluation following the introduction of new technology, organizational changes and the trend towards the harmonization of the terms and conditions of employment for white and blue collared staff.

What is job evaluation?

Job evaluation is a method of establishing the relative positions of jobs in a job hierarchy. Job evaluation schemes do not directly determine rates of pay with the exception of the obsolete factor comparison method. The rate for the job or the salary bracket for a job grade are influenced by a number of factors outside the scope of most schemes. These include market rate pressures, trade union negotiations and traditional patterns of pay differentials between jobs.

Job evaluation schemes set out to measure the relative value of the job, not of the job holder. Ideally, the performance of the individual should not enter into job evaluation, although in practice it may be difficult to dissociate individuals from their jobs where they have been in a position to influence what they do. This applies particularly to senior or specialist jobs where the position has been built round the personal strengths of the job holders.

Job evaluation is concerned with relationships, not absolutes. It cannot measure in definitive terms the inherent value of a job to the organization. It is essentially a comparative process: comparisons with other jobs, comparisons against defined standards, or comparisons of the degree to which a common criterion or factor is present in different jobs.

Job evaluation schemes

The main types of job evaluation schemes are:

1. *Non-analytical schemes:* ranking, paired comparison (a refined process of ranking) and job classification.
2. *Analytical points rating schemes:* where the jobs are analysed and compared by reference to different factors.

Ranking

Ranking is the simplest form of job evaluation. It is a non-analytical approach which aims to judge each job as a whole and determine its relative place in a hierarchy by comparing one job with another and arranging them in order of importance.

Method of comparison

Jobs may be compared by reference to a single criterion or factor such as responsibility, which might be defined as the particular obligations that have to be assumed by any person who carries out the job; or evaluators may be asked to define several facets of the job, for example:

1. Decisions: difficulty, judgement required, extent to which the tasks are prescribed (amount of discretion allowed).
2. Complexity: range of tasks to be carried out or skills to be used.
3. Knowledge and skills: what the job holder is required to know and be able to do.

A list of factors to be considered may be helpful because it steers thinking towards definable aspects of the content of the job rather than dealing with overgeneralized concepts such as responsibility. But there are dangers. Ranking may be distorted because evaluators will attach different weights to the factors, emphasizing some and not others. But they will do this anyway. Without a defined list, they will, consciously or unconsciously, evaluate by reference to their own choice of factors and weight them according to their own whim or prejudice.

Ranking procedure

The ranking procedure is to:

1. Analyse and describe the jobs, bringing out in the description those aspects which are to be used for comparison purposes.
2. Identify key or benchmark jobs; the most and least important jobs, a job midway between the two extremes, and others at the higher or lower intermediate points.
3. Rank the other jobs round the jobs until all jobs are placed in their rank order of importance.
4. Divide the ranked jobs into grades. In effect, this means that the grades are now defined by the jobs that have been placed in them. In future, new jobs can be graded or existing jobs regraded by reference to the established gradings on a job-to-job basis.

Grading jobs in a ranking exercise

There are no fixed rules for determining grade boundaries or the number of grades required. At this stage, job evaluation becomes even less objective than it has been before. The aim will be to produce grades which are administratively feasible and which conform to broad levels of responsibility in the organization. Their purpose is to collect jobs of comparable responsibility into broad bands before pricing the structure by attaching salary brackets to the bands.

Some guidance on the division of jobs into grades may be provided by a natural promotion ladder: junior clerk to clerk, to section leader, to group leader and so on. The danger of this approach is that the existing hierarchy may simply be reproduced, which could defeat the purpose of the scheme.

Pay structures do not necessarily have to have rigidly defined job grades (see Chapter 23). But grades have their advantages. Grouping jobs together into a grade means that they are considered to be roughly equal and can be priced within the same salary range. This helps to overcome the fundamental problem of ranking, that of placing closely related jobs one above the other on the basis of subjective judgements which cannot be validated.

The process of job grading means that a dividing line has to be placed between adjacent jobs in the rank order. This division can be invidious if, as is often the case, the difference between the importance of the two jobs on either side of the boundary is not significant. This problem is shared by all forms of job evaluation although, in theory at least, points schemes enable divisions to be made where there are natural breaks between bunches of points. This problem can be alleviated by the use of overlap between salary ranges, ie where the maximum salary of a lower range extends beyond the minimum point of the next range above.

Advantages of ranking

Ranking produces a hierarchy without having to analyse the job content or parts of a particular job individually. This means that the evaluation can be done very quickly and if the final order is acceptable, the structure can be implemented easily, without excessive cost in terms of cost or resources.

Those who favour ranking claim that the process of assessing the overall importance of the job as a whole to the organization is, in practice, what people do even when they go through the analytical motions of assessing the different facets of a job in a points rating scheme.

Ranking schemes can be used as a check on the results obtained by other more sophisticated schemes to ensure that the hierarchies produced are 'felt-fair'.

Disadvantages of ranking

The disadvantages of ranking are:

1. There is no rationale to defend the final rank order if it is challenged. Ranking one job higher or lower than another becomes a matter of opinion, although, to a degree, even the more sophisticated methods of job evaluation do no more than channel opinions into specified areas. The opinion is confined to one aspect of the job and guidance is given in how to exercise it, but ultimately, it is still an opinion. However, ranking systems cannot, for this reason, be used convincingly to deal with equal value problems.
2. Judgements become multi-dimensional when a number of jobs have to be placed in order of importance. Inconsistencies can occur because different individuals will give more weight to one

factor than to others because they do not know what complex of factors is operating or what the balance is between them.

3. While it may be easy to establish the extremes in a rank order, it may be difficult to discriminate between the middling jobs. Consensus on the correct rank order may therefore be hard to obtain.

4. Ranking does not provide a clear basis for grading or re-grading jobs and a graded salary structure is, after all, often the main reason for having a job evaluation scheme.

To try to overcome these formidable disadvantages, paired comparisons, job classification or points schemes can be used.

Paired comparisons

Paired or forced comparisons are a refinement of job ranking. This approach introduces an element of scoring to give an indication of the degree of importance between two jobs. As with job ranking, the method is more appropriate for smaller organizations or where jobs within a similar job family are being assessed.

Specially designed score charts are necessary and the use of a computer to correlate the results will reduce the time an evaluation takes. The method is easily understood and is quick. As with job ranking, the approach is hard to defend rationally, even though decisions represent the consensus when an evaluation was done.

How the method is used

As with job ranking, the job evaluation panel analyses each job as a whole. The panel then goes on to compare it with all other jobs in turn (this may not be necessary with basic job ranking). If a job is considered more demanding it scores two points, if it is as demanding it scores one point and if it is less demanding it scores nothing. By totalling up the scores a rank order is produced, as illustrated below:

Job	A	B	C	D	E	Total score	Rank order
A	—	0	2	0	2	4	2
B	2	—	2	2	2	8	1
C	0	0	—	2	0	2	5
D	2	0	0	—	1	3	3
E	0	0	2	1	—	3	3

Number of calculations

One problem with paired comparisons is that as the number of jobs increases, the number of paired comparisons rises rapidly so that to evaluate fifty jobs will involve 1,225 comparisons. With the use of a computer, however, this need not be a great drawback.

Advantages

This method combines the advantages of ranking, notably speed and simplicity, with a more efficient way of checking the consistency of the ranking. The number of individual assessments, which may be inconsistent due to bias, is reduced.

The advantages can be summarized as:

- quick and easy to understand;
- jobs are assessed as a whole so that more general questions such as creativity or financial responsibilities can be considered without attempting to quantify each particular job factor.

Disadvantages

Paired comparisons may help to eliminate some of the subjectivity and inconsistencies of whole job ranking but it still fails to answer why a job is necessarily more important or more demanding. While analysing jobs as a whole does give an important 'feel' for the job, paired comparisons assume that everyone reaches the same conclusions about each job – if this consensus does not exist then it becomes hard to justify where the job should be placed.

The disadvantages can be summarized as:

- difficult to justify why jobs are considered more important;
- the number of calculations will be impractical for a large number of jobs unless computer facilities are available;
- the evaluation relies on the team's ability to come to a consensus on where a job should be ranked.

The paired comparison method can be applied to all types of jobs. It is well suited to manual jobs where there is already an established feeling about how important jobs are in comparison with one another, ie where an organization does not have to justify why certain jobs are more demanding or considered more important.

Job classification

Job classification is based on an initial definition of the number and characteristics of the grades into which the jobs will be placed. The grade definitions attempt to take into account discernible differences in skill and responsibility and may refer to specific criteria, such as level of decisions, knowledge, equipment used and education or training required to do the work. Jobs are allotted to grades by comparing the whole job description with the grade definition.

A job classification scheme for clerical jobs may be based on the Institute of Administrative Management's grading scheme. Alternatively, a job classification scheme can be built up within a company following a ranking or points evaluation exercise. The number of grades can be determined along the lines suggested above when grading procedures in ranking schemes were discussed. The ranking or points system will indicate the grades into which the benchmark jobs are placed and the descriptions of these jobs provide guidance when writing grade definitions. The benchmark jobs can then be used as reference points to illustrate the necessarily generalized grade descriptions.

Advantages of job classification

The advantages of job classification are that, first, it is simple to operate and, second, standards of judgement are provided in the form of grade definitions. It is often a good system to use in an organization that wants to introduce job evaluation quickly without elaborate and costly studies and wants an easy method of slotting new or changed jobs into an established structure.

Disadvantages of job classification

The disadvantage of job classification is that it cannot cope with complex jobs which will not fit neatly into one grade. It is less suitable for senior positions where grade definitions have to become so generalized that they provide little help in evaluating borderline cases. It also tends to be inflexible in that it is not sensitive to changes in the nature and content of jobs.

The problem with job classification is that even with clerical jobs, where it seems to have more relevance, it is still better in practice to evaluate by comparing jobs with jobs rather than by comparing jobs with job descriptions. Once the initial grades into which the benchmark jobs have been slotted are established, the system is usually expendable. In addition, like ranking or paired comparisons, job classification cannot readily be used in equal pay for work of equal value cases.

Points rating

Points rating schemes are based on an analysis of separately defined characteristics or factors which are assumed to be common to all the jobs. It is further assumed that differences in the extent to which the characteristics are found in the jobs will measure differences between the jobs. Points schemes are sometimes loosely called factor comparison schemes, although strictly speaking this term should be used for an out-dated approach which apportions agreed rates of pay between factors in accordance with the extent to which the factor is present in the job.

The factors selected in points schemes are those considered to be most relevant in assessing the comparative value of jobs. Typical factors include skill (of various kinds), responsibility, decisions, complexity and contacts with other people.

Each factor is given a range of points so that a maximum number of points is available. The relative importance or 'weighting' of a factor is determined by the maximum number of points allotted to it. In each factor, the total range of points is divided into degrees according to the level at which the factor is present in the job. The characteristics of each degree in terms of, say, level of complexity, are defined as yardsticks for comparison purposes.

Points rating procedure

Jobs are evaluated by studying job descriptions containing analyses of the degree to which the factor is present in the job and comparing them with the factor level definitions. The jobs are graded for each factor and the points for each grading are added to produce a total score. This score can then be related to the scores of other jobs to indicate the rank order. For example, an evaluation of two jobs using a typical scheme could produce the results shown in Table 21.1.

Factor	Job A		Job B	
	Level	*Points*	*Level*	*Points*
Resources	4	20	5	25
Decisions	4	60	4	60
Complexity	5	25	3	15
Knowledge and skills	3	15	3	15
		120		115

Table 21.1 *Points rating evaluation*

Grading jobs in a points rating exercise

To develop a grade structure, the points scored are plotted against salaries. Any clustering of scores will help to establish the divisions between job grades, and when the salary ranges have been fixed with the help of information on market rates, the dimensions of each grade can be re-evaluated and slotted into the structure according to their points rating.

Advantages of points schemes

The advantages of points schemes are listed below:

1. Evaluators are forced to consider a range of factors which, as long as they are present in all the jobs and affect them in different ways, will avoid the oversimplified judgements made when using non-analytical schemes.
2. Points schemes provide evaluators with defined yardsticks which should help them to achieve some degree of objectivity and consistency in making their judgements.
3. They at least appear to be objective even if they are not, and this quality makes people feel that they are fair.
4. They provide a rationale which, however specious, helps in the design of graded salary structures.

Disadvantages of points schemes

Points schemes have three disadvantages:

1. They are complex to develop, install and maintain.
2. They give a spurious impression of scientific accuracy, though it is still necessary to use judgement in selecting factors, deciding on weightings, defining levels within factors, and interpreting information about the jobs in relation to the often rather generalized definitions of factors and factor levels.
3. They assume that it is possible to quantify different aspects of jobs on the same scale of values and then add them together. But skills cannot be added together in this way.

Characteristics of job evaluation schemes

The characteristics and advantages and disadvantages of each type of evaluation scheme are summarized in Table 21.2.

Pros and cons of job evaluation

Each of the schemes described in Table 21.2 has its advantages and disadvantages, but before choosing between them it will be useful to consider in general the points for and against formal job evaluation schemes.

Pros

The main point made in favour of the more formal types of job evaluation systems, especially analytical schemes, is that they are objective. This means, according to the *Oxford English Dictionary*, 'treating a

Scheme	Characteristics	Advantages	Disadvantages
1 Ranking	Whole job comparisons made to place them in order of importance	Easy to apply and understand	No defined standards of judgement: differences between jobs are not measured
2 Paired comparisons	Panel members individually compare each job in turn with all the others being evaluated. Points are awarded according to whether the job is more, less or equally demanding than each of the jobs with which it is being compared. These points are added to determine the rank order, usually with the help of a computer. The scores are analysed and discussed in order to achieve consensus amongst the members of the panel	Ranking is likely to be more valid on the principle that it is always easy to compare a job with one other job rather than with the whole range of disparate jobs	As with ranking, the system neither explains why one job is more important than another nor assesses differences between them
3 Job classification	Job grades are defined and jobs are slotted into the grades by comparing the whole job description with the grade definition	Simple to operate and standards of judgement are provided in the shape of the grade definitions	Difficult to fit complex jobs into a grade without using elaborate grade definitions
4 Points rating	Separate factors are scored to produce an overall points score for the job	The analytical process of considering separately defined factors gives the impression that the evaluation is objective. Consistency in judgement is helped by having defined factor levels	Complex to install and maintain. Objectivity is more apparent than real: subjective judgement is still required to rate jobs of different factors

Table 21.2 *Characteristics of evaluation schemes*

subject as to the actual facts, not coloured by the feelings or opinions of the writer'. This claim cannot be substantiated. The only factual basis for job evaluation is the job description, but this can never convey the full flavour of a job, however carefully written. And no existing system of job evaluation can eliminate the colouring provided by the feeling or opinions of the evaluators.

It is also claimed that job evaluation provides the basis for a logical pay structure. This is a true statement, as far as it goes, but there is no proof that the more elaborate forms of job evaluation produce more logical salary structures.

Perhaps the most convincing claim that can be made for formula job evaluation schemes is that they are demonstrably more fair than entirely subjective managerial judgements, as long as the schemes are fully disclosed to staff who participate in them. This is where the more elaborate approaches come into their own. Points, guide charts, paired comparisons and multiple regression analysis with the help of a computer all give the impression that schemes are accurate, scientific and, above all, objective. They are felt to be fair, whether they are or not, and that is what counts when gaining acceptance of the results they produce.

Cons

The main point made against the more elaborate job evaluation schemes is that they can be costly to install and maintain. The installation costs include management consultants' fees, if they are used, which can be considerable, plus the time spent by management and staff working with the consultants or designing a company scheme. When job evaluation is used to develop a new pay structure or to revise an old one, inevitable costs arise when staff are slotted into new grades. If any jobs are downgraded, it is most unusual for the people concerned to suffer any reduction in salary. Instead they are 'red circled' by being given personal-to-job-holder gradings which mean that they retain their present salary and expectations of fixed increments if they are on a scale. When jobs are upgraded, however, it is customary to increase salaries at least to the minimum of the new grade. If the costs are really exceptional, it may be possible to phase increases over a period of time, but this is only deferring the expense. New or revised structures therefore increase the pay of some staff (and the number could be considerable) without balancing this increase by decreases elsewhere. The cost may be a 3% increase in the paybill or more, if considerable changes are made to the pay structure.

Maintenance can also be expensive, especially if job evaluations are carried out by committees.

Moreover, job evaluation is not the universal panacea that some companies think it to be. Handling its introduction can be a very delicate matter, especially if trade unions are involved. Evaluations can upset long-standing differentials and gradings and thus create more problems than they solve.

The disadvantages mentioned above mainly arise from the operation of job evaluation schemes, but there are more serious limitations to the process of job evaluation itself.

1. No scheme has been proved to be valid in that it measures what it sets out to measure, or reliable in that it produces consistent results. An act of faith is required to believe in job evaluation.
2. 'Whole-job' comparison schemes look wrong because they seem to oversimplify, but analytical systems are equally suspect – apples and pears cannot be added together. The quantification of subjective judgements does not make them any more objective.
3. Job evaluation relies on human judgement. Its methodology may be logical and it may provide guidelines on the exercise of judgement, but these are subject to different interpretations and varying standards among assessors, and their preconceived notions will ensure that subjectivity creeps in. This tendency to make *a priori* judgements about how jobs should be ranked or graded means that the deliberations of evaluators often take the form of a series of self-fulfilling prophesies.
4. Averaging a group of subjective judgements, as in consensus schemes, does not make them any more objective.
5. All evaluation schemes deteriorate as the organization changes and as evaluators become more skilled at manipulating the system. Grade drift – unjustified upgradings as a result of the manipulation – occurs and the pay structure is no longer equitable.

To sum up, job evaluation attempts to impose objectivity on a process of subjective judgement. It can never succeed in the task. In the last analysis, all job evaluation schemes boil down to organized rationalization.

Job evaluation strategy

Is job evaluation necessary?

The pros for job evaluation as given above appear to be self-evident, but the cons are formidable and reading them prompts the question, 'Is job evaluation really necessary?' The answer is, of course, yes. You cannot avoid evaluating jobs. That is what you do every time you decide on what one job should be paid in relation to another. The question needs to be re-stated as, 'Is a formal system of job evaluation necessary?'

Informal or formal?

A completely informal approach means relying on judgement without the benefit of any form of job analysis or a systematic analysis of market rates. Except in the smallest organizations, it is unlikely to work.

A semi-formal system can work for some companies. This involves job analysis, so that even if internal comparisons are fairly crude, they are at least based on fact rather than opinion. Additionally, market rate information is collected regularly and, where the market place is competitive, these rates will have a dominant influence on the structure. They will largely determine differentials between jobs in different market groups or jobs within a hierarchy where there are well established market rates at different levels. For example, this will apply in marketing organizations where there are clearly defined rates for different grades of product or brand managers.

A semi-formal approach linked to market rate intelligence often works well in loosely structured, dynamic, market orientated or fairly small companies, and it can form the basis for a 'spot-rate' pay structure as described in Chapter 23. But in larger organizations which are less subject to change and in which equity is a more important consideration, a more formal method is desirable to establish fair and sensible differentials and to achieve consistency in grading jobs. When deciding on what approach is required the following questions need to be answered:

1. Who should be covered?
2. How many schemes?
3. Should the scheme(s) be specially designed for the company? or
4. Should one of the standard schemes offered by consultants (the 'proprietary brands') be used and if so, which one?

Who should be covered?

Ideally, every job should be evaluated so that comparisons can be made at best throughout the organization or at least between staff in comparable occupations at different levels. Some companies, however, exclude directors and possibly senior management on the grounds that their salary levels are largely determined on a personal basis. Senior jobs are often built round the skills of particular individuals and they can change, sometimes quite radically, when one manager leaves or is promoted and is replaced by another. Where this happens, job evaluation would clearly be about evaluating the individual, not the job.

How many schemes?

The tendency has been to have different systems for, say, managers, clerical staff and manual workers because of the difficulty of designing a scheme which is equally applicable at all levels of responsibility or for completely different types of work. Job evaluation is based on explicit or implicit factors or criteria which are believed to define the relative value of jobs. The factors typically used in executive jobs are unlikely to be appropriate for manual workers. But the attempt to introduce common factors too often results in a scheme which will not discriminate effectively at different levels. And even if a 'whole job ranking' system is used (as described on page 353) comparisons at all levels may still be difficult because the criteria that are implicitly used in such schemes are seldom universally applicable.

Attempts are, however, being made, although it is not easy, to extend a single scheme to all or at least a wider range of employees. There are two reasons for this. First, the equal value legislation in the UK has made it necessary to compare levels of responsibility across the previously rigidly separated boundaries of clerical and manual staff. The second reason is the drive to harmonize conditions of employment for white and blue collar employees. Such extensions are probably most effective when different occupational categories need to be evaluated which are at roughly equivalent levels in the organization structure, although the type of work and conditions of employment are dissimilar. In other words, schemes can be extended horizontally without too much difficulty. The problems arise when vertical integration is attempted. This is why many organizations still have one scheme for managerial staff and another for clerical and manual workers. A compromise found in some large organizations is to use the same approach from top to bottom but to vary the factors in a tailor-made points rating scheme to meet the evaluation needs at different levels.

Tailor-made scheme?

The main advantage of a scheme specially designed for the company is clearly that it can take into account any unique features of the organization such as the need to cover different categories of staff. Special factors can be introduced at different levels and appropriate weightings can be applied. Tailor-made schemes can also be designed to fit the salary administration systems of the firm. They are not necessarily less expensive to introduce than a proprietary brand because account has to be taken of the opportunity costs in the shape of the considerable amount of executive time that has to be spent in designing, developing and introducing a special company scheme. This time can be reduced by getting a firm of management consultants to design a tailor-made scheme.

What type of scheme?

When developing a tailor-made scheme, the choice is between using a 'whole job' ranking, paired comparison or job classifications system or introducing a more complex points scheme. The natural way to evaluate jobs is to compare one whole job with another – people do this almost instinctively. However carefully factors are analysed and however carefully they are told to compare jobs factor by factor, evaluators will bring to the table their preconceived ideas of the overall relativities between jobs. These intuitions will inevitably colour their judgements. The tendency is to manipulate points scores to produce a result which coincides with the views that people have already formed, ie the process of organized rationalization mentioned above. In the light of this phenomenon, there is much to be said for a ranking or classification approach which is realistic enough to recognize that nothing will stop people behaving in this way.

Points schemes may be used in complex situations where it is felt that only a highly analytical approach will provide an acceptable basis for evaluation, and they can provide a useful basis for designing a salary structure. Their elaborate nature may make them difficult to understand and their objectivity may be suspect. But their use may be justified if it is considered that staff are going to be favourably impressed both by the sheer quantity of time and trouble involved in introducing a scheme, and by the apparent fairness or the process of analysis.

Points schemes have been steadily increasing in popularity, partly because they are thought to be the best way of dealing with equal value problems, but also because of their 'face validity'. People *feel* that they are scientific so they must be all right. They may, of course, work as well as any other approach, given thorough job analysis, the effective training of evaluators and the joint determination of management, staff and trade unions to see the exercise through. But no one should be starry-eyed enough to believe that, given these inputs, a points scheme will in itself produce more accurate results than other methods.

Introducing job evaluation

Having decided on the approach to be adopted, the steps required to introduce a scheme are to:

- Inform staff and agree on how they should be involved.
- Clarify trade union attitudes, where appropriate.
- Select benchmark jobs.
- Plan the job evaluation programme.

Informing and involving staff

Staff must obviously be informed about the exercise. It affects them deeply and their help will be required in analysing jobs. The objectives and potential benefits should be discussed and it should be made absolutely clear that it is the jobs which are to be evaluated and not the people carrying out the jobs. The way in which staff are consulted will depend on the company's normal policies for consultation and negotiation.

There is much to be said for involving staff in the job evaluation programme. They can assist in selecting, analysing and evaluating benchmark jobs. It is becoming increasingly common to set up job evaluation committees to establish and maintain the scheme and to hear appeals.

Trade union attitudes

If the company is unionized, the form in which consultation and participation takes place will be strongly influenced by union attitudes. Staff unions may insist on being involved in the job evaluation programme, although they might not be prepared to commit themselves in advance to accept its findings. The guidelines on job evaluation issued by one major union are:

1. A preliminary meeting should be held between management and union to establish the need for job evaluation and the method to be used.
2. A job evaluation committee should be set up to define the scheme's terms of reference and the extent and method of communication between management and union.
3. A decision should be made as to which union members should take an active part in the scheme.
4. An appeals procedure should be set up.
5. Revision of the scheme should be carried out at regular intervals in order to identify changes both in individual jobs and in company objectives.

One union has stated very firmly that no job evaluation scheme should be allowed to undermine the traditional role of collective bargaining in determining pay. The function of job evaluation, according to this union, is to deal with the job structure. The pay structure is a matter for negotiation.

Another union produced the following list of reservations about job evaluation:

1. Error-prone management judgements will replace negotiations and weaken the joint determination of wage rates and structures.
2. The wage system arrived at can be rigid, whereas wage systems should be dynamic and part of a continuous process.
3. Job evaluation can emphasize 'the rate for the job' and overlook the importance of 'the rate for the ability to do the job'.
4. At the time of introduction there is the possibility that the new pay structure will involve no more than a rearrangement of the old structure and not include any increase or benefit for employees as a whole.

These guidelines and attitudes are typical. They should be taken into account in any organization where staff are represented by unions or by staff associations with negotiating rights.

Select benchmark jobs

In any exercise where there are more than 30 or 40 jobs to be evaluated it is necessary to identify and select a sample of benchmark jobs which can be used for comparisons inside and outside the organization. The benchmark jobs should be selected to achieve a representative sample of each of the main levels of jobs in each of the principal occupations.

The size of the sample depends on the number of different jobs to be covered. It is unlikely to be less than about 5% of the total number of employees in the organization and it would be difficult to produce a balanced sample unless at least 25% of the distinct jobs at each level of the organization were included. The higher the proportion the better, bearing in mind the time required to analyse jobs (seldom less than one man day for each job).

Draw up job evaluation programme

The points to be covered in a job evaluation programme are:

1. *Staffing:* who is responsible for analysis, evaluation, pay comparisons and the design of the salary structure.
2. *Briefing:* of management, staff and unions on the objects of the exercise and how they are to be achieved.
3. *Procedures:* the terms of reference, membership and methods of working of any job evaluation committee.
4. *Training:* the training to be given to full and part-time analysts and evaluators. This is a vital part of the programme. If training is carried out thoroughly, many of the limitations of job evaluation referred to earlier can be minimized.
5. *Pay comparisons:* methods of conducting market rate surveys and the timetable for completing them.
6. *Job evaluation:* methods and procedures, including appeals, and the timetable for completing the programme.
7. *Job analysis:* the methods to be used in job analysis, the jobs to be covered and the timetable for completing the programme.
8. *Design the structure:* the methods to be used and the timetable for completing the design.
9. *Communication and negotiation:* the approach to communicating the results of the exercise to staff and for negotiating the structure with unions. It is highly desirable to produce a booklet explaining the scheme.
10. *Maintenance:* the procedures for maintaining the scheme, including regradings and appeals.

When the programme has been drawn up, the detailed work of job analysis, pay comparisons and design of the structure can be carried out.

Staffing the job evaluation exercise

Responsibility for the overall co-ordination of the introduction of job evaluation should be in the hands of a senior executive who can then report on progress to the board and advise it on ensuing salary policy developments.

Where there is a developed personnel function the personnel manager will take control. In larger organizations with a salary administration department the executive in charge of this function will normally take responsibility for the introduction and maintenance of the scheme. Provided adequate training is given at the outset, job analysis is an excellent way for new personnel or other company trainees to familiarize themselves with the company and the work done in its different departments. Many larger organizations expect their personnel trainees to spend a year or more working on job analysis as an essential addition to their background experience. Analysts will need to be taught the basic skills of interviewing and the elements of a concise descriptive style for writing job descriptions.

The use of analysts either to write job descriptions or check on those written by job holders and their supervisors often greatly improves the quality of job descriptions submitted for evaluation.

Staffing the job evaluation committee is a fairly delicate exercise. A balance has to be struck between the different divisions or departments in the organization and the different levels of staff covered by the scheme. Again the process of job evaluation is an excellent training ground because it exposes committee members to a detailed analysis of the kinds of work done elsewhere in the organization and to an extended period of discussion and negotiation with other staff of different levels. Where trade unions are involved it is usual for them to nominate an agreed number of representatives balanced by management nominees and a mutually acceptable chairman, often the personnel manager.

Briefing for job evaluation

Effective briefing of all staff involved at the introduction stage of a job evaluation scheme is usually crucial to its success. This can be done at a meeting or series of meetings at which the executive responsible for the introduction of the scheme outlines its aims and emphasizes the long-term benefits for both company and staff of a properly evaluated basis for the new salary structure. A simple question and answer sheet given out at the meeting and covering the common, if basic, questions employees normally ask will also help remove any misgivings that may arise. Some of the most common questions are:

- What is job evaluation?
- Why does this company need job evaluation?
- How will it work?
- How does it affect promotion policy?
- How will the system be kept up to date?
- Does job evaluation mean that everyone whose job is in the same grade gets the same rate of pay?
- How does the publication of job grades and salary bands affect confidentiality?
- How does the system cater for additions to or alterations in jobs?
- What happens if an individual disagrees with his grading?
- How quickly will appeals on grading be dealt with?
- How will the company go about grading new jobs created as the result of change or expansion?

Answers should be tailored to proposed company practice.

Briefing the job evaluation committee

Much of the success of a job evaluation committee depends on how it is briefed and the way in which an *esprit de corps* is developed. The first meeting should discuss the collective responsibilities of the committee, answer members' questions and perhaps try a few 'practice runs' before formal gradings get under way.

Briefing is usually the chairman's responsibility or that of the personnel manager if he is not chairman. The main points that need to be covered at the first meeting are:

- Restatement of the purpose of job evaluation.
- Detailed briefing on every aspect of the company's own scheme.
- Reminders that the committee has the right to go back to the individual or supervisor for further details and clarification as often as necessary and the right not to evaluate any job until they are completely satisfied that the job description is adequate.

Committee proceedings are usually confidential but minutes summarizing the reasons for grading each job should be kept.

How much time is involved?

However much the company may want to get the scheme fully implemented it is unwise to rush job evaluation. Even the keenest evaluation committee can only grade a limited number of jobs in a day: eight is probably a realistic average maximum. After this the quality of evaluation tends to drop and more time has to be spent later in checking and assessing the validity of grading. The final review of all the grades allocated to check that no inconsistencies have occurred should be done meticulously and with enough time allowed for re-evaluation if necessary. Extra time devoted at this stage will help reduce appeals to the inevitable few. Careful preparation for the communication of job grades and of the handbooks or other documents describing the scheme and its operation will also assist acceptance.

Appeals procedure
Even the most committed and highly trained job evaluation committees make mistakes. Add to this 'political' considerations such as managers who expect the people they supervise to be more highly graded as a reflection of departmental status and individuals who feel the importance of their job has been undervalued, and the need for an appeals procedure is inevitable. Unions will want to negotiate the basis for appeals when the introduction of job evaluation is agreed. A fairly typical appeal sequence covering unionized and non-unionized staff would be:

1. Appeal goes to supervisor.
2. Supervisor and employee appeal to grading committee.
3. If the decision is not acceptable:
   (a) unionized staff involve branch officials
   (b) non-unionized staff go through their own grievance procedure to higher authority.
4. Ultimately the appeal goes to a top management committee for final decision.

Equal value

Under the equal value amendment to the British Equal Pay Act, *any* woman can claim equal pay with *any* man if she believes her work is equally demanding under such factors as 'effort, skill and decision-making'. Equal value claims can be made whether or not job evaluation schemes exist and they can cut across traditional boundaries so that blue collar workers can compare their jobs with those of white collar workers and *vice versa*. Vulnerability to claims is highest where traditional sex-based job-segregation exists.

Claims are heard by industrial tribunals who may ask 'independent experts' appointed by ACAS (the Advisory Conciliation and Arbitration Service) to assess equality of value between claimant and comparator. The experts carry out their evaluation by applying sets of factors to the job analysis such as:

- responsibility, effort, skills, 'know-how';
- physical demands, environment, planning and decision-making, skill and knowledge;
- skills and experience, working conditions, effort.

The independent experts start with the job description to identify any areas where the content of the job is the cause of conflict. They attempt to get agreement on the facts and ask the employer to justify the differential. A precise point rating for each factor is usually considered neither necessary nor appropriate, but a general statement comparing the demands of each job under each factor heading is essential.

The existence of a company job evaluation scheme which assigns values to the jobs under review can only be used to prove that no discrimination is taking place if the scheme itself is non-discriminatory. Job evaluation schemes can be discriminatory either in the choice of factors and/or in the weightings attached to the factors and also in the grading process – reflecting underlying discrimination. The Equal Opportunity Commission has stated that job evaluation should not give a spurious objectivity to the *status quo*: 'A commitment to a fair job evaluation may require that some traditional assumptions are changed regarding the value attributed to work predominantly carried out by women.' It also advises that extremely high or low weightings should not be given to factors which are exclusively found in jobs performed predominantly by one sex.

Once factors are selected and weightings applied so that sex bias is avoided, the administration of the scheme should be in line with good personnel practice. Hay Management Consultants have published a useful code of practice, the main points of which are summarized below:

● Formation of steering and review panels should have regard to the distribution of men and women across the organization.
● Where it may not always be easy to persuade women to be involved, appropriate education should be provided in order to bring home the importance of active participation.
● Individuals involved should be thoroughly trained in the techniques and approaches they are required to assess and monitor and should be briefed to avoid sex bias (both direct and unintentional).
● Allocation of jobs across more than one evaluation panel should avoid adherence to any traditional occupational/grading or historical difference in the sex of job holders.
● An appointed chairperson should monitor panel operation and encourage active involvement of all panel members in the process.
● Evaluators should possess the qualities of open mindedness and fair judgement and, in addition to being thoroughly trained in the job evaluation method, they should be specifically briefed on guarding against sex bias in their interpretation of job descriptions and subsequent evaluation.
● Evaluation of jobs should be the result of panel consensus based purely on job content without reference to job holders or historical position in the pecking order.
● Evaluations should be updated to reflect changes in jobs and

results should be regularly audited to ensure sex bias does not creep in over time.

- Where a series of 'benchmark' jobs is fully evaluated and other jobs are subsequently positioned within that framework, the benchmark sample should be equally representative of typically female and typically male-dominated jobs and where possible include jobs populated by both.
- Evaluation and appeals panels should comprise a cross-section of individuals representative of the range of job groups/occupations to be evaluated and reflect the distribution of men and women.
- Detailed descriptions of all jobs should be prepared using a uniform format.
- Where job analysts are involved in the preparation of job descriptions both men and women should be selected with reference to their distribution across the range of jobs.
- All individuals involved in the preparation of job descriptions should, in addition to receiving appropriate training in the approach to collection and presentation of information, be briefed to avoid sex bias in discussion, interpretation and choice of words used to describe jobs.
- Job descriptions should be agreed as representative of the job by job holders, line management and, where appropriate, the job analyst and union/staff association representative.
- Job titles appearing on job descriptions should avoid any indication of sex of job holder (eg not 'manageress').
- The name and gender of the job holder should be avoided on copies of descriptions put forward for panel evaluation.

Chapter 22
Establishing Market Rates

Competitive salary levels and pay structures can only be developed and maintained if the external market is regularly and systematically checked. This can be done using a range of sources from large-scale, formal salary and benefits surveys to job advertisements, companies' annual reports, informal confidential contacts and other forms of market intelligence.

Job evaluation schemes can be used to determine internal relativities, but in themselves they cannot put a price to the job. To a large extent pay levels are subject to market forces which have to be taken into account in negotiations and in fixing the rates for particular jobs. Some specialized jobs may not be subjected to the same external pressures as others, but it is still necessary to know what effect market rates are likely to have on the pay structure as a whole before deciding on internal pay differentials which properly reflect levels of skill and responsibility. It has also to be accepted that market pressures and negotiations will affect differentials within the firm. An employer may be unwilling to submit to individual pressure because of the danger that it will distort the structure. But it may sometimes be necessary to recognize the compelling force of market or union demands in one area and adjust rates accordingly. Wherever possible such adjustments should be regarded as special measures and an attempt should be made to contain their influence on other scales by isolating them as exceptions ('red-circling').

The purpose of both published and privately conducted surveys is to provide accurate and representative data on the current range of salaries or wage rates paid for the jobs or levels of responsibility in question. These need to be looked at in relation to company size, industry type, ownership, location, and other factors such as particular market pressures which affect what the market is prepared to pay.

Despite great improvements in sampling and analysis, salary surveys and other forms of pay analysis can sometimes be misleading and should perhaps never be taken entirely at face value. The concept of the market rate, even in the local labour market, is an inexact one. It is noticeable that for identical jobs there is always a range of rates paid by different employers. This is particularly so in managerial jobs and other occupations

374

where duties can vary considerably between companies, even if the job title is the same. It is therefore only possible to use pay surveys to provide a broad indication of market rates. Judgement has to be used in interpreting the results of special inquiries or the data from published surveys. There is usually plenty of scope for selecting evidence which supports whatever case is being advanced.

Information on the rates paid by other firms can come from the following sources:

- company surveys;
- club surveys;
- local surveys conducted by employers, unions or other bodies;
- general published surveys;
- analyses of job advertisements.

Company surveys

Company surveys are conducted when specific information is required of the pay and benefits provided by comparable companies for similar jobs. The steps required to conduct a company survey are to:

1. Draw up a list of suitable companies which are compatible with regard to industry, size and the sort of jobs they are likely to have.
2. Approach each company. It is clearly best to maintain a list of friendly contacts who from experience are known to give reliable information. These may develop into a 'club' which can operate at various levels of formality in exchanging information on a regular or an as-required basis. If such contacts or a club are not readily available it may be necessary to approach a company out of the blue and ask them for information. This has obviously to be provided on a reciprocal basis and it may sometimes be possible to offer the *quid pro quo* of an anonymous summary of the results. In making such contacts the messages that have to be got across are that:

   - a responsible individual is conducting the survey;
   - the survey will be carried out competently and in confidence;
   - the reciprocal information provided will be relevant and useful;
   - the company being approached will not be put to too much trouble.

3. Prepare job data and, if necessary, survey forms. It may be possible to obtain the information required over the telephone, but it is necessary to have information about the jobs ready to ensure that like is being compared with like. If a postal survey is

being conducted it is even more necessary to provide basic data about the duties and responsibilities of the jobs to assist in making valid comparisons. A pro forma may be prepared by the surveying company for completion by the participating company to save time and trouble and to help in the subsequent analysis. The form should provide spaces for the information required on pay scales, actual salaries paid, overtime earnings and, for wage earners, details of basic rates, regular total earnings, variations in earnings, the make up of total earnings (base rates, bonuses, overtime, shift payments, etc) and hours worked.

4. Where it is difficult to make valid comparisons by telephone or post by reference to outline job descriptions it may be possible to carry out on-the-spot inquiries, if other companies are willing to participate. Much more can be got out of a face-to-face discussion which will clarify any differences in responsibilities that may affect comparisons. The best results will be obtained if the parties agree to benchmark jobs being analysed and compared using a common method of job evaluation which compares agreed factors as in a points or factor comparison scheme.

5. Analyse the information obtained from the survey, ensuring that so far as possible like jobs are being compared and that the details provided on pay distinguish between basic rates and piecework, overtime, and shiftwork earnings. It is also important to establish that the earnings are regular and not distorted by special circumstances. If, when comparing earnings, they are brought down to an hourly rate to eliminate the effect of overtime, it is worth remembering that a simple division of the total earnings by the hours will not remove the impact of overtime if the effect of overtime premiums is not discounted.

6. Present the analysis in a form which can be easily assimilated and reveals the range of rates of pay or earnings for the jobs covered by the survey. The presentation may show the range of pay or earnings from highest and lowest, the median rate and the upper and lower quartile. The median is the middle item in the distribution of salaries or wage rates – 50% of the jobs will be paid more than the median and 50% of the jobs will be paid less. The upper quartile is the rate above which 25% of the jobs are paid more, the lower quartile is the rate below which 25% of the jobs are paid less.

Club surveys

Salary clubs have been around a long time and employers seem to place a high value on them. It was in 1974 that the Government's Pay Board wrote:

> Our studies showed most employers used quite a number of surveys – indeed it was exceptional for an employer to rely on one or two. However, where employers belong to a 'pay club' we found that the information obtained from the 'club' was regarded as more relevant than that contained in the general surveys partly because the other club members were considered to be the main competitors for that type of staff.

Clubs may be administered either by management consultants or by companies themselves. Clubs tend to operate in single industries, although some cover a range of industries – a survey of 'blue chip' companies, for instance. Many cover all managerial and professional grades, although there are those which cover only one employee category – graduates for example, within one industry. When a single employee category is chosen, this will normally be because there is strong competition for people with skills which are in demand.

The major advantage of running a salary club is that participants to the survey know who the other participants are and that their data are relevant. When members of the same club are in the same industrial sector they may be thought of as competitors for the same type of staff in the same salary market. This is particularly true for managers and specialists whose skills are easily transferable from one company to another in a similar line of business. At managerial level, members of the same club typically employ a rather homogeneous group of staff in terms of the experience required, the demands of the job and their qualifications. Some clubs exchange salary information only on managerial and specialist grades, eg from first line to senior management, while others cover technical and professional grades, clerical, or indeed only manual employees.

The establishment of a salary club may start from a more informal exchange of salary information between two or more companies who employ similar types of staff. A club may be the result of individual initiatives by one or two compensation specialists within companies. In some industries, the computer industry for example, there is a more regular exchange of salary information than in others. Some consultants specialise in club survey work in certain industrial groups. If the target group is sufficiently finely defined, as for example, in the international banking sector and the pharmaceutical industry, then not only are a homogeneous group of employees being surveyed, but also a very high proportion of the potential number of participants will probably take part.

General published surveys

The number of surveys continues to grow, but the quality of data they provide varies enormously. Both the Top Pay Unit of Incomes Data Services and the Pay and Benefits Bulletin published by Industrial Relations Services publish regular reviews of these surveys and analyses of the trend data they contain. The Top Pay Unit also publishes a *Directory of Salary Surveys* every couple of years which is essentially a consumer's guide to the salary survey market. It gives full information on the jobs covered, sample data, cost and availability as well as comments on the quality and reliability of the data.

General surveys such as those produced by Remuneration Economics, Monks/Charterhouse, Inbucon, Reward and the Executive Compensation Service (now part of the Wyatt Company) are based on data collected from as large a number of participating organizations as they can attract — typically from mailshots to a large number of employers. They cover base salary and total earnings levels paid on a given date and a certain amount of data on benefits entitlements. The most usual company analyses are by industrial sector, and size in terms of annual sales turnover and/or numbers of employees. Most surveys include some indication of regional variations and can be expected to add to this given the interest in regional pay differences for jobs; here local market influences are more important than national trends. Clerical and shopfloor jobs that are recruited using local sources need local pay analyses to give an acceptable picture of the market – especially among smaller organizations. National data will always be needed however for jobs which are recruited on a national basis. It is important to remember that where, for instance, there appear to be regional differences in management pay, this will almost always turn out on deeper analysis to be related to the size of the job and the nature and age of the industry rather than the location. Traditional engineering companies tend to pay less than their high-tech counterparts and they tend to be located in different parts of the country. They are also often not demanding the same academic background and level of skills from the managers they employ. Nor, sadly, are some of them in a position to afford higher pay – for better qualified managers able to improve profitability through innovation and improved financial management.

Most surveys also provide data on annual salary movement.

Advertisements

Advertisements are often used to give information on salary or wage levels. But they should be treated with caution. The rates quoted may be inflated to attract candidates and the information about the job may be too imprecise to permit useful comparisons to be made.

Analysing and presenting the results

As survey returns come in they should be checked carefully to ensure that acceptable matching or pricing has been given for each job. Any doubtful figures should be referred back to participants and discussed with them. Where comparisons turn out not to be close enough to be acceptable, the data should be rejected – preferably with the agreement of the participant concerned.

Salary club surveys can generally be processed very quickly and participants typically expect a report within a month of sending in their returns. Strict deadlines usually have to be set and enforced to ensure this is possible. Whoever is responsible for the survey should ensure that the analysis of results can begin as soon as the first few returns have come in and been checked.

The methods used in the analysis and presentation of survey results will depend on the number of returns received and the degree of sophistication in salary policy of both the survey producer and the participants. It can therefore vary from simple histograms (bar charts) either set out on graph paper or drawn by computer showing the salary scales or actual ranges paid by participants and coded company by company, to complex statistical analyses producing computer printouts which present the data in relation to a number of different variables. In selecting which forms of analysis will yield the most meaningful results and present the data in a way which helps the salary policy decision-making process, it helps to concentrate on what the data are actually based on and who will use the findings. The use of multiple regression analysis, correlations and standard deviations looks very sophisticated and is therefore sometimes seductive. For data based on large samples such techniques have their value and can be used to effect. But the application of sophisticated statistical techniques to rather tentative data collected in a small-scale salary survey has all the subtlety of a sledgehammer crushing a nut. What matters most is to present a limited amount of directly relevant market data in a way which shows what the actual operating salary range for any given job is where the extremes of practice lie as well as the midpoint – backed by a brief commentary on the underlying influences affecting the distribution.

A statistical summary of research data might look like that shown in Table 22.1.

Job title	Salary range (£)			Actual salary (£)		
	Lower quartile	*Median*	*Upper quartile*	*Lower quartile*	*Median*	*Upper quartile*
Production manager	16100-18800	18000-20200	19500-22300	17800	19100	20200

Table 22.1 *Summary of salary data: production managers*

Salary data can also be represented graphically in various ways. Figure 22.1 illustrates the relationships between salary ranges and actual salaries for a number of companies and the relative position of the originating company. This approach has considerable visual impact and is also particularly useful for internal salary policy decision making.

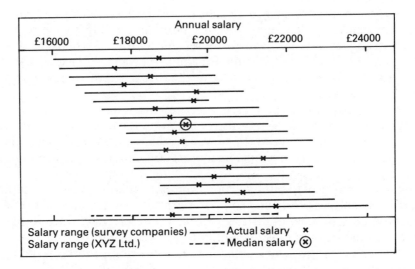

Figure 22.1 Salary survey data presented graphically

Using survey data

The translation of salary market data into an acceptable company salary structure is a process based on judgement and compromise. The aim is to extract a derived market rate based on effective estimates of the reliability of the data, and to strike a reasonable balance between the competing merits of the different sources used. However 'scientific' the approach, this is essentially an intuitive process. Once all the data available has been collected and presented in the most accessible manner possible (ie job by job for all the areas the structure is to cover), a proposed scale midpoint has to be established for each level based on the place in the market the company wishes to occupy, ie its 'market posture'. The establishment of this midpoint will be based not only on assessment of current and updated salary data, but on indications of movement in earnings and the cost of living which are likely to affect the life of the whole structure. For organizations needing to stay ahead of the market this point will often be around the upper quartile; for others closer alignment with the median is adequate.

Chapter 23
Pay Structures

Definition

A pay structure consists of an organization's pay levels or scales for single jobs or groups of jobs. In a graded pay structure, these will be defined by the minimum and maximum rates of pay in each grade for the jobs placed in the grade. Within each grade there will be scope for progression according to merit or service or a combination of the two (salary progression systems are described in Chapter 24). However, a system of individual job rates without any defined grades but, possibly, with scope to earn more by merit or by means of a payment by results scheme, could equally well be described as a pay structure.

In one organization there may be a wage structure for manual or hourly paid workers and a separate salary structure for white collared staff who are paid monthly or, less frequently, by the week. Harmonization of terms and conditions for all employees in the shape of single-status companies is, however, becoming more common. Traditional status symbols are, rightly, going, and the only distinction made between employees is their rate of pay, which is governed by the value of their contribution and by the market rate for their job. Unified grading systems occur in high-tech firms and where overseas companies, particularly Japanese firms, are setting up factories in Great Britain.

This chapter starts by considering the criteria for any pay structure – wage, salary or unified, and the considerations affecting the number of structures. It continues to deal with the main types of pay structures:

1. Graded salary structures.
2. Individual job range structures.
3. Spot rate structures.
4. Benefit grade structures.
5. Progression curve structures.
6. Rate for age scales.

Criteria for pay structures

The criteria that should be used when selecting or modifying a pay structure are that it should:

- be appropriate to the needs of the organization, in terms of its culture, its size, the degree to which it is subject to change, the need for employee mobility and the type and level of employees to be covered;
- be flexible in response to internal and external pressures, especially those related to market rates and skill shortages;
- provide scope for rewarding high flyers while still providing appropriate rewards for the bulk of employees on whom the organization depends;
- ensure that rewards are given in line with performance and achievement;
- provide a basis for career planning which will motivate ambitious employees;
- facilitate consistency in the treatment of varying levels of responsibility and performance.

How many structures?

The advantage of having one structure to cover all grades of employees is that a consistent approach to gradings, differentials and control can be adopted from top to bottom. The problems of borderline cases between two structures are avoided and the overall structure is easy to explain and understand.

It may not, however, be feasible to have one structure covering all staff which satisfies all the criteria listed above. It may be necessary to separate senior managers from the rest because their terms and conditions of employment are different or because more scope is needed to recognize variations in responsibility and performance than would be possible in a conventional graded structure used for other staff. At this level, each job might have its own salary bracket or 'spot rate'. At the other end of the scale, it might be necessary to separate junior staff, either because they are paid a rate for age or because they are in jobs where the opportunity to improve performance is limited and should therefore be paid a flat rate or placed within a fairly small salary bracket.

Separate structures for different occupations may be necessary because the salaries of some categories of employees are negotiated with trade unions, or because there are special market rate pressures which make it difficult to fit them into the general salary structure. Some salary systems have a number of different structures for 'market' groups such as computer staff, brand managers or accountants. The salaries for these groups are fixed primarily by reference to market rates and the salaries in one group are not compared specifically with those in other groups. However, a consistent approach to the salary structure may be used across the company with regard to differentials within groups and the width of salary brackets.

Graded salary structures

A graded salary structure consists of a sequence of salary ranges or grades, each of which has a defined minimum and maximum. It is assumed that all the jobs allocated into a range are broadly of equal value, although the actual salaries earned by the individuals in a range will depend on their performance or length of service.

Main features of a graded salary structure

The main features of a typical broad-banded salary structure are:

1. All jobs are allocated into a salary grade within the structure on the basis of an assessment of their internal and external value to the organization.
2. Each salary grade consists of a salary range or band. No individual holding a job in the grade can go beyond the maximum of the salary range unless he or she is promoted.
3. The jobs allocated to a salary grade are assumed to be broadly of the same level. In other words, they normally have the same minimum and maximum rates, which correspond with the grade boundaries.
4. The number of salary ranges or grades will depend on: (a) the salary levels of the highest and lowest paid jobs to be covered by the structure, which give the overall range of salaries within which the individual salary ranges have to be fitted, (b) the differentials between grades, and (c) the width of the salary ranges.
5. There is a differential between the midpoints of each salary range which provides adequate scope for rewarding increased responsibility on promotion to the next higher grade but does not create too wide a gap between adjacent grades or reduce the amount of flexibility available for grading jobs. This differential should normally be 15-25%, but 20% of the midpoint of the lower grade is a typical differential.
6. The salary ranges are sufficiently wide to allow recognition of the fact that people in jobs graded at the same level can perform differently, and should be rewarded in accordance with their performance. To allow room for progression, the ranges at junior

clerical level need be no wider than 15-20% of the minima for the grade. At senior levels, however, where there is more scope for improvements and variations in performance, the ranges could be 35-60%, although the most typical width is about 50%, or plus or minus 20% of the midpoint of the range.

7. There is an overlap between salary grades which acknowledges that an experienced person doing a good job can be of more value to the company than a newcomer to a job in the grade above. Overlap, as measured by the proportion of a grade which is covered by the next lower grade, is usually 25-50%. A large overlap of 40-50% is typical in companies with a wide variety of jobs, where a reasonable degree of flexibility is required in grading them. It results in a larger number of grades than is required for a typical promotion ladder within a department, and implies that in some circumstances a grade can be jumped following promotion.

8. The midpoint of the range is the salary level which represents the value to the organization of any job in that grade in which the performance of the job holder is fully acceptable. It may be regarded as the 'target salary' for the grade, which would be the average salary of the staff in the grade assuming a steady movement of people through the range.

9. The midpoint of the range is aligned to the market rates for the jobs in the grade. The salary policy or 'posture' of the organization will determine whether the midpoint is equated to the median market rate or whether it is related to another point, for example, the upper quartile market rate or 10% above the median market rate.

10. General increases in salary levels following negotiations or changes in the cost of living (usually expressed in percentage terms) are dealt with by proportionate increases to the midpoints of each salary range. Assuming that the policy is to maintain range widths, this would result in proportionate increases to the maxima and minima of each grade.

11. Jobs can be regraded within the structure when it is decided that their value has altered because of a change in responsibilities or a pronounced movement in market rates. In the latter case, it is necessary to note that this is a special market rate for the job imposed by external circumstances and does not imply that jobs previously placed by job evaluation at the same level should also be regraded.

12. Progression within a grade depends on the performance of the individual. It would generally be assumed that all fully competent individuals in any jobs in a grade would eventually reach the normal maximum for a grade, if they are not promoted

out of it. Less competent individuals may stop progressing at some point below the grade maximum. In some circumstances, provision may be made for exceptional individuals to receive more than the grade maximum if there are no immediate opportunities for promotion but the company wishes to retain their services and maintain their motivation.

Structure design features

Make-up of a salary grade
A basic principle of a salary structure is that individuals advance through the structure either by progressing within the salary grade for the job as they improve their performance, or by promotion.

In the simplest structure, people move more or less steadily from the entry point of the grade (which might be above the minimum if they have already gained relevant experience elsewhere or within the firm) to the upper limit, unless they move to a higher grade. It is possible, however, to distinguish three stages into which this progression is divided, and for salary administration purposes it is helpful to divide the grade into three zones which correspond to these stages.

The three zones are:

1. *The learning zone*, which covers the period when a person is on his 'learning curve', familiarizing himself with the knowledge and skills required if he is to become fully competent. The length of time to go through this zone will vary according to the individual's experience, competence and ability to learn. It would be accepted that someone might enter the range at any point in this zone, from bottom to top, depending on experience.
2. *The qualified zone*, which covers the period when the job holder continues to increase his capacity to do the work and to improve his performance. The minimum salary in this zone should be the market rate for the job, so far as this can be ascertained, the assumption being that the market rate is the salary level required to attract a competent individual from another job to join the company. The mid-point in this zone, which is also the midpoint of the grade, is the salary level which all competent employees would be expected to achieve. This is above the market rate in order to retain these individuals. An employee who is no more than competent could stop at this point, but most would continue to advance until they reach the top of the qualified zone, which would be regarded as the normal maximum for the job. Many such employees would in any case be promoted to a higher grade before they reach the upper limit of this zone.
3. *The premium zone*, which is reserved for those employees, especially in the higher grade jobs, who achieve exceptional

results but for whom suitable promotion opportunities do not exist. This zone enables outstanding staff to be given additional rewards and encouragement. In some salary structures, the published salary grades for each job only cover the learning and qualified zones, the premium zone being reserved for use in special cases. Progression through that zone would not be regarded as normal by management or staff.

A 50% salary grade made up according to these principles is illustrated in Figure 23.1.

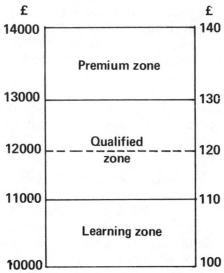

Figure 23.1 Make-up of a salary range

Relationships between grades

Figure 23.2 illustrates the relationships between grades if a differential of 20% is established between them. Promotion could take place between grades one and two or between grades one and three. In the former case, the existence of the new job in the next higher grade implies some overlap in the knowledge and skills required and it might be appropriate to pro-mote someone to the starting point of the qualified zone, or even in exceptional cases, into the qualified zone, as long as there is still reason-able scope for salary progression within the grade. A jump in grades implies that the promoted employee would have quite a lot to learn in his new job and is likely to start at the minimum salary, which still allows a reasonable promotion increase even if he is some way through the quali-fied zone in the lower grade. An example of a salary structure designed in accordance with these principles is shown in Figure 23.3.

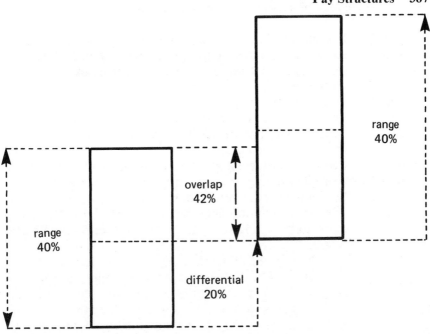

Figure 23.2 Relationship between two salary grades

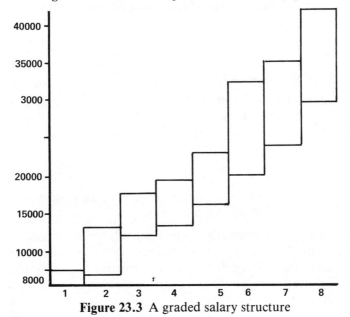

Figure 23.3 A graded salary structure

Designing the salary structure

The simplest and therefore the best way to design a salary structure is to take the following steps:

Step 1:   Establish by market rate surveys and studies of existing structures and differentials the salary levels of the most senior and most junior jobs to be covered by the structure.

Step 2:   Draw up a salary grade structure between the upper and lower limits, as established in step 1, according to policies for differentials, the width of salary grades and the size of overlap between grades.

Step 3:   Conduct a job evaluation exercise, preferably by means of a simple ranking scheme, although this could be refined by using paired comparisons.

Step 4:   Obtain market rate data, bearing in mind that there is likely to be a range of market rates rather than a precise figure.

Step 5:   Slot the jobs into the grade structure in accordance with the results of both the job evaluations and the market rate surveys. It is here that judgement is required. While some decisions on grades will be obvious, others will be more difficult. If in doubt, re-evaluate the borderline cases to help make the final marginal decision. One advantage of an overlapping structure is that such decisions are less critical.

Advantages of graded salary structures

The advantages of this type of structure are that:

1. The relative levels of jobs in different functions can be readily assessed and recognized.
2. Consistent methods of grading jobs and establishing differentials between them can be maintained.
3. A well defined and comprehensible framework exists within which pay and career progression can be planned and controlled.
4. Better control can be exercised over pay for new starters, merit increments and promotion increases.

The only potential disadvantage is that a graded structure inhibits flexibility. It can be more difficult to react quickly to market rate changes and the imposition of a rigid ceiling on an individual's pay progression in a job may limit the ability to reward exceptional performance.

Individual job range structures

Where the content of jobs is widely different, or where flexibility in response to rapid organizational changes or market rate pressures is vital, an individual job range system may be preferable to a graded structure.

In these circumstances, differences should not be blurred by the procrustean process of forcing a number of dissimilar jobs within the rigid confines of a salary grade.

Individual job range systems simply define a salary bracket for each job. The midpoint of the range is related to market rates and the limits are expressed as plus or minus a percentage of the midpoint salary, typically, at senior levels, plus or minus 20 per cent.

The advantages of individual job ranges are that they are more flexible and avoid the inevitable problems which occur when positions are evaluated just below grade boundaries. But they are more difficult to control and require more administrative time and effort.

Individual job ranges are probably best for senior jobs or for rapidly growing companies where a conventional grade structure would be too stultifying. They are often associated with points job evaluation schemes which provide a basis for assessing relativities between jobs and fixing benefits.

Spot rate structures

In its simplest form, a spot rate or job rate system allocates a specific rate for a job. There are no salary brackets. The rate is fixed by reference to market rates or by negotiation with trade unions – spot rate structures are almost universal for manual workers. Job evaluation can be used to establish the hierarchy but this may not be the case if rates are negotiated or if there are considerable market pressures.

Modifications to the spot rate system

The basic system as described above can be modified in one or more of the following ways:

1. Performance-related bonuses can be earned on top of the basic rate.
2. Additional payments can be made to the spot rate for special skills or responsibilities. This is common in structures for manual workers.
3. Scope may be allowed for some discretion to pay people below the spot rate if they are not fully qualified to do the job. The assumption is that the spot rate is the market rate the company has to pay to attract and retain someone who is fully capable of meeting the standards expected by the company. If those standards are higher than in the outside world, then the company spot rate would be higher than the external market rate, for example, it would be located at the upper quartile of the distribution of market rates. People appointed or promoted to a

job which they are not yet qualified to do at the level required could be paid up to, say, 10% less than the spot rate and progressed towards that rate as quickly or as slowly as their progress warrants. This salary could stop below the rate if they are not going to make it, in which case their continued retention by the company would be under question.

Benefit grades

It may be necessary to superimpose a benefit grade structure on top of a job grade or spot rate system. Each benefit grade will define the benefits that can be obtained such as a company car or an improved pension scheme. Jobs can be slotted into benefit grades by means of job evaluation or by a more subjective assessment of what benefits are required to provide increased rewards for greater responsibility or to compete with market rates.

A benefit grade structure is shown in Table 23.1.

Management grade	Salary range (mid point) £	Company car (retail price pre-1987 value) £	Petrol	Pension scheme	Medical insurance
1	30,000 to 40,000	17,500	Yes	Senior fund 2/3 of final salary after 20 years service	Yes
2	22,500 to 30,000	12,500	Yes	Senior fund 2/3 of final salary after 30 years service	Yes
3	17,500 to 22,500	7,500	No	Normal fund 2/3 of final salary after 40 years service	Yes

Table 23.1 *Benefit grade structure*

A benefit grade structure superimposed on an individual job range structure is illustrated in Figure 23.4.

Salary progression curves

Salary progression curves, sometimes called maturity curves or career curves, aim to link increases in salary over a fairly long period to increased maturity or experience. They are best used for professional, scientific or other highly qualified staff who are carrying out work in which their contribution is almost entirely related to their professional capacity rather

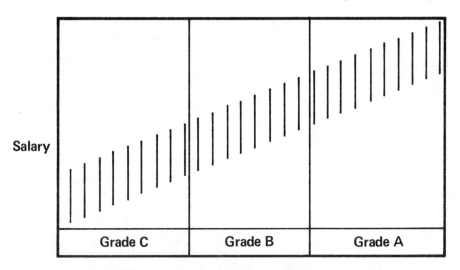

Figure 23.4 Individual job ranges and benefit grades

than to a more or less fixed set of duties that enable their job to be firmly placed in a rigid hierarchy.

Progression curves are mostly used for professional or scientific staff whose starting salary is linked to the market rate for their degree or to a professional qualification. The system assumes that they will develop within their discipline at some standard rate or rates as a result of their experience.

A single progression curve is illustrated in Figure 23.5. This is almost a rate for age curve except that progression is not inevitable – the curve is only a guideline and some may advance more rapidly than others. Another

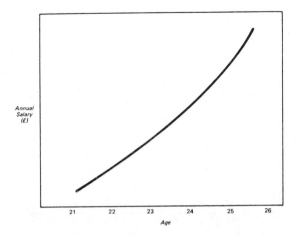

Figure 23.5 Salary progression curve

difference is that progression curves are, or should be, determined by reference to a salary survey which indicates the salaries people carrying out professional or scientific work can expect to get at certain ages. A scatter-graph of market rates, as shown in Figure 23.6, can indicate the appropriate rate of progression if a 'line of best fit' is drawn which represents the trend between the two variables of salary and age.

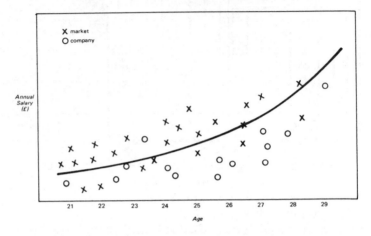

Figure 23.6 Salary survey and progression curve

More than one rate of progression may be provided where it is felt that there should be some scope to reward and encourage individuals according to their performance and potential. The approach is illustrated in Figure 23.7 where there are three different starting rates, A, B and C, which might be related to level of qualification; for example, post-graduate qualification, first or upper second degrees, lower second or pass degree.

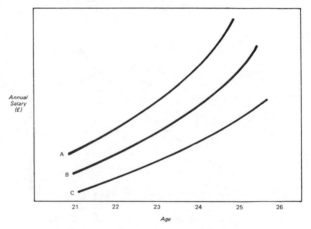

Figure 23.7 Graded progression curves

Thereafter, the curves A, B and C represent the expected rate at which an individual with the relevant starting qualifications may be presumed to progress with increased experience. Of course, the initial qualification does not guarantee that performance will be maintained at the same level. People with lower qualifications may rapidly catch up or overtake those with higher qualifications and would be moved towards or on to a higher scale than that on which they started.

A progression curve system designed along these lines must be used flexibly or it will defeat its purpose. The aim is to allow plenty of scope to advance people according to their contribution. The curves should only be used as guidelines to assist in salary planning – ensuring that individuals advance in salary at a rate appropriate to their performance and potential.

Rate for age

A rate for age system is an incremental scale in which a specific rate of pay or a defined pay bracket is linked to each age for staff in certain jobs. Rate for age scales are usually reserved for young employees under training or for junior clerical or laboratory staff carrying out routine work. The assumption behind rate for age scales is that the staff are on a learning curve which means that their value to the company is directly linked to increased experience and maturity.

The simplest structure consists of one rate for each age as shown in Figure 23.8.

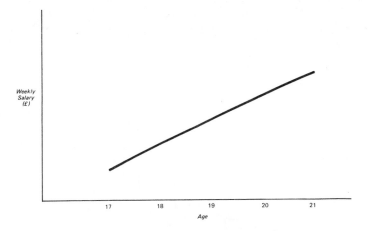

Figure 23.8 Rate for age structure

A more complex structure to accommodate three different job grades is shown in Figure 23.9.

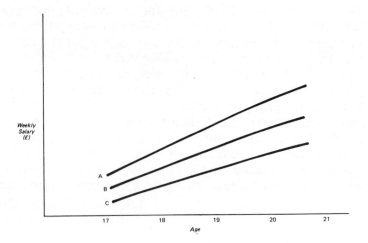

Figure 23.9 Rate for age structure for three job grades

It may be thought desirable to allow some scope for merit at each age and Figure 23.10 shows how merit can be catered for in a rate for age scale.

Rate for age scales of the basic type illustrated in Figure 23.8 are inflexible but they may have to be used because they are a tradition in the local labour market and with a highly mobile form of labour it is essential to keep pace with market rates. Their great advantage is that they are easy to administer – invidious decisions about the relative merit of people under training do not have to be made and the scales achieve complete equity. They may be worth retaining for these reasons, but there is a lot to be said for relating pay to age *and* performance as in Figure 23.10 rather than to the arbitrary criterion of age.

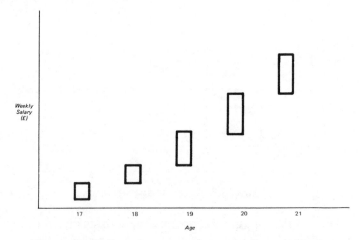

Figure 23.10 Rate for age structure with merit bands

Chapter 24
Salary Progression Systems

The concept of salary progression

Salary progression in a job takes place at a rate which depends on merit, experience or incremental increases in responsibility which do not constitute promotion or justify regrading.

In a graded salary structure or a job grade system as described in Chapter 23, progression takes place within a defined salary bracket. A spot rate structure will not normally allow for salary progression unless a feature of its system is the scope to start people at a level below the spot rate.

Salary progression in a career usually takes place between jobs and as a result of promotion and career planning. In a graded structure this would happen as illustrated in Figure 24.1.

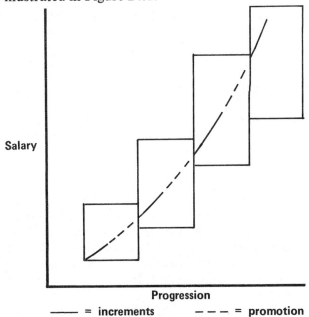

Figure 24.1 Salary progression over a career in a graded salary structure

For some specialist or professional jobs, such as scientists in research and development organizations, advancement is not necessarily a matter of promotion from a job in one grade to another clearly differentiated job in a higher grade. It is equally likely to be a case of steady progression as additional skill and expertise is gained and more important projects can be undertaken, possibly without any additional managerial responsibility. In these circumstances, salary progression curves such as those described in Chapter 23 can be used. Alternatively, the fluid grading system of the British Scientific Civil Service can be adopted. This recognizes that scientific careers unfold over a longer period than the normal grading system allows, and that scientists should therefore be allowed to progress smoothly through successive grades in accordance with their individual performance and value to the organization rather than in relation to steps on a promotional ladder which is irrelevant to their normal career progression.

But these are special cases and the salary progression systems described in this chapter are mainly concerned with progression in a salary range. There are two basic approaches, each with variants, to the way in which salaries can be progressed within ranges:

1. *Incremental systems* where fixed increments are given at regular intervals. These can be modified to allow some variation according to performance.
2. *Performance-related systems* where progression is entirely related to performance, although the degree to which progress is controlled may vary.

Incremental systems

In the basic fixed incremental system, the individual moves through the salary range by predetermined steps related to service, as shown in Figure 24.2, where, in a 40% range, eight increments of 5% of the range minimum salary are given.

This approach is widely used in the British Civil Service and other parts of the public sector where there is an emphasis on service and experience. To some, including many trade unionists, its uniformity has the advantage of eliminating any bias on the part of management. Some managements prefer the system because it is completely under control. The inevitability of the annual award appeals to many staff, especially at junior levels, where there is less scope for variation in performance.

One of the reasons why fixed incremental systems achieved a measure of popularity in the days of incomes policies was that they were allowed by the government on the grounds that such systems are self-financing. This assumption is based on the concept of attrition, which occurs when the costs of merit increases are eroded during the course of a year because,

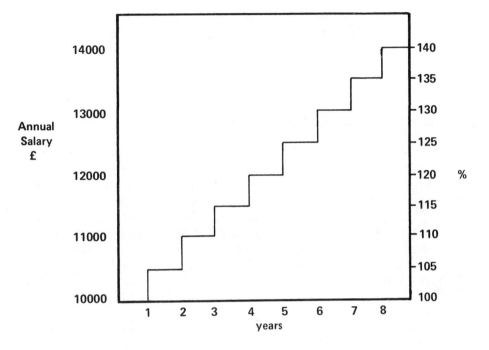

Figure 24.2 Salary progression within limits

normally, the average salary of leavers in a company exceeds the average salary of joiners. In theory, this process can entirely wipe out the cost of merit increments, but this depends on the unlikely event of the difference between the salaries of leavers and joiners equalling or exceeding the costs of increments. In practice this only happens in special circumstances such as in a steady situation where the numbers going out at the upper ends of salary ranges are exactly balanced by the numbers coming in at the lower end, or when turnover is greater among high earners than low earners. It is unlikely that attrition will fund more than 40% of expenditure on merit payments.

The principle of the fixed reward may be free of bias in that the amount given does not depend on a merit assessment which could be influenced by the prejudices of the assessor. But it can hardly be called fair if fairness involves, as it should do, paying people in line with their performance. Any organization which believes in rewarding staff according to merit should not adopt a fixed incremental system unless it feels either that this is the only way in which it can control salary costs, or that merit pay would not be acceptable to a trade union. Neither of these is a sufficient reason. Salary costs can be controlled using the methods described in Chapter 27. Trade unions can sometimes be persuaded that merit pay is desirable and that performance appraisal systems can operate fairly. This is particularly the case for more senior staff where merit pay is most valid. At lower levels, if trade unions are adamant, fixed increments over a limited period of time do less damage to the process of performance management.

It is, however, possible to modify the rigidity of a fixed incremental system in the way described later in this chapter.

The pressure for performance-related systems

The current climate is very much in favour of the performance management approach or PRA – payment for results and achievement. This has been partially caused by the decline in the rate of inflation. Merit payments falling between 2 and 4% look puny alongside inflation rates and 'cost of living' increases of as much as 20% which occurred as recently as 1979. When inflation is 4 or 5% and the merit element becomes the 'real' pay increase or even the total pay increase, its impact is enhanced. This fact was not lost on many boards of directors and there has been a change from pay increases based on input in the form of seniority, experience and qualifications to pay increases based on individual output measured against the achievement of agreed targets.

The pressure for performance-related pay has also been engendered by the enterprise culture which has become a major feature of British life. The days of incomes policies which restricted the development of merit pay systems seem to have gone for ever.

Merit pay as a motivator

The attitude of the Conforederation of British Industries to merit or performance-related pay is as follows:

> Our view on merit and performance-related payments, and the philosophy behind them, is that where they provide a genuine link between work performance and responsibilities and reward they are well worth while. To keep them operating to best effect, they do of course need regular attention. But we view them as having an important place as part of the route towards the improved international labour cost competitiveness which we so badly need. More generally the CBI believes that financial incentives combined with good employee involvement and communication can lead to greater employee commitment to their company and greater understanding of business realities.

Clearly, many top managers wish pay within their organization to be more closely related to performance – both corporate and individual. But there is no consistent research evidence that performance-related pay systems actually influence performance standards. Offering the prospect of extra cash, particularly at senior levels, is not of itself likely to produce substantial tangible performance improvements. The Office of Manpower

Economics, reporting on a survey they conducted in 1980 of Pay Systems for Senior Managers said:

> Adjustments in pay are not the only way in which the organizations taking part in this study seek to improve or reward performance. Job content and job satisfaction are often at least as influential as adjustments to pay. Executives welcome recognition by the organization of their performance and contribution. At least for senior managers, promotion is considered in the majority of organizations to be a particularly powerful motivator so long as promotion opportunities exist. Training and career development also have an important role to play.

In Walter Goldsmith and David Clutterbuck's book *The Winning Streak*,[1] the authors argue that most of the successful companies they describe are among the highest payers within their respective industry sectors. However, there are some notable exceptions: GEC's Lord Weinstock, for example, is quoted as saying: 'A lot of people may not be motivated by more money'. Academic research on theories of motivation and the extent to which money acts as an incentive, is certainly not conclusive on this point. Nevertheless, there are those in senior management, and in management consultancy, who believe that merit and other performance-related pay can encourage a more entrepreneurial approach among managers. Peter Brown of Reward Regional Surveys is quoted by Goldsmith and Clutterbuck as saying:

> We have to get back to merit as the basis for annual increments . . . The evidence we have suggests that the most profitable companies have face-to-face discussions about performance with individual managers and a fair amount of discrimination about how much each person gets.

Union attitudes

As with the management side, there cannot be said to be a uniform trade union view of merit pay – although suspicion about them is fairly widespread. This is because merit systems confer on management the right to determine unilaterally aspects of terms and conditions which, according to the unions, should be negotiable.

Public sector unions, faced with proposals to introduce merit pay, have traditionally tended to view these moves as part of a general strategy to weaken their collective bargaining strength. On the other hand, they have not been opposed to the process of performance appraisal, when it is used for assessing promotional potential and training/development needs.

Performance-related merit systems

Performance-related systems provide for the rate at which an individual's salary progress is to be determined by an assessment of their merit and their present and future value to the organization.

Basis of performance-related systems

Performance-related systems will be based on the performance management procedures described in Chapter 28. While an important aim of these procedures' purpose is to provide information which will assist in career planning and in assessing development and training needs, they can also be used to provide an overall assessment of performance which can help to determine merit pay. To avoid the vexed question of pay prejudicing the developmental purpose of performance appraisal, it is best to hold the performance and career counselling sessions at a different time, preferably in advance of the salary review. Managers can then 'read across' from the appraisal, but the process of using this in a reward review need not affect the counselling or performance that has already taken place.

Qualities of a successful performance-related system

In a survey conducted by the Top Pay Unit of Incomes Data Services in conjunction with the Institute of Personnel Management[2] the views of personnel managers were sought on what they thought were the essential qualities of a successful performance-related system. They thought it should be:

- based on a fair and equitable method of measuring performance using a formal performance appraisal system;
- as fair and consistent as possible between individuals performing at the same level – and seen to be so;
- flexible enough to help managers tie decisions into business needs – good performers have to feel they have been given significant increases;
- easy to understand – for both managers and the personnel department;
- straightforward to operate and monitor;
- based on the firm foundations of a good basic salary/wages and benefits package within the framework of good overall personnel practice;
- supported by a clearly defined staff/management development policy.

Typical merit payments at different levels of performance

The Incomes Data Services survey showed that the number of ratings companies used in their merit schemes, and the flexibility to award different increases at the same standard of performance varies considerably. Companies which have a single merit-based review are likely to have more flexibility in this respect than where merit is paid in addition to a general increase. For example, at IBM, managers have a 5% discretion in deciding the level of subordinates' salary, once the performance rating has determined the appropriate part of the salary band for the individual. By contrast, at United Dominions Trust, which agrees a general award each year with its staff union, the merit payment at each performance rating is a fixed percentage.

Research on executive pay awards suggests that whereas most merit policies make provision for a nil increase to be awarded this is a severe and a relatively rare sanction – in practice often restricted to employees whose performance is much below standard, and who are likely to be disciplinary cases. A more usual increase for the individual performing 'barely adequately' has tended to be at the same level as the rate of inflation and a typical increase for an outstanding performer is between 10 and 15%, including the general increase if paid.

Types of performance-related systems

The main performance-related systems are:

1. *Fixed scales with limited flexibility* – essentially a fixed incremental scale with the scope to award double increments or to withhold increments.
2. *Fixed parallel scales* as illustrated in Figure 24.3 where increments are predetermined according to performance.

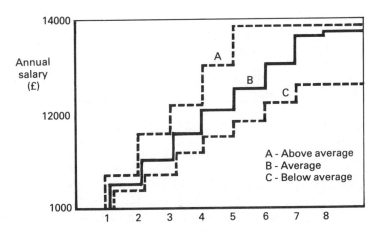

Figure 24.3 Incremental system with fixed parallel scale

3. *Variable progression within limits.* This commonly used approach differs from the semi-fixed or fixed parallel scale systems in that there are no fixed incremental points but some constraints are applied to the exercise of management discretion. The award of increases is determined in a systematic manner which is related to

a performance assessment procedure and is subject to control to ensure consistency of treatment as well as the observance of over-all financial limits. In some cases the individual can expect to move through the whole range for the job or grade provided his performance is satisfactory, but the rate at which he progresses towards the maximum will depend on his performance. In other cases, particular zones within the range are related to specific levels of performance and points are established within the ranges as the maxima for performance at different levels. The operation of this system is illustrated in Figure 24.4.

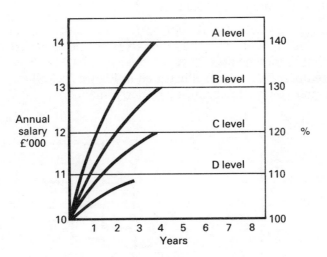

Figure 24.4 Progression lines within limits

Some companies provide guidelines for management such as those in Table 24.1 but these are not mandatory as in the fixed parallel scale system. The rates at which staff progress to the maximum attainable in their salary range may be varied at management's discretion subject to keeping within their merit increase budget.

In some organizations an extra 'premium zone' has been added to the top of the salary range to cater for exceptional staff.

4. *Variable progression guidelines.* Guidelines can be provided for progression over a fairly long period according to performance as in the salary progression curve system. This is described in

Performance	Annual increment	Maximum attainable in range (% of base rate)	Years to maximum
A Outstanding	10	140	4
B Very effective	7.5	130	4
C Satisfactory	5	120	4
D Barely satisfactory	3 (if any)	110	3
E Unsatisfactory	Nil	—	—

Table 24.1 *Example of guidelines in a variable progression system*

Chapter 23 but in essence, it provides for different rates of progression through performance zones. Progress is governed by merit ratings.

5. *Variable progression without guidelines.* In this type of system, management discretion in the award of increments and determination of their size tends to be restricted only by the maximum of the range and is not based on formalized procedures. Overall financial constraints may, however, be applied which limits the total sum available for increments in any given period, and some guidance may be given on the maximum award that can be paid. For example, managers responsible for reviewing individual salaries might be told that the maximum individual award should be 10% of salary.

6. *Variable progression to a 'spot rate'.* In modified versions of the 'spot rate' salary structure as described in Chapter 23, staff may be recruited at a rate below the spot rate (defined as the rate for a fully qualified and competent job holder and which is competitive with market rates, and will enable the organization to attract and retain suitable people), when they are not yet fully qualified to earn the full rate for the job. In these circumstances they would be progressed to the spot rate in accordance with the speed at which they learn their job and can meet its demands in full. Above the spot rate, performance-related merit bonuses can be earned.

7. *Variable progression without defined ranges.* This approach is characterized by a belief in the need to determine an appropriate salary at a point in time as a flat rate for the job. Increments are then given on an entirely individual basis so that the level of pay can be matched to performance in the job, usually on the basis of a largely subjective assessment. Control is often achieved by centralizing all decisions on increments. The ad hoc, arbitrary

and autocratic nature of this method has little to commend it, although it is typical of many small businesses.

8. *Merit bars.* Merit bars or control points can be part of any fixed or variable system. They are based on the belief that individuals take time to become experienced in their job and can usually be expected to perform satisfactorily for several years. They can be used with or without fixed service-related increments to the midpoint. They may also be used at the upper quartile of a scale, instead of the midpoint, after which variable progression begins. The part of the salary scale between the merit bar and the maximum is sometimes called the 'premium zone' since its use is restricted to high performers. Premium zones are also used for those in receipt of special market rate premia where external pressures require higher salaries to be paid within a range than would be justified on the basis of merit alone.

9. *Merit bonuses.* Merit bonuses can be paid as additional non-consolidated rewards for outstanding performance at any point on the salary progression curve. They are also useful for rewarding people at the top of the scale for continuing good performance in a job where there are no immediate opportunities to be promoted to a higher scale. Merit bonuses have been introduced experimentally for senior grades in the Civil Service, which is an area where promotion possibilities have become more restricted, and where the number of high performing individuals at the top of their range is increasing.

Choice of approach

The ideal system should:

1. Fit the corporate culture – the style of the company. A bureaucratic or mechanistic organization which believes – rightly or wrongly – in the maximum centralization of decision taking and in exercising strict control over managerial judgements might prefer a fixed incremental system, although it could allow for some discretion by using parallel scales. On the other hand, a less autocratic organization which believes in delegating as much authority as possible while retaining a reasonable degree of control might prefer to adopt the guideline approach, which allows for variable progression in a range.

2. Match the type of jobs it is meant to cover. A fixed incremental system, with possibly some room to reward special merit is often appropriate for junior clerical jobs, while a variable progression scheme would be more suitable for managerial jobs. There is no

reason why both approaches should not be used in one organization, if different levels of staff have to be catered for.

3. Provide scope for rewarding different levels of performance within jobs.
4. Facilitate the planning of salary progression in accordance with estimates of potential.
5. Enable management to retain a reasonable degree of control over its operation.
6. Operate fairly and consistently.
7. Be easy to communicate to staff so that they can be convinced that it is fair and can be motivated by receiving some indication of their possible line of progression.

None of the systems described above could satisfy all these criteria but as long as the approach enables progression to be varied according to performance but within clearly defined guidelines it should be possible to adapt it to the specific needs of the organization.

Getting results out of performance-related pay

The greater danger in running a performance-related pay system is that it does not fulfil its function or that it is not used effectively to improve performance. Too often increments or bonuses are given away. Even more often, staff are not provided with the incentive of knowing what they can earn if they improve their performance in specified ways and achieve specified results. The first step in getting more out of performance pay is to develop a salary planning system.

Salary planning

The aim of salary planning is to ensure that individuals are correctly placed in their salary range in relation to their performance and that they move through and between salary grades at a rate appropriate to their progress and potential. Most salary planning decisions are short-term ones in that they are concerned with deciding on the next increment to be paid because of merit or promotion. Longer-term salary plans are closely linked with career planning procedures (see Chapter 31), and the advantage of a formal salary structure is that it is possible to forecast future salary progression in the event of promotion.

Salary planning in the short term can be carried out by means of a variable increment system with guidelines which show the various rates at which people can progress through a zoned salary range. It is then possible to take a view on the likely or desirable rate at which someone's salary should advance by reference to an assessment of performance and an estimate of potential.

There are no fixed principles for doing this. The approach should be, first, to compare what an individual is being paid with what his level of performance suggests he should be paid. This will indicate what his immediate increase should be, although if his salary is considerably below what he should be getting it may be necessary to phase his increases. Secondly, consideration should be given to his potential and the salary progression that would be appropriate if he is to be given further encouragement to develop and remain with the company. There is no question of predetermining future increases at this stage, but it may be necessary to adjust the current increase to which he would normally be entitled. This could be higher than usual if it is thought that potential should be recognized now before it is too late and the individual has left the company. It could be lower than usual if it is felt that the increments to which he is entitled in his present salary range should be spread over an extra year or two so that he does not come to a grinding halt too soon.

Salary planning is greatly assisted if salary progression curves can be used to compare where the individual has got to with the standard curves and with his contemporaries. In the simplified example in Figure 24.5 the fact that Mr Y has fallen behind is clearly revealed and steps can be taken to find out if this is deserved or whether he should be given a higher increment or increments to restore him to his rightful place.

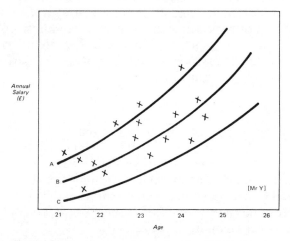

Figure 24.5 Progression curves and salary planning

An illustration of how salary planning takes place within a range according to performance assessments and the range parameters is given in Table 24.2.

In this example, the salary range is divided into four sections and the assessments indicate the sections in which individuals should eventually be placed in the range, assuming they maintain the same standard of performance and are not promoted. Those people who are given a satisfactory rating after a year in the job, having started at the bottom of the scale, could be told that they will progress to a maximum of £24,000 in three years time if their performance remains satisfactory, assuming a 5% increase each year.

Assessment	Range section (for a range where the span is 40% above the minimum)	Salary limits (for a range of £20,000 to £28,000)
A Outstanding	30% of minimum to maximum	£26,000-£28,000
B Very effective	20% to 30%	£24,000-£26,000
C Satisfactory	10% to 20%	£22,000-£24,000
D Barely satisfactory	0% to 10%	£20,000-£22,000

Table 24.2 *Salary planning in a range*

More importantly, however, they could be told that if they step up their performance to a very effective rating, they would get as far in two years at the rate of 7.5% a year. Similarly, outstanding staff could be given the exciting and stimulating news of how far and fast they can go if they maintain that level of performance. This approach can be used in any scheme but it is particularly appropriate in a salary progression curve system as described in Chapter 23.

Using performance pay to motivate

The salary planning process described above can be used to create expectations of the rewards that can follow from behaving in a particular way. This is in accordance with the expectancy theory of motivation which emphasizes that it is what people hope *and* expect to get if they behave in a certain way that motivates them, not what they know will come to them whatever they do. The procedure for assessing performance and 'reading across' from the assessment to the reward must, therefore, include deliberate steps to inform people of how they can benefit and what they must do about it.

References

1. Goldsmith, W and Clutterbuck, D *The Winning Streak.* Weidenfeld and Nicolson, London, 1984.
2. *The Merit Factor – Rewarding Individual Performance.* IDS Top Pay Unit and the Institute of Personnel Management, London, 1985.

Chapter 25

Payment by Results Systems

Payment by results systems relate the pay or part of the pay received by manual workers to the number of items they produce or the time they take to do a certain amount of work. They can operate on an individual or a group basis and although they usually provide for pay to fluctuate with performance in the short term, they can, as in measured day work, provide for a longer-term relationship. This chapter is divided into six parts:

1. A review of the background against which payment by results systems should be considered, covering:
   - arguments in favour and against;
   - criteria for success.
2. A brief description of the main types of scheme:
   - individual straight money piecework;
   - individual straight time piecework;
   - individual differential piecework;
   - group incentive schemes;
   - factory-wide incentive or 'gain-sharing' schemes;
   - measured day work.
3. An examination of how and why payment by results schemes degenerate and what can be done about it.
4. An analysis of the steps required to select a payment system.
5. A review of the methods of installing a payments by results scheme.
6. A final analysis of what should be done to monitor the system.

Arguments in favour and against payments by results systems

In favour

The main argument put forward by those in favour of any payment by results system is, of course, that people work to make money – the more money they make the happier they are and they will work harder if, and only if, they are paid more money. Higher output becomes what both management and workers want and everyone is happy. Underlying this argument is the assumption that piecework operators have the power to control the amount of effort they put into the job and that they adjust their effort solely or mainly in relation to the monetary return they get from it.

Against

Arguments against the 'economic man' philosophy of piecework and its practical effects have been gaining ground over a number of years, especially since a number of research projects into what actually happens on the shop floor have exposed the inadequacies of the system – for example, those carried out by Tom Lupton.[1]

The argument against the 'economic man' rationale for payment by results schemes is that it is a naive view of motivation. People at work have much more complicated goals than the simple pursuit of money and are not so many donkeys as to react as required to the carrot or the stick. One of the earlier formulations of this argument came from Douglas McGregor who wrote:

> The practical logic of incentives is that people want money, and that they will work harder to get more of it. Incentive plans do not, however, take account of several other well-demonstrated characteristics of behaviour in the organizational setting: (1) that most people also want the approval of their fellow workers and that if necessary they will forego increased pay to obtain this approval; (2) that no managerial assurances can persuade workers that incentive rates will remain inviolate regardless of how much they produce; (3) that the ingenuity of the average worker is sufficient to outwit any system of controls devised by management.[2]

The more specific arguments against payment by results systems are that they:

(a) are not effective in themselves – they do not increase effort or output;

(b) cause more trouble than they are worth in the shape of conflict between management and men, arguments about rates, jealousies between those on piecework and those on lower time rates, damage to pay structures where carefully calculated relativities are upset because one group of workers is fortunate enough to benefit from a loose rate, and frustrations to workers who suffer from unstable and unpredictable earnings;

(c) are a major cause of wage drift – the inflation of earnings outside the normal pattern of negotiated pay settlements.

Conclusion

The argument that people will only work harder if they can earn more money may appear to be simplistic. But Goldthorpe[3] in his research on what motivated car workers found that they preferred their repetitive, boring jobs which paid higher wages to the much more interesting jobs for lower pay available to them nearby. Of course, people work for other things besides money, but money can be an effective motivator because it provides the means for satisfying so many needs. Incentive schemes do work if they satisfy the criteria for success set out below.

Criteria for success

The criteria for the success of a payment by results scheme are that:

1. It should be appropriate to the type of work carried out and the workers employed.
2. The reward should be clearly and closely linked to the effort of the individual or group.
3. Individuals or groups should be able to calculate the reward they get at each of the levels of output they are capable of achieving.
4. Individuals or groups should have a reasonable amount of control over their efforts and therefore their rewards.
5. The scheme should operate by means of a defined and easily understood formula.
6. The scheme should be properly installed and maintained.
7. Provision should be made for controlling the amounts paid to ensure they are proportionate to effort.
8. Provision should be made for amending rates in defined circumstances.

Types of payment by results systems

Straight piecework

The most common of the schemes of payment by results which are purely individual in character is what is called straight piecework. This means payment of a uniform price per unit of production and it is most appropriate where production is repetitive in character and can easily be divided into similar units.

Straight piecework rates can be expressed in one of two main forms, 'money piecework' or 'time piecework'. In the case of money piecework, the employee is paid a flat money price for each piece or operation completed. In the case of time piecework, instead of a price being paid for operation, a time is allowed (this is often called a time-allowed system). The worker is paid at his basic piecework rate for the time allowed, but if he completes the job in less time he gains the advantage of the time saved, as he is still paid for the original time allowed. Thus, an operator who completes a job timed at 60 hours in 40 hours would receive a bonus of 50% of his piecework rate, ie ((60-40)/40) x 100.

Piece rates may be determined by work study using the technique known as effort rating to determine standard times for jobs. In situations where work is not repetitive, especially in the engineering industry, times may be determined on a much less analytical basis by ratefixers using their judgement. This often involves prolonged haggles with operators.

Differential piecework

Straight piecework systems result in a constant wage cost per unit of output, and management objections to this feature led to the development of differential systems where the wage cost per unit is adjusted in relation to output. The most familiar applications of this approach have been the premium bonus systems such as the Halsey/Weir or Rowan schemes. Both these systems are based on a standard time allowance and not a money piece rate, and the bonus depends on the time saved. Unlike straight piecework, the wages cost per unit of production falls as output increases, but the hourly rate of workers' earnings still increases, although not in proportion to the increased output. For obvious reasons, these systems are viewed with suspicion by unions and workers and many variations to the basic approach have been developed, some of which involve sharing the increments of higher productivity between employers and workers. For a fuller description of the various types of individual and group incentive schemes reference should be made to *Incentive Payment Systems* by R Marriott.[4]

Measured day work

In measured day work the pay of the employee is fixed on the understanding that he will maintain a specified level of performance, but the pay does not fluctuate in the short term with his performance. The arrangement relies on work measurement to define the required level of performance and to monitor the actual level. Fundamental to measured day work is the concept of an incentive level of performance, and this distinguishes it clearly from time rate systems. Measured day work guarantees the incentive payment in advance thereby putting the employee under an obligation to perform at the effort level required. Payment by results, on the other hand, allows the employee discretion as to his effort level but relates his pay directly to the output he has achieved. Between these two systems are a variety of alternatives that seek to marry the different characteristics of payment by results and measured day work, including banded incentives, stepped schemes and special forms of high day rate.

Measured day work seeks to produce an effort-reward bargain in which enhanced and stable earnings are exchanged for an incentive level of performance. The criteria for success in operating it are:

- total commitment of management, employees and their unions, which can only be achieved by careful planning, joint consultation, training, and a staged introduction of the system;
- an effective work measurement system, and efficient production planning and control and inventory control procedures;
- the establishment of a logical pay structure with appropriate differentials from the beginning of the scheme's operation – the structure should be developed by the use of job evaluation and in consultation with employees;
- the maintenance of good control systems to ensure that corrective action is taken quickly if there is any shortfall on targets.

Group incentive schemes

Group or area incentive schemes provide for the payment of a bonus either equally or proportionately to individuals within a group or area. The bonus is related to the output achieved over an agreed standard or to the time saved on a job – the difference between allowed time and actual time.

Group bonus schemes are in some respects individual incentive schemes written large – they have the same basic advantages and disadvantages as any payment by results system. The particular advantages of a group scheme are that it encourages team spirit, breaks down demarcation lines and enables the group to discipline itself in achieving targets. In addition, job satisfaction may be achieved through relating the group more closely to the complete operation. Group bonuses may be particularly useful where groups of workers are carrying out interdependent tasks and when individual bonus schemes might be invidious because workers will have only limited scope to control the level of their own output and will be expected to support others, to the detriment of their personal bonus.

The potential disadvantages of group bonus schemes are that management is less in control of production – the group can decide what earnings are to be achieved and can restrict output. Furthermore, the bonus can eventually cease to be an incentive. Some opponents of group schemes object to the elimination of personal incentive, but this objection would only be valid if it were possible to operate a satisfactory individual incentive scheme, which is not always the case.

Group schemes may be most appropriate where people have to work together and teamwork has to be encouraged. They are probably most effective if they are based on a system of measured or controlled day work where targets and standards are agreed by the group, which is provided with the control information it needs to monitor its own performance.

Gainsharing

Gainsharing schemes provide a bonus for all workers in the company or factory which is related to an overall measure of performance. They are sometimes called share of production plans or factory-wide incentive schemes. The overall measure may be output or, more frequently, added value, which is usually defined as:

(a) *income* from sales of the product or service (output); less
(b) *expenditure* on materials and other purchased services (input); leaves
(c) *added value* which is either distributed as wages, salaries, pensions, interests on loans, taxes, and dividends, or retained in reserves or for investment and depreciation.

Gainsharing schemes using the added value concept can operate as in the original Rucker plan by establishing over a period the proportion of added value which is represented by payroll costs (typically 40 to 50%) and then calculating the amount distributed as follows:

Added value is:	£800,000
40% of added value is:	£320,000
Actual payroll is:	£280,000
Distributed to employees:	£40,000

A variant of this example is to agree that the employee savings, that is, £40,000, should be divided on an agreed basis, say 50% for employees and 50% for the company, the latter proportion being needed by the company to provide amongst other things for a return on new investment.

An added value scheme operating in Perkin Elmer is based on the proportion of value added that had in practice been distributed to employees in the form of pay – the employee's share. Over a period of five years this was remarkably constant at 47.9%. Value added is then calculated quarterly and if the employee share is greater than the pay already distributed, 75% of that surplus is distributed in the form of a bonus. The remaining 25% is transferred to a reserve account which accumulates throughout the year and provides a buffer against quarters in which the employee share of value added may be found to be less than the money that has already been paid. Any surplus remaining in the reserve account at the end of the year is then finally distributed as a terminal bonus. Bonuses have averaged about 20%. Any deficit is absorbed by the company, so that a new reserve account is always started with the new financial year.

An important feature of the Perkin Elmer plan, which is an essential feature of gainsharing schemes, is the extensive involvement of employees in analysing performance and, jointly with management, agreeing on ways to improve productivity and thus increase their share. John Leare of Perkin Elmer has said that the single most important benefit of operating the plan has been:

The identification of a common purpose for both management and employee. Morale is high and there is much wider trust and co-operation. The annual pay negotiations have lost their edge since total remuneration is already agreed and any increases in basic rates of pay, which are already automatically linked to the Retail Price Index, merely lead to a corresponding reduction in bonus levels.[5]

The main argument against any type of factory-wide incentive scheme is that it does not provide a direct incentive because the link between individual effort and the eventual reward is tenuous. A gainsharing scheme can, however, be effective if it provides reasonably high bonuses, 10% or more, and includes arrangements for participation in jointly analysing the factors that have contributed to the size of the added value and what can be done to improve the share allocated to employees. Such schemes can minimize the problems of degeneration and constant bickering between employees and management which plague most conventional payment by results systems.

Selecting a payment system

As Bowey and Thorpe have commented: 'Many managers still believe that as long as an incentive scheme is designed, maintained and 'operated' correctly, higher performances will follow automatically.'[6] But managers will usually admit that decay is inevitable and seem prepared to accept this uncomfortable fact.

Both these assumptions can be challenged. A payment by results scheme will only work if it is appropriate and if full consultation has taken place during its introduction. Degeneration can be controlled but, again, this is only possible where the scheme fits the circumstances, although control action as described in the later section of this chapter dealing with degeneration may still be required.

A contingency approach

A contingency approach, as advocated by Bowey and Thorpe[6] on the basis of extensive research into the operation of payment by results schemes, involves making a diagnosis of:

- environmental conditions;
- structures;
- features of the work;
- the behavioural system;
- the operating system.

This method, however, is not sufficient to guarantee success. According to Bowey and Thorpe, management must first clarify its objectives and must also use a participative approach in installing the scheme.

Initial steps

The initial steps required to select an incentive payment scheme are therefore:

1. Define objectives and assumptions.
2. Analyse the existing situation.
3. Evaluate alternative systems.

Define objectives and assumptions

Everyone starts by wanting a system which will help with the recruitment of good quality employees and which will reduce labour turnover. Managements also want the system to provide direct incentives to increase output, although some may recognize the limits to which this can be done in their environment and attach importance to one or more of the following objectives:

- obtaining consistency in performance;
- containing labour costs;
- reducing pay disputes;
- improving product quality;
- improving delivery times;
- improving equipment utilization;
- obtaining a lower level of rejects;
- reducing the level of work in progress;
- gaining control over the pay structure to reduce wage drift and problems of differentials;
- improving methods, planning, work loading and labour flexibility.

The analysis of objectives should define priorities and assess how far they are being achieved by the present payment system. But it is also necessary to examine and if necessary challenge the assumptions that management holds about payment systems. Rightly or wrongly it may be assumed that 'the workers in this plant are only interested in money', or that 'the existing system is the best one we've got, so why change it?', or 'all we need to do is to tighten up the loose rates' (rather than find out why the rates are loose in the first place), or 'that's the way the men want it', and so on.

Analyse the existing situation

The existing situations should be analysed by obtaining answers to the following questions:

1. What is the system of work – batch, mass production, flow-line process?
2. How long is the average work cycle?

3. To what extent is the work high- or low-tech, skilled, semi-skilled, unskilled, repetitive or varied?
4. Is the flow or cycle steady or intermittent and is the work method constant or varied?
5. To what extent do changes in methods occur?
6. How often does the type of work carried out change because of new products or design modifications?
7. Is work carried out mainly on an individual basis, or are workers operating together in teams?
8. What proportion of workers will be able to participate individually or in groups in a direct incentive scheme?
9. What is the incidence of wasting time?
10. To what extent is the pace of work tightly controlled by, for example, the production line?
11. How tightly are workers supervised?
12. What is the general climate of employee relations – co-operative, hostile, neutral?
13. What level of productivity/work rate is being achieved now?
14. What is the scope for increasing existing work rates?
15. If productivity can and should be increased, is an incentive scheme the best or the only way to do it?
16. Have the alternatives of improved work organization, methods or supervision been considered?
17. Will managers and supervisors be capable of controlling an incentive scheme?
18. Has the firm the resources required in the shape of industrial engineers to install and maintain the scheme? If not, can they be obtained?
19. What is the union's attitude to incentive schemes?
20. How likely are employees to respond positively to a payment by result system?

Evaluate alternatives

The main alternatives should be evaluated in general against the criteria given earlier in this chapter (page 410) and the particular points relating to each system as given below:

Individual piecework
This may be appropriate when individual effort clearly determines output and:

(a) the job cycle is short;
(b) the number of modifications is small;
(c) the work requires purely manual skills and/or only single purpose hand tools or simple machine tools are used;

(d) product changes and modifications are limited;
(e) job stoppages are small;
(f) a high proportion of tasks is specified;
(g) effective work measurement techniques are in use;
(h) good quality work study and rate fixing staff are available;
(i) reasonably stable industrial relations are maintained on the shop floor.

Group piecework

Group piecework systems may be suitable if collective effort clearly determines output and the other features necessary for individual piecework systems are present.

Gainsharing

Factory-wide incentive schemes are appropriate when:

(a) the company believes that jointly created wealth should be shared with employees;
(b) a conventional piecework system would be difficult to manage;
(c) there is scope for participation in considering methods of improving productivity – and willingness on all sides to get involved;
(d) added value or some other measure of overall performance can be easily calculated and the relationship between individual performance and eventual results can be clearly established.

Measured day work

Measured day work may be appropriate where individual effort largely determines output and:

(a) conditions are inappropriate for individual piecework;
(b) operations are of the process type or assembly line;
(c) the job cycle is long;
(d) accurate work measurement of operations is possible so that acceptable standards can be agreed;
(e) high quality work study staff are available;
(f) high quality management negotiators are available;
(g) the unions are responsive to the advantages of measured day work and there is a reasonable chance of reaching agreement on the system and the standards adopted.

Time rate systems

If none of these approaches appears to be satisfactory, consideration will have to be given to using a time rate system. Time rate, also known as day rate, day work, flat rate or hourly rate, is the system under which operators are simply paid a predetermined rate per week, day or hour for the actual time they have worked. The basic rate for the job is fixed by negotiation, by reference to local rates, or by job evaluation, and only varies with time, never with output or performance.

In some circumstances, what are termed high day rates are paid which are higher than the agreed minimum rates. The high day rate may include a consolidated bonus element and is probably higher than the local going rate in order to attract and retain labour. High day rates have been a feature in some parts of the British motor industry where above minimum earnings are expected because of a history of payment by results, and where there is a high proportion of machine control of output. They are most appropriate in assembly lines where workers can be trained to produce work of a specified standard and to maintain a fixed working pace determined by work study.

Time rates are most commonly used where it is thought that it is impossible or undesirable to apply a payment by results system, for example, in maintenance work. But they may also be adopted as an alternative to an unsatisfactory piecework system. From the point of view of operators, the advantages of time rates are that earnings are predictable and steady and they do not have to engage in endless arguments with supervisors and ratefixers about piece rate or time allowances.

The obvious accusation made against time rates is that they do not provide the motivation of a direct incentive relating the reward to the effort. The logical point is that people want money and will work harder to get more of it. The argument is a powerful one, and explains the high proportion of workers on payment by results schemes – for example, one half of manual workers in the British engineering industry. But it ignores all the problems associated with piecework, which are discussed below, and pays insufficient attention to the other motivating factors intrinsic to the job or provided by management. It is true, however, that time rate systems, especially high day rates, make greater demands on management and supervision.

Time rates may be appropriate where:

(a) individual or group effort does not determine output;
(b) it is difficult to determine accurate standards by means of work measurement;
(c) there are many modifications or design changes;
(d) product changes are numerous;
(e) job stoppages may be numerous;
(f) there is a tradition of unsatisfactory shop floor relations.

Designing the system

The following factors should be taken in to account in designing the system:

1. How performance will be measured.
2. The employees who will take part in the scheme and who will therefore have part of their pay directly linked to their own performance or that of their group.
3. The employees who will not take part in the scheme (supervisors, maintenance workers, inspectors, etc) and how they will be compensated. In the case of immediate supervisors, there should at least be a reasonable differential, say 10 to 20%, between their pay and the average pay for a standard week including bonus earned by the people they supervise.
4. Whether or not the scheme will be an individual one or linked to group performance.
5. Whether the bonus payments will be related to basic pay and therefore higher for those on higher basic rates, as in individual schemes, or whether bonus payments will be equal for all members of the group, as in group schemes.
6. The proportion of pay which can be earned as bonus. This may have to be fixed as a percentage for standard performance, say 33.33%, and as an upper limit, say 50%.
7. The full basic rate – this could be the basic rate, but some schemes allow a minimum bonus payment of, say, 10%.
8. The relationship between output/effort and reward, ie the extent to which, if at all, there is a differential built into the scheme which shares the results of higher productivity between the company and the workers.
9. The basis upon which employees not earning bonuses will be paid when, for example, they are on waiting time, attending meetings on company business, or working on a new job which has not yet been rated, or on holiday or sick. Shop-average bonus is a fairly typical method of payment, although individual average bonuses are also paid.
10. The timings of bonus payments (the period of work for which bonuses are paid) and the lapse of time before payments are made.
11. The arrangements, if any, to alleviate the problems of large fluctuations in bonus payments.
12. The methods to be used to maintain the scheme and to inform employees of their earnings.

Installing a payment by results scheme

1. Define the objectives of the payment system and list and, if necessary, challenge the assumptions held about the purpose of the system and how it should operate.

2. Collect facts about the existing system: the pay structure, the types of payment schemes in use, the number of people paid under each arrangement, the levels of earnings in different occupations, and the make up of earnings, including overtime payments.
3. Analyse the circumstances in which the payment system operates.
4. Compare the existing or proposed arrangements against the criteria for evaluating systems listed above.
5. Analyse the effectiveness of the pay structure and payment systems by:
   (a) comparing the results achieved with the objectives of the system under such headings as ability to attract and retain staff, effect of productivity, effect on management/ employee relationship;
   (b) identifying particular problem areas where the system is producing anomalies in pay or earnings between occupations or units, where the requirements of equal pay legislation are not met or where rates of pay are not competitive with local going rates.
6. Consider conducting an attitude survey to obtain the views of workers, rate fixers and supervisors about the present system and what changes need to be made.
7. Consult as required with unions and employees on the present arrangements and what needs to be done about them.
8. Conduct pay surveys as required to establish local market rates.
9. Conduct job evaluation studies as required in consultation with unions to establish correct relativities and to provide the basic data for designing a logical pay structure.
10. Develop pilot tests and install any revised or new individual, group or measured day work payment systems that may be required in consultation with unions.
11. Revise the pay structure as necessary in the light of the actions taken in steps 8 to 10 and in consultation with the unions or employee representatives. In a unionized concern, revisions to the pay structure would, of course, have to be negotiated with the unions.
12. Ensure that information is available which will enable the effectiveness of a revised pay system or structure to be monitored.

Prerequisites for success

Following their research into payment systems and productivity, the Pay and Rewards Research Centre, Strathclyde University, concluded that three essential prerequisites for introducing a successful incentive scheme were:

1. The top of the organization is committed to a programme of change.
2. A team of managers is developed who know what is required of them and have the enthusiasm to make it work.
3. The rest of the work force is convinced that the project is worthy of their support, is shown how to make it work and is assisted in its operations.

The importance of participation

Bowey and Thorpe[6] emphasized the importance of the last of these requirements – a participative approach. There is no point in introducing a scheme which aims to increase productivity without involving employees in discussing how to obtain improvements and how they will benefit financially from them. It is equally necessary to discuss at each development stage the design of the scheme and how it will operate. Work measurement techniques should be demonstrated, and many companies train selected employee representatives in work measurement so that they can agree timings and, importantly, re-timings. It is essential at this stage to prepare employees for the fact that rates will have to be altered as a result of changes in work, work mix and methods. Any agreement should spell out and indicate how re-timing will be made in consultation with representatives and employees. Management has to be completely open about the scheme while making it clear that it will not allow it to deteriorate. The latter point is vital, as will be seen from the following analysis of why payment by results schemes degenerate.

Degeneration of bonus schemes

Bonus schemes degenerate. The consultants and work study engineers say they shouldn't but they do. In an ideal situation they would not. Managers and supervisors would execute control in the way that consultants tell them to. But the latter do not always live in the real world where there are always numerous opportunities for bonus workers to gain more from the scheme than they have earned, which is what is meant by degeneration. It is sometimes called wage or earnings drift.

Causes of degeneration

The main causes of degeneration are:

1. *Special allowances.* All schemes have allowances for the payment of shop average earnings or some other figure which includes a premium over the base rate in certain circumstances. The most common are for unmeasured work or waiting time. Clearly the higher the proportion of this time when pay is unrelated to effort,

the more the scheme degenerates. Allowances are in theory controllable by management but supervisors closer to the shop floor have been known to make their life easier by granting allowances too easily. And this can be done on an hour-to-hour basis and in small increments which can all too readily be missed by more senior managers.

Allowances can also be manipulated by, for example, workers booking in waiting time rather than time on a difficult job which earns less than average bonus.

2. *Erosion of standards.* The type of work or the work mix can change almost imperceptibly over a period of time. It may not be possible to point to a change in method significant enough to justify a re-timing of the job under the rules of the scheme.

The original ratings, although not slack, may not have been particularly tight – workers themselves and their representatives will have seen to that. As time goes on workers learn how to take short cuts (sometimes risky ones) which increase or maintain earnings for less effort.

3. *Cross-booking.* Workers sometimes cross-book from different tasks to easier ones from a bonus earning point of view. Work measurement is not an exact science, whatever work study engineers may say, and some ratings are easier than others. The ability of work people to get to know ways round the scheme should never be underestimated. An important American study by Donald Roy[7] showed that productivity could be held back even when a payment by results scheme was in operation. He observed that in a time allowed scheme where bonus is directly linked to the amount of time saved in doing the task from the original time allowed, some timings were inevitably tighter than others. If there is a reasonably generous fall-back rate (the basic rate paid, whatever the effort or results), which there frequently is, employees may work more slowly and thus save their effort on the difficult jobs, but still earn a reasonable standard rate, while working hard and fast on the easier jobs to achieve the bonus earning they wanted. Research studies have frequently shown that workers set their own level of bonus earnings and adjust their effort accordingly. Sometimes, they can be under pressure from their fellow workers not to work too hard and thus bust the rate, or at least inspire management to indulge in a rate cutting exercise.

To prevent management becoming aware that some jobs are easier than others workers sometimes do not record all their time on these jobs, thus keeping earnings down. Workers then allocate their time to other jobs to raise them into the bonus earning range, or then simply take it easy. They operate, as it were, on borrowed time.

Tom Lupton[1] in the 1960s observed similar ways in which workers 'beat the system' and Richard Thorpe[8] confirmed that this practice continues in a more recent British participative study (1980) in an engineering works where he found that he had to learn how to 'skive' and take part in cross-booking practices. He and his co-workers kept their output low on the 'tight' jobs where they could not earn bonuses and worked fast on the easy jobs, allocating the time saved to other jobs or wasting it. Higher productivity did not enter into their picture.

Remedies

To avoid degeneration it is necessary to:

1. Introduce a bonus scheme only where the following conditions apply:
   - short cycle repetitive work;
   - changes in work mix, tasks or methods are infrequent;
   - workfloor hold-ups are rare and not prolonged;
   - management and supervision are capable of controlling the scheme, not only technically, but also from the point of view of being able to prevent manipulation and skiving; and/or
   - productivity is so low that the stimulus of a bonus scheme, even when it might create problems later, is still worth while.

2. Take care in introducing the scheme to use the best work study engineers available so that accurate and even standards are obtained.

3. Ensure that the rules of the scheme as agreed with a trade union allow for re-timings because of changes in the task, (including, importantly, work mix) changes in method or errors in the original bonus calculation.

4. Institute recording systems or rules for booking time on no-bonus earning activities which minimize the risk of allowance manipulation or cross-booking.

5. Train managers, supervisors and industrial engineers in how to manage and control the scheme. Impress on them that they will be held accountable for productivity and for ensuring that the scheme does not degenerate.

6. Continuously monitor bonus performance and crack down on any drift. Ensure that new jobs are timed properly and the implications of any changes in work mix or methods are understood and deflected in altered standards.

7. Keep on emphasizing to managers and supervisors their responsibility for controlling the scheme and take them to task if they do not.

Monitoring the payment by results system

The steps that should be taken to avoid degeneration have already been discussed in this chapter. To ensure that the operation of the system is properly monitored, the following information is required regularly.

Any payment system can erode or decay, however carefully its installation was managed. It is essential to review the system in operation regularly to ensure that it continues to achieve its objectives. The review should consider labour unit costs and performance as well as measuring earnings in different sections and jobs in order to spot anomalies. It may be particularly important to analyse overtime earnings as these are often responsible for creating semi-permanent distortions in the earnings structure when overtime is not controlled properly. Attention might also be directed towards shift premiums and other special allowances for dirty or dangerous work or unsocial hours, to ensure that they are reasonable and in tune with market rates. Finally, a review should consider the equal pay situation to ensure that the arrangements conform with equal pay legislation – in Britain, that separate male and female rates should not exist and women should be paid the same as men if they are employed on the same or broadly similar work as men or on work of equal value.

A review of the payment system could include an analysis of present arrangements as described earlier in this chapter. The other matters that could be looked at specifically include:

- labour cost per unit of output;
- output figures and performance levels;
- the proportion of bonus to total pay;
- levels of earnings in different departments and jobs;
- percentage of time paid on average bonus when normal bonus work was available;
- percentage overtime worked;
- percentage shift premium in total pay;
- average earnings compared with the salary levels of first line supervisors.

The aim of the review should be to ensure that management is prepared to take corrective action in good time when the payment system is not operating effectively.

References

1. Lupton, T *On the Shop Floor*. Pergamon Press, Oxford, 1963.
2. McGregor, D *The Human Side of Enterprise*. McGraw-Hill, New York, 1960.
3. Goldthorpe, J H *The Affluent Worker: Industrial Attitudes and Behaviour*. Cambridge University Press, Cambridge, 1968.
4. Marriott, R *Incentive Payment Systems*. Staples Press, London, 1969.

5. Leare, J 'The Value-added Approach to Sharing Company Wealth', *Personnel Management*, October, 1987.
6. Bowey, A M and Thorpe, R *Payment Systems and Productivity*. Macmillan, London, 1986.
7. Roy, D 'Quota Restrictions and Goldbricking in a Machine Shop', *American Journal of Sociology*, Vol 67, No 2, 1952.
8. Thorpe, R *The Relationship Between Payment Systems, Productivity and the Organization of Work*. Unpublished MSc thesis, Strathclyde University, 1980.

Chapter 26
Other Forms of Remuneration and Benefits

The forms of remuneration and benefits other than basic pay described in this chapter are:

- profit sharing schemes;
- bonus schemes;
- incentive schemes for sales staff;
- employee benefits.

These form the total remuneration employees receive and the concept of total remuneration is discussed at the end of the chapter.

Profit sharing

Definition

Profit sharing is a plan under which an employer pays to eligible employees, as an addition to their normal remuneration, special sums in the form of cash or stock related to the profits of the business. The amount shared is determined either by an established formula, which may be published, or entirely at the discretion of management. Profit sharing schemes are generally extended to all employees of the company except directors.

Objectives of profit sharing

Most companies which operate profit sharing schemes have one or more of the following objectives in mind:

- to encourage employees to identify themselves more closely with the company by developing a common concern for its progress;
- to stimulate a greater interest amongst employees in the affairs of the company as a whole;
- to encourage better co-operation between management and employees;
- to recognize that employees of the company have a moral right to share in the profits they have helped to produce;

● to demonstrate in practical terms the goodwill of the company towards its employees.

It is generally recognized that schemes which share profits according to some universal formula amongst all or most employees will not provide any real incentive because they fail to satisfy the three basic requirements of an incentive scheme, namely:

(a) that the reward should bear a direct relation to the effort;
(b) that the payment should follow immediately or soon after the effort;
(c) that the method of calculation should be simple and easily understood.

Types of schemes

The main types of profit sharing schemes are:

1. *Cash* – a proportion of profits is paid in cash direct to employees. This is the traditional and still the most popular approach.
2. *Stock* – a proportion of profits is paid in stock. This is much less popular, especially since the advent of the approved deferred share trust scheme with its considerable tax advantages.
3. *Approved deferred share trust (ADST)* – the company allocates profit to a trust fund which acquires shares in the company on behalf of employees.
4. *Mixed schemes* – an ADST scheme is sometimes offered in addition to a cash scheme, or the latter is made available to staff before they are eligible for ADST shares or as an alternative to ADST shares.

In addition, the British government introduced in 1987 its profit-related pay (PRP) scheme which provides income tax relief for approved schemes.

A survey of profit sharing in 356 firms published by the Glasgow University Centre for Research into Industrial Democracy and Participation revealed that in the two-thirds of the survey firms which operated profit sharing, the most popular scheme, especially amongst the smaller firms, was the simple cash-based option. The ADST type scheme is, however, gaining in popularity. Profit sharing was much more common among US-based companies (64%) than their European counterparts (29%), and the schemes were more prevalent in London and the South than in the Midlands and the North.

Cash schemes

The main characteristics of typical cash schemes can be analysed under the following headings, which are discussed below:

(a) eligibility;
(b) formula for calculating profit shares;
(c) method of distributing profit shares;
(d) amount distributed;
(e) timing of distribution.

Eligibility

In most schemes all employees except directors are eligible. The normal practice is to require one year's service to be completed before a share in profits can be received. Profit shares are then usually paid in relation to the pay earned or the time served between the date on which one year's service was completed and the date on which the profit shares are paid.

Formula for calculating profit shares

There are three basic approaches to calculating profit shares. The first is to use a predetermined formula for distributing a fixed percentage of profits. This formula may be published to staff so that the company is committed to using it. The advantages of this approach are that it clarifies the relationship between company profits and the amount distributed and demonstrates the good faith of management. The disadvantages are that it lacks flexibility and the amount paid out may fluctuate widely in response to temporary changes in profitability.

The second approach is for the board to determine profit shares entirely at its own discretion without the use of any pre-determined or published formula. The decision is based on a number of considerations, including the profitability of the company, the proportion of profits that it is felt should reasonably be distributed to employees, estimates of the expectations of employees about the amount of cash they are going to receive and the general climate of industrial relations in the company. This is the more common approach and its advantages are that it allows the board some flexibility in deciding the amount to be distributed and does not commit it to expenditure over which it has no control. Random fluctuations can be smoothed out and the profit-sharing element of remuneration can be adjusted easily in relation to other movements in pay within the company. The disadvantage is that a secret formula or the absence of a formula appears to contradict one of the basic reasons for profit sharing: the development amongst employees of a firmer commitment to the company because they can identify themselves more clearly with its successes and appreciate the reasons for its set-backs. The scheme is no longer a completely realistic profit sharing device if employees feel that they are insufficiently rewarded for improved performance or insulated from reverses. These arguments against flexibility are powerful ones but, on balance, a flexible approach is to be preferred because it does not commit the company to distributing unrealistically high sums when profits are shared out.

The third approach is a combination of the first and second methods. A formula exists in the sense that a company profit threshold is set below which no profits will be distributed. A maximum limit is set on the proportion of profits that will be distributed, for example, 5% and/or that percentage of salary that will be distributed as a profit share, for example, 10%.

Methods of distributing profit shares
The main ways of distributing profit shares in cash schemes are to:

(a) distribute profits as a percentage of basic pay with no increments for service. This is a fairly common arrangement and those who adopt it do so because they feel that profit shares should be related to the individual contribution of the employee, which is best measured by pay. Service increments are rejected because the level of pay received by an individual should already take into account the experience he has gained in the company;

(b) distribute profits as a percentage of earnings with payments related to length of service. This approach is also frequently used and its advocates argue that it will ensure that loyalty to the company will be suitably encouraged and rewarded. They claim that to rely on pay as the sole arbiter of profit shares would be unjust because many valuable employees have, through no fault of their own, limited opportunities to move out of their present occupation or grade;

(c) distribute profits in proportion to pay and some measure of individual performance. This approach is rare below board level because of the difficulty of measuring the relationship between profits and performance and because it is considered that individual effort should be rewarded directly by merit increments or promotion;

(d) distribute profits as a fixed sum irrespective of earnings or service. This completely egalitarian approach is rare.

The choice of approach is usually between distributing profit shares either in relation to pay or in relation to pay and service. The arguments for and against each approach are finely balanced but there is a good case for providing some uplift for longer service staff in any situation where a company relies on its experienced staff to contribute their specialized skills and knowledge to its success and cannot ensure that its normal policies for paying merit increments or promoting staff will adequately reward their loyalty to the organization.

Amount distributed
A survey conducted by Incomes Data Services in 1986 revealed that

rather more than half of the companies surveyed leave the amount to be distributed to 'directors discretion'. Others provide limits within which the directors decide. A maximum of 5% of profits is typical, but this may only be paid if it is triggered by profits reaching a defined level. At British Home Stores, for example, there is a maximum of 5% of profit, providing profits exceed £23 million.

Other surveys into the amounts distributed in British profit sharing schemes have indicated that the proportion of pay shared out can vary from as little as 2% to 20% or more. The Glasgow University survey showed that in 60% of the firms surveyed which had profit-sharing schemes, the share amounted to less than 6% of pay. Ideally, however, the share should be somewhere between 5 and 10% of pay in order to be meaningful without building up too much reliance on the amount to be distributed.

Timing of distribution

Most schemes distribute profits annually, although a few share out profits twice a year. Distribution is usually arranged to fall in good time for either the summer holidays or Christmas.

Employees' attitudes

The Industrial Participation Association (IPA) recently questioned 2,700 employees in 12 companies about their attitudes to profit sharing. The results of the survey are summarized in Table 26.1.

	Agree strongly	Agree	Don't know	Disagree	Disagree strongly
	%	%	%	%	%
1 Profit sharing created a better attitude in the firm	10	55	16	18	1
2 It is popular because people like to have the bonus	24	69	4	3	—
3 It strengthens people's loyalty to the firm	6	41	12	34	2
4 It makes people try to work more effectively so as to help the firm to be more successful	6	45	15	31	3
5 It is good for the company and its employees	14	72	11	3	—

Table 26.1 *Attitudes to profit sharing –*
Industrial Participation Association

The IPA believes that the survey 'suggests that profit sharing does significantly improve employee attitudes and employee views of their company.' They reach this view essentially by adding together the percentages recorded under Agree Strongly and Agree.

However, in the Incomes Data Services 1986 study of profit sharing the comment was made that: 'Another interpretation would be to add up all the responses except those under Agree Strongly, the one clear positive statement. This would suggest that most employees do not have a particularly positive attitude.'

Of course, employees like the cash, but their gratitude to the company is probably short-lived. Company profits are remote figures to people in the offices and on the shop floor. They will express some interest in their size, because it affects the hand-out, but the idea of working harder to generate more profit for someone else will not necessarily appeal to them.

Benefits of profit sharing

Profit sharing and profitability
A survey carried out by Wallace Bell and Charles Hanson in 1985-86[1] sought to establish a correlation between profit sharing and profitability. 113 profit sharing companies and 301 non-profit sharing companies were surveyed and their performance compared on the basis of nine economic ratios over a period of eight years. Taking the composite results of all 414 companies, the average performance of the profit sharers over the eight years was better than that of the non-profit sharers on every one of the nine economic ratios used. And taking an average of averages, the average of ratios of the profit sharers were 27% higher than those of the non-profit sharers. Of course, as Bell and Hanson say, the profit sharing companies were not better just because they had profit sharing. It was because they were good companies that they introduced profit sharing.

The particular features of how these companies achieved success were that managers:

- had clear and defined objectives and the ability to harness the resources needed to achieve them;
- recognized that their most important resource is people;
- saw employees not in terms of 'them and us', as adversaries, but as part of a team that should be working together for the success of the enterprise and sharing in its success;
- were able to generate a reciprocal attitude among the employees and thus overcome the 'them and us' feelings that are found equally, and sometimes more strongly, among employees towards management;
- were able to generate a commitment to success.

Profit sharing and industrial relations
The Glasgow University survey referred to earlier expressed the more

pessimistic view that the influence of profit sharing on industrial relations is marginal. The researchers concluded that profit sharing was used by employers as an effort-reward operation and not as an attempt to involve employees more closely in the decision-making apparatus. Yet, the evidence that profit sharing does increase effort hardly exists at all and that is simply because, as was mentioned earlier, the link between effort and reward is so tenuous. What, therefore, is the point of having a profit-sharing scheme if it is not used to increase productivity by means of involving employees and mounting a communications campaign pointing out how *they* benefit from increased output and profitability?

Conclusions

It is worth noticing that a number of companies have introduced profit sharing primarily because they feel that it is their duty to share their prosperity with their employees. If this view is held, then any uncertainty about the benefits arising from profit sharing is not an argument against its introduction. It is, of course, possible to take the opposite view; that profits are the wages of capital and that a company is not under any moral obligation to share profits with its employees, although it has the duty of treating them fairly and providing them with the rewards, benefits and conditions of employment that are appropriate to the contribution they make.

For anyone contemplating the introduction of profit sharing or wondering whether to continue an existing scheme the fundamental question is, 'do you consider that in addition to all the benefits already provided by the company to its employees, it has a moral obligation to share its prosperity with them?' If the answer to this question is in the affirmative, a profit-sharing scheme is what you want. If the answer is in the negative, alternative means of rewarding employees and increasing their identification with the company should be sought as described elsewhere in this book.

Bonus schemes

Bonus schemes provide an award, usually in the form of a lump sum payment, which is additional to basic salary and is related in some way to the performance of the individual or group of individuals receiving the bonus. Bonus schemes should be distinguished from profit sharing schemes, as described, which share out a proportion of profits to all or most staff on the basis of a formula or management decision which is seldom related to individual performance, although the profit share is usually paid in proportion to salary.

Aims of bonus schemes

The principal aim of a bonus scheme is to provide an incentive and a reward for effort and achievement. Executive bonus schemes linked to company profits can also aim to make senior managers feel that their personal prosperity is linked to the performance of their company or unit.

Bonus schemes are supplementary to basic salary and are most appropriate where they apply to entrepreneurial types such as chief executives, marketing men and sales staff who, it is assumed, will strive for material reward, and whose results upon which their bonus depends can be clearly linked to their personal efforts and achievements.

Bonus schemes criteria

When assessing whether or not a bonus scheme is appropriate, the following criteria should be used:

- The amount of the award received after tax should be sufficiently high to encourage staff to accept exacting targets and standards of performance. Standard bonuses should not be less than 10% of the basic salary and, if an effective incentive is wanted, the standard bonus should be around 20% to 30% of salary.
- The incentive should be related to quantitative criteria over which the individual has a substantial measure of control.
- The scheme should be sensitive enough to ensure that rewards are proportionate to achievements.
- The individual should be able to calculate the reward he can get for a given level of achievement.
- The formula for calculating the bonus and the conditions under which it is paid should be clearly defined.
- Constraints should be built into the scheme which ensure that staff cannot receive inflated bonuses which may not reflect their own efforts.
- The scheme should contain provisions for a regular review, say, every two or three years, which could result in its being changed or discontinued.
- The scheme should be easy to administer and understand, and it should be tailored to meet the requirements of the company.

Executive bonus schemes

There are innumerable formulae for executive bonus schemes, and each company must adopt one which suits its own circumstances. The simplest formula is for a percentage out of net profits before tax to be paid *pro rata* to the executive's basic salary. In some schemes, dividend payments and provisions for reserves are deducted from net profits before the distribution of bonuses and there is usually an upper limit to the amount of bonus that can be paid. These schemes are crude but provide a direct incentive as long as results are directly influenced by the actions of the executives in the scheme. They can get out of hand unless an upper limit is strictly applied, and their emphasis on profits may make some executives seek short-term gains at the expense of the longer-term development of the company.

Other schemes are based on a formula which measures company performance. Bonuses are paid when a target figure is attained and increased further as the target figure is exceeded. The increase of bonus may be on a straight-line basis, ie directly proportionate to the improvement in results. Alternatively, it may be geared either by decreasing the rate of bonus the more the target is exceeded, which is generally regarded as poor practice, or by increasing the rate, which could be an expensive device. A straight-line progression is to be preferred.

The formula in some schemes is directly applied to the executive's salary. In other schemes, a percentage of profits on an increasing scale is released into a bonus pool which is distributed in proportion to salary.

Incentive schemes for sales staff

Where it is felt that sales staff need to be motivated by an incentive commission scheme the majority of companies find that the best approach is a basic commission on sales volume or, in more sophisticated firms, on the contribution to fixed costs and profits of the sales of each product group or product. The standard commission is typically set at about one-third of salary to provide a noticeable incentive without adversely affecting feelings of security.

A successful sales commission plan should satisfy all the criteria listed above for bonus schemes. But it is particularly necessary to ensure that:

(a) the reward is fair in relation to the efforts of the sales representative. This means that attention has to be paid to setting and agreeing realistic and equitable targets, making allowances for special circumstances outside the control of the sales representative which might affect sales, and splitting commission fairly when more than one person has contributed to the sale;

(b) the scheme directs sales effort in accordance with management's policy on the product mix and does not encourage the representative to concentrate on what is easiest to sell;

(c) the scheme does not encourage high pressure selling which results in an unacceptable level of returns, cancellations and complaints;

(d) the scheme does not encourage representatives to neglect their indirect selling activities, such as servicing customers.

These criteria are not always easy to satisfy and a cautious approach is therefore needed before introducing an incentive scheme. A straight salary may be more appropriate where there is a wide range of products, a highly technical product, a high proportion of non-selling activities such as merchandizing to be carried out, or when flexibility is required in allocating salesmen to customers, territories or products.

Employee benefits

Employee benefits consist of any items or rewards that are provided by employers for the benefit of their employees which are not part of normal pay. They are sometimes called 'fringe' benefits, but some benefits are so essential that the use of the word 'fringe' seems quite inappropriate. These include pensions, sick pay, and holidays. Others, such as cars, housing benefits, medical benefits and the range of benefits that can be made available to executives can be regarded as optional extras.

Pension schemes

Pension schemes are designed to provide employees with security by currently building up rights which will give a guaranteed income to the employee or his dependants on retirement or death. Pensions are financed by contributions from the company and in most, but not all, cases the employee.

Pensions are generally regarded as the most important employee benefit after basic pay, although many employees, especially younger ones, express little interest in their pension arrangements until in many cases it is too late.

The need to ensure that the pension arrangements are the best the company can afford arises for three reasons:

1. A company has a moral obligation to do the best it can to provide a reasonable degree of security for its employees, especially its longer-service employees.
2. A good pension scheme demonstrates that the company has the long term interests of its employees at heart.
3. A good scheme will help to attract and retain high quality staff, especially older staff employed at senior levels who are likely to be most interested in pension rights.

Main features of pension schemes
Pension schemes are usually complex affairs and their provision can vary considerably. Professional advice from pensions specialists is always required when reviewing pension arrangements to assess what the company needs, what it can afford and all the legal and tax considerations

surrounding pension schemes. The following is a list of the main features that have to be dealt with when reviewing pension schemes.

Pension formulae. There are four main types of formulae for determining pensions on retirement:

1. Final salary (salary service), where the pension is calculated as a fraction of the salary at retirement or as an average over the closing years or months of service. If the arrangement is to pay one sixtieth of final salary for every year's service the formula would be described as n/60ths. In this case, someone on retirement with 40 years' service would obtain 40/60ths of his final salary as a pension, the maximum allowed in the UK under the Inland Revenue code of approval for pension schemes.
2. Average salary (salary graded), where fixed amounts of pension are given for each year spent in a salary bracket.
3. Flat rate, where a flat rate payment is made which is quoted as a given rate for each year of service.
4. Money purchase, where contributions are fixed and accumulate in a 'pool' for each employee.

A final salary scheme is clearly preferable for the employee because the pension will be based on earnings just before retirement, which should keep pace with increases in the cost of living. But in inflationary times, which are always with us, a final salary scheme can be very costly.

Contributions. Schemes can be either contributory – requiring contributions from both the employer and the employee – or non-contributory, in which case only the employer makes the contribution. The contributions of employees tend to average about 5% to 6% of basic salary.

The arguments advanced in favour of a contributory scheme are that sharing the cost means that more money is available to buy better benefits, and that employees appreciate benefits more when they have had to pay for them. The arguments in favour of non-contributory schemes are that they are an attraction to employees, are more flexible in response to change and cost less to run.

Entry age. The entry age can be fixed at 25 or, preferably, 21. There is usually a qualifying period of six months to a year.

Post-retirement pension increases. Pension schemes can be more or less inflation-proofed by the process of escalation – allowing for increases in pensions in response to change in the cost of living. This is a highly desirable but potentially expensive feature.

Lump sum on retirement. Pension schemes can offer the right of commutation of pension on retirement which allows the exchange of part of the pension for a tax free lump sum. This provides a useful aid to those wanting to buy a retirement home, or it can be used for special purchases or investment.

Widows' benefits. Pension schemes support a widow whose husband has died in service either by providing a lump sum, a reduced widows' pension or a combination of the two. If wisely invested, a lump sum can often provide a better income than a pension. During his working life a man should know that there will be adequate provision for his dependants.

Arrangements for paying a widow's pension after the husband's death in retirement vary widely. The best method is to provide a pension of up to two-thirds of the husband's pension.

Early and late retirement. Early retirement pensions are usually calculated at a reduced rate and schemes may define the reduction that will apply for each year between the year of early retirement and the normal retiring age. If an employee retires early through ill-health he or she should at least be entitled to the pension earned up to retirement age. A more favourable arrangement would be to pay an improved pension which would take account of potential service up to normal retirement age.

There may be situations in which the company wants employees to stay on after normal retiring age, but their continued service should be reviewed regularly from the point of view of their health. Pension schemes should always provide for a 'late retirement increment' under which an employee who continues to work after his normal retirement date can receive an enhanced pension without any further contributions from himself or his employer.

'Top hat' arrangement. A 'top hat' arrangement is one in which a pension scheme for directors or senior staff is topped up by means of an additional non-contributory scheme. A 'top hat' scheme is offered when a company wishes to provide a greater benefit to individuals over and above that supplied under its main fund. Such benefits could usually be provided by augmentation within the fund but there are sometimes internal company reasons for requiring a separate policy.

Additional voluntary contributions. A good scheme will include provisions for additional voluntary contributions (AVCs) which enable employees to top-up their pension to the Inland Revenue limits, although the amount they can contribute is restricted at present to 15% of their pay. This is a very tax-effective form of saving for the future. AVCs can now be made outside the company's schemes through an insurance company.

Funding. All schemes have to be funded so that the money is available to pay the promised benefits. The usual arrangement is to build up funds by contributions which are invested in securities or in an insurance policy or both. The basic choice is between running a private self-administered fund through trustees or operating a scheme through an insurance company. Private schemes require considerable investment expertise and administrative effort to organize, although some large companies feel they can run a better and less costly scheme if they go it alone with specialist actuarial advice. The majority of schemes are designed and administered for their clients by insurance companies who have the actuarial, investment and administrative skills required.

Pensions legislation

The British government has made some significant changes to pension arrangements in the Social Security Act 1985, as follows:

- Personal pensions will be contracted out of the state earnings related pension scheme (SERPS), which means that at retirement age anyone who has taken out a personal pension will only receive the basic state old-age pension plus whatever personal pension they have been able to provide.
- At present, for those with SERPS benefit, employees pay 2.15% of certain earnings and employers pay 4.1%. Instead of that money being deducted from their income and passed to the state, it will be deducted and passed to a personal pension scheme if that is what the employee wants.
- As an incentive, the state will pay an additional 2% of salary into a personal pension scheme for a five-year period from 1988 to 1991 to all those who start a personal pension during that time, provided they have not been in an employer's contracted-out scheme.
- All new employees will be able to choose freely whether or not they join the company's pension scheme.
- Existing employees will be given the choice of staying with the employer's scheme or opting out.

Choice of scheme

Pension schemes are complicated affairs and are subject to a number of legal and fiscal considerations. The choice of what goes into the scheme in the shape of alternative types and levels of benefits will depend largely on what the company can afford to pay. It may be necessary to trade off one benefit against another by, for example, reducing the pensions formula from n/60ths to n/80ths in order to introduce a 50% widows' pension. If there is any choice within a budget, employees should be consulted about their preferences.

The cost of pension schemes can be anything up to 25% of pay-roll, so it is worth taking care in setting them up and maintaining them. They should be reviewed regularly with the help of expert advice to ensure that they are properly funded (although in periods of high inflation this is difficult) and that a reasonable mix of benefits is being provided for the money subscribed by the company and its employees.

Sick pay

For junior staff most companies provide sick pay on a sliding scale according to service. A reasonably generous but not untypical arrangement would be:

Up to 1 year's service	– 4 weeks' full pay
1 to 5 years' service	– 13 weeks' full pay
5 years plus	– 13 weeks' full pay plus 1 week for each year of service.

For managerial staff, the majority of companies in the UK give full pay for six months or more.

Many companies seem to adopt an ungenerous approach to sick pay because they feel it could be costly with large numbers of staff and because they are unlikely to get much credit for their generosity. These arguments are not usually advanced on firm grounds and perhaps more credit at small cost could be obtained from an increase in sick pay allowance than most companies realize.

Holidays

Most staff in the UK now receive at least four weeks' paid annual holiday and, for management five or more weeks is increasingly becoming the rule. There has traditionally been a differential between staff holidays and those given to manual workers and this has been maintained to a certain degree as manual worker holidays have increased. But the move towards harmonization (single status organizations) is resulting in the increasing equalization of this and other benefits. In the EEC countries, holidays tend to be longer than in the UK but in North America, executives' holidays lag behind – many still have only two weeks a year.

Cars

After pensions and holidays, which are usually taken for granted, cars have been the most highly regarded fringe benefit in the UK. The provision of a company car saves the executives both the capital costs of acquisition and, usually, the heavy running costs, but this advantage has been reduced by recent UK legislation. From the company's point of view, the provision of a car can still be less costly than paying the extra salary needed to compensate the executives for not having a car when allowance is made for tax. And in the UK at least, where over 90% of top management have company cars, it has been almost impossible to be competitive without giving a car or the equivalent net salary.

But there are some disadvantages. A car is a very visible sort of benefit and great care has to be taken to ensure that the size or cost of cars accurately reflects differentials. It is also costly to administer a car fleet. A further point to consider is that not all people like to have a company car imposed upon them. Many would prefer to spend the equivalent money as they wish.

Housing assistance

Housing assistance falls into three categories:

1. Allowances to transferred staff, including removal expenses, travelling expenses for visits, lodging allowances, settling in grants or disturbance allowances, and assistance with conveyancing and estate agents' fees.
2. Allowances to new employees which may include assistance with removal, travelling and lodgings.
3. Assistance with house purchase which can include arrangements with a building society or insurance company to obtain a mortgage on preferential terms and to reserve funds for company employees, or various forms of long term or bridging loans at reduced interest rates.

Medical benefits

The most popular form of medical benefit is medical insurance, and a large number of UK companies participate in schemes such as BUPA or Private Patients' Plan.

Other benefits

There is a long list of other benefits that can be provided, many of them being reserved for executives as special rewards. These benefits include:

- low interest loans;
- help with education;
- payment of professional subscriptions;
- free or heavily subsidized meals;
- subsidized accommodation;
- service agreements for executives.

The danger of an over-liberal approach to executive benefits is that they enlarge the gap between the 'haves' and the 'have nots' and can therefore be divisive, and the material advantages conferred by these benefits can be considerably reduced if they are taxed at the full rate.

Other allowances

The main allowance that can be paid to staff is for overtime. Normally this is reserved for junior staff although union pressures have extended its application in some companies. Where normal overtime is worked it is usual to pay for overtime at a flat rate, adding a premium of, say, an extra 50% if excessive overtime is worked. The approach differs considerably between companies and some organizations have adopted premium payments for all overtime. Other premiums may be given to employees who work unsocial hours or on regular shifts.

Total remuneration

The total remuneration concept is based on the belief that all aspects of pay and employee benefits should be treated as a whole, the different parts of which can be adjusted according to the needs of the company and the individual. This means that, in setting levels of remuneration, account is taken of the value to employees and the cost to the company of each of the benefits to which job holders are entitled as well as their basic salary and bonus payments. Remuneration is thereby treated as a total package so that employees can be told about the complete value of what they are getting, valid comparisons can be made with other companies and an appropriate balance is achieved between the different components of remuneration.

The concept applies to all levels of staff, but it is of more importance at higher levels because of the tax advantages that may be achieved by providing certain benefits as an alternative to basic salary. Although, as tax authorities tighten up on their regulations, the scope for tax planning to reduce the incidence of income tax on higher earnings is becoming increasingly restricted.

Total remuneration and the company

The approach to total remuneration should be to decide on the mix of basic pay, bonuses and other employee benefits that should be provided at different levels by reference to company policies on differentials and external comparisons. Ideally, the value of each element should be assessed in terms of the benefit received by individuals – gross and net of tax – at different salary levels and the cost to the company, also gross and net of tax. By comparing remuneration on both a gross and net basis the scope for using fringe benefits to reduce the effect of progressive taxation can be identified. It is unlikely that benefits other than basic salary, especially pensions, will take up an increasing proportion of total remuneration as responsibility increases.

Total remuneration and the individual

Everyone starts off with wanting a good basic salary to provide for the necessities of life and satisfy the basic needs in Maslow's hierarchy of human needs – to survive and to achieve security. Thereafter other needs become more important, and these are the ones that can best be satisfied by the intrinsic motivators present in the work itself.

At the same time people begin to seek alternative means of providing for their needs and, particularly at higher levels, may not find the package offered by the company fully acceptable. This is why what has been termed the 'cafeteria' system has been devised whereby people can choose from the benefits on display as long as they are within their budget. In its simplest and most readily applicable form, the 'cafeteria' system might offer a straight choice between an improved benefit such as a bigger car or an augmented pension, and the equivalent increase in gross salary. More elaborate versions will give a range of benefits to choose from, and one method works out the value of the benefits, expresses them in points terms and allocates so many points to an executive to deploy as he wishes. Such approaches have only limited application, but the least a company can do is to avoid the mistake of forcing benefits on people who may not appreciate them. If money is to motivate, it should satisfy needs that the individual actually possesses rather than those he is assumed to have.

Reference

1. Wallace Bell, D and Hanson, C G *Profit Sharing and Profitability*. Kogan Page, London, 1987.

Chapter 27
Salary Administration

Salary administration procedures

Salary administration procedures are concerned with the implementation and control of salary policies and with the control of salary costs against budgets. Control is an essential element of salary administration, and this section will therefore begin with a general discussion of the desirable features of a control system. It will then deal more specifically with the following procedures:

- salary budgets;
- cost of living or general reviews of salary levels;
- individual salary reviews;
- fixing salary levels on joining the company or on promotion;
- salary control.

Desirable features of control

To achieve effective salary control the salary administration procedures should have the following features:

1. Defined ranges with minima and maxima to which all jobs are allocated on the basis of their value, with all employees paid within the ranges for the jobs performed.
2. Defined methods of progress within the range based on specific criteria.
3. A detailed salary budget based on the number of staff required to carry out the forecast volume of work; forecast salary levels taking into account the effects of general and incremental increases; forecasts of promotions and promotional increases and numbers joining and leaving the organization; and forecasts of the likely effect on salary costs of changes in the numbers employed and of differences between the salary levels of those joining or leaving.

4. Clear statements of the degree of authority at each management level to award or to confirm increments with arrangements for authorizing proposed salary changes and checking their consistency with policy.
5. Clear salary review guidelines defining the limit to which the payroll costs of each department can increase as a result of merit awards, together with other instructions on, for example, the maximum awards that can be given and the distribution of awards according to performance and between the population in each salary grade.
6. Procedures for auditing increases and salary levels to ensure that they are in accordance with salary policies, and for monitoring actual salary costs against budgeted costs.

Salary budget

A salary budget is a statement in quantitative and usually financial terms of the planned allocation and use of resources to meet the operational needs of the company. All budgets are based on a planned level of activity or volume of output which determines the resources required. In the case of the salary budget, the forecast levels of activity indicate the number of different categories of staff that are needed for the budget period. The annual salary budget is a product of the numbers of staff to be employed and the rates at which they will be paid.

The salary budget has to take account of the financial resources available to the company. This will affect the ability to pay general or individual merit increases, or the numbers employed, or both. Salary budgets in large organizations are prepared by departmental managers in accordance with instructions issued by the accounts department. They are often based on current salary levels and are inflated at a later stage when decisions are made about how much money can be allocated for individual and general salary increases. An example of a budget form is shown in Figure 27.1.

Historical control over salary costs is achieved by comparing budgeted costs with actuals, analysing any variances, and deciding on corrective action; which could take the form of a reduction in manning levels or in the budget for merit increases if salary costs are over the budget. A cost comparison form is illustrated in Figure 27.2.

But backward looking controls are not enough. It is also necessary to ensure that the salary policies and guidelines laid down by management are implemented, and the procedures required for this purpose are described below.

General and market rate salary reviews

General salary reviews take place when it is necessary to increase all or

				Salary budget for year ending					
Department:				Proposed by:			Approved by:		
Actual — previous year...........				Forecast — forthcoming year.........					
No.	Salary cost	Overtime cost	Total cost	Category of staff	No.	Salary cost	Overtime cost	Total cost	Increase or decrease in total cost
				Managers					
				Supervisors					
				Clerical staff					
				Temporary staff					
				Total					
Reasons for forecast increase/decrease over previous year:									

Figure 27.1 Salary budget form

Department				COST COMPARISON STATEMENT	Quarter ending:				
This quarter				Category of staff	Year to date		Forecast for year		
Number		Pay-roll cost			Pay-roll cost		Pay-roll cost		
Actual	Variance	Actual	Variance		Actual	Variance	Actual	Variance	
				Managers					
				Supervisors					
				Clerical staff					
				Temporary staff					
				Total					
Reasons for variance and proposed actions:									

Figure 27.2 Salary cost comparison form

most salaries in response to increases in the cost of living or in market rates, or as a result of settlements affecting either staff or hourly paid employees.

General reviews tend to be an annual event, although external market pressures may mean that they have to take place at different times of the year to individual merit reviews. Changes in market rates generally, or, which is more likely, to particular market groups, may require adjustments to pay as and when necessary, rather than in accordance with a fixed timetable. If market pressures are acute for an important category of employee, then it does not make sense to delay a review until it is too late and key staff have been lost. In competitive situations, a flexible approach to salary administration is essential.

Companies without staff unions who operate a secret salary policy often try to differentiate between a general and merit increase. Their staff receive their annual award and do not know how much is general or how much is particular to them. Companies pursue secrecy in salary policies because it enables them to exercise complete control until, that is, the staff lose patience and move into the ever-welcoming arms of the trade unions. Companies are frightened of divulging their salary structure or review policies to staff because they feel that this may open the door to recognition claims and pay negotiations. The other reason for not publishing salary scales, which is not admitted to so freely, is that the structure is so illogical that it would be impossible to explain or to justify it to the staff.

It is difficult to reconcile this point of view, especially with regard to merit increments, with the equally prevalent view that money is the great motivator. How can money motivate effectively if everyone is kept in the dark about the relationship between effort and reward?

The best approach is to distinguish between general and individual increases, even if they are paid at the same time. The general increase is paid to everyone, although some companies reserve the right to withhold general increases or give smaller increments to staff whose performance is below average or overpaid. At the same time, the salary brackets are adjusted, usually at both ends, by the same amount. It is equally important to keep individuals informed of how they stand in the salary structure and the rewards they are getting or can obtain.

Individual salary reviews

The purpose of an individual salary review is to decide on the merit increments that should be given to staff. The usual practice is to have one annual review for all staff, with the possibility of a half-yearly review for younger staff with high potential who need encouragement more than once a year. Some companies phase increases throughout the year on birthdays or on the anniversary of staff joining the company. This, they say, enables more individual attention to be paid to staff and removes the emotional atmosphere that surrounds the annual review. But phased reviews are more difficult to administer and control except where a fixed increment system is in use, and most organizations prefer one or two fixed dates for a review. Individual salary reviews require the preparation of budgets and guidelines for management in accordance with the principles of salary control as set out at the beginning of this chapter.

Salary review guidelines

Salary review guidelines are necessary to inform managers of what they can pay and how they should distribute it amongst their staff. The aim should be to give managers the maximum amount of authority to determine merit increments within a budget as long as this freedom does not result in unacceptable inconsistencies in the awards given to staff. It has to be faced that any merit review system which relates rewards to performance and not to a time-scale will result in inconsistencies. Even if rigid guidelines are laid down on the amount and distribution of awards, the ultimate decision on who gets what will depend on the largely subjective judgement of someone. It is best, however, for this judgement to be exercised by people in direct charge of staff rather than by remote control.

The various types of guidelines available are:

1. *Overall cost guidelines* where a budget of, say, 4% of pay-roll is imposed for merit reviews. This is the essential guideline and managers may be left to distribute the pool as they please, or they may be subjected to various degrees of control on the grounds that they might otherwise make eccentric awards such as giving everyone exactly the same small amount or giving a limited number of people excessively high increases.

2. *Guidelines on maximum and minimum increases* where managers are told that they cannot give an increase of more than, say, 10% or less than, say, 3% on the grounds that too high an increase could produce inequities and too low an increase is meaningless – 3% or 4% is generally regarded as the minimum worthwhile increase. These limiting guidelines are not too restrictive and can easily be added to the basic budget figure to produce a reasonable balance between excessive control and excessive freedom.

3. *Guidelines on the relationship between performance and reward* where it is laid down that awards should be related to an overall assessment of performance on a scale like this:

Assessment	Increment (%)
A – outstanding	9-10
B – very satisfactory	7-8
C – satisfactory	4-6
D – barely satisfactory	3*
E – unsatisfactory	0

*but only if there is hope of improvement and the individual needs encouragement.

The problem with this approach is that the assessments are entirely subjective. There will be no common standards of judgement between departments and the distribution of awards will be as inconsistent as ever. All that such guidelines can do is to provide some indication to managers about how they might distribute the pool of money made available to them amongst their staff.

4. *Guidelines on the distribution of increments* where, in an attempt to overcome the varying standards of judgement leading to an 'all my geese are swans' approach to rewarding staff, managers are required to conform to a forced distribution of merit increases. For example, they are not allowed to give an increase of 9% to more than 10% of their staff. The distribution scale may be related to the guidelines on increments like this:

Assessment	Increment %	Distribution %
A – outstanding	9-10	10
B – very satisfactory	7-8	20
C – satisfactory	4-6	40
D – barely satisfactory	3	20
E – unsatisfactory	0	10

In this example a normal distribution is followed, but this may be rejected, quite rightly, by managers as an entirely arbitrary device. They will claim that their departments are exceptional and will refuse to accept any contention that the abilities of their staff conform to the normal distribution of the population as a whole. They will claim, and they might even be right, that they have trained and developed a body of exceptional men and women and that they have taken great care both to avoid selecting duds and to remove anyone who has slipped through the net. Distributions can, of course, be altered to conform to this viewpoint by increasing the proportion of higher increments, thus conceding that the normal distribution of abilities does not apply. But this is still an entirely arbitrary process.

5. *Guidelines on rates of progression* where managers are helped to plan salary progression by being given an indication of the number of years it should take staff at different levels of performance to reach the top of the grade and, in a zones salary range, the limits within the range which can be reached according to their performance. For example:

Assessment	Limit in grade	Years to limit from grade minimum
A	Grade maximum	7-8
B	Qualified zone maximum	7-8
C	Midpoint	8-9
D	Learning zone maximum	5 or more
E	Not normally retained	—

Again, such guidelines may be helpful in salary planning but it would be wrong to apply them too rigidly.

There is a danger of going too far with guidelines and imposing so much rigidity on the system that it collapses under the strain. There is a limit to the extent to which it is appropriate or possible to direct increments in any situation where decisions are not all made centrally. Constraints in the form of budgets and upper and lower limits can and should be applied, but the other guidelines on amounts and distribution should never be used as mandatory controls. They can be helpful in showing managers how the system can work but as examples only.

The best form of guideline, other than the essential budget limits, is the briefing and training that should be given to managers who are recommending increments. Thereafter, guidance should be based on an analysis of recommendations from the centre so that managers who adopt a seemingly eccentric approach can be asked to justify it. If they cannot, they must be persuaded to think again and to do better next time.

Procedures for grading jobs

The procedures for grading or re-grading jobs should lay down that new jobs or jobs where the responsibilities have changed can only be graded or re-graded when a job evaluation has taken place. This should require the preparation of job descriptions which can be matched with other jobs and grade definitions, or can be used as a basis for an analytical job evaluation.

Managers who wish to re-grade a job or increase a salary because of market rate pressures or because a member of staff is 'holding a pistol at their heads' by threatening to leave for a higher salary, should be required to produce evidence to support their case. The evidence should be positive. It is not enough to refer to one or two carefully selected advertisements. And it is always dangerous to succumb to blackmail, however, valuable the individual appears to be. Panic measures should be avoided by keeping a careful watch on market rate trends and taking any necessary action in good time.

Fixing salaries on appointment or promotion

Control over starting salaries should be exercised by providing guidelines on the policies to be followed and by defining who has the authority to approve salaries. The guidelines should state that the normal practice is to start inexperienced staff at the bottom of the range, but salaries up to, say, 15% above the minimum can be offered if this would not cause embarrassment by appointing an outsider at a higher salary than existing staff. Appointments at a salary above this level would only be made with the approval of a higher authority.

Promotions should be dealt with as they arise rather than being left to the annual review. The increase should be meaningful, say, 10% or more, and the starting point in the new salary grade should provide adequate scope to reward performance in the new job. Ideally, therefore, the starting point should not be higher than 15% or so above the minimum rate for the grade.

Salary control procedures

Salary control procedures are concerned with:

- salary review budgets;
- generating and using control information;
- monitoring gradings within the salary structure by the use of compa-ratios;
- understanding and using the principle of salary attrition.

Salary review budgets

The best way to plan and control the individual or merit review is to determine the increase to the pay-roll that can be allocated for merit payments. The review budget can then be expressed as, say, 5% of pay-roll costs, and this is the limit given to each manager for increasing the pay-roll. The following factors influence the size of the budget:

- The salary policies of the company on the rates at which staff of different levels of ability should progress through their salary ranges.
- The extent to which the actual salaries in each grade differ from the target salary, which is usually the mid-point in the grade and, ideally, should correspond to the average salaries of the job holders in the grade. The information used for this purpose is the compa-ratio as described below.
- The potential effect of what is termed salary attrition on average salaries over the year. Attrition is the reduction in salary costs which can take place over a period of time as a result of staff

joining the company at a lower salary than those who leave. This process is also discussed below.

● The amount the company thinks it can afford to pay on the basis of forecasts of revenue, profits and pay-roll costs and an analysis of the effects of salary attrition on costs.

● The effect of government regulations on pay increases.

Control information

In a smaller or even medium sized organization, control over the implementation of individual salary reviews is easily achieved by checking through recommendations and ensuring that they appear to be reasonable and that the total increase to the pay-roll does not exceed the budget.

In a larger organization it may be advisable to exercise control by means of a salary review form for each department such as the one illustrated in Figure 27.3.

Overall control can be maintained quite simply by requiring each department to produce a summary of the individual recommendations which shows the percentage increase to the pay-roll and the distribution of merit awards of different amounts. A more elaborate approach, suitable only for organizations which want to exercise close central control, is to use a summary sheet showing details of average salaries and increments in each grade as illustrated in Figure 27.4.

Compa-ratios

A compa-ratio (short for comparative ratio) is a measure of the extent to which the average salaries in a grade deviate from the target salary. It is used to compare actual averages with the target salary to indicate the extent to which salary levels are high or low, and thus suggest where action may have to be taken to limit increases or to adopt a more generous policy. The formula for calculating a compa-ratio is:

$$\frac{\text{Average of all salaries in the grade}}{\text{Midpoint of the salary range}} \times 100$$

A compa-ratio of 100 would indicate that the average salary is aligned to the midpoint of the salary grade and that no corrective steps need to be taken. An average salary of £9600 compared with a midpoint of £12,000 would produce a compa-ratio of 80 and would indicate the need to investigate why average salaries were low and possibly no longer competitive. This could have arisen because of an influx of new staff or those promoted into a salary grade.

A compa-ratio of 120 arising if average salaries were £14,400 in a grade where the midpoint was £12,000 would suggest either there were a lot of long-service staff in the grade (which could be a cause of congratulation

FUNCTION/DEPARTMENT						PROPOSED BY					DATE		APPROVED BY			DATE	
		Date			Job grade	Last increase			Present salary	Assess-ment (2)		Proposed increase		Approved increase		Comments
Name	Job title	of birth	of joining	started present job		Amount	Date	Reason (1)				Amount	New salary	Amount	New salary	
(1)	(2)	(3)	(4)	(5)	(6)	(7)	(8)	(9)	(10)	(11)		(12)	(13)	(14)	(15)	(16)
Total number								Total		Totals						

NOTES

1. Reasons for last increase:
   M = merit
   P = promotion

2. Assessment
   A – Outstanding   C – Satisfactory
   B – Very satisfactory   D – Barely satisfactory
                  E – Unsatisfactory

Figure 27.3 Individual salary review form

DEPARTMENT   PROPOSED BY   DATE   APPROVED BY   DATE

Grade	No. in grade	Present		Proposed											
		Salary bill £	Average salary £	Distribution of merit increments (number)			Number not receiving increment			Distribution in grade (number)			Salary bill £	Average salary £	% Increase
				A	B	C	Assessed D/E	On maximum	On mid-point	Premium zone	Qualified zone	Learning zone			
	(1)	(2)	(3)	(4)	(5)	(6)	(7)	(8)	(9)	(10)	(11)	(12)	(13)	(14)	(15)
1															
2															
3															
4															
5															
6															
7															
8															
9															
10															
11															
12															
13															
14															
15															
16															
17															
18															
Total															
Approved total															

Figure 27.4 Salary review summary sheet

or alarm) or that staff were being overpaid and increases needed to be modified. Compa-ratio analysis can therefore reveal a situation where earnings drift has taken place – the natural but not necessarily appropriate tendency for salaries to drift towards the upper range or top of a salary range irrespective of the merits of the individuals concerned.

Information on compa-ratios and changes in the average salaries can be recorded on a form such as the one illustrated in Figure 27.5 and used for manual comparisons and to provide guidance on the likely effects of salary attrition.

		Number in grade		Average salary		Compa-ratio	
Grade	Salary range	Last year	This year	Last year	This year	Last year	This year

Figure 27.5 Compa-ratio summary form

Salary attrition

Attrition to the costs of awarding merit increments takes place when the average salary of leavers in a company exceeds the average salary of joiners. This is the normal situation and it means that an increase in the salary bill of, say, 3% at the beginning of a year could be steadily eroded during the year as a result of the inflows and outflows of staff.

In practice, the difference between the salaries of leavers and joiners is not likely to correspond exactly with the cost of the merit increase. But if there are movements in and out of a company or a salary grade and if the salaries of leavers are higher than joiners, which is highly probable, then there must be some attrition.

The importance of attrition for salary control purposes is that it is possible to assume that it will finance the cost of merit increases wholly or in part during the year. Alternatively, it can be assumed that merit increases in a fixed incremental system, where people are likely to be moving steadily into, out of and through grades, are not inflationary.

Some companies have developed attrition models which they use to determine in advance the cost of merit awards. Other companies adopt the less sophisticated approach of calculating attrition as the residual figure which remains after general and merit increases, expressed as a percentage of pay-roll, have been subtracted from the percentage increase in average salaries.

Computerized salary administration

The scope for computerizing salary administration systems is covered in Chapter 19.

Salary problems

No system of reward management can ensure that a company is not faced with salary problems. Reward management takes place in dynamic conditions and unpredictable changes are inevitable. Salary levels and grading ultimately affect employees, collectively and as individuals. Salary policies and reviews arouse strong feelings which must be dealt with.

Most of the likely problems have been considered in earlier chapters, but at the risk of some repetition it is felt that it would be useful to review the main issues in this chapter to highlight the pressure points that occur in salary systems. The problems discussed below are:

- Absorbing market rate pressures.
- Widening differentials.
- Performance pay.
- Staff reaching the top of their salary league.
- Statutory salaries.
- Deteriorating job evaluation schemes.

Absorbing market rate pressures

Market rate forces – the 'hidden hand' in remuneration policies, to paraphrase Adam Smith – produce the perennial problem of reconciling the need to keep pace with what other companies pay with the need to preserve equitable internal relativities. The problem arises when general and individual salary reviews have not enabled the company's salary levels to keep pace with increases in market rates. It is exacerbated if the company is expanding and is compelled to obtain key staff who are in short supply.

The problem occurs in its most acute form when the grading given to specialist jobs such as computer programmers within the company does not place them on a salary range which is competitive with market rates. If this is genuinely the case, there are five possible courses of action that can be taken:

1. Create a separate 'market group' structure for these jobs. This isolates the problem to a degree but invidious comparisons can still be made within the company and a proliferation of salary structures can cause administrative difficulties.

2. Create a special salary range for the jobs which need not correspond with any existing job grade salary range. Again, this does not prevent comparisons and intermediate salary ranges of this kind can destroy the integrity of the structure if indulged in to excess. But this method provides a measure of isolation without the administrative complexities of a completely separate structure.

3. Pay a market rate premium to job holders who retain the original grading given to their jobs. This is a variation of the second choice which in certain circumstances may be easier to justify and administer. It is also easier to remove a premium than to abolish a grade.

4. Placing the jobs in question in a higher grade but identifying them as special cases, known in the trade as 'red circling'. This can be quite an effective way of dealing with isolated cases, but one of the earlier three choices provides a more easily controllable method of dealing with a large number of similar jobs.

5. Recruiting staff at a higher point in the salary range. This is the easiest solution, but it can only be used as a short-term expedient because it restricts salary progression and may be difficult to justify to staff in other jobs in the grade.

None of these choices presents the ideal solution because no such solution exists. The circumstances will indicate whether a short-term or a longer-term method is best and the degree to which isolation on a permanent basis is necessary.

Widening differentials

Differentials are widening between and within companies in the following areas:

1. Between high- and low-paying organizations – the variations in prosperity between differing sectors of industry and commerce and between different regions are major contributors to this problem.

2. Between companies paying bonuses or incentives and those paying straight salaries – this arises not just because of the bonus element but also because the bonus-paying companies tend to have higher base salaries, a reflection of their policy of demanding results but expecting to have to pay over the odds to get the extra performance they require.

3. Between top and middle management within companies – this is partly incentive led, bonuses are given more readily to top management and the amounts tend to be considerably higher as a

proportion of the base salary. But the widening of differentials has also taken place because of a deliberate policy of redressing the situation of the 1970s when differentials were squeezed and 'head room' was lacking. This increase in differentials as a response to the more onerous demands made on top management is usually desirable, but it has sometimes meant that middle managers have felt neglected, and they are still important.

4. Between executives recruited by search and those with a one-company career, key people in short supply are increasingly being recruited by executive search consultants or head-hunters. The best executives will already be paid in the upper quartile of the salary range for their jobs before they are offered a 20% or higher increase to move companies.

To a degree, the widening of differentials is a fact of life that everyone working in an enterprise culture has to accept. When it happens between companies or sectors the problem is one of market pressure and can only be dealt with by one of the methods suggested earlier. Within companies the aim should be to ensure that differentials are justified; that they truly reflect differences in contribution and that they properly reward achievement.

Performance pay problems

The emphasis in the 1980s on performance-related pay is an appropriate response to the ever increasing pressure for results. However, bonus schemes and merit awards can be divisive if they are only awarded to top people and the favoured few whose results can be measured. The supporting staff who do the hard work should be remembered too, but companies often neglect them. It can, of course, be difficult to develop performance-related pay schemes for clerical or other junior staff, a problem which is very evident in the Civil Service. But there are means of varying progression according to merit as described in Chapter 24 and these should be used wherever possible.

Performance-related pay can also cause problems because merit assessments are too often based on subjective and biased judgements. This can only be avoided by the intensive training of assessors and by carefully monitoring the appraisal scheme.

Staff reaching the top of their salary range

Staff who reach the top of their salary range may feel demotivated if there are no prospects of promotion. The blow will be softened if they are fully aware of the policy of the company on limiting progression to the top of the salary range and can be told that the company's policy of relating the salary range midpoint to market rates means that they are well paid compared with what they could earn elsewhere. Feelings of disappointment can be further reduced, if not eliminated, by assuring staff that every attempt will be made to maintain the purchasing power of their salaries and that jobs will be regraded if there is a sufficient increase in responsibilities.

It is possible to deal with this problem by introducing a premium zone on top of the normal salary range which is reserved for outstanding staff whose promotion is blocked. This may provide for a 10% or more up-lift in salary. The use of premium zones must be controlled very carefully.

However, the problem returns when staff get to the top of their premium zone. They may have been told clearly that they are now paid well above the going rate but, especially if they have been used to regular increments, they may still feel aggrieved if they come to a grinding halt. One solution to the problem is to pay non-consolidated bonuses for exceptional work. But these must not be handed out too liberally or they will lose any incentive effect they might have had. People at the top of their scale should already be well paid. If they want more they must earn it.

Starting salaries

The problem of starting new staff at higher rates than existing employees should, in theory, be minimized if internal salary levels are regularly reviewed in comparison with market rates. In practice, especially when a government imposes pay restrictions, salaries within a company often lag behind those outside, and anomalies are almost inevitable. If normal salary structure review and control procedures fail to control this problem, the anomalies should be noted and special steps taken to overcome them at the time of the next salary review by giving higher increases to those left behind, or by restricting the increases of the higher paid staff, unless their performance justifies the retention of their differential.

Deteriorating job evaluation schemes

Job evaluation schemes can deteriorate for a number of reasons. The scheme may not have been controlled properly so that grade drift occurs through unjustifiable upgradings as a result of pressures from managers or staff. Or the scheme may have lost credibility because it no longer gives acceptable solutions. Or the administration of the scheme has become so bureaucratic that the time taken to produce answers is unduly prolonged.

The facile answer to these problems is to say that effective administration should prevent grade drift, remove doubts and speed up results. But the evaluation scheme itself may be at fault because it is no longer appropriate (if it ever was), or because it is difficult to administer. Job evaluation systems are inherently prone to these defects because they are subjective and rely on large acts of faith backed up by time consuming analysis.

Simple schemes, even if they are rather crude, are often more effective in the long run.

It is tempting to scrap the existing scheme when it goes wrong and replace it with a new and much more elaborate system. This temptation should be resisted unless the situation is desperate. New schemes are expensive to introduce and they can cause more trouble than they are worth because of the expectations they create amongst staff, which are often disappointed. It is preferable to make a determined effort to tighten up controls and speed up administration, making only minor modifications to the scheme itself. These changes should be in the direction of simplification.

Part VII
Human Resource Development

The process of human resource development starts from the strategic plans of the enterprise which define where the business is going and, broadly, the resources required to get there. These strategies are translated by human resource planning into more specific definitions of how many and what sort of people will be needed in the future. Simultaneously, the business plan will be defining what levels of performance are required to achieve objectives.

Human resource development starts, therefore, with performance management, as discussed in Chapter 28. The prime aim of this process is to improve individual and therefore organizational performance – now and in the future. To achieve this aim, performance appraisal systems assess how effectively people are working in their present jobs and what they need to do and to know to perform even better. This information provides the basis for the three main areas of human resource development which are discussed in the next three chapters:

1. *Training* – the systematic development of the knowledge, skills and attitudes required to carry out a task or a job.
2. *Management development* – improving the performance of managers and giving them opportunities for growth and development.
3. *Career management* – ensuring that the organization has the people it needs to provide for growth and management succession, and that individual managers are given the guidance and help they require to realize their potential and develop their abilities.

Chapter 28
Performance Management

What performance management is about

Performance management is about getting better results through people. It consists of a range of activities, the primary aim of which is to help managers obtain improved performance from their staff, who will be rewarded accordingly. Performance management, however, also looks to the future. It is very much concerned with the development of potential so that people are capable of taking on greater responsibility and can thus earn even higher rewards.

Link with reward management

Performance management activities provide the information needed to determine levels of reward in relation to contribution, and to plan salary increases in relation to progress and potential. They also ensure that appropriate intrinsic incentives and rewards are given for achievement. These include recognition, status and opportunities for advancement. A full description of performance-related systems of salary progression is given in Chapter 24.

Performance management activities

The five performance management activities are:

1. Performance review.
2. Potential review.
3. Performance improvement programmes.
4. Career development programmes.
5. Reward review.

Performance review

The purpose of a performance review is to analyse what a person has done and is doing in his job in order to help him or her to do better, by developing strengths or by overcoming weaknesses. The phrase 'performance review' suggests a deliberate stocktaking exercise. Some people deny that this is necessary. They claim that managers must be making judgements about their subordinates all the time – why go through the artificial and, to some, painful process of summing up in a few platitudinous phrases how well or how badly someone is doing? He ought to know anyway.

The answer to this objection is that managers do not know – they only obtain a series of random impressions. They need to take time off, not only to analyse and record their impressions systematically, but also to think about how they can help their subordinates to improve. Even when managers have formed a balanced view, they often find it difficult to carry out the most important task of conveying it to their subordinates unless they are stimulated into doing so.

But it is not easy to do well. Assessing people properly is a difficult task not simply because, in McGregor's phrase, 'Managers are uncomfortable when they are put in the position of playing God'[1] – everyone forms judgements about other people, and are quite happy to; what they do not like is to justify their views in writing or, worse still, face to face with the person they are assessing. The fundamental problems are:

- the development and understanding of characteristics and standards against which people can be assessed objectively and consistently, which means that those who develop and use performance review procedures must appreciate the factors affecting assessments of people;
- the method of recording judgements, when the task is to choose a performance review technique which encourages managers to set out their views within an understood framework, but does not impose an unreasonable burden of form filling;
- ensuring that counselling sessions do take place between managers and their subordinates which make good use of the appraisal to show the way to improvements in performance.

Factors affecting assessments

Assessments require the ability to judge people, and good judgement is a matter of using fixed standards, considering only relevant evidence, avoiding projection (the process of ascribing to other people one's own unacceptable wants and faults) and combining probabilities in their correct weight.

The factors affecting assessments are those arising from:

- the characteristics of the manager, including his ability to judge people, and his attitudes to the process of assessment;
- the interaction between the manager and the interviewee;
- the way in which the person being assessed is regarded by the manager – stereotyping;
- the methods used to measure performance.

Characteristics of the manager

Most managers think they are good judges. One seldom if ever meets anyone who admits to being a poor judge of people, just as one seldom hears anyone confessing that he is a bad driver – although accident rates suggest that bad drivers do exist – and mistakes in selection, placement and promotion indicate that some managers are worse than others at judging people.

Differences in personality characteristics will affect the type of judgements made and also the consistency and fairness of the judgements. As a result, the attitudes of managers to their staff will vary so that different managers will appraise the same people quite differently. One manager will, for example, rate everyone very strictly so that the average level of his ratings will be much lower than that of another manager who is less strict. A major reason for differences in level arises because managers do not have common standards to judge by.

It has also been discovered that if two managers are required to rate the same people, not only do they tend to rate against different standards, but the spread or scatter of their ratings will vary. One person, for example, will tend to produce ratings that group fairly closely around the man, whereas another judge's ratings will be much more widely scattered. It has been found that people who make snap judgements or jump to conclusions quickly tend to produce a wider scatter of judgements than people who are more deliberate and painstaking. It has also been found that people who produce a wide scatter in judgements tend to see things in extremes – as black or white rather than in shades of grey. The well-known 'halo effect' or its less known opposite, the 'horns effect', are associated with the spread factor. These effects arise when the manager is aware of some prominent or recent example of good or bad performance and assumes from this that all aspects of the job holder's performance are equally good or bad.

Knowledge of these factors has strongly influenced the design of the various performance review systems described later in this chapter. In an attempt to ensure consistency in judgements, assessment characteristics have been defined and scales have been drawn up against which the ratings are made. Elaborate statistical devices have been developed to eliminate variations.

These systems have universally failed and the emphasis has turned to improving managers' skills in judging by:

- encouraging them to define and agree standards and measures of effectiveness beforehand with those concerned;
- encouraging and training people to avoid jumping to conclusions too quickly by consciously suspending judgement until all the relevant data available have been examined;
- providing managers with practice in exercising judgements which enable them to find out for themselves their weaknesses and thus improve their techniques.

Interaction between the manager and the interviewee

Assessments are made by observation and discussion during interviews. But their validity is affected by the following problems:

- poor perception – not noticing things or events for what they are;
- wishful thinking – noticing only those things one wants to see;
- poor interpretation – putting one's own interpretation on information;
- projection – seeing one's own faults in other people.

Empathy is required to obtain an accurate interpretation of a person's behaviour. Empathy is the ability to put oneself into someone else's shoes when trying to understand why he or she is behaving in a certain way.

The development of an effective performance review system is more a matter of overcoming the problems of making assessments and of improving empathy than of introducing elaborate procedures, whether these are traditional merit rating-schemes, or slightly more up-to-date management by objectives programmes. There is a limit to which empathy can be induced – it is a skill and an attitude which people have mainly to develop for themselves. But they can be helped to improve their ability to understand others by gaining a greater knowledge of the forces and drives that affect people and by being given practice in using skills of gathering and analysing information about them carefully, objectively and systematically.

Performance appraisal is a skilled process which, unfortunately, many managers are not very good at. Training is necessary to develop the skills required and to encourage an attitude of mind which ensures that managers will give this important aspect of their duties the emphasis it deserves.

Stereotyping

Judgements are affected by the universal tendency to stereotype. We all tend to carry around with us a collection of mental pictures of what we imagine certain people to be like, and these preformed pictures or stereotypes are used as an easy way to classify those with whom we come into contact. Familiar stereotypes include curates, retired colonels and students. It is difficult to avoid stereotyping people as typical salesmen, accountants or personnel managers, but managers should be encouraged to control a tendency to stereotype because it is only when they can learn to see people as individuals that they are able to make an objective assessment of performance.

Factors affecting the measurement of performance

Appraisal schemes have been in existence since before World War I, when W D Scott invented the man-to-man comparison scale. Various schemes of merit rating were developed, mainly in the USA between the wars, and came into increasing use in the UK after World War II. To a large extent, however, they are greeted by line management with hostility or indifference as an administrative burden imposed on them by a power-seeking personnel department. In particular, managers resist them because of:

- a mistrust of the validity of the scheme itself;
- a dislike of criticising subordinates to their face;
- lack of skill in handling appraisals and interviews;
- dislike of new procedures.

As Douglas McGregor pointed out, this resistance was met by imposing controls; but assessments are then done as a matter of routine and the forms gather dust in the personnel department – forgotten and ignored. McGregor suggested in his highly influential article 'An Uneasy Look at Performance Appraisal'[1] that the emphasis should be shifted from appraisal to analysis:

> This implies a more positive approach. No longer is the subordinate being examined by the superior so that his weaknesses may be determined; rather he is examining himself; in order to define not only his weaknesses but also his strengths and potentials . . . He becomes an active agent, not a passive 'object'. He is no longer a pawn in a chess game called management development.

MrGregor went on to suggest that the emphasis should be on the future rather than the past in order to establish realistic targets and to seek the most effective ways of reaching them. The accent of the review is therefore on performance, on actions relative to goals:

> There is less tendency for the personality of the subordinate to become an issue. The superior, instead of finding himself in the position of a psychologist or a therapist, can become a coach helping the subordinate to reach his own decisions on the specific steps that will enable him to reach his targets.

In short, the main factor in measuring performance should be the analysis of the behaviour required to achieve agreed results, not the assessment of personality. This is, in effect, management by objectives, which is concerned with planning and measuring results in relation to agreed targets and standards. It is possible, however, that McGregor and others overstated their case when they placed so much emphasis on planning for the future. Surely, future behaviour cannot be determined without an analysis of what is right or wrong with current behaviour. Results are what count, but it is still necessary to consider how better results can be achieved by changing behaviour and by acquiring new knowledge and improved skills.

The factors affecting the measurement of performance were also studied in the UK by Kay Rowe[2] who carried out an extensive research project into the effectiveness of the more traditional methods of appraisal which use largely subjective ratings of personality traits. This study confirmed that managers did not like using these schemes and were using them badly. She noted that assessors were required to answer such questions as 'Is he tactful?', 'Has he a pleasant personality?', 'Is he vindictive?' and commented: 'No appraiser has the moral right to press judgement on such matters, except in so far as they are directly and demonstrably relevant in the subordinate's job.'[2] The view was reaffirmed that if appraisals are meant to help people to improve their performance they must consider how the results were achieved. It was suggested that one of the bonuses of results-orientated appraisals is that they would be more acceptable to both appraiser and appraised.

Performance review techniques

There has been a steady growth in the use of results-orientated appraisals over the past seven years, largely due to the influence of management by objectives. There is no doubt that, properly conducted, this is the best approach. It is necessary, however, to review briefly the other techniques available before considering how results-orientated schemes can be made to work. The main types are:

- overall assessment;
- guideline assessment;
- grading;
- merit rating;
- critical incident;
- results-orientated.

Overall assessment
This approach simply asks a manager to write down in narrative form his comments about the employee. He may be given a checklist of personality characteristics to consider such as reliability, enthusiasm, appearance, acceptability and, with a slight bow to the McGregor philosophy, he may be asked to comment on results achieved against targets.

This is the simplest approach and at least ensures that managers have to collect their thoughts together and put them down on paper. But different people will consider different aspects of performance and there will be no conspiracy in the criteria selected for assessment. The value of the exercise will also depend on the ability of the manager to express himself in writing. And he will tend to be evasive. As Kay Rowe reported on the comments made in the six schemes she studied:

> A few suggested careful thought and a conscientious effort to say something meaningful but the vast majority were remarkable for their neutrality. Glib, generalized, enigmatic statements abounded. Typical of such statements was 'a loyal, conscientious and hard-working employee'. Such a statement may well have been true but it is not very revealing.[2]

Guideline assessment

The guideline assessment approach is an attempt to obtain more specific judgements from assessors who are asked to comment separately on a number of defined characteristics; for example, industry and application, loyalty and integrity, co-operation, accuracy and reliability, adaptability, knowledge of work and use of initiative. When assessing a characteristic such as industry and application, managers might be asked to: 'Consider his application to work and the enthusiasm with which he approaches a task. Does he work quickly and stick to the job or is he slow and inclined to slack if not watched?'

In theory this method should help managers to be more precise but in practice the guidelines are so vague that comments are uninformative, especially if they are about generalized characteristics such as industry and application.

Grading

Grading is a further development of the guideline approach which attempts to provide a framework of reference by defining a number of levels at which the characteristic is displayed and asking managers to select the definition which most closely describes the individual they are assessing. For example, in rating effective output the manager in a typical grading scheme is asked to choose between:

(a) Outstanding – outstanding output of high quality work.
(b) Satisfactory – satisfactory level of output and effort.
(c) Fair – completes less than the average amount of effective work.
(d) Poor – low output and poor worker.

In themselves, definitions of this type are not particularly helpful – they are generalized and fail to establish actual standards against which judgements can be made. Assessments are therefore just as subject to variations and inconsistencies as in the other schemes.

Merit rating

Merit rating is similar to grading except that numerical values are attached to the judgements so that each characteristic is rated on a scale of, say, one to 20. The ratings are then added up to produce a total score.

A variation of this approach is the graphic rating scale in which the assessor ticks the place on a line running from very high to very low to indicate the employee's standing on each quality. In its most Machiavellian form, this method requires an *eminence grise* in the personnel department to attach values to ratings and adjust them when it is thought that a manager is tending to over- or under-assess his staff.

These schemes have rightly been discredited. Their only reason for survival is that they satisfy those people who are not happy unless they can quantify everything, even the patently unquantifiable judgements of personality characteristics. The other problem with this type of scheme, as with all the others, is that it does not ensure that the assessor bases his judgements on systematic and objective observations of the job behaviour of the people he is asked to describe.

Critical incident method

The critical incident method is an attempt to overcome the fundamental defect of the other schemes by focusing attention on behaviour. It is based on Flanagan's technique of defining jobs in terms of the typical behaviour of job holders.[3] The method asks managers familiar with a job to record critical incidents of successful or less successful job behaviour. After a large number of such incidents have been collected, they are categorized to form an overall picture of the typical types of behaviour that indicate either effective or ineffective performance. Ideally, this analysis should be carried out with the managers who are going to conduct the appraisals. They can then become familiar with the approach and recognize how it can help them to make more objective assessments by comparing the actual behaviour of their staff with the realistic examples they have contributed.

In a scheme developed by the writer for agricultural salesmen, this technique was used to collect a wide range of critical incidents, such as, for product knowledge: 'Makes a point of talking to technical liaison staff about special features of products', 'Is sometimes caught out on technical points by a customer'. From these incidents, definitions were made of different levels of behaviour; for example, the definition of above standard behaviour for product knowledge: 'Carries out an analysis of the selling points of each product, on the basis of regular contacts with research and development staff, careful study of relevant technical literature, comparative assessments of the strengths and weaknesses of competitors' products and recorded observations of the needs and reactions of customers.'

The advantage of this approach is that it is firmly rooted in observations about actual job behaviour. The disadvantages are the time and effort required to develop a scheme and its limitations to large groups of people in fairly homogeneous jobs. It is for this reason that it has never been adopted on a large scale, but the principles on which it is based are sound and the technique can be useful in defining standards of performance.

Results-orientated appraisal

Results-orientated appraisal is based on quantitative, measurable and specific targets which are agreed jointly by superior and subordinate. Instead of requiring the manager to rate his subordinates on historical evidence in relation to vaguely defined characteristics, under this approach each subordinate is requested to establish, for himself, short-term targets for output, quality, or the introduction of a new procedure or ways in which he can improve his own efficiency or that of his department. Together, the superior and the subordinate talk over what is required to meet these targets and to adjust them so that they are consistent with the targets of other subordinates and the department as a whole. At the end of a set period (say, six months) they meet again to evaluate how all these targets have been met, to discuss what could be done better and to set new targets for the next period.

Where it is not possible to set quantifiable targets, performance standards are agreed by the manager with his subordinate which define the observable behaviour that will indicate whether the task is being well or badly done. A definition is also agreed of the behaviour that will indicate whether or not the individual has potential for promotion. In some areas the standard may be the achievement of specific quantity or quality targets. In other areas, however, a more generalized statement has to be made. But this is expressed in terms of actual job requirements, behaviour and the tasks to be done, rather than by referring to personality factors.

The advantages of this procedure are that:

(a) the subordinate is given the opportunity to make his own evaluation of the results he obtains. When he is discussing results he is actually appraising himself and gaining some insight into how he might improve his performance;

(b) the job of the manager shifts from that of criticising the subordinate to that of helping him to improve his performance;

(c) it is consistent with the principle that people work better when they have definite goals which they must meet in specified periods.

The difficulty most people meet is that of defining realistic and specific targets or standards and it is still necessary when appraising performance to analyse why the result was a success or failure as well as measuring what the result was.

The results will be affected by external circumstances beyond the control of the individual, and these should be identified and discounted. However, although everything else seems to be under the individual's control, it should be remembered that results may be affected by the basic personality traits which might be very difficult if not impossible to change. The aim of the review should not be to produce personality changes, which is difficult if not impossible, but to influence those aspects of behaviour which affect performance which an individual can control. It should be remembered that while a change in behaviour can help to change attitudes, it is almost impossible to change attitudes and thereby change behaviour. Some analysis of how the job was done as well as what results were achieved is, however, necessary, and the headings under which it might be appropriate to analyse a manager's job performance includes:

- professional and technical knowledge in relation to job requirements;
- judgement – problem solving, decision making, deciding priorities;
- initiative – resourcefulness, enterprise, energy;
- co-operation – involvement, contribution to team effort;
- leadership – motivation and development of staff.

A checklist on managerial standards of performance is set out at the end of this chapter.

Results-orientated schemes are based on the principle of management by objectives (see Chapter 30). A variation of this approach which is linked to the data collected on principal accountabilities in using the Hay method of job evaluation, is the scheme developed in Book Club Associates which is called the System of Accountable Management, SAM for short. This system is described in Figures 28.1 and 28.2. The performance appraisal form used as part of this system is illustrated in Figure 28.3 and an example of a statement of accountabilities is given in Appendix C.

Potential review

The review of potential is concerned with forecasting the direction in which an individual's career should go and the rate at which he is expected to develop. It provides information to the company on which it can base management succession plans, and to the individual on his future with the company which may encourage him to stay and to improve his abilities still further.

The assessment of potential requires the analysis of existing skills, qualities and how they can be developed to the mutual advantage of the company and the employee, as well as the identification of any weaknesses which must be overcome if the employee's full potential is to be achieved. There is also an important counselling aspect to the review of potential which consists of discussions with the individual about his

Book Club Associates
System of Accountable Management

Purpose

1. The system of accountable management is a method of management, the overall aim of which is to improve BCA's results by improving the performance of its managers.

2. This aim is achieved by ensuring that:
   (a) managers know what they are going to be held responsible for;
   (b) the results obtained by managers are measured and monitored by their superiors *and* themselves so that action can be taken as necessary to improve performance.

3. Although better understanding of responsibilities and improved guidance and control (self control as well as control exercised from above) are the primary purposes of the system, it has three subsidiary aims:
   (a) to assist in career development and in making promotion decisions;
   (b) to identify training needs;
   (c) to provide the basis for performance-related pay decisions.

Operation

4. The system of accountable management is based on two main documents which are prepared for each managerial position:
   (a) a statement of accountabilities;
   (b) a statement of objectives expressed in the form of targets, tasks or standards.

   Notes on the preparation of these documents are given below.

5. These documents will form the basis for a system of performance appraisal which will assess the results obtained against objectives.

Approach

6. The system of accountable management is essentially a joint effort between the manger and his/her subordinate. The documents referred to above are prepared following discussions between the two parties concerned. This means that the accountabilities, performance indicators and, above all, the actual objectives, have to be agreed.

7. It is important also to appreciate that, although the system will provide for a regular stocktaking performance review, the process of measuring, monitoring and amending objectives is continuous. And this process is carried out by the individual, as well as by his or her manager, in the light of a clearer understanding of what has to be achieved.

8. The overall system is illustrated in the chart shown in figure 28.2.

Preparing statements of accountability

Content
9. The statement of accountability contains:

   (a) *A definition of overall accountability* — the purpose of the job as a whole as measured by the end results that the job holder is expected to achieve.
   (b) *Definitions of specific accountabilities* — the key result areas in the job, normally not more than ten, one of which will always be a general accountability for managing the job holder's area.
   (c) *Criteria for assessing performance* — these are defined for each accountability and are expressed as the types of objectives, targets or standards to be achieved. Where objectives can be quantified or are variable, this statement will only name the criterion to be used (e.g. new member acquisition budget) rather than the actual target figures (these are set out separately as specific objectives).

10. Note that the statement indicates what the job holder is expected to *achieve*. It does not set out *how* the job is achieved: that is the purpose of a job description.

11. Methods of preparing the statement are given below.

Overall accountability statement
12. This is a concise statement, preferably expressed in one sentence, which starts with an infinitive — 'to . . .' — and summarizes the essential characteristics of the job in terms of its overall purpose and, in general, the results expected of the job holder. The statement should convey the essence of the job so that it is instantly recognizable.

13. The following are some examples of statements of overall accountability:

   (a) *Chief Executive:* 'To plan, direct and control all BCA's activities and to achieve results which meet the owners' objectives for the business.'
   (b) *Personnel Director:* 'To develop and implement personnel strategies which make a major contribution to achieving BCA's objectives, and to provide the personnel and administrative services required by BCA.'
   (c) *Overseas Marketing Manager:* 'To achieve targets for member recruitment, sales, and profit for EBC operations, to manage export sales, and to assist in the development of new markets.'

Specific accountabilities

14. The overall accountability is in effect segmented into a number of key result areas which, if they are met, will ensure that the purpose of the job will be achieved. Each of these specific accountabilities represents a finite area of the job to which specific objectives or standards can be attached.

15. In order to facilitate concentration on the key areas of accountability, it is essential to restrict them to no more than ten, preferably seven or eight. For managers one of these will always be 'Manages operations and (where appropriate) the staff of the department/section to fulfil the above accountabilities in accordance with BCA's management guidelines.'

16. Most people find that the best way to prepare the list of specific accountabilities is to:

    (a) think through each aspect of the job and then jot down, at random, specific tasks to be carried out or possibly results to be achieved;
    (b) review the initial list and, if necessary, group related tasks together into single key result or accountability areas in order to produce a list of headings;
    (c) place the accountability areas in a logical order which relates, where feasible, to some form of sequence such as plans-operates-monitors-controls;
    (d) write each specific accountability in the style described below;
    (e) number specific accountabilities sequentially.

17. A specific accountability statement starts with an active verb to eliminate superfluous words. Use verbs which clearly express the actual responsibility to get things done e.g. achieves, implements, prepares, completes, ensures that.

18. The following are some examples of specific accountability definitions:

    (a) 'Prepares financial plans and budgets for approval by the Board.'
    (b) 'Implements the system of accountable management.'
    (c) 'Sets pricing levels for one-shots and catalogues items to maximize revenue and gross margin.'

Criteria for assessing performance

19. The criteria for assessing performance spells out the factors that are used to measure the extent to which a specific accountability has been met. They can refer to:

    (a) the quantitative budget or target area that has to be achieved or not exceeded, e.g. recruitment budget, subsidy, trading budget, inventory target, or
    (b) the standards required in completing special projects or tasks (not continuing responsibilities), e.g. 'Project X is to be completed by Y to meet in full the objectives set for the project' or
    (c) qualitative standards of performance which are used when quantification or reference to a specific project is not possible. The statement should start with the phrase: 'Performance is up to standard if ...' For example:

(i) 'Performance is up to standard if realistic media schedules are produced and presented effectively with a media mix that is likely to generate acceptable ROCPOs.'

(ii) 'Performance is up to standard if both oral and written briefs are clear and given on time.'

(iii) 'Performance is up to standard if lead lists are accurate and produced on time and lead books are up-to-date.'

Objectives

20. The specific objectives in the form of quantified budgets, targets or tasks to be completed over a period are agreed at appropriate intervals between the manager and the subordinate.

21. At the same time, the qualitative standards of performance as set out under the performance indicator heading are reviewed and any amendments required are agreed.

Performance review

22. The review of performance against agreed objectives and standards is a continuous process. At least once a year, however, a 'stocktaking' exercise is carried out which appraises overall performance. This review is also used as a basis for assessing potential.

Figure 28.1 *The system of accountable management in Book Club Associates*

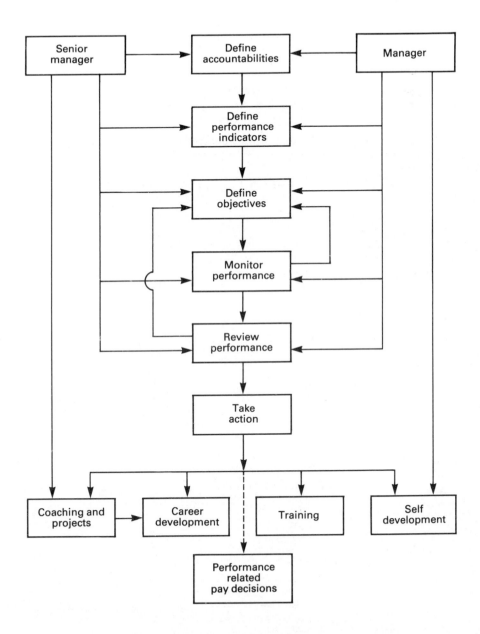

Figure 28.2 Flow-chart – system of accountable management

CONFIDENTIAL

PERFORMANCE AND POTENTIAL ASSESSMENT

NAME:

_____

JOB TITLE:

_____

DEPARTMENT:

_____

PERIOD OF ASSESSMENT:

_____

PERFORMANCE ASSESSMENT

ACHIEVEMENT OF OBJECTIVES

Comment on results achieved in the period against agreed objectives, targets and standards of performance as derived from the statement of accountabilities.

FACTOR ASSESSMENT

Comment on and assess performance in relation to each of the following factors as they affect the achievement of objectives.

Ratings:
A = excellent B = highly acceptable C = acceptable D = not entirely acceptable E = unacceptable.

	RATING
PROFESSIONAL AND TECHNICAL KNOWLEDGE in relation to job requirements	
JUDGEMENT – problem solving, decision making, deciding priorities	
INITIATIVE – resourcefulness, enterprise, energy	
CO-OPERATION – involvement, contribution to team effort	
LEADERSHIP – motivation and development of staff	

OVERALL PERFORMANCE ASSESSMENT   ✓

A	Far exceeds requirements in all areas	
B	Consistently exceeds requirements in most areas	
C	Meets requirements	
D	Does not meet requirements in all areas	
E	Fails to meet requirements	

COMMENTS ON OVERALL ASSESSMENT

POTENTIAL ASSESSMENT   ✓

A	Very considerable potential – a high flyer	
B	Definite potential for promotion to at least one level higher	
C	Some potential for promotion	
D	No potential	
X	Too early to assess	

COMMENTS ON POTENTIAL ASSESSMENT

PROPOSED ACTION

Training requirements and/or additional experience

Assessment carried out by: Date:

COMMENTS BY ASSESSOR'S MANAGER

Signed   Date aspirations and how these can best be matched to the future foreseen for him. These discussions are, in fact, a vital part of the procedure because they can provide the manager with information about his employee's feelings on this subject, which may have a marked effect on plans for development including training and job rotation. They can also provide employees with additional motivation and the encouragement they may need to remain with the company.

Assessing potential, however, is not easy. It has to start with a review by the immediate manager who can only base his judgement on what he can observe about performance on the present job. This will not necessarily indicate that the individual is going to be capable of carrying greater responsibility in the future when the demand may be quite different. Hence the 'Peter Principle', invented by L J Peter, which advances the somewhat pessimistic view that managers tend to be promoted to the level of their own incompetence.[4]

To avoid this difficulty, some companies insist on evaluations of potential being made by managers at one level higher than the immediate manager on the grounds that they can take a more detached and knowledgeable view on the basis of some direct knowledge of the individual as well as the views of the latter's boss. Assessment centres, as described in Appendix L, can also be used to determine potential.

The following is a checklist of the points to be considered in assessing potential:

1. Has the job holder been long enough in the present job to form an assessment?
2. Will the job itself grow or change?
3. What are the job holder's views about the present job?
4. In the light of the answers to (1), (2) and (3), how long should the job holder continue in the present job?
5. What sort of things can the job holder do well?
6. What sort of things is the job holder less good at?
7. What are the job holder's interests and ambitions?
8. In the light of (5), (6) and (7), what jobs could the job holder move to, in the short and longer term?
9. What further training and experience does the job holder need to fit him/her for promotion?
10. Can the job holder get the training and experience required in the present job or have special arrangements to be made?

Performance improvement programmes

Performance improvement programmes are largely in the hands of the manager, who guides, counsels, coaches and recommends further training. The manager also informs his staff at the time of the reward review of the rewards they can expect in the shape of salary increases, bonuses or extra fringe benefits. He can also tell them about the non-financial rewards in the forms of increased status and recognition.

Counselling

Counselling is a vital part of performance improvement programmes if they are to achieve their prime purpose of helping people to improve and develop. But it is difficult to do well and many managers are reluctant to do it at all. In one unpublished study conducted by the writer it was found that more people were dissatisfied after their counselling session than they were before. Even where a results-orientated approach is adopted, a clumsy interviewer can allow the discussion to degenerate into pointless arguments about where blame should be attached for something that has gone wrong.

There are three approaches to performance counselling:

1. *The tell and sell method* in which the manager seeks first to let the employee know how he is doing, then to gain his acceptance of the evaluation, and finally to get him to follow the plan outlined for his improvement. The problem with this method is that considerable and unusual skill is required to get people to accept criticisms and to change in the required manner. There are occasions when people have to be told, but it may not always be possible to provide the motivation required for change, unless resort is made to crude threats or inducements.

2. *The tell and listen method* in which the evaluation is communicated to the employee who is then allowed to respond to it. Instead of the interviewer dominating the discussion he sits back and becomes a non-directive counsellor during the second part of the interview. The employee is encouraged to think things out for himself and to decide on what needs to be done, and the assumption is that he is more likely to change in these circumstances than if he had been told what to do. A further advantage of this approach is that the interviewer will profit more from the interview by receiving feedback from the employee on how the job may be improved with regard to supervision, work methods and job assignments. But the method requires considerable skill on the part of the interviewer in listening, reflecting feelings and summarizing opinions.

3. *The problem-solving approach* in which the interviewer abandons the role of judge and becomes a helper. The appraisal is not communicated to the employee. Instead a discussion takes place of the work problems of the employee, who is encouraged to think through his own solutions to them, including the changes he has to make to his behaviour to achieve improvement. This

approach motivates original thinking because it stimulates curiosity. It also provides the intrinsic motivation that can be derived from work itself and the process of tackling work problems. Job satisfaction can be improved by reorganizing or enlarging the job, by changing the employee's perception of his role and by increasing the superior's ability to provide guidance and help in the form it is needed. Again, this approach needs skill, but it is the most fruitful method and it is one which can clearly be linked to results-orientated review techniques.

Training

To conduct effective appraisal and counselling sessions requires the use of skills which few managers are likely to acquire in the normal course of their work. It is essential, therefore, that training should be given in conducting interviews. Without such training, managers may do more harm than good.

The training should include information on the mechanics of the system, but its main purposes will be first, to ensure that managers are convinced of the value of the appraisal and counselling process and secondly, that they know how to do it and are given confidence by practising the skills required. The use of role playing sessions and videos is therefore an important part of a good training course. The training will concentrate on interactive skills and will have the following features:

1. It is based on the assumption that the primary limitation on supervisory or managerial effectiveness lies not within each job boundary, but on the interface between jobs.
2. There are no preconceived rules about how people should interact. It is assumed that the way interaction happens is dependent upon the situation and the people in it – this is what has to be analysed and used as a basis for the programme.
3. The training takes place through groups which enable people to practise interactive skills – such skills can only be acquired through practice.
4. Participants have to receive controlled and systematic feedback on their performance – this is achieved by using specially developed techniques of behaviour analysis. Videos are used to help them see the realities for themselves.

These general principles are applied to performance management training by first analysing the processes involved – the interactions that take place when agreeing targets, reviewing results and counselling on the improvements required. Further research then takes place on the factors involved in making assessments so that managers understand not only the procedures they have to follow but also appreciate the criteria they should use when analysing results achieved and the behaviour that led to those results. Finally, trainees are given extensive practice in conducting appraisal and counselling interviews with feedback on their performance.

Career development programmes

Career development programmes also start with the manager, who gives feed-back from the potential review, indicating how the employee's career may develop and what he, the employee should do about it, as well as how the company will help. Career advisors or mentors as desribed in Chapter 31 can give a more general view about career opportunities and the steps the employee can take to exploit them. Again, the rewards resulting from future promotions should be spelt out to provide additional motivation.

Career counselling

Career counselling as part of a career development programme involves advising individuals on their possible career paths and what they must do to achieve promotion. This does not mean that a long-range plan consisting of a number of predetermined steps can be revealed. It is seldom, if ever, possible to be precise about long-term career prospects. Even if it were possible it would be dangerous either to raise expectations which might not be fulfilled or to induce a feeling of complacency about the future. It may be feasible to talk about the next step but, beyond that, the wisest approach is to do no more than provide – in planning jargon – a scenario of the opportunities that might become available. Career counselling should not be concerned with making what might turn out to be empty promises. Its main aim should be to help the individuals concerned to develop themselves by giving them some idea of the direction in which they ought to be heading. (See also Chapter 31).

Reward review

The reward review translates the performance review and, to an extent, the potential review into action. There are some people who believe that performance appraisals should be entirely divorced from salary reviews. If, as they say, it is seen simply as a way of fixing the annual hand-out, then the other aims will be neglected because of the over-riding and emotional importance all concerned will attach to any discussion which might affect monetary rewards. The fact remains, however, that the size of these awards will be affected by the manager's opinion of his subordinate. Salary reviews cannot, therefore, be completely separated from performance assessments. It is no good conducting a thorough performance review at one time and agreeing conclusions with the individual concerned only to recommend a salary increase which is quite inconsistent with the assessment.

The best approach is to take the heat out of the main performance review session by conducting it at a different period of the year from the salary review. The earlier performance appraisal is consulted at the time of the salary review and the overall assessment is reviewed in the light of any subsequent developments. This means that the 'read-across' is out in the open and where performance has improved then an improved merit increase can reinforce changed and more effective behaviour.

Performance management procedures

Timing

Performance and potential reviews are usually conducted annually within a fixed period throughout the organization. Some companies conduct rolling reviews on birthdays or anniversaries of joining the company. This spreads the load and allows more individual attention to be given to the review but is less easy to control than a general review.

Basic approach

Performance management procedures should be based on the results-orientated approach, as long as this allows for a review of why the result was achieved as a basis for agreeing what needs to be done in the future. The procedure should be as simple as possible – the use of a multiplicity of elaborate forms should be avoided. It should require managers to see their subordinates to discuss and agree targets and standards, to review performance, and to provide guidance and encouragement which will enable the individual to take action himself to develop his strengths or overcome his weaknesses. It should identify for managers what they as individuals, and the company, should do to help in the process of training and development.

Assessment reviews

Provision should be made for assessments to be reviewed by the assessor's own superior, so that the individual being appraised does not feel he is at the mercy of a prejudiced boss. It may be desirable to allow for formal appeals against assessments, or at least to let people know that they have the right to discuss their assessment informally with a higher authority if they feel it is unfair.

Records

A performance appraisal procedure can operate without any standard forms at all, as long as managers know what to do and are motivated to do it. Targets and action plans can be jotted down and agreed on blank sheets of paper. Management development activities and training needs can be based on the follow-up discussions between whoever is responsible for these functions and the departmental managers. If the company is large or complex, it might be preferable to ask for a brief report on training and development needs and an indication of who has potential for promotion, but this does not need an elaborate form. However, maintaining records allows the personnel department to analyse the consistency of appraisals which can be to everybody's benefit. It is critical to emphasize the confidentiality of appraisal documents and also to allow employees to leave periods of low performance firmly behind them when their work improves. Some organizations maintain strict limits on the time for which appraisals are kept, eg a maximum of two years to emphasize the constructive and forward-looking approach of performance management.

Computerized personnel information systems are being increasingly used as described in Chapter 19 to record data on performance and potential assessments which can be linked to overall career management systems (see Chapter 31).

Checklist – managerial standards of performance

1. Leadership

- Develops cohesive groups and teamwork.
- Guides others to the accomplishment of objectives and responsibilities.
- Resolves conflicts.
- Provides direction under uncertain conditions.

2. Managing skills

- Delegates work responsibility among employees for maximum efficiency.
- Monitors employees' performance to achieve organizational goals and maintain control.
- Sets clear, understandable objectives and priorities for department, self and *with* each employee.
- Schedules and develops contingency plans.
- Motivates people toward effective, co-operative group and individual efforts.

3. **Human resource development**

- Conducts performance reviews according to established guidelines.
- Praises and recognizes positive performance of employees; builds confidence in employees by supporting their appropriate decisions and actions.
- Takes corrective measures when employees' performance needs improvement.
- Encourages and assists individuals through coaching, training and other methods to acquire knowledge and skills necessary for effective job performance and promotion.

4. **Decision making**

- Recognizes critical situations and takes appropriate action.
- Investigates situations adequately and appropriately for the circumstances prior to making decisions and/or recommendations.
- Willing to accept responsibility for decisions whatever the outcome.
- Involves others in the decision making process.
- Considers the whole organization when making decisions.

5. **Problem solving**

- Identifies and anticipates potential problems.
- Solves problems efficiently and effectively.
- Solicits and encourages ideas and input from others.
- Looks for, evaluates and considers alternatives and options in solving problems.
- Personally recommends action.

6. **Innovation/creativity**

- Recommends new methods and ideas.
- Accepts ideas and builds on them; adds value to given efforts.
- Questions constructively why things are done in a particular way.

7. **Flexibility/adaptability**

- Willing to accept new assignments and complete them according to set standards.
- Can handle a wide variety of assignments.
- Willing to consider new ideas and methods.
- Open to constructive criticism and suggestions.

8. Co-operativeness

- Collaborates with other internal departments.
- Interfaces professionally and effectively.
- Procures co-operation from others.

9. Responsiveness

- Understands and responds to needs and requests in an appropriate, timely manner.
- Makes his/her expertise available to others.
- Represents the department's services and products in a precise and appropriate manner.

10. Communication

- Communicates all matters of importance up and down the organization in an accurate, timely manner.
- Provides complete and reliable information.
- Participates easily and influentially in meetings.
- Listens carefully to others.
- Writes clearly, concisely, accurately and persuasively.
- Speaks clearly, concisely, accurately and persuasively.

References

1. McGregor, D 'An Uneasy Look at Performance Appraisal', *Harvard Business Review* Vol 35, No 3, May - June 1957, pp 89-94.
2. Rowe, K H 'An Appraisal of Appraisals', *Journal of Management Studies* Vol 1, No 1, March 1964, pp 1-25.
3. Flanagan, J C 'The Critical Incident Technique', *Psychological Bulletin* Vol 51, 1954, pp 237-58.
4. Peter, L J *The Peter Principle*, William Morrow & Co, New York, 1972.

Chapter 29
Training

Aims

The aims of training are to:

- shorten learning time so that new recruits reach their peak of efficiency as quickly and economically as possible;
- improve the performance of existing employees;
- help people to develop their capacities so that the company can meet most, if not all, its future requirements for managers, supervisors and higher grade professional, technical, sales or production staff from within the organization.

These aims can be achieved by adopting a systematic approach, as suggested below, concentrating mainly on 'on the job' and 'do-it-yourself' training. For detailed descriptions of these types of training, see Appendix K.

The process of systematic training

Training is the systematic development of the knowledge, skills and attitudes required by an individual to perform adequately a given task or job. The key word in this definition is 'systematic'. Systematic training is training which is specifically designed to meet defined needs. It is planned and provided by people who know how to train. Training programmes can all too easily be irrelevant. It is easy to fall into the trap of training for training's sake. It is necessary to adopt a systematic approach, which need not be elaborate or costly and which involves:

- defining training needs;
- deciding what sort of training is required to satisfy these needs;
- using experienced trainers to plan and implement training;
- following up and evaluating training to ensure that it is effective.

Training involves learning in three areas: knowledge, skills and attitudes. Learning may be something that the trainees want to do for themselves, or it may be necessary to provide it for them. If training is provided, individuals may need to be given an incentive – to be motivated – to learn and to apply their learning. Even if no incentive is required – if trainees are self-motivated – it may still be necessary to provide the guidance and training facilities which will help them to channel their enthusiasm towards a worthwhile end.

People learn by being taught, but they also learn through experience. In fact, it can be said that training is essentially the modification of behaviour through experience. But experience is more effective if it is planned and if people are helped to make the most of it.

Therefore training is, or at least can seem to be, a complex process and the techniques used can vary almost infinitely according to the situation. There are, however, certain fundamental concepts and principles upon which all training should be based and, in this chapter, these will be reviewed before consideration is given to their application to the training for different occupations.

The first area that will be covered is learning theory, because all training is, or should be, based upon an understanding of how people learn.

The essential components of the sequence of training as shown in Figure 29.1 will then be dealt with. These consist of:

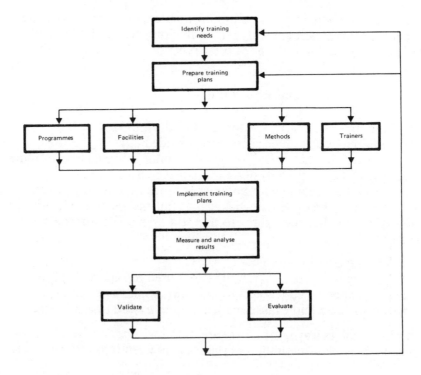

Figure 29.1 The sequence of training

- the identification and analysis of training needs – all training must be directed towards the satisfaction of defined needs; for the company as a whole, for specific functions or groups of employees, or for individuals;
- the definition of training objectives – training must aim to achieve measurable goals expressed in terms of the improvements or changes expected in corporate, functional, departmental or individual performance;
- the preparation of training plans – these must describe the overall scheme of training and its costs and benefits. The overall scheme should further provide for the development of training programmes and facilities, the selection and use of appropriate training methods and the selection and training of trainers;
- the implementation of training plans, including the maintenance of training records;
- the measurement and analysis of results, which require the *validation* of the achievements of each training programme against its objectives and the *evaluation* of the effect of the whole training scheme on company or departmental performance;
- the feedback of the results of validations and evaluations so that training plans, programmes and techniques can be improved.

Continuous development

The Institute of Personnel Management's 1987 code of practice on continuous development states that:

If learning activity in an organization is to be fully beneficial both to the organization and its employees, the following conditions must be met:

- the organization must have some form of strategic business plan. It is desirable that the implications of the strategic plan, in terms of the skills and knowledge of the employees who will achieve it, should be spelled out
- managers must be ready and willing (and able) to define and meet needs as they appear, all learning needs cannot be anticipated; organizations must foster a philosophy of continuous development
- as far as practicable, learning and work must be integrated. This means that encouragement must be given to all employees to learn from the problems, challenges and successes inherent in their day-to-day activities
- the impetus for continuous development must come from the chief executive and other members of the top management team (the board of directors, for example). The top management team must regularly and formally review the way the competence of its management and workforce is being developed. It is important too that one senior executive is charged with responsibility for ensuring that continuous development activity is being effectively undertaken
- investment in continuous development must be regarded by the top management team as being as important as investment in research, new product development or capital equipment. It is not a luxury which can be

afforded only in the 'good times'. Indeed, the more severe the problems an organization faces the greater the need for learning on the part of its employees and the more pressing the need for investment in learning. Money spent within the organization on research and development into human resource development itself is money well spent. An evaluation of current human resource development procedures can confirm the effectiveness of current practice or point the way towards necessary change. Such research is as valuable as technical research.

Successful continuous development demands:

- rapid and effective communication of priority operational needs
- the availability of appropriate learning facilities and resources as a normal part of working life
- recognition by each employee that he or she shares ownership of any organizational collective learning plan
- recognition by each employee that he or she is able to create some personal development plan
- all strategic and tactical operational plans fully take into account the learning implications for the employees affected
- clear understanding, by everyone, of their responsibilities.

Learning theory

Learning theory provides the background against which training programmes and techniques should be developed and used. A knowledge of the basic concepts of how people learn is essential to anyone who plans or conducts training. Even during the initial phase of the training sequence – when training needs are being identified – it is still necessary to be aware of learning theory as this will help to direct inquiries towards those areas where training is most likely to be effective.

Conditions required for effective learning

Learning theory suggests that there are ten main conditions required for learning to be effective:

1. *Individuals must be motivated to learn.* They should be aware that their present level of knowledge or skill, or their existing attitude or behaviour, needs to be improved if they are to perform their work to their own and to others' satisfaction. They must, therefore, have a clear picture of the behaviour they should adopt.
2. *Standards of performance should be set for learners.* Learners must have clearly defined targets and standards which they find acceptable and can use to judge their own progress.
3. *Learners should have guidance.* Learners need a sense of direction and 'feedback' on how they are doing. Self-motivated individuals may provide much of this for themselves, but the trainer should still be available to encourage and help when necessary.

4. *Learners must gain satisfaction from learning.* Learners are capable of learning under the most difficult circumstances if the learning is satisfying to one or more of their needs. Conversely, the best training schemes can fail if they are not seen as useful by the trainee.
5. *Learning is an active not a passive process.* Learners need to be actively involved with their trainer, their fellow trainees and the subject matter of the training programme.
6. *Appropriate techniques should be used.* Trainers have a large repertory of training tools and materials. But they must use these with discrimination in accordance with the needs of the job, the individual and the group.
7. *Learning methods should be varied.* The use of a variety of techniques, as long as they are equally appropriate, helps learning by maintaining the interest of the trainee.
8. *Time must be allowed to absorb the learning.* Learning requires time to assimilate, test and accept. This time should be provided in the training programme. Too many trainers try to cram too much into their programmes and allow insufficient scope for practice and familiarization.
9. *The learner must receive reinforcement of correct behaviour.* Learners usually need to know quickly that they are doing well. In a prolonged training programme, intermediate steps are required in which learning can be reinforced.
10. *The need to recognize that there are different levels of learning and that these need different methods and take different times.* At the simplest level, learning requires direct physical responses, memorization and basic conditioning. At a higher level, learning involves adapting existing knowledge or skill to a new task or environment. At the next level, learning becomes a complex process when principles are identified in a range of practices or actions when a series of isolated tasks have to be integrated or when the training deals with inter-personal skills. The most complex form of learning takes place when training is concerned with the values and attitudes of people and groups. This is not only the most complex area, it is also the most difficult and dangerous.

The learning curve

When planning and implementing training programmes account must be taken of the phenomenon known as the learning curve. This refers to the fact that it takes time for an inexperienced trainee to achieve a reasonable standard of skill in a task – this is usually called the 'experienced worker's standard' (EWS).

The standard learning curve is shown in Figure 29.2.

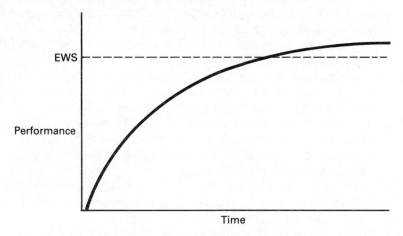

Figure 29.2 A standard learning curve

But rates of learning vary, depending upon the effectiveness of the training, the natural aptitude of the trainee and the latter's interest in learning. Both the time taken to achieve the experienced worker's standard and the speed with which learning takes place at different times will affect the shape of the curve, as shown in Figure 29.3.

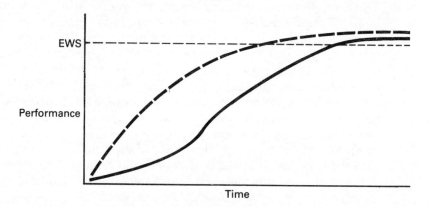

Figure 29.3 Different rates of learning

Learning is often stepped with one or more plateaux while further progress is halted. This may be because the trainees cannot continually increase their skills or speed of work and need a pause to consolidate what they have learnt. The existence of steps such as those shown in Figure 29.4 can be used when planning training to provide deliberate reinforcement periods when newly acquired skills are practised in order to achieve the expected standards. When planning a training module which describes the training required to acquire a particular skill it is often desirable to proceed step by step, taking one task at a time, re-inforcing it and then progressively adding other parts, consolidating at each stage. This is called the progressive parts method of training.

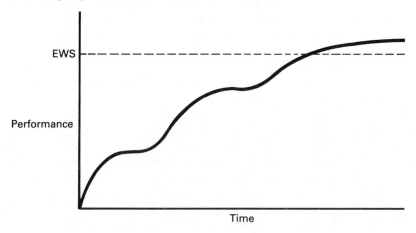

Figure 29.4 A stepped learning curve

Applying learning theory

Each of the ten conditions required for learning described above and the existence of the learning curve needs to be applied in planning training and ensuring that it is effective. Particular attention should be given to motivation, providing satisfaction from learning, making training an active process, and reinforcement. Training is about changing behaviour and all these factors are important if change for the better is to take place. Hence the importance of what has been termed the behaviour modelling approach to training.

Behaviour modelling

The behaviour modelling approach is based on the logic that training begins with the learning of new behaviour. Contrary to the opinion of many trainers, Campbell[1] has shown that attempts to change behaviour by verbal persuasion or logic do not always succeed. The main block to attitude change is the existence of defence mechanisms which come into action when customary beliefs or attitudes are threatened. Under press-ure, temporary changes in attitudes may result from training. But it may not be transferred to successful changes in behaviour on the job after training has been completed. And one of the main problems in training is achieving 'transfer'. It is too easy for trainees at the end of the course to be full of knowledge and enthusiasm following their classroom or training centre experiences. Unfortunately, it is even easier for them to come up against obstacles (sometimes self-induced) and indifference back at work which make it difficult to apply what they have learned. Action learning, do-it-yourself training and training on the job may help to overcome the problem, but off the job training must still take place, and where it involves changes in attitudes as well as behaviour, the technique of behaviour modelling has a part to play.

The training theory incorporated in behaviour modelling is based on reinforcement to obtain retention of learning and the transfer of behaviour. Reinforcement as a principle developed by behaviourists such as Skinner[2] is defined as any consequence which strengthens or increases a behaviour which it follows. From this basic concept Bandura[3] developed his social learning theory. Social learning is based on observing the behaviour of other people. In a sense it is vicarious reinforcement. A model is formed of desirable behaviour by observation and this is reinforced by practising the new behaviour with other members of the training group. Behaviour modelling procedures are quite different from many other traditional training approaches in that they do not rely on changing attitudes first and then hoping that behaviour will fall into line with these new attidudes. Instead, these procedures are aimed at directly changing behaviour without relying on the tactics of attitude change.

The foundation of behaviour modelling is the modelling of a set of desirable behaviour patterns live, on video tape or on film. Steps are taken to ensure that the trainee can retain sufficient knowledge of the model behaviour to be able to tackle the next stage, in which he practises or rehearses the desired behaviour. The final stage, which is the key to success, is to achieve social reinforcement by getting the trainee involved with other trainees in practising the new behaviour. This active and joint process enables trainees to observe the other participants and learn from their behaviour. To ease transfer from the classroom to the job, the model and the rehearsals are made to look as much like the job as possible.

Social modelling uses existing techniques of role playing and simulation but places these methods in the context of a much more structured attempt to ensure reinforcement from the behaviour of other trainees and to relate what is being learned off the job to the behaviour required on the job.

Identifying training needs

Training will not be effective unless it is based on an understanding of learning theory. But training must have a purpose and that purpose can only be defined if the training needs of the organization and the groups and individuals within it have been identified and analysed. Put like that, this seems a trite and obvious statement. Too much training in industry and commerce, however, has been training for training's sake. In effect, people have said: 'Training is a good thing, let there be training.' Perhaps the major contribution of the industrial training boards in Great Britain was to emphasize the importance of an analytical and systematic approach to training. And analysis starts at the beginning, with the study of training needs.

Training needs analysis – aims

The analysis of training needs aims to define the gap between what *is* happening and what *should* happen. This is what has to be filled by training (see Figure 29.5).

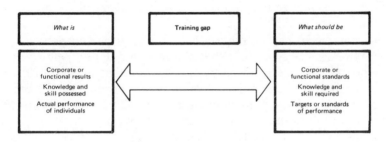

Figure 29.5 The training gap

The gap may consist of the difference between:

- how the company or a function within the company is performing and how it should perform;
- what people know and can do and what they should know and do;
- what people actually do and what they should do.

Training needs analysis – areas

Training needs should be analysed first for the company as a whole – corporate needs; secondly for departments, functions or occupations within the company – group needs; and thirdly for individual employees – individual needs. These three areas are inter-connected, as shown in Figure 29.6. The analysis of corporate needs will lead to the identification of training needs in different departments or occupations, while these in turn will indicate the training required for individual employees. The process also operates in reverse. As the needs of individual employees are analysed separately, common needs emerge which can be dealt with on a group basis. The sum of group and individual needs will define corporate needs, although there may be some super-ordinate training requirements which can only be related to the company as a whole – the whole training plan may be greater than the sum of its parts.

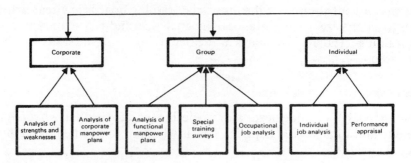

Figure 29.6 Training needs – areas and methods

Corporate needs can be determined by analysing company strengths and weaknesses – a procedure that should normally be part of the corporate planning process. These should be examined in each of the main activity areas: for example, development, production, marketing, finance, personnel, and management services. The aim should be to identify those problems that can be attributed to weaknesses or gaps in the knowledge, skill and capacities of managerial, technical, clerical and production staff. This is necessarily a broad brush approach. It may do no more than highlight areas within functions or departments where further study is required.

Corporate training needs should also be recorded by the manpower plan, which will indicate the numbers and types of people required in the future. In fact, the manpower planning process, as described in Chapter 10, should provide a major source of information on longer term training requirements.

Group needs can be identified by analysing functional or departmental manpower plans or by conducting special surveys using questionnaires and interviews, as discussed below. Job analysis can be used to determine the knowledge and skills required in specific jobs and this information can be supplemented by analysing the results obtained from the assessment of individual needs.

Individual needs can be assessed by the use of job analysis and by analysing the information obtained from performance reviews, as discussed below.

Training needs analysis – methods

Surveys to identify training needs can be conducted by questionnaire or by interview or preferably by a combination of these two methods. They may use job analysis on a comprehensive or sample basis, or they may rely upon broader questions designed to reveal problem areas. Training surveys may complement more analytical investigations by seeking to identify general training needs which might not be revealed, except with a great deal of effort, by looking at individual jobs. They may also provide a framework for the training plan and the more detailed studies that follow. Their aim should be to define manpower problems that can be solved by training. Training is always more relevant, and therefore more effective, if it ensures that trainees understand and take the action required to overcome the actual problems they meet when carrying out their work. Training should be problem-based and action-orientated.

The simplest method of conducting training surveys is to go round asking managers and supervisors what they think are the training priorities in their departments. The results obtained may be subjective but, as long as the surveys are comprehensive and the answers are analysed carefully, they will provide a useful starting point for more detailed analysis. They will also ensure that management and supervision feel involved from the beginning – they are more likely to help with job analysis and to support the training programme if they have been consulted about their requirements.

If a general survey is being carried out for the first time and in the absence of any other information, it should obtain details of:

- numbers and types of employees;
- future manpower requirements;
- any difficulties experienced or anticipated in obtaining adequate staff in sufficient quantities;
- any operating problems which can be attributed to shortages of manpower or poor quality performance;
- specific jobs or occupations where gaps in knowledge or lack of skill are producing unsatisfactory results;
- high labour turnover, absenteeism or grievance rates which may indicate that employees have not been properly trained or that additional training for managers and supervisors is required;
- present training arrangements and their adequacy;
- the priorities for improving or instituting training schemes.

Follow-up surveys, which aim to audit training arrangements, should concentrate on analysing the effectiveness of training schemes in solving management's problems, and on up-dating the information on manpower plans and training priorities.

The results of the training surveys should be used to define objectives, priorities and the likely pay-off of any proposed schemes.

Job analysis

Of all the stages in the systematic training process, job analysis is probably the most important. Good training is synonymous with relevant training. By defining the duties, responsibilities, tasks, knowledge and skills which make up a job – and specifying training accordingly – relevance must result.

Job analysis is the process of examining a job in order to identify its component parts and the circumstances in which it is performed. It can be a highly detailed and expensive procedure, or it can embrace no more than a broad study of duties and training requirements. The stages required in a detailed study are:

- *a broad analysis* of the requirements of the job and any special problems surrounding it as seen by the job holder, his superior and, possibly, his colleagues;
- an analysis of the particular skills needed to do the job;
- a detailed study of the responsibilities, duties and tasks carried out which forms the basis for a *job description*;
- an analysis of the knowledge and skills required by the job holder which forms the basis for a *job specification*;
- a description of the training requirements for the job – the *training specification*.

The broad job analysis

The aim of the broad analysis is to get an overall picture of the demands of the job and the problems job holders meet in doing their work which will provide a basis for the subsequent more detailed study. It should also place the job in its organizational setting and establish relationships with other jobs so that linked training schemes can be planned and priorities determined.

The broad analysis should provide information on:

- the overall purpose of the job – a brief summary of what the job holder does and how the job fits in with other functions;
- the main knowledge and skills required;
- how training is carried out at present – and how effective it is;
- the problems facing the job holders – in learning the job, in carrying it out, in relating to other people;
- any weaknesses in performance – general, or particular to individual employees;
- action required.

Skills analysis

Skills analysis starts from the broad job analysis. It goes into further detail, however, about what workers have to be able to do and the particular attributes they need to do it.

The techniques used in skills analysis are:

1. Job breakdown.
2. Manual skills analysis.
3. Task analysis.
4. Faults analysis.

Job breakdown

The job breakdown technique analyses a job into separate operations, processes or tasks which can be broken down into manageable parts for instructional purposes.

A job breakdown analysis is recorded in a standard format of three columns. These are:

1. *The stage column.* The different steps in the job are described – most semi-skilled jobs can easily be broken down into their constituent parts.
2. *The instruction column.* Against each step a note is made of how the task should be done. This, in effect, describes what has to be learned by the trainee.
3. *The key points column.* Against each step any special points such as quality standards or safety instructions are noted so that they can be emphasized to a trainee learning the job.

Manual skills analysis

Manual skills analysis is a technique developed by W D Seymour from work study. It isolates for instructional purposes the skills and knowledge employed by experienced workers performing tasks which require a high degree of manual dexterity. It is used to analyse short-cycle, repetitive operations such as assembly tasks and other similar factory work.

The hand, finger and other body movements of an experienced operative are observed and recorded in great detail as he/she carries out his/her work. The analysis concentrates on the tricky parts of the job which, while presenting no difficulty to the experienced operative, have to be analysed in depth before they can be taught to trainees. Not only are the hand movements recorded in great detail, but particulars are also noted of the cues (vision and other senses) which the operative absorbs when performing the tasks. Explanatory comments are added when necessary.

Task analysis

Task analysis is a systematic analysis of the behaviour required to carry out a task with a view to identifying areas of difficulty and the appropriate training techniques and learning aids necessary for successful instruction. It can be used for all types of jobs but is specifically relevant for clerical tasks.

The analytical approach used in task analysis is similar to those adopted in the job breakdown and manual skills analysis techniques. The results of the analysis are usually recorded in a standard format of four columns as follows:

1. *Task*. A brief description of each element.
2. *Level of importance*. The relative significance of each task to the successful performance of the whole job.
3. *Degree of difficulty*. The level of skill or knowledge required to perform each task.
4. *Training method*. The instructional techniques, practice and experience required.

Faults analysis

Faults analysis is the process of analysing the typical faults which occur when performing a task, especially the more costly faults. It is carried out when the incidence of faults is high.

A study is made of the job and, by questioning workers and supervisors, the most commonly occurring faults are identified. A faults specification is then produced which provides trainees with information on what faults can be made, how they can recognize them, what causes them, what effect they have, who is responsible for them, what action the trainees should take when a particular fault occurs, and how a fault can be prevented from recurring.

Benefits of skills analysis

Skills analysis is an essential element in systematic training. It is only by breaking down the job into its constituent parts and identifying what the worker needs to know and be able to do to complete each task satisfactorily that relevant training programmes can be prepared.

Skills analysis enables instruction to be based on the progressive part method in which the trainee is taught and practises each part until it can be done at target speed and at an acceptable level of quality. When two successive parts can be done separately in the target time they are practised jointly until the required speed is attained. Then a third part is added and so on, until the complete job has been learned. This is by far the best method of extending training in any job where there is more than one task to do, to the point at which trainees attain the training objective by achieving the experienced worker's level of output and quality.

Job description

The material for job descriptions can be assembled by questionnaires, interviews, observation, activity sampling or diary sheets. The choice of methods will depend on the type of job, the circumstances in which the information has to be obtained, and the amount of time and money available.

For training purposes the job description should contain information on:

- the job title;
- organization position – immediate superior and subordinates;
- the main role – the overall purpose of the job;
- the main activities and tasks carried out;
- the standard or measures of performance for each activity;
- the contacts made with other given departments;
- the limits of authority given to the job holder.

Job specification

A job specification is a product of job analysis. It breaks down the broad duties contained in the job description into the detailed tasks that must be carried out. It then sets out the characteristics that the worker should have in order to perform these tasks successfully. These characeristics are:

- *Knowledge* – what the worker needs to know. It may be professional, technical or commercial knowledge; or it may be about the commercial, economic or market environment, the machines to be operated, the materials or equipment to be used or the procedures to be followed, the customers, clients, colleagues and subordinates he or she is in contact with and the factors that affect their behaviour; or it may refer to the problems that will occur and how they should be dealt with.
- *Skills* – what the worker needs to be able to do if results are to be achieved and knowledge is to be used effectively. Skills are built gradually by repeated training or other experience. They may be manual, intellectual or mental, perceptual or social.
- *Attitudes* – the disposition to behave or to perform in a way which is in accordance with the requirements of the work.

Training specification

The training specification is a detailed statement of what the trainee needs to learn based on a comparison between the job specification and the trainee's present level of performance. For the inexperienced recruits, the job specification is, in effect, the training specification, although it might have to be presented in a different form to be of use as the base of a training programme. For more experienced people, the training specification should describe what training is required to fill the gaps between what they should know and do know, and between what they should do and can do.

General training specifications for new starters or for workers transferred to new jobs normally assume no previous knowledge or experience. Individual training programmes would then have to be modified to take account of existing skills.

Planning training programmes

Training plans derive directly from the process of analysis that has just been described. The steps required are as follows:

1. Summarize training needs.
2. Formulate training policies.
3. Decide where training should take place.
4. Decide on the training techniques to be used.
5. Set objectives.
6. Determine methods of evaluating training.

Summarizing training needs

The summary of training needs should establish the main areas and priorities for training. The summary should be supported by the detailed training specifications for each occupation.

Where large numbers of apprentices or other trainees are to be trained, the summary should show the numbers to be trained and the expected output of the training schemes. Similarly, an indication should be given of the numbers to be trained in any of the more specialized areas, including supervisor and management training. The summary may list individual requirements for training or present them on a departmental or functional basis.

The overall summary should set out for each category of employee:

● the number employed at present;
● the number of those requiring training;
● the number of new entrants expected;
● training required (cross referenced to detailed training specifications);
● a broad indication of priorities.

Training policies

Training policies should be developed which will provide guidelines on the detailed planning of training by defining the scope and aims of the training schemes, the basis of training plans, the procedure for developing formal training schemes, and methods of evaluating and controlling training.

Where should training take place?

There are three places where training can take place: in company, on the job, off the job; and external, off the job. Each has its uses, its advantages and disadvantages.

In company, on the job
In company, on the job training may consist of teaching or coaching by

managers, supervisors or trainers at the desk or at the bench. It may also consist of individual or group assignments and projects. It is the only way to develop and practise managerial, supervisory, technical, selling, manual, and clerical skills. It has the advantage of actuality and immediacy. The trainee works, learns and develops expertise at the same time. Theory is put into practice immediately and its relevance is obvious. The disadvantages are that the effectiveness of the learning is strongly influenced by the quality of the guidance and coaching provided on the job. Many managers and supervisors are unskilled at training and disinclined to carry it out or to encourage it. Relying on fellow employees – 'sit by me' or 'sitting by Nellie' training – has equally obvious disadvantages. The instruction may be inadequate and the training may perpetuate bad habits. Above all, the trainee may be distracted by the environment and find it difficult to acquire the basic skills quickly.

In company, off the job
In company, off the job training can take place on special courses or in training areas or centres which have been specially equipped and staffed for training. It is the best way to acquire advanced manual and clerical skills and to learn about company procedures and products. It helps to increase the identification of the trainee with the company as a whole, and the use of systematic training techniques, special equipment and trained trainers means that the basic skills and knowledge can be acquired quickly and often economically. The main disadvantage arises when trainees are transferred from the training course to a job to apply their knowledge and skills in practice. On a full-time manual skills course in a training centre, they will have been sheltered from the realities of the rough and tumble in most workshops, especially in batch production factories. At manager and supervisor level the problem of transferring from the 'training situation' to 'real life' may be even more difficult.

External training
External training is useful for the development of managerial, supervisory, technical and social knowledge and skills, especially if the courses cover standard theory and practice which can easily be translated from the general to the particular. External training should be able to supply the quality of instruction which it might be uneconomic to provide from internal resources. It can be used to implant highly specialized knowledge or advanced skills and has the added advantage of broadening the horizons of those exposed to it. The main disadvantage is that of transferring learning into practice – even more acute with external courses. However effective the training, the knowledge and skills acquired may be quickly dissipated unless they are used immediately. It may also be difficult to select relevant courses from the bewildering variety available.

The art of designing training programmes is to select the right blend of on the job and off the job training. There are no rules for doing this. Each programme has to be considered individually. But the emphasis should always be towards putting learning into practice and, therefore, first consideration has to be given to what happens on the job. Off the job courses, whether internal or external, should be regarded as complementary and supplementary activities which may stimulate learning or provide knowledge and skills that cannot be obtained internally; but they are always subsidiary to what an individual does and learns in his normal place of work.

Training techniques

There are many training techniques, and the choice will depend on the training situation in which it is to be deployed. The techniques available are analysed in Appendix K.

Setting objectives

It is essential to define the objectives of the training programme. Objectives can be defined as 'criterion behaviour', ie the standards or changes of behaviour *on the job* to be achieved if training is to be regarded as successful. This should be a definition of what the trainee will be able to *do* when he goes back to work on completing the course, in other words, terminal behaviour. Transfer of training is what counts and behaviour on the job is what matters. Training objectives are best expressed as follows:

> On completing the training (or this part of the course) the trainee will be able to . . . (read a balance sheet, program a micro-computer, operate a word processor, work to a high degree of accuracy, etc.).

Evaluation of training

It is at the planning stage that the basis upon which each category of training is to be evaluated should be determined. At the same time, it is necessary to consider how the information required to evaluate courses should be obtained and analysed.

The process of evaluating training has been defined by Hamblin as: 'Any attempt to obtain information (feedback) on the effects of a training programme, and to assess the value of the training in the light of that information.'[4] Evaluation leads to control which means deciding whether or not the training was worthwhile (preferably in cost/benefit terms) and what improvements are required to make it even more cost-effective.

Evaluation is an integral feature of training. In its crudest form it is the comparison of objectives (criterion behaviour) with effects (terminal behaviour) to answer the question of how far training has achieved its purpose. The setting of objectives and the establishment of methods of measuring results are, or should be, an essential part of the planning stage of any training programme.

Evaluation is difficult because it is often hard to set measurable objectives and even harder to collect the information on the results or to decide on the level at which the evaluation should be made.

Evaluation levels

Hamblin,[4] has suggested that there are five levels at which evaluation can take place:

1. *Reactions.* The reactions of trainees to the training experience itself: how useful or even how enjoyable they feel the training is, what they think of individual sessions and speakers, what they would like put in or taken out, and so on.
2. *Learning.* Evaluation at the learning level requires the measurement of what trainees have learned as a result of their training – the new knowledge and skills they have acquired or the changes in attitude that have taken place. This is the terminal behaviour that occurs immediately after the training has finished.
3. *Job behaviour.* At this level, evaluation attempts to measure the extent to which trainees have applied their learning on the job. This constitutes an assessment of the amount of transfer of learning that has taken place from an off the job training course to the job itself. If the training is carried out on the job there should be little difference between learning and job behaviour.
4. *Organization.* Evaluation at this level attempts to measure the effect of changes in the job behaviour of trainees on the functioning of the organization in which they are employed. The measurement might be in such terms as improvements in output, productivity, quality, morale (if that can be measured), contribution, or sales turnover. In effect, the question answered by this type of evaluation is not simply what behavioural changes have taken place, but what good have those changes been for the unit or department in which the employee works.
5. *Ultimate value.* This is a measure of how the organization as a whole has benefited from the training in terms of greater profitability, survival or growth. But it might also be defined in terms of the trainee's personal goals rather than those of the organization which sponsored him. This could be a legitimate company goal for training if it is believed that what is good for the individual is good for the organization, or if the company feels that it has a social duty to educate and train its employees to the maximum of their capacity. Fundamentally, however, evaluation at this level is related to the criteria by which the organization

judges its efficiency and its success or failure. The difficulty is assessing how far training has contributed to the ultimate results.

As Hamblin points out, the five levels are links in a chain: training leads to reactions, which lead to learning, which leads to changes in job behaviour, which lead to changes in the organization, which lead to changes in the achievement of ultimate goals. But the chain can be snapped at any link. A trainee can react favourably to a course – he can 'enjoy it' – but learn nothing. He can learn something, but he cannot, or will not, or is not allowed to, apply it. He applies it, but it does no good within his own area. It does some good in his function, but does not further the objectives of the organization.

Evaluation can start at any level. Ideally, some people might say, it starts and finishes at levels four and five; organizational and ultimate value. This is all that really matters, they claim. But it may be difficult, if not impossible, to measure the effect of training in these respects. In any case, it may be desirable to work backwards to find out what went wrong at earlier levels if the ultimate benefits arising from training are inadequate.

Sources of information

The sources of information for training evaluation as listed by Easterby-Smith[5] are given below.

Observation
Trainers should be able to observe who is contributing and who is not. They gain fairly clear impressions of how much is being absorbed and how interested the trainees are in learning by noting reactions to the trainer and reactions between themselves.

Observations can be carried out more analytically by using the Bales interaction process analysis categories (Table 29.1) to classify statements made by trainees in group discussions.

Easterby-Smith notes that one feature which has become increasingly common in management training is the feedback of interaction analysis to trainees as part of the process of encouraging them to try out new forms of behaviour. He gives as an example (Table 29.2) a checklist of types of interaction in a lecture which members of the audience are asked to complete.

Most training programmes will generate written reports and comments and these can be collected and used for evaluation purposes by the trainer.

Informants
The judgements of individuals who have attended the course, qualified observers, the managers of trainees and senior managers in general are an

Positive socio- emotional	1.	Shows solidarity
	2.	Shows tension release (jokes, laughs)
	3.	Agrees (understands, complies)
Gives task help	4.	Gives suggestion (direction)
	5.	Gives opinion (analysis, feelings)
	6.	Gives orientation (information, classification)
Requests task help	7.	Asks for orientation
	8.	Asks for opinion
	9.	Asks for suggestion
Negative socio- emotional	10.	Disagrees
	11.	Shows tension
	12.	Shows antagonism

Table 29.1 *Bales interaction process analysis categories*

Try to recall specific examples from the lecture to illustrate some of the following:

1 A clear explanation of a point – how was this done; what use was made of examples/illustrations?

2 An explanation of a point – how was this done; what use was made of examples/illustrations?

3 Summarizing something in the middle of the lecture before moving on to the next point.

4 Use of pauses and/or silence.

5 Bodily activity: one time when (s)he was very active; another time when (s)he was very still.

6 Variations in tempo and themes.

7 Other approaches to maintaining interest and attention: jokes, stories, games, etc.

8 An attempt to gain involvement from the audience. How did (s)he do it?

Table 29.2 *Observational checklist for delivery/ interaction during a lecture*

(Source: Easterby-Smith, M *Evaluation of Management Education, Training and Development.* Gower, 1986)

obvious and important source of material for observations. But these judgements are likely to be subjective and should not be relied upon entirely.

Data collection methods

The main data collection methods are:

Objective tests

Tests such as the Myers-Briggs or 16-PF personality tests can be used in the early diagnostic stages of a course to identify the personality traits of participants so that the training and, later, the evaluation can be adjusted to the training needs of those attending the course. This type of test should not, however, be used to measure before and after personality traits. A good test should produce similar results when administered on separate occasions to the same people. The training course should not therefore affect test performance; which only goes to show that training not only should not but also cannot change personalities (it can only modify attitudes and get people to reconsider and possibly change their values).

Attitude scales

Attitudes are enduring systems of beliefs about an object, feelings about the object, and tendencies to want to take action with respect to the object. An attitude scale will take a range of subjects covered in a training session or course, one of which could be delegation, and ask trainees to answer a series of *yes* or *no* questions about them, for example:

Can you delegate responsibility?   Yes   No

Attitude scales can be administered before and after the training session and used not only to evaluate how much learning has taken place but also to reinforce points that do not seem to have got across. Evaluation is only worthwhile if it leads to action which supplements, improves or reinforces learning or indicates where modifications are needed to training methods.

Rating scales

A rating scale can be used to evaluate reactions to:

1. The *inputs* to the course in the form of subject matter.
2. The *outputs* to the course in the form of what the trainee has learnt.
3. The *processes* of the course in the form of the effectiveness of the training.
4. The *impact* of the course in the form of what trainees are now going to do which they did not do before.
5. The *overall effectiveness* of the course – the extent to which trainees felt it had achieved its objectives.
6. The *administration* of the course.

A typical rating question could be:

The last session was:

Relevant to my work 1   2   3   4   5   6   7   Irrelevant to my work

Attainment tests

Attainment tests focus on the outcomes of training in the shape of increases in knowledge or skills. They can be administered before and after the course and often take the form of multiple choice questions as in Table 29.3.

Which of the following factors is likely to have the most effect on an individual's performance at work:

(a) the value of the rewards for improved performance (eg promotion, increased pay, higher status);

(b) the extent to which he feels that the reward will be related to the effort he puts into the work;

(c) his ability to do the work;

(d) the extent to which he understands and accepts his responsibilities?

Table 29.3 *A multiple choice question*

Questionnaires

End-of-course questionnaires typically ask such questions as:

- What specific changes would you suggest to improve this course?
- Were there any particular high or low points on this course and what do you think caused them?
- What was the most significant thing you learnt on this course and how did you learn it?
- What specific action(s) will you take following this course on return to work?

Questionnaires get data quickly and cheaply, but they can be subjective and partial.

Interviews

A two-way exchange of information about the impact of a course can be the most effective method of evaluation. An interview can be structured or open – the results of the former may be more consistent, while the latter may be more revealing. In any interview, whether or not it is structured, interviewers will get most out of it if they:

- know what they want to find out;
- ask the right questions;
- give feedback to the person being interviewed;
- phrase questions in such a way that they encourage the informant to open up, rather than simply answering 'yes' or 'no'.

Conducting training programmes

The only general rule for conducting training programmes is that the courses should continually be monitored to ensure that they are proceeding according to plan and within the agreed budget. This is the job of the head of training who should be required to report on progress against plan at regular intervals.

There are, however, a number of considerations which affect the conduct of training for specific occupations, and those concerning managers and supervisors (these considered jointly because the basic principles are similar), sales staff, craftsmen and clerical staff are discussed briefly below. Industrial relations training is dealt with in Chapter 32 and communications training in Chapter 34.

Management and supervisory training

As the old saying goes, managers learn to manage by managing under the guidance of a good manager. The emphasis should therefore always be towards on the job training, by planned experience, coaching or assignments. This can be supplemented – but never replaced – by off the job training to extend knowledge, fill in gaps, develop skills or modify attitudes.

In his report on the experienced manager, Alastair Mant[6] said, on the basis of extensive research, that:

- the majority of managers do not benefit greatly from external management courses;
- managers benefit more from well designed and well conducted internal courses variously termed 'in-company', 'in-plant' or 'in-house', which are linked to the job and involve problem-orientated project work;
- the organization and not the individual should be regarded as the main consumer of management training, the aim of which is to secure better results for the company.

Professor Revans[7] has taken the same standpoint consistently over many years in developing his concept of 'action learning'. Action learning is based on the conviction that, valuable though specialist knowledge may be as a tool, the most effective resources available to those who want to improve performance are their own talents and experience. Action learning aims to help individuals and groups to recognize and develop these natural resources and put them to good use. It is described in more detail in Appendix K.

Project training is a particularly valuable method of providing managers and supervisors with new experience and the opportunity to extend their knowledge over a wider range of problems and to exercise their analytical skills in solving them.

Training courses

Courses should be used judicially. They can provide:

- concentrated knowledge;
- an opportunity to acquire new skills or to develop and practice existing skills;
- a framework for analysing past experience;
- the chance to reflect on ways in which better use can be made of future experience;
- a means of having new ideas accepted and changing attitudes through group activities not available on the job.

Internal courses

An important spin-off from internal courses, especially resident ones, is that the participants get to know more about their company and their colleagues. Their sense of identification with the organization is thereby increased.

The essential characteristics of an effective formal internal course are threefold. First, it should be problem-based. It must help participants to overcome the actual problems that have been identified as those most likely to prevent good performance. Secondly, it should be action-orientated. It must result in positive action which produces improvements in performance. The effectiveness of the course is primarily measured by the extent to which the desired action has resulted from it. Thirdly, senior management should be involved in the course, thus demonstrating their support of the manager or supervisor and their recognition of his responsibilities and importance.

It goes without saying that the course should be highly participative, making the maximum use of discussion, case studies and group exercises. Throughout the programme participants should be compelled to list the action points to which they will give attention when they return to their jobs. The course may aim to impart knowledge, but the emphasis should be on the skills required to make effective use of the knowledge the participants have or acquire on the course.

External courses

External general management courses should be used with caution. They can broaden the knowledge and skills of those attending and they can serve as a sort of accolade to demonstrate that someone has 'arrived' or is about to 'arrive'. But the problem of transferring learning back to work can be a formidable one.

The purpose of an external general management course should be to develop the natural ability of managers and to build upon their experience by helping them to:

- think more clearly and critically about all aspects of their jobs;

- understand more about the management techniques that are available so that they can appreciate the ways in which these techniques overlap and are inter-dependent and how they can be used to get results;
- obtain a broader understanding of business and organizational problems, thus overcoming any tendency towards insularity or a narrow departmental viewpoint.

Continuity

Whatever form of training is used, management and supervisory training should be seen as a continuous process. One of the greatest fallacies of the typical one-week internal management course, as described above, is that this is sufficient. This applies equally to longer external courses. The management and supervisory training programme should therefore be established as a continuing activity at all levels of management to avoid the dissipation of interest and enthusiasm that follows an isolated course, and to promote the progressive development of managerial and supervisory skills as new experiences are encountered and as conditions change.

Sales training

The aim of sales training should be to equip the salesman with the knowledge, skills, attitudes and habits required to meet or exceed his sales targets.

The first requirement is knowledge of the company and its products, customers, competitors and sales administration procedures.

Secondly, he has to acquire and develop skills: prospecting, making the approach, making presentations, handling objections, closing the sale, and handling complaints. Perhaps the most important skill to be developed, however, is analytical ability. The salesman must be taught how to analyse his product into its technical characteristics and, most important, its selling points – those aspects of the product that are likely to appeal to particular customers. He must also be taught how to analyse his customers from the point of view of their buying habits and the features of the product that are most likely to appeal to them. In addition, he must be able to analyse himself – his own strengths and weaknesses as a salesman so that he can exploit his strengths and overcome his weaknesses.

Thirdly, training should aim to develop attitudes: of loyalty to the company and belief in its products, and of understanding and tolerance with regard to potential and existing customers. The salesman has to believe in himself, he must be given confidence and provided with the motivation to go out and sell – a task which requires courage, determination and persistence.

The fourth requirement is to develop sound work habits: organizing time, planning activities, following up leads, maintaining records and submitting reports.

Sales training, like any other form of training, should be based on an analysis of the salesman's job and the problems he is likely to meet. The training programme should be continuous; there can never be a time in any salesman's career when he would not benefit from training. Use should be made of classroom training to provide basic knowledge and an opportunity to practise skills. But most training should be carried out on the job by sales managers or supervisors who can demonstrate sales techniques and observe and comment on the efforts of the salesman.

Classroom training should be highly participative and involve the trainees in practising every aspect of selling. The members of the course should be made to carry out detailed analyses of the selling points of the company's products in comparison with those of competitors. They should also be asked to work out for themselves the sort of sales resistance they will meet and how they should handle objections. Above all, role playing exercises should be used to give each trainee experience in every aspect of selling, and closed circuit television is invaluable as a training aid for this type of exercise. Sales training films are helpful, but they should not be relied upon too much. If one of the main aims of a classroom course is to increase the identification of the salesman with the company and its products, then it is essential for the message to be given by company sales executives and sales training managers.

Field training should be complementary to classroom training. It should be carefully programmed so that area or district sales managers know exactly what sort of training every salesman under their control should be receiving at any point in time. Field sales managers and supervisors therefore need to be thoroughly trained themselves in coaching techniques and in running local sales meetings.

The field training programme should consist of an appropriate mix of live demonstrations with customers, of observations of the salesman at work by the manager followed immediately by 'kerbside' coaching sessions, and of more formal off the job counselling or training sessions. The latter may be restricted to the manager and an individual salesman, or may consist of sales meetings which follow a programme of sales topics laid down by headquarters and supplemented by sessions dealing with local problems. It is essential for the field sales training programme to be monitored from headquarters by the sales training manager. Some field managers recognize the importance of training and are good at it. Others neglect it to pursue sales, or are not particularly effective trainers. These individuals need encouragement, stimulation and help.

Selling is a highly personal business and it is therefore important to recognize and meet individual training needs. A performance review system is required for this purpose which focuses attention on the results achieved and the areas where performance needs to be improved by training to obtain better results. The scheme should be linked to informal counselling and coaching sessions as well as more formal training activities.

Technical and skill or craft training

Technical and skill or craft training schemes can be divided into four main types:

Graduate – post-graduate training usually lasting two years, leading to a professional qualification.

Student – a course of education and practical training leading to a degree or some other qualification as a technologist. In the UK the course may include 'block' release to college for periods of, say, four weeks. Or, more commonly, it is a 'thin sandwich' – periods of up to six months in college and at the works, or a 'thick sandwich' – one year's basic training, three or four years at university and one year's post-graduate training.

Technician – a course of education and training which could last up to three or four years leading to employment as a technician or draughtsman and an appropriate technician's qualification.

Skill or craft – a course lasting up to three or four years depending on the level of skill that has to be attained and often leading to a craft certificate or other record of achievement.

At one time such training schemes were always called apprenticeships and the indenture agreement laid down a fixed period of training. But it did not specify what training should take place or indicate what standards had been achieved.

The old apprenticeship agreement is being replaced by the training agreement. This stipulates the basic and general training, and the skill modules that have to be completed to satisfactory standards before the agreement can be discharged. A skill module will be based on skills analysis and will define what training is required to achieve 'experienced worker's standard' in a particular skill or task. It will set out the exercises to be carried out and how attainments should be tested. The training agreement may also specify the part-time period of further education that has to be completed.

Phases of training

In the major craft industries – engineering, construction and shipbuilding – the practical training for all types of trainees or apprentices consists of the following three phases:

1. *Basic Training* – in which the trainee receives training in basic skills in a basic training workshop. This training should consist of a series of modules such as those drawn up by the Engineering Industry Training Board in Great Britain. Clearly, the standard modules should be chosen on the basis of an analysis of the knowledge and skills required, and additional modules should be

specially developed if necessary. A basic course for an engineering craft apprentice may last a full year, by which time he should be fully equipped with all the basic skills.

Each module should have defined objectives – criterion behaviour. There should also be predetermined methods of measuring terminal behaviour by tests or observations after the module has been completed.

The training should be given by trained instructors in a space set aside for training.

2. *General training* – in which the trainee is given experience in a number of different shops, processes or operations to consolidate his training. If it is already decided that he is to become, say, a tool room turner, he would be given an extended period of familiarization in the tool room. But he would also spend some time in related areas; for example, the jig and tool drawing office, the foundry, the machine shop and various fitting and assembly shops.

Technician, student and graduate trainees in engineering would also spend a general period of training 'round the shops' but would then move into the engineering, design or development departments, depending on their speciality. A production specialist, for example, would spend time in the planning, jig and tool, production control, work study, rate fixing and quality control departments.

During the period, graduate and student trainees should be given special projects which will test their understanding of the design, development, engineering and manufacturing functions. Craft and technician trainees may return to the training school for advanced skill courses in machine operation, draughting or any other speciality.

The biggest danger to avoid in this period of general training is that trainees aimlessly wander from shop to shop and find themselves relegated to a tedious job out of harm's way because no one wants to know about them. The burr bench in a machine shop is a favourite dumping ground for unwanted trainees. To avoid this danger, it is essential to have a syllabus of training in every workshop which is based on an analysis of knowledge and skill requirements. There should be one trained supervisor responsible for training in each workshop and in a large department, such as a machine shop, there may be more than one full-time training supervisor. The training department should also monitor the progress of trainees carefully to ensure that they are following the syllabus and are acquiring the knowledge and skill they need. In a large organization there may be one or more full-time supervisors who spend all their time in the shops chasing shop supervisors and checking on the progress of trainees.

The trainees themselves should know what they are expected to learn at each stage so that they can request a move if they feel they are wasting their time or are not covering the syllabus. They should also be required to keep log-books to record what they have done. These should be seen regularly by their training officer as a check on their progress.

3. *Final training* – in which trainees settle down in the department of choice, or the department for which best fitted. During this period he will probably be doing the same work as experienced craftsmen, technicians or technologists. The aim is to ensure that he is equipped to apply his learning in normal working conditions and at the pace and level of quality expected from a fully experienced and competent individual.

Throughout these three stages the training department has to work closely with the educationists to ensure that, so far as possible, the theory is complementary to the practice.

The length of the period of training at each stage will obviously depend on the level and complexity of the knowledge and skills that have to be acquired and on the type of apprenticeship. Traditional union agreements may lay down the length of training in some cases. The experience of any company conducting training along the lines described above, however, has shown that if the basic training is sufficiently comprehensive and the period of experience is adequately planned and monitored, the length of time to reach a fully experienced worker's standard may be considerably less than the traditional period.

Training for other skilled crafts should follow the same pattern of basic training: familiarization with the application of different aspects of the craft, and final consolidation of knowledge and skills. The basic training period, however, may not be so elaborate and may well be carried out in a local technical college which is better equipped to provide the skilled instruction required.

Integrating education and training
One of the main problems faced in running craft and technical training schemes is that of integrating education and training: that is, ensuring that the theoretical instruction provided by a university, polytechnic or technical college is of practical use. This particularly applies to graduate, student and technician.

It is, of course, impossible to ensure that all college instruction is directly relevant. And it would be undesirable to make the attempt. The aim of technical education should be to train the mind of the apprentice and to equip him with understanding of general principles and concepts which he can put to use. But some parts of the course will deal with applications, and it is in these areas that integration is desirable.

Integration can be achieved by maintaining good liaison with the college, which should have industrial liaison officers for this purpose. It is also a good idea to keep in touch with lecturers and instructors and give them a chance to look at the work carried out by apprentices in the company.

Members of the training department should meet regularly to discuss progress in their studies and how they can make the best use of what they have learned. In some companies it may be helpful to have qualified engineers in the design, development, production engineering and manufacturing departments to act as tutors for groups of graduates, students or technicians. They can arrange individual or collective meetings regularly to discuss practical applications and to provide advice on the course of studies.

Clerical training

Clerical training is the most neglected form of training. Perhaps this is because both line and training managers often despise or at least underestimate the skill content of most clerical work. This feeling has been intensified because of the tendency of O & M analysts to de-skill clerical jobs.

But inefficiency in clerical work can be an important factor in reducing the efficiency of the organization as a whole. A company cannot afford to neglect training in clerical skills and departmental procedures.

Clerical training should be divided into three areas: basic training, further education, and continuation training. During the basic training stage, when the clerk is being taught how to carry out his or her first job, a foundation is being laid for the employee's career. During this period, young clerks and trainees should obtain background knowledge of the company and acquire the basic knowledge and skills they need.

Clerical trainees should be encouraged to follow a further course of studies leading to a professional or commercial qualification. The course of studies should be decided by agreement between the employee, his departmental manager and the training department.

The third area is continuation training. Training and development should be a continuous process. When each trainee has completed his basic training programme and, preferably, has obtained a qualification, his abilities should be developed by providing broader experience within the company and by short technical courses. The aim at this stage should be to ensure that staff with potential are not allowed to stagnate within a department and that they are prepared for greater responsibility.

References

1. Campbell, J P 'Personnel Training and Development', *Annual Review of Psychology* Palo Alto, California, 1971.

2. Skinner, B F *Science and Human Behaviour* Free Press, New York, 1953.
3. Bandura, A *Social Learning Theory* Prentice-Hall, Englewood Cliffs, NJ, 1977.
4. Hamblin, A C *Evaluation and Control of Training* McGraw-Hill, Maidenhead, 1974.
5. Easterby-Smith, M *Evaluation of Management Education, Training and Development* Gower, London, 1986.
6. Mant, A *The Experienced Manager* British Institute of Management, 1970.
7. Revans, R W *Developing Effective Managers* Longman, Harlow, 1971.

Chapter 30
Management Development

What is management development?

Management development is a systematic process which aims to ensure that the organization has the effective managers it requires to meet its present and future needs. It is concerned with improving the performance of existing managers, giving them opportunities for growth and development, and ensuring, so far as possible, that management succession within the organization is provided for.

The objectives of a typical management development programme are to improve the financial performance and long-term growth of the company by:

- improving the performance of managers by seeing that they are clearly informed of their responsibilities and by agreeing with them specific key objectives against which their performance will be regularly assessed;
- identifying managers with further potential and ensuring that they receive the required development, training and experience to equip them for more senior posts within their own locations and divisions within the company;
- assisting chief executives and managers throughout the company to provide adequate succession and to create a system whereby this is kept under regular review.

Role of the organization

The traditional view is that the organization need not concern itself with management development. The natural process of selection and the pressure of competition will ensure the survival of the fittest. Managers, in fact, are born not made. Cream rises to the top (but then so does scum).

The reaction to this can be summed up in John Humble's phrase, 'programmitis and crown princes'.[1] Management development is seen mainly as a mechanical process using management inventories, multi-coloured replacement charts, 'Cook's tours' for newly recruited graduates, detailed job rotation programmes, elaborate points schemes to appraise personal characteristics, and endless series of formal courses.

The true role of the organization in management development lies somewhere between these two extremes. On the one hand, it is not enough, in conditions of rapid growth (when they exist) and change, to leave everything to chance – to trial and error. On the other hand, elaborate management development programmes cannot successfully be imposed on the organization. Because, as Drucker says: 'Development is always self-development. Nothing could be more absurd than for the enterprise to assume responsibility for the development of a man. The responsibility rests with the individual, his abilities, his efforts.'[2] But he goes on to say:

> Every manager in a business has the opportunity to encourage individual self-development or to stifle it, to direct it or to misdirect it. He should be specifically assigned the responsibility for helping all men working with him to focus, direct and apply their self-development efforts productively. And every company can provide systematic development challenges to its managers.

Executive ability is eventually something which the individual must develop for himself on the job. But he will do this much better if he is given encouragement, guidance and opportunities by his company and his manager. In Douglas McGregor's phrase: managers are grown – they are neither born nor made. The role of the company is to provide conditions favourable to faster growth. And these conditions are very much part of the environment and organization climate of the company and the management style of the chief executive who has the ultimate responsibility for management development. As McGregor wrote:

> The job environment of the individual is the most important variable affecting his development. Unless that environment is conducive to his growth, none of the other things we do to him or for him will be effective. This is why the 'agricultural' approach to management development is preferable to the 'manufacturing' approach. The latter leads, among other things, to the unrealistic expectation that we can create and develop managers in the classroom.[3]

Responsibility for management development

Management development is not a separate activity to be handed over to a specialist and forgotten or ignored. The success of a management development programme depends upon the degree to which all levels of management are committed to it. The development of subordinates must be recognized as a natural and essential part of any manager's job. But the lead must come from the top.

The approach to management development

Management development should be regarded as a range of related activities rather than an all-embracing programme. The use of the word 'programme' to describe the process smacks too much of a mechanistic approach.

This does not imply that some systematization is not necessary First, because many managers have to operate in more or less routine situations and have to be developed accordingly; and secondly, because organizations will not continue to thrive if they simply react to events. There must be an understanding of the approaches that can be used to develop managers and means of assessing the existing managerial resources and how they measure to the needs of the enterprise. And plans must be made for the development of those resources by selecting the best of the methods available. But this should not be seen as a 'programme' consisting of a comprehensive, highly integrated and rigidly applied range of management training and development techniques.

The management development activities required will depend on the organization: its technology, its environment and its philosophy. A bureaucratic, mechanistic type of organization, such as a large government department, a nationalized industry, a major insurance firm or a large process manufacturing company, will be inclined to adopt the programmed routine approach, complete with a wide range of courses, inventories, replacement charts, career plans and management by objectives based review systems. An innovative and organic type of organization may rightly dispense with all these mechanisms. Its approach should be to provide its managers with the opportunities, challenge and guidance they require, relying mainly on seizing the chance to give people extra responsibilities, and ensuring that they receive the coaching and encouragement they need. There may be no replacement charts, inventories or formal appraisal schemes, but people know how they stand, where they can go and how to get there.

Management development activities

Management development activities can be divided into seven areas; the first five of which are discussed in this chapter (areas 6 and 7 are dealt with in Chapter 31).

1. Organization review.
2. Manpower review.
3. Performance review.
4. Management by objectives.
5. Training.

6. Succession planning.
7. Career planning.

These activities are interrelated, as shown in Figure 30.1 and, in this sense, it would be possible to talk about a 'programme' of management development where the process consists of education and training, career planning and succession planning activities which are derived from the outcome of the organization, manpower and performance reviews.

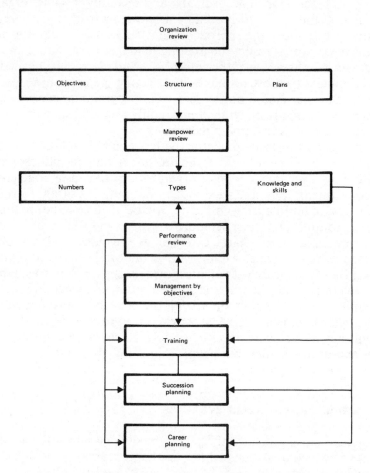

Figure 30.1 The process of management development

Organization review

Management development is closely related to organization development, which focuses attention on people and the social system in which they work – individuals, working groups and the relationships between them – and uses various educational activities which may aim primarily to develop teamwork but also provide training for the individuals concerned. Management development appears to focus attention more on individuals than on groups and relationships, but it must do this within the context of the needs of the organization as a whole.

Management development activities should therefore be founded upon a review of the objectives, plans and structure of the organization and the implications of present weaknesses and future demands on managerial requirements.

Manpower review

The organization review leads naturally into a review of manpower resources. This is the manpower planning aspect of management development and, where the circumstances permit, it implies an analysis of the present resources and future requirements in terms of numbers, types and knowledge and skills. This is a general review, and individual and management succession needs would be analysed separately, although performance reviews will provide information on strengths and weaknesses that affect the overall plan.

It may be impossible to prepare precise forecasts of future requirements, but it is still desirable to give some thought to the general considerations that will affect education and training, career planning and succession planning.

Performance review

Performance review systems are used to identify development needs by highlighting strengths and weaknesses and, so far as this is possible, potential for promotion. They are also a basis for the counselling and coaching activities which should form the most important part of an individual's development within a company. The general approaches available are considered in Chapter 28 but a particular approach – management by objectives – which incorporates a performance review element as well as a number of other features concerned with management development is discussed below.

Management by objectives

Management by objectives has in some quarters been regarded as the key activity in a management development programme. Perhaps it has been oversold as the universal panacea for all management development problems, but it can have a part to play in an integrated programme and its basic philosophy is relevant to anyone concerned with the management of people.

Management by objectives has been defined by John Humble as 'A dynamic system which seeks to integrate the company's need to clarify and achieve its profit and growth goals with the manager's need to contribute and develop himself. It is a demanding and rewarding style of managing a business.'[4]

Management by objectives is essentially a method of managing organizations and people and of improving the performance of managers. The basic processes are:

- Subordinates agree with the managers the objectives of their job – expressed as targets or standards of performance for each key result area. The individual objectives are in line with unit and organizational objectives, and are defined in a way which emphasizes the contribution they make to achieving departmental and corporate plans. So far as possible, the objectives are quantified, and 'job improvement' plans (in Humble's phrase) are jointly developed to indicate what the manager should contribute to the unit's and the company's plans for better performance.
- Performance is reviewed jointly by the manager and the subordinate to compare results with the defined objectives and standards.
- The manager and subordinate agree where improvements are required and how better results can be achieved and, as necessary, re-define targets and standards.

Management by objectives has often developed into a range of elaborate systems and techniques – too elaborate many people say – but it is based upon a fundamental philosophy with which it is difficult to quarrel. Before discussing the systems aspect, which has been the subject of considerable recent criticism, it is desirable to reconsider the basic philosophy that started what can only be described as the management by objectives movement.

Philosophy of management by objectives

If, irreverently, Odiorne in America and Humble in Britain can be described as the high priests of the management by objectives movement, then the messiah must be recognized as Drucker, although McGregor, who followed Drucker in time, cannot be regarded as a mere disciple – he had more of a Pauline role, interpreting and reinterpreting the gospel: in his case, in behavioural science terms.

Drucker coined the phrase in *The Practice of Management*, in which he wrote:

> An effective management must direct the vision and efforts of all managers towards a common goal. It must ensure that the individual manager understands

what results are demanded of him. It must ensure that the superior understands what to expect of each of his subordinate managers. It must motivate each manager to maximum efforts in the right direction. And while encouraging high standards of workmanship, it must make them the means to the end of business performance rather than the ends in themselves.[2]

In Drucker's view, this approach would first ensure that individual and corporate objectives would be integrated. Secondly, it would eliminate the ineffectiveness and misdirection that result from management by 'crisis' and 'drives'. Finally, and most important, it would make it possible for managers to control their own performance. 'Self-control means stronger motivation: a desire to do the best rather than just enough to get by. It means higher performance goals and broader vision.'

McGregor's contribution arose from his Theory Y and Theory X concept. He said that:

The central principal which derives from Theory Y is that of integration: the creation of conditions such that the members of the organization can achieve their own goals *best* by directing their efforts towards the success of the enterprise.[3]

McGregor, however, emphasized that the aim should be to achieve 'management by integration and self-control'. He criticized some interpretations of management by objectives which have led to no more than a new set of tactics within a strategy of management by direction and control. He also stressed that his concept of management by integration and self-control is a strategy – a way of managing people: 'The tactics are worked out in the light of the circumstances. Forms and procedures are of relatively little value ... "Selling" management a program of target setting and providing standardized forms and procedures is the surest way to *prevent* the development of management by integration and self-control'.[3] It is a pity that these words of wisdom in 1960 have been largely ignored by the academics, management consultants and civil servants who have since erected great edifices of forms and systems. All too often these have come crashing down on the heads of those who have tried to live with them because managers rightly revolt against the reduction of their skills to a series of mechanical processes.

But these criticisms are levelled at some applications of management by objectives, rather than the basic concept. It can still play an important part in management development as long as it avoids infecting itself with the disease of 'programmitis' that Humble suggested was endemic in traditional management development schemes.

Using management by objectives

Management by objectives should have the active support of top management. It should not be seen by line managers as yet another form-filling exercise imposed upon them by the personnel department or outside consultants. Their commitment to it as a means of helping them to manage more effectively and thereby helping themselves must be obtained. Management by objectives is most effective when managers recognize for themselves – with or without encouragement – that it is something they can use to their own advantage. It is even more effective if they are allowed the maximum amount of freedom to apply it in their departments in their own way – let them develop their own forms, if they want to use them. If not, let them do without. The agreed objectives can be written out on the back of an envelope if they prefer it that way – as long as they can find the envelope when it comes to a review.

The management by objectives cycle

The management by objectives cycle is a feedback process which requires the definition of corporate objectives from which are derived unit objectives. The next stage is the joint discussion and agreement of the individual manager's key result areas, objectives and action plans. This is followed by the reviews of results which are fed back for the revision of individual, unit and corporate objectives and plans. The process is illustrated in Figure 30.2.

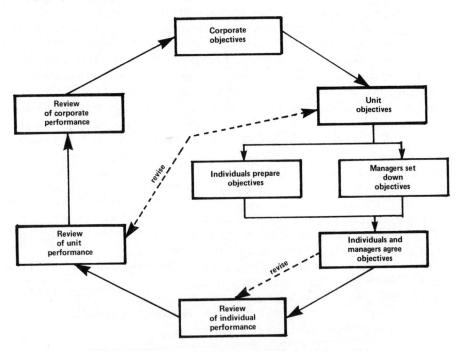

Figure 30.2 The management by objectives cycle

Setting objectives

Individual objectives have to be related to what the job holder is expected to do. The first step, therefore, is to agree on the main job segments for which objectives and standards are set – what Humble refers to as the key result areas. Examples of key result areas for typical management jobs in a light engineering business are shown in Table 30.1.

For each key result area, targets and standards of performance should be agreed in discussion between the manager and his subordinate. At the same time, agreement should be reached on how the results should be measured. The first thoughts might be developed independently prior to a joint discussion, or the targets and standards could be worked out jointly from the start.

General Manager	Works Manager	Sales Manager
1 Profitability	1 Achievement of factory output targets	1 Achievement of sales targets
2 Volume and growth of business	2 Control of costs	2 Contribution to profits and fixed overheads
3 Provision and utilization of fixed assets	3 Utilization of plant and machinery	3 Development of new accounts
4 Provision and utilization of current assets	4 Control of stocks	4 Extension of existing business
5 Product innovation	5 Product quality	5 Customer satisfaction
6 Customer satisfaction	6 Labour productivity	6 Identification of new products
7 Operating costs	7 Industrial relations	7 Introduction of new products
8 Management effectiveness	8 Management effectiveness	8 Effectiveness of sales force
9 Employee productivity and attitude	9 Safety	9 Control of costs

There should not normally be more than ten key result areas.

Table 30.1 *Examples of key result areas**

Wherever possible targets should be quantified in terms of specific results to be achieved. For example:

● sales turnover to be increased by x%;
● no more than y% of orders to be delivered after their promised date;
● scrap rate to be decreased by z%.

If targets cannot be quantified in this way, they may be defined as a task to be achieved in a certain time: eg 'Implement the budgetary control scheme in Department A by 30 November.'

In these cases, and in others where quantitative or time targets cannot be set, it is necessary to agree a standard of performance which will define when the job has been satisfactorily performed. For example, a production controller's key activity was to 'provide an efficient workshop load planning service'. It was then agreed with him that: 'Your performance in carrying out this activity will be considered satisfactory if:

(a) you maintain accurate records of individual loads;
(b) you maintain an accurate record of output targets and actual outputs of individual load centres and departments;
(c) you are fully aware of the delivery position in general, and in particular, where orders are making unusually heavy demands in any load centres or departments.'

There are a number of different sorts of measures of effectiveness. For example:

● positive, ie a hoped-for event, result or other outcome should occur;
● negative, ie an undesirable event or other outcome should not occur;
● measurements in terms of quantity;
● measurements in terms of cost;
● measurements in terms of time;
● measurements that can be compared against a standard item or a specification.

The ground rules for selecting measures: first, each one should be directly concerned with success in performing the task; second, each should be measurable in terms understood by the persons carrying out the work; and third, each one should be independent, ie not easily confused with or seeming to overlap other ones.

Problems in setting objectives usually occur in jobs where it is difficult to set quantifiable targets except in cost terms, which are necessarily negative. The aim should be to provide positive objectives which will increase commitment. In these circumstances, it is wrong to pursue quantification just for the sake of it. The best approach is to agree time targets for getting things done as part of an action plan and, in other areas, to work through what is required to achieve an acceptable standard of performance. The outcome when set down on paper may appear to be somewhat generalized, but it is the process of discussion between the manager and his subordinate in working through each standard which is likely to provide the most beneficial results in that it produces a basis of agreement on what needs to be done and how results will be assessed.

The discussion at this stage should also cover the actions required to achieve results – the 'job improvement plan' in M by O jargon. This is the opportunity for the manager to provide guidance and coaching in advance, although he should avoid *telling* his subordinate how to do it.

His aim should be to help the subordinate to think out for himself what he needs to do to achieve his objectives.

Reviewing performance

The earlier stage in the cycle should ensure that the manager knows what he is supposed to do and how well he is expected to perform. It is now necessary to ensure that he knows how well he is actually performing so that he can take steps to improve his own performance or receive the coaching he needs from his manager.

The review should aim to compare the results achieved with those required. It should be forward rather than backward working. If performance has been below standard the emphasis should be on what needs to be done to improve it. And so far as possible, the manager should encourage his subordinate to review his own performance in order to identify problems and come up with solutions to them.

Implications of management by objectives

Management by objectives in practice has been criticized because it has over-emphasized ends expressed in quantifiable terms. This has led to the pursuit of short term goals at the expense of long term results. Attempts to quantify the unquantifiable have also led managers to reject M by O as unrealistic.

It can also be argued that it is impossible to divorce ends from means. Management by objectives purists say that it is only the results that count. But if managers are to improve their performance they must improve the *way* in which they get results. They should indeed be encouraged to think this out for themselves – and M by O, if conducted properly, should help – but they will also need the guidance of their managers about the means they use as well as the ends they should aim to achieve.

Paradoxically enough, management by objectives in its ripest form is probably best applied in large bureaucratic organizations where its routines fit in with the prevailing climate and management style. In other organizations it provides a basic philosophy of 'management by integration and self-control' which should be an essential part of any management system. For management development purposes the concept of M by O is useful, not for the procedures that surround it, but because it does focus attention on the needs of the individual manager in his job and on the role of his manager in helping him to identify and meet these needs.

Management training

Management development is sometimes seen as primarily a matter of providing a series of appropriate courses at various points in a manager's career. But, as Hawdon Hague[5] suggests, the best definition of training is the 'modification of behaviour through experience', which means that managers will develop best if they receive their training in the 'real' situation, ie in the normal course of their work through coaching, projects and guided self-analysis.

The principal method by which managers can be equipped is by ensuring that they have the right variety of experience, in good time, in the course of their careers. This experience can and should be supplemented, but never replaced, by courses carefully timed and designed to meet particular needs.

The various approaches to management training on the job and on formal courses are discussed more thoroughly in Appendix J. It is sufficient to state now that while training is an important part of management development, it should not be allowed to degenerate into no more than a series of formal courses, even when these are based on elaborate job descriptions, job analyses and performance review systems. This guarantees a static and increasingly irrelevant approach. Formal training courses should only be used when it is essential to supplement what managers are learning on the job. The key management development activity is therefore ensuring that managers are given the chance to learn; and this is primarily a matter of encouraging and stimulating on the job training and providing career opportunities to broaden experience.

References

1. Humble, J 'Programmitis and Crown Princes', *The Manager* December 1963.
2. Drucker, P F *The Practice of Management* Heinemann, London, 1955.
3. McGregor, D *The Human Side of Enterprise* McGraw-Hill Book Company, New York, 1960.
4. Humble, J *Management by Objectives in Action* McGraw-Hill Publishing Company, Maidenhead, 1970.
5. Hague, H *Managements Training for Real* Institute of Personnel Management, London, 1973.

Chapter 31
Career Management

Definition

Career management plans and shapes the progression of individuals within an organization in accordance with assessments of organizational needs and the performance, potential and preferences of individual members of the enterprise.

Overall aims

Career management has three overall aims:

1. To ensure that the organization's needs for management succession are satisfied.
2. To provide men and women of promise with a sequence of training and experience that will equip them for whatever level of responsibility they have the ability to reach.
3. To give individuals with potential the guidance and encouragement they need if they are to fulfil their potential and achieve a successful career with the organization in tune with their talents and aspirations.

Specific aims

The specific aims of career management policies and procedures are to:

- help employees identify the skills and qualities needed for both current and future jobs;
- align and integrate personal aspirations with organizational objectives;
- develop new career paths and plans that point outwards from the individuals in all directions, not just upwards;
- revitalize employees who are experiencing stagnation in their careers;

- provide employees with the opportunity to develop themselves and their careers;
- by the above means, provide mutual benefits for both the organization and individual employees.

Process

The process of career management is illustrated in Figure 31.1. Each of the stages in this process is discussed below.

Career dynamics

Career dynamics describe how career progression takes place – the ways in which people move through their careers and advance upwards, grade by grade, within the organization.

Career progression dynamics

Figure 31.2 illustrates the ways in which career progression take through three main stages:

1. *Expanding* at the start of a career, when new skills are being acquired, knowledge is growing rapidly and aspirations and inclinations are being clarified.
2. *Establishing* the career path, when skills and knowledge gained in the expanding stage are being applied, tested, modified and consolidated with experience, and when aspirations are confirmed or amended.
3. *Maturing* when individuals are well established on their career path and proceed along it according to their motivation, abilities and opportunities.

Through each of these stages people develop and progress at different rates. This means at the maturing stage they either continue to grow, 'plateau-out' (although still doing useful work), or stagnate and decline.

The implications of change

Career management is essentially about managing change – organizationally and individually. In looking at career dynamics it is important to remember that the ability to cope with change varies considerably. Tomorrow's people, as illustrated in Figure 31.3 have no problem in developing their skills in response to change. Those who fail to do so become yesterday's people and decline and fall.

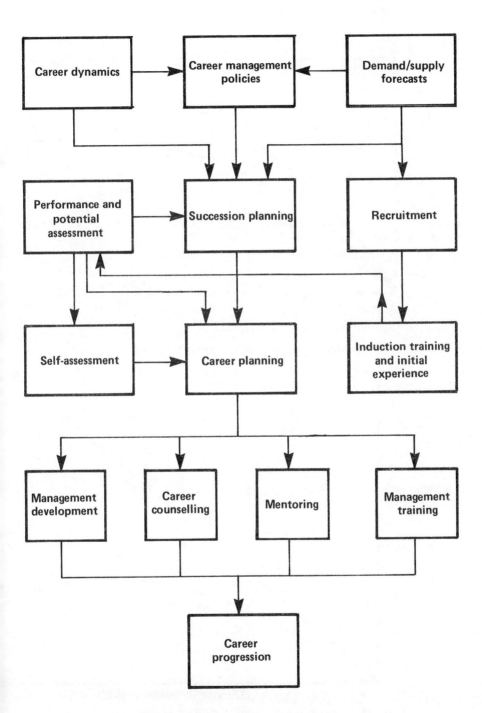

Figure 31.1 The process of career management

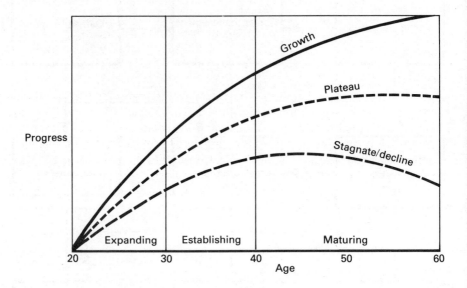

Figure 31.2 Career progression curves

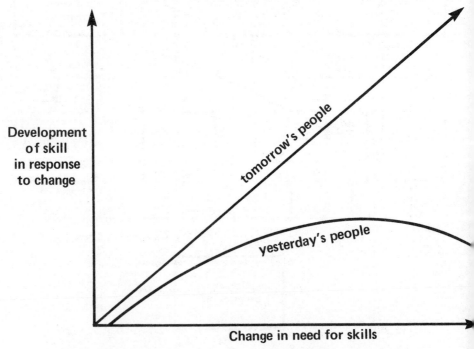

Figure 31.3 Career management – the implications of change

The relevance of career dynamics

The study of career dynamics is a necessary prelude to the formulation of career management policies and the preparation of management succession plans. The study is carried out by analysing the progression of individuals within an organization – function by function – in relation to assessments of performance, as illustrated in Figure 31.4. This can be used to trace typical career progressions in relation to performance assessment and to compare actuals with the model that can be developed from the empirically determined trend lines. An analysis of career dynamics can also point the way towards any actions required to alter career path trends for promising individuals by means of specific career management actions. Finally, the analysis will reveal anomalies such as over-promotions (victims of the 'Peter principle' who have been promoted to the level of their own incompetence) or problems of managers who are stagnating or have gone over the hill.

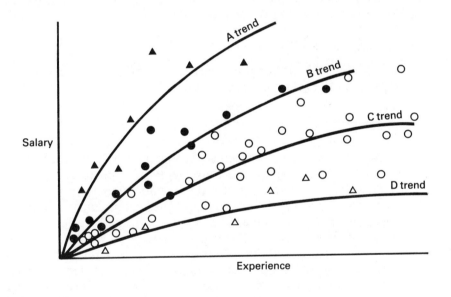

Figure 31.4 Progress analysis

Career management policies

Career management policies cover the following areas.

Make or buy decisions

The organization needs to decide on the extent to which it:

- makes or grows its own managers (a promotion from within policy);
- recruits or buys-in deliberately from outside (bringing 'fresh blood' into the organization) which means adopting a policy that accepts a reasonable amount of wastage and even takes steps in good time to encourage people, fairly gently, to develop their careers elsewhere if they are in danger of stagnating;
- will have to buy-in talent from outside because of future short-falls in the availability of managers as revealed by the demand and supply forecasts.

A make or buy policy may be expressed as: 'We plan to fill about 80% of our management vacancies from within the organization. The remaining 20% we expect to recruit from outside'.

Short or long-term policies

Policies for determining the time scale for investing in careers fall into one or other of the following categories:

- *Short-term performance.* Employers who adopt, consciously or unconsciously, this policy, concentrate on the 'here and now'. They recruit and train high performers who will be good at their present job and are rewarded accordingly. If they are really good, they will get promoted – there are plenty of opportunities – and the enterprise will get what it wants. Deliberately to train managers for a future that may never happen is considered a waste of time. Top managers in this type of organization may well say: 'If we can get good people to do good work, the future will take care of itself. They'll prove and mature their abilities in their present job and be ready and indeed eager to take on extra responsibilities when the occasion arises. The future can take care of itself. If there's no one around at the time, then we'll buy in someone from outside – no problem'!
- *Long-term plans.* Employers who believe in long-term career planning develop highly structured approaches to career manage-ment. They go in for elaborate reviews of performance and potential, assessment centres to identify talent or confirm that it is there, 'high-flyer' schemes, and planned job moves in line with a pre-determined programme.
- *Long-term flexibility.* Employers who follow this policy appre-ciate that they must concentrate on getting good performance now and that in doing so they will, to a considerable extent,

be preparing people for advancement. To this extent they adopt
the same attitude as short-term employers. However, they also
recognize that potential should be assessed and developed by
training which is not job-specific and by deliberately broadening
experience through job rotation or the re-direction of career
paths. This approach avoids the possible short-sightedness of the
here-and-now policy and the rigidity and, often, lack of realism,
inherent in the structured system. In conditions of rapid development and change, how far is it actually possible to plan careers
over the long term? The answer must be to a very limited extent,
except in a static organization which has implicitly recognized
that it provides a 'cradle to grave' career for people who, in
general are willing to wait for 'Buggins' turn'.

As a generalization, the short-term system is likely to be more common
in smallish, rapidly growing 'organic' businesses where form follows
function and the organization is fluid and flexible. The longer-term
system is more prevalent in larger, bureaucratic, 'mechanistic' types of
organization, where accurate forecasts of future needs can be made, significant changes in skill requirements are not likely to take place and
there is a steady flow, according to easily assessed performance, up the
promotion ladder.

Specialists or generalists

Career management policies should cover the extent to which the organization is concerned about developing better and better specialists (broadly
in line with the short-term approach) or whether it attaches equal, or even
more, importance to developing the appropriate number of generalists
who are capable of exercising effectively the managerial functions of
planning, organizing, motivating and controlling. Obviously, all organizations have a mix of these two categories, but it may be a matter of policy to create a dual career structure with separate career ladders for pure
specialists who would be rewarded in accordance with their technical contribution and not in line with their place in a management grade hierarchy. There is no universal law that says a top-rate specialist who is not a
manager and does not want to be one, must be paid less than someone
who happens to have the skills and inclinations to take him or her along
the management route.

Clearly, the policy depends on the type of organization, especially its
technology and the extent to which it is a hierarchy of managers with a
few specialists on the side (for example, an insurance company with a
large branch network but with a select team of actuaries and investment
managers at head office), or is a hi-tech research-based operation where
the technologist is king, or queen, as the case may be.

Dealing with the 'plateaued' manager

As John Davies and Yvonne Deighan have suggested: 'Preoccupied with motivating and retaining our superstars, we have neglected the needs of the vast majority of managers who actually keep the business going. The problem is that, once they know they can rise no higher in the organization, they are likely to experience what Professor John Hunt called the 'managerial menopause'.[1]

These people can fall into three categories as defined by Davies and Deighan:

1. *Contented maturity* – people who have progressed well and feel that they have had a satisfying career in a good company. Although they have been overtaken by high-flyers, they are not too put-out by this and are content to go on doing their job well and find satisfaction outside as well as inside work. In these cases the policy might be to recognize the worth of these 'solid citizens', keep them rewarded appropriately, and strive to enlarge or enrich their jobs when this is possible. They make excellent mentors (mentoring systems are described later in this chapter).

    Many people are not as ambitious as some achievers think they are or ought to be. For those who are in a state of contented maturity, the organization should have a policy of registering how much it values their services and accepting that 'they have done jolly well and need not be driven any further'.

2. *Discontented maturity* – many people who have plateaued but in spite of having progressed reasonably well, believe that they should go further and are under pressure to do so because of their own ambitions (possibly unrealistic), the cult of success in the company or even the expectations of their spouse. Because of their frustrated expectations these people tend to be characterized by low morale, cynicism, staleness and depression. Revitalizing them is again a matter for job enrichment and enlargement as part of a programme for changing job structures, where possible. This approach should become a deliberate policy of the company, but it needs to be backed up by counselling which will help those affected adversely by plateauing to learn to live with it and, perhaps, positively enjoy the feeling that they no longer have to join in the 'rat race'. The policy on counselling should therefore incorporate help to plateaued managers as well as rising stars. Career management may primarily be concerned with development but it also has to take care of those people who are worth taking care of at each stage of their career.

3. *Thwarted rising stars* – people who have started well but are now burning themselves out and not living up to their own expectations or those of the organization. Counselling may help these individuals

to become reconciled to their situation, but it will not necessarily work in this way. It may be necessary to have a policy which recognizes that thwarted rising stars need 'out-placement' rather than job counselling, that is, help in restructuring their careers elsewhere.

Demand and supply forecasts

Demand and supply forecasts are provided by the use of human resource planning and modelling techniques (see Chapter 13). In larger organizations, modelling is a particularly fruitful method to use because it does allow for sensitivity analysis of the impact of different assumptions about the future (answering 'what if' questions). The basic framework for a manager resourcing model is illustrated in Figure 31.5.

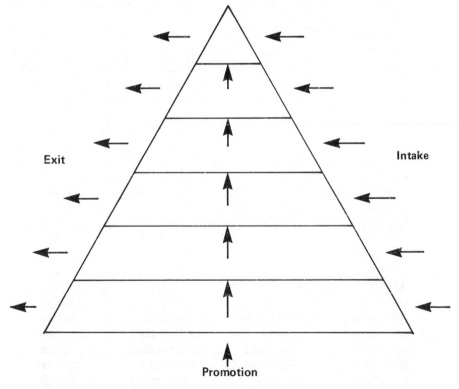

Figure 31.5 Manager resourcing model

Expert systems as described in Chapter 19 can also be used where this is an extensive database on flows, attribute requirements (personnel specifications), and performance and potential assessments. Such systems can establish relationships between the opportunities and the personal attributes they demand so that careers advisors can take a set of personal attributes and identify the most appropriate available opportunities. At the career planning stage they can also identify people with the correct abilities and skills for particular jobs and provide information on the career management programmes required to ensure that attributes and jobs are matched and careers progress at an appropriate rate. Career management systems such as ExecuGROW (Control Data) have been specially developed for this purpose.

Succession planning

The aim of management succession planning is to ensure that as far as possible suitable managers are available to fill vacancies created by promotion, retirement, death, leaving or transfer. It also aims to ensure that a cadre of managers is available to fill the new appointments that may be established in the future.

The information for management succession planning comes from organization reviews and demand and supply forecasts. The succession plans will be influenced by the career dynamics of the organization and also by the performance and potential assessments, which provide information on who is ready now and in the future to fill projected vacancies. This information needs to be recorded so that decisions can be made on promotions and replacements, and training or additional experience arranged for those with potential or who are earmarked for promotion.

The records need not be elaborate. In practice, complex inventories and detailed succession charts replete with colour codes and other symbols are a waste of time, except in the largest and most bureaucratic organizations. All the information required can be recorded on a simple management succession schedule such as the one illustrated in Figure 31.6.

A computerized personnel information system as described in Chapter 19 can, with the help of competency modelling techniques, store inventories of the skills and experience of individual employees together with records of their performance and potential assessments. Lists of attributes for key jobs can also be stored and this information can be linked to the other data mentioned above to provide guidance on who is available to fill present or future vacancies and on any career plans needed to ensure that potential is realized.

Performance and potential assessment

The aim of performance and potential assessment is to identify training and development needs, provide guidance on possible directions in which

MANAGEMENT SUCCESSION SCHEDULE			Department				Director/Manager		
Present Managerial and Supervisory Staff							Possible successors		
Name	Position	Age	Date due for replacement	Rating		If promotable, indicate what position and when	Names (1st & 2nd choice)	Positions	When ready
				Performance	Potential				

Figure 31.6 Management succession schedule

an individual's career might go, and indicate who has potential for promotion. The techniques used are described in Chapter 28 on performance management. In addition to the type of assessment procedures listed there, it may be interesting to categorize employees in one of the four squares set out in Figure 31.7.

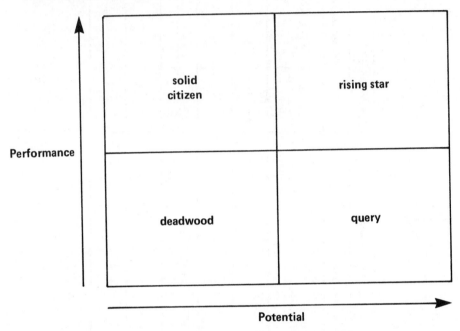

Figure 31.7 Categorization – performance/potential

The rising stars are people with potential, who will benefit from career planning, wider experience and management training. The organization may wish to 'fast track' them by rapid promotion or by offering more challenging opportunities. They should be listed and looked after. This may mean paying over the odds to demonstrate that the company values them and wants to keep them from straying further afield. It does not mean setting up a row of crown princes whose future is guaranteed and whose path to the top is made easy. They have to know that they have only been given these opportunities because they have performed well so far, and that the demands made on them in the future are going to be even greater. There is no easy way to the top and they must realize that they will have to work their passage, and that, while the company has its eye on them and is going to help their development, in the last analysis it will be up to them.

The solid citizens are the people on whom the organization depends to get things done. They are the backbone of the organization. They are sometimes called workhorses, but this is a derogatory term. They are not necessarily going to rise much above their present level, but they are useful and dependable and they still need training in new techniques and skills. They also need the encouragement and motivation provided by varying their responsibilities, introducing new opportunities wherever this can be arranged, and assuring them that they are doing a worthwhile job.

The queries are those managers who for one reason or another do not seem to be making the grade. They may have the ability but not the motivation, or they may have the motivation but not the ability. In the latter case it is worth trying to establish and satisfy training needs. They are clearly worth saving, if that is at all possible. People with ability who lack motivation may present a bigger problem. It is a good thing to find out why they are not motivated and do something about it.

The deadwood are the people – one hopes few in number, if they exist at all – who ought to go. As long as all else in the shape of training and encouragement has failed, there is no point in keeping them – for their sake as well as that of the company. They could do better elsewhere if they can find a nice square hole into which they will fit.

Recruitment

Career management means taking into account the fact that the organization will inevitably need to recruit new managers who will then have to prove themselves while gaining their initial experience and undergoing induction training. As soon as they have been with the company long enough to show what they can do and where they might go, their performance and potential can be assessed and they can be fed into the career management system.

Self assessment

As mentioned in Chapter 30, the best form of development is self-development. Similarly, the most important contribution to individual career planning must come from managers themselves. They must be given the encouragement to assess what they want to do and become and the opportunity to discuss their aspirations and plans with their manager and a career counsellor or mentor.

Career planning

The process of career planning

Career planning is the key process in career management. It uses all the information provided by the organization's assessments of requirements, the assessments of performance and potential and the management succession plans, and translates it into the form of individual career development programmes and general arrangements for management development, career counselling, mentoring and management training.

Career planning models

In bringing all the career management data together at this stage it is useful to develop models to describe the processes involved. Figure 31.8 shows a generalized career progression model which indicates on the basis of an analysis of career dynamics how many years people in different potential categories might take to reach their maximum level in the organization.

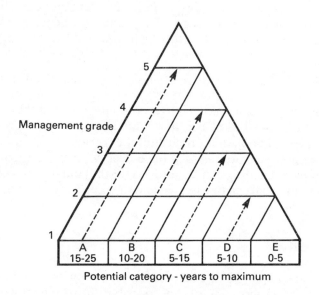

Figure 31.8 Career progression model

This background data can be used to determine the normal stages through which a career planning programme might proceed as illustrated in Figure 31.9. This identifies various aiming points to which careers should be directed and the category of training and experience required to help people to progress from one point to the next and beyond. However, it only defines the phases through which careers develop. The determination of precisely what training and experience is required at each stage obviously depends on assessments of the organization's collective needs, individual needs and individual aspirations.

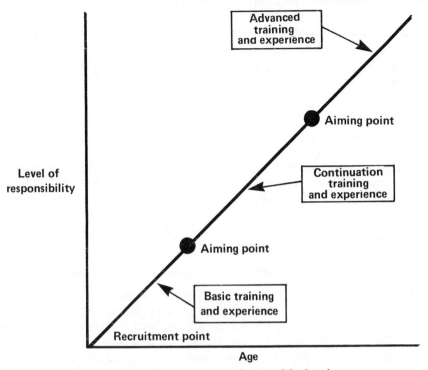

Figure 31.9 Career progression – critical points

Career planning is for solid citizens as well as high-flyers

The philosophy upon which career plans are based refers not only to advancing careers to meet organizational and individual requirements, but also to the need to maximize the potential of the human resources of the organization in terms of productivity and satisfaction under conditions of change, when 'development' does not necessarily mean promotion. As mentioned earlier in the chapter, an obsession with high-flyers and 'fast tracking' may lead to a neglect of the majority of employees who also need to be motivated, encouraged and given every opportunity to use their skills and abilities.

Career planning is for individuals as well as the organization

Career planning procedures are always based on what the organization needs. But they have to recognize that organizational needs will not be satisfied if individual needs are neglected. Career plans must therefore recognize that:

  ● members of the organization should receive recognition as *individuals* with unique needs, wants, and abilities;

- individuals become more motivated by an organization which responds to their aspirations;
- individuals *can* grow, change and seek new directions if they are given the right opportunities, encouragement and guidance.

Career planning techniques

Career planning takes all the information generated by the succession plans, performance and potential assessments and self assessments, to develop programmes and procedures which are designed to implement career management policies, achieve succession planning objectives and generally improve motivation, commitment and performance. The procedures used are those concerned with:

(a) training and management development as described in Chapters 28 and 29;
(b) career counselling and mentoring as described below.

In addition, career planning procedures may cater for the rising stars by 'fast-tracking' them, that is, deliberately accelerating promotion and giving them opportunities to display and enlarge their talents. But these procedures should pay just as much if not more attention to those managers who are following the middle route of steady, albeit unspectacular, progression.

Career counselling

Performance management procedures, as described in Chapter 28, should provide for counselling sessions between individuals and their managers. These sessions should give the former the opportunity to discuss their aspirations and the latter the chance to comment on them – helpfully – and, at a later stage, to put forward specific career development proposals to be fed into the overall career management programme.

Career counselling is, however, a skilled job and the immediate boss is not always the best person to do it, although all managers should be trained in the techniques involved. Some large organizations have appointed specialists whose sole job is to provide a career counselling service to back up the efforts of line managers and to advise on what needs to be done for individuals or, more generally, by the organization as a whole. Mentoring systems, as described in the next section of this chapter, can also be used for this purpose.

The individuals concerned may need an increased level of self-awareness, better access to information about career opportunities and improved decision-making skills. Decision support systems have been developed such as Career Builder (Hopson and Scally[2]), which explores the individual's values and skills, and RESOLVE (Wooler and Wisuda[3]), which is a programme for training in career decision-making. These systems, however, are primarily of interest to young people starting their careers.

Mentoring

Definition

A mentor, according to the Oxford English Dictionary, is 'an experienced and trusted counsellor'. Mentoring is the process of using specially selected and trained individuals to provide guidance and advice which will help to develop the careers of the 'protégés' allocated to them.

Aims

The typical aims of a mentoring programme, as suggested by Clutterbuck[4] are to:

- establish a cadre of broadly trained generalist managers at or just below middle management level;
- speed up and improve the induction of specific types of recruits and reduce wastage during the early period of employment;
- help top management to assess the abilities of both individual young managers and the rising generation of managers as a whole;
- provide equal opportunities for disadvantaged groups of employees.

Some mentoring systems concentrate on the young high-flyers, some offer a company wide service for all junior managers, professional or technical staff with some promise, even if they are not 'stars', while others are only concerned with people entering the organization who need more help and guidance in learning their job and finding their feet than can be provided either by their immediate superior or by formal induction training courses.

Mentoring is aimed at complementing learning on the job, which must always be the best way of acquiring the particular skills and knowledge the job holder needs. Mentoring also complements formal training by providing those who benefit from it with individual guidance from experienced managers who are 'wise in the ways of the organization'.

Mentoring, however, should have as its main purpose that of furthering the careers of individuals with a future in the organization. It is therefore a necessary part of a career management programme, although it is also an excellent training technique.

The role of the mentor

Mentors provide for the person or persons allocated to them (their 'protégés'):

- guidance on how to acquire the necessary knowledge and skills to do a new job;
- advice on dealing with any administrative, technical or 'people' problems individuals meet, especially in the early stages of their careers;
- information on 'the way things are done around here' – the corporate culture and its manifestations in the shape of core values and organizational behaviour (management style);
- coaching in specific skills, especially managerial skills such as leadership, communication and time management;
- help in tackling projects – not by doing it for protégés but by pointing them in the right direction, that is – helping people to help themselves;
- a parental figure with whom protégés can discuss their aspirations and concerns and who will lend a sympathetic ear to their problems.

How mentors carry out their role

There are no standard mentoring procedures. Typically, however, a mentor will be allocated one or more protégés and given a very general brief to carry out the functions described above.

This brief could be more specific with trainees who may be undergoing a fairly prolonged period of training in a number of departments. In these cases there may be a programme of training and a 'syllabus' defining what trainees have to learn. This could take the form of a 'do-it-yourself' training programme using 'discovery' techniques (both these approaches are described in Appendix K). The mentor's job is to meet the trainees regularly to review progress. Trainees report on what they have done and how they have coped with any problems they have met. They inform their mentor of what they have achieved in carrying out projects allocated to them. If they have been given questions to answer on functions they have been learning about, the mentor may test their understanding. Coaching in various management skills may form part of the programme.

With more experienced individuals for whom the mentor is more in a 'counselling' than a 'coaching' role, the arrangements may be more informal. Regular meetings could be held to discuss progress, aspirations and plans, but the mentor's function might often be no more than to act as a resource to whom people can go to for help and advice when they need it.

Launching a mentoring system

The following steps are required to launch a mentoring system:

1. Define objectives.
2. Define the role and functions of mentors.
3. Obtain the support of management, starting at the top.
4. Appoint a senior manager to co-ordinate the mentoring programme.
5. Identify through performance and potential appraisals individuals who will be allocated to mentors as part of a career management programme. Also list the trainees for whom mentors will be appointed.
6. Select mentors who have the following attributes:

   - a reasonable degree of seniority;
   - a sound and seasoned knowledge of the company and its political structure;
   - the ability to encourage and motivate;
   - the ability to create an open, candid atmosphere so that their protégés will confide in and trust them;
   - good interpersonal skills for counselling and coaching;
   - a good record for developing people;
   - a wide range of skills and understanding to pass on;
   - a good network of contacts and influence;
   - above all, an interest in mentoring and a willingness to spend time in doing it well.

7. Train mentors in counselling, and coaching and teaching techniques and ensure that they fully understand their role and how they perform it.
8. Brief the managers of individuals who are to be allocated to mentors on what will happen and how they, the managers, as well as the individuals, will benefit. This is important. Without the support of middle management, mentoring systems fail.
9. Allocate protégés to mentors.
10. Follow-up to ensure that the system is working as planned – that mentors are carrying out their role properly, that protégés are benefiting and that their managers are supportive.

Maintaining a mentoring system

Mentoring systems can be launched on a wave of enthusiasm, but can rapidly sink with all hands unless strenuous efforts are made to keep them steaming away in the right direction – just keeping them afloat is not enough. Top management should be encouraged to take a continued interest in the programme, which they will do if it is effective and they are told about how it is benefiting the organization. Mentors must be encouraged and, if interest is flagging, stimulated to greater activity. If they cannot or will not cope they should be relieved of their responsibility. Mentors will come and go, so it is always useful to have some trained people in reserve.

Benefits of a mentoring system

For the organization
The benefits of a mentoring system to the organization are that it will:

- enhance the efficiency and effectiveness of the training for those taking on new roles or being prepared for promotion;
- improve motivation and commitment and thus reduce the rate at which people that the organization needs in the future are lost;
- provide further information on promising individuals so that career plans can be made for them which will satisfy the organizational requirements for management succession or a flow of well-equipped managers to meet future growth needs.

For individuals
The benefits of mentoring for individuals are that it will:

- enable them to acquire more quickly and comprehensively the skills and understanding they need;
- improve their self-confidence;
- help them to learn how to adjust to the corporate culture and the formal and informal processes that take place in the organization;
- provide them with a means to discuss their hopes and fears, and to realize the former and resolve the latter.

Career progression

A satisfying system of career progression is the overall aim and culminating point of a career management programme. As was demonstrated in Figure 31.1, there is a sequence of events and actions required to reach this point, starting with an understanding of the career dynamics and management requirements of the organization and, having defined career management policies, ensuring that each of the activities is co-ordinated as part of the overall programme.

The benefits of this approach are clear. The organization defines what it needs in the light of an understanding of its situation. Each activity can then be fitted into a systematically prepared action plan. It may never be possible to predict exactly what the organization will need, especially in times of change. Neither can a career management programme like the one described in this chapter guarantee that the organization will get what it wants. But it is much more likely to do so if these methods are used.

References

1. Davies, J and Deighan, Y 'The Managerial Menopause', *Personnel Management* March 1986.
2. Hopson, B and Scally, M *Career Building: A Computer Programme for Managing Your Own Career* Lifeskills Associates/UHA, Leeds, 1984.
3. Wooler, S and Wisuda, A 'An educational approach in designing computer-based career guidance systems', *British Journal of Educational Technology* 16(2), 1985.
4. Clutterbuck, D *Everyone Needs a Mentor* Institute of Personnel Management, London, 1985.

Part VIII
Employee Relations

Employee relations consists of all those aspects of personnel management where employees are dealt with collectively. The primary aims of employee relations policies and procedures are to improve co-operation, to minimize unnecessary conflict, to enable employees to play an appropriate part in decision-making and to keep them informed on matters that concern them.

Wherever there are trade unions, industrial relations will be a major pre-occupation of personnel management. Industrial relations policies and procedures need to be developed and operated in the light of an understanding of the processes at work in collective bargaining, where the 'web of rules' is developed by formal and informal negotiations and by discussions between management and the trade unions. Chapter 32 therefore starts with an analysis of industrial relations as a system of rules developed by formal and informal processes of collective bargaining. It goes on to discuss the framework of industrial relations and the roles of the various parties involved before considering industrial relations strategies, procedural agreements and negotiating techniques.

The remaining chapters in this part then examine the important subjects of participation, consultation and communications and the means available to develop procedures and techniques which will create a climate of employee relations which is more conducive to co-operation and trust.

Chapter 32
Industrial Relations

Industrial relations is concerned with the systems, rules and procedures used by unions and employers to determine the reward for effort and other conditions of employment, to protect the interests of the employed and their employers, and to regulate the ways in which employers treat their employees. The systems and procedures will include the processes of collective bargaining as well as formal procedure agreements. It is concerned also with the roles of the parties involved in the system – management, union officials, shop stewards and employees – and the relationships between them. It covers the industrial relations strategies adopted by management and unions, the procedure agreements evolved to enable the system to operate, and, of course, the processes of negotiating.

Industrial relations is dealt with here under the following headings:

- *Industrial relations as a system of rules* – the basis upon which industrial relations operates.
- *Collective bargaining* – the process of industrial relations which concludes agreements and handles disputes.
- *Industrial relations and the individual.*
- *The framework of industrial relations* – the roles of the government, the trade unions and the employers' associations.
- *The role of management.*
- *The role of shop stewards.*
- *Union membership and the closed shop.*
- *Industrial relations strategy* – especially for union recognition.
- *Procedural agreements* – their purpose and content.
- *Negotiating* – bargaining strategies and techniques.
- *Industrial relations training.*
- *Developments in industrial relations.*

Industrial relations as a system of rules

Industrial relations can be regarded as a system or web of rules regulating employment relations. The essence of the system is that the rules are jointly agreed by the representatives of the parties to employment relations, which makes for readier acceptance than if they are imposed by a third party, such as the state.

The system of rules is not necessarily a formal system. The rules appear in many more or less formal or informal guises: in legislation and statutory orders, in trade union regulations, in collective agreements and arbitration awards, in social conventions, in managerial decisions, and in accepted 'custom and practice'. They may be defined and coherent, or ill-defined and incoherent. Within a plant the rules may mainly be concerned with doing no more than defining the *status quo* which both parties recognize as the norm from which deviations may only be made by agreement. In this sense, therefore, an industrial relations system is a normative system where a norm can be seen as a rule, a standard or a pattern for action which is generally accepted or agreed as the basis upon which the parties concerned should operate.

Types of regulations and rules

Job regulation aims to provide a framework of minimum rights and rules. Internal regulation is concerned with procedures for dealing with grievances, redundancies or disciplinary problems and rules concerning the operation of the pay system and the rights of shop stewards. External regulation is carried out by means of employment legislation, the rules of trade unions and employers' associations, and the regulative content of national or local agreements.

The rules can be of two kinds:

1. *Procedural* which deal with such matters as the methods to be used and the rules to be followed in the settlement of disputes, to regulate the behaviour of the parties to the agreement.
2. *Substantive* which refer to working hours or to other job terms and conditions in the area of employment covered by the agreement. These rules regulate the behaviour of employers and employees as parties to individual contracts of employment.

Procedural rules are intended to regulate conflict between the parties to collective bargaining and when their importance is emphasized a premium is being placed on industrial peace, and less regard is being paid to the terms on which it may be obtained. Substantive rules settle the rights and obligations attached to jobs. It is interesting to note that in Britain the parties to collective agreements have tended to concentrate more on procedural rather than on substantive rules. In the United States, where there is greater emphasis on fixed term agreements, the tendency has been to rely more on substantive rules.

Role of the system

The systems theory of industrial relations, as propounded by Dunlop,[1] states that the role of the system is to produce the substantive and procedural rules which govern how much is distributed in the bargaining process and how the parties involved, or the 'actors' in the industrial relations scene, relate to one another. The output of the system takes the form of:

> The regulations and policies of the management hierarchy; the laws of any worker hierarchy; the regulations, degrees, decisions, awards or orders of governmental agencies; the rules and decisions of specialized agencies created by the management and worker hierarchies; collective bargaining arrangements and the customs and traditions of the workplace and work community.[1]

Systems theory, however, does not sufficiently explain the role of the individual in industrial relations, neither does it take into account the tendency of governments to become more interventionist in dealing with the system as a whole, while intervening less in disputes. These issues are discussed later in this chapter.

Industrial relations and the individual

As Thomason[2] points out, systems theory concentrates on those relationships which establish, contain and apply the rules by which people behave at work. But this traditional approach assumes that the behaviour of people is rule-orientated. The more recent developments in motivation theory such as reactance and orientation theory as discussed in Chapter 8, suggest that individuals are more autonomous than is generally supposed.

Reactance theory states that individuals choose behaviour so as to maximize need satisfaction. They are not passive receivers and responders, instead, they actively strive to make sense of their environment and to reduce uncertainty by seeking to control for themselves factors influencing rewards. Orientation theory emphasizes that people can and do seek certain goals and rewards from work independently of the work and the work context. Because people react in individualistic ways to events and have deeply rooted orientations about what they want to do and how they want to behave, they will not necessarily conform exactly to the established rules, although they will take them into account.

Increasingly, management and trade unions have to learn that they may not be so much in control of the situation as they would like to be. Rules may no longer be sufficient in themselves. What is more important is to develop a corporate culture and organization climate which integrates the needs of the individual and the company while recognizing that workers may still need to protect their interests by collective action.

This view is sometimes described as the *residual theory* of management which sees employers and managers as endowed with all the power and authority which was originally held by the sovereign head or sole proprietor, except that which they may relinquish voluntarily. This unitary view, which is essentially autocratic and authoritarian, is sometimes expressed in agreements as 'management's right to manage'.

In contrast, the *trusteeship theory* regards the manager as the trustee of the many interests in the undertaking: shareholders or political masters, customers or clients *and* employees. This concept suggests that management 'has the *duty* to manage' rather than the right to manage.

Collective bargaining

The industrial relations system is regulated by the process of collective bargaining, defined by Flanders as a 'social process that continually turns disagreements into agreements in an orderly fashion'.[3] Collective bargaining aims to establish by negotiation and discussion agreed rules and decisions in matters of mutual concern to employers and unions as well as methods of regulating the conditions governing employment.

It therefore provides a framework within which the views of management and unions about disputed matters that lead to industrial disorder can be considered with the aim of eliminating the causes of the disorder. Collective bargaining can also be regarded as a joint regulating process, dealing with the regulation of management in its relationships with work people as well as the regulation of conditions of employment. It has a political as well as an economic basis – both sides are interested in the distribution of power between them as well as the distribution of income.

Collective bargaining takes two basic forms, as identified by Chamberlain and Kuhn.[4]

1. *Conjunctive bargaining* which 'arises from the absolute requirement that some agreement – *any* agreement – be reached so that the operations on which both are dependent may continue' and results in a 'working relationship in which each party agrees, explicitly or implicitly, to provide certain requisite services, to recognize certain seats of authority, and to accept certain responsibilities in respect of each other'.
2. *Co-operative bargaining* in which it is recognized that each party is dependent on the other and can achieve its objectives more effectively if it wins the support of the other.

A similar distinction was made by Walton and McKersie[5] when they referred to *distributive bargaining* as the 'complex system of activities instrumental to the attainment of one party's goals when they are in basic conflict with those of the other party', and to *integrative bargaining* – 'the system of activities which are not in fundamental conflict with those of the other party and which therefore can be integrated to some degree.

Such objectives are said to define an area of common concern, a purpose'.

Both forms of collective bargaining emphasize that in industrial relations the parties cannot withdraw, or not for long; they are dependent upon each other for performance of their specialist functions and for their survival (except in the isolated cases where workers' co-operatives independently keep a firm going after its financial collapse). Conjunctive or distributive bargaining is a recognition of this mutual interdependence, but it is limited and negative. Co-operative or integrative bargaining is based on both the mutual interdependence of management and employees *and* their recognition that they can achieve more for themselves by adopting this approach.

The framework of industrial relations

The rule making and regulating processes of industrial relations take place within the framework of government, national, corporate and plant institutions which operate according to certain stated or unstated principles. These principles, and the framework within which they operate, vary substantially from country to country. In the UK the institutions consist of:

1. *The government* which, according to its political persuasion, creates a legal framework which confers rights on employees and duties on employers.

   The British government has established institutions such as the Advisory, Conciliation and Arbitration Service (ACAS) which, besides carrying out the functions set out in its title, has the objective of encouraging the development of collective bargaining and the development and, where necessary, reform of collective bargaining machinery. There is also a network of industrial tribunals to hear unfair dismissal, equal pay and equal opportunity cases and other matters raised where employers are failing to comply with the provisions of employment legislation.

2. *The unions* whose objectives can broadly be defined as being:
   (a) to redress the bargaining advantage of the individual worker *vis-a-vis* the individual employer by substituting joint or collective action for individual action;
   (b) to secure improved terms and conditions of employment for their members and the maximum degree of security to enjoy those terms and conditions;
   (c) to obtain improved status for the worker in his work;
   (d) to increase the extent to which unions can exercise democratic control over decisions that affect their interests by power sharing at the national, corporate and plant level.

The union power is exerted primarily at two levels – at the industry-wide level, to establish joint regulation on basic wages and hours with an employers' association or equivalent; and at the plant level, where the shop stewards organizations exercise joint control over some aspects of the organization of work and localized terms and conditions of employment. Unions are party to national, local and plant procedure agreements which govern their actions to a greater or lesser extent, depending on their power and on local circumstances.

Unions could be said to be in the business of managing discontent and Clive Jenkins referred to the professional union bargainer as sitting on 'a pinnacle of institutionalized indignation'. But it does not follow that unions introduce conflict – Jenkins also suggested that 'a union official is vocationally a gladiator because the work of the union is basically defensive'. It can be said that the role of a union is simply to provide a highly organized and continuous form of expression for sectional interests which would exist anyway. Such conflicts of interest are inherent in working relationships and unions can contribute to their solution by bringing issues out into the open and jointly defining with employers procedures for dealing with them.

There are various types of unions in Britain, including *craft unions*, the oldest kind, which require entry by apprenticeship and try to maintain standards by the joint control of apprenticeships and by resisting 'dilution' of the craft by those who have not become full members of the union; *general unions*, the largest kind, which take in recruits without being concerned about their level of skill, occupation or industry; *industrial unions*, which contain recruitment and representation to one industry; *sectoral unions*, which cater for one sector of employment only, such as the civil service; *manual unions*, which recruit what are normally termed manual workers; and *white collar unions*, a growing field, which include workers who are removed by one or more degrees from direct production or direct service, such as clerks, supervisors, technicians, scientists and managers. These types of unions can be combined or overlap; for example, there are white collar sections in general unions, or unions catering for one sector such as banking which are exclusively for white collared workers.

Most of the unions are federated on a fairly loose basis to the Trades Union Congress which exerts political influence and tries with varying degrees of success to co-ordinate and regulate the trade union movement – a difficult task because of the jealously guarded independence of individual members.

Individual unions are run by full-time central and district officials, with local committees of members. Their organization extends into the place of work by means of shop stewards whose role is discussed later in this chapter.

3. *The employers' associations* which vary enormously in their size and influence over their members. Some will be heavily involved at national and local level in negotiations with unions. Others are mainly advisory in character. Individual employers in manufacturing and some nationalized industries may subscribe to the Confederation of British Industry which exerts political influence and provides advice but does not negotiate, and exerts no control over employers' associations.

The role of management

Management typically sees its function as that of directing and controlling the work force to achieve economic and growth objectives. To this end, it believes that it is the rule making authority. Management tends to view the enterprise as a unitary system with one source of authority – themselves – and one focus of loyalty – the company. It extols the virtue of team work, where everyone strives jointly to a common objective, each pulls his weight to the best of his ability, and each accepts his place and his function gladly, following the leadership of the appointed manager or supervisor. These are admirable sentiments but unrealistic, and they sometimes lead to what McClelland[6] has referred to as an 'orgy of avuncular pontification' on the part of the leaders of industry.

The realistic view, as advanced by Fox,[7] is that an industrial organization is a plural society, containing many related but separate interests and objectives which must be maintained on some kind of equilibrium. In place of a corporate unity reflected in a single focus of authority and loyalty, management has to accept the existence of rival sources of leadership and attachment. Management has to face the fact that in Drucker's phrase,[8] a business enterprise has a triple personality: it is at once an economic, a political and a social institution. In the first, it produces and distributes incomes. In the second it embodies a system of government in which managers collectively exercise authority over the managed, but are also themselves involved in an intricate pattern of political relationships. Its third personality is revealed in the plant community which evolves from below out of face-to-face relations based on shared interests, sentiments, beliefs and values among various groups of employees.

The role of management is to exercise authority as well as to build up team work and it is concerned with the development of rules for this purpose. But management has increasingly to accept that it no longer has absolute authority. To a very great extent management and unions are mutually dependent. For each, the achievement of its own function is dependent upon a working relationship with the other. And there are three factors which are important in this relationship. The first is stability – a firmly established basis for interaction between management and employees. This is why many managers deplore closed shops in theory as an infringement of liberty, but in practice accept that there is less likelihood of trouble if all employees in a job category or unit are members of one union. For the same reason, one union covering all members of the plant may be preferred as a way of reducing the fragmentation of bargaining and of avoiding inter-union rivalries and demarcation – 'who does what' – disputes, even though a monolithic union may be more powerful. The second factor is trust – a belief that when the bargaining is over and the agreement is reached, both parties will keep their word. The third factor is understanding of each other's point of view. This does not mean that the parties must always be at one about the fundamental issues that affect them. But they must know how each side sees these issues if a collective agreement is eventually to be negotiated or if a relatively stable working relationship is to be maintained.

At the highest level, management has often been too remote from the unions and their members. J T Winkler's interesting piece of research on this subject, published under the apt title of *The Ghost at the Bargaining Table*, revealed that: 'Most directors have no significant contact with any manual or clerical staff other than their secretaries . . . Non-contact was also just as much the norm for production directors and for those normally responsible for personnel matters.'[9] According to Winkler, their withdrawal is a coping device which enables low-level compromises with unions to take place on a pragmatic basis which do not threaten any fundamental principles.

Sir Michael Edwardes when he was chairman of British Leyland took a different view from the directors interviewed by Winkler. In *Back from the Brink* Edwardes emphasized his conviction that leadership in industrial relations had to come from the top and had to include direct contact with workers. His objective in tackling the sad state of industrial relations in BL was, as he put it:

> . . . not to destroy or weaken the unions. On the contrary, it was to rebalance the
> whole order of things so that, together with management, national union officials
> would be able to play a proper role without finding their authority eroded by strong
> stewards, weak management, and a lack of understanding of what management
> was trying to achieve. This mixture has led to chaos in the past.[10]

The role of shop stewards

The role of shop stewards is to represent their members to management in all matters that affect them. They negotiate and resolve disputes, but they may also deal with a host of day-to-day issues affecting the interests of their members.

Shop stewards can help management and supervision by squashing unreasonable complaints, or by dealing with issues as they arise on the shop floor, thus preventing escalations into major disputes. Commenting on his study of industrial relations in a British car factory, Clack wrote that 'the convenors and shop steward organization at the factory did not appear as a driving force behind labour unrest, but could more validly be regarded as "shock absorbers" of the industrial relations machinery'.[11]

The popular stereotype of the difficult, aggressive, and often surly shop steward as a common feature of the British industrial scene has been largely dispelled by research such as that carried out by Marsh, Evans and Garcia[12] on workshop industrial relations in over 400 British engineering establishments. This revealed that the overwhelming proportion of the managers in the survey thought that shop stewards were helpful (80%) – 9% thought they were obstructive and the remaining 11% had no firm views on the subject. There are, of course, difficult shop stewards, just as there are difficult managers and supervisors. And shop stewards are militant when they feel they have to be; as Phillip Higgs, convenor of a Midlands engineering factory said: 'It is our job to do more damage to the enemy than he does to us. If you can get a limited objective with very few casualties, you are all the more ready to move on to the next step. With each such advance we secure a little more control, a little more of managerial function is taken from management.[13]

A satisfactory climate of relationships with unions and shop stewards cannot be achieved either by exaggerating militancy or by underestimating it. The approach management should use is to take steps to understand why it exists and to develop strategies, rules and procedures which will enable conflict to be managed by co-operative as well as conjunctive processes of collective bargaining. These approaches are discussed in the next section.

Union membership and the closed shop

As identified by Millward and Stevens[14] there are five types of arrangements for trade union membership:

1. *All* manual workers have to be members of unions in order to get or keep their jobs.
2. *Some* groups of manual workers have to be members of unions in order to get or keep their jobs.
3. Management strongly recommends that *all* manual workers are members of unions.
4. Management strongly recommends, for *some* groups of manual workers, that they are members of unions.
5. No manual workers have to be members of unions nor is it strongly recommended that they are members.

The first two of these categories correspond precisely to the comprehensive or partial closed shop as negotiated in a union membership agreement. This could be pre-entry if applicants have to be a member of the appropriate union before joining the company, or post-entry if employees have to join the union after they have been engaged by the company. The third and fourth categories are referred to as *employer-endorsed* unionism.

Table 32.1 shows the distribution of establishments with people in one or other of these categories of union membership agreements as revealed by the Workshop Industrial Relations Survey of 2019 establishments carried out in 1984 under the auspices of the Department of Employment and other bodies.

	Manual workers (%)	Non-manual workers (%)
1 All members	17	6
2 Some members	3	3
3 Management strongly recommends all members	15	16
4 Management strongly recommends some members	1	1
5 None of the above arrangements	64	74
	100	100

Table 32.1 *Union membership agreement*

For obvious reasons, trade unions prefer a closed shop arrangement. Although some politicians and many libertarians are against the closed shop in principle, managements, as noted earlier, often learn to live quite happily with them and even grow to like the settled state that a closed shop produces.

Millward and Stevens did note, however, that where there was a closed shop for some groups of manual workers, then earnings for manual workers tended to be higher, independently of the general level of trade union membership.

Industrial relations strategy

The relationships that exist between employers and those they employ usually exist in tactical situations. Events happen and management and unions react to them. Employers are disagreeably surprised when they are suddenly faced with a claim for union recognition from their white collared staff. Unions are shocked by the absence of any procedure for dealing with redundancies. Industrial relations too often involves tactics without strategy.

It could be claimed that trade unions do have a general strategy: to protect the interests of their members and to improve their conditions. Many employers could also be said to operate in accordance with a general if somewhat negative strategy: to contain the constant pressure from the trade unions. But these are attitudes not strategies. All too often, there seems to be little evidence that any considered thought has been given to longer range developments and to the plans that are required to create and exploit opportunities to improve relationships or to meet potential threats to industrial harmony.

The aim of the industrial relations strategies of an organization should be to ensure that corporate objectives can be achieved by gaining the maximum amount of co-operation from employees and by minimizing the amount of industrial unrest. The factors influencing industrial relations strategy can be divided between those operating mainly within the organization and those bringing pressure to bear from outside.

Internal factors affecting industrial relations strategy

The main internal factors are as follows:

- The attitudes of management to employees – the extent to which management recognizes that it has a responsibility towards its employees as well as to its shareholders and customers.
- The attitudes of employees to management – the extent to which they are satisfied with the company as an employer and with their work and prospects.
- The attitudes of management to trade unions, which tend to fall into three categories:
  - (a) negative – those who resent the existence of unions either because they feel they unnecessarily interfere with management's authority or because they feel they will damage the paternalistic climate that exists and will erode the loyalty of employees to the company;
  - (b) neutral – those who accept the unions if they are there, possibly as a necessary evil, but do not believe that there is any point in management taking an active interest in promoting good relationships with them;
  - (c) positive – those who believe that unions can play an important role in partnership with management in developing better relationships between the company and its employees.
- The attitude of employees to unions. They can also have negative, neutral or positive feelings about unions.
- The inevitability of differences of opinion between management and unions. The primary role of the unions is to look after the interests of their members, while management is primarily concerned with economic performance. These interests are bound to

clash sometimes over how the earnings of the company should be distributed between its owners and its employees.

- The extent to which management can or wants to exercise absolute authority to enforce decisions affecting the interests of employees.
- The present and likely future strength of the unions.
- The extent to which there is one dominating union or the existence of a number of competing unions which may lead to inter-union and demarcation disputes.
- The extent to which effective and agreed procedures for discussing and resolving grievances or handling disputes exist within the company.
- The effectiveness of managers and supervisors in dealing with industrial relations problems and disputes.
- The effectiveness of shop stewards or employee representatives and the degree of authority they can exercise over their members.
- The prosperity of the company, the degree to which it is expanding, stagnating or running down and the extent to which technological changes are likely to affect employment conditions and opportunities.

External factors affecting industrial relations strategy

The main external factors are as follows:

- The militancy of the unions – nationally or locally.
- The effectiveness of the union and its officials and the extent to which the officials can and do control the activities of shop stewards within the company.
- The authority and effectiveness of the employer's association.
- The extent to which bargaining is carried out at national, local or plant level.
- The effectiveness of any national or local procedure agreements that may exist.
- The employment and pay situation – nationally and locally.
- The legal framework within which industrial relations exists.

Areas covered by industrial relations strategy

Industrial relations strategies cannot be developed in isolation, as an analysis of the internal and external factors affecting them clearly indicates. They must be related to overall business strategies as well as to other personnel policies concerning employment, training, pay and working conditions. The specific areas in which industrial relations strategies can be developed are as follows:

- The improvement of relationships with employees generally

through joint consultation and communications procedures (these are considered in Chapters 33 and 34).

● The improvement of relationships with unions or staff associations by developing better collective bargaining and other industrial relations procedures or by improving the operation of existing procedures.

● The improvement of the competence of managers and supervisors in dealing with industrial relations matters, including communications and joint consultations.

● The education and training of shop stewards or staff representatives (in conjunction with the union or staff association).

In some situations, alternative strategies may have to be considered; for example, when a non-union company is confronted with the possibility of trade unionism. Figure 32.1 is an example of how the alternatives could be set out in the form of a decision tree.

Union recognition

One of the biggest industrial relations problems that can face a company is that of recognition, whether of any union in a non-unionized company, or of additional unions in a company which is already partly unionized. Recognition can take place in two forms: first, representative rights which simply allows the union to represent employees on issues affecting them but does not concede that they have the right to negotiate terms and conditions of employment; second, negotiating rights, which give them full authority, within any national agreement, to negotiate terms and conditions. The unions will naturally want negotiating rights and may only accept representative rights as a second best if they are forced to do so by lack of support from employees or a particularly tough management. Clearly, they regard representative rights as a step towards full negotiating rights.

Recognition strategy in a non-unionized company

Management in a non-unionized company may well feel that they have to resist the unions to the last ditch as a disruptive influence which will erode management's traditional prerogative – the authority to manage its own affairs. This is understandable. Unions may not be so disruptive as they fear, but they certainly reduce the absolute authority of management. And no one voluntarily likes to relinquish long-established authority.

The six main strategies for dealing with potential or actual recognition issues are shown in Figure 32.2. These provide for a steadily increasing degree of formalization and loss of authority by management.

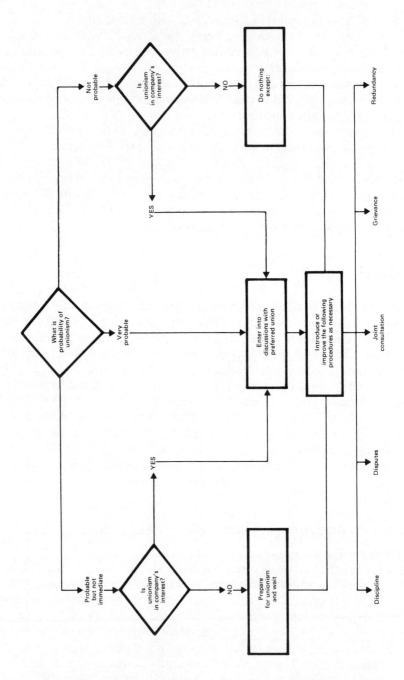

Figure 32.1 Trade Union membership – alternative strategies

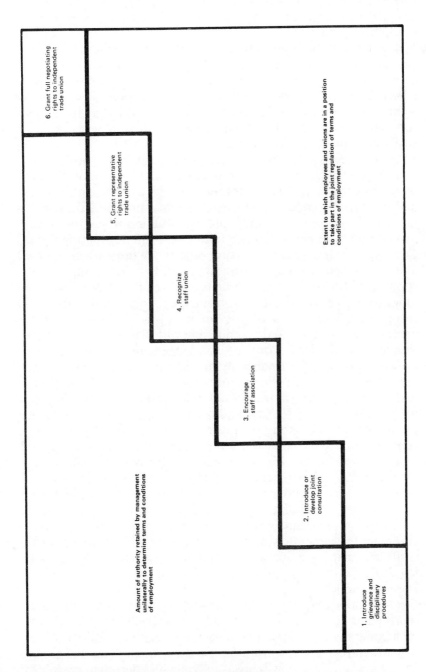

Figure 32.2 Alternative strategies for dealing with potential or actual recognition issues

- *Strategy one* is the minimum that any company should do and, under British law, there have to be published grievance and disciplinary procedures.
- *Strategy two* is an attempt to divert interest by introducing joint consultation. It may work in the increasingly rare situations where staff are totally uninterested in unions but in most cases where there is any pressure for unionization it fails. The failure of joint consultation as a means of holding unions at bay is because too many committees are so emasculated that employees can easily become disillusioned about them.
- *Strategy three* is a diversion strategy for setting up a staff association which has been adopted with some success in Britain by a number of commercial companies such as building societies and insurance companies. It may sometimes only be a delaying tactic and can lead inexorably into the situation where the staff association becomes in effect a union with full negotiating rights.
- *Strategy four* is a stronger version of strategy three when the staff association acquires negotiating rights. In Britain a company sponsored staff union will not be recognized in law as a trade union, which opens the door for outside unions to press for recognition. Irrespective of this factor, it is advisable for management to have as little to do as possible with setting up an association apart from a few words of encouragement, and nothing to do with supporting it financially or with special facilities. If it is seen as a creature of the company, a staff association will soon lose credibility and will totally fail in its objective of keeping other unions at bay. It may, and often does, fail anyhow because the unions are too strong for it, or because the staff have acquired a taste for collective bargaining and decide that they will do better with the backing of a union. A further problem is that management, in its anxiety to appease a staff association and keep out a union, may negotiate 'soft' agreements – softer than they probably would have negotiated with a trade union. The staff association strategy is therefore one which should only be entered into deliberately and with great care when the company is confident that it will work. It should not be used as a last despairing device to keep the unions out – it will always fail in these circumstances.
- *Strategies five and six*, which involve recognizing the union as a representative or a negotiating body respectively, may be forced on a company if its strategies at earlier stages have failed. It is a pity when this happens, not because the company has had to accept a union (which will always be much easier than was anticipated), but because it has been forced to capitulate. This is a bad start to the relationship. It creates initial feelings of resent-

ment and may give the union the impression that management will always be likely to collapse if pressed fairly hard. The bargaining advantage will have moved to the union. If the climate of opinion nationally and within the firm is mainly in favour of recognition, then it is better to concentrate on getting a satisfactory procedure agreement as a basis for co-operative collective bargaining in the future rather than fighting on.

Choice of strategies

The choice of strategies is a management decision in the sense that it depends initially on its assessment of three factors: first, the extent to which it approves or disapproves of unions; second, the strength of the unions inside and outside the company; and third, the consequences of resisting the union. Management's choice may, of course, be limited if the unions are already strong enough to force the company into recognizing them. The aim of the strategy should be to avoid being put under this sort of pressure either by gracefully granting recognition, on good terms, or by adopting one of the other approaches, if they seem appropriate.

The first step management should take before deciding on its strategy is to examine and if necessary revise its assumptions about unions. This could be done by talking to other employers or even by meeting a real live union official or two and finding that horns and tails are not as much in evidence as was thought. The next step should be to assess the strength of feelings of employees and to evaluate the strength of the union, if it still felt that unionization constitutes a threat.

The strength of a possible approach from a union can be assessed informally by keeping ears close to the ground. First line supervisors should know what their groups are thinking, and it is up to higher management to ensure that any reliable information they acquire is passed upwards. There is no point in being taken completely by surprise.

It is necessary to assess at the same time which union, if any, is likely to approach and how strong its attack will be. Employers' associations and local contacts amongst employers of similar categories of staff can provide some guidance. It may be helpful to form some idea of which union would be preferable if there is more than one union on the scene. Steps can then be taken later to provide more encouragement (or less discouragement) to the preferred union.

A union, of course, may make a formal approach to talk to employees about joining them. It is normally unwise to reject such approaches. Facilities can easily be given for the union officials to meet interested employees out of working hours on the company's premises. Many firms have found that the number attending such meetings gives an indication of the feelings of their employees. Arrangements can usually be made for feedback on what went on, which can give valuable clues to the attitude of employees and the strategy being followed by the union. It is important at this stage and all subsequent stages to obtain a realistic view of the strength of the union and the reactions of employees. There is no point in fighting bloody battles if it is inevitable that the war will eventually be lost. This only stores up trouble for the future. On the other hand, it is inadvisable to give in too easily. The union must appreciate now that management can be firm when it wants to be.

The tactics of management now and later should be based on its judgement of present and future union strengths and the direction in which the loyalties of its employees may go. More reliable information on the views of employees can be obtained by conducting an attitude survey, or, as it might more appropriately be termed, a preference survey. This would ask whether or not they wish to be represented by a union, or whether they would prefer an employees' association or some other non-unionized consultative body to represent their interests. Employers often resist the approaches of unions, on the grounds that their employees might not wish to be forced to join or even live with a union. This could be true in some circumstances, where the staff are mainly white collared workers with the typical middle class suspicion of trade unions. But it could be a rationalization of management's own fears about loss of prerogative. No harm can be done by testing reactions – there is no evidence that the mere fact of conducting a survey encourages staff to think about joining a union. The value of a formal assessment is that it provides a reasonably factual basis for deciding on the strategy and tactics that the company should adopt.

At a later stage it may be decided that a ballot should be held to decide whether or not a union should be recognized. Management may feel strongly that recognition should not be given until at least 51% of the relevant employees are actually members of a union. This sounds reasonable, but it may be necessary to concede recognition with a lower percentage if it seems inevitable that more employees will join. There are no guidelines available on what is the minimum percentage for recognition. Each case has to be decided on its merits.

Recognition strategy in a partly unionized company

A partly unionized company may be faced with a claim for recognition by a union representing employees who are not currently covered by a union agreement. Strategies in this case can be developed along the lines suggested for a non-unionized company facing unions for the first time, except that the company can presumably benefit when formulating its approach from the experience it has already gained. This situation is most likely to arise when white collar unions make an approach to clerical, technical, supervisory or management staff. Top management may feel increasingly despondent as their own kind fall into what they might regard as the maw of the unions, but most companies have learned to live with staff unions quite happily.

A more difficult situation arises when an alternative or breakaway union tries to encroach on the membership of existing unions. There are two dangers: first, of the fragmentation of bargaining units and second, inter-union strife. There is everything to be said for minimizing fragmentation. A bargaining unit, in the sense of a body of employees who are represented by one union, should preferably cover all employees of the same status or occupation in one plant. Bargaining units may be stratified according to status or divided according to occupation but they should not overlap. This causes confusion, lack of stability and difficulties in reaching agreements. It is not easy to control a move towards fragmentation when unions are taking the initiative, but management can at least resist recognition claims if they seem to be undesirable.

De-recognition

Management does not *have* to recognize a trade union, although it might find it very difficult to resist recognition if the work force is overwhelmingly unionized. But an employer may feel that there is no point in recognizing a union which only represents a small proportion of employees or is totally ineffective. There are no legal constraints on de-recognition. It is up to management to decide whether it needs to be done and, if so, can it be done without too much bloodshed.

Clearly, employees have to be encouraged to feel that they will not lose anything if they are no longer represented. The company must have demonstrated that it treats people fairly. As was noted in the introduction to Part VI on reward management, companies are increasingly turning towards more flexible pay systems, where rates are agreed individually, market forces prevail, and the annual pay round no longer exists. Firms may indeed be moving in this direction mainly for their white collared employees, or where conditions of employment have been harmonized to remove the invidious class distinction between white and blue collared workers. But if these moves can be seen as advantageous to all concerned, the scope for individual settlements will increase and the need for a trade union will diminish. This may lead to de-recognition.

Closed shop recognition

Closed shops can be pre-entry, when employees are required to join a union before starting work, or post-entry when they have to join the union within a stated period. A company may give *de facto* recognition to either sort of closed shop, or it may conclude a membership agreement with the union. Such recognition is legalized under British law and a company which has a membership agreement with a recognized union can insist on an employee joining the union and dismiss him fairly if he refuses, as long as he does not have genuine religious objections or other deeply held conviction against being a member of a trade union.

Clearly, a closed shop should only be recognized if there is a very large majority of union members and it is possible to avoid serious difficulties over non-union employees who are reluctant to join. The decision may be a difficult one, as it could require balancing the interests of stable relationships with the union against the rights of the individual. The latter may have to be subordinated to the general good, but it could be an unpleasant business. The only answer is to conclude an agreement with the union that those existing employees who have genuine conscientious or religious objections to joining can be allowed to remain, possibly subscribing the normal union dues to a recognized charity. More recently in the UK the government has issued a code of practice on closed shops which defines the circumstances in which closed shops should be set up, provides guidlines on agreements and indicates where dismissal from a closed shop would be unfair. And the 1980 and 1982 Employment Acts provide greater protection to individuals in closed shops.

Procedural agreements

A procedure is an established way of carrying out some piece of business. The aim of a procedural agreement is to ensure that the business conducted between management and union is carried out in an orderly, consistent and generally accepted manner.

Procedural agreements have evolved as a method of exercising joint regulation over matters that affect the interests of both the company and its employees. A procedural relationship is established between an employer and a trade union as soon as the union's right to represent the interests of its membership has been recognized. When that right includes the settlement of terms and conditions of employment by negotiation the active continuity of the relationship is maintained as adjustments are made to meet constantly changing circumstances. The procedural aspects of an act of recognition establishing negotiating rights are usually concerned with defining the area in which the union's representative capacity is acknowledged, indicating the subjects which are brought within the scope of negotiation, the steps by which agreement is to be sought and the procedure to be followed if there is failure to agree.

Procedural agreements may contain the following sections:

1. A preamble defining the objectives of the agreement.
2. A statement that the union is recognized as a representative body with negotiating rights.
3. A statement of general principles, which will include a commitment to use the procedure (a no-strike clause) and may additionally include a *status quo* clause which restricts the ability of management to introduce changes outside negotiated or customary practice.

4. A statement of the facilities granted to unions, including the rights of shop stewards and the right to hold meetings.
5. Provision for joint negotiating committees (in some agreements).
6. The negotiating or disputes procedure.
7. Provision for terminating the agreement.

Preamble – objectives

The objectives of the agreement should be stated in the preamble, for example:

> To use the processes of negotiation to achieve results beneficial to the company and the employees.
>
> To provide a framework which will enable discussions to take place at all levels on ways of continuing the development of good industrial relations in the company.
>
> To provide an arrangement through which matters of concern to both employers and management can be discussed and negotiated at an appropriate level.
>
> To provide a means of negotiation and consultation on all matters directly and indirectly affecting the company's employees with the objective of achieving sound and constructive relations between the management and the employees.

Union recognition

The recognition section should confirm the right of the signatory union or unions to represent specific categories of employees within an agreed bargaining unit. The rights may be defined as being:

> To represent and to negotiate wages and conditions of employment on behalf of its members who are employed by the company.

Reference may also be made in this section to union membership. A general phrase would be used such as:

> The company and the union recognize that it is in the interests of good industrial relations that all employees in agreed bargaining units should become and remain members of the union.

This reference to union membership could be accompanied by an undertaking from the company to encourage employees to join the union. It could be further developed into a closed shop agreement, although those words would never be used, by a statement to the effect that all existing employees in the defined bargaining unit should become members of the union within, say, four weeks of the date of the agreement unless they have genuine religious objections. The agreement could go on to state that all new employees should join the unions within, say, two weeks of starting with the company. In the more extreme cases, where a pre-entry closed shop is in force, the agreement would state that the company undertakes only to engage men or women who are already members of the union, unless they have genuine religious objections.

Reference might be made in these circumstances to the payment by those with religious objections of the equivalent of the union dues to a charity agreed with the union.

General principles

The statement of general principles should indicate how the parties to the agreement are going to work together to achieve its objectives. The following points should be included:

- A statement of common purpose – 'The company and the union have a common objective in using the processes of negotiation and consultation to achieve results beneficial to both parties'.
- A definition of the role of the unions as recognized by management – 'The company recognizes that effective industrial relations are best realized through fully representative unions capable of authoritative negotiation'.
- A definition of the role of management as recognized by the unions – 'The unions for their part recognize that management has the prime responsibility to manage the undertaking in order to achieve its objectives efficiently'.
- An undertaking not to take industrial action until the agreed procedures are exhausted (a commitment to use procedure or no-strike clause) – 'The company and the unions agree that mutually satisfactory conditions are best achieved through the process of negotiation. The company therefore agrees to refrain from lock-out, and the union from stoppage of work or other restrictions on production until the procedure for resolving disputes prescribed in this agreement (and the national agreement) has been exhausted'.
- An undertaking may be included not to change the *status quo* without prior consultation – 'Prior consultation will take place before any change in working practices or methods of payment is implemented. Should the change result in a dispute between the management and the unions, the practice shall revert to what it was prior to the dispute and the change shall only be made subsequently should it be agreed through the negotiating procedure'.

Union facilities

The agreement on union facilities should cover the following three areas:

1. *Rights and duties of shop stewards* – it is necessary to define:
   - The right of employees to elect shop stewards – 'Employees of the company who are members of the union will elect representatives to act on their behalf in accordance with this agreement'.

- What a shop steward is – 'For the purpose of this agreement a shop steward is an accredited representative of the union who has been recognized by the company'.
- Eligibility – the agreement may define a minimum length of service before becoming eligible for election as a steward. It may also state that the company will recognize shop stewards elected in accordance with the agreed procedure but reserves the right, after consultation with the district or regional union organizer, to withhold or withdraw recognition from any particular individual.
- The number of shop stewards – 'The company and the union will agree the number of shop stewards to be elected each year and the areas of production or groups of people whom they will represent'.
- Election arrangements – 'Elections by secret ballot may be held at a mutually convenient time and the company will assist in providing ballot facilities if required'.
- Notification arrangements – 'When a shop steward has been elected the company will be notified officially by the union'.
- Provision for a senior shop steward – 'The shop stewards may elect a senior shop steward'.
- The duties of shop stewards – 'Shop stewards will act in accordance with agreements between the union and the company, so far as these affect the relations between the company and its employees. They will be subject to the control of the union in trade union matters'.
- Facilities for shop stewards – 'Facilities will be afforded to shop stewards by the company to carry out their functions within the framework of this agreement to deal with questions and problems in the department or section represented by the shop steward'.
- Arrangements for shop stewards leaving work and holding meetings and discussions – 'A shop steward wishing to leave his work to investigate a grievance, contact a union official, meet other shop stewards or carry out any other union business will first obtain the permission of his foreman or other person in authority. Should he wish to visit a department other than the one for which he is the elected representative, he will also obtain permission of the foreman or other person in authority in that department or section. Such permission will not unreasonably be withheld'.
- The basis upon which shop stewards are paid while carrying out their duties – 'Shop stewards will suffer no financial loss through the discharge of their duties as shop stewards'.
- Training arrangements – 'The parties agree on the need to

provide suitable training for shop stewards to achieve the skills required to carry out their duties'.

● Protection of employment rights – 'Action taken by shop stewards in good faith in pursuance of their duties, shall not in any way affect their employment with the company'.

● Arrangements for transferring or dismissing shop stewards – 'Before a shop steward is transferred from a department or section he represents, and before he is dismissed from the company, the transfer or dismissal will be brought to the notice of the branch secretary by management'.

2. *Union meetings and communication facilities* – for which the agreement should define:

● Arrangements for meetings between the company and the union – 'Meetings between representatives of the company and the union will normally be held during working hours and on the company's premises'.

● Arrangements for union meetings – 'The company recognizes that on certain occasions union meetings can with advantage be held on the company's premises outside working hours. Permission to hold such meetings should be obtained in advance from the company'.

● The use of notice-boards by unions – 'The union will be allowed the reasonable use of company notice-boards for union announcements'.

3. *The collection of union dues* – the agreement may specify a 'check-off' arrangement for the company to collect union dues – 'It is agreed that a check-off system will operate whereby the company agrees to deduct union dues (but not entrance fees or special levies) from the wages of union members and to pay them to the union. This will only apply to employees who have previously authorized the deductions in writing'.

Joint negotiating committee

Provision for a joint negotiating committee is not a necessary part of a procedural agreement. Many, if not most, companies would prefer to avoid formalizing negotiating arrangements in this way. A joint negotiating committee, however, is sometimes set up when a large company agrees that terms and conditions of employment should be determined by collective bargaining within the company or plant, and prefers to regularize negotiating procedures rather than engage in a series of *ad hoc* trials of strength.

The terms of reference of a company joint negotiating committee should cover the following points:

1. *Objective.* To provide the means of negotiation and consultation

on all matters directly and indirectly affecting the hourly paid employees in the company's establishment.

2. *Terms of reference*
    (a) To negotiate company-wide wage systems, hours of work, overtime rates and other conditions of employment.
    (b) To provide a means of joint consultation on production, safety, welfare matters and on general company problems.
    (c) To review the operation of domestic disputes and disciplinary procedures and to decide on any changes necessary.

3. *Composition*
    (a) Numbers of shop stewards and management representatives.
    (b) Constituencies of shop steward members.
    (c) Method of election of accredited shop stewards.

4. *Officers.* Chairman and secretary of management and union sides.

5. *Meetings.* Arrangements for regular ordinary meetings and extraordinary meetings (when agreed by both chairmen).

6. *Agenda.* Arrangements for placing items on the agenda and raising additional items.

7. *Minutes.* Arrangements for chairmen to agree minutes and for distributing same.

8. *Failure to agree.* Procedure to be followed if the committee fails to agree. This could include bringing in full-time union officials and employer's officials for a works conference and, if this fails, progression through the normal negotiating procedure for the industry or some form of conciliation process. In Britain this could be provided by the Advisory, Conciliation and Arbitration Service (ACAS).

Disputes procedure

A domestic disputes procedure should describe each of the stages for dealing with disputes in the company from when an issue is first raised on the shop floor until, assuming it is not settled at an earlier stage, it is either referred to outside conciliation or is dealt with in accordance with the agreed procedure for avoiding disputes in the industry. A disputes procedure of this nature is, in effect, a grievance procedure for employees who are members of a union.

The domestic procedure should state the principle that no strike or lockout should take place until the procedure has been exhausted, unless this has already been stated as a general principle in the procedural agreement. Time limits should be given for moving from one stage to the next of the procedure in the event of a failure to agree.

The following is an example of a typical staged disputes procedure in a medium sized plant where there is no national agreement.

Domestic disputes procedure

Stage 1

1. All queries and grievances should in the first place be raised by the employee with his foreman. If the employee chooses to approach the shop steward in the first instance concerning the matter, they may subsequently jointly discuss it with the foreman, or the shop steward may raise the matter on the employee's behalf with the foreman. (The latter sentence goes further than many procedures which lay down that the shop steward should only become involved on individual issues if the employee has failed to get satisfaction. In practice, however, shop stewards do become involved in the first instance and it is realistic to allow for this in the procedure.)

2. If the issue affects a group of union members in the same department or section, the shop steward raises the matter with the foreman.

3. The foreman will do his best to resolve the issue and give an answer within *three* working days of the matter being raised with him. However, if the issue is one on which he cannot give a decision he will immediately refer the matter to stage 2 of the procedure.

Stage 2

4. If the employee or shop steward is not satisfied with the answer provided by the foreman, the latter will refer the issue to the departmental manager who will discuss the matter with the shop steward. The departmental manager may ask the personnel manager to attend this meeting and the shop steward may be accompanied by the senior shop steward of his union.

5. The departmental manager, following discussions with the personnel manager, will give his answer within *three* working days of the matter being raised with him (ie within six working days of the matter being raised initially).

Stage 3

6. If the shop steward is not satisfied with the answer given by the departmental manager, the departmental manager will refer the matter to the works manager who, together with the personnel manager, will discuss the matter with the shop steward and the senior shop steward.

7. The works manager will give his answer within *three* working days of the matter being raised with him (ie within nine working days of the matter being raised initially).

Stage 4

8. If the union is dissatisfied with the answer provided by the works manager a conference should be held to discuss the matter within the company at which a director of the company, other appropriate members of management, the senior shop steward and, if required, the district officer of the union will be present.

Stage 5

9. If a mutually satisfactory agreement is not reached in stage 4 the matter will be referred to conciliation and, if that fails, arbitration. The means of conciliation or arbitration will be agreed between the company and the district officer of the union.
10. The recommendations of the conciliation body, or the decision of the arbitration body, will not be regarded as final and binding on either the company or the union. However, both parties will use these findings as a basis for further negotiation.

General

11. No lockout, stoppage of work or other unauthorized action will take place as a result of any complaint, grievance or dispute in which the company and union members are concerned. Any such action before the procedure has been exhausted will be a breach of this agreement.

Records

12. Records will be maintained by company foremen or managers of the details of the complaint and decisions made at each stage of the procedure. Copies of the records will be given to shop stewards or union officials concerned.

Disciplinary procedure

It is normal to include a disciplinary procedure in a formal procedural agreement. The points that should be covered and an example of a procedure are given in Chapter 15 and Appendix H.

Termination of the agreement

It is usual in Britain not to specify a terminal date for the procedural agreement but to state that it would be subject to, say, six months' notice of termination from either side.

Redundancy procedures

It is not common practice for redundancy procedures to be incorporated in a procedural agreement, mainly because it is difficult to obtain complete agreement in advance on the precise criteria for redundancy and the compensation to be offered. Such procedures are often discussed separately and informal agreement reached that they should be used as guidelines for action in the event of redundancy. The points that should be covered in redundancy procedures are considered in Chapter 15 and Appendix I.

Industrial relations procedures for non-unionized companies or employees

In non-unionized companies, or for categories of employees who are not members of a union there is, of course, no formal negotiating procedure. There may be arrangements for joint consultation (see Chapter 33) and the terms of reference of joint consultative committees or works councils might possibly allow reference to conditions of employment, but it is most unlikely that such committees would be allowed to negotiate on pay matters. A company may decide to encourage an employees' association and negotiate with it, but this is tantamount to a union, especially if the company keeps at arm's length from the association.

A non-unionized company should at least have a disciplinary procedure (Appendix H) and a grievance procedure (Appendix G). Both are required in Britain under the Employment Protection Act. In addition, it may be advisable to have a redundancy procedure (Appendix I), even if this is not announced to staff.

Grievance procedure

Grievance procedures for individual employees should aim to settle the grievance fairly and as near as possible to the point of origin. They should be simple and rapid in operation. The procedure should be in writing and state that:

(a) the grievance should normally be discussed first between the employee and his or her immediate superior;

(b) if satisfaction is not achieved at this level the employee should have the right of appeal to the next higher level of management and, if he wishes, may be accompanied by another member of the company's staff to help him put his case;

(c) there should be a further right of appeal to the highest level in the company if satisfaction is not achieved at an earlier stage.

Negotiations

Negotiations take place when two parties meet, one or both aiming to win as much as they can from the other while giving away as little as possible. Negotiating can be a war game. It is a battle in the sense that the bargainers are pitting their wits against each other while also bringing in the heavy artillery in the shape of sanctions or threatened sanctions. As with other battles, the negotiation process can produce a pyrrhic victory in which both sides, including the apparent winner, retire to mourn their losses and lick their wounds. It is a game in the sense that both sides are trying to win, but there are various conventions or rules which the parties tacitly adopt or recognize, although in practice they may break them in the heat of the battle.

Negotiations can normally be broken down into four stages:

1. Preparing for negotiation: setting objectives, defining strategy and assembling data.

2. Opening.
3. Bargaining.
4. Closing.

Before analysing these stages in detail it may be helpful to consider the process of bargaining and list the typical conventions that operate when bargaining takes place.

The process of bargaining

The process of bargaining consists of three distinct, though related, functions. First, bargainers state their bargaining position to their opposite numbers. Second, they probe weaknesses in the bargaining position of their opposite numbers and try to convince them that they must move, by stages if this is inevitable, from their present position to a position closer to what the bargainer wants. Third, they adjust or confirm their original estimate of their own bargaining position in the light of information gleaned and reactions from their opposite number, so that, if the time comes to put an estimate of bargaining position to the test, the ground chosen will be as favourable as possible.

The essence of the bargaining process was well put by Peters in *Strategies and Tactics in Labour Negotiations*. He comments:

> In skilful hands the bargaining position performs a double function. It conceals and it reveals. The bargaining position is used to indicate – to unfold gradually, step by step – the maximum expectation of the negotiator, while at the same time concealing, for as long as necessary, his minimum expectation. By indirect means, such as the manner and timing of the changes in your bargaining position, you, as a negotiator, try to convince the other side that your maximum expectation is really your minimum breaking-off point ... Since you have taken an appropriate bargaining position at the start of negotiations, each change in your position should give ever-clearer indications of your maximum expectation. Also, each change should be designed to encourage or pressure the other side to reciprocate with as much information as you give them, if not more.[15]

Bargaining conventions

There are certain conventions in collective bargaining which most experienced and responsible negotiators understand and accept, although they are never stated and, indeed, may be broken in the heat of the moment or by a tyro in the bargaining game. These conventions help to create an atmosphere of trust and understanding which is essential to the maintenance of the type of stable bargaining relationship that benefits both sides. Some of the most generally accepted conventions are listed below:

1. Whatever happens during the bargaining, both parties are using the bargaining process in the hope of coming to a settlement.
2. Attacks, hard words, threats and (controlled) losses of temper are perfectly legitimate tactics to underline determination to get one's

way and to shake the opponent's confidence and self-possession. But these are treated by both sides as legitimate tactics and should not be allowed to shake the basic belief in each other's integrity or desire to settle without taking drastic action.

3. Off-the-record discussions are mutually beneficial as a means of probing attitudes and intentions and smoothing the way to a settlement. But they should not be referred to specifically in formal bargaining sessions unless both sides agree in advance.

4. Each side should normally be prepared to move from its original position.

5. It is normal, although not inevitable, for the negotiation to proceed by alternate offers and counter-offers from each side which lead steadily towards a settlement.

6. Concessions, once made, cannot be withdrawn.

7. Firm offers must not be withdrawn, although it is legitimate to make and withdraw conditional offers.

8. Third parties should not be brought in until both parties are agreed that no further progress would be made without them.

9. The final agreement should mean exactly what it says. There should be no trickery, and the terms agreed should be implemented without amendment.

10. If possible, the final settlement should be framed in such a way as to reduce the extent to which the opponent obviously loses face or credibility.

Preparing for negotiation

Negotiations take place in an atmosphere of uncertainty. You do not know how strong your employees' bargaining team is and what it really wants. The members of that team do not know how much you are prepared to concede or the strength of your convictions.

In a typical wage negotiation the union or representative body making the claim will define three things:

● the target it would like to achieve;
● the minimum it will accept;
● the opening claim which will be most likely to help them achieve the target.

You as the employer will define three related things:

● the target settlement you would like to achieve;
● the maximum you would be prepared to concede;
● the opening offer you will make which will provide you with sufficient room to manoeuvre in reaching your target.

The difference between their claim and your offer is the negotiating range.

If your maximum exceeds their minimum this will indicate the settlement range. This is demonstrated in Figure 32.3. In this example the chance of settlement without too much trouble is fairly high. It is when your maximum is less than their minimum, as in Figure 32.4, that the trouble starts. Over a period of time a negotiation where a settlement range exists proceeds in the way demonstrated in Figure 32.5.

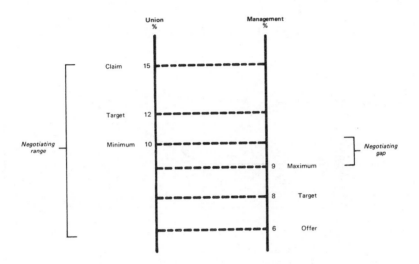

Figure 32.3 Negotiating range with a settlement zone

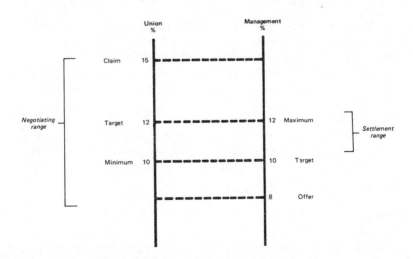

Figure 32.4 Negotiating range without a settlement zone

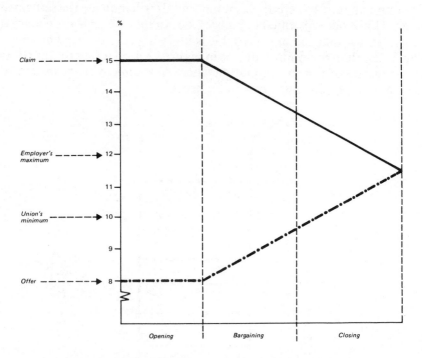

Figure 32.5 Stages of a negotiation

Objectives
Your objectives should be defined in the form of your target settlement and your initial and maximum offers. These will be conditioned by:

- the relative strengths of your case and that of the union;
- the relative power of the company *vis-a-vis* the union;
- the size of the union's claim and whether it is realistic;
- the likely target and minimum acceptable offer set by the union;
- the amount of room for negotiation you want to allow;
- your ability to pay;
- the going rate elsewhere;
- the rate of inflation. Although you should never concede that it is your job to protect your employees from inflation, the cost of living will usually be one of the chief arguments advanced by a union for an increase.

Strategy
Your strategy should clearly be designed to achieve your target settlement, with the maximum you are prepared to concede being your fall-back position. You need to decide two things:

1. The stages you would ideally like to follow in moving from your

opening to your closing offer. This is dependent on the amount of room for negotiation you have allowed.

2. The negotiating package you want to use in reply to whatever package the union has put forward. Your aim should be to provide scope for trading concessions during the course of negotiations. There is also much to be said for having in reserve various conditions which you can ask the unions to accept in return for any concessions you may be prepared to make. You might, for example, ask for an extended period before the next settlement in return for an increase in your offer.

Preparation

It is essential to prepare carefully for negotiations so that you do not, in Aneurin Bevan's phrase, 'go naked to the conference table'. The following steps should be taken:

1. List the arguments to be used in supporting your own case.
2. List the likely arguments or counter-arguments that your opponent is likely to use.
3. List your own counter-arguments to the arguments of your opponent.
4. Obtain the data you need to support your case.
5. Select the negotiating team. This should never have fewer than two members, and for major negotiations should have three or more: one to take the lead and do most of the talking, one to take notes and feed the negotiator with any supporting information he requires, and the others to observe opposite numbers and play a specific part in negotiations in accordance with their brief.
6. Brief the members of the negotiating team on their roles and the negotiating strategy and tactics that are to be adopted. If appropriate, prepared statements or arguments should be issued at this stage to be used as required by the strategic plan.
7. Rehearse the members of the team in their roles. They can be asked to repeat their points to other members and deal with responses from them; or someone can act as devil's advocate and force the leader or other members of the team to handle awkward points or negotiating ploys.

At this stage it may be possible to meet the opponent informally to sound out his position, while he sounds out yours. The 'early warning' system can be used to condition the opponent to modify his likely initial demands by convincing him of the strength of your own position or your determination to resist.

Opening

Your tactics when opening the negotiation should be as follows:

1. Open realistically and move moderately.
2. Challenge your opponent's position as it stands; do not destroy his ability to move.
3. Explore attitudes, ask questions, observe behaviour and, above all, listen in order to assess your opponent's strengths and weaknesses, his tactics and the extent to which he may be bluffing.
4. Make no concessions of any kind at this stage.
5. Be non-committal about proposals and explanations (do not talk too much).

Bargaining

After the opening moves you begin the main bargaining phase during which you narrow the gap between the initial positions and try to persuade your opponent that your case is sufficiently strong to force him to close at a less advantageous point than he had planned. Employ the following tactics:

1. Always make conditional proposals: 'If you will do this then I will consider doing that.' The words to remember are: 'if . . . then . . .'.
2. Never make one-sided concessions: always trade off against a concession from the other party: 'If I concede x then I expect you to concede y.'
3. Negotiate on the whole package: do not allow your opponent to pick you off item by item, and keep the issues open to extract the maximum benefit from your potential trade-offs.

Closing

When and how you close is a matter of judgement, and depends on your assessment of the strength of your opponent's case and his determination to see it through. There are various closing techniques:

1. Making a concession from the package, preferably a minor one which is traded off against an agreement to settle. The concession can be offered more positively than in the bargaining stage: 'If you will agree to settle at x, then I will concede y.'
2. Doing a deal: splitting the difference, or bringing in something new, such as extending the settlement time-scale, agreeing to back payments, phasing increases, making a joint declaration of intent to do something in the future (eg introducing a productivity plan).
3. Summarizing what has happened to date, emphasizing the concessions that have been made and the extent to which you have moved, and stating that you have reached your final position.
4. Applying pressure through a threat of the dire consequences which will follow if your offer is not accepted.
5. Giving your opponent a choice between two courses of action.

Do not make a final offer unless you mean it. If it is not really your final offer and your opponent calls your bluff, you will have to make further concessions and your credibility will be undermined. He will, of course, attempt to force you into revealing the extent to which you have reached your final position. Do not allow him to hurry you. If you want to avoid committing yourself and thus devaluing the word 'final', state as positively as you can that this is as far as you are prepared to go.

Industrial relations training

Industrial relations training is required for four categories of people in a company: managers, supervisors, shop stewards and employees. The training should be planned along the lines suggested in Chapter 29 which means that it should be based on an analysis of training needs and should include specific objectives to be achieved by the course as a whole and by each session in a course. Training for shop stewards and employees can be usefully carried out jointly with the trade union, but it is even more important to train managers and supervisors.

Management training

Managers are often taught about 'human relations' on courses but are seldom given training in collective bargaining or education in the role of the unions. This shows up in two ways: first, at the conference table where inexperienced managers are often completely outgeneralled by well-trained and experienced union officials and, secondly, in the un-cooperative attitude taken by some managers to unions because they fail to understand company policy on industrial relations or the useful part that unions can play in achieving stable industrial relations.

Negotiating skills are mainly acquired by experience and practice, but it is dangerous to allow inexperienced managers to practise negotiating techniques with experienced shop stewards or union officials. The answer is to run special company courses, or to have separate sessions on existing courses, which deal with negotiating skills and allow managers to practise them in role playing exercises. They can also be required to analyse industrial relations case studies to determine the tactics that should be used. The case studies should preferably be based on actual problems that have occurred within the company.

Developments in industrial relations

Recent developments in industrial relations have been concerned with:

1. Government interventions.
2. The role of the trade unions.

3. Overall changes in workplace industrial relations.
4. The closed shop.
5. The impact of harmonization.
6. The impact of new technology.
7. The move towards individualism.
8. Involvement.
9. Bargaining structures.
10. New-style agreements and final-offer arbitration (pendulum agreements).

Government interventions

Government policy in the 1980s has been to influence union-management behaviour by legislation while maintaining a flood of employment rights for individuals. The aim has been to curb the unions, to democratize their procedures and to make them more liable for the acts of their members. The scope given to employers to place injunctions on unions taking or supporting what is now illegal action has allowed some managements to take some steps towards redressing the balance of power between them and the unions.

The role of the trade unions

Membership of trade unions declined catastrophically in the early 1980s, although losses have been slowing down recently. Some unions fought major wars with employers and lost them. What has been called the 'new realism' emerged, especially in unions such as the EETPU (Electrical, Electronic, Telecommunication and Plumbing Union). This accepts the need to adjust union strategies and tactics to changes in technology, company organization and the economic circumstances which affect company performance. New realism means being in favour of partnership based on single-union, strike-free, single status flexibility agreements, and also seeking every opportunity to achieve greater harmonization and industrial democracy. The 'new-style' agreements discussed later in this section are part of this approach. The new realism movement has been dismissed by Donald Macintyre[16] as no more than new pragmatism, and many unions will have nothing to do with it, perhaps because it seems to them to fit in too well with what management wants.

Overall changes in workplace industrial relations

The recession of the 1980s has been reflected in an overall reduction in strike activity (except in coal mining and newspaper publishing), lower pay settlements, attempts by management to regain prerogatives lost in times of over-full employment, and claims from the Government that the spirit of new realism was spreading rapidly. This has led to the development of 'macho-management' tactics in some organizations, but this is probably a short-lived phase which will be increasingly difficult to sustain in a period of economic recovery, for example, the Ford Motor Company strike in 1988.

Where trade unions are strongly entrenched there has been a move within companies towards greater formalization in the conduct of industrial relations. Formal procedures for dealing with such matters as discipline and dismissals, grievances and conditions of employment have become widespread. In these situations there is still a potentially powerful role for employee representation, but as Colin Hawksworth wrote:

> This will not necessarily mean representation through trade unions; although where unions are already recognized, most employers will be prepared to build on the working relationships which already exists. But in all changes which take place, consultation will be more significant than negotiation. The dominance of collective bargaining over the last few years, and its divisive effects, has moved managers firmly away from joint regulation.[17]

The closed shop

Closed shops grew rapidly in Great Britain from the early 1960s, when there was an estimated membership of 3.75 million workers, to 1978 when there were at least 5.2 million members. Employers learned to live with them during this period because on the whole they felt that they made their life easier.

This situation, however, changed in the 1980s. There has been a concerted Government attack on the closed shop and more employers are taking the view that it is an illiberal and counter-productive feature of the industrial relations scene. This is partly a reflection of the overall trend in workshop industrial relations, but other factors such as the impact of harmonization and new technology are changing employment structures and relationships with employers and are contributing to a decline in the importance of the closed shop, although not to its fall.

The impact of harmonization

More companies are harmonizing terms and conditions of employment for all their employees and this has been coupled with a move towards integrated pay structures. Employers who have set up single-status organizations and who have a number of unions, are trying to achieve a single-union agreement covering all grades of employees. This, however, is not an easy option, not least because it may involve the end of closed-shop agreements and be seen by the union as a threat to their continued existence in the firm. New-style agreements as discussed later, often contain provisions for a single union.

The impact of new technology

A comprehensive survey of workplace industrial relations and industrial change was conducted by the Policy Study Institute in 1984. In his report on the results of the survey, Daniel[18] commented that British workers, especially office workers, generally experience and accept a very high level of major technical change. Such change was usually popular among the workers affected, but both shop stewards and full-time union officials tended to support changes even more strongly than the ordinary workers they represented. Where there was resistance to change by workers and union representatives, it was most frequently provoked by organizational changes introduced independently of any new technology. So great was the support for change that even major innovations have been introduced with surprisingly little consultation.

The results of the survey also provided support for those who have argued that the spread of advanced technology would enrich the jobs of the workers. The tendency is for companies to employ more highly skilled staff and to pay them better. There were some job losses, but they were small in proportion to the losses arising from declining economic performance in those other companies which were not taking advantage of new technology.

In general, the introduction of new technology is likely to enhance skills, promote flexibility and multi-skilling, encourage harmonization and lead to even greater pressure from employers to deal with their staff on an individual basis.

The move towards individualism

In the 1970s the survey into industrial relations sponsored by the Department of Employment, the Policy Studies Institute and the Social Science Research Council, revealed that there was a growth of union recognition, membership and activity within the workplace which was shown, in certain cases, to have taken place with management compliance. This trend has been reversed in the 1980s, with more employers derecognizing unions and seeking to establish individual and direct relationships with their employees. This shift in direction has been encouraged by Government legislation, increased competition – nationally and internationally – the drive towards privatization of nationalized industries and the ethos summed up in the phrases 'market economy' and 'enterprise culture'. New and more flexible pay structures are being developed which favour individual rather than collective bargaining (specially for white collared workers), payment for performance (measured individually) and alignment to market rates. But it cannot be assumed that unions will not fight back to protect their rights and, as they perceive them, those of their workers, as was shown at Fords in 1988.

Adrian Cadbury has suggested that the reason for the opening up of more individual choice over pay and conditions is the existence of the 'third force', which is the determination of individuals to exercise more control over their own lives: 'The shift in the focus of power is from institutions to the units within them and from collective organizations to individuals'.[19]

Involvement

Employers are increasingly concerning themselves with building commitment, sharing their values with employees, and ensuring that staff know where the company is going, are proud of it, and want to be a part of its future. This 'hearts and minds' approach is achieved by following the participation/involvement/direct communication route, using such means as quality circles, team briefing and intensive but participative training to develop a climate of mutuality. Indoctrination programmes (only they are never called that) are part of this process.

Involvement often takes the form of a direct appeal to individual workers. It by-passes the traditional trade unions completely, and they often resent this. Joint consultation may continue to exist as part of the normal employee relations machinery, but management may well prefer to rely on immediate contacts rather than on operating at one stage removed from the office or shop floor.

Bargaining structures

There has been a tendency to decentralize bargaining so that pay settlements are made at local rather than corporate or national level. But this process has not always been accompanied by a relaxation in the central control of industrial relations policy and decisions. This trend was revealed in a 1986/7 survey funded by the Economic and Social Research Council which, as reported by Paul Marginson, found that 'over a range of important personnel and industrial relations decisions, a significant number of enterprises allocate their establishments no role in decision-making: they issue instructions. And only a small minority give total autonomy over these decisions'.[20]

New-style agreements and final offer arbitration

During the 1980s a major union, the Electrical, Electronic, Telecommunication and Plumbing Union (EETPU) and a number of Japanese firms with plants in the UK (Toshiba, Sanyo, Hitachi and Nissan) developed and applied the concept of what many people prefer to call 'new style' agreements. These agreements aim to make strikes unnecessary – they do not claim to eliminate the possibility altogether; hence 'new style' rather than 'no-strike'. Their culminating point is what has come to be known as 'pendulum' or 'one-or-the-other' arbitration, which means that the arbitrator has to choose between the final offers of the two parties, without compromising. Pendulum arbitration is also known as final-offer arbitration, or straight choice arbitration, which describes the process more accurately than 'pendulum', which implies a swing back and forwards between two alternatives rather than a choice of one or the other.

Theoretical background

The theoretical background to the new style agreements starts from a distinction between rights and interests. Questions of rights relate to the application of rules to particular situations. Issues of interest arise in the absence of rules, for example during claims and counter-claims on new terms and conditions of employment. The new style agreements are based on the mutually accepted rights of parties, expressed in the recognition agreement. The stated intention of the parties is to reconcile the few remaining differences of interest, especially pay, by in-company negotiations. Where a difference of 'interest' persists, pendulum or final offer arbitration takes place. However, reaching this final stage is regarded as a failure to meet the spirit of the agreement.

In his important article 'Is Compulsory Arbitration Compatible with Bargaining'[21] Stevens argued that a strike was a technique for imposing a cost of disagreement on the parties. He took as a starting point Kahn-Freund's contention that the strike is an essential feature of collective bargaining: 'Collective bargaining as we understand it is unthinkable without social sanctions . . . collective bargaining cannot work without the ultimate sanction of the strike and lock out'. Stevens' contention was that if a strike occurs, the outcome of the strike negotiations becomes the 'particular solution' – a solution that should and could be open to the parties without the strike: 'The expected cost of a strike will serve as a standard against which each party may weigh the expected cost of any given concession and hence determine the least favourable terms which will be acceptable to him'. His solution was the one-or-the-other approach, which would perform as a strike-like institution. This would involve in its first phase direct negotiations between the parties with no third party intervention. If that failed, a hearing would be held before an arbitrator to whom the parties would present their cases and who would come down on one side or the other.

Principles

The new style agreements are based on the following principles:

1. *Single-status* – all conditions the same except salary.
2. *Community of interests or mutuality* – explicit statements may be included in the agreement to the effect that the well-being of employees is dependent upon the company's success.
3. *Involvement* – the company accepts that employees have a genuine 'say' in terms of consultation and advice and the

company will also be willing to disclose the necessary information.

4. *Flexibility* – flexibility is an accepted method of working, particularly in high-tech companies, but this requires effort on the part of the company to train and retrain staff.

5. *Inexhaustible disputes procedure* – this overcomes the inherent problems of normal disputes procedures, which, although they may include a peace clause restraining the parties from taking industrial action while the matter is 'in procedure', specifically or implicitly allow for the procedure to become exhausted without the dispute being resolved. A new style agreement is 'inexhaust-ible' in that the compulsory final stage of pendulum arbitration provides for a binding solution to the dispute. However, a comprehensively worded peace clause may still be included.

6. *Unnecessary strikes* – the aim of a new style agreement is to make strikes unnecessary. It does not usually attempt to outlaw strikes because of the contractual complications of making such agreements legally enforceable. As a strike substitute, the final offer agreement can threaten to impose an unacceptable penalty (the other party's offer) if agreement is not reached, and risk-averse negotiators prefer to avoid this outcome.

7. *Responsible negotiation* – conventional negotiations are subject to what have been termed 'narcotic' or 'chilling' effects. The narcotic effect happens when there is compulsory arbitration and negotiators are in danger of turning to it as an easy and habit-forming release from the obligation to conduct hard, responsible negotiations. The chilling effect on the parties' determination to reach agreement occurs when they know a normal 'split the difference' type of arbitration may happen at the last stage and there is therefore an incentive to maintain excessive demands. Final offer arbitration is designed to avoid these effects. The parties have an incentive not to hold everything back for the arbitration and it is hoped that the final offers will be sufficiently close together to be accepted by the losing party. As Giles Burrows wrote, 'The fairness of the procedure is its symmetry. The parties do not risk the uncertainty of the arbitrator fashioning an award, possibly with additional elements, which turns out to be unworkable in practice'.[22]

Advantages

Wyn Bevan, Executive Councillor, EETPU, claimed at the Institute of Personnel Management conference in 1987 that the new style agreements, (single-union, strike-free, single status, flexibility) offered the following advantages:

● *For the trade union:*
'The opportunity for harmonization, greater industrial democracy, improved public image, increased membership, recognition in areas that would otherwise become non-union, better productivity, hence better job prospects, the ability to resolve disputes without loss of wages, or union funds, better training for its members, and therefore increasing their ability to "sell their skills" on the jobs market.'

● *For the employer:*
'Flexibility – an end to demarcation, machinery to solve disputes without loss of production, a better trained, motivated and involved workforce, and the opportunity, fast disappearing though it could be, of ending confrontational industrial relations once and for all, before history's well-recorded cycle of capital versus labour swings back to favour unions. As manufacturing pulls back to 1979 levels of growth and output, the so-called British disease will undoubtedly re-assert itself to everyone's disadvantage.'[22]

Disadvantages
Perhaps the main argument used against final offer arbitration is that it is based on the false assumption that arbitrators 'split the difference'. However, the fact that the assumption is false may not influence the 'chilling effect'. It is the strength of the assumption that counts, not its validity.

The other problem about new style agreements is that conventional trade unions dislike them intensely as removing their major weapon – the strike – and providing for more advantages to employers than themselves. It is because of this entrenched attitude that new style agreements are not making much headway in traditional areas of industry, which is a pity.

References

1. Dunlop, J T *Industrial Relations Systems* Holt, New York, 1958.
2. Thomason, G T *A Textbook of Industrial Relations Management* Institute of Personnel Management, London, 1984.
3. Flanders, A *Management and Unions: The Theory and Reform of Industrial Relations* Faber and Faber, London, 1970.
4. Chamberlain, N W and Kuhn, J W *Collective Bargaining* McGraw-Hill, New York, 1965.
5. Walton, R E and McKersie, R B *A Behavioural Theory of Labor Negotiations* McGraw-Hill, New York, 1965.
6. McClelland, G *British Journal of Industrial Relations* June 1963, p 278.
7. Fox, A 'Industrial Sociology and Industrial Relations', *Royal Commission on Trade Unions and Employers' Associations Research Paper No 3* Her Majesty's Stationery Office, London, 1966.

8. Drucker, P *The New Society* Heinemann, London, 1951.
9. Winkler, J T 'The Ghost at the Bargaining Table: Directors and Industrial Relations', *British Journal of Industrial Relations* Vol XII, No 2, July 1974.
10. Edwardes, Sir Michael *Back from the Brink* Collins, London, 1983.
11. Clack, G *Industrial Relations in a British Car Factory* Cambridge University Press, Cambridge, 1967.
12. Marsh, A L, Evans, E O and Garcia, P *Workplace Industrial Relations in Engineering* Kogan Page, London, 1971.
13. Higgs, P 'The Convenor', *Work 2* Penguin Books, Harmondsworth, 1969.
14. Millward, N and Stevens, M *British Industrial Relations 1980-84* Gower, London, 1986.
15. Peters, J *Strategies and Tactics in Labour Negotiations* Duckworth, New York, 1968.
16. Macintyre, D 'Eclipse of the New Realism', *Personnel Management* September 1984.
17. Hawksworth, C 'Labour Relations in the 80s', *Personnel Management* November 1984.
18. Daniel, W W *Workplace Industrial Relations and Industrial Change* Frances Pinter, London, 1987.
19. Cadbury, A 'The 1980s – a Watershed for British Industrials', *Hitachi Lecture* University of Sussex, 1986.
20. Marginson, P 'How Centralised is the Management of Industrial Relations?', *Personnel Management* October 1986.
21. Stevens, C M 'Is Compulsory Arbitration Compatible with Bargaining?', *Industrial Relations* February 1966.
22. Burrows, G *No-strike Agreements and Pendulum Arbitration* Institute of Personnel Management, November 1984.

Chapter 33
Participation and Joint Consultation

What is participation?

Participation takes place when management and employees are jointly involved in making decisions on matters of mutual interest where the aim is to produce solutions to the problems which will benefit all concerned. Participation does not mean that the parties subordinate their own interests entirely. But it does mean that they aim to achieve objectives which are not in fundamental conflict with those of the other party, and which can therefore be integrated to some degree. Participation does not require total and bland agreement all the time, and bargaining about issues is not excluded. It is akin to integrative or co-operative bargaining where the parties find common or complementary interests and solve problems confronting both of them.

Participation should be distinguished from negotiation which, although it involves joint decision-making, does this by a process of distributive or conjunctive bargaining where the sole aim is to resolve pure conflicts of interests.

Participation is more than joint consultation, which is the process by which management seeks the views, feelings and ideas of employees through their representatives, prior to negotiating or making a decision. Although joint consultation may involve the discussion of mutual problems and is a necessary aspect of participation, it leaves with management the ultimate responsibility for making decisions. Participation is also more than communications, which is the process of keeping people informed about intentions, opinions, results or decisions on matters that interest them, although effective two-way communications are necessary to successful participation and joint consultation.

The purpose of participation

The purpose of participation should be to advance the well-being of all concerned – owners and managers in addition to workpeople. It should be

600

a means of enabling the enterprise to achieve its objectives, as long as it is understood that those objectives include acting in a socially responsible way to employees as well as the maximization of profits.

The objective of participation is not, therefore, simply to provide people with job satisfaction because they feel that they are involved. This is an important and legitimate aim, but it is not the only one. Participation should do more than help people to feel good. It should provide them with the means of identifying their own interests with those of the enterprise in which they work, so that both can flourish. Participation should therefore provide employees with the opportunity to contribute to the success of the organization by involving them in decision-making and by means of joint consultation, productivity committees, suggestion schemes and, the latest development, quality circles.

Participation and industrial democracy

Are participation and industrial democracy the same thing? To some, industrial democracy is an alternative way of describing more or less traditional forms of joint consultation. To others, it comprises the joint regulation or control by unions and management of decisions and actions which affect the present and future conduct of the business. This implies trade union participation in decision-making at all levels in the enterprise, including the highest level, the board. This view, as held by trade unionists, rejects conventional joint consultative arrangements or paternalistically based profit-sharing schemes as a charade of participation which gives workpeople none of the substance of control that has been firmly based with the leading shareholders. The demand for two-tiered board structures and for union representation on the board arises from this latter viewpoint.

The debate on industrial democracy has often been concerned with means rather than with ends. It is the *form* and extent of participation that has caused most argument, not the objective. There has been a fair measure of agreement on both sides of industry with the following definition of the two basic purposes of industrial democracy prepared by the Industrial Participation Association (Great Britain) for its evidence to the Committee of Inquiry on Industrial Democracy:

(a) That it is both reasonable and just that the employees of a company should have the means to influence the major decisions that may determine the conditions of their own working lives, and thereby the lives of their families – decisions that are commonly taken at a level where at present it is not usual for employees to be directly involved or represented.

(b) That an essential purpose of industrial democracy must be to improve the efficiency and productivity of the enterprise, by enabling employees at all levels to make a more effective contribution – increased productivity being the context in which employees' interests, as well as the interests of other parties, can best be advanced.[1]

Forms of participation

Participation can vary according to the level at which it takes place, the degree to which decision-making is shared, and the mechanisms of a greater or lesser degree of formality which are used.

Levels of participation

Participation takes various forms at different levels in an enterprise. These levels were classified by the Industrial Society[2] as:

- job level;
- management level;
- policy-making level;
- ownership level.

Participation at the job level involves the supervisor and his immediate group, and the processes include the communication of information about the work, the delegation of authority, and the interchange of ideas about how the work should be done. These processes are essentially informal.

Participation at management level can involve sharing information and decision-taking about issues which affect the way in which work is planned, co-ordinated and controlled, and the conditions under which the work is carried out. There are limitations. Management as a whole, and individual managers, must retain authority to do what their function requires. Participation does not imply anarchy. But it does require some degree of willingness on the part of management to share their decision-making powers. At this level, participation becomes more formalized, through consultative committees, briefing groups or other joint bodies involving management and trade unionists.

At the policy-making level, where the direction in which the business is going is determined, total participation implies sharing the power to make the key decisions on investments, disinvestments, new ventures, expansions and retractions which affect the future well-being of both the company and its employees. Ultimately, it means that such decisions are made fairly by directors who represent the interests of the owners, the management, and the workpeople. The proposal to have a supervisory board upon which worker representatives have the power to veto major investment decisions, mergers or take-overs, closures or major redeployment is not full participation, but it is in accordance with the reality of the divided loyalties that worker representatives would have if they had to share the responsibility for unpopular decisions by becoming full board members in the accepted sense.

At the ownership level, participation may imply a share in the equity, which is not meaningful unless the workers have sufficient control through voting rights to determine the composition of the board. Workers' co-operatives are also participative in the sense that the workers, including managers and supervisors, *are* the management and must therefore be involved in joint decision-making at board level.

The degree to which decision-making is shared

At the one end of the scale management can make decisions unilaterally; at the other end, much more rarely, workers decide unilaterally. Between these extremes there is a range of intermediate points which can be expressed (Figure 33.1) as a scale.

The point on this scale at which participation should or is able to take place at any level in an organization will depend on the attitudes, willingness and enthusiasm of both management and employees. Management may be reluctant to give up too much of its authority except under duress from the unions, or legislation aimed at developing industrial democracy (the political term for participation). Unions may prefer not to be over-involved in decision-making so that they can shoot from the side-lines when they want to.

Mechanisms for participation

At the job level participation should be as informal as possible. Groups may be called together on an *ad hoc* basis to consider a particular problem, but formal committees should be avoided in small departments (say, less than 250 people) or at section level. Team briefing (see Chapter 34) can be used to provide for informal two-way communications.

At the next higher level, more formality may be appropriate in larger organizations. There is scope for the use of joint consultative committees or joint negotiating committees with carefully defined terms of reference on the matters they can discuss.

At the policy-forming level, participation becomes more difficult to organize. This is when management will be most reluctant to abandon its prerogatives unless forced to by legislation. Unions, as already mentioned, do not like to be put in a position where they may have to endorse unpopular decisions. Works councils may be given the chance to discuss policy issues, but if the final decision on any matter which is clearly not negotiable is made at board level, the works council may be seen as an ineffectual body.

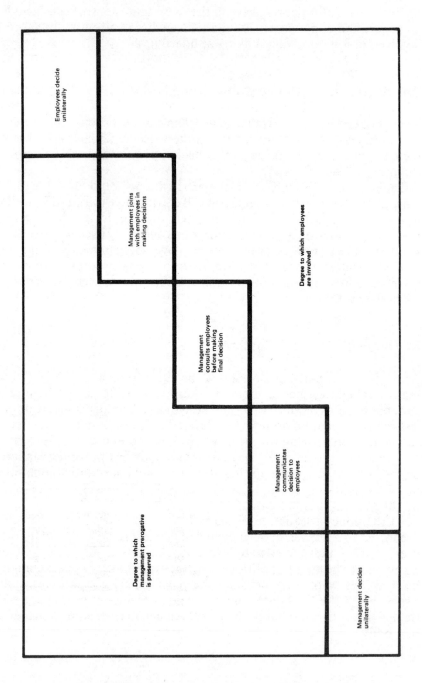

Figure 33.1 Scale of participation

Arguments for and against participation

The arguments for and against participation are not evenly balanced; they cannot be. They represent totally different points of view or, to put it more plainly, prejudice. And there is prejudice on both sides. Essentially, the favourable arguments are optimistic about human nature while the unfavourable ones are pessimistic. It would be a pity if the pessimistic view prevailed in this as in other spheres. But a favourable view on participation should not be allowed to develop into idealism.

In favour

- It satisfies the individual's basic need for involvement in affairs that affect him or her.
- It makes better use of the skills and capacities available in the enterprise.
- It gives people the opportunity to influence events which will have a direct or indirect effect on their present and future prosperity and security.
- It recognizes the reality of life today in which traditional authoritarian patterns of behaviour are being steadily eroded.
- It is better to develop a participative system within an organization in a planned and orderly way rather than have it forced upon the company by the government or the unions.

Against

- The board must exercise direction and control, and management must manage – managers cannot be effective unless they are allowed to exercise their authority with the minimum of interference.
- Direction and management are specialized skills which are not shared amongst all employees. The extent to which workers' representatives at board level and elsewhere can make a real contribution is limited.
- Power-sharing implies information-sharing – the necessarily confidential nature of much top management decision-making would be seriously impaired if workpeople were involved.
- The unions do not want it because it might impair their negotiating power or put them in an invidious position if they have to support unpopular management decisions.
- Employees do not want increased participation, either because they are apathetic or because they do not see any advantage to themselves in it.
- Participation may drive key decisions under cover if directors or managers form secret cabals or starve workers' representatives of the information they need to make a proper contribution.

A touch of realism along the lines suggested by the pessimists is required to make participation work.

Requirements for successful participation

Irrespective of the level at which participation takes place or the degree to which it is formalized, there are ten basic requirements for success:

1. The objectives of participation must be defined, discussed and agreed by all concerned.
2. The objectives must be related to tangible and significant aspects of the job, the process of management or the formulation of policies that affect the interests of employees. They must not relate to peripheral matters such as welfare or social amenities, ie in Herzberg's phrase, they should not be concerned with the 'hygiene' factors alone.
3. Management must believe and must be seen to believe in participation. Actions speak better than words and management must demonstrate that it will put into effect the joint decisions made during discussions.
4. The unions must believe in participation as a genuine means of advancing the interests of their members and not simply as a way of getting more power. They should show by their actions that they are prepared to support unpopular decisions to which they have been a party.
5. Joint consultation machinery should be in line with any existing systems of negotiation and representation. It should not be supported by management as a possible way of reducing the powers of the union. If this naive approach is taken it will fail – it always does. Joint consultation should be regarded as a complementary process of integrative bargaining to the distributive bargaining that takes place in joint negotiating committees. A separate consultative system may not be necessary in a well-organized 100% union establishment.
6. If management does introduce joint consultation as a means of keeping unions out, it should be prepared to widen the terms of reference as much as possible to cover issues which might normally be the subject of negotiation with unions. This approach can backfire if the staff representatives acquire a taste for negotiation and turn to the unions if they find they are not getting what they want. It is an approach which should be used with extreme caution. It has been known to work with white collar unions but, it can be difficult to resist strong union demands for recognition. It would be a pity in these circumstances to lose face by abandoning a management sponsored system.
7. Joint consultative committees should always relate to a defined working unit, should never meet unless there is something specific

to discuss, and should always conclude their meetings with agreed points which are implemented quickly.
  8. Employee and management representatives should be properly briefed and trained and have all the information they require.
  9. Managers and supervisors should be kept in the picture.
  10. Consultation should take place *before* decisions are made.

Joint consultation

Joint consultation is the most obvious method of participation. It is essentially a means for management and employees to get together to discuss and, where appropriate, determine matters affecting their joint or respective interests.

In its simplest form joint consultation is the informal exchange of views between individual employees and their managers, and takes place all the time in a well-run enterprise. But where the number of employees, or a complex organization, makes access from employees to management or from management to employees difficult, then informal methods need to be systematized.

Objectives of joint consultation

The objectives of joint consultation should be to provide a means of jointly examining and discussing problems of concern to both management and employees. It involves seeking mutually acceptable solutions through a genuine exchange of views and information. Joint consultation allows management to inform employees of proposed changes which affect them and employees to express their views about the proposed changes. It also provides a means for employees to contribute to their own views and knowledge on such matters as productivity and safety.

Topics for joint consultation

Joint consultation does not mean power-sharing – involving employees in policy decisions on such matters as investments, marketing and product development plans, and mergers. These would only be the subject of joint decision-making if full participation at board level were to take place.

The terms of reference to joint consultative committees often exclude the discussion of basic terms and conditions of employment such as wage rates and premium payments, hours of work and holidays. These are either regarded as part of management's prerogative in a non-unionized plant or are dealt with through the normal negotiation machinery. This leaves matters such as methods of work, job evaluation, works rules and safety as usual – and important – topics for joint consultation.

Joint consultation and negotiation

There are dangers in having two separate systems of employee representation. If the firm is strongly unionized, the unions will dominate the consultative committee, which is wasteful and often leads to the consultative committee system dealing with trivialities and falling into disrepute. It may be useful to have a place where people can argue about the quality of the sausages in the canteen, but if that is all they ever talk about (and sometimes this appears to be the case) then it would be better to abandon formal joint consultation altogether and rely on other channels. A reverse situation can sometimes occur when companies set up joint consultation as an alternative to a union negotiating committee. What may happen is that the joint consultative committee members persuade or force management to negotiate with them with the result that there are two competing negotiating bodies, which is a recipe for disaster.

The argument in favour of keeping negotiating issues outside the terms of reference of joint consultation committees is that it gives the latter more opportunity to deal calmly with non-controversial matters. Negotiating committees may get into so many conflict situations that they are no longer capable of looking dispassionately at even the least controversial issues. There is some truth in this argument, but the ideal approach in a strongly unionized plant is to have one system of representation, and for all concerned to do everything in their power to develop a co-operative climate for consultation as well as negotiation.

When a company is involved in negotiations there is no easy answer to the problem of reconciling the machinery required for that purpose with the system most appropriate to joint consultation. It is no good, however, clinging to an effete joint consultative arrangement if all the real decisions are made with union representatives through the negotiating machinery. Separate joint consultation arrangements should be maintained only if they do provide proper representation for non-unionists and a genuine opportunity for employee representatives to discuss real issues which might be neglected in the hurly-burly of negotiations.

An interesting approach to solving this problem was developed at Glacier Metal by Wilfrid Brown[3] with the help of Elliott Jaques.[4] In *The Changing Culture of a Factory* the latter described the process of working through problems in the developing representative system, while in *Exploration in Management* Brown describes how the representative, legislative and appeals system functioned. The representative system was the basic machinery through which employees could express their views, but a legislative system was established above, and not in parallel to the representative system which 'comprises councils ... in which the executive and representative systems meet and by means of which every member can participate in formulating policy and in assessing the results of the implementation of that policy'.[3]

Constitution

Before deciding on detailed terms of reference it is necessary to determine the aims and scope of joint consultation, paying particular attention to the question of the extent to which committees can become involved in policy or negotiating issues. It is also necessary to consider who should be covered by the committee system. A choice will have to be made. It could only cover non-managerial or supervisory employees, or supervisors and even managers could be catered for separately. Finally, decisions will have to be made on the committee structure, which in a large organization often consists of separate councils for each major department or group of departments and an overall works council. It is sometimes best to start in a modest way with one or two pilot schemes in large departments before setting up too elaborate a system. Some large companies, however, have restricted the system to one works council on the grounds that departmental matters are best dealt with informally by local management.

The following points should be covered in the constitution of a consultative committee:

- The objectives of the committee.
- Its terms of reference – the matters which it can and cannot discuss.
- Its composition:
    - employee representatives (number, constituencies)
    - management representatives
    - co-option provisions
    - officers.
- The period of office of members and arrangements for their retirement.
- Election procedure:
    - who organizes
    - when held
    - qualifications of candidates and voters
    - nominations
    - voting arrangements.
- Committee meetings:
    - frequency
    - where held
    - procedures for placing items on the agenda
    - arrangements for minutes.
- Facilities for committee members:
    - liaising with constituents
    - payment while attending meetings.

Quality circles

It can be argued that one of the greatest failings which result from the 'top-down' type of management prevailing in the UK and many other Western countries is that it ignores the knowledge that exists at the lowest level in the organization. Many investigators who have been trying to establish the secret of the success of Japan's industry have decided that a major ingredient is the degree to which collective or group management is practised.

One of the techniques of group involvement used successfully in Japan (although the idea originated in the United States in the 1950s) is quality circles. Quality circles grew out of Japan's great need in the early 1960s to lose its post-war reputation as a clever producer of shoddy copies of Western products and to raise the quality of its goods. The approach owes a lot to the strong attachment to working in cohesive groups which exists in Japan. The first circle was registered in 1963 within the Nippon Telegraph and Telephone Public Corporation, and now there are hundreds of thousands of circles operating in Japan. Virtually all big companies use them.

Definition

Quality circles are small groups of volunteers who are engaged in related work and who meet regularly to discuss and propose ways of improving working methods or arrangements under a trained leader.

Aims

The aims of quality circles are to:

- give those doing the job more scope to use their experience and know-how;
- provide opportunities to tap the knowledge of employees, who may know more about work problems which are hidden from more remote managers and supervisors;
- improve productivity and quality;
- improve employee relations;
- win commitment to the organization.

Essential features

The essential features of quality circles are that they:

- consist of volunteers;
- have a trained leader, usually not always a superior;
- hold regular meetings which are strictly limited in duration – often one hour;
- have five to ten members;

- usually select which problems to tackle but may be steered away from problems which are clearly beyond their scope or are already being dealt with;
- use systematic and analytical techniques in which they have been trained to solve problems;
- may use brainstorming to identify possible solutions (brainstorming involves the group listing as many solutions as they can think of – some good, some not so good – and then refining them and ranking them in merit order);
- present their results to management;
- implement accepted proposals.

Prerequisites for success

Management support
The first prerequisite is that top management believes in the value of quality circles and is committed to their success. Middle management and supervision must also be involved in its introduction. They are the people who are most likely to have reservations about quality circles because they can see them as a threat to their authority and reputation – for example, when a problem is overcome by a circle rather than the supervisor.

Trade unions
Trade unions should also be informed of the plan to introduce quality circles. Some unions are hostile because they feel that quality circles can reduce their influence and power, and that management is deliberately introducing them for this purpose.

Facilitator
The introduction and maintenance of a quality circle needs a 'facilitator' who trains, encourages and guides quality circle members, ensures that they are given the resources they need and sets up presentation sessions. The facilitator is often a line manager rather than a personnel officer or a trainer. This vital role also involves encouraging the circles and ensuring that top management backing continues by keeping them informed of the benefits provided by quality circles – publicity on their achievements is important. The facilitator can also deal with any problems quality circles meet in getting information or in dealing with management.

Training
Training is an important part of the quality circles. Team leaders need an initial two- to three-day training course in the analytical techniques they will use and in team building and presentation skills. They also need refresher training from time to time. Team leaders, with the help of facilitators, also train the members of their team. This training effort is a valuable spin-off from a quality circle programme. Instruction in leadership,

problem-solving and analytical skills is a useful way of developing exist-ing or potential supervisors. Membership of a quality circle is also a means of developing skills as well as getting more involved.

Typical projects

The University of Manchester Institute of Science and Technology's (UMIST) 1983 research into quality circles in Great Britain[5] classified the proportions of projects in different areas as follows:

- quality improvement 18%
- cost reduction 15%
- production processes 14%
- productivity improvement 12%
- waste prevention 10%
- plant improvements 9%
- communications 6%
- service processes 5%
- safety 4%
- other 7%

Maintenance of a quality circle programme

The facilitator, as mentioned earlier, has the key task of keeping the pro-gramme going – encouraging the quality circles and ensuring that man-agement is told about their achievements. The UMIST survey established that the major obstacles to quality circle programmes, as established by the reasons for failure, were:

- suspicion 19%
- slow management response to proposals 14%
- lack of support 14%
- over-ambitious projects 13%

It is up to top management and the facilitator, but especially the latter, to overcome these problems.

Benefits

The UMIST research listed the following benefits in the order of import-ance given by management:

- increased involvement of employees 25%
- improvement of communications 21%
- improvement of quality and productivity 17%
- reduction in barriers between management and shop floor . . . 17%
- reduction in operating costs 10%

● encouraging employees to establish an identity 9%
● encouraging labour to become more flexible 1%

Suggestion schemes

Suggestion schemes can provide a valuable means for employees to participate in improving the efficiency of the company. Properly organized,
they can help to reduce the feelings of frustration endemic in all concerns
where people think they have good ideas but cannot get them considered
because there are no recognized channels of communication. Normally,
only those ideas outside the usual scope of employee's duties are considered and this should be made clear, as well as the categories of those eligible for the scheme – senior management are often excluded.

The basis of a successful suggestion scheme should be an established
procedure for submitting and evaluating ideas, with tangible recognition
for those which have merit and an effective system for explaining to employees without discouraging them that their ideas cannot be accepted.

The most common arrangement is to use suggestion boxes with, possibly, a special form for entering a suggestion. Alternatively, or additionally, employees can be given the name of an individual or a committee to
whom suggestions should be submitted. Management and supervision
must be stimulated to encourage their staff to submit suggestions, and
publicity in the shape of posters, leaflets and articles in the company
magazine should be used to promote the scheme. The publicity should
give prominence to the successful suggestions and how they are being
implemented.

One person should be made responsible for administering the scheme.
He should have the authority to reject facetious suggestions, but should
be given clear guidance on the routing of suggestions by subject matter to
departments or individuals for their comments. The administrator deals
with all communications and, if necessary, may go back to the individual
who submitted the suggestion to get more details of, for example, the savings in cost or improvements in output that should result from the idea.

It is desirable to have a suggestion committee consisting of management and employee representatives to review suggestions in the light of
the comments of any specialist functions or executives who have evaluated them. This committee should be given the final power to accept or
reject suggestions but could, if necessary, call for additional information
or opinion before making its decision. The committee could also decide
on the size of any award within established guidelines, such as a proportion of savings during the first year; usually not less than 10% and not
more than $33\frac{1}{3}$%. There should be a standard procedure for recording
the decisions of the committee and informing those who made suggestions of the outcome – with reasons for rejection if appropriate.

Planning for participation

The form of participation appropriate for a company will depend upon the attitudes and relative strengths of management and unions, its past experience of negotiation and consultation, and the current climate of employee relations. The form may also be affected by government legislation; but whatever method is adopted it is essential to take into account the requirements for successful participation listed earlier in this chapter and to plan its introduction or development in the following stages:

1. Analyse and evaluate the existing systems of consultation, communication and other formal and informal means of participation.
2. Identify the influences within and without the company which affect the climate of industrial relations and suggest the most appropriate form in which participation should take place.
3. Develop a plan for improving or extending participation in whatever form is appropriate to the company.
4. Discuss the plan in depth with all concerned – management, supervisors, workpeople and unions. The introduction of improved participation should itself be a participative process.
5. Brief and train those concerned with participation in their duties and how they should be carried out.
6. Introduce new schemes on a pilot-scheme basis – do not expect immediate results and be prepared to modify them in the light of experience.
7. Keep the whole system under continuous review as it develops to ensure that it is operating effectively.

References

1. *Industrial Democracy – The Way Forward* Industrial Participation Association, London, 1976.
2. *Practical Policies for Participation* The Industrial Society, London, 1974.
3. Brown, W *Exploration in Management* Heinemann, London, 1960.
4. Jaques, E *The Changing Culture of a Factory* Tavistock Productions, London, 1951.
5. Dale, B G and Ball, T S *A Study of Quality Circles in UK Manufacturing Organizations* Department of Management Sciences, University of Manchester Institute of Science and Technology, 1984.

Chapter 34
Communications

The nature of communications

Communications are concerned with the creation, transmission, interpretation and use of information. The communication can be on a person-to-person basis, as when a boss tells someone what to do and when a subordinate reports back to his superior, or it can be on a departmental/corporate basis when general instructions or pieces of information are passed down the line, and reactions, reports and comments float, more or less effectively, up again.

Communications start with the communicator wanting to say something; he then decides how it is to be said and transmitted. The communication arrives with the recipient who forms an impression of what he has heard and interprets it against his own background of attitudes and experiences (Figure 34.1).

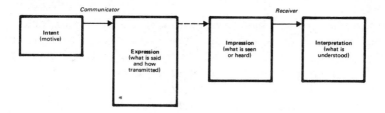

Figure 34.1 The process of communication

The basic problem in communications is that the meaning which is actually received by one person may not be what the other intended to send. The communicator and the receiver are two people living in different worlds; any number of things can happen to distort the messages that pass between them. People's needs and experiences tend to colour what they see and hear. Messages they do not want to hear are repressed. Others are magnified, created out of thin air or distorted from their original reality.

The importance of communications

Organizations function by means of the collective action of people, yet each individual is capable of taking independent action which may not be in line with policy or instructions; or may not be reported properly to other people who ought to know about it. Good communications are required to achieve co-ordinated results.

Organizations are subject to the influence of continuous change which affects the work employees do, their well-being and their security. Change can only be managed by ensuring that the reasons for and implications of change are communicated to those affected in terms they can understand and accept.

Individuals are motivated by the extrinsic reward system and the intrinsic rewards that come from the work itself. But the degree to which they are motivated depends upon the amount of responsibility and scope for achievement provided by their job, and upon their expectations that the rewards they will get will be the ones they want and will follow from the efforts they make. Feelings about work and the associated rewards depend very much on the effectiveness of communications from their boss and within the company.

Above all, good two-way communications are required so that management can keep employees informed of the policies and plans that affect them and employees can react promptly with their views about management's proposals and actions. Change cannot be managed properly without an understanding of the feelings of those affected by it, and an efficient system of communications is needed to understand and influence these feelings.

But the extent to which good communications create satisfactory relationships rather than simply reduce unsatisfactory relationships can be exaggerated. A feature of management practices during this century is the way in which different management theories become fashionable or influential for a while and then decline in favour. Among these has been the 'good communications' theory of management. This approach to dealing with management problems is based upon the following assumptions:

1. The needs and aims of both employees and management are, in the long run, the same in any organization. Managers' and employees' ideas and objectives can all be fitted together to form a single conceptual framework.
2. Any differences in opinion between management and employees are due to misunderstandings that have arisen because communications are not good enough.
3. The solution to industrial strife is to improve communications.

This theory is attractive and has some validity. Its weakness is that the assumptions are too sweeping, particularly that the ultimate objectives of management and workers are necessarily identical. Experiences in countries, such as Yugoslavia, which have had long experience of industrial democracy have suggested that workers' representatives who are appointed to the board of a company concern themselves mainly with pay and conditions and are not greatly interested in other aspects of the company's business. The good communications theory, like paternalism, seems to imply that the company can develop loyalty by keeping people informed and treating them nicely. But people working in organizations have other and, to them, more important loyalties elsewhere; and why not?

The existence of different loyalties and points of view in an organization, however, does not mean that communications are unimportant. If anything, the need for a good communications system becomes even greater when differences and conflict exist. But it can only alleviate those differences and pave the way to better co-operation. It cannot solve them.

Communication problems

Communication problems fall into four main categories:

1. People are not aware of the need to communicate.
2. People do not know what to communicate.
3. People do not know how to communicate.
4. Proper facilities for communicating are not available.

These problems are equally important, although inadequacy in any one area can lead to communication failures, and they are not easy to solve. To overcome them it is necessary to formulate a strategy for communications which will form the basis for developing communications systems, and to maintain a continuous programme of education and training in communication techniques. The strategy, systems and training programmes should, however, be founded on an understanding of the barriers to communication.

Barriers to communications

So many barriers exist to good communications that the constant cry in all organizations that communications are bad is hardly to be wondered at – it is amazing that any undisturbed messages get through. Some of the main barriers are summarized below.

Hearing what we expect to hear
What we hear or understand when someone speaks to us is largely based on our own experience and background. Instead of hearing what people tell us, we hear what our minds tell us they have said. We all tend to have preconceived ideas of what people mean: when we hear something new we tend to identify with something similar that we have experienced in the

past. People like predictability and 'one of the most time-consuming passions of the human mind is to rationalize sentiments and to disguise them as logic' (Roethlisberger and Dickson).[1]

When people receive a communication which is consistent with their own beliefs they will accept it as valid, seek additional information and remember accurately what is heard.

Ignoring information that conflicts with what we already know

We tend to ignore or reject communications that conflict with our own beliefs. If they are not rejected, some way is found of twisting and shaping their meaning to fit our preconceptions. Communications often fail when they run counter to other information that the receiver already possesses, whether that information is true or false.

The technical term for what happens when people receive irreconcilable information is *cognitive dissonance*, a theory developed by Festinger, which asserts that an individual experiences discomfort when he holds logically inconsistent 'cognitions' (a person's individual views or images of events which shape his social behaviour) about an object or an event, and that he is thus motivated to reduce the discomfort or dissonance by changes to his views or his attitudes. Cognitions are selectively organized to reflect an individual's own environment, experience, wants and goals, and his physiological structure. This provides the frame of reference against which the properties of a particular object or piece of information are judged. People resist change or the communication asking them to change because the new ideas are outside their frame of reference.

Where communication is inconsistent with existing beliefs, the receiver rejects its validity, avoids further exposure to it, easily forgets it and, in his memory, distorts what he hears.

Perceptions about the communicator

Not only does the receiver evaluate what he hears in terms of his own background, but he also takes the sender into account. Experience or prejudice may ascribe non-existent motives to the communicator. Some people see every collective action as a conspiracy. Others look behind the message to read into it all sorts of different motives to those apparent on the surface. It is extremely difficult for us to separate what we hear from our feelings about the person who says it.

Influence of reference group

The group with which we identify – the reference group – influences our attitudes and feelings. 'Management' and 'the union' as well as our family, our race, our political party and our religious beliefs (if any) constitute a reference group and colour our reactions to information. What each group 'hears' depends on its own interests. Shared experiences and common frames of reference will have much more influence than exhortations from management, where people with whom employees feel they have nothing in common hand on messages containing information which conflicts with what they already believe.

Words mean different things to different people

This is the problem of semantics. As Strauss and Sayles put it: 'Essentially language is a method of using symbols to represent facts and feelings. Strictly speaking we can't convey *meaning*, all we can do is convey *words*. And yet the same words may suggest quite different meanings for different people. The meanings are in the people not the words.'[2]

Words may have symbolic meanings to some people with the result that they convey a quite different impression from the one intended. 'Profits' to management are an essential prerequisite to survival and growth: to employees, they represent ill-gotten gains as a result of keeping down pay or over-pricing. 'Closed shop' to a trade unionist means an appropriate device for maintaining stability and strength and ensuring that employees contribute to the organization: to managers, 'closed shop' may suggest a fundamentally illiberal device restricting the freedom of both management and workers.

In short, do not assume that something which has a certain meaning to you will convey the same meaning to someone else.

Jargon

All professions and trades develop their own special language or 'jargon'. It is a convenient way of communicating technical terms between those who know the jargon, but it is an effective and irritating barrier between those who know and those who do not.

Non-verbal communication

In trying to understand what people are saying to us we use many cues besides language – what has come to be called 'body language'. Looking at the eyes, the shape of the mouth, the muscles of the face, even bodily posture, may tell us more about what the other person really thinks than the words he uses. In a sense, this is an aid to communication if the real meaning of what we are saying is conveyed by the expression on our face rather than by the actual message. But it can become a barrier if people misinterpret our 'body language'.

Emotional context

Our emotions colour our ability to convey or to receive the true message. When we are insecure or worried, what we hear and see seems more threatening than when we are secure and at peace with the world. When we are angry or depressed, we tend to reject out of hand what might otherwise seem like reasonable requests or good ideas. During arguments, many things can be said which are not understood or are badly distorted.

Noise

'Noise' in the sense of outside factors interfering with the reception of the message is an obvious barrier. It may be literal noise, which prevents words being heard, or figurative noise in the shape of distracting or confused information which distorts the message. The forms in which messages are communicated – unclear syntax, long unwieldy sentences with numerous 'hanging' clauses, polysyllabic words – all help to produce noise.

Size
The sheer size and complexity of modern organizations is one of the main barriers to communication. Messages have to penetrate layer upon layer of management or move between different functions, units or locations. They thus become distorted or never arrive. Reliance is placed more on the written rather than the spoken word to get the message through, and this seriously restricts the effectiveness of the communication.

With size goes formality, and with formality go restrictions to the freedom with which communication can take place. E F Schumacher has suggested that 'small is beautiful' and this certainly applies to communications. His theme was applied more to the encouragement of creativity than to the development of good communications, but it is equally relevant to both. On the question of creativity he wrote that:

> In any organization, large or small, there must be a certain clarity and orderliness: if things fall into disorder nothing can be accomplished. Yet, orderliness as such is static and lifeless; so there must be plenty of elbow-room and scope for breaking through the established order, to do the thing never done before, never anticipated by the guardians of orderliness, the new, unpredicted and unpredictable outcome of a man's creative idea.[3]

Organizations, he wrote, have to strive continuously for the 'orderliness of *order* and the disorderliness of creative freedom'. He did not say, but well might have, that a free flow of communication is essential to bridge the gap.

Overcoming barriers to communication

The overall implication of this formidable collection of barriers is that no one should assume that every message sent will be received in the form that he intended it to be. But communications can be improved, even if perfect understanding between people is impossible.

Adjusting to the world of the receiver
When communicating, the tendency is to adjust to oneself. You have the need to say something and to say it in a particular way. But to get the message across, you have to adjust to the receiver. This means thinking ahead and trying to work out how he will perceive the message – understanding his needs and potential reactions. It also means using feedback and reinforcement techniques as discussed later.

The effective communicator tries to predict the impact of what he is going to write or say on the receiver's feelings and attitudes. He tries to tailor the message to fit the receiver's vocabulary, interests and values, and is aware of the possible ways his information can be misinterpreted because of the symbolic meanings attached to phrases, the influence of the reference group and the tendency for people to reject what they do not want to hear.

Overcoming barriers requires *empathy* – the ability to put oneself in someone else's shoes and understand how he is likely to hear and interpret the message.

Using feedback

Feedback is the process of obtaining information on performance in order to take corrective action where this is necessary. In communications, feedback means ensuring that the communicator gets a message back from the receiver which tells him how much has been understood. This is why face-to-face communications are so much more effective than the written word, as long as the communications are truly 'two-way'; in other words, the receivers are given adequate opportunity to respond and react.

Using reinforcement

The message may have to be presented in a number of different ways to get it across. Good speakers know that if they can get more than three important ideas across in a thirty-minute talk, they are lucky, and they must repeat each idea at least three times in different ways to ensure that the message has been received and understood. In giving complicated directions, it is wise to repeat them several times, perhaps in different ways, to guarantee successful transmission.

Using direct, simple language

This seems so obvious as hardly to be worth stating. But many people seem unable to express themselves clearly and without the use of jargon or an excessive number of adjectives, adverbs and sub-clauses.

Reinforcing words with actions

Communications are only effective if they are credible. If management says a thing then it must do it. Next time, it is more likely to be believed. The motto should be 'suit the action to the words'.

Using face-to-face communication

Face-to-face communication is more effective than the written word for the reasons already mentioned. First, the sender is able to experience direct feedback from the receiver on what the latter is or is not hearing. The way in which the message is presented can then be adjusted by being expressed in different terms or reinforced. If necessary, the message itself can be changed in the light of immediate reactions. Secondly, most people express themselves more clearly and directly when they use the spoken rather than the written word. Thirdly, a spoken message can be delivered in a much more human and understanding way – this helps to get over prejudices against the speaker. It also means that criticisms can be expressed in a more constructive manner. A written reproof seems much more harsh and condemnatory than one delivered orally.

Using different channels of communication

Some communications have to be in writing to get the message across promptly and without any danger of variations in the way in which it is delivered. But wherever possible, written communications should be supplemented by the spoken word. Conversely, an oral briefing should be reinforced by a written confirmation.

Reducing problems of size

Communication problems arising from size can be reduced structurally by cutting down the number of levels of management, reducing spans of control, ensuring that activities are grouped on the basis of ease of inter-communication on matters that concern them, and decentralizing authority into smaller, self-contained although accountable units. An appropriate degree of informality, in relationships within the structure can be encouraged, and organization development programmes can be used to increase trust and understanding. Techniques such as briefing groups, as described later in this chapter, can be used to get oral communications more effectively disseminated throughout the organization.

Making communications work

Overcoming barriers to communication can be a slow and, for long periods, an unrewarding task. Communications can only be effective in an atmosphere of trust and co-operation. A sudden conversion to the 'good communications' philosophy resulting in a massive communication campaign will not convert a bad situation into a good one overnight. Trust and understanding have to be built up over a long period during which management demonstrates that it really believes in explaining and listening to people about the things that concern them.

To achieve good results, communication should be seen as a strategic matter to be planned, developed and controlled on the basis of a full understanding of the requirements, the problems, and the needs of everyone in the organization.

Communications strategy

The starting point for the formulation of a communications strategy should be an analysis of the different types of communication with which the strategy should be concerned. Communication studies embrace all human activities in an organization, and the analysis must narrow the field down to well-defined areas in which action can be taken. The main areas and the objectives to be attained in them are set out in Table 34.1.

	Communication Area	Objectives
I. MANAGERIAL	1. The communication downwards and sideways of corporate or functional objectives, policies, plans and budgets to those who have to implement them.	To ensure that managers and supervisors receive clear, accurate and prompt information on what they are expected to achieve to further the company's objectives.
	2. The communication downwards of direct instructions from a manager to a subordinate on what the latter has to do.	To ensure that the instructions are clear, precise and provide the necessary motivation to get people into action.
	3. The communication upwards and sideways of proposals, suggestions and comments on corporate or functional objectives, policies and budgets from those who have to implement them.	To ensure that managers and supervisors have adequate scope to influence corporate and functional decisions on matters about which they have specific expertise and knowledge.
	4. The communication upwards and sideways of management information on performance and results.	To enable management to monitor and control performance so that, as necessary, opportunities can be exploited or swift corrective action taken.
II. INTERNAL RELATIONS	5. The communication downwards of information on company plans, policies or performance.	To ensure that (i) employees are kept informed of matters that affect them, especially changes to working conditions, and factors influencing their prosperity and security; (ii) employees are encouraged to identify themselves more completely with the company.
	6. The communication upwards of the comments and reactions of employees to what is proposed will happen or what is actually happening in matters that affect them.	To ensure that employees are given an opportunity to voice their suggestions and fears and that the company is in a position to amend its plans in the light of these comments.
III. EXTERNAL RELATIONS	7. The receipt and analysis of information from outside which affects the company's interests.	To ensure that the company is fully aware of all the information on legislation and on marketing, commercial, financial and technological matters that affect its interests.
	8. The presentation of information about the company and its products to the government, customers and the public at large.	To exert influence in the interests of the company, to present a good image of the company and to persuade customers to buy its products or services.

Table 34.1 *Communication areas and objectives*

Employee relations are mainly affected by managerial and internal communications, although external communications are an additional channel of information. The strategy for managerial communications is concerned with planning and control procedures, management information systems and techniques of delegating and giving instructions. These matters are outside the scope of this book, except insofar as the procedures and skills can be developed by training programmes.

The strategy for internal communications, which is the main concern of this chapter, should be based on analyses of:

● what management wants to say;
● what employees want to hear;
● the problems being met in conveying or receiving information.

These analyses can be used to indicate the systems of communication that need to be developed and the education and training programmes required to make them work. They should also provide guidance on how communications should be managed and timed. Bad management and poor timing are frequently the fundamental causes of ineffective communication.

What management wants to say

What management wants to say will depend upon an assessment of what employees need to know which will, in turn, be affected by what they want to hear.

Management should aim to achieve three things: first to get employees to understand and accept what management proposes to do in areas that affect them; secondly, to get employees to act in the way management wants; and thirdly, to get employees to identify themselves more closely with the company and its achievements and to help them appreciate more clearly the contribution they make to those achievements.

Communications from management should therefore be about plans, intentions and proposals (with the opportunity for feedback from employees) as well as about achievements and results. Exhortations should be kept to a minimum if used at all. No one listens to them. It is better to concentrate on specific requirements rather than resorting to general appeals for such abstract things as improved quality or productivity. The requirements should be phrased in a way which emphasizes how all concerned will actually work together and the mutual benefits that should result.

What employees want to hear

Clearly, employees want to hear and to comment upon the matters that affect their interests. These will include changes in working methods and conditions, changes in the arrangements for overtime and shift working, company plans which may affect pay or security, and changes in terms and conditions of employment. It is management's job to understand what employees want to hear and plan their communications strategy accordingly. Understanding can be obtained by making formal inquiries, by means of attitude surveys, by asking employee representatives, by informally listening to what employees say, and by analysing grievances to see if improved communications could modify them.

Analysing communication problems

Specific examples of employee relations problems where communication failures have been the cause or a contributory factor should be analysed to determine exactly what went wrong and what needs to be done to put it right. The problems may be any of those listed earlier in this chapter, including lack of appropriate channels of communication, lack of appreciation of the need to communicate, and lack of skill in overcoming the many formidable barriers to communication. Problems with channels of communication can be dealt with by introducing new or improved communications systems. Lack of skill is a matter for education and training.

Communication systems

Communication systems can be divided into those using the written word such as magazines, newsletters, bulletins and notice-boards, and those using oral methods such as meetings, briefing groups and public address systems. The aim should be to make judicious use of a number of channels to make sure that the message gets across.

Magazines

Glossy magazines or house journals are an obvious way to keep employees informed about the company and are often used for public relations purposes as well. They can extol and explain the achievements of the company and may thus help to increase identification and even loyalty. If employees are encouraged to contribute (although this is difficult) the magazine can become more human. The biggest danger of this sort of magazine is that it becomes a public relations-type exercise, which is seen by employees as having little relevance to their everyday affairs.

Newsletters

Newsletters aim to appear more frequently and to angle their contents more to the immediate concerns of employees than the glossier form of house magazine. To be effective, they should include articles specifically aimed at explaining what management is planning to do and how this affects the company. They can also include more chatty 'human interest' material about the doings of employees to capture the attention of readers.

Correspondence columns can provide an avenue for the expression of employees' views and replies from management, but no attempt should be made to censor letters (except those that are purely abusive) or to pull punches in reply. Anonymous letters should be published if the writer gives his name to the editor.

The key factor in the success of a newsletter or any form of house magazine is the editor. He should be someone who knows the company and its employees and can be trusted by everyone to be frank and fair. Professional expertise is obviously desirable but it is not the first consideration, as long as the individual can write reasonably well and has access to expert help in putting the paper together. It is often a good idea to have an editorial board consisting of management and employee representatives to advise and assist the editor.

Companies often publish a newsletter in addition to a house magazine, treating the latter mainly as a public relations exercise and relying on the newsletter as the prime means of communicating with employees.

Bulletins

Bulletins can be used to give immediate information to employees which cannot wait for the next issue of a newsletter; or they can be a substitute for a formal publication if the company does not feel that the expense is justified. Bulletins are only useful if they can be distributed quickly and are seen by all interested employees. They can simply be posted on noticeboards or, more effectively, given to individual employees and used as a starting point for a briefing session if they contain information of sufficient interest to merit a face-to-face discussion.

Notice-boards

Notice-boards are an obvious but frequently misused medium for communications. The biggest danger is allowing boards to be cluttered up with uninteresting or out-of-date material. It is essential to control what goes on to the boards and to appoint responsible people to service them by removing out-of-date or unauthorized notices.

A more impressive show can be made of notices and other material if an information centre is set up in the canteen or some other suitable place where the information can be displayed in a more attractive and compelling manner than on a typical notice-board.

Consultative committees

Joint consultative committees as discussed in Chapter 33 exist to provide a channel for two-way communication. Sometimes, however, they are not particularly effective, either because their thunder has been stolen by union negotiation committees, or because their proceedings are over-formalized and restricted. It is essential to disseminate the information revealed at committees around the offices and works, but it is impossible to rely on committee members to do this. Minutes can be posted on notice-boards, but they are seldom read, usually because they contain too much redundant material.

Team briefing

The concept of team briefing (previous called briefing groups), as developed by the Industrial Society, is a device to overcome the restricted nature of joint consultative committees by involving everyone in an organization, level by level, in face-to-face meetings to present, receive and discuss information. Team briefing aims to overcome the gaps and inadequacies of casual briefings by injecting some order into the system.

John Garnett, the former Director of the Industrial Society, has defined the team briefing system as: 'A simple checkable routine or drill where explanations can be given at each level by the boss of each work group on a regular basis. Subjects briefed in the group are those matters which help people to co-operate.'[4]

Team briefing should operate as follows:

1. *Organization*
   - cover all levels in an organization;
   - fewest possible steps between the top and bottom;
   - between 4 and 18 in each group;
   - run by the immediate leader of each group at each level (who must be properly trained and briefed in his task).
2. *Subjects*
   - policies – explanations of new or changed policies;
   - plans – as they affect the organization as a whole and the immediate group;
   - progress – how the organization and the group is getting on: what the latter needs to do to improve;
   - people – new appointments, points about personnel matters (pay, security, procedures).
3. *Timing and duration*
   - a minimum of once a month for those in charge of others and once every two months for every individual in the organization – but only meet if there is something to say;
   - duration not longer than 20-30 minutes.

The merit of team briefing is that it enables face-to-face communications to be planned and, to a reasonable degree, formalized. It is easy, however, for it to start on a wave of enthusiasm and then to wither away because of lack of sufficient drive and enthusiasm from the top downward, inadequately trained and motivated managers and supervisors, reluctance of management to allow subjects of real importance to be discussed throughout the system, and insufficient feedback upwards through each level.

A team briefing system must be led and controlled effectively from the top, but it does require a senior manager with specific responsibility to advise on the subject matter and the preparation of briefs (it is important to have well-prepared material to ensure that briefing is carried out consistently and thoroughly at each level), to train managers and supervisors, and to monitor the system by checking on the effectiveness and frequency of meetings.

Education and training in communications

Communication is ultimately one person passing on a message to another and listening to their reply. Formal channels of communication have to be provided for, but their effectiveness depends on the attitudes, skills and enthusiasm of those responsible for using the system.

Education and training programmes are required to develop the attitude that communication is an important part of management and thus to ensure that a prime consideration when making any decision is how, where and to whom it should be communicated. Communicators need to be made aware of the barriers to communication and the skills of perception and analysis they need to overcome them. Finally, training should be given in specific communication skills – speaking, writing, running meetings and, most important, listening. The training in many of these skills can be conducted by means of more or less traditional courses but the maximum use should be made of group exercises and role playing so that people can practise and develop their skills. Sensitivity or 'T-Group' training (see Appendix K) is one method of increasing the individual's understanding of the impact he or she makes on other people and the way in which they hear what he or she has to say. Such training, as its name implies, should make people more sensitive to the effect they have on others as well as providing them with new tools to analyse the interactions that take place when people are working together.

Twelve rules for internal communications

To sum up, the following are the twelve golden rules for internal communications:

1. There is no such thing as a stone cold certainty in business decisions and it is important everyone in a business realizes this.

2. If a Board cannot or will not clearly spell out its business strategy employees are entitled to assume it does not have one.
3. Assume that in an information vacuum, people will believe the worst.
4. Never take it for granted that people know what you are talking about.
5. Always take it for granted that people doing a job know more about it than you do.
6. Telling people something once is not much better than not telling them at all.
7. Never assume that people will tell you anything that reflects unfavourably upon themselves.
8. Remember that employees read newspapers, magazines and books, listen to the radio and watch TV.
9. Do not be afraid to admit you were wrong; it gives people confidence that you know what you are doing.
10. Asking for help, taking advice, consulting and listening to others are signs of great strength.
11. Communicating good news is easy but even this is not often done by management; bad news is often left to rumours and the grapevine.
12. Changing attitudes to change behaviour takes years – changing behaviour changes attitudes in weeks.

References

1. Roethlisberger, F and Dickson, W *Management and the Worker* Harvard University Press, Cambridge, Mass, 1939.
2. Strauss, G and Sayles, L R *Personnel: The Human Problems of Management* Prentice-Hall, Englewood Cliffs, New Jersey, 1972.
3. Schumacher, E F *Small is Beautiful* Blond and Briggs, London, 1973.
4. Garnett, J *The Work Challenge* Kogan Page, London 1988.

Conclusion

The introduction to this book reviewed the changing scene of personnel management and, against this background, the following 34 chapters described current thinking and practice in each area of the subject. The rate of change has shown no sign of slackening and the purpose of this concluding part is to review where these trends are likely to take personnel management in the 1990s.

Chapter 35
Trends in Personnel Management

The future of personnel management

The following four factors, which are discussed in the first part of this chapter, will govern the future trends of personnel management in the 1990s:

1. Future government policies.
2. The future of the economy.
3. The future of organizations.
4. The future of work.

The second part of the chapter examines how these factors will affect each of the main areas of personnel management.

Future government policies

In the United Kingdom, a Conservative government is likely to be in power into the 1990s. Even if it is then replaced by an administration of a different political persuasion, it seems probable that the influence of Conservative policies will be left for some time to come. The market economy is here to stay, the enterprise culture will prevail, everything that can be privatized will have been, in a way that no other government could unravel, and excessive trade union power will still be constrained.

The future of the economy

The trend has been towards the high-tech and service industries which broadly have favoured the South against the North. Manufacturing industry will thrive, as it does now in part, but only if it accepts and implements technological and organizational change, and adapts its human resource management policies to current thinking, rather than living in the past.

Market economies, of course, do not always run smoothly, as many people found out on 19 October 1987 – black Monday. Prosperous countries which have relied on one product, for example oil, have got into difficulties in the past and might do so again in the future and this could happen here, although the British economy is, fortunately, not unduly dependent on North Sea oil.

The future of organizations and the future of work, which are considered below, are obviously affected to a considerable degree by government economic policy and trends in both world and home markets. The future of organizations, work and, therefore, personnel management, is just as unpredictable as the economic future. But it does not seem unreasonable to suppose that, give or take a few hiccoughs, present trends will continue.

The future of organizations

In 1988, Peter Drucker, as trenchant as ever after all these years, wrote:

> The typical large business 20 years hence will have fewer than half the levels of management of its counterpart today, and no more than a third the managers. In its structure, and in its management problems and concerns, it will bear little resemblance to the typical manufacturing concern, circa 1950, which our textbooks still consider the norm . . . . The typical business will be knowledge-based, an organization composed largely of specialists who direct and discipline their own performance through organized feedback from colleagues, customers and headquarters.

Organizations of the future will be information-based. They will require more specialists than the command-and-control organizations we are used to. The number of management levels and the number of managers can be sharply cut because, as Drucker says, at present ' . . . whole layers of management neither make decisions nor lead. Instead, their main, if not their only, function is to serve as "relays" – human boosters for the faint, unfocused signals that pass for communication in the traditional pre-information organizations.'[1]

The trend towards flatter, leaner organizations is already here. But it will accelerate in the future and this means that many ideas developed in the fifties, sixties and seventies about organization structures, job design, motivating techniques, remuneration policies, management development and industrial relations will become increasingly irrelevant. They are being replaced by a more flexible approach which treats organizational members more as individuals who get their satisfaction from opportunities to use and develop their skills in a more fluid 'organic' environment, who are rewarded according to their individual contribution, who are less concerned about careers within a job hierarchy, who accept that traditional methods of managing are no longer appropriate, and who can tolerate a little ambiguity about where they are going because they know that their skills are in demand and, in any case, they have the capacity to make and enjoy their own future, in or out of work.

The future of work

The future of work is clearly a function of the changes in the economy and organizations mentioned above. High levels of unemployment, caused by increases in the labour supply and by the dual effects of new technology and the recession, seem inevitable in the medium term. Skill shortages still exist but the unemployed will continue to be those who are poorly qualified or those whose skills have become obsolete.

Charles Handy[2] has stated that future developments in the nature of work will include:

- many more people than at present not working in an organization – an increase in out-workers and sub-contracting facilitated by information technology in the shape of computer networks and electronic mail;
- shorter working hours;
- fewer mammoth bureaucracies, more federal organizations and more small businesses;
- more requirements for specialists and professionals in organizations;
- more importance given to the informal, uncounted economy of the home and the community;
- a manufacturing sector that is smaller in terms of people but larger in terms of output;
- a smaller working population and a larger dependent population;
- a greatly increased demand for education, often provided by distance learning;
- new forms of social organization to complement the employment organization.

Trends in personnel management

Personnel management will have to adjust itself to tomorrow's world. Tyson and Fell have suggested that already the personnel function is being:
'... redefined and expanded from the role of being a control-orientated supplier of labour to an overall human resource planning, development and utilization agency.'[3]

The particular areas of personnel management that will be affected by these changes are:

- *Organization planning.* The old principles of organization – span of control, unity of command, the role of line and staff – which were based on the organization of the Roman Catholic church or the Army, no longer apply. Organization design will be governed by information technology. There will be a continuous attack on unnecessary layers of management. Managers will be expected to use the instant information available to them, and to exploit their capacity to communicate quantities of data immediately to any quarter of the globe so that they can concentrate on their roles as leaders and co-ordinators of much larger teams than they could handle before.

● *Organization development.* The importance of shared values will become increasingly recognized. The emphasis will be on gaining commitment by using the 'hearts and minds' approach. The 'flower people' idea, generated in the sixties that organizations exist to make people happy will finally vanish. Organizations exist to get work done, but job satisfaction will be created by providing challenging and rewarding work. Good performance produces job satisfaction, not the other way round.

● *Job design.* Autonomy based on the use of information technology will increase, whether it is individuals working in what Alvin Toffler calls their 'electronic cottages' or autonomous working groups. High-performance work design will become the most frequently used job design technique. This approach will stress the performance requirements of jobs in terms of objectives, targets and standards, and jobs will be designed around individuals or autonomous working groups with these requirements uppermost in people's minds. Job enrichment, with its implication that jobs only exist to enrich the lives of people rather than the concept that people exist in organizations to do jobs, will no longer be fashionable. High-performance design should provide all the challenge and opportunity required to meet the needs of employees for growth and achievement.

● *Human resource planning.* A strategic view of personnel management will become the rule rather than, as tends to be the case now, the exception. People will increasingly be regarded as *the* key resource for which investment plans have to be made which are fully integrated with the longer-term strategies of the business.

● *Recruitment.* Personnel specifications in the new organizations will place greater emphasis on adaptability and the need to 'fit' the corporate culture. Pre-employment education will have to be broad and should develop a range of basic skills so that trainees have a good foundation upon which they can build quickly. Aptitude, attainment, interest and personality tests will become even more sophisticated and will increasingly be used to match people to appropriate jobs. Career guidance will also become more effective so that school and university leavers will have a better chance of setting off in the right direction.

● *Employment.* More use will be made of contract staff and out-workers. Job sharing may not expand as quickly as some people have believed but working hours will be more flexible to meet both operational and individual needs. Terms and conditions of employment will almost universally be harmonized. Single-status will be the norm.

- *Work.* The move towards multi-skilling will accelerate. Flexibility at work will be all-important and employees will have to be able to adapt themselves more quickly to technological change.
- *Databased management.* Computerized personnel information systems will use personnel databases more comprehensively for decision support, as in the areas of human resource planning (with the help of models) and competency modelling. Expert systems will be developed to store, manipulate and present managers with information they need to know for organization and job design, performance management and career planning.
- *Reward management.* The rigid, multi-graded salary structure with fixed increments will be a thing of the past. Pay will be fixed individually in relation to contribution and the market value of the employee. Payment will be for performance rather than simply for 'being there'. Payment by results schemes will still have a valid role in spite of the criticisms that have been levelled at them over the years. But the schemes will be designed more carefully to fit the situation, using the contingency approach. And they will be adaptable to changes in technology, work methods and work mix.

    Fringe benefits will be distributed equally to all employees in line with the principle of harmonization. The tax advantages provided by company cars will disappear and the reward system will depend on money alone to recognize different levels of contribution and achievement.
- *Performance management.* Systems for assessing and improving performance will concentrate on measuring and developing all-round excellence. The highest ratings will be given to those who can make things happen, manage change and adjust rapidly to new challenges and opportunities. Performance improvement programmes will be designed not only to increase productivity but also to encourage flexibility and the acquisition of new skills.
- *Training.* More sophisticated techniques will be devised to identify training needs, set training objectives, use a wider range of training methods (for example computer-based training and distance learning) and evaluate the impact of training more thoroughly.
- *Career management.* The traditional idea of a career developing through the successive levels of a management hierarchy will largely disappear. Dual career ladders will become common,

allowing top specialists to advance just as far and as fast, if not faster, than their managerial colleagues. The equally traditional idea of one career will also vanish. People will have to be prepared to change direction at least once, possibly two or three times, during their working life. New methods of career management such as coaching, counselling and mentoring will replace the concept of management development with that of manager development.

● *Employee relations.* Although some trade unions are unlikely to abandon their traditional ways, 'new style' agreements with their emphasis on single-status, single-union organizations and their belief in conjunctive rather than disjunctive bargaining, will help to achieve replacement of industrial action (properly, industrial inaction) by industrial harmony. Management will recognize generally that it has the *duty* to manage, not the right to manage, and 'mutuality' in the form of joint involvement in problem-solving and decision-making will prevail.

The trade unions will still have a role to play in looking after the collective interests of their members and in protecting their rights. But individualism in employee relations will become more important as a result of the changing nature of organizations and work.

Human resource management

All these changes serve to reinforce the need to adopt the human resource management approach. In the words of Tyson and Fell:

> A human resources management philosophy comes about in an organization... with the perception that labour is not an expense of doing business, but that people are the only resource capable of turning inanimate factors of production into wealth. People provide the source of creative energy in any direction the organization dictates and fosters.[3]

Human resource management is an attitude of mind rather than a substantially new set of techniques for personnel managers to use. The attitude required is a belief in the importance of people as a key resource and a determination to integrate the management of that resource with the strategic planning processes of the organization. This approach provides the basis for developing personnel objectives, strategies and policies which fit or are contingent on the circumstances of the enterprise and meet organizational needs. The effectiveness and value of the contribution of the personnel function to organizational success depends upon its ability to adopt and implement this approach to the management of human resources.

References

1. Drucker, P F 'The coming of the new organization', *Harvard Business Review* January-February 1988.
2. Handy, C *The Future of Work* Blackwell, Oxford, 1984.
3. Tyson, S and Fell, A *Evaluating the Personnel Function* Hutchinson, London, 1986.

Appendices

Appendix A
Personnel Policies

Book Club Associates
Statement of Overall Personnel Policy

1 Book Club Associates recognizes that its prime resource is its staff. It is upon their commitment and effort that the firm depends for its continued prosperity and growth. The principles which govern the application of BCA's personnel policies are set out below.

Equity

2 Employees are treated fairly and justly and an evenhanded approach is adopted. This is applied by:

(a) rewarding staff according to their contribution;

(b) providing equal opportunities for employment and promotion;

(c) applying the principles of natural justice when dealing with issues concerning individuals.

Involvement and participation

3 Staff are regarded as partners in the enterprise. They are involved in decisions affecting them and are encouraged to contribute their skills and knowledge to improving performance.

Communication

4 BCA adopts an open approach which discloses and communicates information to help staff to understand the economics of the business and how they can contribute to increasing its prosperity.

Management Style

5 It is expected that managers will exercise effective leadership but BCA encourages a democratic management style. Managers are both approachable and visible. The emphasis is on team work and cooperation. An atmosphere of mutual trust is fostered.

Consideration

6 It is accepted that to obtain the best performance and support from staff consideration should be given to them as individuals when making decisions which affect their prospects, security and job satisfaction.

Social responsibility

7 Care is taken for the welfare of staff — serving and retired — and support and encouragement is provided where hardship occurs.

Quality of Working Life

8   BCA endeavours to provide agreeable working conditions for its staff and to enrich jobs wherever possible to add interest and increase involvement. The firm is fully conscious of the need to maintain a healthy and safe work environment and systems of work.

Continuous Training and Development

9   BCA requires staff to be fully trained for their jobs in order to ensure that the firm's activities are carried out expertly.

10   The development of the abilities of staff to their full potential is a continuous process to which all managers are expected to contribute.

Opportunity

11   Staff will be given every opportunity to advance their careers in BCA. So far as possible, promotion will be from within the firm.

Performance

12   BCA expects a high level of performance from its staff.

Book Club Associates
Employment Policy

Human Resource Planning

1   Book Club Associates is committed to planning ahead in order to maximize the opportunities for employees to develop their careers within the firm and to minimize the possibility of redundancies.

Quality Staff

2   BCA deliberately sets out to recruit and develop good quality staff who have the ability to meet the high standards of performance that will be expected of them.

Promotion

3   The policy of BCA is to promote from within wherever possible, and to this end, when appropriate, vacancies will be advertised internally. Employees will not be held back from promotion by their manager.

4   It is recognized, however, that it may sometimes be necessary to replace staff or fill new jobs by recruiting from outside the firm when there are no suitable staff available. It must also be appreciated that a vigorous organization like BCA will need 'fresh blood' from time to time.

Equal Opportunity

5   BCA is an equal opportunity company. A separate document sets out this policy in more detail.

Redundancy

6   The firm will use its best endeavours to avoid involuntary redundancy through its human resource planning, re-deployment and re-training procedures.

7   However, should redundancy be absolutely unavoidable, BCA will give the maximum amount of warning possible and will provide help in obtaining suitable alternative work.

Discipline

8   Employees have the right to know the company's rules of conduct and what could happen if they are infringed. In handling disciplinary cases the firm will treat employees in accordance with the principles of natural justice, which are:

   (a) the employee should be informed clearly of the nature of the complaint;

   (b) the employee should be given the chance to explain;

   (c) the employee should be given the opportunity to improve, except in particularly gross cases of incapability or misconduct;

   (d) the employee should be warned of the consequences if specific improvements do not take place;

   (e) the manager's decision to take disciplinary action should be based on sufficient evidence;

   (f) the manager should take any mitigating factors into account;

(g) the disciplinary action should be appropriate to the nature of the offence or misbehaviour;

(h) the employee should have the right to appeal against disciplinary action.

Grievances

9 Employees have the right to raise any grievance with their managers and can, if they wish, be accompanied by another employee of the firm to act as their representative. Appeals can be made to a higher level if employees are not satisfied that their grievance has been dealt with adequately.

Book Club Associates
Equal Opportunity Policy

1 Book Club Associates is an equal opportunity employer. This means that the firm does not permit discrimination of any kind against any other person on grounds of:

(a) colour;

(b) creed or religion;

(c) race or ethnic origins;

(d) nationality or national origin;

(e) sex;

(f) marital status;

(g) disability.

2 Direct discrimination is defined as treating a person less favourably than others are, or would be, treated in the same or similar circumstances.

3 Indirect discrimination occurs when a requirement or condition is applied which, whether intentional or not, adversely affects a considerably larger proportion of people of one race, sex or marital status than another and cannot be justified on grounds other than race, sex or marital status.

4 The firm regards discrimination, as defined in paras 2 and 3 above, as gross misconduct and any employee of the firm who discriminates against any other person will be liable to instant dismissal.

5 The firm will ensure that equal opportunity principles are applied in all its personnel policies and in particular in the procedures relating to the recruitment, training, development and promotion of staff. In applying the policy to the disabled the proviso is that the disability does not prevent the function of the job from being carried out.

Book Club Associates
Human Resource Development Policy

Preamble

Book Club Associates recognizes that the future prosperity of the firm largely depends on the knowledge, skills, expertise and motivation of its human resources.

Aims

The aim of the human resource development programmes of BCA is to provide the firm with the quality of human resources it needs — now and in the future — by:

(a) training employees to achieve maximum effectiveness in the shortest possible time;

(b) developing a multi-skilled work force capable of operating flexibly and responding rapidly to changes in business and organizational needs or skill requirements;

(c) improving performance in their present jobs;

(d) ensuring that the best use is made of the natural abilities of employees by developing their skills and capacities for the benefit of the organization and their future career;

(e) developing commitment to BCA by:

    (i) using the process of training to increase pride in the firm and its products and to inculcate the core values of BCA, especially those concerned with the pursuit of excellence, professionalism, entrepreneurship, market and customer orientation and the belief in an open and democratic management style;

    (ii) ensuring that all employees are aware of the opportunities presented to them by BCA's training policies and programmes.

POLICIES FOR ACHIEVING THE AIMS

1 Development and training is a continuous and systematic process. All training is based on the identification of relevant training needs for the enterprise as a whole, the functions within the firm and individual employees.

2 The relevance of training is directly proportional to the extent to which it contributes to achieving the strategic objectives of BCA.

3 The best training takes place in the 'real' situation, ie in the normal course of work through training on-the-job, coaching, counselling and self-managed projects. This means that line managers have the main responsibility for training their staff, with the support and guidance of the human resource development function within the personnel department.

4 The best form of development is self-development and BCA's training policies are designed to help staff to improve their own performance and to develop their own skills and knowledge. The system of accountable management plays an important part in the process.

5 It follows from points (3) and (4) above that the principal method by which

managers and staff can be equipped to do their jobs and to develop their potential is by ensuring that they have the right variety of experience, in good time, during their careers. This experience can and should be supplemented, but never replaced, by courses carefully timed and designed to meet particular needs.

6   To ensure that development and training programmes make a proper contribution to improving BCA's performance, a continuous process of evaluation takes place, on the basis of which changes are made to increase relevance and effectiveness.

Book Club Associates
Pay Policy

Staff should be correctly rewarded in relation to:

1 The contribution they are expected to make towards achieving the firm's objectives.

2 The results they achieve — in accordance with the principle of paying for performance.

3 The performance of the firm.

4 The value placed on comparable jobs within the firm.

5 The value placed on comparable jobs in other companies, ie. market rates.

6 The differentials required between levels of responsibility in order to:
   (a) recognize seniority;
   (b) provide incentives for career progression within the firm;
   (c) reflect the skills and qualifications needed in different jobs.

7 The economic and commercial environment as it affects the firm and its staff.

Book Club Associates
Involvement and Participation Policy

Aims

1 The aims of Book Club Associates' involvement and participation policy are as follows:

   (a) to generate commitment of all employees to the success of the enterprise.

   (b) to enable BCA better to meet the needs of its customers and adapt to changing market requirements, and hence to maintain its future prospects and the prospects of those who work in it.

   (c) to help the organization to improve performance and productivity and adopt new methods of working to match new technology, drawing on the resources of knowledge and practical skills of all its employees.

   (d) to improve the satisfaction employees get from their work.

   (e) to provide all employees with the opportunity to influence and be involved in decisions which are likely to affect their interests.

Principles

2 The principles of the involvement and participation policies of BCA are as follows:

   (a) *Management must lead* – senior management must provide the lead, and managers at all levels be involved in the action necessary to establish and maintain effective participation. Participation is not to be expected to occur or develop of its own accord.

   (b) *All employees are included* – all employees, including managers, should have the opportunity to participate, and its success will depend on their widespread response. For this they must know that their views are sought and taken into account by management. This will depend largely on individual employees' relationships with their own supervisors and managers, and the extent to which they are involved in the way objectives are set and achieved in their own work area.

   (c) *Education and training* – employees and their representatives, as well as managers, will need appropriate education and training so as to be able to fulfil their participation role in a constructive manner in the interests of the organization and all its employees. Management will provide the resources to do this.

   (d) *The role of employee representatives* – employee representatives have a key role to play in implementing the participation policies by their involvement in staff or works councils and through the operation of the normal representational system.

   (e) *The role of management* – management has the duty to manage the enterprise to satisfy the requirements of its owners, the demands of its customers and the needs of its employees. Whatever arrangements and procedures for involvement and participation may be established, managers remain responsible for making business and organization decisions falling within the area of their own accountability and for communicating such decisions, with relevant background information, to employees.

(f) *The role of communications* – an open policy of communications about business plans (subject to confidentiality), programmes and performance is an essential part of the process of involvement and participation.

Book Club Associates
Communications Policy

1 Book Club Associates believes that it is essential that its staff are informed on the progress, policies, plans and financial state of the firm.

2 The firm recognizes its staff as partners in the business and as such will encourage them to make their opinions known on issues which affect them directly.

3 In pursuing an effective communication policy, Book Club Associates aims to help staff achieve a better understanding of the firm's objectives and policies and to gain their commitment to them.

4 It is recognized that:

   (a) it is important to create a climate within the firm which is conducive to effective communication.

   (b) communication is a two-way process and management has the responsibility of ensuring that staff are able to communicate their views as well as to communicate to them.

   (c) in certain cases, however, there may be a need to preserve confidentiality, which could impose constraints upon communication.

5 The communication policy is closely linked to BCA's policies on involvement and participation and on employee relations.

Book Club Associates
Employee Relations Policy

1 Book Club Associates will strive to ensure that it maintains good relations with its staff in order to protect the interests of both parties.

2 In its dealings with staff representatives or other representative bodies the firm will be frank and fair and aim to create an atmosphere of mutual trust, credibility and consistency.

3 BCA is committed to involvement, participation and open communication to build and maintain a co-operative climate within the firm. Its approach in these areas is set out in more detail in the separate policies for involvement and participation and for communications.

4 The firm recognizes that there will be issues which concern staff collectively and its staff council system is designed to provide a medium for the exchange of views on these issues and the resolution of any problems.

Book Club Associates
New Technology Policy

1 Book Club Associates is committed to the introduction of new technology wherever this is cost-effective; i.e. in general benefits the firm and provides an appropriate return on investments, and in particular furthers BCA's needs to improve profitability, productivity or the level of customer service.

2 The firm appreciates that the introduction of new technology is a matter of concern to its staff from the point of view of changes in work and skill requirements and future security of employment.

3 Recognizing this concern, BCA undertakes to consult with staff on programmes for developing new technology. The reasons for introducing it will be explained as well as its benefits.

4 The consultation process will include discussions on the implications of new technology to staff. Joint consideration will be given to training or re-training needs and policies for re-deployment where this is necessary.

5 The firm will use its best endeavours to avoid involuntary redundancy as a result of new technology. To this end it undertakes to plan its introduction well ahead and to take full account during this planning process of the implications for staff. If, as a result of these plans, any surpluses are forecast, steps will be taken to absorb these so far as possible by re-deployment, re-training or natural wastage.

Book Club Associates
Health and Safety Policy

Overall policy

1 Book Club Associates regards the promotion of industrial safety and hygiene within its business as an essential part of its responsibilities. Furthermore, it regards the promotion of health and safety matters as a mutual objective of every manager and employee.

2 It is, therefore, the firm's policy to do all that is reasonably practical to prevent personal injury and damage to property and to protect everyone from foreseeable work hazards, including the public insofar as they come into contact with the firm or its products.

The responsibility of management

3 Book Club Associates will:

(a) Provide and maintain safe and healthy working conditions at each of its locations, in accordance with the relevant statutory requirements.

(b) Provide safety training for all employees.

(c) Provide all safety devices and protective equipment required by statute and supervise their use.

(d) Ensure that articles and substances purchased for use at work have been so designed and constructed as to be safe and without risk to health and that full information is made available by the suppliers where additional safety precautions are required.

(e) In particular, maintain a constant and continuing attention to all aspects of safety by:

(i) making regular location safety inspections;

(ii) seeking and stimulating consultation and contributions from employees on safety matters;

(iii) ensuring that each location is given adequate health and safety cover by a person well versed in safety requirements relating to the firm's activities;

(iv) ensuring that all means of access and of egress are known to persons either on or using the premises;

(v) setting up safety committees consisting of management and staff representatives which meet regularly;

(vi) providing and maintaining a place of work that is, so far as is reasonably practical, safe, without risks of health, and has adequate facilities for the welfare of all employees.

The responsibility of employees

4 Every employee has the responsibility:

(a) to take reasonable care for the health and safety of themselves and of all persons they come into contact with at work;

(b) to co-operate with management to enable them to carry out their statutory duties with the object of raising and maintaining a high standard of safety and health at work;

(c) report all incidents that have led, or may lead to injury;

(d) co-operate in the investigation of accidents with the object of introducing measures to prevent a recurrence.

Appendix B
Statement of Core Values

The core values of Book Club Associates are:

1 *Excellence* — anything we do well now we can do better.

2 *Profitable growth* — the profitable expansion of the business to generate the return our owners want on their investment and to ensure the continued prosperity and security of our employees.

3 *Enterprise* — we thrive by innovation, by creativity and by seizing opportunities whenever they arise.

4 *Customer service* — we depend on our customers and maintaining and improving levels of service to them is a continuing priority.

5 *Reward* — achievement brings reward to everyone involved in BCA.

6 *Teamwork* — we rely on teamwork to get results.

7 *Professionalism* — the effective and dedicated use and development of skills is a prime requirement.

8 *Productivity through people* — higher productivity and profitability achieved by effective leadership and the development of a committed and well trained work force.

9 *Partnership* — all employees are treated as partners in the enterprise, to be involved in matters that affect them and to be told the results and future plans.

10 *People* — employees are treated fairly and as responsible human beings. They are given the opportunity to develop their skills and careers and the firm is constantly aware of the need to improve the quality of their working life.

Appendix C
Example of a Statement of Accountabilities for a Personnel Manager

Overall accountability

To contribute to the achievement of the personnel objectives and strategies of the firm by:

(a) preparing and managing programmes for obtaining, maintaining, motivating and developing the firm's human resources;

(b) providing the personnel services required;

(c) advising and assisting management in the preparation and implementation of the firm's personnel policies.

Specific accountabilities

Organization development

1 Contributes to the development of an effective organization by advising on the design of jobs and by preparing and introducing organization development programmes.

Performance indicators

Organization development

1 Performance is up to standard if:
(a) jobs are designed to meet management requirements;
(b) agreed organization development programmes are implemented within predetermined budgets and time scales which meet their objectives of improving performance and teamwork and helping to manage change.

659

Human resource planning

2 Prepares in the light of the firm's corporate strategies:
   (a) forecasts of human resource requirements:
   (b) plans for the acquisition, retention and motivation of employees.

Human resource planning

2 Performance is up to standard if:
   (a) corporate plans are analysed and used to provide the basis for the realistic anticipation of the firm's future human resource requirements;
   (b) a pro-active approach is used in making proposals to management on how human resource management programmes can help to achieve their objectives for improving organizational and operational performance;
   (c) reactions to proposals from senior managers for improvements in the use and motivation of human resources are prompt, convincing and, ultimately, effective;
   (d) human resource acquisition, retention and motivation plans achieve the objectives set for them.

Employment

3 Provides the advice and administrative services in the fields of recruitment and employment practices needed to satisfy the requirements for human resources of the firm as a whole and of its individual managers.

4 Provides guidance, administrative services and, as required, technical direction in all areas where the firm has legal and social obligations towards its employees (eg health and safety).

Employment

3 Performance is up to standard if recruitment systems and standards are laid down and monitored in a way which ensures that management requirements are satisfied efficiently.

4 Performance is up to standard if statutory obligations affecting employment are fulfilled so that the firm is not held liable for any transgressions, and procedures are operated which achieve the firm's personnel policies concerning social responsibility, health and safety.

Human resource development

5 Administers the performance management procedures (system of accountable management) at levels up to and including senior management.

6 Plans and implements relevant training and development programmes designed to improve performance and develop potential.

Reward management

7 Advises in the light of the firm's pay policy on pay systems, reward management procedures and pay levels and ensures that the systems and procedures are administered effectively.

Employee relations

8 Provides advice and services on day to day employee relations issues and on programmes for involvement, participation and communications within the framework of employee relations strategies and policies.

Human resource development

5 Performance is up to standard if the system of accountable management is implemented in accordance with agreed objectives and programmes.

6 Performance is up to standard if training and development programmes are prepared and implemented which satisfy identified needs within agreed budgets.

Reward management

7 Performance is up to standard if reward management systems are operated which:
   (a) are in line with the firm's pay policies;
   (b) are cost effective in that they satisfy requirements to attract, retain and motivate staff within agreed cost parameters.

Employee relations

8 Performance is up to standard if:
   (a) day-to-day issues with employees and their representatives are resolved without dissent or disruption;
   (b) the firm's policies and programmes for involvement, participation and communications are maintained and implemented according to plan and in a way which satisfies corporate objectives for increasing the motivation and commitment of employees.

Appendix D
Job Analysis Checklist: Clerical Staff

The following are examples of the questions that might be asked in analysing a clerical job. The questions would not necessarily be put in exactly these words or in this order and it would be necessary to ask a number of supplementary questions to clarify replies.

Job title
1 What is the title of the job?

Responsible to
2 To whom are you directly responsible?

Responsible for
3 Are there any staff directly responsible to you? If so, describe briefly the main purpose of the jobs of each of your immediate subordinates.
4 Have your immediate subordinates any staff responsible to them? If so, what is the total number of staff under your control?

Main purpose of job
5 What is the main purpose of your job, i.e. what, in general terms, are you supposed to do?
6 How does your job fit in with the work of your section or department as a whole?
7 How can the results you achieve in the job be measured or assessed?

Main tasks
8 What tasks or duties do you carry out? Describe them either in chronological order (that is the order in which you do them during the day or week), in order of importance or in order of frequency.
9 Where does your work come from? e.g.:
   - From outside the organization by post or telephone
   - From another department or section
   - From your superior
   - From colleagues.
10 Where does your completed work go to?

Volume
11 How often and in what quantities, is your work received, e.g. does it reach you as a single item, in batches or continuously?
12 For each of your main tasks or group of tasks:
   (a) How often has the work to be done – continuously, daily, weekly, monthly or intermittently?

(b) What is the volume of work you are expected to complete per hour, day or week, as appropriate?

(c) Approximately how long does it take to complete the work?

Forms and equipment

13 Do you have to complete or maintain any forms or records? If so, give examples and describe how they are completed.

14 Do you use any machines or equipment? If so, give details of the machines used and how often you use them.

Contacts

15 To what extent does your work bring you into contact with:

- Members of other departments?
- Other organizations
- Members of the public?

In each case indicate the frequency of the contacts and descrbe what they are about.

Discretion

16 Is the way you do your work laid down in a procedure manual or in any other written instructions? If so, give details.

17 To what extent are you able to vary:

- The methods of work you use
- The order in which you carry out your tasks?

18 Whom would you go to if you were in difficulties over an aspect of your work?

Checking

19 Who checks your work and how frequently?

20 How is your work checked?

Supervision received

21 On what matters and how frequently do you receive direct instructions from your supervisor or manager?

22 What matters have to be referred by you to your supervisor or manager either for him or her to deal with or to obtain approval for an action you propose to take?

23 How often do you have to refer matters to your supervisor or manager?

Supervision given

24 What authority have you got in respect of your subordinates to:

(a) Assign work

(b) Check work

(c) Correct and discipline

(d) Deal with grievances

(e) Recommend appointments, salary increases, transfers, promotions, discharges

(f) Assess their performance?

Working conditions

25 What are the conditions under which you carry out your work?

26 What qualifications and experience do you think are necessary to carry out your work?

27 What specific training is needed to carry out your work?

28 How long did it take you to learn to do the work?

Appendix E
Example of a Job Description

Job title: Works manager

Responsible to: Production director

Responsible to him:
- Production superintendent
- Production controller
- Chief inspector
- Personnel officer

Main role:
To achieve agreed budgets, quality standards and delivery requirements by the efficient control of manufacturing operations, by developing and maintaining good labour relations and by ensuring that his staff work together as a team.

Main activities

PLANS
1   Develops manufacturing plans and budgets in line with estimated market demands and ensures that production capacity, equipment and labour are available to achieve agreed output and forseeable additional demands.

DEVELOPMENT
2   Continually seeks to improve production methods and techniques and to this end makes full use of company engineering research and development services.

OPERATIONS
3   Maintains close liaison with company production control to ensure economic loading on the works and to progress availability of supplies.
4   Ensures that production scheduling fulfils its objectives of meeting programmed delivery dates and optimizing wastage, downtime and stock levels.
5   Ensures that all production operations are progressed and the distribution department is informed of expected departures from programmed delivery dates.
6   Maintains the security of the works and all property, stocks and other assets within it and takes suitable precautions against fire.
7   Maintains in good order the works and the equipment in it.

PERSONNEL
8 Ensures that the works organization is the most appropriate for achieving company objectives.
9 Recruits, trains and develops effective personnel to meet present and future needs.
10 Implements company personnel policies and national agreements.
11 Maintains sound labour relations and morale.

CONTROL
12 Develops an effective reporting system on works performance and directs a continuous programme of monitoring productivity, quality and costs.
13 Ensures that corrective action is taken where required to meet budgets and standards and reports deviations outside agreed control limits to the production director.

Job analysis

Job title: Works manager

Resources controlled:
- Assets: £765,000
- Turnover: £3,100,000
- Personnel: 750

Decisions:
- The basic production technologies are determined by the company engineering department. The works manager is simply concerned with ensuring that the equipment operates as specified and that it is maintained properly. He can introduce changes to meet special requirements but these are minor modifications which do not affect the basic technology and can be installed within one or two days by maintenance craftsmen.
- The overall production programme and quality and cost standards are laid down at company level. The works manager, however, has complete authority to schedule production within the works.
- Buying is conducted centrally but the works manager is responsible for ensuring that stocks are maintained at the minimum level required to maintain an economic production flow and an agreed standard of customer service.
- The works manager has authority to spend on revenue items within the agreed annual company budget. Capital expenditure has to be authorized by the production director.
- The works manager has complete authority to recruit, discipline and, where necessary, dismiss hourly and weekly paid staff in accordance with company personnel policies and procedures. He also has authority to deal with union issues, except those affecting terms and conditions of employment which are dealt with at company level. He must report any major issue to the production director.

Complexity
- The product is not a highly technical one and most of the production employees, except in the foundry and in the development shop, are semi-skilled

assembly line employees. There are nine product lines and three main processes. Some problems are caused when product lines are changed but they are fairly easy to overcome if scheduling is carried out carefully.

- The main difficulty to overcome is ensuring that quality standards are maintained and that downtime is minimized. Maintenance is a key factor and fairly complex procedures have had to be developed to overcome serious problems in the past.
- Labour relations do not present a problem.

Knowledge and skills

- The technical knowledge required is not very high. Anyone with experience in controlling assembly lines or a flow process operation should quickly be able to understand the techniques involved. The main requirement is skill in planning and controlling a high output, fairly high quality plant to meet critical delivery schedules and in motivating a labour force which is engaged on monotonous although well paid work.

Appendix F
Example of a Personnel Specification

Job title — Works Manager

1	Physical characteristics	Essential	— Fit — Able to work long hours in fairly demanding conditions
2	Attainments	Essential	— Time-served apprenticeship — HNC or equivalent
		Desirable	— Graduate apprenticeship — Degree in production engineering
3	Intelligence	Essential	— Top third of population
4	Special aptitudes/ knowledge	Essential	— Comprehensive knowledge of production planning and control techniques in a high-tech environment — Evidence of well developed leadership and teambuilding skills — A practised and successful negotiator
		Desirable	— Experience in the application of modern capacity and aggregate planning and resource allocation techniques
5	Interests	Desirable	— Practical interests (getting things done) — Interested in keeping up-to-date with relevant management techniques — A self-developer
6	Disposition	Essential	— Self-starter — Accepts, indeed seeks, responsibility gladly — Capable of withstanding pressure
7	Circumstances	Desirable	— Willing to travel within reason.

Appendix G
Grievance Procedure

Policy

1 It is the policy of the company that members of the staff should:
   (a) be given a fair hearing by their immediate supervisor or manager concerning any grievances they may wish to raise;
   (b) have the right to appeal to a more senior manager against a decison made by their supervisor or manager;
   (c) have the right to be accompanied by a fellow employee of their own choice, when raising a grievance or appealing against a decision.

The aim of the procedure is to settle the grievance as nearly as possible to its point of origin.

Procedure

2 The main stages through which a grievance may be raised are as follows:
   (a) The employee raises the matter with his immediate supervisor or manager and may be accompanied by a fellow employee of his own choice.
   (b) If the employee is not satisfied with the decision, the employee requests a meeting with a member of management who is more senior than the supervisor or manager who initially heard the grievance. This meeting takes place within five working days of the request and is attended by the manager, the manager responsible for personnel, the employee appealing against the decision and, if desired, his representative. The manager responsible for personnel records the result of the meeting in writing and issues copies to all concerned.
   (c) If the employee is still not satisfied with the decision, he may appeal to the appropriate director. The meeting to hear this appeal is held within five working days of the request and is attended by the director, the manager responsible for personnel, the employee making the appeal and, if desired, his representative. The manager responsible for personnel records the result of this meeting in writing and issues copies to all concerned.

Appendix H
Disciplinary Procedure

Policy
1 It is the policy of the company that if disciplinary action has to be taken against employees it should:
   (a) be undertaken only in cases where good reason and clear evidence exist;
   (b) be appropriate to the nature of the offence that has been committed;
   (c) be demonstrably fair and consistent with previous action in similar circumstances;
   (d) only take place when employees are aware of the standards that are expected of them or the rules with which they are required to conform.
   (e) allow employees the right to be represented by a shop steward or colleague during any formal proceedings;
   (f) allow employees the right of appeal against any disciplinary action.

Rules
2 The company is responsible for ensuring that up-to-date rules are published and available to all employees.

Procedure

INFORMAL WARNING
3 A verbal or informal warning is given to the employee in the first instance or instances of minor offences. The warning is administered by the employee's immediate supervisor or manager.

FORMAL WARNING
4 A written or formal warning is given to the employee in the first instance of more serious offences or after repeated instances of minor offences. The warning is administered by the employee's immediate supervisor — it states the exact nature of the offence and specifies any future disciplinary action which will be taken against the employee if the offence is repeated within a specified time limit. A copy of the written warning is placed in the employee's personnel record file but is destroyed 12 months after the date on which it was given, if the intervening service has been satisfactory. The employee is required to read and sign the formal warning and has the right to appeal to higher management if he thinks the warning is unjustified.

FURTHER DISCIPLINARY ACTION
5 If, despite previous warnings, an employee still fails to reach the required standards in a reasonable period of time, it may become necessary to consider further disciplinary action. The action taken may be up to three days' suspension

without pay, or dismissal. In either case the departmental manager should discuss the matter with the personnel manager before taking action. Staff below the rank of departmental manager may only recommend disciplinary action to higher management, except when their manager is not present (for example, on night-shift), when they may suspend the employee for up to one day pending an inquiry on the following day. Disciplinary action should not be confirmed until the appeal procedure (paragraphs 7 and 8) has been carried out.

SUMMARY DISMISSAL

6   An employee may be summarily dismissed (i.e. given instant dismissal without notice) only in the event of gross misconduct, as defined in company rules. Only departmental managers and above can recommend summary dismissal and the action should not be finalized until the case has been discussed with the personnel manager and the appeal procedure has been carried out.

Appeals

7   In all circumstances, an employee may appeal against suspension, dismissal with notice or summary dismissal. The appeal is conducted by a member of management who is more senior than the manager who initially administered the disciplinary action. The personnel manager should also be present at the hearing. If he wishes, the employee may be represented at the appeal by a fellow employee of his own choice. Appeal against summary dismissal or suspension should be heard immediately. Appeals against dismissal with notice should be held within two days. No disciplinary action which is subject to appeal is confirmed until the outcome of the appeal.

8   If an appeal against dismissal (but not suspension) is rejected at this level, the employee has the right to appeal to the chief executive. The manager responsible for personnel and, if required, the employee's representative should be present at this appeal.

Appendix I
Redundancy Procedure

Definition
1 Redundancy is defined as the situation in which management decides that an employee or employees are surplus to requirements in a particular occupation and cannot be offered suitable alternative work.
2 Employees may be surplus to requirements because changes in the economic circumstances of the company mean that fewer employees are required, or because changes in methods of working mean that a job no longer exists in its previous form. An employee who is given notice because he or she is unsuitable or inefficient is not regarded as redundant and would be dealt with in accordance with the usual disciplinary procedure.

Objectives
3 The objectives of the procedure are to ensure that:
   (a) employees who may be affected by the discontinuance of their work are given fair and equitable treatment;
   (b) the minimum disruption is caused to employees and the company;
   (c) so far as possible, changes are effected with the complete understanding and agreement of the unions and employees concerned.

Principles
4 The principles governing the procedure are as follows:
   (a) The trade unions concerned will be informed as soon as the possibility of redundancy occurs.
   (b) Every attempt will be made to:
      (i) absorb redundancy by the natural wastage of employees;
      (ii) find suitable alternative employment within the company for employees who might be affected, and provide training if this is necessary;
      (iii) give individuals reasonable warning of pending redundancy in addition to the statutory period of notice.
   (c) If alternative employment in the company is not available and more than one individual is affected, the factors to be taken into consideration in deciding who should be made redundant will include:
      (i) length of service with the company;
      (ii) age (especially those who could be retired early);
      (iii) effective value to the company;
      (iv) opportunities for alternative employment elsewhere.

   The first three of these factors should normally be regarded as the most important; other things being equal, however, length of service should be the determining factor.

Procedure

5 The procedure for dealing with employees who are surplus to requirements is set out below.

REVIEW OF MANPOWER REQUIREMENTS

6 Management will continuously keep under review possible future developments which might affect the number of employees required, and will prepare overall plans for dealing with possible redundancies.

MEASURES TO AVOID REDUNDANCIES

7 If the likelihood of redundancy is foreseen, the company will inform the union(s), explaining the reasons, and in consultation with the union(s) will give consideration to taking appropriate measures to prevent redundancy.

8 Departmental managers will be warned by the management of future developments which might affect them so that detailed plans can be made for running down staff, retraining or transfers.

9 Departmental managers will be expected to keep under review the work situation in their departments so that contingency plans can be prepared and the manager responsible for personnel warned of any likely surpluses.

CONSULTATION ON REDUNDANCIES

10 If all measures to avoid redundancy fail, the company will consult the union(s) at the earliest opportunity in order to reach agreement.

SELECTION OF REDUNDANT EMPLOYEES

11 In the event of impending redundancy, the individuals who might be surplus to requirements should be selected by the departmental manager with the advice of the manager responsible for personnel on the principles that should be adopted.

12 The manager responsible for personnel should explore the possibilities of transferring affected staff to alternative work.

13 The manager responsible for personnel should inform management of proposed action (either redundancy or transfer) to obtain approval.

14 The union(s) will be informed of the numbers affected but not of individual names.

15 The departmental manager and the manager responsible for personnel will jointly interview the employees affected either to offer a transfer or, if a suitable alternative is not available, to inform them they will be redundant. At this interview, full information should be available to give to the employee on, as appropriate:
   (a) the reasons for being surplus;
   (b) the alternative jobs that are available;
   (c) the date when the employee will become surplus (that is, the period of notice);
   (d) the entitlement to redundancy pay;
   (e) the employee's right to appeal to an appropriate director;
   (f) the help the company will provide.

16 An appropriate director will hear any appeals with the manager responsible for personnel.

17 The manager responsible for personnel will ensure that all the required administrative arrangements are made.

18 If the union(s) have any points to raise about the selection of employees or the actions taken by the company they should be discussed in the first place with the manager responsible for personnel. If the results of these discussions are unsatisfactory a meeting will be arranged with an appropriate director.

ALTERNATIVE WORK WITHIN THE COMPANY
19 If an employee is offered and accepts suitable alternative work within the company it will take effect without a break from the previous employment and will be confirmed in writing. If the offer is refused the employee may forfeit his or her redundancy payment.

ALTERNATIVE EMPLOYMENT
20 Employees for whom no suitable work is available in the company will be given reasonable opportunities to look for alternative employment.

Appendix J
Promotion Policy and Procedure

Policy
1 The promotion policy of the company is based on three main principles:
   (a) whenever possible, vacancies shall be filled by the most effective people available from within the company, subject to the right of the company to recruit from outside if there are no suitable internal candidates;
   (b) the excellence of an employee's performance in his or her present job in the company or the absence of a suitable replacement shall not be a valid reason for refusing promotion to a suitable post, provided that the procedure set out below is complied with;
   (c) promotion is not affected by race, creed, sex or marital status.

Procedure
1 When a vacancy arises, the head of the department concerned shall obtain the necessary authority, according to company regulations, and notify the personnel department, which will be responsible for submitting suitable candidates. The departmental manager has the final decision in accepting or rejecting a candidate.
2 Except for the circumstances set out in paragraph 5, the personnel department shall advertise supervisory, managerial or specialist posts in grades C and above (works) and 3 and above (staff) on company notice-boards for at least three days.
3 The personnel department, with the agreement of the departmental head, can advertise the vacancy concurrently outside the company.
4 Applications from employees should be sent to the personnel department, which will carry out the following actions:
   (a) notify departmental managers of the departments in which candidates are employed;
   (b) notify the application to the manager of the department in which the vacancy occurs;
   (c) notify candidates whether or not they are required for interview;
   (d) notify candidates of the result of the interview.
5 Internal advertising can be dispensed with where management considers that:
   (a) there is a natural successor (who may have been specially trained to fill the vacancy); or
   (b) because of unusual requirements there is no suitable candidate within the company; or
   (c) the vacancy can be filled by the transfer of an employee of equivalent grade.
6 Where a departmental manager feels that the loss of an employee to another department would vitally affect the efficiency of his department he can appeal to the personnel manager against the transfer, provided that:

(a) the employee has served less than 12 months in his present occupation and grade; or

(b) the rate of transfer from his department of employees of similar grade has exceeded 1% per calendar month over the previous six months.

If the personnel manager is unable to resolve the matter the appeal should be submitted to an appropriate director.

7 Except in the event of a successful appeal against a transfer on the grounds stated in paragraph 6, no employee shall be refused a transfer within a reasonable time by his departmental manager. The date of the transfer should be determined between his present and future departmental managers. A failure to agree on a suitable date should be referred to the personnel manager for resolution or, if that fails, for reference to an appropriate director.

Appendix K
Training Techniques

The training techniques analysed in this Appendix are classified into three groups according to where they are generally used:

1 *On the job techniques* — demonstration, coaching, do-it-yourself training, job rotation/planned experience.
2 *On the job or off the job techniques* — action learning, job (skill) instruction, question and answer, assignments, projects, guided reading, computer-based training, instructional systems development, interactive video, video;
3 *Off the job techniques* — lecture, talk, discussion, 'discovery' method, programmed learning, case study, role playing, simulation, group exercises, group dynamics (team-building), distance learning.

On the job techniques

Demonstration
Demonstration is the technique of telling or showing a trainee how to do a job and then allowing him to get on with it. It is the most commonly used — and abused — training method. It is direct and the trainee is actively engaged. Reinforcement or feedback can be good, if the supervisor, trainer or colleague (that well-known character, Nellie, by whom the trainee sits) does it properly by clearly defining what results have been achieved and how they can be improved. But demonstration in its typically crude form will not provide a structured learning system where the trainee understands the sequence of training he is following and can proceed by deliberate steps along his learning curve. This is more likely to happen if job (skill) instruction techniques are used, as described later.

Coaching
Coaching is a personal on the job technique designed to develop individual skills, knowledge and attitudes. The term is usually reserved for management or supervisory training where informal but planned encounters take place between managers and subordinates.

The agenda for such meetings may be based on a performance review system which includes some elements of management by objectives or target setting. This would identify strengths to be developed or weaknesses in performance to be overcome, and the counselling sessions that should be part of the performance review process would indicate career development needs and the additional knowledge or skills that can be acquired on the job.

Coaching is even more effective if it can take place informally as part of the normal process of management. This type of coaching, as suggested by Hawdon Hague, consists of:

676

- making a subordinate aware of how he is managing by, for example, asking questions on how well he has thought through what he is doing;
- controlled delegation;
- using whatever situations which arise as teaching opportunities;
- setting individual projects and assignments;
- spending time in looking at higher level problems as well as discussing the immediate job.

Coaching may be informal, but it has to be planned. It is not simply going from time to time to see what a subordinate is doing and advising him how to do it better. Neither is it occasionally telling a subordinate where he has gone wrong and throwing in a lecture for good measure. So far as possible, coaching should take place within the framework of a general plan of the areas and direction in which the subordinate should be developed.

Coaching should provide motivation, structure and effective feedback, if the coacher is skilled, dedicated and able to develop mutual confidence. Its success depends on a clear definition of work and training objectives, and this can be a time-consuming process; ultimately, success depends upon managers and supervisors recognizing that it is one of their key responsibilities and they should be encouraged and trained to do it.

Do-it-yourself training
Do-it-yourself training aims to apply the principles of the discovery method (see below) to training on the job. The principle behind it is that people will learn and retain more if they find out for themselves, as long as they are given direction on what to look for and help in finding it.

Do-it-yourself training operates by:

- starting from a definition of what someone needs to know and do to perform a job;
- establishing where the information required is available;
- giving the trainee an outline of the information he has to obtain and where and from whom he can get it. He may be given questions to answer or mini-projects to complete.
- briefing those concerned (mainly the trainee's boss and his colleagues, but also people in other departments) on the help they should give the trainee;
- preparing a timetable for the learning programme;
- arranging for someone (the trainee's boss or the executive responsible for training) to monitor his progress. This should include periodic meetings to check on what has been learned and to provide extra encouragement and guidance.

It is not quite as simple as it may appear to implement do-it-yourself training techniques. They must still be based upon job analysis leading to a full understanding of the knowledge and skills required to do the job. The trainee should be given careful guidance on how to set about getting the information required, and he has still to be motivated to understand the reasons for getting this information and how he or she will benefit.

The managers or supervisors of those under training should be prepared to spend time and trouble helping and coaching their staff. And it is not always easy to persuade busy people to do this, as every training officer knows. The only way is to convince them that this approach will produce better results more quickly and cheaply than other methods. They have to be persuaded that the technique will have a measurably beneficial effect on the performance of the individuals concerned and on the performance of the department as a whole. Training managers have to be salesmen – they have to demonstrate the benefits of the product rather than describe its inherent features.

The only other drawback to do-it-yourself training is that it is more applicable to the development of knowledge than skills. It is therefore more likely to be useful for managers, supervisors and administrative staff than for training machine operators or those in occupations where manual skills are of primary importance. Nonetheless, do-it-yourself training as an embodiment of the voluntary spirit as well as a practical application of learning theory can play an important part in a training programme, especially when shortage of funds precludes any more elaborate approach.

Job rotation/planned experience

Job rotation aims to broaden experience by moving people from job to job or department to department. It can be an inefficient and frustrating method of acquiring additional knowledge and skills unless it is carefully planned and controlled. What has sometimes been referred to as the 'Cook's tour' method of moving trainees (usually management trainees) from department to department has incurred much justified criticism because of the time wasted by trainees in departments where no one knew what to do with them or cared.

It may be better to use the term 'planned sequence of experience' rather than 'job rotation' to emphasize that the experience should be programmed to satisfy a training specification for acquiring knowledge and skills in different departments and occupations. It can be argued in support of job rotation that if it is by experience that adults learn, then that experience should be planned.

Success in using this method depends on designing a programme which sets down what the trainee is expected to learn in each department or job in which he gains experience. There must also be a suitable person available to see that the trainee is given the right experience or opportunity to learn, and arrangements must be made to check progress. For apprentices this will mean the use of training supervisors within departments to see that the training syllabus is followed, and the use of log-books to record what experience has been gained. The syllabus within a department should include specific assignments or projects. A good way of stimulating trainees to find out for themselves is to provide them with a list of questions to answer. It is essential, however, to follow up each segment of experience to check what has been learnt and, if necessary, modify the programme.

On or off the job techniques

Action learning

Action learning, as developed by Professor Revans, is a method of helping managers to develop their talents by being exposed to real problems. They are required to analyse them, formulate recommendations and then, instead of being satisfied with a report, actually take action. It accords with the belief that managers learn best by doing rather than being taught.

This approach conforms to the principle on which all good training should be based – ie it is problem-based and action-orientated. It recognizes that the most perplexing task managers face is how to achieve change – how to persuade their colleagues and others to commit themselves to a different way of doing things. An action-learning programme therefore concentrates on developing the skills which managers need to take action effectively, without ignoring the need for knowledge of relevant techniques.

The concept of action learning is based on six assumptions:

1 Experienced managers have a huge curiosity to know how other managers work.
2 We learn not so much when we are motivated to learn, as when we are motivated to learn something.
3 Learning about oneself is threatening and is resisted if it tends to change one's self-image. However, it is possible to reduce the external threat to a level which no longer acts as a total barrier to learning about oneself.
4 People only learn when they do something, and they learn more the more responsible they feel the task to be.
5. Learning is deepest when it involves the whole person – mind, values, body, emotions.
6 The learner knows better than anyone else what he has learned. Nobody else has much chance of knowing.

A typical action learning programme brings together a group or 'set' of four or five managers to solve a problem. They help and learn from each other, but an external consultant or 'set adviser' sits in with them regularly. The project may last several months and the set meets frequently, possibly one day a week. The adviser helps the members of the set to learn from one another and clarifies the process of action learning. This process involves change embedded in the web of relationships called the 'client system'. The web comprises at least three separate networks; the power network, the information network and the motivational network (this is what Revans means by 'who can, who knows and who cares'). The forces for change are already there within the client system and it is the adviser's role to point out the dynamics of this system as the work of diagnosis and implementation proceeds.

The group or set has to manage the project like any other project; deciding on objectives, planning resources, initiating action and monitoring progress. But all the time, with the help of their adviser, they are learning about the management processes involved as they actually happen.

Job instruction
Job instruction techniques should be based on skills analysis and learning theory as discussed in Chapter 29. The sequence of instruction should follow four stages:

- Preparation
- Presentation – explanation and demonstration
- Practice and testing
- Follow-up.

Preparation for each instruction period means that the instructor must have a plan for presenting the subject matter and using appropriate teaching methods, visual aids and demonstration aids. It also means preparing the trainee for the instruction that is to follow. He should want to learn. He must perceive that the learning will be relevant and useful to him personally. He should be encouraged to take a pride in his job and to appreciate the satisfaction that comes from skilled performance.

Presentation should consist of a combination of telling and showing – explanation and demonstration.

Explanation should be as simple and direct as possible: the trainer explains briefly the ground to be covered and what to look for. He makes the maximum use of films, charts, diagrams and other visual aids. The aim should be to teach first things first and then proceed from the known to the unknown, the simple to the complex, the concrete to abstract, the general to the particular, the observation to reasoning, and the whole to the parts and back to the whole again.

Demonstration is an essential stage in instruction, espcially when the skill to be learned is mainly a doing skill. Demonstration takes place in three stages:

1   The complete operation is shown at normal speed to show the trainee how the task should be carried out eventually.
2   The operation is demonstrated slowly and in correct sequence, element by element, to indicate clearly what is done and the order in which each task is carried out.
3   The operation is demonstrated again slowly, at least two or three times, to stress the how, when and why of successive movements.

Practice consists of the learner imitating the instructor and then constantly repeating the operation under guidance. The aim is to reach the target level of performance for each element of the total task, but the instructor must constantly strive to develop co-ordinated and integrated performance; that is, the smooth combination of the separate elements of the task into a whole job pattern.

Follow-up continues during the training period for all the time required by the learner to reach a level of performance equal to that of the normal experienced worker in terms of quality, speed and attention to safety. During the follow-up stage, the learner will continue to need help with particularly difficult tasks or to overcome temporary set-backs which result in a deterioration of performance. The instructor may have to repeat the presentation for the elements and supervise practice more closely until the trainee regains his confidence or masters the task.

JOB INSTRUCTION GUIDELINES. These are the most important guidelines to follow in giving job instruction:

- Keep instruction and practice within reasonable time limits to avoid boredom and fatigue.
- Arrange demonstration and practice so that trainees can experience some success early in training, thus maintaining interest and providing incentive.
- Ensure that trainees know how they are getting on, but present feedback in an an encouraging and constructive way.
- Provide useful and productive tasks to do.
- Recognize that all learners do not develop at the same rate.
- Provide ample opportunity for practice so that trainees can become used to carrying out the job at the experienced worker's standard of quality and speed and in complete safety.

Question and answer

The question and answer technique consists of an exchange between trainer and trainees to test understanding, stimulate thought or extend learning. It may take place during a job instruction programme or as part of a discussion period on a formal management course. It can be used to increase involvement, to check progress and to explore attitudes to learning. Considerable skill is required to use this method. The questions should be open – they should not lead to 'yes'/'no' answers, but they should also be clear and concise. They should always be asked in an encouraging and supportive manner.

Assignments

Assignments are a specific task or investigation which an individual does at the request of his trainer or manager. The assignment may be used as a test at the end of a training session and, as long as it is realistic, it should help to transfer learning to the work situation. The trainer may still have to provide some guidance to the trainee to ensure that the latter will not lose confidence if he meets difficulties in completing the task.

Assignments may also be given by managers to their subordinates as a means of extending their experience. They should be linked to a coaching programme so that the lessons from the assignment are fully absorbed.

Projects

Projects are broader studies or tasks which trainees are asked to complete, often with only very generalized guidelines from their trainer or manager. They encourage initiative in seeking and analysing information, in originating ideas and in preparing and presenting the results of the project. For apprentices, especially students and graduates, the project can be a practical exercise in which the trainees are required to design, manufacture and test a piece of equipment. Projects for managers may consist of an investigation into a company policy issue or operating problem.

Like assignments, projects give trainees or managers an opportunity to test their learning and extend their experience, although the scope of the study is likely to be wider and the project is often carried out by a group of people.

Guided reading

Knowledge can be increased by giving trainees books, hand-outs or company literature and asking them to read and comment on them. Guided reading may take place before a course when the members are asked to read 'pre-course' literature. They seldom do. Or it may be given during a training course and used as reinforcement. The beautiful hand-outs that lecturers prepare are often allowed to gather dust when the course is over. They can be far more effective if they are distributed at appropriate points during or immediately after the lecture and those attending are required to discuss specific questions arising from them.

Reading as part of a development programme may be a valuable way of broadening knowledge as long at the material is seen by the trainee as relevant and there is follow-up to ensure that learning has taken place. The best way is to ask the trainee to read a handbook or one of two chapters from a longer text and then come back to the trainer or his manager to discuss the relevance of the material and how he can use his knowledge.

Computer-based training

Computers can be used for training in the following ways:

1 To simulate actual situations so that trainees can 'learn by doing'. For example, technicians can be trained in troubleshooting and repairing electronic circuitry by looking at circuit diagrams displayed on the screen and using a light-pen to measure voltages at different points in the circuit. When faults are diagnosed, 'repairs' are effected by means of a light-pen, this time employed as a soldering iron.

2 To extend programmed learning texts to provide diagrammatic and pictorial displays in colour and to allow more interaction between the trainee and the information presented on the screen.

3 To provide a data base for information which trainees can access through a computer terminal.

4 To measure the performances of trainees against predefined criteria.

5 To provide tests or exercises for trainees. The technique of *adaptive testing* uses a program containing a large number of items designed to test a trainee's comprehension of certain principles. But it is not necessary for him to work through all of them or even to satisfy them sequentially in order to demonstrate his understanding. His responses to a limited number of questions will show whether or not he has grasped the appropriate concepts to satisfy given training objectives. The process of testing can thus be speeded up considerably and prove less frustrating for the trainee.

Instructional systems development

Instructional systems development (ISD) techniques as developed by the American services are used to provide a coordinated approach to the training system as a whole. They tabulate the steps required at each stage of the training process to provide training guides to line managers as well as to professional trainers.

The sequence of stages in the ISD approach are:

1 *Analysis* — training needs are determined for the requirements of each task or job. Performance criteria and learning objectives are established, the latter defining what workers have to be able to do to meet the experienced worker's standard.

2 *Design* — the structure and sequence of training required to meet performance criteria and learning objectives are defined and tests or other methods of evaluating training are devised.

3 *Development* — learning media and methods are selected and training materials prepared to add to the basic design in order to prepare the full instructional plan.

4 *Implementation* — the instructional plan is put into effect.

5 *Control* — training is evaluated and the system modified as necessary.

Interactive video

Interactive video is based on the fusion of two powerful training technologies — computer-based training and video — combined so that the sum is greater than the parts.

Computer-based training (CBT) is individualized and interactive. It is able to accommodate each trainee's needs and pace with the software. Video is effective when realistic sound and pictures are essential and a moving camera angle can compensate for the flatness of the screen, helping to portray three-dimensional reality. But video is limited as a training medium. It cannot be individualized. Watching video is a passive activity and the sequence of instruction is always linear.

Interactive video offers the trainer the best of both worlds. It is individualistic, interactive and random-access like CBT, but interactive video can also present, like video, realistic still or moving pictures without sound.

Interactive video is expensive but its benefits are considerable in a number of different applications, such as:

● *For distance learning* — where trainees are widely scattered.

● *For trainees with learning difficulties* — many people, especially those without much formal education find it difficult to absorb information from large blocks of text. As long as the interactive video programme is carefully constructed on the basis of a thorough task and skills analysis, and is designed to meet the requirements of learning theory, it will be an effective way of helping people to take in and use complex instructions.

● *Where there is a scarce training resource* — this might include skilled trainers or the real equipment that a trainee must operate, such as a robot system or an aircraft.
● *Where interpersonal skills are important* — interactive video is much better than print or CBT in improving interpersonal skills such as interviewing, dealing with difficult customers, counselling or handling people problems.
● *When training time is at a premium* — interactive video can cut the time required to achieve learning objectives.

Video
The ability of video to present information visually is an obvious aid to training where the printed word is often limited as a medium and there is a shortage of good trainers to get the message across. Videos can be used to present prepared material in the same way as films. They are most effective if they are backed up by a trainer's guide which ensures that the passive nature of screenwatching is followed up by active learning.

With the help of video cameras, video can provide instant feed-back when training is taking place in such interactive skills as interviewing, counselling, selling, running meetings, and instructing.

Off the job techniques

Lecture
A lecture is a talk with little or no participation except a question and answer session at the end. It is used to transfer information to an audience with controlled content and timing. When the audience is large, there may be no alternative to a 'straight lecture' if there is no scope to break it up into discussion groups.

The effectiveness of a lecture depends on the ability of the speaker and the way in which he presents his material with judicious use of visual aids. But there are several limits on the amount an inert audience can absorb. However effective the speaker, it is unlikely that more than 20% of what he said will be remembered at the end of the day. And after a week, all will be forgotten unless the listener has put some of his learning into practice. To maximize its effectiveness, the lecture must never be longer than 30 or 40 minutes; it must not contain too much information (if the speaker can convey three new ideas, which more than one half of his audience understands and remembers, he will have been successful); it must reinforce learning with appropriate visual aids (but not too many); and it must clearly indicate the action that should be taken to make use of the material.

Talk
A talk is a less formal lecture for a smaller group of not more than 20 people which gives plenty of time for discussion. The encouragement of participation and interest means that more learning is likely to be retained than in a lecture, but the discussion may be dominated by the more articulate and confident members of the group unless carefully controlled.

Discussion

The objectives of using discussion techniques are to:

- get the audience to participate actively in learning;
- give people an opportunity of learning from the experience of others;
- help people to gain understanding of other points of view;
- develop powers of self-expression.

The aim of the trainer should be to guide the group's thinking. He may, therefore, be more concerned with shaping attitudes than imparting new knowledge. He has to stimulate people to talk unobtrusively, guide the discussion along predetermined lines (he must have a plan and an ultimate objective), summarize the discussion from time to time, and sum up at the end.

The following techniques should be used to get active participation:

- Ask for contributions by direct questions.
- Use open-ended questions which will stimulate thought.
- Check understanding; make sure that everyone is following the argument.
- Encourage participation by providing support rather than criticism.
- Prevent domination by individual members of the group by bringing in other people and asking cross-reference questions.
- Avoid dominating the group yourself. The leader's job is to guide the discussion, maintain control and summarize from time to time. If necessary, 'reflect' opinions expressed by individuals back to the group to make sure they find the answer for themselves. The leader's job is to help them reach a conclusion, not to do it for them.
- Maintain control — ensure that the discussion is progressing along the right lines towards a firm conclusion.

Discovery method

The discovery method is a style of teaching that allows the pupil to learn by finding out principles and relationships for himself. The essence of the method is that the training designer thinks out the progression of problems which the trainee is required to solve, relates this progression to the capacity of the trainee, and ensures that learning is based on intrinsic rather than extrinsic factors. In other words, the trainee does not need to rely on previous knowledge and experience, nor does he depend on outside assistance (ie extrinsic factors). The learning, however, is not a random process. The trainee progresses through a series of planned steps, using the intrinsic information provided at each stage.

The discovery method is a demanding one to develop properly. It goes far deeper than skills analysis which simply lists all that has to be learned. Instead, it first identifies the crucial concepts and removes all the non-essentials so that the training material can be appreciated in its most simple form. The next stage is the most difficult: the training designer has to bet inside the learning situation to decide what are the principal obstacles to understanding and to find out why trainees have problems in learning. The next stage is to design a discovery programme specially for the needs of a group of trainees.

The best results from discovery training techniques are achieved with middle-aged and older learners and on tasks that demand the development of concepts and understanding. The method has three main advantages:

1 *Motivation* — the adult is more motivated towards discovery learning because he is involved from the start and involved on his own terms.

2 *Control* — the discovery method reveals the trainee's progress and level of understanding to the instructor and enables easier control to be exercised over performance.
3 *Retention* — learning from experience is easier for adults than learning from words; there is no stress on memorizing, hence this sort of learning is remembered.

The main disadvantage of the discovery method is that it has to be specially designed for limited groups. A further disadvantage is that its benefits are not as evident in the short term as more conventionally based training schemes. But where real understanding and retention of knowledge about the whole job is required for older trainees or people undergoing re-training, the discovery method has a lot to offer.

Programmed learning

Programmed learning consists of a text which progressively feeds information to trainees. After each piece of information, questions are posed which the trainee should answer correctly before moving on.

The basic principles of programmed learning are as follows:

- The subject matter is presented in small units called frames.
- Each frame requires a response from the trainee. Thus he is actively involved in the learning process.
- The trainee is told if his answer is correct at once. This rapid feedback gives immediate reinforcement to the trainee or immediately corrects a misunderstanding.
- The units of information are arranged in correct subject matter sequence and pose increasingly difficult questions. This means that the designer has had to analyse the learning steps required with great care.
- Trainees work independently and at their own pace. Thus they work as quickly or as slowly as they like.

Programmed instruction is primarily a method of systematic presentation which relies a great deal on the self-motivation of the trainee. In its usual form it is quite different from discovery learning which is more concerned with skills than knowledge and allows the trainee greater scope to find out for himself.

Programmed texts may result in an over-mechanical learning process and this could hinder retention. But there are considerable advantages in using this method in conjunction with others as a means of ensuring that the trainee is ready, willing and able to deal with the material confronting him and take an active part in learning.

Case study

A case study is a history or description of an event or set of circumstances which is analysed by trainees in order to diagnose the causes of a problem and work out how to solve it. Case studies are mainly used in courses for managers and supervisors because they are based on the belief that managerial competence and understanding can best be achieved through the study and discussion of real events.

Case studies should aim to promote inquiry, the exchange of ideas and the analysis of experience so that the trainees can discover underlying principles which the case study is designed to illustrate. They are not light relief. Neither are they a means of lightening the load on the instructor. The trainer has to work hard in defining the learning points that must come out of each case and he must work even harder to ensure that these points do emerge.

The danger of case studies is that they are often perceived by trainees to be irrelevant to their needs, even if based on fact. Consequently, the analysis is superficial and the situation is unrealistic. It is the trainer's job to avoid these dangers by ensuring that the participants are not allowed to get away with half-baked comments. He has to challenge assumptions and pin people down to justify their reasoning. Above all, he has to seize every chance to draw out the principles he wants to illustrate from the discussion and to get the group to see how these are relevant to their own working situation.

Role playing

In role playing the participants act out a situation by assuming the roles of the characters involved. The situation will be one in which there is interaction between two people or within a group. It should be specially prepared with briefs written for each participant explaining the situation and, broadly, their role in it. Alternatively, role playing could emerge naturally from a case study when the trainees are asked to test their solution by playing the parts of those concerned.

Role playing is used to give managers, supervisors or sales representatives practice in dealing with face-to-face situations such as interviewing, counselling, coaching, dealing with a grievance, selling, leading a group or running a meeting. It develops interactive skills and gives people insight into the way in which people behave and feel.

The technique of 'role reversal', in which a pair playing, say, a manager and a supervisor run through the case and then exchange roles and repeat it, gives extra insight into the feelings involved and the skills required.

Role playing enables trainees to get expert advice and constructive criticism from the trainer and their colleagues in a 'protected' training situation. It can help to increase confidence as well as developing skills in handling people. The main difficulties are either that trainees will be embarrassed or that they will not take the exercise seriously and will overplay their parts.

Simulation

Simulation is a training technique which combines case studies and role playing to obtain the maximum amount of realism in classroom training. The aim is to facilitate the transfer of what has been learned off the job to on the job behaviour by reproducing in the training room situations which are as close as possible to real life. Trainees are thus given the opportunity to practise behaviour in conditions identical to or at least very similar to those they will meet when they complete the course.

Group exercises

In a group exercise the trainees examine problems and develop solutions to them as a group. The problem may be a case study or it could be a problem entirely unrelated to everyday work. The aims of an exercise of this kind are to give members practice in working together and to obtain insight into the way in which groups behave and arrive at decisions.

Group exercises can be used as part of a team building programme and to develop interactive skills. They can be combined with other techniques such as the discovery method to enable participants to work out for themselves the techniques and skills they need to use.

For example, a course run for managers in a large firm of chartered accountants dealt with problem solving in the following way:

1 The course was divided into three groups of six, all sitting in the same room.
2 Each group was given three linguistic/mathematical problems to solve and was then asked to discuss how the problem should be tackled.
3 Each group was then asked to develop a better problem-solving method which could be used in future.
4 Further exercises were given to the groups for them to test out their problem-solving method – the exercises were again abstract problems, unrelated to work. Managers were selected in each group to act as observers and to feedback to the other members how they behaved and how effective their problem-solving method was.
5 After each exercise, the observers from each group were asked to summarize their observations to the whole course, and a general discussion took place on the lessons learnt.
6 The groups were then asked to get together and work out between them a problem-solving method incorporating the best elements of the three group methods. Again, observers were appointed to report on how effectively this negotiating exercise was conducted.
7 The jointly agreed problem-solving method was tested on further case studies which became progressively more realistic. Some of these were developed into role playing exercises, each designed to illustrate the use of management skills such as working in groups, leadership, delegation, coaching, appraising performance and handling disciplinary problems.

Group exercises may be introduced as part of a formal off the job management or supervisory training course. They are also an essential element in an organization development programme, as described in Chapter 4. Group exercises use many of the principles of group dynamics training, as discussed below, and may constitute a major part of a group dynamics course.

Group dynamics

Group dynamics training is largely based on the work of Kurt Lewin and the Research Centre for Group Dynamics at MIT in 1946. It has three interconnected and often overlapping aims: first to improve the effectiveness with which groups operate (team building); second, to increase self-understanding and awareness of social processes; and third, to develop interactive skills which will enable people to function more effectively in groups. Group training can also help in modifying individual attitudes and values.

Group dynamics programmes may emphasize one of these aims more than the others, and they come in a number of forms. The basic variety is 'T-group' training, but this approach can be modified for use in courses primarily designed to improve interactive skills. There are also various packaged group dynamics courses, of which the best-known are Blake's Managerial Grid and Coverdale Training.

T-GROUP TRAINING. 'T-group' stands for 'training group', which is not a very helpful description. It is also referred to as sensitivity training, group dynamics and group relations training. T-group has three aims:

1 To increase *sensitivity* – the ability to perceive accurately how others are reacting to one's behaviour.

2. To increase *diagnostic ability* — the ability to perceive accurately the state of relationships between others.
3. To increase *action skill* — the ability to carry out skilfully the behaviour required by the situation.

In a T-group, the trainer will explain the aims of the programme and may encourage discussion and contribute his own reactions. But he does not take a strong lead and the group is largely left to its own devices to develop a structure which takes account of the goals of both the members of the group and the trainer and provides a climate where the group are sufficiently trusting of one another to discuss their own behaviour. They do this by giving 'feedback' or expressing their reactions to one another. Members may not always accept comments about themselves, but as the T-group develops they will increasingly understand how some aspects of their behaviour are hidden to them and will, therefore, be well on the way to an increase in sensitivity, diagnostic ability and action skill.

The design of a T-group 'laboratory' may include short inputs from trainers to clarify problems of group behaviour, inter-group exercises to extend T-group learning to problems of representation, negotiation and conflict management, and application groups where members get together to decide how they can best transfer what they have learned to their actual job behaviour. As much opportunity as possible will be given to members to test out and develop their own behavioural (interactive) skills — seeking or giving information, enlisting support, persuading and commanding.

Follow-up studies have noted three principal areas of change following the attendance of trainees at an external T-group laboratory:

1. Increased openness, receptivity and tolerance of differences.
2. Increased operational skill in inter-personal relations, with overtones of increased capacity for collaboration.
3. Improved understanding and diagnostic awareness of self, others and interactive processes in groups.

T-groups have been attacked because of the possibility of negative or detrimental effects. But none of the follow-up studies has detected any significant problems. A more valid basis for doubt is that it has been difficult to prove that they have been cost-effective for organizations who have used them in company or have strongly supported external programmes.

This criticism could be levelled at any other form of group training or, indeed, most off the job training. The degree to which it can be invalidated will depend on the effectiveness of the training design and of the trainer.

T-group laboratories in their purest form are unlikely ever to become a major part of company training programmes, but the group dynamics approach has valid uses in the modified forms described below.

INTERACTIVE SKILLS TRAINING. Interactive skills training is defined by Rackham as: 'Any form of training which aims to increase the effectiveness of an individual's interaction with others.'[1]

As developed by Rackham and others at the British Overseas Airways Corporation in 1968, interactive skills training has the following features:

● It is based on the assumption that the primary limitation on supervisory or managerial effectiveness lies not within each job boundary, but on the interface between jobs.

- There are no preconceived rules about how people should interact. It is assumed that the way interaction happens is dependent upon the situation and the people in it — this is what has to be analysed and used as a basis for the programme.
- The training takes place through groups which enables people to practise interactive skills — such skills can only be acquired through practice.
- Participants have to receive controlled and systematic feedback on their performance — this was achieved by using specially developed techniques of behaviour analysis.
- The analysis of behaviour was used to structure groups to avoid the restrictions on behaviour change which might result from relying on arbitrarily composed groups.

A typical design for an interactive skills programme as developed by Rackham consists of three stages:

1 *The diagnostic stage* in which the groups undertake a wide range of activities. These are designed to provide reliable behaviour samples which the trainer records and analyses.
2 *The formal feedback stage* in which the trainer gives groups and individuals feedback on their interactive peformance during the diagnostic phase.
3 *The practice, monitoring, feedback stage* in which the group undertakes further activities to develop and practise new behaviour patterns and receives feedback from the trainer to gauge the success of attempts at behaviour change.

COVERDALE TRAINING. Coverdale training is a more structured form of interactive skills training which is described as: 'a system of planned experience, by which people may begin to discover for themselves certain lessons — and then go on learning from their subsequent experience.' The four main characteristics or principles of Coverdale Training are that:

- managers learn by doing — practising the skills they need to get things done;
- the training is centred around practical tasks — tasks which are actually performed rather than just talked about;
- managers learn a systematic approach to getting things done;
- learning takes place in groups.

THE MANAGERIAL GRID. The managerial grid training as developed by Blake[2] and his colleagues consists of a simple diagnostic framework provided to members to aid them in describing one another's behaviour. The basic philosophy of grid training is that the task of the individual manager is to achieve production through people. In achieving this task, the manager has to show concern both for productivity and people.

Blake suggests that managers can be characterized by their location on a two-dimensional grid — the managerial grid — one axis of which is labelled concern for production and the other concern for people. Each axis is a scale with nine points and so the location of a manager on the grid can be specified by two co-ordinates. Five principal managerial styles are described in Blake's grid:

1,1 *Impoverished management* — exertion of minimum offer to get done the work required to maintain membership of the organization.
9,1 *Task management* — where a person is high in task efficiency but low in human satisfaction.
1,9 *Country club management* — high human satisfaction but low work tempo.

5,5 *Middle of the road management* — adequate task performance while maintaining morale at a satisfactory level.

9,9 *Team management* — high task achievement from committed people. Production is achieved by the integration of task and human requirements into a unified system.

A grid seminar is used to teach each participant to see his managerial style. Trainees are first familiarized with grid language and theory and then work in groups through a series of exercises and case problems which allow each individual to exhibit his management style. This behaviour then becomes the object of feedback. Trainees acquire skills in the perception of their own and other people's style of behaviour, and the aim is to move them towards the 9,9 region of the grid.

Grid training consists of a series of seminars intended to develop the application of the message throughout the organization. In this respect, it is a type of organization development 'intervention' designed to increase organizational effectiveness rather than to concentrate on the improvement of individual interactive skills.

The grid has sound theoretical foundations, being based on a number of research studies. It recognizes the importance of developing an appropriate management style to obtain results by the effort and commitment of work groups. It has plenty of face validity — ex-grid trainees usually speak highly of it — but research studies are only partially conclusive on its overall effectiveness.

Distance learning
Distance learning enables trainees to learn, often in their own time and at home, from instruction material prepared and sometimes presented elsewhere.

The most familiar method of distance learning is the correspondence course. This is normally conducted by post and so suffers from a time lag between the student sending in work and receiving it back marked by the tutor. These delays could be protracted, which is a disadvantage when what is really required to enable learning to take place is a dialogue between pupil and teacher. Success in taking a correspondence course relies on the tenacity of the student as well as the quality of instruction and the speed with which correspondence is turned round.

In the UK, the Open University provides a highly developed form of distance learning with some elements of the correspondence course, but a lot is added to this basic approach by the use of television, radio and video as well as highly sophisticated teaching texts which often rely on the discovery method or a form of programmed learning. Computer-based training techniques are also used and there is the opportunity to be exposed directly to the Open University tutors at summer schools.

The recently introduced Open Tech programme aims to widen training and re-training opportunities for adults, with particular reference to technical, supervisory and managerial skills. Training is open to everyone and learning can take place at home, at work or at an education or training establishment.

References
1 Rackham, N, Honey, P and Colbert, M *Developing Interactive Skills* Wellens Publishing, Northampton, 1967.
2 Blake, R R, Mouton, J S, Barnes, J S and Greiner, L E 'Breakthrough in Organizational Development', *Harvard Business Review* Vol 42, 1964, pp 133-35.

Appendix L
Assessment Centres

An alternative method, which has been developed to overcome the problems of evaluating potential, is the use of assessment centres where the aim is to provide a broad approach to the identification of executive or supervisory potential. In an assessment centre, the multiple assessment of several individuals is carried out by a group of trained assessors using a variety of techniques such as games, simulations, tests and group discussions.

Assessment centres use the group selection techniques described in chapter 14. A programme may last anything from one to four days, although the longer programmes are also used as management development activities in themselves.

The characteristics assessed in a typical programme include assertiveness, persuasive ability, communicating ability, planning and organizing ability, self-confidence, resistance to stress, energy level, decision-making, sensitivity to the feelings of others, administrative ability, creativity and mental alertness. It is a formidable list and one cannot help wondering how accurately such factors can be measured even over four days and with lots of trained observers and psychologists.

The programme may consist of such activities as questionnaires filled in by participants about their attitudes to their work and the company and their aspirations, written tests, video taped ten-minute speeches, role playing exercises requiring leadership and group participation, in-basket exercises requiring participants to handle typical problems in a supervisor's in-tray, various interview simulations, management decision games, self-appraisal and peer rating, and depth interviews. Everything is observed and assessed by trained assessors.

A review by Ungerson[1] of the research findings on assessment centres concluded that there is good reason to believe that well-conducted assessment centres can and do achieve better forecasts of future performance and progress than judgements made by line managers in the normal unskilled way. Face-validity is high — everyone is impressed by the proceedings. So is reliability. He emphasized, however, that these favourable findings arose from centres run by highly trained full-time professional members using paper and pencil tests as well as subjective judgemental procedures.

The problem with assessment centres is their cost. They are not worth doing unless they are done well, and this means that amateur efforts or the use of packaged systems without proper training are to be avoided. In all but the largest organizations they are unlikely to be cost-effective. Most companies will have to rely on their normal assessment procedures, although these should ensure that judgements about potential are checked by trained managers who are aware of the qualities needed for advancement and how these can be assessed by measuring performance in the current job.

1. Ungerson, B 'Assessment Centres: A Review of Research Findings' *Personnel Review Vol 3, No 3, Summer 1974, pp 5-13.

Index of Authors Cited

693

Index